The
Hallucinogens

THE
HALLUCINOGENS

A. Hoffer

FORMERLY,
DEPARTMENT OF PUBLIC HEALTH
PSYCHIATRIC RESEARCH
UNIVERSITY HOSPITAL,
SASKATOON, CANADA

H. Osmond

NEUROPSYCHIATRIC INSTITUTE
PRINCETON, NEW JERSEY

WITH A CONTRIBUTION BY

T. Weckowicz
Department of Psychiatry
College of Medicine
University of Alberta
Edmonton, Canada

1967

ACADEMIC PRESS   New York and London

ACADEMIC PRESS, INC.
111 Fifth Avenue, New York, New York 10003

United Kingdom Edition published by
ACADEMIC PRESS, INC. (LONDON) LTD.
Berkeley Square House, London W.1

LIBRARY OF CONGRESS CATALOG CARD NUMBER: 66–30086

Third Printing, 1969

PRINTED IN THE UNITED STATES OF AMERICA

Preface

In 1954 we designated mescaline, lysergic acid diethylamide, and adrenochrome as hallucinogens. The only other substances which we classed as hallucinogens were the active principals from marijuana, harmala alkaloids, and ibogain, not at that time identified chemically for certain. In the past decade so many additional hallucinogens have been discovered, studied, and described and so many new publications have appeared that this may be the last time it will be possible to give a detailed description of the hallucinogens in a single volume. Within another five to ten years each hallucinogen may well require its own monograph.

The term "hallucinogen" is not completely satisfactory since it over-emphasizes the perceptual elements of the response to these drugs, and perceptual changes are often minor; changes in thought and mood are much more important. Other terms have been suggested but they, too, have faults. Thus, psychotomimetic has been used as a general description, but these compounds do not necessarily make the subject psychotic. The term delirients seems no better since subjects given these compounds are seldom delirious. Psychedelic, Osmond's word, refers to a particular kind of drug reaction, as does, of course, psychotomimetic, or delirium. For these reasons it seems appropriate to continue using the term hallucinogens for a variety of substances which can produce reactions which may be psychotomimetic, psychedelic, or delirient, depending upon many other factors.

Hallucinogens are then chemicals which in nontoxic doses produce changes in perception, in thought, and in mood, but which seldom produce mental confusion, memory loss, or disorientation for person, place, and time. These latter changes are characteristic of organic brain reactions following intoxications with alcohol, anesthetics, and other toxic drugs.

This work has been written for chemists, biochemists, psychologists, sociologists, and research physicians. It cannot, therefore, satisfy each group fully, but we believe that it is sufficiently comprehensive and well documented so that each group can use it as a springboard for future enquiry into these fascinating chemicals.

The use of hallucinogens has been described as one of the major advances of this century. There is little doubt that they have had a massive

impact upon psychiatry, and may produce marked changes in our society. The violent reaction for and against the hallucinogens suggests
that even if these compounds are not universally understood and ap-
proved of they will neither be forgotten nor neglected.

A. HOFFER[*]
H. OSMOND

September, 1967

[*] Present address: 800 Spadina Crescent East, Saskatoon, Canada.

Contents

PREFACE v

Chapter I. Plant β-Phenethylamines

Introduction 1
Mescaline 1
Mescaline Analogs 45
Amphetamines 46
Methylenedioxyamphetamines 47
Asarone 55
Kava Kava 57
Safrole 62
Sympathomimetic Amines 63
References 75

Chapter II A. d-Lysergic Acid Diethylamide

Introduction 83
Sources of LSD 83
Chemistry of LSD 88
Pharmacology 89
Biochemistry of LSD 90
Neurophysiological Effects 91
Comparison of Some Ergot Alkaloids for
  Psychotomimetic Activity 93
Toxicology of LSD 95
Complications When LSD Is Given 96
Dose and Psychological Activity 103
Effect of LSD on Normal Subjects 104
Psychotomimetic Reaction to LSD 128
The Psychedelic Experience 131
Effect of LSD on Schizophrenic Patients 139
Use of LSD in Psychotherapy 148
Rapid Personality Change and LSD 196

Criticisms of LSD Therapy and Rebuttal 197
Modifiers of the LSD Experience 205
How Does LSD Work 211
Some Consequences of LSD's Introduction to Psychiatry 233

Chapter II B. Ololiuqui: The Ancient Aztec Narcotic

History and Identification 237
Taxonomy of Convolvulaceae Containing Ergot Alkaloids 239
Chemistry 240
Psychological Properties 241
References 252

Chapter III. Adrenochrome and Some of Its Derivatives

Introduction 267
Chemistry 269
Chemical Properties 271
Biochemical Properties 272
Formation and Metabolism of Adrenochrome 322
Psychological Properties of Adrenochrome 343
Adrenolutin 366
Prolonged Reactions to Adrenochrome and Adrenolutin 397
Anxiety and Adrenochrome 415
Anxiety and Adrenolutin 416
5,6-Dihydroxy-N-methylindole 419
Adrenochrome Monosemicarbazone 432
References 433

Chapter IV. Indole Hallucinogens Derived from Tryptophan

Introduction 443
Tryptophan 444
Tryptamine 448
Cohoba, the Narcotic Snuff of Ancient Haiti 450
Dimethyl- and Diethyltryptamines 458
Effect of Bufotenine, Dimethyltryptamine (DMT),
   and Diethyltryptamine (DET) on Animal Behavior 461
Cross-Tolerance of DMT 464
α-Methyltryptamine 465
α-Ethyltryptamine 466
Methyl-2-methyltryptamine 468
Iboga Alkaloids 468
Harmine 472
Psilocybin 480
Yohimbine 500
How Tryptamine Hallucinogens Act 502

Serotonin 503
Drugs and Central Serotonin or Noradrenaline 506
References 511

Chapter V. **Hallucinogens Related to Parasympathetic Biochemistry**

Introduction 517
Factors Which Produce Synaptic Depression 519
Factors Which Produce Excitation 519
Acetylcholine 522
Acetylcholinesterase 523
Anticholinesterases as Hallucinogens 524
Cholinergic-Blocking Hallucinogens 525
Benactyzine 528
Cholineacetylase Inhibitors as Antihallucinogens 538
Anesthetic Hallucinogens 538
References 544

Chapter VI. **Taraxein**

Introduction 547
Biochemistry of Taraxein 547
Psychological Properties 551
How Does Taraxein Work 553
References 553

Chapter VII. **Animal Studies of Hallucinogenic Drugs**

T. Weckowicz

Introduction 555
Studies in Invertebrates 556
Lower Vertebrates 558
Higher Vertebrates 563
General Effect of Hallucinogenic Drugs Introduced
    Intrasystemically 563
Intracerebral Effect of Hallucinogenic Drugs 571
Behavioral Correlates of Electrophysiological Effects
    of Hallucinogens 575
Effects of Hallucinogenic Drugs on Learning and
    Other Higher Cognitive Functions 578
Summary and Conclusions 589
References 590

AUTHOR INDEX 595

SUBJECT INDEX 613

Chapter I

Plant β-Phenethylamines

Introduction

The final determination of the structure of adrenaline aroused great interest in a large series of amines with similar structure. Many of these were examined by Barger and Dale (1910) including some only recently identified as normal plant constituents. Mescaline was isolated by Heffter in 1896 from mescal buttons. This is the dried material obtained from a cactus which grows in the southern and central Americas. Bernadino de Sahagun first recorded in 1560 the use of peyote by the Mexican Indians. He wrote "it produces in those who eat or drink it, terrible or ludicrous visions; the inebriation lasts for two or three days and then disappears." But this information remained known only to the Indians and perhaps come Christian missionaries. In 1886, while traveling in America, Louis Lewin became familiar with the plant. He examined specimens of the cactus which Hennings named lewinii (a new species of *Anhalonium*). Lewin (1888a, 1894a,b, 1964) extracted several alkaloids from peyote and crystallized anhalonine.

Two members of this class of chemicals, mescaline and adrenaline, typify the main properties of these compounds. Both were known over 60 years ago but only in the past few years have they been studied as psychochemicals which might lead into some of the causes of schizophrenia. It is surprising that the idea was so slow in arriving in psychiatric research. It is not suprising they are chemically close for they are biogenetically related to the amino acids phenylalanine, tyrosine and 3,4-dihydroxyphenylalanine.

We will treat these compounds under two main subsections. The first will consist of a review of the hallucinogen, mescaline, its close analogs and peyote. The second will review all the other known plant β-phenethylamines.

Mescaline

INTRODUCTION

Mescaline, one of the active alkaloids of the American peyote plant, is historically the most interesting hallucinogen. Its use probably extends backward in time as long as the hallucinogenic mushrooms, and it has been known by Western man for nearly 100 years. The native American Church of North America, a Christian-derived religion based upon the regular use of peyote as a sacrament, is widespread among North American Indians. It is nearly 100 years old. Like many new religions it has had to contend with much persecution and opposition, chiefly directed against the use of peyote.

As a result of mescaline's hallucinogenic properties the first clear formulation was made that there was, if not a similarity, a parallelism between certain drug-induced mental states and psychotic mental states. Freud could have drawn the same conclusion for cocaine which he was the first to use as a euphorient. But instead it was Lewis Lewin who arrived at this conclusion in a series of papers which culminated in his great book, long out of print, being reprinted.

This is what Lewin said—

If, in order to investigate how these internally caused perceptions appear and to which cause we must attribute them—false projection of ideas, unreal happenings, or nonexistent objects—we limit the problem to what we can actually observe, we are immediately faced with a tangible cause to which psychologists and alienists ignorant of the facts have paid little attention, and which for this reason has not been allowed out to its final consequences—I mean the action of chemical substances capable of evoking such transitory states without any physical inconvenience for a certain time in persons of perfectly normal mentality who are partly or fully conscious of the action of the drug. Substances of this nature I call Phantastica. They are capable of exercising their chemical power on all the senses, but they influence particularly the visual and auditory spheres as well as the general sensibility. Their study promises one day to be of great profit for the understanding of the mental states above mentioned. Many years ago I indicated the part played by chemical substances of another kind in the appearance of mental disturbances of some duration, and very recently in the case of a gas, carbon monoxide, I pointed out briefly how genuine permanent mental diseases may be produced by a disturbance of the chemistry of cerebral life. The solution of many problems may be expected in this direction, as the issue of my own investigations in the sphere of the hallucinants or phantastica shows.

The problem is as follows. Taking for granted what we know of the phantastica and of their action as chemical substances on the brain in the form of sensorial illusions, may we go further, and suppose that in those cases where hallucinations and visions transitorily appear in perfectly sane persons they are due to the chemical action of bodies produced for some reason in the human organism itself? We may presume that there is a certain mental predisposition present at the time. We may base our affirmative response on facts. I know of organic products of disintegration which actually cause temporary excitation of certain points of the brain. I know of others which bring about somnolence and sleep and even mental disorders. Even if other causes are brought forward to explain hallucinations, if they are interpreted as the consequence of the excitation of certain central nerves, all these interpretations do not exclude the possibility of the chemical action of certain bodies produced in the organism being the direct cause of the excitation and the indirect cause of the series of consequences.

The importance of the Phantastica or Hallucinatoria extends to the sphere of physiological, semiphysiological, and pathological processes. It throws light on the concept of excitation, not easily accessible by science, on which so many strange manifestations of the cerebral functions are founded, by giving it an explanation without which it would be void, an explanation which accounts for the various effects by the chemical action of chemical substances produced in the organism itself. An objection to this point of view should not be found in the rapid appearance and eventual rapid cessation of the phenomena and the restitution of normal sense-perceptions. There are many chemical and especially chemico-catalytic reactions which develop in the same manner. I am convinced that it is the chemical action of organic decomposition products which causes the hallucinations so frequently met with in febrile diseases, hallucinations which the patient shows in such abundance and in such a variety of forms even when he has not completely lost consciousness. If any light is ever to be shed on the almost absolute darkness which envelopes these cerebral processes, then such light will only originate from chemistry, and never from morphological research. Morphology indeed has succeeded hitherto in giving but few explanations of vital processes. It has given no explanations of the extremely delicate action of certain chemical substances on living beings, especially on their nervous system, and will in all probability remain equally sterile in the future.

The point of view here put forward does not pretend to be the only one applicable to known processes of life. Others assume, in my opinion with equal justification, that a religious impulse, for instance, a truly divine emotion which makes the soul vibrate in its most profound depths, may be transmitted as a wave of excitation, and may influence centers which call forth internal impressions, false perceptions, hallucinations, etc. I know from events of everyday life that very violent emotions may under certain favorable conditions give rise to certain changes in the cerebral functions. These emotions are not only such as may be considered as abreactions of the intelligence, fear, anguish, fright, horror, but also the repulsive instincts such as disgust, loathing, abhorrence. The disorders of the brain which these sensations evoke are most various, collapse, delirium, convulsive trembling, troubles of the vascular system, etc. They may even terminate in death through the secondary reactions of vital organs. These consequences certainly appear more frequently than is supposed, but the mechanism to which they are to be traced is extremely difficult to perceive.

By the end of the first half of the twentieth century everything that could have been said about the psychological changes which followed the ingestion of mescaline had been said. The next decade witnessed a change in emphasis from the purely phenomenological to the biochemical, pharmacological, and the clinical uses of mescaline.

Lewin (1888b), Prentiss and Morgan (1895, 1896a,b, 1896–1897, 1918), Mooney (1896), Mitchell (1896), and Ellis (1897, 1898, 1902) were the first experimenters who used peyote or its main hallucinogen for self-experimentation. They were struck by the brilliant visual perceptual changes by peyote but white man does not relish the chewing of fibrous woody buttons, nor enjoy their soapy bitter taste. Vomiting was even more common than after mescaline and even though the experience was, on the whole, intensely exciting and interesting there was little desire to repeat it again and again. Thus Mitchell wrote, "These shows are expensive . . . The experience, however, was worth one such headache and indigestion, but was not worth a second." William James took one button only and was "violently sick for 24 hours, and had no other symptom whatever except that and the Katzenjammer the following day." He saw no visions, but no one would on one button (less than 25 mg of mescaline).

The isolation of the alkaloid mescaline from the peyote plant ensured that intensive studies would continue for the bitter alkaloid dissolved in water is much more suitable for the white man's palate and may be given parenterally. Knauer and Maloney (1913) gave 150 to 200 mg mescaline sulfate subcutaneously. Beringer (1923, 1927, 1932) used up to 600 mg parenterally. The usual doses ranged between 200 to 500 mg. By 1940 detailed studies were reported by Fernberger (1923, 1932), Lewin (1888b), Mayer-Gross and Stein (1926), Serko (1913), Kluver (1926, 1928), Guttmann (1936), M. G. Smith (1934), and Stockings (1940).

Louis Lewin may be considered as the first scientist who introduced mescaline to Western science. In 1931 in the translation of his 1924 monograph Lewin wrote the following:

"In the action of peyote, as in every case of man's reaction to an influence, one factor must be taken into account as an essential element in the form taken by the reaction: the individuality of the subject. There are no means of foreseeing this form. It is impossible to lift even a corner of the veil that shrouds the physiological process in the diversity of the functional modifications of cerebral life subject to the influence of one of these substances. Hallucinations of vision, such as we shall shortly describe, may be completely absent, and hallucinations of hearing and disorders of the feeling of location in space may take their place. I consider it important that no single component of the plant, mescaline for instance, represents its total action. The other substances present in the anhalonium, which in part may act differently, cooperate and exercise an influence on the total results.

"Influenced by the quantity imbibed—more than 9 gm have been taken—the effects appear after 1 to 2 hours and may last 4 or more hours. After an injection of mescaline the effects generally last 5 to 7 hours. They come about in darkness or when the eyes are closed, but may also continue if the subject passes into another room.

It is not always possible to distinguish sharply between the different stages. The first phase, generally accompanied by unimportant physical sensations, consists in a kind of removal from earthly cares and the appearance of a purely internal life which excites astonishment. In the second phase appear images of this exclusively internal life, sense-hallucinations, miracles which affect the individual with such energy and force that they appear real. During the greater part of the time they are accompanied by modifications of the spiritual life which are peculiar in that they are felt as gladness of soul or similar sensations, impossible to be expressed in words and quite foreign to the normal state, but nevertheless full of delight. No disagreeable sensations disturb these hours of dreamlife. The troubles which are liable to occur in the sense-illusions of certain mental diseases, sensations of fear or disturbances of action, never appear. The individual is usually in a state of extreme good humor and full of a feeling of intellectual and physical energy; a sense of fatigue rarely occurs, and then, as a rule, only during the latter course of the toxic action.

"The sense-illusions are the interesting factor at these stages. Quite ordinary objects appear as marvels. In comparison with the material world which now manifests itself, the ordinary world of everyday life seems pale and dead. Color-symphonies are perceived. The colors gleam with a delicacy and variety which no human being could possibly produce. The objects bathed in such brilliant colors move and change their tints so rapidly that the consciousness is hardly able to follow. Then after a short time colored arabesques and figures appear in endless play, dimmed by black shadows or brilliant with radiant light. The shapes which are produced are charming in their variety; geometrical forms of all kinds, spheres and cubes rapidly changing color, triangles with yellow dots from which emanate golden or silver strings, radiant tapestries, carpets, filigree lacework in blue or on a dark background, brilliant red, green, blue and yellow stripes, square designs of golden threadwork, stars with a blue, green, or yellow tint or seeming like reflections of magic crystals, landscapes and fields bright with many-colored precious stones, trees with light yellow blossoms, and many things besides. As well as these objects, persons of grotesque form may frequently be seen, colored dwarfs, fabulous creatures, plastic and moving or immobile, as in a picture. At the end of a psychosis one man saw with his eyes open white and red birds, and with closed eyes white maidens, angels, the Blessed Virgin, and Christ in a light blue color. Another patient saw her own face when she closed her eyes. An increase of sensibility to variations of light can be ascertained as in the case of strychnine (Beringer, 1922).

"These internal fantastic visions may be accompanied by hallucinations of hearing. These are more rare than the former. Tinkling and other sounds are heard as from very far away or are perceived as the singing of a choir or a concert, and are described as wonderfully sweet and harmonious. Sometimes agreeable odors are perceived or a sensation as if fresh air were being fanned toward the subject; or unusual tastes and feelings are experienced. The general sensibility may be affected, and then the subject has the illusion of being without weight, of having grown larger, of depersonalization, or of the doubling of his ego. The body of an epileptic had become so insensible that he did not know whether he was lying down or where and how he was lying. The sense of time is diminished or is completely lost.

"It is significant that in all these abnormal perceptions due to functional modifications in the cerebral life the individual preserves a clear and active consciousness, and the concentration of thoughts takes place without any obstacle. The subject is fully informed as to his state. He exhibits a desire for introspection, asks himself, for example, whether all the strange things he experiences are real. But he rejects this idea, well knowing that he has taken anhalonium. Nevertheless, the same phantasms impose themselves upon him once more. A man to whom the preparation had been given said to the physician: 'I know I am in my senses and I thank God for having let me see such beautiful visions. They ought to be shown to jewelers and artists, they might be inspired by them.' This was the man who believed himself to be in the heavenly kingdom and who had seen among others the Blessed Virgin of Czenstochova.

"The most important fact in the whole mechanism of the cerebral cortex is the modification of the mental state, the modification of psychological life, hitherto unknown spiritual experiences compared with which the hallucinations lose in importance. An unprejudiced physician (mescaline) gave the following detailed description of his wonderful experiences.

. . . My ideas of space were very unusual. I could see myself from head to foot as well as the sofa on which I was lying. All else was nothing, absolutely empty space. I was on a solitary island floating in the ether. No part of my body was subject to the laws of gravitation. On the other side of the vacuum—the room seemed to be unlimited in space—extremely fantastic figures appeared before my eyes. I was very excited, perspired and shivered, and was kept in a state of ceaseless wonder. I saw endless passages with beautiful pointed arches, delightfully colored arabesques, grotesque decorations, divine, sublime, and enchanting in their fantastic splendor. These visions changed in waves and billows, were built, destroyed, and appeared again in endless variations first on one plane and then in three dimensions, at last disappearing in infinity. The sofa-island disappeared; I did not feel my physical self; an everincreasing feeling of dissolution set in. I was seized with passionate curiosity, great things were about to be unveiled before me. I would perceive the essence of things, the problems of creation would be unraveled. I was dematerialized.

Then the dark room once more. The visions of fantastic architecture again took hold of me, endless passages in Moorish style moving like waves alternated with astonishing pictures of curious figures. A design in the form of a cross was very frequent and present in unceasing variety. Incessantly the central lines of the ornament emanated, creeping like serpents or shooting forth like tongues towards the sides, but always in straight lines. Crystals appeared again and again, changing in form and color and in the rapidity with which they came before my eyes. Then the pictures grew more steady, and slowly two immense cosmic systems were created, divided by a kind of line into an upper and a lower half. Shining with their own light, they appeared in unlimited space. From the interior new rays appeared in more luminescent colors, and gradually becoming perfect, they assumed the form of oblong prisms. At the same time they began to move. The systems approaching each other were attracted and repelled. Their rays were broken into infinitely fine molecules along the middle line. This line was imaginary. This image was produced by the regular collision of the rays against one another. I saw two cosmic systems both equally powerful in appearance and the difference of their structure, and in perpetual combat. Everything that happened in them was in an eternal flux. At the beginning they moved at a giddy speed which gradually changed to a quiet rhythm. I was possessed with a growing feeling of liberation. This is the solution of the mystery, it is on rhythm that the evolution of the world is finally founded. The rhythm became more and more slow and solemn and at the same time more strange and indescribable. The moment drew near when both the polar systems would be able to oscillate together, when their nuclei would combine in a tremendous construction. Then everything would become visible to my eyes. I would experience everything, understand all, no limits would bind my perception. A disagreeable trismus tore me away in this moment from the supreme tension. I gnashed my teeth, my hands perspired and my eyes burnt with seeing. I experienced a very queer muscular sensation. I could have detached separately every single muscle from my body. I felt great unhappiness and profound discontent. Why had physical sensations torn me from the supremacy of my soaring soul?

However, I had one unshakable conviction: Everything was ruled by rhythm, the ultimate essence of all things is buried in rhythm, rhythm was for me a medium of metaphysical expression. Again the visions appeared, again the two cosmic systems, but at the same time I heard music. The sounds came from infinity, the music of the spheres, slowly rising and falling, and everything followed its rhythm. Dr. B. played music but it did not harmonize with my pictures and disturbed them. It came again and again, that mighty tension of the soul, that desire of solution, and then each time at the decisive moment the painful cramping of the muscles of the jaw. Crystals in a magic light with shining facets, abstract details of the theory of knowledge appeared behind a misty vaporous veil which the eye sought to pierce in vain. Again forms appeared fighting one another: in concentric circles, from the middle Gothic, from the outside Romanesque forms. With an increasing jubilation and daring the Gothic pointed arches penetrated between the Romanesque round arches and crushed them together. And again, shortly before the decision, the gnashing of teeth. I was not to penetrate the mystery. I was standing in the midst of the evolution of the universe, I experienced cosmic life just before its solution. The impossibility of understanding the end, this refusal of knowledge was exasperating. I was tired and experienced bodily suffering.

Thus does the character and extent of the action of this marvelous plant present itself. It will easily be understood that, as I have already stated, it will evoke in the brain of an Indian the idea that it is a personification of God. The phenomena to which it gives rise bring the Indian out of his apathy and unconsciously lead him to superior spheres of perception and he is subjected proportionately to the same impressions as the cultivated European who is even capable of undertaking an analysis of his concomitant state. The physical phenomena which occur in either subject, such as, for example, nausea, a feeling of oppression in the breast, heaviness of the feet, muscular spasms in the calves of the leg or the masticatory muscles, are unimportant and without consequence. It is at present not possible to state to what extent the habitual administration of this substance will produce an inner desire to prolong its use, or whether anhalonism, like morphinism, produces a modification of the personality by a degradation of the cerebral functions, as I consider probable.

Thus anhalonium constitutes a large field for research work as to the physiology of the brain, experimental psychology, and psychiatry. It is necessary that this work should be carried out, by reason of the richer scientific results we may expect from it than from experiments on animals.

Knauer and Maloney gave mescaline to themselves and to other physicians in Kraepelin's Clinic. They completed 23 experiments. Beringer used physicians and medical students in about 60 studies.

These early scientists were interested chiefly in the visual perceptual phenomena which followed the ingestion of mescaline. Thus, Weir Mitchell took 3 drachm of an extract altogether (equivalent to 3 mescal buttons). Mitchell was remarkably sensitive to peyote or else he used very large buttons for he consumed probably less than 100 mg of mescaline. About 4½ hours after he took his first dose he found himself "deliciously at languid ease" and later he reported as follows:

The display which for an enchanted two hours followed was such as I find it hopeless to describe in language which shall convey to others the beauty and splendor of what I saw. Stars . . . delicate floating films of color . . . then an abrupt rush of countless points of white light swept across the field of view, as if the unseen millions of the Milky Way were to flow a sparkling river before the eyes . . . zigzag lines of very bright colors . . . the wonderful loveliness of swelling colors of more vivid colors gone before I could name them. Then, for the first time, 'definite objects associated with colors' appeared. A white spear of grey stone grew up to huge height, and became a tall, richly finished Gothic tower of very elaborate and definite design, with many rather worn statues standing in the doorways or on stone brackets. As I gazed every projecting angle, cornice, and even the face of the stones at their joinings were by degrees covered or hung with clusters of what seemed to be huge precious stones, but uncut, some being more like masses of transparent fruit. These were green, purple, red, and orange, never clear yellow and never blue. All seemed to possess an interior light, and to give the faintest idea of the perfectly satisfying intensity and purity of these gorgeous color-fruits is quite beyond my power. All the colors I have ever beheld are dull in comparison to these. As I looked, and it lasted long, the tower became of a fine mouse hue, and everywhere the vast pendant masses of emerald green, ruby reds, and orange began to drip a slow rain of colors.' After 'an endless display of less beautiful marvels I saw that which deeply impressed me. An edge of a huge cliff seemed to project over a gulf of unseen depth. My viewless enchanter set on the brink a huge bird claw of stone. Above, from the stem or leg, hung a fragment of the same stuff. This began to unroll and float out to a distance which seemed to me to represent Time as well as immensity of Space. Here were miles of ripped purples, half transparent, and of ineffable beauty. Now and then soft golden clouds floated from these folds, or a great shimmer went over the whole of the rolling purples, and things, like green birds, fell from it, fluttering down into the gulf below. Next, I saw clusters of stones hanging in masses from the claw toes, as it seemed to me miles of them, down far below into the underworld of the black gulf. This was the most distinct of my visions.' In his vision, Mitchell saw the beach of Newport with its rolling waves as 'liquid splendors, huge and threatening, of wonderfully pure green, or red or deep purple, once only deep orange, and with no trace of foam. These water hills of color broke on the beach with myriads of lights of the same tint as the wave.' Again, the author considers it totally impossible to find words to describe these colors. 'They still linger visibly in my memory and left the feeling that I had seen among them colors unknown to my experience.'

Havelock Ellis wrote—

The visions never resembled familiar objects; they were extremely definite, but yet always novel; they were constantly approaching, and yet constantly eluding, the semblance of known things. I would see thick, glorious fields of jewels, solitary or clustered, sometimes brilliant and sparkling, sometimes with a dull rich glow. Then they would spring up into flowerlike shapes beneath my gaze and then seem to turn into gorgeous butterfly forms or endless folds of glistening iridescent, fibrous wings of wonderful insects . . . According to Rouhier the second type of visions is represented by familiar objects, landscapes, faces, etc., whereas the visions of the third type, which are supposed to be especially characteristic of mescal, cannot be traced back to events of the past. Monstrous forms, fabulous landscapes, etc., appear. Mitchell's visions are cited for illustration. The phenomena of the fourth type are said to have remarkable similarity with those produced by hashish. It seems to us that any scheme which, in a detailed manner, assigns different kinds of visions to successive stages of the mescal state must be viewed as extremely arbitrary. The only thing that is typical with regard to sequence is that very elementary visions are followed by visions of a more complex character. In general, the phenomena observed first are seen by pressing upon the eyeballs. Thereafter, visions appear with closed eyes without such stimulation. Then, they may be seen with open eyes in the dark room and even in broad daylight. It is to be noted, however, that in some cases pressure on the eyeballs is entirely ineffective.

Kluver (1926) observed the following sequence of changes—

12:30 noon. Clouds from left to right through optical field. Tail of a pheasant (in center of field) turns into bright yellow star; star into sparks. Moving scintillating screw; 'hundreds' of screws. A sequence of rapidly changing objects in agreeable colors. A rotating wheel (diameter about 1 cm) in the center of a silvery ground. Suddenly in the wheel a picture of God as represented in old Christian paintings— Intention to see a homogeneous dark field of vision: red and green shoes appear. Most phenomena much nearer than reading distance.
12:35. The upper part of the body of a man, with a pale face but red cheeks, rising

slowly from below. The face is unknown to me. While I am thinking of a friend (visual memory-image) the head of an Indian appears.

12:45. Wavy spongy ground of greenish black color.—Glowing coals turn into pin heads of brilliant white color.

1:05. Wonderfully cut deep red jewels constantly changing in size, shape, color, and distance from each other. Sometimes covered with silvery or greenish drops. The whole very symmetrical. The design on a background the color of which changes frequently.—Try to see the experimenter, but: blue clouds, a church, the dim face of an old man on background, blue arabesques. The whole seen through a steel veil the meshes of which are constantly changing in size and form.

1:10. Bright yellowish sparks irregularly distributed in the whole field.

1:15. Beads in different colors. Colors always changing: red to violet, green to bright gray, etc. Color so bright that I doubt that the eyes are closed.—Yellow mass like saltwater taffy pierced by two teeth (about 6 cm in length).

1:20. Eyes open: the pupils alternately dilate and contract in daylight; difficulties in forcusing objects. Closing the eye: arches in violet. Black quatrefoils with three corners. The fourth corner seems to be lacking. Impossible to 'get' the fourth foil: the quatrefoils begin moving to the left and disappear—Silvery water pouring downward, suddenly flowing upward—Landscape as on Japanese pictures: a picture rather than a real landscape,—sparks having the appearance of exploding shells turn into strange flowers which remind me of poppies in California.

1:25. Again the quatrefoil. Cannot get the fourth foil.

1:30. Open the eyes for a few seconds, look at the experimenter and close them: positive after-image of the face of the experimenter. His hair turns into hair of a cat, his eyes get a bright yellowish color. Then the head of a cat (natural size); hereafter the whole field filled with yellow eyes. (No change in size of the eyes during the modifications.)—Then a brilliant blue wheel rotating in left upper field. Blue wheel turns into red sparks.

1:35. Spiral rapidly revolving in center of field drawn out away from me.—(Blinders taken off, eyes remain closed) field turns red, red jewel motive appears; jewels now very small (diameter perhaps 0.3 mm). Elephant (size on picture) turned upside down.

1:45. Pheasant tails filling the whole field.—Red jewel motive.—Colored threads running together in a revolving center, the whole similar to a cobweb.—A number of silvery forms in the midst of the field.—Gorgeous vine leaves colored as in Fall, on violet ground,—Arabesques, ornaments, designs changing kaleidoscopically.—Feeling that eyes are open.

1:55. Scintillating gem (size of a nut) deep red in color in center surrounded by greenish dark ground.—Steel veil of gorgeous bluish-violet color.—Visual memory—image of red candy: field turns green.

2:05. Moving rings in different colors.—In center bright light as coming from an electric bulb. Bulb seems to be incomplete. Then brilliant bluish form running through the field; seems to be incomplete in a certain way. In both cases unable to state what is lacking and how the impression of incompleteness arises.—Green sun (diameter about 3 cm) in bluish dark field; no motion. Then revolving system of splinters of glass; system illuminated from within.

2:15. Homogeneous dark ground with bright patches in left upper field. Suddenly very intense bright light as if produced by an exploding shrapnel (apparently a few cm distant from the eyes). Almost simultaneously jerky movement of hand to make sure whether blinders are on.

2:25. Darkish figures revolving around a center in a counterclockwise direction.

(Eyes open): streaks of green and violet on the wall. Then a drawing of a head changing into a mushroom (both of natural size). Then a skeleton (natural size) in lateral view turned about 30° to the left. Head and legs are lacking. Try to convince myself that there are only shadows on the wall, but still see the skeleton (as in X-ray).

2:45. (Eyes closed). Soft deep darkness with moving wheels and stars in extremely pleasant colors.—Nuns in silver dresses (about 3 cm height) quickly disappearing.—Collection of bluish ink-bottles with labels.—Red, brownish and violet threads running together in center.—Autumn leaves turning into mescal buttons.—Different forms emitting intense greenish light.—Forms in different colors; contours often dark.

3:05. (Eyes open): the walls covered with squares (about 2×2 cm): shadowy dark contours. The corners of the squares: red jewels (three-dimensional). This design followed by similar mostly more complicated designs in various colors. Sometimes not sure whether the phenomena are localized at the distance of the walls.

3:20. (Eyes closed): on dark ground a red flag on pole waving to the left.—Designs as on rugs.—From now on, the opening of the eyes does not necessarily banish the visionary design. The designs seem to be localized on walls, on the floor, etc. The opening of the eyes does not change the magnitude of the forms.

3:35. (Eyes closed): marvelous explosion of scintillating yellowish light mass in center of the field). (Diameter of exploding mass about 4–5 cm). Very agreeable.

3:45. (Eyes open): impossible to look at the walls without seeing them covered with visionary phenomena. Various designs, then the upper part of the body of an Egyptian woman (two-dimensional, but natural size). (Eyes close): a jewel design turns into dark background with symmetrically arranged golden sixes which move from the right to the left.

3:55. Strange animal (length perhaps 10 cm) rapidly turns into arabesques.—Gold rain falling vertically.

4:05. On stationary background rotating jewels revolving around a center. Then, with a certain jerk, absence of all motion.—Regular and irregular, forms in iridescent colors reminding of radiolaria, sea urchins, and shells etc., in symmetrical or asymmetrical arrangement.—Shells illuminated from within radiating in different colors, moving towards the right, turned about 45° towards the right and somewhat towards me. A little piece in every shell is broken out.—Slow majestic movements along differently shaped curves simultaneous with 'mad' movements.—Feeling there is 'motion per se'—Man in greenish velvet (height about 7–8 cm) jumping into deep chasm.—Strange animal turns into a piece of wood in horizontal position.

4:15. (Eyes opened): visionary phenomena on the walls. Moving the eyes, I notice that the scotoma which I have in my left eye moves before the designs.

From 4:30 PM on various experiments were conducted. The visionary phenomena, however, lasted until retiring and could always be seen in the dark room with open eyes. Arabesques, ornaments, various geometric patterns were dominating. On the following day, October 19, after a period of sleep, there was still a great sensitivity to colors, but visions could not be detected with closed or open eyes. On October 20, 10:00 AM, I saw one of the designs with closed eyes at the moment when the dentist began drilling one of my bicuspids.

Kluver (1928) completed the most comprehensive analysis of the visual and other changes induced by mescaline. The initial visual changes were mainly changes in elementary brightness and color visions. These were then succeeded by forms and form combinations which Kluver found were common to all the mescaline accounts. Subjects saw symmetrical geometric forms in brilliant and bright colors, transparent Oriental rugs, filigreed objects of art, wallpaper designs, cobweblike figures, Gothic domes, buttresses, modern patterns, spirals, screws, and prisms. These are the form constants which Kluver found in all mescaline visions; atypical visions upon closer examinations were often variations of these form constants.

Form Constants

CRYSTALLINE FORM CONSTANTS. These were the gratings, lattices, fretworks, honeycomb or chessboard designs listed by Kluver. We have called them crystalline because they are repetitive two- or three-dimensional patterns much as atoms are arranged in chemical crystals. One of Beringer's physicians constantly saw a fretwork and eventually became part of it. One of our subjects had similar crystalline patterns after taking lysergic acid diethylamide. He saw a square screen or lattice before him. At each node on the screen there was a nude girl dancing in time to the music. He saw this pattern until he fell asleep late that night. It was more fascinating to him than a TV show his friends were watching. The form constants described by mescaline are probably common to the visual hallucinogens like LSD-25, psilocybin, dimethyl- and diethyltryptamine. They are not found commonly in the adrenochrome and adrenolutin experiences.

COBWEB FORM CONSTANTS. These were "colored threads running to together in a revolving center, the whole similar to a cobweb", "immense areas over which gigantic cobwebs were spread."

TUNNEL FORM CONSTANTS. These form constants have also been described as funnels, alleys, cones or vessels, for example "long narrow tunnels . . . the ends of which appear in the distance as brilliant points."

THE SPIRAL. For example, "A procession coming from the lower right, moved slowly in spiral turns to the upper left."

Color and Illumination

Kluver found that no one color was related to mescaline changes. All colors were observed but many subjects noted a marked increase in brightness or in apparent illumination for example, "very intense bright light as if produced by an exploding shrapnel."

An outstanding characteristic was the unusual saturation of colors. Ellis was impressed not only "by the brilliance, delicacy, and variety of colors, but even more by their lovely and various textures."

Not only were objects more vividly illuminated but the source of the illumination was localized or unknown. One of Beringer's subjects reported, "The illumination . . . seemed to come from an unknown invisible source of light" "somehow they seemed to be illuminated from behind, the light coming from afar."

Huxley (1956) referred to certain well-marked characteristics of the mescaline experiences. "The most striking of these common characteristics is the experience of light. There is a great intensification of light; this intensification is experienced both when the eyes are closed and when they are open. Light seems preternaturally intense in all that is seen with the inward eye. It seems also preternaturally strong in the outside world.

"With this intensification of light there goes a tremendous intensification of color and this holds good of the outer world as well as of the inner world."

Visual Patterns

Most subjects have reported a symmetry of visual patterning. Often the geometric center of the field was also the center of the patterned imagery. There was no uniformity in the localization of the patterns. Sometimes the phenomena were localized on the walls, on the floor, or whatever the subjects were looking at. Occasionally the visual phenomena floated in the air, or were said to be "in the eyes" or "in the head."

The objects seen were either two or three dimensional. Objects were seen very clearly in three dimensions but could rapidly alter to blurred drawings. In size, the visionary objects varied from "gigantic" domes to Lilliputian figures. The objects sometimes appeared singly and thereafter became multiple, for example, "A small wooden face appears, it has the form of a small apple . . . suddenly there are three, four faces in one row."

Kluver raised the important question of whether it was possible to influence visions by thinking. Most of the subjects reviewed could not do so. Some were able to influence visions. Only a few could call forth objects at will.

Huxley (1956) aptly states "Intensified light, intensified color, and intensified significance do not exist in isolation. They inhere in objects. When the eyes are closed, visionary experience begins with the appearance in the visual field of living, moving geometrics. These abstract three-dimensional forms are intensely illuminated and brilliantly colored. After a time they tend to take on the appearance of concrete objects such as richly patterned carpets, or mosaics, or carvings. These, in turn, modulate into rich and elaborate buildings, set in landscapes of extraordinary beauty. These things are all new. The subject does not remember or invent them; he discovers them, 'out there,' in the psychological equivalent of a hitherto unexplored geographical region."

Afterimages

Kluver found changes in the afterimage—

While fixating a stimulus object, e.g., a paper-square, in order to produce an after-image, the background which consisted of one of Hering's gray papers was most of the time covered with ever-changing designs. The stimulus object was also covered with varying forms and colors. Now and then, the phenomena on the background appeared in the complementary color of the square which we were fixating. Sometimes we could observe the normal marginal contrast, but it was more pronounced than usual. The hues of the after-images obtained did not differ from those seen under normal conditions. In some instances, the visions prevented the appearance of after-images entirely; in most cases a sharply outlined after-image appeared for a while. Then the after-image became a part of the visionary design. Measurements of the size of after-images under various conditions did not reveal anything exceptional. While the visionary phenomena were stationary, the afterimages moved with the eyes.

Mayer-Gross and Stein (1926) reported periods of prolonged afterimages alternated with periods when there was no afterimage. Kluver found that visionary phenomena, afterimages, and real objects were strikingly similar. Knauer and Maloney (1913) found afterimages were "much more material and real than the most vivid of the hallucinations produced by mescaline." The majority of subjects found afterimages finally blended with images.

Perception of movement was changed very often. Very commonly a continuous movement of an object was seen as successive appearance at different places. "The perception of a moving burning cigarette was a great surprise to me. Not a continuous line or circle . . . but a number of small glowing balls. At the end of the movement I could still see the entire movement as if it were fixed by a number of glowing balls standing in air." Perhaps some of these phenomena are due to a prolongation of the afterimage (see Chapter II).

Apparent Movement in Stationary Objects

Kluver reported further—

It is theoretically interesting that the occurrence of apparent movements in the mescal state depends to a certain extent on the nature of the stimuli. Certain observations show that small objects are more easily displaced than large ones; objects which together with their surroundings form an optical 'whole' and which are so to speak definitely anchored in optical respects are less likely to move than those which seem to be detached from their background; objects, the contours of which 'suggest' movement, are more likely to move than those with definite, well-marked contours; objects, the appearance of which gives the impression of weight, are less likely to be displaced than those which appear light. It is to be noted that even under normal conditions our apparently stable world involves optically certain tendencies to movement. Whereas in everyday life we may be aware of only this tendency we find that in the mescal state this tendency, this implicit dynamite, is transformed into actually perceived movement. At this point we have to insist on the fact that it is not necessary at all that the subject be consciously aware of the above mentioned qualitative aspects of the phenomena. It is not necessary, for example, that he consciously judge a given object to be a 'very small' object; what matters is not the judgment but the fact that 'smallness' or the dynamic aspects above referred to phenomenally exist. If they exist, then, apparent movement is likely to occur. Expressed differently: we find empirically that apparent movement is likely to occur as soon as certain optical characteristics are present.

Transformations

There were gradual transformations of a stimulus object into an illusory object. The middle of a wall could become a spot seen as a house. One of Beringer's subjects saw the following:

The middle of the wall was a spot interpreted as a house; small spots made the whole, without effort, into a long, castle-like building; I could see the windows and the ramp. Before them there was an elegant line which represented the shore of a pond in a very plastic way. The castle was reflected in the water. When my interpretative effort weakened, the whole picture persisted for a while, then other ever-changing pictures appeared, forming themselves slowly. At first the lines became always more distinct until something turned up without my being conscious of influencing the whole process . . . it was not possible any more to see nothing but lines, there was always something . . . I did not succeed in seeing something intentionally without having the lines as a basis.

Changes in Other Senses

Kluver reported that there were changes in all the senses but he considered the predominant changes occurred in the visual sense.

Kluver's brilliant studies can be said to have marked an end to an epoch of pioneering, extremely interesting, and valuable studies with one hallucinogenic compound. The monograph by Kluver marked the conclusion of one epoch and the beginning of another. The vast number of mescaline studies since then have done little more than to add some detail although most papers were less well written with descriptions of lesser value than those given by the pioneer researchers. But Kluver's work also marked the beginning of the modern era in which there was a shift in direction. No longer were scientists content merely to describe. They became interested in examining the phenomena in relationships to similar phenomena recorded by the mentally ill. Some were more impressed by differences between the mescaline experience and the schizophrenic experience and others were equally impressed by the many similarities. Kluver wrote in 1928—

> On account of its specific effects on the optical sensorium, mescal is an excellent instrument of research for the psychologist. It is a very handy tool especially in the descriptive and genetic analysis of space and color phenomena. Utilizing this drug we may study profitably various aspects of normal and abnormal visual perception, simultaneous and successive contrast, different types of colorblindness, entoptic phenomena, dreams, illusions, pseudo-hallucinations, hallucinations, synesthesia, Sinnengedachtnis, the relation of peripheral to central factors in vision, the role of visual elements in thinking and the psycho-genesis of 'meaning.' Owing to the subjectification of the 'objective' world in the mescal state, an investigation of the last problem seems especially promising. The study of eidetic imagery and of subjective visual phenomena in general may also consider with profit the nature and the behavior of visual phenomena experimentally produced with drugs. Systematic experimentation undertaken with the view to obtaining a complete picture of the optical and non-optical effects in eidetic and non-eidetic individuals, in different constitutional types, in children, in primitives and in individuals of different social levels cannot fail to yield definite results. The psychiatrist will be interested in the effects of mescal not only as a means for a more adequate appreciation of the visual disturbances in various diseases, but also as a possible avenue to a psychology of schizophrenia. The anthropologist studying the origin and the varieties of 'visions' in different areas or the ornamental art of various tribes will be greatly interested in the existence of certain super-individual form-constants as found in mescal visions.
>
> In general there is no doubt that the form of the visual experiences in the mescal state differs radically from the general form of the visual phenomena caused by other drugs; but in some respects certain drugs lead to remarkably similar visual effects. Psychology, ophthalmology, psychiatry, and anthropology are in need of a detailed analysis of the optical effects of various drugs. In fact, a differential pharmacopsychology of form-constants is a desideratum. Unless we know these form-constants, we cannot consider those aspects of the visual phenomena which are due to the personality of the subject. Although at present there seems to be no uniformity in the way personality affects the character of the intoxication, it seems possible that some day the study of mescal effects will give us information about what Miller has called 'the hinterland of character' (cf. Miller, 1926).

This has been a long introduction to a most interesting subject but it is essential to know one's history if progress is to be made.

THE CACTUS ALKALOIDS

Extraction and Isolation

According to Reti (1950) the plants are best dried immediately after they are collected. They should be cleaned, the spines extracted, and the residue cut into thin slices and either sun dried or dried at 40°–60°C. The ground material may then be stored safely.

Powder is extracted with 85–95% ethyl alcohol. The extract is filtered and reduced *in vacuo* to a small volume. Water is added and all alcohol removed by evaporation under vacuum. The decanted solution is extracted several times with ether to remove some impurities. It is then made alkaline with ammonia or sodium carbonate and the alkaloids are extracted into ether or chloroform.

The crude solution may be further purified by various extractions described by Reti. The extracts from various species of cacti have been found to contain twelve characterized β-phenethylamines and may contain some not yet identified. A second major class of substances is also found, the tetrahydroisoquinolines. These are apparently easily derived from the phenethylamines by the introduction of another carbon on the terminal nitrogen with simultaneous ring closure. Only within the past few years have similar compounds appeared in psychiatry as psychoactive drugs.

Mescaline is β-3,4,5-trimethoxyphenethylamine with the empirical formula $C_{11}H_{17}O_3N$ and the structure shown in Fig. 1. It is a colorless alkaline oil or oily crystalline material with a melting point of 35°–36°C. It is soluble in water, alcohol, and chloroform but less soluble in ether. Mescaline sulfate is insoluble in alcohol, slightly soluble in cold water, but very soluble in hot water. The sulfate or chloride salts form colorless crystals. Because the mescaline salts are more soluble and more easily handled they have been used in the majority of psychological experiments.

The empirical formula was discovered by Heffter (1894a,b, 1898a,b, 1901) and the correct structural formula was determined by Spath and his colleagues in a series of important papers (1919, 1934). Reti (1950) listed several methods of synthesizing mescaline. Two close analogs of mescaline have been isolated from peyote, N-methylmescaline and N-acetyl mescaline (Spath and Becke, 1934).

Other mescaline derivatives are probably psychotomimetic in man but they have not been studied. De Jong examined a series of compounds and found they produced experimental catatonia in his animals. One of them, 3,4-dimethoxyphenylethylamine, was a more powerful substance than mescaline. Some of the compounds are shown in Fig. 1.

It seems that three hydroxyls or one or more methoxyl groups on the ring are sufficient to impart catatonic properties to the phenylethylamine group, that is, when the carbon of the side chain is not hydroxylated.

The latter compounds are adrenalinelike compounds. De Jong reported that adrenaline was the strongest catatonizing compound. Ephedrine (phenylpropanolmethylamine), which has no ring hydroxyls, was much less active.

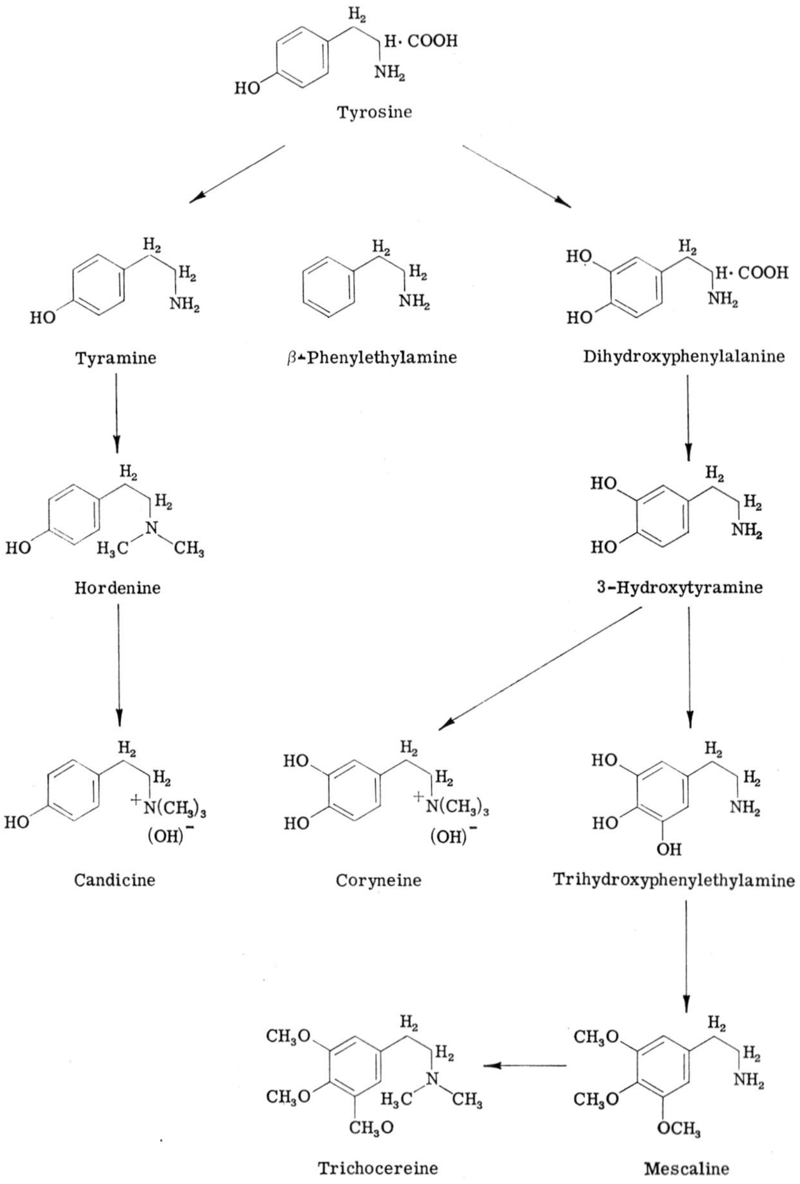

Fig. 1. Some phenylethylamines.

Thus it appears a phenylethylamine with one or more methoxyl groups on the ring and either an hydroxyl or methoxyl group on the β-carbon of the side chain should confer the greatest psychotomimetic property to the compound.

We have conducted a few experiments with hydroxymescaline synthesized by Dr. Heacock. There were indications it was psychotomimetic in humans but it seemed not to be as strong as mescaline. However, many additional experiments remain to be done.

OTHER PHENYLETHYLAMINES

The first four of the following compounds have been found in other plants but not in the cactus. The latter four are all present in peyote.

1. Phenylethylamine
2. *N*-methylphenylethylamine
3. Tyramine
4. 3-Hydroxytyramine
5. Hordenine (or anhaline). This is found in the cactus and in cereal seedlings
6. Candicine
7. Coryneine
8. Trichocereine (*N*-dimethylmescaline)

The structures of some of these compounds are shown in Fig. 1.

Apparently all the cactus alkaloids are biogenetically linked to the naturally occurring amino acids tyrosine, phenylalanine and 3,4-dihydroxyphenylalanine. In Fig. 1, Reti (1950) has shown a simple scheme.

This scheme includes only simple and biologically known types of reactions. Ring closure with formaldehyde or acetaldehyde could lead to the formation of the tetrahydroisoquinolines not shown in Fig. 1. (Spath, 1919, 1921a,b, 1922, 1934, 1936, 1938).

Evidence for this relationship is as follows:

1. The simultaneous occurrence of both phenylethylamines and isoquinolines in the same species of plants
2. The completely hydrogenated side chain
3. The natural phenylethylamines and tetrahydroisoquinolines carry free or methylated phenolic groups in the same ring positions 4; 3,4; or 3,4,5
4. The ease with which closure occurs *in vitro*

Apparently only mescaline is psychotomimetic. However there have been few studies with most of this series. De Jong (1945) found that neither tyramine nor hordenine produced experimental catatonia in mice. Luduena in one self-experiment (1933) found trichocereine did not produce any sensory changes. Most of the substances have sympathomimetic properties which differ in some detail from those of adrenaline or noradrenaline.

BIOCHEMISTRY

Bernheim and Bernheim (1938) studied the oxidation of mescaline and other amines by various animal tissues. Using conditions they had previously found were optimal for oxidation of tyramine, they found rabbit liver oxidized mescaline very rapidly, but rat and guinea pig liver and rabbit kidney oxidized it very slowly. Rat and guinea pig kidney and cat and dog liver and kidney were inactive. It was possible to make preparations which oxidized tyramine (and β-phenylethylamine, β-phenyl-β-oxyethylamine and isoamylamine) but not mescaline but every preparation which oxidized mescaline also oxidized tyramine.

The differences in rates of oxidation were not due to a lesser affinity of mescaline for the oxidase. In fact the affinity constant of mescaline was 0.25×10^{-3} M, somewhat greater than the one for tyramine—0.5×10^{-3} M.

Tyramine absorbed somewhat less than two atoms of oxygen per molecule but mescaline took up two atoms (also β-phenylethylamine and β-phenyl-β-oxyethylamine). Mescaline sulfate, 100 mg, was oxidized by 50 ml of rabbit liver preparation. It yielded 56% of trimethoxyphenylacetic acid.

The oxidation of mescaline was inhibited by 0.001 M KCN. Tyramine oxidation (and the other amines tested) was not altered by this concentration. Pyrophosphate and 0.008 M borate also inhibited mescaline oxidation. Increasing the concentration of oxygen increased the oxidation of mescaline several times, as it did oxidation of the other amines.

Bernheim and Bernheim (1938) suggested that the presence of some heavy metal was essential for tyramine oxidase to oxidize mescaline. This system would be different from the cytochrome–indophenol oxidase system.

Slotta and Muller (1936) had given mescaline to rabbits a few years earlier and found they could recover about half of the dose as trimethoxyphenylacetic acid. The rabbits were 70 times as tolerant for mescaline as humans in terms of dose. Excretion continued up to 48 hours. They did not find any mescaline in the urine of dogs or man after mescaline administration. They also found some 3,4,5-trimethoxyphenyl formaldehyde, some trimethoxyphenylethyl alcohol and other unidentified substances containing a methoxy group in rabbit urine.

Trimethoxyphenylacetic acid was not excreted in man and it was relatively nontoxic for animals and man. No physiological or behavioral changes were seen in rabbits or dogs with 800 mg doses. About 60% of the ingested dose was recovered unchanged in the urine.

Slotta and Muller reported that mescaline produced less strong psychological changes in normal subjects than in schizophrenics but that the 2,3,4-trimethoxy isomer induced much stronger changes in schizophrenics. The first finding has been amply documented, that is, that schizophrenics tend to react less strongly to mescaline but we have not seen any further reports on Slotta and Muller's second statement. When corroborated this could lead to interesting biochemical speculations on the nature of the toxin present in schizophrenia.

Moller (1935) in contrast to the above authors did find mescaline in human urine. He recovered 94% of a dose he had himself taken. Psychiatric patients did not excrete such a large proportion. Richter (1938) recovered 53% of an intravenous dose and 58% of an oral dose given to humans. Salomon *et al.* (1949) recovered 9–39% of the dose of mescaline given to 5 schizophrenic and 1 neurotic subject. Two schizophrenics given 276 mg of mescaline base excreted 20%. The one neurotic subject excreted 36%. This supports Moller's finding but the question needs to be reexamined.

Harley-Mason *et al.* (1958) isolated 3,4-dihydroxy-5-methoxyphenylacetic acid from human urine after the consumption of mescaline. They also considered the possibility that a portion of the mescaline could be converted into an indole derivative. Ratcliffe and Smith (1959) found 3,4-dimethoxy-5-hydroxyphenethylamine as a minor metabolite of mescaline.

Goldstein *et al.* (1961), and Friedhoff and Goldstein (1962) gave rats 400 μg/kg of mescaline-1-^{14}C and isolated some 3,4,5-trimethoxyphenylethanol. Pretreatment of the rats with iproniazid decreased deamination of mescaline to the phenylacetic acid derivative and increased the excretion of the alcohol. Pretreatment with calcium carbamide which inhibited further oxidation of the aldehyde also increased the excretion of the alcohol. They believed mescaline is normally metabolized by oxidation to 3,4,5-trimethoxyphenylacetaldehyde which may then be oxidized to the acid or reduced to the alcohol. Spector (1961) also found that the acid was a major metabolite when he gave dogs 20 mg/kg of labeled mescaline.

Friedhoff and Goldstein found that the alcohol alone was much more active in altering animal behavior than mescaline. In rabbits 2.5 mg/kg was more active than 10 mg/kg of mescaline. Pretreatment with calcium carbamide (a dehydrogenase inhibitor) potentiated the action of both.

They suggested that in animals 3,4,5-trimethoxyphenylacetaldehyde was the active mescaline metabolite which produced the changes in behavior. If this is true one would expect that pretreatment with iproniazid which decreased the formation of aldehyde whould reduce the severity of the mescaline reaction. However, it did not either potentiate or antagonize and the question still remains open. Inhibitors of enzymes alter metabolic pathways. It is probable the mescaline pathways in untreated animals are not quantitatively the same but this technique does prove certain pathways are possible. The alcohol may be considered an analog of ethyl alcohol. The same quantity of alcohol, that is 2.5 ml/kg IV or in a human over 150 ml would certainly produce major psychological changes. This question of the active derivative will depend upon measurements *in vivo* of the concentration of the alcohol in blood following administration of mescaline.

Daly *et al.* (1962) further examined the methylation and demethylation possibilities of mescaline *in vitro*. Enzymatic O-methylation of 3,4,5-trihydroxyphenethylamine with rat catechol O-methyltransferase produced 3,5-dihydroxy-4-methoxyphenethylamine and small quantities of 3,4-dihydroxy-5-methoxyphenethylamine and 3,4-dimethoxy-5-hydroxyphenethylamine. Mescaline was demethylated by rabbit liver preparation to form small quantities of 3,4-dimethoxy-5-hydroxyphenethylamine and 3,5-dimethoxy-4-hydroxyphenethylamine. Daly *et al.* also found that rabbit liver enzyme preparations deaminated mescaline to 3,4,5-trimethoxyphenylacetic acid. This reaction was inhibited by iproniazid, semicarbazide, and by nicotinamide.

We have found that nicotinamide does not alter the intensity of the mescaline reaction in human subjects. Apparently deamination of mescaline is not essential for the psychological activity of mescaline.

Friedhoff and Winkle (1962a,b) isolated 3,4-dimethoxyphenylethylamine from schizophrenic urine in 15 out of 19 cases. It was not present in 14 normal controls. This suggests that excessive methylation is a factor in the biochemical pathology of schizophrenia.

Cochin *et al.* (1951) gave 20 mg/kg of mescaline to dogs by oral, intramuscular, and intravenous routes. Following IV administration there was a rapid decrease in plasma levels to concentrations between 6 and 10 μg/ml in 2 to 30 minutes. There was then a slower loss of mescaline and no more was found after 8 hours. After intramuscular injections, plasma decay curves were similar but the plasma levels did not reach the same high peak. With oral administration plasma levels reached their peak at about 1 hour. The concentration reached was about half the intravenous peak. There was then a linear decrease in concentration up to 10 hours when some was still present.

About 28–46% of the dose was recovered in the urine with a 24-hour collection period. One half of the total quantity excreted in urine occurred in the first 3 hours.

The distribution between various tissues was studied after IV administration of 25 mg/kg. Kidney, liver, and spleen had from three to six times as much during the first 4 hours than did plasma or cerebral cortex. But cerebral cortex at 4 hours had nearly twice as much as plasma. The erythrocyte plasma ratio was 1 : 3 to 1 : 0. Vogt (1935) also found much higher levels of mescaline in liver and kidney than in either blood or brain.

Spector (1961) gave dogs anesthesized with pentobarbitone sodium 20 mg/kg of ^{14}C-mescaline intraperitoneally. The dogs were catheterized and urine was collected for 13 hours. They excreted 55–62% of the radioactivity. Peak excretion occurred after 2 hours. About 40% of the radioactivity appeared to be mescaline and the rest was trimethoxyphenylacetic acid. Their work clearly indicated mescaline was partially deaminated with the formation of a carboxylic acid derivative. Block (1953a,b,c, 1954a,b, 1958; Block and Block, 1952, 1954; Block, Block, and Patzig, 1952a,b,c) in a series of biochemical studies used ^{14}C-labeled mescaline in order to discover which tissues incorporated it. Mescaline was incorporated into all protein, but phosphorylation, glycolyses, and mitochondrial respiration apparently was not required. Oxygen had to be present. They used mice because mouse liver does not contain a specific mescaline oxidase and so resembles man more closely.

When given a 2 mg IP injection there was a biphasic excretion. After from 5 to 7 hours about half of the activity was accounted for in urine and feces. Over the next 2 hours there was a marked increase in the rate of excretion until at 11 hours, 80% was excreted. At 15 hours about 90% was excreted.

The mice also showed two psychological phases. Ten minutes after the injection of mescaline, cramplike spasms developed which lasted from 1 to 3 hours. Two hours after the injection the mouse lapsed gradually into a sleepy phase for about 4 to 6 hours. The first autonomic phase coincides with the maximum concentration of mescaline in the body. During the second phase only minimal quantities were present but liver protein reached its highest mescaline content.

Liver homogenates readily incorporated mescaline. Humans and mice do not have a specific mescaline oxidase so that the mescaline can circulate in the body unchanged for a long time. In contrast phenylethylamine is rapidly broken down to phenylacetic acid.

Incorporation of mescaline was not dependent upon amine oxidase activity. The incorporation was enzymatic. Heating liver tissue to 60°C destroyed these enzymes, but at temperatures about 100°C, chemical incorporation (nonenzymatic) became marked. There was also an anti-incorporation factor. When liver homogenate was heated to 55°C for a short time the anti-incorporation enzyme was destroyed and incorporation became marked. The addition of tyramine also accelerated incorporation.

Block believed the body was protected against toxic amines, for example tyramine, by containing active oxidases which would detoxify them and anti-incorporation enzymes which would prevent them from being bound and so protected from their oxidases. But since mescaline is not a natural animal constituent no animal defenses have been developed. Adding tyramine to tissues bound the anti-incorporation factor and so allowed the incorporation of mescaline.

Block further reported that incorporation was effected by isolated cell nuclei without the addition of activators. Mitochondria and microsomes reacted as did total homogenate. Incorporation was not increased in nuclei by tyramine or by heating. The inhibitor factor apparently is localized in mitochondria and microsomes.

Quastel and Wheatley (1933) found that mescaline inhibited oxidation of brain tissue when the substrates were glucose, lactate, pyruvate, and glutamate. Oxidation of succinate was not inhibited. Schueler (1948) corroborated these findings but he found mescaline inhibited brain tissue respiration only after it had been incubated for 2½–3 hours in the absence of substrate.

Blaschko (1944) found that rabbit liver amine oxidase had only a slight oxidative action on mescaline. Secondary octyl alcohol and methylene blue, both inhibitors of amine oxidase, did not interfere with the oxidation of mescaline.

Lewis and McIlwain (1954) found that electrically stimulated guinea pig brain slices were more sensitive to mescaline than the same tissue respiring at a resting level. Mescaline had little effect on resting tissue. When the tissue was stimulated with electrical stimuli in the form of condenser pulses there was a twofold increase in the rate of respiration. Mescaline markedly reduced the rate of respiration and the rate of glycolysis. The inhibition was observed with 10^{-3} M mescaline (50% inhibition of respiration): this concentration is close to the quantities of mescaline which are active *in vivo*. Lewis and McIlwain suggested mescaline (and also LSD-25) prevented changes in level of activity normally caused by applied pulses.

Deltour *et al.* (1959) reported that mescaline and LSD had no effect on glutamic acid decarboxylase of brain tissue. Adrenochrome is an inhibitor of this enzyme but its monosemicarbazone was an activator.

Dengler *et al.* (1961) found that cat cortex slices took up DL-norepinephrine. This was inhibited 32% by 10^{-6} M mescaline. But reserpine, chlorpromazine, and cocaine were much more effective inhibitors. Isoreserpine, acetylcholine, and serotonin had no effect.

Mescaline has a few nonspecific effects on biochemical processes in the body. Hollister (1961) found that mescaline (5 mg/kg) increased free fatty acids of blood, reduced urinary phosphorus, and decreased total circulating eosinophils. Creatinine levels, alkaline phosphatase, copper oxidase, and serum glutamic oxalopyruvic transaminase levels were not altered. The mescaline effect in elevating free fatty acids resembles the action of adrenaline as does its effect in decreasing eosinophils. However, the reduction in urinary phosphorus is more comparable to the action of adrenolutin and LSD.

Bradley *et al.* (1961) reported that 100 mg/kg of mescaline did not alter the nonprotein sulfhydril concentration of brain. But according to De Ropp and Snedeker (1961) 240 mg/kg increased free alanine levels in rat brain.

Rafaelsen (1961) found that glucose uptake by isolated rat diaphragm and isolated rat spinal cord was not altered by mescaline.

Other biochemical changes were investigated by Denber (1961a,b) and Denber *et al.* (1962). A series of subjects were given 500 mg of mescaline. There was a slight decrease in blood amino acid levels and a small rise in blood glucose was most marked one hour after administration. There were no changes in cholesterol, bilirubin, calcium, creatinine, nor urea levels. Cephalin cholesterol flocculation and thymol turbidity liver function tests were unaltered. This contrasts with Georgi *et al.* (1949) and Fischer *et al.* (1951) who, using Quick's hippuric acid excretion test found there was some liver abnormality after the ingestion of mescaline.

Runge *et al.* (1961) discovered a curious property of mescaline. They found that lyophilized human serum from schizophrenic patients had a peculiar infrared spectrum. This unusual absorption spectrum was found in few comparison controls. When 20 mg of mescaline was added to 3 ml serum the schizophrenic type of absorption curve was reproduced. In this, it resembled adrenochrome which also reproduced the schizophrenic absorption curve at the same concentration.

PHYSIOLOGY

Mescaline apparently blocks the neuromuscle complex. Schopp *et al.* (1961) anesthetized dogs with pentobarbital sodium, then prepared the peroneal tibialis anticus nerve muscle preparation. When mescaline was injected into a close arterial vessel it had no anticurare activity. It pro-

duced a striking depression in contraction adding to the depression produced by curare. When it was given alone 4–5 mg/kg of mescaline
caused a transient (10–30 second) depression. When larger doses were
studied the depression was more prolonged and more time was required
for the preparation to recover. There was an overresponse on recovery.
A potassium chloride solution (2 ml of 1.15%) partially reversed the
mescaline-induced depression. Adrenaline solution (1–2 ml 1/50,000) also
reversed the depression partially. After mescalinization, it was possible
to stimulate the muscle using direct stimulation. Chronically denervated
preparations did not respond to mescaline.

Grace (1934) stimulated the isolated frog gastrocnemius muscle
preparation every 3 minutes. Mescaline concentrations of less than 1 part
in 500 had no effect. Greater concentrations shortened the muscle and
diminished contractions. After 50 minutes, the muscle preparation was
sometimes paralyzed.

Costa (1956) found that 0.1 mg/kg of mescaline facilitated serotonin
activity on uterine muscle preparations. Higher doses caused contraction. One μg/liter of LSD antagonized the mescaline response but lower
doses (0.2 μg/liter) facilitated the mescaline effect.

Mescaline alters the pattern of cerebral electrical activity and also of
deeper brain centers. Takeo and Himwich (1965) and Wikler (1954)
found a slight increase in alpha frequency on the surface electroencephalogram. There was a shift in pattern in the direction of desynchroniza-
tions. This was sometimes associated with anxiety, hallucinations, and
tremor. Changes in the direction of synchronization occurred when subjects were euphoric, relaxed, or drowsy.

Smythies *et al.* (1961) injected 5–40 mg of mescaline into rabbits who
carried in dwelling electrodes in the optic cortex. At low doses there
was a potentiation of waves but at higher doses there was an initial
period of inhibition.

Himwich *et al.* (1959) found that mescaline activated the mesodiencephalic activating system.

Marrazzi (1960) measured the effect of many substances on transmission across certain central synapses. He injected the test chemical
into the common carotid artery. Despite the circle of Willis there is a
unilateral distribution of blood so that there is a rapid ipsilateral increase in concentration of the chemical. After dilution into the general
blood stream the concentration used becomes subthreshold for most
peripheral effects and so prevents a barrage of afferent signals coming
from the periphery to the brain.

Distortion of synaptic transmissions can be either in the direction of
excessive stimulation or excessive inhibition. Most of the substances

tested were depressants. The most potent depressants were serotonin and bufotenine. The weakest depressants were mescaline, adrenochrome, adrenolutin, and noradrenaline. LSD, adrenaline, and GABA were intermediate in inhibitor activity.

Curtis and Davis (1962) measured the effect of several phenylethylamines including mescaline on neurons of the lateral geniculate nucleus of the cat anesthesized with pentobarbitone. They had low activity compared to serotonin. Dopamine and mescaline had one sixth the potency of serotonin but the duration of this inhibition was twice as long. Tyramine and noradrenaline had one twelfth the activity of serotonin. Phenylethylamine, ephedrine, phenylephrine, adrenaline, and isoprenaline had less than one twelfth the activity of serotonin.

Rovetta (1956) discovered that mescaline applied directly to the surface of the brain cortex acted as a convulsant. This was corroborated by Ochs *et al.* (1962). They applied 1% solutions of mescaline to intact cerebral cortex of rabbits and cats and to cortical island preparations. When one drop of mescaline solution was placed on the cortex the negative direct cortical response became smaller in amplitude and longer in duration. After 6 minutes mescaline spikes appeared which became larger until they reached several times the height of the direct cortical response. Spikes were found in acute or chronic island preparations and over several cortical areas. The latency varied up to 100 milliseconds and depended upon the strength of the stimulus. GABA rapidly blocked both the direct cortical response and the spike and produced an inversion of the former but not of the spike. When GABA was washed off with Ringers solution, spike activity returned rapidly. Intravenous injections of pentobarbital blocked the spike but not the direct cortical response.

The most pertinent studies were completed by Monroe *et al.* (1957). They gave 500 mg of mescaline to 5 chronic schizophrenic patients and to one who suffered from paralysis agitans. The patients carried cortical implanted electrodes. One patient who had a marked clinical response to mescaline developed paroxysmal 10 per second activity from the left anterior hippocampal region. On the second occasion, he developed episodes of up to 20 seconds of high amplitude delta activity in the right anterior cortex accompanied by sharp high amplitude spikes in the right septal and hippocampal area and in the right cortex.

Another subject who had a pronounced visual reaction to mescaline developed high amplitude delta activity in the septal region with low amplitude diphasic spikes sometimes followed by low amplitude slow waves in the hippocampal region.

All the electroencephalograms revealed some response to mescaline (also to LSD). A generalized response sometimes predominated in cortical leads, that is, alpha disappeared and fast activity in the beta range increased. If there was rhythmic theta or underlying delta before mescaline was given, this also decreased and was replaced by fast beta. There were similar changes in the subcortical areas (caudate, amygdaloid, hippocampal, and septal areas).

Monroe *et al.* felt that most significant changes occurred in the subcortical areas. Here, paroxysmal activity appeared limited to the septal, anterior hypothalamic, or amygdaloid–hyppocampal regions. Bursts lasted 1–10 seconds. These were similar to those seen in these areas in schizophrenic patients who had not been given mescaline. These changes correlated with the psychological responses and somatic changes. They found that mescalinized subjects and schizophrenics could have paroxysmal electroencephalographic abnormalities in the rhinecephalon which were not reflected in the corticograms and which correlated with psychotic behavior.

Mescaline increased body temperature in rabbits. Pletscher (1957) found that 50 mg/kg given subcutaneously increased rectal temperature 0.33°C. After pretreatment with iproniazide (100 mg/kg) the temperature increased 1.93°C. In this, mescaline resembled reserpine, serotonin, adrenaline, phenylethylamine, and tyramine.

Fellows and Cook (1957) reported that mescaline increased scratching in mice, but not in the rat, guinea pig, cat, pigeon, hamster, rabbit, dog, or monkey. The amount of scratching was increased. The mice had episodes of scratching the back of neck with the hind foot for 1–2 seconds. A dose of 10 mg/kg by mouth produced 5 scratches in a fifteen-minute period. A dose of 100 mg produced 100 scratches. Doses in between were related in a linear manner to scratching behavior. Chlorpromazine, resperpine, serotonin, and morphine antagonized the scratch induced behavior. Anticonvulsants and barbiturates did not. Promazine had one fourth the activity of chlorpromazine.

Haley (1957) injected mescaline into brain ventricles and found that it produced scratching. Serotonin had similar properties.

TOXICOLOGY

Acute Toxicology

Speck (1957) reported that the LD-50 for mescaline given intraperitoneally to unfasting male albino rats was 370 mg/kg. Similar toxicity was found for white mice, guinea pigs, and frogs. Death was preceded by flexor convulsions, respiratory arrest, then cardiac arrest. Curare or decamethonium did not block convulsions. Mescaline produced hypo-glycemia and bradycardia. The bradycardia was marked in half an hour but was normal in 1 hour. There was marked vasoconstriction. The animals became indifferent to pinprick, to tail snipping, or touch. At the height of the cardiac arrest transient cyanosis was seen.

The LD-50 dose of mescaline depressed glucose at 1 hour from 97 mg % to 25 mg in unfasted rats. It remained low for 4 hours and was normal again in 24 hours. These rats (who survived) did not suffer any clonic–tonic convulsions, nor coma.

When animals were returned to their cage they were hyperreactive to noises. Frequently the animals hind limbs were weak, they trembled and developed exophthalmos. They did a lot of chewing, sniffing, and sneezing. The next day they were drowsy and the third day they were normal. There was a synergestic effect on the death rate of insulin by mescaline.

Adrenaline (0.12 mg) blocked the effect of mescaline on glucose. It also partially blocked bradycardia but the LD-50 was not altered. Physo-stigmine (1 mg/kg) given with 30 mg/kg of mescaline killed all the animals.

Chronic Toxicity

Speck gave 50 mg/kg daily to rats for 1½ months. They then had ruffled coats, squealed when handled, and they were apprehensive. Auditory stimulation produced excitation but not convulsions during the first week. No tolerance developed with respect to hypoglycemia and bradycardia. There was a small increase in weight in the liver and the adrenal gland. There were small hemorrhages in lung and liver but other organs were not altered. Mescaline had a chronic nonspecific stressing effect and no tolerance developed.

Prolonged Reactions to Mescaline

Morselli (1936) took 750 mg of mescaline alone in his apartment. He suffered a severe psychotomimetic reaction lasting about 16 hours. But for the next two months he had the delusion that a man in one of the pictures in his apartment was alive and was haunting him with hostile intentions. Removing the portrait did not help. At times his anxiety was so great he slept somewhere else. After two months he was finally normal.

Stevenson and Richards (1960) reported two prolonged reactions to mescaline. One subject was given 400 mg of mescaline with the usual re-action. Twice that day he was injected with sodium succinate intravenously and that night he was normal. Two weeks later he again took 400 mg. Eleven hours later he seemed well enough to go home. After sleeping the subject felt normal the next day, but after working hard for 12 hours he noted a return of feelings of unreality. The next morning he was apathetic and in a daze. He forgot to carry out his assignments and he was indifferent to his unfinished work. For the 11 days following his mescaline reaction he was like a paranoid schizophrenic with changes in perception and changes in thought, apathy, disinterest, and depression. On the morning of the twelfth day, he awakened feeling normal. But this subject had from early childhood used his inner world of phantasy during periods of stress, and for two years after his prolonged experience he remained passive, lacking in ambition, apathetic to a mild degree, forgetful, and negligent in his work and suffered inappropriate anxiety.

The second subject, a 22-year-old female, received 400 mg of mescaline. She had an unpleasant paranoid reaction with severe impairment of her thought processes. After 10 hours she appeared normal. The following morning her reaction continued. She suffered impaired attention, reduced emotional expression, and her thinking was accelerated and paranoid. For several days afterwards, she had visual and auditory hallucinations.

Tolerance to Mescaline

ANIMALS. Freedman *et al.* (1958) studied the development of tolerance to mescaline in rats. Each day they were given 10 mg/kg and their gross behavioral and rope-climbing performance was observed. The behavioral changes came on after 10 minutes, reached a peak at 20 minutes and were gone after 60 to 90 minutes. Tolerance developed more slowly than with LSD but was present in most of the animals by the fifth day.

Cross-Tolerance between Mescaline, LSD, and Psilocybin

Balestrieri (1957a, 1961a,b) found a highly significant cross-tolerance between LSD and mescaline. That is, subjects given either one no longer responded with the same intensity to an active dose of the other. There was somewhat less cross-tolerance between LSD and psilocybin. Wolbach *et al.* (1962) corroborated these findings. They used 10 opiate addicts serving sentences who had some experience with LSD or mescaline. When they were given from 0.75 to 1.5 μg/kg of LSD daily they developed a tolerance for LSD and a cross-tolerance for mescaline. When 2½–5 mg/kg of mescaline was given daily similar tolerance for mescaline and cross-tolerance to LSD developed.

PSYCHOLOGICAL CHANGES PRODUCED BY MESCALINE IN ANIMALS

Friedhoff and Goldstein (1962) studied the behavior of rats given mescaline. Below 10 mg/kg there was no consistent effect. At this dose level minimal effects such as licking, chewing, and motor incoordination were seen. When more mescaline was given, the initial hyperactivity was followed by depression of activity, marked hind leg incoordination, pupillary dilatation, and cyanosis. When 200 mg was given, the rats developed severe weakness and became semistuporous with frequent myoclonic jerks. Pretreatment with iproniazid did not increase or decrease the reaction. In contrast, pretreatment with calcium carbamide which would increase the concentration of ethyl alcohol potentiated the mescaline effect. Pure alcohol (2.5 mg/kg) given intravenously was as active as 10 mg/kg of mescaline in rabbits. The potentiation by calcium carbamide suggests that 3,4,5-trimethoxyphenylacetaldehyde is responsible for its activity.

One of the earliest structure activity studies of mescaline analogs was completed by Gunn *et al.* (1939). They compared 4-methoxy,3-methoxy-3,4-methylenedioxy and 3,4-dimethoxy derivatives of phenylethylamine for central activity and effect on blood pressure, in mice, rabbits, and cats. The first three compounds were central nervous system stimulants and had 1/300 the blood pressure elevating activity compared to adrenaline. The last compound was a central depressant. On the basis of their studies they concluded as follows:

1. With the same phenyl nucleus the isopropylamine side chain made the compound more toxic and it had more stimulatory potency on the central nervous system.
2. The methylene dioxy compound was even more toxic and a greater stimulant.
3. An hydroxyl on position 4 made the compound less toxic and less stimulant to the central nervous system than either a hydrogen or methoxy group.
4. An additional phenyl group on the methoxy group at 3 or 4 increased the central stimulant activity.
5. 3,4-Methylenedioxyphenyl isopropylamine was a more powerful central nervous stimulant than benzedrine.

Chorover (1959) gave 25 mg/kg mescaline sulfate intraperitoneally to albino rats. There was a rapid extinction of the conditioned avoidance response to sound. A dose of 25–50 mg depressed spontaneous activity and impaired performance of previously learned conditioned avoidance responses to auditory and visual stimuli. It impaired the performance of

rats trained to run or freeze to avoid electroshock for three days. Chorover (1961a,b) reported 25 mg/kg mescaline given intraperitoneally
produced an immediate and persistent suppression of the conditioned
avoidance response in Wistar rats. Escape responses and spontaneous
locomotor activity in the open field test were not affected. Orienting
responses showed the animals heard the buzzer. The effect of mescaline
on the behavior of mice was examined by Fekete *et al.* (1961) and
Borsy *et al.* (1961). Using the hot plate method they found that 100
mg/kg of mescaline had an analgesic effect in 87.5% of the animals.
Trimethoxybenzoyl morpholine, 200–400 mg/kg given intraperitoneally,
did not modify the effect of 200 mg/kg mescaline on mice. Given alone
at a dose level of 50 mg/kg, 16.5% of the animals had analgesis. When
both compounds were given together only 68% of the mice had analgesia
for heat.

When mice were given 100 mg/kg mescaline the degree of excitation
was decreased 50% by 12.5 mg/kg of trioxazin and inhibition was enhanced by 25 mg/kg. Spontaneous activity was diminished below the
base line by 50 mg/kg.

Mescaline enhanced the orientation reflex to 140% over the base line.
Trioxazin (12½ mg/kg) reduced this to 70% and 25 mg/kg abolished it.

Greenblatt and Osterberg (1961) found that mice motor (exploratory)
overactivity, as measured by the actophotometer, was not sustained. Ray
and Marrazzi (1961) reported that 11–15 mg/kg of mescaline blocked
positively motivated behavior with only a slight slowing of negative
motivated response. The effect lasted 60–90 minutes.

De Jong (1945) reported his extensive experiments with mescaline on
animals. He removed the entire cerebellum from one cat. Nearly one
month later the animal had marked motor incoordination and some
increase in muscle tone in the hind limbs. Two months after the operation the cat was given 100 mg mescaline sulfate subcutaneously. In 14
minutes the cat had developed typical catalepsy. Mescaline also produced catatonia in mice, in a normal cat, a monkey, a pigeon, and in
frogs. The monkey required 270 mg (2.5 kg per animal). De Jong tested
a series of methoxylated phenylethylamine compounds for their
catatonizing effect on some animals. His results are shown in Table 1 and
the structure of some of the compounds in Fig. 2.

The evaluation of the catatonizing power and fear-producing power
is ours derived from de Jong's protocols. It is apparent that the number
4 position is important, for only when a substituted group was present,
was there any catatonizing power. Position 3 seems more important than
position 5. The ethoxy group on 4 reduces activity. An additional group

on the β side chain position increases activity. Furthermore ethoxy groups at position 4 made the compound very toxic or produced more intense fear. Perhaps fear is a result of more vivid hallucinations. De Jong's data suggest that of all the methylated derivatives studied by Daly *et al.* (1962) 3,5-dihydroxy-4-methoxyphenylethylamine would be the most active psychologically.

TABLE 1

The Catatonizing Action of Some Phenylethylamine Derivatives[a]

Derivative			Position	Catatonizing	Fear-producing
3	4	5	B	power	power
CH_3O	CH_3O	CH_3O	H_2	Strong[b]	Moderate
CH_3O	CH_3O	H	H_2	Strong	Moderate
CH_3O	C_2H_5O	CH_3O	H_2	Moderate	Strong
CH_3O	CH_3O	C_2H_5O	H_2	Moderate	Strong
C_2H_5O	C_2H_5O	CH_3O	H_2	Very toxic	
H	CH_3O	H	H, CH_3O	Moderate	Slight
CH_3O	CH_3O	H	H, CH_3O	Moderate	Slight
CH_3O	CH_3O	CH_3O	H, CH_3O	Moderate	Slight
CH_3O	$C_6H_5CH_2O$	CH_3O	H_2	Moderate	Slight
CH_3O	$C_6H_5CH_2O$	CH_3O	H, CH_3O	Strong	Slight
CH_3O	HO	CH_3O	H_2	None	None
HO	HO	HO	H_2	Slight	Slight
H	HO	HO	H_2	None	None

[a] Summarized from de Jong (1945).
[b] Mescaline.

Smythies *et al.* (1958) gave cats a series of mescaline analogs at a dose level of 25 mg/kg. Four of the compounds, the 3-methyl, 4-methyl, 4-chloro, and 3,5-dimethyl, 4-methoxy derivatives of phenylethylamine, produced strong rage reactions with growling, hissing, aggressive behavior, and withdrawal.

Two compounds, the 3,4,5-triethoxy and 3,5-dimethoxy derivatives were inactive. Intermediate in activity were the derivatives with ethyl, isopropyl, or butyl groups on the number 4 position. As the side group became heavier, less rage was produced in the cats. Using the Winter and Flataker rope-climbing test with rats they also found that removing the 5-methoxyl group reduced activity 50%. Loss of the 5-hydroxy group eliminated activity but placing a benzyloxy group on position 5 increased activity.

Ernst (1962) corroborated de Jong's (1945) results on some mescaline analogs. The 4-methoxy and 3,4-dimethoxy analogs produced a striking

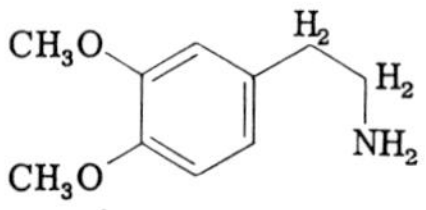

3,4-Dimethoxy-
phenylethylamine

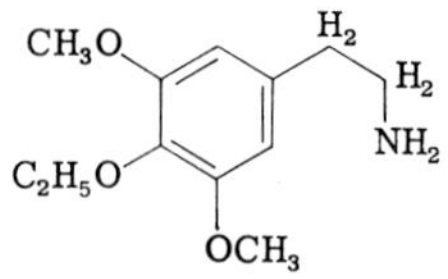

3,5-Dimethoxy-
4-ethoxyphenylethylamine

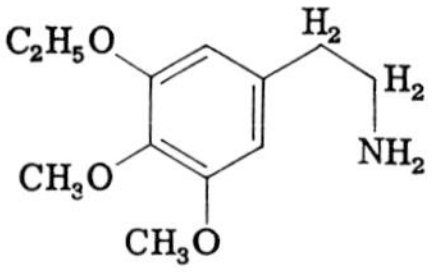

3,4-Dimethoxy-
5-ethoxyethylamine

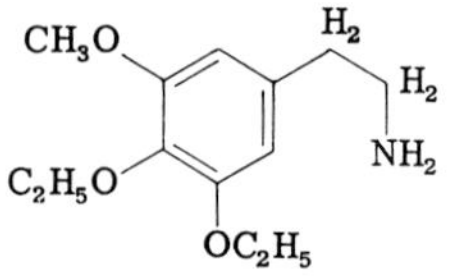

3,4-Diethoxy-5-methoxy-
phenylethylamine

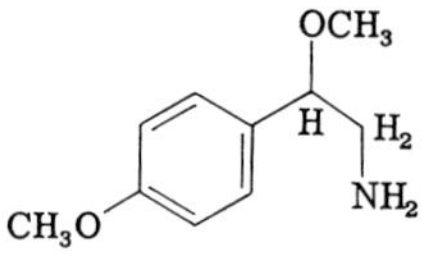

p-Methoxyphenyl-β-
methoxyethylamine

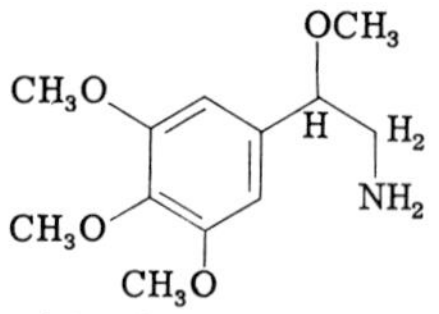

β-Methoxymescaline

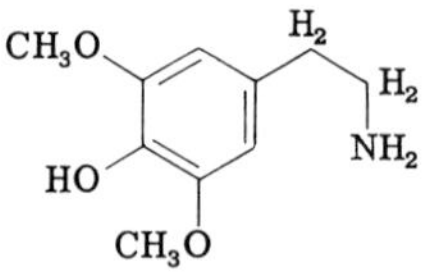

3,5-Dimethoxy-
4-hydroxyphenylethylamine

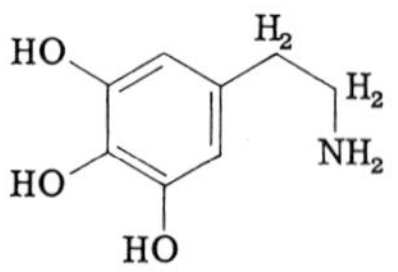

3,4,5-Trihydroxy-
phenylethylamine

Fig. 2. Some methoxylated phenylethylamines.

hypokinetic rigid syndrome in cats. De Jong found that the 4-methoxy derivative was less potent than mescaline but also found the 3,4-dimethoxy derivative was as potent as mescaline. Ernst (1962) further found that removing the methyl group from position 4, that is, 4-hydroxy and 3,5-dimethoxyphenylethylamine produced an inert substance, again confirming de Jong. Ernst suggested abnormal methylation of dopamine could lead to similar substances and could play a role in the production of catatonia.

Friedman *et al.* (1963) compared the toxic effect of hydroxymescaline, hydroxy-*N*-methylmescaline, mescaline, and the isoquinoline derivative of mescaline. In Albino Swiss mice the LD-50 intraperitoneally of mescaline was 400–800 mg/kg. The other 3 compounds had similar LD-50. Hydroxymescaline subdued the mice more than mescaline. In a few preliminary experiments we found that hydroxymescaline in one human subject had much less activity than mescaline. Of the 3 substances examined by Friedman *et al.* the isoquinoline most resembled mescaline.

Saxena *et al.* (1962) treated Betta with mescaline and LSD and studied their interaction with serotonin and dopa. Drugs were injected intramuscularly in 0.05 ml and the fighting response was studied after 30 minutes. They used 0.1–0.3 μg per fish. After 35 minutes there was a phase of excitation with rolling and jerking movements of the fish. They then gradually calmed down and would neither notice nor attack an intruder. The response toward the intruder became smaller and smaller in time and lasted about 4–5 hours. After 24 hours they were normal when small doses were used but after large doses 3 to 5 days were required. Prolonged administration of mescaline produced reduced awareness which was characterized by the animal swimming against the beaker wall, and loss of equilibrium. Then the fish reduced food consumption, became emaciated, and died.

The fish could withstand prolonged administration of mescaline, up to 23 days. After the fourteenth day fluctuations in after-drug responses stopped and the fish did not attack the intruders.

There was some interaction between serotonin and mescaline. Serotonin given ½ hour and 3½ hours after mescaline produced a violent reaction which was more or less random. If stupor occurred they did not recover. When mescaline and serotonin were given simultaneously a milder reaction occurred, marked chiefly by an increased awareness without fighting of the environment. When serotonin was given 2 hours before the mescaline the fish recovered from the mescaline more quickly. This data suggests serotonin may have partially protected these fish against the mescaline. Dopa had neither an antagonistic nor synergistic effect on mescaline.

Mescaline also affects the spinning behavior of spiders. Christiansen *et al.* (1962) found that 1 gm/kg of mescaline caused female spiders to spin webs with 30% shorter threads. The webs had a smaller catching area and more irregular angles. A higher dose diminished web building. Psilocybin was ten times more active than mescaline.

PSYCHOLOGICAL EFFECT OF MESCALINE ON HUMAN SUBJECTS

We have already given a comprehensive description of the effect of mescaline on normal volunteers at the beginning of this section. Since the effect of all the hallucinogens on humans is remarkably similar the detailed and extensive description of the LSD experience which follows in a subsequent chapter sufficiently describes mescalines action on normal subjects.

Mescaline and Schizophrenia

Mescaline and other hallucinogens were interesting to psychiatrists primarily because they allowed normal subjects to experience for a short time what they might experience for a long time had they become schizophrenic. These chemicals altered cerebral and nervous function in such a way that the final psychological reaction was classifiable with schizophrenia rather than with the neuroses or psychopathic states. In short, models of the natural diseases were not available in the laboratory. Scientists used models to highlight similarities or differences depending upon objectives, knowing the models are not the natural phenomenon. For many years there was a rather futile debate as to whether the mescaline experience was real schizophrenia. The debate was continued by those who stated that the experience was a model, not schizophrenia, and by those who maintained it was not schizophrenia but stoutly insisted that those who claimed it was a model really inferred it was the natural schizophrenia. Fortunately, this type of discussion did keep alive interest in mescaline and served some useful purpose.

Comparisons between schizophrenia and the mescaline experience had been made for many years but a major impetus to do something about this similarity followed the study by Osmond and Smythies (1952). They showed that there was a remarkable identity of symptoms for both conditions. This is shown in Table 2 which is reproduced here.

Schizophrenic patients react to mescaline in much the same way as do normals except that larger quantities are required. The number of variables which influence mescaline and LSD reactions in normal subjects is great. When a subject also has schizophrenia an additional large number of variables are added. Some of these include the duration

TABLE 2

A Comparison between the Psychological Effects of Mescaline and the Symptoms of Acute Schizophrenia[a]

Effects	Mescaline		Acute Schizophrenia	
	Illusions	Hallucina-tions	Illusions	Hallucina-tions
1. Sensory disorders				
a. Vision	XXX	XX	XX	XX
b. Hearing	X	X	XX	XX
c. Body image	XXX	—	XX	—
d. Smell and taste	XXX	XXX	XX	XX
e. Skin sense	XX	—	XX	—
f. Temperature	XX	—	XX	—
g. Synaesthesia	XXX	—	?	—
2. Motor disorders				
a. Catatonia	XX		XXX	
3. Behavior disorder				
a. Negativism	XX		XXX	
b. Withdrawal	XX		XXX	
	(Big doses)			
c. Antisocial violence	Reported		XX	
4. Thought disorder				
a. Pressure	XX		XX	
b. Disturbed association	XXX		XXX	
c. Blocking	XX		XXX	
d. Substitution of primi-tive thinking in the form of visual images for conceptual thought	XXX		XXX	
e. Neologisms	X		XX	
5. Disorders of interpretation				
a. Ideas of influence	XX		XXX	
b. Paranoid ideas	XXX		XXX	
c. Heightened significance of objects	XXX		XX	
6. Delusions	XX[b]		XXX	
7. Splitting	XX[b]		XXX	
8. Depersonalization	XX		XX	
Derealization	XXX		XXX	
9. Mood disorders				
a. Fear and terror	XXX		XXX	
b. Depression	X		X	
c. Indifference and apathy	XX[b]		XXX	
d. Manic symptoms	X		X	
e. Euphoria	XXX		XX	
f. Schizoid humor	XX		XX	
10. Insight	Sometimes absent[b]		Sometimes present	

[a] Key to symbols: X, occurs; XX, marked when it occurs but not always present; XXX, marked and frequent; —, not relevant.

[b] Time factor.

and treatment already given to patients. One would not expect an acute schizophrenic who has been ill one week to react in the same way as one who has been ill in a mental hospital for twenty years.

Thale *et al.* (1950) gave 200 to 400 mg of mescaline orally to 5 schizophrenic subjects. Unfortunately they selected subjects who had not had visual hallucinations at any time before. This, in our opinion, would make it difficult to draw valid comparisons. Furthermore, the dose used was rather small for schizophrenic patients. None of the schizophrenic subjects had any changes in perception during the experience but one patient reported the next morning that he had seen terrifying changes in the features of the examiner and that he had seen strange things he would not describe. Thale *et al.* gave their patients an imagery test before and during the mescaline experience. In this test subjects were asked to report in which sensory mode they imagined 130 stimulus situations. The visual imagery scores of the schizophrenic subjects was initially higher than the control group of normal subjects. Mescaline reduced the scores by 25%. In contrast scores for normal subjects increased 20% on repetition of the test. The increase in normal subjects was possibly a practice effect. Mescaline decreased visual imagery markedly. This is not surprising because mescaline by altering vision and increasing afterimage could reduce visual memory.

This experiment demonstrated that schizophrenics who did not have visual hallucinations normally did not develop them when given small doses of mescaline.

Hoch (1951, 1952, 1955) and Hoch *et al.* (1952) gave mescaline to three different clinical types of schizophrenics. One group were overt nondeteriorated schizophrenics. With very few exceptions they suffered a marked accentuation of their symptoms and much disorganization. Some patients were able to differentiate the mescaline perceptual changes from their natural ones. In general, mescaline made obvious underlying schizophrenic symptomatology. Group two were chronic deteriorated patients. Where affect had not been blunted the reaction was similar to group one. But schizophrenics with marked emotional blunting, apathy, and indifference did not complain of any increase in the severity of their symptoms. The third group, pseudoneurotic schizophrenics, became more markedly schizophrenic with less awareness of reality and much more intellectual disorganization. There was marked underscoring of their emotional patterns and a heightening of anxiety to panic occurred. These patients were dominated by their mescaline experiences and behaved toward them as would schizophrenics. Hoch believed mescaline precipitated a transient schizophrenic episode in this group. Hoch concluded that normal subjects responded to mescaline with organiclike reactions containing some features of schizophrenia, whereas in schizophrenics the psychoses was deepened in intensity.

Denber and Merlis (1955) and Merlis (1957) gave 500 mg of mescaline sulfate intravenously to 25 schizophrenic patients. The experience reached its maximum within an hour. At the fourth hour acute anxiety and most of the mental changes were gone but patients remained antagonistic, hostile, and negativistic. They had regained their previous mental state in 24 hours. The hostility of the patients, in our opinion, may not be a mescaline phenomenon. These authors do not state how patients were selected, whether they were given a choice of not taking the drug, whether they had been properly prepared, etc. It is likely any subject given mescaline against his will, or without proper preparation, would remain resentful and hostile after recovering.

Mescaline produced the usual unpleasant autonomic effects such as nausea, vomiting, sweating, changes in awareness of heat or cold, pain, etc. The most frequent affective changes were a marked increase in anxiety and tension often culminating in panic. In general there was a marked accentuation of the schizophrenic symptomatology. Denber and Merlis stated that mescaline produces a clinical picture almost indistinguishable from the schizophrenic state.

Twelve of the patients were given a series of 12 ECT. Eight were improved. These subjects were given mescaline a second time. In 10 patients, the psychosis was reactivated. It was qualitatively similar to the previous experience but less intense.

Denber and Merlis (1955) measured changes in EEG after mescaline sulfate was injected into schizophrenic patients. For the first hour % time alpha decreased in over half the group. All alpha activity disappeared in 5 patients within 39 minutes. At the fourth hour 13 patients still had these changes. At 24 hours the EEG's were normal in 10 and not quite normal in 6 cases. Nonspecific random beta activity frequently appeared. No delta waves or focal abnormalities were seen.

Merlis and Hunter (1955) examined post-ECT EEG changes following mescaline injection in 8 schizophrenic patients. At the first and fourth hour there was a symmetrical suppression of high voltage, slow wave activity. By 24 hours, the patterns were normal.

Effect of Mescaline on Epileptics

Denber (1955) gave 500 mg of mescaline sulfate intravenously to 12 epileptic patients. The predominant clinical reaction was drowsiness, lethargy, apathy and/or sleep in 8 patients. Two subjects developed somatic delusions. The sensorium remained clear in all. One patient developed an acute panic reaction with agitation, restlessness, fear, and anxiety. She did not have any perceptual changes but became disorganized and paranoid. Twenty-four hours later she was depressed and withdrawn and had amnesia for her mescaline experience. Later it was found that this patient had both schizophrenia and epilepsy.

The EEG changes in these epileptic patients were similar to those found in schizophrenics. Alpha activity increased in some, decreased in some and disappeared in others. Delta activity was decreased in 6 and completely suppressed in 6. High-voltage slow wave bursts were diminished in frequency and amplitude in 3 cases and completely suppressed in 9. Spike wave discharges disappeared temporarily in 2 cases for 50 minutes after injection. One patient developed petit mal for 24 hours. After 24 hours, 4 records had returned to premescaline state. In 4 others recovery had not occurred.

Sensory Deprivation and Mescaline

Mescaline has not been given to subjects who were also placed in sensory deprived environments. This has been done for LSD and it was found that deprivation decreased the intensity of the LSD experience. It is likely sensory deprivation would also decrease the intensity of mescaline's reaction.

Sampaio and Igert (1961) gave 300 mg mescaline to a 57-year-old woman who had been blinded 10 years before. She had become depressed, suicidal, and developed visual hallucinations. When given mescaline she had sensory hallucinations but they were not as clear as the ones she had had before and were unrelated to them.

Comparison of LSD and Mescaline

Matefi (1952) compared the effect of LSD and mescaline on the same subject. In this subject LSD produced a hebephrenic type of reaction and mescaline produced a catatonic kind of reaction. Frederking (1955) also gave both LSD and mescaline to the same subject. In this subject 500 mg of mescaline produced a very powerful experience characterized by a mood alteration between despair and euphoria. A year later he was given 60 μg of LSD which produced a much more circumscribed reaction. This subject reported that the mescaline effect was more profound. Frederking felt there were clear differences between these two compounds.

Schwarz *et al.* (1955) compared the effect of 50 μg of LSD on 11 normal subjects against the effect of 400 mg of mescaline on another group of 13 subjects. The frequency with which changes occurred is shown in Table 3.

Szara (1957) compared mescaline, LSD, dimethyltryptamine, and diethyltryptamine in a series of self-experiments. The duration of the experience was 8–10, 7–8, 2–3, and 1 hour, respectively. The four compounds produced qualitatively similar experiences but in the author the affective reactions were not the same.

Rinkel *et al.* (1961) compared the effect of mescaline (500 mg), LSD (70 μg). and psilocybin (10 mg) on some normal volunteers. They were able to relate the kind of response they elicited to the Sheldonian types.

TABLE 3

COMPARISON OF LSD AND MESCALINE[a,b]

Process	Mescaline (13 tested)	LSD (11 tested)
Perception		
Visual changes	12	10
Auditory changes	2	2
Body image changes	11	11
Synethesias	1	9
Thought		
Blocking	4	6
Loosening of associations	8	4
Neologisms	1	1
Pressure	1	3
Affect		
Anxiety	7	4
Depression	0	3
Manic symptoms	11	3
Withdrawal	4	7
Suspicion	2	3

[a] Taken from Schwartz *et al.* (1955).

[b] Numbers refer to the number of subjects showing change.

Mesomorphs (athletics) developed marked physiological disturbances, euphoria, and very few somatic changes. The intellectual (aesthetic) types suffered mental confusion, disruption of mental function, and few physiological changes but many somatic complaints. Similar changes were found with psilocybin and LSD but they were most pronounced with mescaline.

The Response to Repeated Administration of Mescaline

The kind of experience which comes to subjects when they take mescaline depends upon a variety of factors already described. One of the variables which is very important has been ignored by the vast majority of investigators. This is the effect of repeated administration which should be sharply differentiated from tolerance studies where the drug is given so frequently there is no chance to recover physiologically or psychologically between sessions.

All theories of personality breakdown here for each experience differs so much from the preceding that the simple personality drug theories become untenable. Anyone who has given repeated doses to the same subject is aware of these major differences between experiences. Richards and Stevenson (1961) gave mescaline to each of 16 volunteers twice. On the second administration the subjects were less anxious, more communicative, had more depersonalization, and more perceptual disturbances. Subjects who were high or low on depersonalization and perceptual disturbances tended to have similar changes both times. There was no consistency with respect to mood, communicativeness, imagery, fantasy, perception of body, and paranoid ideation.

Substances Which Potentiate Mescaline

Few substances are known which potentiate the mescaline experience. Tripod (1957) reported that atropine increased the effect of mescaline in increasing the motility of mice. Balestrieri (1957a) found that 20–30 mg of amphetamine, given intravenously at the height of the mescaline experience, intensified the reaction. Methedrine and other amphetamine-like compounds have also been used by therapists to prolong LSD reactions in subjects who might benefit from the prolongation of the experience. Denber (1959) found diethazine (Diparcol) is a potentiator of mescaline.

Substances Which Antagonize Mescaline

Most of the tranquilizers, sedatives and antitension compounds have some blocking action on the mescaline experience. This is not surprising since any chemical which reduces awareness or reduces the level of consciousness should, to some degree, ameliorate the experience induced by mescaline. The fact that so many of these compounds do block the mescaline experience reduces their theoretical interest. For those who are interested in knowing how and where mescaline acts, it is much more important to study substances like succinic acid which blocks the mescaline experience without being either a tranquilizer, sedative, or antitension substance.

BARBITURATES. Before tranquilizers became popular, barbiturates were used to reduce the mescaline experience. Hoch (1951) found that the simplest way to counteract the action of mescaline was to inject sodium amytal intravenously. The affective changes became normal sometime before sleep occurred. Similarly, Vogel (1951) found that intravenous barbiturates were very effective antagonists.

FRENQUEL. Fabing (1955) found that (4-piperidyl)-benzhydrolhydrochloride (Frenquel) was a potent antagonist of mescaline. Two subjects were pretreated with 4 doses (50 mg) beginning two days before they were given 400 mg of mescaline sulfate. Neither subject had any perceptual changes. One had some disruption of his continuity of thought. Two other subjects were pretreated with placebo. They had the normal reaction to mescaline. At the height of their experience they were injected with 100 mg of Frenquel intravenously. Within a few minutes they were nearly normal.

Himwich (1956) found that Frenquel also blocked the mescaline effect in rabbits where it blocked the altering response of the electroencephalogram. But Monroe *et al.* (1957) found in their experiments that Frenquel had little blocking either psychologically or as measured by the EEG.

SUCCINATE. Schueler (1948) confirmed Quastel and Wheatley's (1933) finding that mescaline inhibited respiration of brain tissue when glucose, lactate pyruvate, or glutamate were substrates. The oxidation of succinate was not inhibited. Schueler, therefore, gave succinate to some normal subjects who had received mescaline. Within 5 to 10 minutes of an intravenous injection of 3.5–6.0 gm of sodium succinate, perceptual changes, including visual disturbances and distortions of time and space, were markedly decreased while mood became normal. After ½ to 1 hour the symptoms returned. Hoch (1951, 1956a,b) did not find succinate very useful as an antidote for mescaline. Presumably, he tried it only on schizophrenic subjects so there may be no disagreement between these authors. Stevenson (1957) and Stevenson and Sanchez (1957) corroborated Schueller but they used normal volunteers and larger doses of succinate. The effect was quite variable and in some it did little. In other subjects visual hallucinations and illusions seemed to melt away. Colors lost their quality of intense saturation, became dull, and finally faded. They pointed out that since succinate is rapidly oxidized *in vivo*, it would lose its antidotal action after a short period of time and allow the subjects to reenter the experience.

TRANQUILIZERS. Many workers found that chlorpromazine and later most of the other tranquilizers antagonized the mescaline effect. Schwarz *et al.* (1955) gave one subject, a 30-year-old physician, 400 mg of mescaline sulfate. Three hours later he had a typical mescaline experience with many perceptual changes. Five minutes after he received 25 mg of chlorpromazine intramuscularly, the visions disappeared and the alpha rhythm and amplitude returned to its pretreatment values. Fifteen minutes later he was normal. Hoch (1956a, 1957, 1958) made similar observations.

Denber (1959) compared several tranquilizers as mescaline antagonists. Nonpsychotic psychiatric subjects in a mental hospital were used. Each subject was given 500 mg of mescaline sulfate intravenously. One hour later they were given the tranquilizer being examined intramuscularly. Twenty-five subjects were given 50 mg of chlorpromazine. The mescaline reaction was blocked completely 10 minutes after the injection. Tension decreased sharply as well as anxiety, restlessness, and agitation. The intense emotional reaction diminished, and motor restlessness subsided. After ½ hour the subjects were able to lie quietly. One hour later they were all normal but 3 hours later they were lethargic, drowsy, and some fell asleep. Monroe *et al.* (1957) also found that chlorpromazine blocked mescaline psychologically and on the EEG.

Denber also reported that triflupromazine in doses of 40–60 mg was as effective as chlorpromazine. Prochlorperazine and thiopropiazate were only moderately active but promazine and promethazine were not antidotes. These latter two compounds produced drowsiness and sedation up to 1 hour, but when this disappeared the mescaline experience reappeared.

Diethazine aggravated the experience in 5 out of 6 subjects. From these experiments Denber concluded that the most active phenothiazines had a halogen on position 2 and a 3-carbon linkage between the ring and the terminal nitrogen. Removing the halogen removed the antimescaline effect but left the sedative effect; adding a piperazine ring to the side chain tended to remove the sedative action while leaving the antimescaline effect. Diethazine which has a 2-carbon internitrogen link and lacks a halogen made the mescaline reaction worse, that is, it was a potentiator. This may be related to its atropinelike and anti-Parkinsonism effect.

ELECTROCONVULSIVE THERAPY. Hoch (1951) reported that the mescaline experience was not altered by ECT.

LOBOTOMY AND MESCALINE. Hoch (1951) found that mescaline reactivated schizophrenic psychosis in lobotomized patients but the intensity of the response was much less.

DIBENAMINE. Parker and Hildebrand (1962) found that 5–10 mg of mescaline given intravenously to cats caused a rapid rise in blood pressure. The cat pretreated with 20 mg/kg dibenamine was protected against all the gross effects of mescaline.

MISCELLANEOUS ANTAGONISMS. Tripod (1957) gave a series of compounds to mice and then gave them mescaline. He used motor activity as his criterion of response. Mescaline antagonized the effects of serpasil, chlorpromazine, promazine, meprobamate, azocyclanol, and serotonin. The effect of doriden, phenobarbital sodium bromide, atropine, and benactyzine was potentiated.

MESCALINE AS A PSYCHOTHERAPEUTIC AGENT. All the substances which produce experiences like LSD or mescaline have been used for treating both normal and mentally sick subjects. We would expect that the results would be similar with all these chemicals where other conditions are the same except where the duration of treatment is important. Mescaline produces the longest reaction and so may be more useful in certain illnesses than psilocybin which induces a much shorter reaction. On the other hand, a series of shorter experiences may better fit into the therapists' therapeutic situation and to the patient's needs. Comparative therapeutic studies of mescaline and the other psychotomimetic and psychedelic drugs have not been reported.

Frederking (1953, 1955) recommended that mescaline could be used for facilitating therapy. One subject was cured of sexual impotence with one mescaline experience. Psychoanalysis had failed to cure this patient. Frederking felt the mescaline experience was more overpowering than the LSD one and was indicated where a strong emotional reaction was desired.

Mescaline Analogs

3,4,5-Trimethoxyamphetamine (TMA)

Peretz *et al.* (1955) studied the effect of 3,4,5-trimethoxyamphetamine on animals and on man. TMA in doses up to 80 mg/kg did not produce death in mice. The mice developed tremor, intermittent scratching of their ears. A dog rapidly given 24 mg of TMA developed an acute catatonic reaction for 2 to 3 hours. The animals had all four limbs on the ground, their heads cocked, and a marked droop to their head. Then they swayed but did not fall. They did not respond to calling. After 40 minutes the animal would lie down. A large dose given intravenously slowly developed marked ataxia but no catatonia.

They gave 9 normal volunteers 50–100 mg of TMA by mouth. One to two hours later they were giddy. This was followed by increased movement, an increase in communicativeness, and a decrease in inhibitions. This phase of excitement lasted 3–4 hours. After 6–7 hours they were normal. No visual or other hallucinations were reported. If, however, subjects were exposed to a stroboscope they saw visual hallucinations very similar to those produced without stroboscopic stimulation in subjects given mescaline. Once the subjects had been stimulated with the stroboscope some were able to have visual hallucination without further stroboscopic stimulation. Shulgin *et al.* (1961) with similar doses found similar changes but did not use a stroboscope and elicited no visual hallucinations. But when they gave about 200 mg to 5 subjects quite a different syndrome developed. After one-half hour there was autonomic distress with sweating, tremor, chills, nausea, and dizziness.

For the next 7 hours there were psychological changes which were qualitatively similar to the mescaline reaction but they were less pronounced. The emotional response was very marked. Anger, hostility, and megalomaniac euphoria were dominant. All subjects reported visual imagery. These authors were much impressed with the antisocial nature of the patient's response.

Amphetamines

Connell (1958) collected a series of 42 cases of subjects who became psychotic from the use of amphetamine. Eight took only single doses of the drug and of these, 4 took single doses from 75 to 325 mg (mean 193 mg). Case 1 became paranoid. Case 2 became violent, attacked nurses, and hallucinated cockroaches and worms crawling on the wall. He was paranoid. Case 3 became paranoid and felt so aggressive he sought protection to avoid doing harm to someone. Case 8 was very agitated and paranoid. She sat on the bed and shouted out against the doctors who were persecuting her.

The remaining 34 patients took amphetamine over a period of time, ranging up to many months. In general, the reactions of the total group of 42 were fairly similar.

For a long time it has been taught that amphetamine psychosis was a toxic confusional psychosis characterized by disorientation. But only 3 of the subjects were disoriented and in 2 of these there were complicating factors. The remainder of the group had psychosis very similar to schizophrenia. In fact, 4 patients were given insulin coma treatment which is usually given only to schizophrenics.

The typical clinical picture was a paranoid psychosis with delusions and auditory hallucination. Visual hallucinations were of minor importance and less disturbing than the auditory hallucinations. Out of the 42 patients, 29 had auditory hallucinations, and 21 visual. According to Connell (1958) and Evans (1959) similar psychotic reactions are produced by phenmetrazine (Preludin). Other observors have reported similar psychoses following administration of an amphetamine including Alles, Fremont-Smith, Heath, and Seevers (see Alles, 1959) and Herman and Nagler (1954).

Tolentino (1957) observed 9 cases of β-phenylisopropylamine addiction. Eight of them were psychotic.

Khat (Kat)

Because khat contains ephedrinelike compounds it seems best included in this section. Lewin (1931) gave a brief account of khat and how it was used. Apparently it was taken socially to produce excitation, banish sleep, and promote communication. It was used as a stimulant to dispel feelings of hunger and fatigue.

The natives chewed young buds and fresh leaves of catha edulis (*Celastrus edulis*). This is a large shrub which can grow to tree size. It originated in Ethiopia and spread until its use covered Kenya, Nyasaland, Uganda, Tanganyika, Arabia, the Congo, Rhodesia, and South Africa. The khat trees are grown interspersed between coffee trees.

Khat was used in Yemen even before coffee and it was immensely popular. Lewin described khat markets to which khat was brought in bundles of branches from the mountains.

Khat contains cathine (*d*-norisoephedrine), cathidine, and cathinine. Cathine is also one of the alkaloids found in *Ephedra vulgaris*. It is fortunate, perhaps, that khat is also very rich in ascorbic acid which is an excellent antidote to amphetamine-type compounds.

In animals, khat produces excitation and increased motor activity. In humans, it is a stimulant producing a feeling of exaltation, a feeling of being liberated from space and time. It may produce extreme loquacity, inane laughing, and eventually semicoma. It may also be an euphorient and used chronically can lead to a form of delirium tremens. Galkin and Mironychev (1964) reported that up to 80% of the adult population of Yemen use khat. Upon first chewing khat, the initial effects were unpleasant and included dizziness, lassitude, tachycardia, and sometimes epigastric pain. Gradually more pleasant feelings replaced these inaugural symptoms. The subjects had feelings of bliss, clarity of thought, and became euphoric and overly energetic. Sometimes khat produced depression, sleepiness, and then deep sleep. The chronic user tended to be euphoric continually. In rare cases the subjects became aggressive and overexcited. Galkin and his colleague observed 51 subjects who had taken khat. Of these, 27 became excited, 18 became somnolent, and 6 remained unchanged. The respiratory rate and pulse rate were accelerated and the blood pressure tended to rise. The subjects also had a decrease in the functional capacity of the cardiovascular system.

Methylenedioxyamphetamines

Alles (1959) studied 3,4-methylenedioxyphenylethylamine and 3,4-methylenedioxyphenisopropylamine in some self-experiments. A dose of 36 mg of the second compound produced no change, but an additional

90 mg initially produced increased tension and jitteryness. At 45 minutes, visual hallucinations of curling gray smoke rings were seen. Sounds were remarkably clear and apparently minor sounds were exaggerated. Ales had the out-of-the-body experience common to the hallucinogens. There was a generalized feeling of well-being. The pupils were widely dilated and accommodation was defective.

Alles had different reactions to amphetamine and stated there was a distinct difference between these and the dioxyamphetamines. Hoffer (1962) found that one mg of 3,4-methylenedioxyaminomethylbenzyl alcohol oxalate placed within the ventricles of two cats produced no behavioral changes. The work by Gunn *et al.* (1939) with 3,4-methylenedioxyphenylisopropylamine has already been discussed.

NUTMEG

Nutmeg, available in any grocery store, is one of the most widely distributed natural plant hallucinogens. No public action was needed to control its use because very few people knew it had these interesting properties. However, it has been known and used by some prisoners unable to obtain their more favored drugs and, according to one intelligent informant from the beat areas of New York City, it is regularly used by many interested people seeking different worlds of reality. Toxicological literature suggests that two nutmegs taken at one time can produce very severe physiological reactions and even death. But nutmeg users have taken up to six or more nutmegs in order to gain the desired experience.

Perhaps nutmeg pastry is popular because of the myristicin it contains. A feeling of well-being, following the ingestion of these cakes, might easily lead to a conditioned reaction to this pastry. In the same way it is likely that adrenoxyl is used by surgeons because of the feeling of well-being it induces in their patients, and not because it is a valuable hemostatic agent (Hoffer and Osmond, 1960). The euphorient or relaxant properties of nutmeg and of myristicin should be examined carefully. Too little attempt has been made by modern man to discover safe plant antitension and euphorient remedies.

The active substance is myristicin, a methylenedioxy-substituted compound which differs from mescaline in not having a terminal nitrogen on the side chain. Its powerful psychological activity raises the question of whether the amide group on mescaline is really required for psychological activity.

Schultes (1963a,b) reported that Indians in Venezuela used a snuff prepared from trees of the genus *Virola* of the *Myristicaceae* family. It was called Yakee or Parica. This was prepared from *V. calophylla* and *V. calophylloidea.* The bark was stripped off in the morning before the day became too hot. A blood-red resin, which oozed from the inner surface of the bark, was scraped off and boiled for hours until a thick paste formed. This was dried and pulverized and mixed with ashes of the stems of a wild cacao species.

Nutmeg is the spice representing the kernel of the seed of a dioecious evergreen tree *Myristica fragrans.* Nutmeg is harvested chiefly from the Molucca Islands. The trees yield fruit in about eight years, reach their maturity in about 25 years, and bear seed for 60 years or so. The ripe fruit is about 2 inches in diameter. When mature it splits into two, exposing a crimson aril about a single seed. The dried aril forms commercial mace. The dried kernel is the nutmeg which is freely available.

The seed contains a volatile fragrant oil which varies in content between 5 and 15% by weight. The principal constituent of the oil is myristicin.

Nutmeg extract has been used for many years by alcoholics and addicts when their own preferred chemical was unavailable. Marcovitz and Myers (1944) described a series of 32 marihuana addicts giving 5 case histories. Two of these include statements regarding the use of nutmeg. Thus in Case 4, "In prison and in the guardhouse he took nutmeg extract"; in Case 5, "In addition to marihuana he took 'yellow jackets,' barbital, and nutmeg."

Krantz became aware of three cases of nutmeg intoxication in one year (Truitt *et al.,* 1961). Green (1959) described one case of severe nutmeg poisoning in a 28-year-old woman who ingested 18.3 gm of nutmeg.

Dale (1909) reported that the volatile oil was the active constituent of nutmeg. Cats were very sensitive and were killed by 5 to 10 gm. In man, there was narcosis with excitation and delirium. Power and Salvay (1908) found that dogs were insentitive to nutmeg but Christomanos (1927) fed dogs large quantities of myristicin daily and saw an increase in fat deposits in the liver.

Toxicology

Truitt *et al.* (1961) found that the LD-50 in white male rats when myristicin was given intraperitoneally was about 1000 mg/kg. The LD-50 for East Indian and West Indian nutmeg was 500 mg/kg and 70 mg/kg respectively. After steam distillation the LD-50 increased to 1720 and 1730 mg/kg.

Twelve young male white rats were fed 10 mg/kg myristicin daily for 26 days. The treated rats grew at the same rate as the control comparison group. At autopsy, no abnormalities were found.

Payne (1963) reported two cases of nutmeg poisoning in two students seen at the University of North Carolina Student Health Service. Each student ate about two nutmegs each. After 5 hours, they developed autonomic changes and feelings of unreality. One student was hyperactive and agitated and talked incoherently. Both were "red as beets." They became drowsy after 12 hours and the drowsiness lasted for another 24 hours.

Pharmacology

Truitt *et al.* (1961) found that 100 mg/kg of myristicin given intraperitoneally diminished the mean sleeping time of ten rats given 120 mg/kg of phenobarbital from 162 to 144 minutes. Five ml of a 10% suspension in 6% acacia given intravenously lowered blood pressure about 20 mm of Hg in each of 2 mongrel dogs for 10 minutes.

Monkeys given 100 mg/kg showed respiratory arrest but were revived by artificial respiration.

Animal Behavioral Changes

Doses of 50 to 75 mg/kg IV produced ataxia and disorientation in monkeys but they were not altered otherwise. After 2 to 3 hours they were completely normal. In one monkey, given 1 mg/kg of chlorpromazine one-half hour later, the myristicin masked the typical response. Given by mouth 5 gm of nutmeg produced no change in another monkey.

One cat pretreated with 2 mg/kg of morphine sulfate IP was given 50 mg/kg of myristicin 35 minutes later IP. Within a few hours the cat became catatonic and depressed and the next morning it was dead.

Schultes (1963a,b) inhaled one-third of a teaspoonful of snuff using the V-shaped bird-bone snuffing tube. This was one-quarter of the usual native dose. After 15 minutes, he felt a drawing sensation over his eyes, then a tingling in his fingers and toes. Then he suffered a headache and later his feet and hands became numb. Walking was difficult. For about 3 hours he was nauseated and experienced uneasiness and lassitude. Then he was drowsy and 4½ hours after snuffing it (1:30 PM) fell asleep. The headache was present until noon. His pupils were widely dilated.

Psychotomimetic Properties

Truitt *et al.* (1961) gave 10 normal subjects 2 capsules, one containing 400 mg of myristicin and one an inert substance. Three substances reported no change to either dose. One had a mild euphoric reaction to placebo. Two subjects had questionable responses to myristicin. One subject had the usual psychotomimetic experience with changes in perception (a sense of lightheadedness, a feeling of being detached, distances were more variable), changes in thought (more talkative, some insensitivity to others, difficulty in concentrating) and euphoria with a good deal of laughing. This experience might be compared to the psychedelic experience produced by LSD-25, etc.

Two subjects had clearly unpleasant reactions consisting of anxiety, tension, tremor, and somatic complaints.

One of the authors (Enoch Calaway, III) took 15 gm of nutmeg in acacia suspension at 9:00 AM. One hour later he noted some euphoria and he felt flushed and warm.

The pleasant elated feeling increased. I had been angry about a particular situation. By 10:30 the anger was dispelled and I felt at peace with the world. I wandered out to a leisurely lunch with some friends and felt quite unconcerned about my work. This is unusual for me. After lunch I went to a store downtown and then took the specification for a piece of marble to a stone cutter, and especially returning, I noticed that I was having difficulty concentrating. I experienced increasing feelings of being detached and somewhat depersonalized. My mouth was becoming noticeably dry. After parking my car, I went to my office and lay down on my couch, only to have the very strange feeling of being completely lost. At this point I discovered that I had a pulse of about 124, and so called to some of my colleagues for help. I was apparently highly suggestible because one person suggested a drink of whiskey and I took a small drink of whiskey. Another suggested a dextroamphetamine and I took a methamphetamine tablet. Another person suggested dimenhydrinate and I took one of those tablets.

By this point I was unable to think clearly. When people tried to talk to me I had the sensation of watching a television commercial with the sound turned off. I was aware of sound but I simply could not make any sense out of what was being said to me. I had complete lapses of attention although I remained conscious. I was driven home, and on arriving there I experienced considerable emotional lability, bursting into tears at one point. I ate very little supper, having no appetite at all, and then went to bed. At bedtime my temperature had fallen to 94°, my pulse was still around 100. I was pale and clammy and my mouth was gone dry, but my pupils were constricted.

Although the dry mouth and the inability to concentrate were annoying, I slept off and on through the next day. On Friday, I was aware that I had not had a bowel movement in 24 hours and took a dose of Epsom salt. I was by this point suffering from lower abdominal distension. The feeling of vague detachment continued although I was unable again to drive a car or get about much.

Friday was spent almost solely in bed. I was unable to concentrate, think, or do much effective work around the house. I was quite content to lie still and look at nothing. By Friday evening at supper time I was feeling a good deal better. I had a drink before dinner and went to bed promptly after dinner and slept through the evening again. By Saturday morning I was feeling quite well and was able to drive the car again, although some vague feelings of detachment and unreality were detectable from time to time.

Ten grams of nutmeg with the volatile component removed produced in two other subjects some undesirable effects such as lower intestinal discomfort, unusually heavy sleep in one case, and insomnia in the other. The authors concluded that the other constituents must contribute to the psychological effect of the whole nut.

Recently one of our former alcoholic patients was asked about his experiences with nutmeg. We were especially concerned about any information he might have regarding its toxic properties. His account of its toxicity and its effect upon him follows.

Toxicity. Subjective account by Subject P. R.

With regard to the bad effects of using nutmeg, it's difficult to recall the bad effects of anything one has taken for the pleasure it evokes. I do recall quite vividly some of the bad effects—if that's what they are. One is that once the drug takes control of the body and mind, one becomes very conscious of the heart beat. The drug demands that the user recline as it becomes almost impossible to stand, walk, or even sit. All one wants to do is lie flat on the back for hours and hours with the eyes closed and the mind in a complete state of surrender. Suddenly the heart beat thuds itself into your consciousness. It begins to reverberate inside one like a big pounding drum. What can be very frightening at times is the deadening slowness of its beat. It seems to be an eternity between one pounding beat and the next. Almost as though it were a metronome you find yourself concentrating on each beat and tensely waiting for the next thud that seems to be never coming.

Another recollection I have is the sense of feeling terribly flushed. The head and face become very tight and the flushed feeling gives the impression that a high fever is occurring. On one or two occasions I've looked in the mirror and saw that the face was beet red, the eyes horribly inflamed and the pupils almost non-existent.

I think one could become mentally disturbed if the drug was taken long enough. Most people who use it are prison inmates. They only use it on weekends, and then may go long periods with none. I've only known one man who went on a bat that lasted about a month. He became very vague after the first week. Then he became quite paranoiac and began babbling like an idiot. His condition kept getting worse so that at the end of the month he was completely insane, attacked guards and prisoners both, and was taken out to the mental hospital in a straitjacket. He came back in about six months but was never the same again. Occasionally I see him yet and he's still quite mad, very obsessive about ideals of living and still very suspicious of the world and its people. However, this may not have been wholly due to nutmeg, I don't know.

I don't know if I told you or not that when one takes nutmeg it becomes very difficult to urinate or have a bowel movement. This is also true of being 'high' on any of the opiates. Other than the severe gnawing aches in the bones and muscles I can't recall anything else uncomfortable about taking the drug.

PSYCHEDELIC ACCOUNT. Subject Mr. P. R.

NUTMEG: The Unknown Drug. On the kitchen shelf of most homes sits a tin of the most potent drug, innocently and unknown, a drug sold in every grocery store, used by every cook and ignored by sleuths of the narcotics division of the justice department. Even the hipsters in their frantic search for new kicks overlook its potential for creating dreams and stirring sensuality. This strange exotic drug from the Orient is a household byword and yet within its innocent spiciness lurks a chemical capable of drugging one completely out of the world of reality and sending him into a hypnotic trance where a world of golden dreams and euphoric bliss wraps itself around him.

This drug is found in the common kitchen spice known as nutmeg.

Never have I found anyone who could tell me how the rare individual who has lost himself for days or weeks in the unreal world this spice can induce first discovered that nutmeg was a narcotic as well as a kitchen spice. Maybe some seaman stumbled upon its secret when beachcombing on a tropical isle where it grows? Or maybe the natives use it in their mystical religious rites in the way the North American Indian communicates with the spirit world through the trance of peyote? I don't know. All I know is that it is horrible to take but once digested it gives the individual a peace of mind and body never found in heroin or morphine.

For some strange reason nutmeg is a drug that seems to be used only in prison, and then only by the rare individual. I believe the reasons for this is that in the first place it is a revolting concoction to take. One has to have between six and eight tablespoonfuls. This is mixed into a mug of hot water. It is stirred frantically until the water turns a milky brown. Drinking this mixture is only the beginning. The nutmeg does not dissolve and the user then has to spoon the horrible bitterness into his rebellious stomach as quickly as possible. For the next half hour his stomach tries to get rid of it but heroically the user fights the nausea and doesn't vomit it back up.

After approximately 45 minutes the user finds himself giggling in a silly manner at everything. Regardless what is said; what is done; what is thought; it all seems so ridiculously humorous. Anyone who has smoked marijuana has experienced this complete inability to control laughter at sometime. Some even have had this experience with LSD.

After 30 to 60 minutes of this gut-tearing silliness the mouth and throat begin to dry up as though one had taken atropine. I believe the whole system becomes dehydrated because one may go 36 hours without a bowel movement or a desire to urinate. When the dehydration sets in then the laughter stops and a great lethargy creeps over one. Although one might think they'll lie down and read this is impossible because the eyes become dry, red, contracted to pinpoints and it's impossible to keep them open. The natural thing to do is lie down.

A strange thing happens when one begins to 'coast' on nutmeg. I've taken it in solitary confinement where the bed was only the hard cement floor; and I've taken it where I had a comfortable bed and mattress to lie on. It didn't matter. Once the lethargy took over both felt like I was resting on a cloud. It seems that one has a tendency to lie flat on the back and the lethargy is so great not even a finger or a muscle will be moved unless forced to.

It's when the drug really takes over that beautiful visions replace reality. These are usually very exotic visions. Mine, possibly because I lived in the Far East and still love it, immediately take me back to some tropical isle. But now is when the nutmeg begins to have many of the characteristics of an LSD session. The visions and dreams one experiences begin to lose their continuity and come in chunks of unrelated experiences. One may find his childhood becomes his reality except that it is invariably a happy childhood. Then his visions will jump into a whole vortex of revolving, unexplainable colors. Suddenly, as though it is coming from thousands of miles, music will take on such sweetness and lucidity and color that one becomes lost in it. You find yourself hung up on a bar and then hurry like hell to catch up with the rhythm and notes again. Usually the music you've been listening to is from the prison radio. Sometimes, just as in marijuana, one can hear a whole symphony played in the most exquisite manner when there's no music being played at all. Voices, speaking to you, are also part of the experience.

Unlike both LSD and marijuana—I'm speaking only of my own experiences now—when someone speaks to me while in a nutmeg coma I can wrench myself back to reality and know what they're saying. The only problem is that it seems like ten minutes between their question and my answer and my speech is very slow and thick.

Time loses all meaning just as in LSD. One also likes themselves when under nutmeg and almost becomes childlike in the ability to understand yourself and forgive yourself. The user becomes very sensual under its influence and although the effects are with him from 24 to 36 hours he usually has an erection most of the time.

I've only taken it once when a free man and this was once I was very sick with a heroin habit. I got many of the same results as I did in prison except that the heroin sickness made it wear off quickly and I found I was ten times as sick afterwards with my habit.

To get back to the sensuality one experiences, sex images become very vivid and pulsating. With no conscious thought of whether a guard will catch you or not, one finds himself fondling his penis with the greatest pleasure he's ever experienced. Soon he begins to masturbate and the sex images become so real they're in the cell with you. It seems to take hours and hours before the final orgasm but in all those hours one has the sensation that he is having an orgasm except there's no ejaculation. When ejaculation does occur, it also seems to be prolonged for at least an hour and although marijuana can give one a tremendous sensation during sexual intercourse, I know of nothing that creates such sexual pleasure as nutmeg. I've never had actual intercourse under its influence but I feel sure if a man and woman both experienced the same sensuality as the convict does in prison masturbating under its influence, one of them would go insane with pleasure.

Another similarity to marijuana that one experiences with nutmeg is the development of a voracious appetite, especially for sweets. And just as one gets the 'chuck-horrors' under the influence of marijuana so that even a bite of dry bread tastes like the most delightful food in the world, the same thing happens with nutmeg.

I've never had a desire for food with LSD although, like nutmeg, I've had a huge thirst for fruit juices.

Whether the drug of nutmeg stays with one 24 or 36 hours one really doesn't sleep. But he is in a sleep stupor and capable of shutting out all noises that are obnoxious. There seems to be no sensation of cold when high. Although many nights in the 'hole' were horror to me because of the cold and I had no covers, on the days or nights that a buddy was able to smuggle in nutmeg I felt no discomfort at all. Neither does it matter whether one is in a lighted place or in pitch darkness. The eyes are closed and one sees most of the visions in erotic colors anyway. I think possibly the greatest similarity nutmeg has to LSD is the sensation of going back and back in time to ages one has only read about. Another is the complete loss and the lack of need for time as we know it.

When the drug finally wears off one sinks into a deep slumber. But the awakening is torture. The after-effects of nutmeg are actually painful. Every bone and muscle in the body aches as though one had malaria. The eyeballs set up a throbbing pain all their own. The nose runs frantically and a great deep depression sets in. Although in prison—unless in solitary confinement—one has to go to work if he is not so sick that it's impossible. No one reports sick to the doctor with a nutmeg hangover. But to save your soul it's impossible to work. All one can do is find a quiet spot and t⁻ ⁻ to massage the ache out of the legs, shoulders and arms. I think possibly this also accounts for the fact that very few convicts ever indulge. When you do, you time it for a weekend.

Strangely, you rarely see a narcotic drug addict or an alcoholic reverting to nutmeg in prison. It's usually those who have smoked considerable hashish or marijuana and this is the closest kick they come to it. Never have I known anyone who used it daily and was addicted; and I've never seen anyone take it on the outside.

3-Methoxy-4,5-methylenedioxyamphetamine

Shulgin (1964) synthesized this compound from myristicin. When given to mice it affected them quantitatively and qualitatively as if given trimethoxyamphetamine. In human subjects there was some activity at 1 mg/kg. With 2 mg/kg it was like mescaline. It had three times the potency of mescaline. When an ethylene bridge group was used the activity was reduced markedly.

Asarone

Acorus calamus is a plant known in Asia, Europe, and North America for its medicinal properties. It was also known as flag root, rat root, and sweet calomel. During the great depression of the 1930's it was chewed in England by people unable to buy tobacco.

Recently one of our informants well acquainted with the habits of the Indians of northern Canada, reported his personal experiences with rat root collected in northern Alberta by the Cree. He reported that nearly all the Indians over age 40 used rat root regularly but the younger Indians were unfamiliar with it and its use was discouraged by physicians who practiced there. Rat root users seemed to be healthier, and were not subject to alcoholism. The Indians used rat root (a) as an antifatigue medicine (they chewed about 1 inch of the dried root which had a diameter equal to a pencil); (b) as an analgesic for relieving toothache, headache, etc; (c) for relief of asthma; (d) for oral hygiene, and (e) to relieve hangover.

Our informant had over the years tested these medicinal qualities and generally confirmed them. It was particularly effective for alleviating fatigue. On one occasion, he walked 12 miles in the northern woods to fight a forest fire. He was out of condition and was exhausted at the end of the march. He chewed and swallowed 2 inches of rat root. Within 10 minutes the fatigue vanished and on the return march he seemed to be walking 1 foot above the ground and felt wonderful. The effect was very unlike amphetamine. On his return home he was very exhausted but after a night's sleep was normal.

The informant and his wife, a trained psychiatric nurse, were both sophisticated subjects with hallucinogens. They had taken LSD several times in well-controlled experiments at one of our research laboratories. They had both taken 10 inches of rat root 5 times and both agreed it produced an experience very similar to LSD.

The active principals in *A. calamus* are asarone and β-asarone, isolated by Baxter and Kendel (1961).

1, 2, 4-Trimethoxy-5-
propenylbenzene

The pharmacology of asarone and β-asarone has been examined by Sharma *et al.* (1961), Chaudhury *et al.* (1957), Dandiya and Sharma (1962), and Das *et al.* (1962).

Asarone relaxed isolated ileum of rat, guinea pig, and rabbit. It was weaker than papaverine. Its antispasmodic action against acetylcholine, histamine, and barium chloride was weaker than papaverine. But it had a slight relaxant effect on dog trachea preparations comparable to papaverine. Finally, it protected a guinea pig against experimental asthma produced by acetylcholine or histamine aerosoles. Its use in Ayurvedic medicine as a sedative and for bronchitis, asthma, diarrhea, and dysentery is not so far-fetched.

Another source of asarone was the wild carrot fruit collected in Central Asia (Pigulevskii *et al.*, 1961; Pigulevskii and Kovaleva, 1962). The *Daucus carota* contained asarone but caucasian plants did not. The Asian carrot fruit also contained *l*-pinene, -myrcene, -bergamotene, -β-bisabolene, -asarone, and -carotol.

Recently Dandiya and Menon (1965) found that asarone antagonized the action of mescaline on rats. It also protected them against *d*-amphetamine more effectively than did chlorpromazine.

Kava Kava

Kava kava (also kawa, awa, yagona, kawa kawa, and wati) is one of the psychologically active plants in common use in the islands of the Pacific. Natives in main areas of the South Pacific have used kava kava as a national beverage to relax, to ease pain and to produce sleep.

According to Steinmetz (1960), the Swedish botanist Daniel Carl Solander and the artist Sydney Parkinson accompanied Captain James Cook on his first voyage in 1768–1771. These three were the first white men to observe the kava kava ceremonies and its effect upon man. Lewin (1886) was the first psychopharmacologist to study it in detail.

When used in moderation kava kava is a mild social euphorient and from the published accounts it is somewhat less dangerous than alcohol. After alcohol was introduced into the South Seas the use of kava kava which was much less potent decreased temporarily. But recently kava kava beverage has come back into general use. Many alcoholics residing on the Pacific were cured when they replaced alcohol with kava kava. In large doses kava kava is hallucinogenic. The structure of the active alkaloids extracted from kava kava is very similar to myristicin found in nutmeg and asarone found in rat root.

Geographical Distribution

According to Lewin (1931) kava kava was confined to the inter-tropical zone between 23° north latitude to 23° south latitude and from 135° east longitude to 130° west longitude. It was grown and used in New Guinea where the inebriating beverage was called keu, in the Carolines where missionaries jealously destroyed many plantations, in the Solomon Islands in the New Hebrides, Fiji Islands, Samoa, the Society Islands, Sandwich Islands, and in Tahiti where by 1930 it was no longer known to the natives. In 1908 Samoa exported over 70,000 lb. It is no longer grown in Tahiti or in the Philippine Islands (Steinmetz, 1960).

Botany

Kava kava is prepared from the plant *Piper methysticum* Forst. It grows best up to 1000 feet above sea level in cool, moist highlands. It reaches a height of 6–8 feet here. Where summer temperatures are between 80° and 90°C with sufficient sunlight it will grow densely to 20 feet. The plant bears fruit in 2½ to 3 years and is propagated by cuttings. It is a commercial crop in Fiji and in other islands.

Five varieties are cultivated in Fiji, 3 white and 2 black. The white varieties are considered the best source, but they mature 1 year later. The black varieties are preferred for the commercial crop.

Allied species are present in other regions; *Piper excelsum* Forst in New Zealand used by the Maoris as an infusion for headache, *Piper latifolium* Forst in the Marquesas islands called avavahai, *Piper planta-giveum* Schleit in West Indies and Mexico used like kava kava as a narcotic.

HARVESTING THE ROOTSTOCK

The rootstock is just below the surface of the ground. It reaches 3–5 inches thick in 2½–4 years after planting. Older root patches become heavy and knotted and gather strength and flavor. After 6 years, the rootstocks may reach 20 lb; after 20 years they may weigh 100 lb.

After harvesting, the rootstocks are scraped, cut into pieces, and dried in the sun or placed on platforms.

Preparation of Kava Kava

The customs of preparing and drinking kava kava was intimately bound to the social and religious practices of the natives. Before the missionaries interfered with the native use of kava kava the plantations were divided into 3 parts. The best was reserved for evil gods and was taboo. The second was reserved for the Atu, the gods of sleep and the last part was reserved for the family. More recently the gods have been given very little.

Old or young roots were cleaned, debarked, and cut into small pieces. The roots were then masticated (Tonga method) or crushed between stones (Fiji method). The chewers, young men or women, first cleaned their hands and mouths, then chewed the roots slowly until the root was fine and fibrous. They were not allowed to swallow any. After adequate chewing the material was place in large wooden bowls whose capacity was 2–6 liters. At the start of the ceremony these were filled with water. After the chewed root had been steeped for some hours the residue was removed and the infusion was ready for drinking.

The infusion was a dirty grayish brown or grayish white liquid which still contained a fair amount of fibrous detritus. On settling the liquid was a light or dark brown color. Lewin described the taste of this drink as insipid to very bitter, aromatic biting, soapy or astringent. The more thoroughly the roots were chewed or crushed the more resin was extracted and the more intense the taste. We have drunk small quantities of kava kava extract several times and can confirm Lewin's apt descriptions.

The Ceremony

Kava was consumed during festivals and ceremonies for example when planting trees, palavering with other tribes discussing public affairs, entertaining guests. It was also used as a medicine and as a daily beverage. Samoans drank kava kava before medicines. During festivals held to honor foreigners kava kava feasts were sometimes held at night. The new Hebrides had public kava kava houses and in Samoa a public square was used. The ceremonies varied from area to area. In the Fiji Islands natives sang and danced while brewing the kava kava. Few places still retain their ancient customs. The ceremonies have been abbreviated or even abolished possibly to avoid the critical scrutiny of the white missionaries.

The Hawaiians used kava kava for inducing relaxation. The nobles used it socially for pleasure, the priests ceremoniously and the working class for relaxation. It was given to mediums and seers to enhance their psychic powers. It was used to increase inspiration and to assist contemplation. It seems to have been employed in the way some investigators have tried to use LSD and psilocybin.

Psychological Activity

According to Lewin (1931), kava when carefully prepared and in small quantities produced mild euphorient changes. It reduced fatigue, and brightened the intellect. Appetite was improved. Some visitors preferred it to champagne.

Larger quantities produced a carefree and happy state with no mental or physical excitation, Lewin classed it as a real euphorient which in the beginning made speech more fluent and lively and increased sensibility to subtle sounds. The subjects were never angry, agressive and noisy.

When very large doses or extremely potent kava kava was used the beverage was narcotic or sedative, kava drinkers' legs became tired and weak, their muscles were controlled poorly; their gait unsteady, and they appeared to be drunk. There were visual and auditory changes, but not often of an unpleasant kind. Kava drinkers eventually fell asleep. Many white men have described their magical feeling while their legs were paralyzed, followed by sleep lasting a few minutes to many hours accompanied by incoherent dreams. Many white men became habitués of kava.

KAVA KAVA PREPARED BY CHEWING. In moderation, it is a narcotic. Sensory nerves are paralyzed. Muscles are first stimulated, then paralyzed, but it does not impair mental alertness. In contrast to alcohol, the person under the influence of kava kava is quiet, tranquil, and friendly.

If large quantities are consumed, vision is disturbed, pupils are dilated, walking is difficult, gait is staggering, and the subjects wish only to sleep. According to Steinmetz, kava kava has been described as the most powerful soporific in existence. But it is a spinal depressant, not a cerebral depressant. A glass of kava kava beverage will produce sound sleep within one half hour. After a few hours the subject awakens feeling normal. There are no hangover effects.

KAVA KAVA PREPARED BY GRATING OR POUNDING. This preparation produces a very different effect. The effect is primarily tonic and stimulant. Although its taste is pungent, it has an agreeable lilaclike odor. This drink is given to the sick and those convalescing.

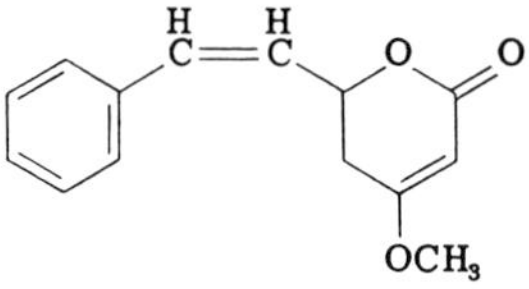

Kawain 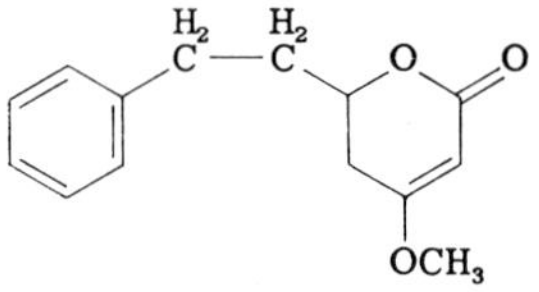   Dihydrokawain

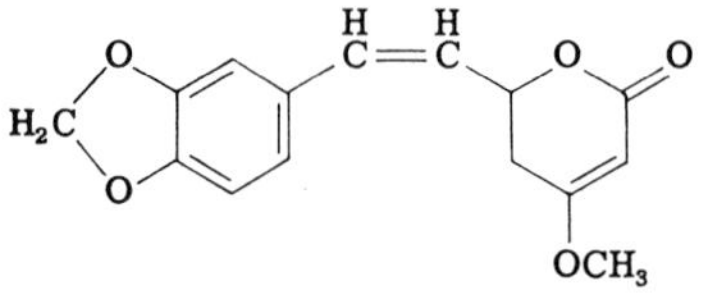

Methysticin 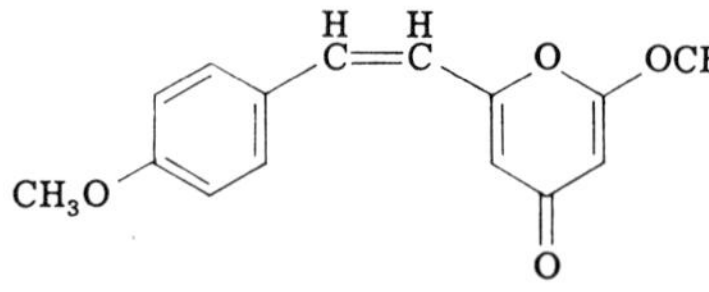   Yangonin

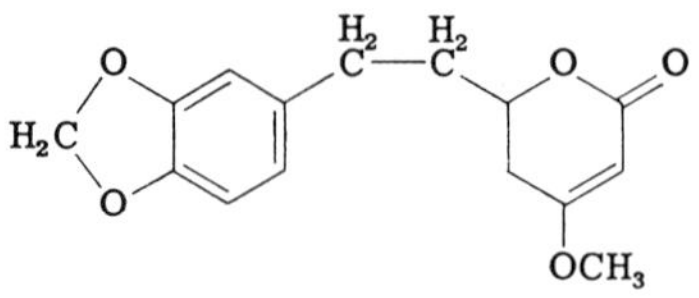

Dihydromethysticin

FIG. 3. Some compounds found in kava kava.

Chemistry

The chemistry of kava kava has been described by Steinmetz (1960) and Klohs *et al.* (1959a,b). The compounds isolated from kava kava are shown in Fig. 3.

Apparently dihydrokawain and dihydromethysticin are the two active ingredients of kava kava. The active structure. is as follows:

The saturated lactone ring is chiefly responsible for the narcotic property of these kawain chemicals.

Pharmacology

Klohs *et al.* (1959b) found that a chloroform extract of *Piper methysticum,* methysticin, and dihydromethysticim were quite effective in protecting mice against the lethal effect of strychnine when yangovin afforded no protection. All the compounds prolonged pentobarbital sleeping time, but dihydromethysticin was the most active. A dose of 60 mg/kg prolonged sleeping time over 400%. There was a marked synergistic effect when several of the compounds were combined which explained the marked potency of crude extracts.

Additional pharmacological data was provided by Keller and Klohs (1963). Dihydrokawain and dihydromethysticin were sedative for mice, rats, cats, and rabbits. For cats the dose was 50 mg/kg. Higher doses produced atixia. The animals slept 2 to 10 hours. There was no change in blood pressure or heart rate. In the rabbit dihydrokawain increased spindle action in the electroencephalogram and narcotic doses produced slow waves.

Hart *et al.* (1960) prepared a water percolate of kava kava root. (1 gm/ml). Intraperitoneal administration of 0.1–0.5 ml/kg of the percolate increased ease of handling mice and reduced activity cage counts to one half without producing depression. Intracarotid injection of 0.2 ml in a cat given pentobarbital produced cortical synaptic inhibition in the transcallosal preparation. It was equivalent to 40 μg serotonin. These effects were similar to those found for LSD and were consistent with a CNS inhibitory effect found for other psychotomimetics, euphorients, and tranquilizers.

Meyer and Meyer-Burg (1964) found that dihydromethysticin and dihydrokavain were anticonvulsant for mice and rats at doses which produced few symptoms. A single dose of 25 mg/kg of dihydromethystium (or 60 mg/kg of dihydrokavain) intraperitoneally, elevated the threshold to maximal electroshock seizure. Diphenylhydantoin, mysoline, and phenobarbital were more active anticonvulsants but as their toxicity was higher the protective indices were about the same. The dihydromethysticin protected animals for 6–8 hours.

Clinical Uses of Kava Kava

Kava kava is available in some pharmacies as an alcoholic extract of Rhizoma methystici. It has been considered to have antibacterial properties. Steinmetz (1960) suggested that a combination of antiseptic and narcotic properties would warrant clinical studies for a variety of conditions. Keller and Klohs (1963) gave 500 mg of dihydromethysticin per day to some schizophrenics. It did not help them. It did have mild tranquilizing effects. We would suggest that clinical trials would be best made for anxious tense or depressed patients.

Toxicity

Lewin described the following changes in those who chronically took large quantities of kava, mental weakness, red, inflamed, blood shot, dull bleary eyes, extreme emaciation, marked tremor of the hands, and numerous skin eruptions. Chronic intoxication was called kawaism. Keller and Klohs (1963) reported that schizophrenic subjects on a dose of 300–800 mg per day developed an exfoliative dermatitis characterized by a dry scaly skin.

Kava kava can be addicting especially for chewers. Kava kava addicts develop inflamed eyes, a scaly ulcerous skin, and are generally physically deteriorated. Habitual drinkers become intoxicated more quickly than occasional ones (Gatty, 1955–1956).

Safrole

Another chemical in this series is safrole, the principal component of oil of sassafras, Brazilian sassafras oil and oil of *Illicium parviflorum*. It is also a minor component of cinnamon leaf oil, California laurel oil, American wormseed oil, camphor oil, and nutmeg. It was very commonly used in the United States until 1960 as a flavoring agent for the beverage root beer and of course, was present in sassafras tea. Its structure is given here.

Safrole is very similar in structure to myristicin and asarone. For this reason we would expect it to have psychological effects such as euphoria in small doses and the hallucinogenic experience in large doses.

However, it is no longer allowed in foods. Long *et al.* (1963) reported they had confirmed its carcinogenic properties in animals where it increased the incidence of tumors. It had been known it was hepatatoxic. For these reasons its use in foods was prohibited.

Cases of poisoning in children have been reported by Abbott *et al.* (1961) and Craig (1953). Craig reported toxic quantities killed by central paralyses of respiration. Symptoms appeared in 10–90 minutes. Vomiting and shock were common. Five children under age 2½ were poisoned. Three were very dizzy, 2 became stuporose and 1 was ephasic. One child responded dramatically to an injection of nikethamide.

Sympathomimetic Amines

Only within the past two decades has there been some clarification of the relative roles of noradrenaline and adrenaline in nervous activity. But there have been very few published studies which deal with their central psychological activity. This is not surprising since noradrenaline became available very recently and adrenaline was too toxic to use for human studies. Cannon's work clearly implicated adrenaline as a mediator of anxiety, perhaps of affect. There was some reluctance to accept the fact that the manifestations of anxiety which followed the injection of adrenaline were indeed a "real" anxiety. Landis and Hunt (1935) believed adrenaline did produce a real anxiety, that there was a genuine emotional change. All the physiological components of anxiety were produced but whether or not the subject accepted the subjective changes as real anxiety depended upon their ability to equate the experience with previous nondrug anxieties.

For the vast majority of humans there rarely is a dissociation between the feeling of being anxious and its physiological or sociological reason and there is a satisfactory explanation for their discomfort. Humans are uncomfortable when the situation which should produce anxiety does not (as do some schizophrenias, or tranquilized subjects) or when anxiety is felt when there is no adequate reason (as in many anxiety states, schizophrenia, and other psychiatric conditions). Thus Landis (1924) and Cantril and Hunt (1932) reported that most of their experimental subjects given adrenaline injections demanded a satisfactory reason for emotion before the experience could be felt as complete.

Lindemann (1935) gave 1 mg of adrenaline to various psychiatric groups by injection. Four patients in a manic excited stage became less excited and appeared clinically improved. Eight neurotics felt a marked increase in tension. Seven schizophrenics became more excited, 4 showed no change in behavior and 2 depressed patients became suicidally depressed. Its chief effect was to increase anxiety, self-concern, and tension and in exaggerating instinctual needs with aggravation of conflict. There should be no further quarrel with the finding that adrenaline can induce anxiety (Altschule, 1954). There is no doubt adrenaline is the first member of a class of chemicals which produce models of anxiety. Perhaps a useful term for this experimental neuroses would be model neuroses. This could be defined as any chemical which in nontoxic doses produce anxiety or tension in the absence of changes in perception or in thought. The chief change is in the areas of affect, mood, interest, drive, etc. All hallucinogens in very low doses have a similar activity but they are excluded because of the major changes in perception or thought which follow ingestion of larger doses.

Noradrenaline does not produce anxiety. Swan (1952) found that noradrenaline produced mild symptoms usually unfamiliar to the subjects although fear was occasionally reported.

It is not surprising therefore that compounds similar in structure to adrenaline have interesting psychological properties, that inhibitors of enzymes which destroy adrenaline are euphorients, or deterrents or energizing compounds (Hoffer, 1959).

ADRENALINE METHYL ETHER

These are substances with an ether link on the β-hydroxyl of the side chain of adrenaline (see Heacock and Scott, 1959). One, adrenaline methyl ether, has been studied by Page and Hoffer (1964). Since a free hydroxyl must be present on the β-carbon for the marked pressor qualities to be present, Heacock synthesized the methyl ether as a compound which might have much less autonomic activity. In fact, it has only about 1/300 the blood pressure elevating effect on adrenaline. This made it possible to administer larger quantities. This compound was found to be a mild stimulant of the amphetamine type.

In vitro the steric properties of adrenaline methyl ether prevent its conversion into an adrenolutinlike compound but it can easily be converted into a dihydroxyindole. This, therefore, suggests adrenaline methyl ether should be a safe substance much less likely to produce psychotic reactions than the amphetamines. It is likely it is more rapidly destroyed in the body. However, very little is known about this interesting compound.

Of all the compounds described, adrenaline methyl ether resembles adrenaline most closely. It is a nontoxic stimulant, but whether or not it is hallucinogenic, is not known. We have used it for several years in treatment trials for apathetic schizophrenics, neurotic depressions, and other conditions where we believe there was an insufficiency of adrenaline (see Hoffer and Osmond, 1960). With over 20 cases we have not seen any increase in psychosis using doses up to 15 mg per day. It was not effective in one case of narcolepsy (C. M. Smith, 1963). When 1 mg was placed within the ventricles of a couple of cats with permanent indwelling cannula there was an activation of behavior. They were affectionate, overly active, and much more playful.

A comprehensive account of adrenaline methyl ether (AME) was given by Page and Hoffer (1964). AME is less toxic than adrenaline, produces significant stimulation of the central nervous system but is less active on peripheral cardiovascular and respiratory mechanisms. A dose 100 times as great as for adrenaline is required to produce cardiovascular effects. But the central nervous stimulant effect is apparent at a dose about ten times that required for adrenaline.

The behavioral effects on mice differed from amphetamine and nialamide and was quantitatively similar to imipramine. The acute toxicity in mice was less than 1/20 of adrenaline. The LD-50 IP was 425 mg/kg.

AME, given intraperitoneally, decreased motor activity of mice and salivation produced more rapid respiration and finally clonic convulsions and death. It produced slight ataxia but no sedation at nontoxic doses, whereas adrenaline produced sedation but no ataxia. AME was 1/50 as effective subcutaneously as adrenaline in activating reserpine induced ptoses and 1/20 as effective as amphetamine.

Page and Hoffer (1964) found that AME was clinically useful as a stimulant for depressed patients. It was given in controlled trials to 148 depressed patients. Of the patients, 40% were of a home and hospital for the aged, 36% were long-term mental patients and 24% were out-patients in a clinic. Another 31% suffered from reactive depressions, 28% from chronic brain syndrome with cerebroarteriosclerosis. All had failed to respond to prolonged extensive treatments with various psychic stimulants. The dose ranged from 5 mg (for the very old) to

50 mg per day, with an average of 10 mg per day for the aged and 30 mg per day for the others. The chronic institutionalized mental patients were treated for 15 days to 4 months, the aged patients 4 months and the out-patients 3 months.

Regular evaluations established that 67% experienced a definite stimulation of the central nervous system in 4 weeks or less. Of the aged 90% were less depressed. Overstimulation was seen in nearly half the cases but this was readily controlled by daily mean oral doses of 235 mg of promazine. No cardiovascular reactions were seen.

The psychic effect of AME was within the general class of methylphenidate.

AME is therefore indicated for treatment of depression in nonpsychotic aged patients, in institutionalized and out-patients suffering from reactive depressions and motor retardations, and in mixed neuroses and personality disorders. However, in two cases with severe psychoses depression subsided dramatically. There were few side effects. Occasionally insomnia occurred which was readily controlled with barbiturates.

AME is also indicated for what might be termed the chronic housewife syndrome. This occurs in many normal women raising their families and is characterized by a general malaise and fatigue worse in the morning just after arising but which gradually improves during the day. By evening they are much more alert and cheerful (at a time when many husbands are tired and disinclined to engage in further strenuous or stimulating adventures).

These subjects also suffer from irritability and nervousness because they are unable to cope with their daily work in a manner to which they had become accustomed. One such subject, age 42, was treated in a double blind design with 5 mg as follows (Hoffer, 1964):

Design

She was given 10 packages numbered from 1 to 10. Each package contained seven 5-mg capsules of either placebo or of AME, that is, she would take either one or the other for the entire week. Each day the subject kept a diary in which she recorded her response. She was told that two new forms of the same compound which had previously been helpful were being tested but it was impossible to tell by their appearance which capsules were placebo or active. The daily diary consisted of reports on the following: fatigue, irritability, mood, ability to work, tension, desire to eat, and general impression. The subject was continuously at home and did not receive any psychotherapy at any time. At the end of each week she mailed her report to Dr. Hoffer.

Scoring

The following scoring scheme was used. For any day for each category, she was given a score of zero if she reported changes as "no," "none," "normal," or "not much"; ½ if the following adjectives appeared: "some," "a bit more," "unhappy for a short while," "not so good," "a bit," "unhappy for a short while," or "once," but all for a sufficient psychological reason. She was given a score of 1 if the description "yes," or "once," without sufficient reason occurred.

For example her report for Sunday of the second week appears in the following tabulation.

Category	Change	Score
Fatigue	None	0
Irritability	None	0
Mood	Unhappy for a short while	½
Ability to work	Good	0
Tension	Once (after E's call)	½
Desire to eat	Not much	0

The call referred to an episode when her young daughter flying home from Chicago was landed at a strange airport because of flying conditions and phoned her mother long distance. Thus her total score for Sunday was 1.

Results

The scores for each of the 11 weeks of the study are shown in Table 4. On the eleventh week she took the same preparation she had taken earlier and which she knew to be active.

The first week she did not follow the items listed but described her reactions in general terms. Her score was therefore estimated. The first week's scores are omitted from all calculations.

The scores for individual categories are shown in Table 5.

When total scores only are considered there is no overlap whatsoever and the score alone correctly predicts whether placebo or adrenaline methyl ether was used that week. In the eleventh week the total score reached 8 on AME. During this week the subject's husband was running for a major political office in his locality and the subject was much involved in this. Her husband was defeated. During this eleventh week on AME, her score approaches her best week while on placebo.

Low scores indicate greater normality. It is seen the subject was less fatigued, less irritable, less depressed. and less plagued by hunger

TABLE 4

WEEKLY SCORES DURING DOUBLE BLIND STUDY OF ADRENALINE METHYL ETHER
TOTAL SCORE FOR WEEKS

	1 Pa	2 AME	3 P	4 AME	5 AME	6 P	7 AME	8 P	9 P	10 AME	11 AME
Fatigue	3	½	½	0	2	1½	0	4½	1	½	2
Irritability	3	0	5	0	0	2½	2½	1	3	1	3
Mood	3	½	½	0	0	1½	0	0	2	0	1
Ability to work	3	½	0	0	1½	0	0	0	1½	0	0
Tension	3	2	0	2	1½	½	½	1½	½	3	2
Desire to eat	3	½	2	½	2	2	0	3	0	½	0
Total	18	4	8	2½	5½	8	3	10	8	5	8

a P indicates placebo.

(desire to eat) when she regularly took AME. However, during this interval she was as tense as during placebo weeks. That is, AME controlled all the symptoms but tension. It appears that in this subject AME has not lost the adrenalinelike tension inducing properties.

There is no doubt that AME is a useful stimulant (and much superior to placebo) for this subject. She has continued to take AME for two years at a dose of 5 mg per day and she has remained normal. For the first time in years, she has been able to carry on with minimal interference from fatigue and irritability.

TABLE 5

MEAN SCORES AND THEIR RANGE FOR ADRENALINE METHYL ETHER AND PLACEBO[a]

Category	Mean weekly score		Range	
	Placebo	AME	Placebo	AME
Fatigue	1.9	0.6	0.5–4.5	0–2
Irritability	2.9	0.7	1–5	0–2.5
Mood	1.0	0.1	0–2	0–0.5
Tension	0.6	1.8	0–1.5	0.5–3
Desire to eat	1.8	0.7	0–2	0–2
Total score	8.5	4	8–10	2.5–5.5

[a] For ten-week period only.

Since AME was a definite useful stimulant in this person there must be many more who would respond in the same way since the hypothesis that this subject is unique is untenable (see Chassan, 1960, 1961) and in fact we have seen similar good results on several other subjects.

AME is also useful for stimulating acute schizophrenic patients when combined with either nicotinic acid or nicotinamide. We have treated several such cases with very good results. Mr. T. O., for example, was first seen in January 1960, complaining of extreme nervousness of 3 years' duration. He found it most difficult to carry on his profession and was considering leaving it since he blamed his anxiety on it. He had noted slight visual perceptual changes, his thinking process had become slow, but his affect was appropriate and tense and depressed. He was diagnosed as a chronic anxiety neurosis. He was treated with mild antitension compounds to which he made a moderate response. He continued without medication over the summer but late in 1960 he was seen again in much the same condition as he had been previously. He was started on AME 15 mg/day and did not show any substantial improvement. In January 1962, his condition was reassessed and he was rediagnosed as having pseudoneurotic schizophrenia. He was started on nicotinic acid 3 gm per day on January 5, 1962 without AME. One week later he was much improved, less shaky, with better color and his thinking was clearer. However, the flush embarrassed him in his duties with the public. He was started on nicotinamide 3 gm per day and because he was still depressed he was also given Marplan 10 mg t.i.d. for one week, then 10 mg b.i.d. on February 24, 1962. On March 10, 1962 his mood had not improved. The Marplan was discontinued and his nicotinamide was reduced to 1½ gm per day. He was started on AME, 5 mg t.i.d. on April 21, 1962, he had reduced the nicotinamide to ½ gm per day. He was complaintive, irritable, and paranoid and began to blame other people for his symptoms. He was advised to increase the nicotinamide to 1½ gm per day. One month later he was much improved, cheerful and optimistic and he enjoyed his work. Since then he was continued to take nicotinamide 1½ gm per day regularly and has taken 1 to 3 capsules of AME as needed, that is, whenever he is somewhat fatigued or low. When seen in June, 1963, he was normal, that is, completely free of symptoms and signs and happy with the same kind of work he had much earlier found so depressing.

Several other schizophrenics have shown similar responses to this combined therapy. According to the adrenochrome hypothesis of schizophrenia, AME should be relatively safer for them than other sympathomimetic amines since it probably cannot be converted *in vivo* into adrenolutin.

DISCUSSION

Mescaline is a phenylethylamine and has some similarity in structure to adrenaline. Because noradrenaline and adrenaline seem to be intimately involved in the reaction of the brain it seems logical to relate the known psychotomimetic phenylethylamines to adrenaline. Adrenaline, itself, is a psychotomimetic if it should get into the brain. The presence of the 3 hydroxyl groups gives it its powerful pressor properties and this effectively prevents the use of enough adrenaline to test its central activity as a psychotomimetic. The modification of any one of the hydroxyls lowers the pressor properties and allows the psychological properties to become manifest.

The following modifications in the adrenaline molecule may be made:

1. Addition of methoxyl groups at positions B. These produce the methylated derivatives of phenethylamine related to mescaline and include asarone.
2. Removal of hydroxyls from the benzene ring. This produces the amphetaminelike compounds and ephedrines.
3. The hydroxyls at (B) may be bridged by methylene groups, for example methylenedioxyamphetamines and myristicin.
4. Groups (D) and (C) may be linked to form isoquinolines which are psychologically active.
5. New groups may be added at (A) to form adrenaline ethers, for example, adrenaline methyl ether.
6. Group (C) may join to form indoles, for example adrenochrome, adrenolutin, etc.

There are striking similarities and differences between the four classes of phenylethylamines. The simplest compounds are mild antidepressants in low doses but in single high doses or with constant use with lower doses they are clearly hallucinogenic. They are, however, strong sympathomimetics and have other effects on body chemistry and physiology. Finally they are addictive. The dioxy bridge compounds are less-strong autonomic substances. The few experiments completed suggest that they are centrally active in a slightly different way that they can produce psychotomimetic changes. They have not been used sufficiently to know whether they are addictive. The methoxy derivatives have lost most of their sympathomimetic effect but are more clearly catatonic producing in animals or hallucinogenic in man. TMA which is a methoxylated amphetamine derivative seems to have characteristics of both. It is an hallucinogenic substance in small doses when the subjects are stimulated visually with a flashing light. In larger doses, there is a marked increase in rage, anger, or hostility, but no increase in visual phenomena. The anger rage reactions of TMA are similar to the paranoid states so frequent with amphetamine psychosis. Thus, one can conclude that the phenylethylamine nucleus produces euphoria in low doses, rage in high doses with autonomic effects. Adding methyl groups to the phenol hydroxyls markedly reduces the rage but increases the intensity of visual and other perceptual changes. However, these must remain tentative conclusions since too little is known about the amphetamines. They have not been studied as hallucinogens. It is quite possible subjects given amphetamine and stimulated with the stroboscope would have visual hallucinations. In fact, one of our normal psychiatric nurses developed pronounced visual changes each time she took the usual, that is 5 mg, doses of amphetamine. Another severely neurotic woman developed a paranoid psychosis after a methedrine interview for which she had been given 20 mg IV. She required admission to a mental hospital where she remained several months before her psychosis cleared. She had not taken any amphetamine before.

Finally, there are paradoxical reactions which are mysterious. There are young people and some adults who react to amphetamines with relaxation and ease as if they were sedated. The amphetamines should be reexamined as hallucinogens by giving larger doses to normal subjects who have been treated to block the blood pressure and other autonomic effects. In one case adrenaline methyl ether was given to a female subject who had consistently reacted previously to amphetamine with marked excitation. But adrenaline methyl ether produced a profound sedation and relaxation. She felt completely relaxed and at ease, but was too languid to perform her normal activities and so did not like the effect.

The phenylethylamine molecule could interfere with the biochemical and physiological role of the sympathomimetic amines. Adrenaline is a very reactive chemical which has weak central properties and very strong peripheral effects. There are several ways of altering its structure.

In each case there is a marked reduction in its autonomic properties. This makes it possible to give much larger quantities until pronounced central effects become apparent. The possible compounds are shown in Fig. 4.

1. Psychotomimetic indoles such as adrenochrome and adrenolutin
2. Anti-tension compounds such as 5,6-dihydroxy-N-methylindole and 5,6-dihydroxy-N-isopropyl indole. Adrenochrome can be converted into a nontoxic relaxant quinone indole by the formation of semicarbazides
3. Methoxylated derivatives such as mescaline, etc.
4. Methylene bridge compounds such as myristicin
5. Ethers such as adrenaline methyl ether
6. Isoquinolines

Phenylethylamines probably produce their stimulant effect by replacing amines like dopamine, noradrenaline and adrenaline in some central nervous system neuroses. The duration of this activity will depend upon the rapidity with which these substances are altered by enzymatic action or removed. It is also possible products formed by enzymatic action alter the stimulant properties and cause different effects. In 1954, Hoffer, Osmond, and Smythies suggested a fraction of the mesca-

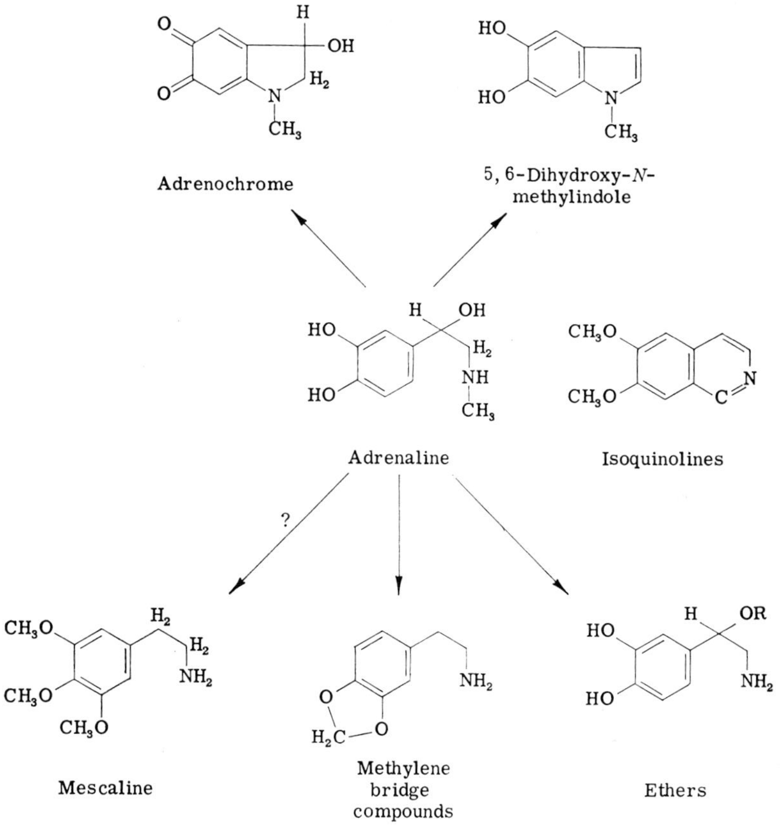

FIG. 4. Some derivatives of phenylethylamine.

line given human subjects could be converted into an indole. Others like Leyton (1963) and Cerletti (1963) have considered this possibility.

The biphasic activity of 3,4-dimethoxyphenylethylamine, Smythies and Sykes (1966) might be an expression of indolization of an amine. The first peak could be due to the stimulant activity of the amine while the second peak could be the activity of its indole. Bergen (1965) found that adrenochrome produced a delayed response in rats about where the second 3,4-dimethoxyphenylethylamine peak was found. The negative findings of Hollister and Friedhoff (1966) might be due to a lack of oxidizing enzymes in his subjects so no indole was formed. In addition, N,N-dimethyl mescaline would be much less easily indolized since the terminal nitrogen is fully saturated. According to Smythies and Sykes (1900) it is a stimulant only as would be expected if indolization discussed here did play a role.

BULBOCAPNINE

Many of the adrenergic compounds are related chemically to the sympathomimetic amines. The peyote plant contains a large number of compounds which are very similar to mescaline and another group which may have been synthesized from phenethylamines. These are the isoquinolines. They have been introduced recently into psychopharmacology. Tetrabenazine is one of the newer psychochemicals. Another isoquinoline is bulbocapnine which is very similar in structure to isocorydine. Bulbocapnine should be a well-known hallucinogenic compound since it was the second one, after mescaline, to receive thorough scientific study. But De Jong's (1945) classical animal studies with bulbocapnine are out of print. In fact, very few copies were sold when the book first appeared and the rest were destroyed because they could not be sold. There have been several human studies by de Jong (1945, 1956), de Jong and Schaltenbrand (1925), and Henner (1928).

A large group of alkaloids are derived from phenethylamines. They include isoquinolines, benzylisoquinolines, protoberberines, aporphins, protopines, narcotine, aconitum the highly toxic delphinium poisons. All of the compounds have an effect on the central nervous system but they require much more careful and systematic examination. Anhalonidine is reported to be an hallucinogen by Lewin. Pellotine produced convulsions in dogs and cats and carnegine caused excitability and convulsions. Benzoquinolizines were nonhypnotic sedatives and decreased brain serotonin and noradrenaline levels (Pletscher, 1957; Pletscher *et al.*, 1958). Isocorydine produced catatonia in animals (Manske, 1954) and in cats it caused catalepsy, salivation, tremor, plaintive mewing, terror, hostility, and apparently, hallucinations (Waud, 1958; Waud and Lam, 1959). Larger doses caused hyperkinesis and later convulsions.

It is not impossible that similar compounds could, in rare cases, be formed in the body. Buzard and Nytch (1959) found that noradrenaline could combine with pyridoxal phosphate to form a tetrahydroisoquinoline *in vitro*. According to Lewis, in de Jong's (1945) monograph, the discovery of experimental catatonia was considered one of the greatest discoveries of modern medicine. Perhaps this was why de Jong's work was ignored so asiduously for so long.

De Jong compared animal catatonia to human catatonia. They were both defined by the following changes:

A. Hypokinetic phenomena including—
   (1) diminished motor initiative
   (2) catalepsy
   (3) physiological negativism
B. Hyperkinetic phenomena and
C. Autonomic phenomena

De Jong found that bulbocapnine produced catatonia in chimpanzees. Two animals were given 10–15 mg/kg. One of them developed typical animal catatonia. It also caused catatonia in the dog, cat, and in birds.

More recently Wada (1962) and Wada *et al.* (1963) placed bulbocapnine into the brain ventricles of two monkeys. After 1–6 mg there was no immediate effect but after 2–2½ minutes they became restless, and responded poorly to the environment. After 5–6 minutes they became drowsy. EEG changes also appeared. The drowsy state was episodic. The behavioral and EEG changes were very similar to those produced by adrenaline, acetylcholine and psilocybin.

Schaltenbrand (see de Jong, 1956) took bulbocapnine himself in 1925 and according to de Jong became catatonic. The film shown at the Society of Biological Psychiatry Meeting, Chicago 1955, by de Jong (1956) was quite convincing. This compound did produce a form of catatonia. A stupor which lasted one hour was produced by 150–200 mg of bulbocapnine injected by vein.

Bulbocapnine was first isolated from *Corydalis cava.* Recently Bin and Kuo-Chang (1964) studied alkaloids extracted from a related plant *Corydalis ambigua* cham et Ech. They compared the pharmacological activity of tetrahydropalmatine with tetrahydroberberine. The structures are as shown below:

Tetrahydropalmatine   Tetrahydroberberine

These compounds produced sedation in mice which was not altered by pretreatment with a monoamine oxidase inhibitor. Evoked potentials from the reticular formation were inhibited. The mode of action was different from tetrabenazine and apparently did not involve either serotonin or noradrenaline mechanisms.

REFERENCES

Abbott, D. D., Parkman, E. W., Wagner, B. M., and Harrisson, J. W. E. (1961). *Pharmacologist* 3:62.

Alles, G. A. (1959). *In* "Neuropharmacology" (H. A. Abramson, ed.), Josiah Macy, Jr. Found., New York.

Altschule, M. D. (1954). *New Engl. J. Med.* 251:476.
Balestrieri, A. (1957a). In "Psychotropic Drugs" (S. Garattini and V. Ghetti, eds.), Elsevier, Amsterdam.
Balestrieri, A. (1961a). In "Neuro-Psychopharmacology" (E. Rothlin, ed.), p. 581. Elsevier, Amsterdam.
Balestrieri, A. (1961b). "Patologia Mentale E. Farmacologia." Padova, Italy.
Balestrieri, A., and Fontanari, D. (1959). *Arch. Gen. Psychiat.* 1:279.
Barger, G., and Dale, H. H. (1910). *J. Physiol. (London)* 41:19.
Bergen, J. (1965). "The Molecular Basis of Some Aspects of Mental Activity." A NATO Advanced Study Institute, Drammen, Norway.
Beringer, K. (1922). *Experimentelle Psychosen. durch Mescalin,* Vortrag auf der sudwestdeutschen Psychiater-Versammlung in Erlangen.
Beringer, K. (1923). *Z. Ges. Neurol. Psychiat.* 84:426.
Beringer, K. (1927). "Der Meskalinrausch. Seine Geschichte und Erscheinungsweise." Springer, Berlin.
Beringer, K. (1932). *Z. Ges. Neurol. Psychiat.* 140:52.
Bernheim, F., and Bernheim, M. L. C. (1938). *J. Biol. Chem.* 123:317.
Bin, H., and Kuo-Chang, K. (1964). *Sci. Sinica (Peking)* 13:601.
Blaschko, H. (1944). *J. Physiol. (London)* 103:13P.
Block, W. (1953a). *Z. Naturforsch.* 8b:440.
Block, W. (1953b). *Z. Physiol. Chem.* 294:1.
Block, W. (1953c). *Z. Physiol. Chem.* 294:49.
Block, W. (1954a). *Z. Physiol. Chem.* 296:1.
Block, W. (1954b). *Z. Physiol. Chem.* 296:108.
Block, W. (1958). "Chemical Concepts of Psychosis." (M. Rinkel, ed.). McDowell Obolensky, New York.
Block, W., and Block, K. (1952). *Chem. Ber.* 85:1009.
Block, W., and Block, K. (1954). *Angew. Chem.* 64:166.
Block, W., Block, K., and Patzig, B. (1952a). *Z. Physiol. Chem.* 290:160.
Block, W., Block, K., and Patzig, B. (1952b). *Z. Physiol. Chem.* 290:230.
Block, W., Block, K., and Patzig, B. (1952c). *Z. Physiol. Chem.* 291:119.
Borsy, J., Fekete, M., and Csizmadia, Z. (1961). *Acta Physiol. Acad. Sci. Hung.* 19:27.
Bradley, C. A., Miya, T. S., and Yim, G. K. W. (1961). *J. Neuropsychiat.* 2:175.
Brown, M. L., Lang, W. J., and Gershon, S. (1965). *Arch. Intern. Pharmacodyn.* 158:439.
Buzard, J. A., and Nytch, P. D. (1959). *J. Biol. Chem.* 234:884.
Cantril, H., and Hunt, W. A. (1932). *Am. J. Psychol.* 44:300.
Cerletti, A. (1963). In "Hallucinogenic Drugs and Their Psychotherapeutic Use" (R. A. Sandison and A. Walk, eds.), p. 1. H. K. Lewis, London.
Chassan, J. B. (1960). *Psychiatry* 23:173.
Chassan, J. B. (1961). *Behavioral Sci.* 6:42.
Chaudhury, S. S., Gautam, S. R., and Handa, K. L. (1957). *Indian J. Pharm.* 19:183.
Chorover, S. L. (1959). *Psychopharm. Abstr.* 1:648.
Chorover, S. L. (1961a). Ph.D. Thesis, New York University, Dept. Psychol.
Chorover, S. L. (1961b). *J. Comp. Physiol. Psychol.* 54:649.
Christiansen, A., Baum, R., and Witt, P. N. (1962). *J. Pharmacol. Exptl. Therap.* 136:31.
Christomanos, A. A. (1927). *Arch. Exptl. Pathol. Pharmakol.* 123:252.

Cochin, J., Woods, L. A., and Seevers, M. H. (1951). *J. Pharmacol. Exptl. Therap.* **101**:205.

Connell, P. H. (1958). "Amphetamine Psychosis. The Institute of Psychiatry." Chapman & Hall, London.

Connell, P. H., and Rodnight, R. (1957). *Proc. Biochem. Soc. B.J.* **65**: Part 1, 7P.

Costa, E. (1956). *Proc. Soc. Exptl. Biol. Med.* **91**:39.

Craig, J. O. (1953). *Arch. Disease Childhood* **28**:475.

Curtis, D. R., and Davis, R. (1962). *Brit. J. Pharmacol.* **18**:217.

Dale, H. H. (1909). *Proc. Roy. Soc. Med.* **2**:69.

Daly, J., Axelrod, J., and Witkop, B. (1962). *Ann. N.Y. Acad. Sci.* **96**:37.

Dandiya, P. C., and Menon, M. K. (1965). *Life Sci.* **4**:1635.

Dandiya, P. C., and Sharma, J. D. (1962). *Indian J. Med. Res.* **50**:46.

Das, P. K., Malhotra, C. L., and Dhalla, N. S. (1962). *Arch. Intern. Pharmacodyn.* **135**:167.

De Jong, H. H. (1945). "Experimental Catatonia." Williams & Wilkins, Baltimore, Maryland.

De Jong, H. H. (1956). *J. Clin. Exptl. Psychopath. & Quart. Rev. Psychiat. Neurol.* **17**:388.

De Jong, H. H., and Schaltenbrand, G. (1925). *Neurotherapie* 6.

Deltour, G. H., Ghuysen, J. M., and Claus, A. (1959). *Biochem. Pharmacol.* **1**:267.

Denber, H. C. B. (1955). *Psychiat. Quart.* **29**:433.

Denber, H. C. B. (1959). *In* "Biological Psychiatry" (J. H. Massermann, ed.), p. 203. Grune & Stratton, New York.

Denber, H. C. B. (1961a). *Psychiat. Quart.* **35**:18.

Denber, H. C. B. (1961b). *Neuropsychopharmacol.* **2**:25.

Denber, H. C. B., and Merlis, S. (1955). *Psychiat. Quart.* **29**:421, 430 and 433.

Denber, H. C. B., Teller, D. N., Rajotte, P., and Kauffman, D. (1962). *Ann. N.Y. Acad. Sci.* **96**:14.

Dengler, H. J., Spiegel, H. E., and Titus, E. O. (1961). *Nature* **191**:816.

De Ropp, R. S., and Snedeker, E. H. (1961). *Proc. Soc. Exptl. Biol. Med.* **106**:696.

Ellis, H. (1897). *Lancet* **I**:1540.

Ellis, H. (1898). *Smithsonian Inst., Ann. Rept.* p. 537.

Ellis, H. (1902). *Popular Sci. Monthly* **41**:52.

Ernst, A. M. (1962). *Nature* **193**:178.

Evans, J. (1959). *Lancet* **II**:152.

Fabing, H. D. (1955). *Neurology* **5**:319.

Fekete, M., Borsy, J., and Csak, Z. (1961). *Acta Physiol. Acad. Sci. Hung.* **18**:85.

Fellows, E. J., and Cook, L. (1957). *In* "Neuro-Psychopharmacology" (S. Garattini and V. Ghetti, eds.), p. 397. Elsevier, Amsterdam.

Fernberger, S. W. (1923). *Am. J. Psychol.* **34**:267.

Fernberger, S. W. (1932). *J. Abnormal Soc. Psychol.* **26**:367.

Fischer, R., Georgi, F., and Weber, R. (1951). *Schweiz. Med. Wochschr.* **81**:817.

Frederking, W. (1953). *Psyche Stuttgart* **7**:342.

Frederking, W. (1955). *J. Nervous Mental Disease* **121**:262.

Freedman, D. X., Aghajanian, G. K., and Ornitz, E. M. (1958). *Science* **127**:1173.

Friedhoff, A. J., and Goldstein, M. (1962). *Ann. N.Y. Acad. Sci.* **96**:5.

Friedhoff, A. J., and Winkle, E. V. (1962a). *Nature* **194**:867.

Friedhoff, A. J., and Winkle, E. V. (1962b). *J. Nervous Mental Disease* **35**:550.

Friedman, O. M., Parameswaran, K. N., and Burstein, S. (1963). *J. Med. Chem.* **6**:227.

Galkin, V. A., and Mironychev, A. V. (1964). *Federation Proc.* **23**: Suppl., T741.

Gatty, R. (1955–1956). *Econ. Botany* **910**:241.

Georgi, F., Fischer, R., and Weber, R. (1949). *Schweiz. Med. Wochsch.* **79**:121.

Goldstein, M., Friedhoff, A. J., Pomerantz, S., Simmons, C., and Contrera, J. F. (1961). *J. Neurochem.* **6**:253.

Grace, G. S. (1934). *Z. Pharmacol. Exptl. Therap.* **50**:359.

Green, R. C. (1959). *J. Am. Med. Assoc.* **166**:1342.

Greenblatt, E. N., and Osterberg, A. C. (1961). *Federation Proc.* **20**:397.

Gunn, J. A., Gurd, M. R., and Sachs, I. (1939). *J. Physiol. (London)* **95**:485.

Guttmann, E. (1936). *J. Mental Sci.* **82**:203.

Haley, T. J. (1957). *Arch. Intern. Pharmacodyn.* **110**:239.

Harley-Mason, J., Laird, A. H., and Smythies, J. R. (1958). *Confinia Neurol.* **18**:152.

Hart, E. R., Ray, O. S., Furgiele, A. R., and Marrazzi, A. S. (1960). *Pharmacologist* **2**:72.

Heacock, R. A. (1959). *Chem. Rev.* **59**:181.

Heacock, R. A., and Scott, B. D. (1959). *Can. J. Biochem.* **37**:1087.

Heffter, A. (1894a). *Arch. Exptl. Pathol. Pharmakol.* **34**:65.

Heffter, A. (1894b). *Ber. Deut. Chem. Ges.* **27**:2975.

Heffter, A. (1896). *Ber. Deut. Chem. Ges.* **29**:216.

Heffter, A. (1898a). *Arch. Exptl. Pathol. Pharmakol.* **40**:385.

Heffter, A. (1898b). *Ber. Deut. Chem. Ges.* **31**:1193.

Heffter, A. (1901). *Ber. Deut. Chem. Ges.* **34**:3004.

Henner, K. (1928). Ceska Graficka Unie S. A. Prague.

Herman, M., and Nagler, S. H. (1954). *J. Nervous Mental Diseases* **120**:268.

Himwich, H. E. (1956). *In* "Lysergic acid Diethylamide and Mescaline in Experimental Psychiatry" (L. Cholden, ed.), Grune & Stratton, New York.

Himwich, H. E., Van Meter, W. G., and Owens, H. (1959). *In* "Biological Psychiatry" (J. H. Masserman, ed.), p. 27. Grune & Stratton, New York.

Hoch, P. H. (1951). *Am. J. Psychiat.* **107**:607.

Hoch, P. H. (1952). "The Biology of Mental Health and Disease." Harper (Hoeber), New York.

Hoch, P. H. (1955). *Am. J. Psychiat.* **111**:787.

Hoch, P. H. (1956a). *In* "Studies in Routes of Administration and Counteracting Drugs" (L. Cholden, ed.), Grune & Stratton, New York.

Hoch, P. H. (1956b). *20th Intern. Physiol. Congr., Brussels, 1956, Abstr. Rev.*

Hoch, P. H. (1957). *J. Nervous Mental Disease* **125**:442.

Hoch, P. H. (1958). *Res. Publ., Assoc. Res. Nervous Mental Disease* **36**:335.

Hoch, P. H., Cattell, J. P., and Pennes, H. H. (1952). *Am. J. Psychiat.* **108**:579.

Hoffer, A. (1959). *Ann. N.Y. Acad. Sci.* **80**:772.

Hoffer, A. (1962). *Intern. Rev. Neurobiol.* **4**:307.

Hoffer, A. (1964). *Mind* **2**:166.

Hoffer, A., and Osmond, H. (1960). "The Chemical Bases of Psychiatry." Thomas, Springfield, Illinois.

Hollister, L. (1961). *Clin. Res.* **9**:181.

Hollister, L. E., and Friedhoff, A. J. (1966). *Nature* **210**:1377.

Huxley, A. (1956). "Heaven and Hell," Chatto & Windus, London.

Keller, F., and Klohs, M. W. (1963). *Lloydia* **26**:1.

Klohs, M. W., Keller, F., and Williams, R. E. (1959a). *J. Org. Chem.* **24**:1829.

Klohs, M. W., Keller, F., Williams, R. E., Toekes, M. I., and Cronheim, G. E. (1959b). *J. Med. Pharm. Chem.* **1**:95.

Kluver, H. (1926). *Am. J. Psychol.* **37**:502.

Kluver, H. (1928). "Mescal—The Divine Plant and Its Psychological Effects." Kegan Paul, London.

Knauer, A., and Maloney, W. J. M. A. (1913). *J. Nervous Mental Disease* **40**:397.

Landis, C. (1924). *J. Comp. Psychol.* **4**:447.

Landis, C., and Hunt, W. A. (1935). *J. Exptl. Psychol.* **18**:505.

Lewin, L. (1886). Uber Piper Methysticum (Kava kava). Monograph, Berlin.

Lewin, L. (1888a). *Arch. Exptl. Pathol. Pharmakol.* **24**:401.

Lewin, L. (1888b). *Therap. Gaz.* **4**:231.

Lewin, L. (1894a). *Arch. Exptl. Pathol. Pharmakol.* **34**:374.

Lewin, L. (1894b). *Ber. Deut. Botan. Ges.* **12**:283.

Lewin, L. (1931) "Phantastica, Narcotic and Stimulating Drugs." (Translation of 1924, German edition.) Routledge and Kegan Paul, London.

Lewin, L. (1964). "Phantasteca: Narcotic and Stimmulating Drugs, Their Use and Abuse." Dutton, New York.

Lewis, J. L., and McIlwain, H. (1954). *Biochem. J.* **57**:680.

Leyton, G. (1963). *In* "Hallucinogenic Drugs and Their Psychotherapeutic Use." (R. A. Sandison and A. Walk, eds.), p. 23. H. K. Lewis, London.

Lindemann, E. (1935). *Am. J. Psychiat.* **91**:983.

Long, E. L., Nelson, A. A., Fitzhugh, O. G., and Hansen, W. H. (1963). *Arch. Pathol.* **75**:595.

Luduena, F. P. (1933). *Compt. Rend. Soc. Biol.* **114**:809; *Rev. Soc. Arg. Biol.* **9**:335.

Manske, R. H. F. (1954). *In* "The Alkaloids" (R. H. F. Manske and H. L. Holmes, eds.), Vol. 4, p. 78. Academic, New York.

Marcovitz, E., and Myers, H. J. (1944). *War Med.* **6**:382.

Marrazzi, A. S. (1960). *Recent Adv. Biol. Psychiat.* **2**:333.

Matefi, L. (1952). *Confinia Neurol.* **12**:146.

Mayer-Gross, W., and Stein, H. (1926). *Z. Ges. Neurol. Psychiat.* **101**:354.

Merlis, S. (1957). *J. Nervous Mental Disease* **125**:432.

Merlis, S., and Hunter, W. (1955). *Psychiat. Quart.* **29**:430.

Meyer, H. J., and Meyer-Burg, J. (1964). *Arch. Intern. Pharmacodyn.* **148**:97.

Miller, E. (1926). "Types of Mind and Body. Psyche Miniatures."

Mitchell, S. W. (1896). *Brit. Med. J.* **II**:1625.

Moller, A. G. (1935). *Acta Psychiat. Neurol.* **10**:405.

Monroe, R. R., Heath, R. G., Mickle, W. A., and Llewellyn, R. C. (1957). *Electroencephalog. Clin. Neurophysiol.* **9**:623.

Mooney, J. (1896). *Therap. Gaz.* **20**:7.

Morselli, G. E. (1936). *J. Psychol.* **33**:368.

Ochs, S., Dowell, A. R., and Russell, I. S. (1962). *Electroencephalog. Clin. Neurophysiol.* **14**:878.

Osmond, H., and Smythies, J. (1952). *J. Mental Sci.* **98**:309.

Page, J. A., and Hoffer, A. (1964). *Diseases Nervous System* **25**:558.

Parker, J. M., and Hildebrand, N. (1962). *Federation Proc.* **21**:419.

Payne, R. B. (1963). *New Engl. J. Med.* **269**:36.

Peretz, D. I., Smythies, J. R., and Gibson, W. C. (1955). *J. Mental Sci.* **101**:317.

Pigulevskii, G. V., and Kovaleva, V. I. (1962). *Akad. Nauk SSSR* **5**:15; See *Chem. Abstr.* **56**:11727.

Pigulevskii, G. V., Kovaleva, V. I., and Motskus, D. V. (1961). *Soveshch. Vilnyus* p. 153; see *Chem. Abstr.* **55**:15842.

Pletscher, A. (1957). *In* "Psychotropic Drugs" (S. Garattini and V. Ghetti, eds.), 468. Elsevier, Amsterdam.

Pletscher, A., Besendorf, H., and Bachtold, H. P. (1958). *Arch. Exptl. Pathol. Pharmakol.* **232**:499.
Power, F. B., and Salvay, A. H. (1908). *Am. J. Pharm.* **80**:563.
Prentiss, D. W., and Morgan, F. P. (1895). *Therap. Gaz.* **19**:577.
Prentiss, D. W., and Morgan, F. P. (1896a). *Therap. Gaz.* **20**:4.
Prentiss, D. W., and Morgan, F. P. (1896b). *Med. Record* **50**:258.
Prentiss, D. W., and Morgan, F. P. (1896–1897). *Nat. Med. Rev.* **6**:147.
Prentiss, D. W., and Morgan, F. P. (1918). *Indian Rights Assoc.* No. 114.
Quastel, J. H., and Wheatley, A. H. M. (1933). *Biochem. J.* **27**:1609.
Quastel, J. H., and Wheatley, A. H. M. (1934). *Biochem. J.* **28**:1521.
Rafaelsen, O. J. (1961). *Psychopharmacologia* **3**:185.
Ratcliffe, J., and Smith, P. (1959). *Chem. & Ind.* (*London*) p. 925.
Ray, O. S., and Marrazzi, A. S. (1961). *Psychologist* **16**:453.
Reti, L. (1950). *In* "Progress in the Chemistry of Organic Natural Products." (L. Zechmeister, ed.), Springer, Berlin.
Reti, L. (1953). *In* "The Alkaloids" (R. H. F. Manske and H. L. Holmes, eds.), Vol. 3, p. 313. Academic, New York.
Richards, T. W., and Stevenson, I. P. (1961). *Southern Med. J.* **54**:1319.
Richter, D. (1938). *Biochem. J.* **32**:1763.
Rinkel, M., Dimascio, A., Robey, A., and Atwell, C. (1961). *In* "Neuro-Psychopharmacology" (E. Rothlin, ed.), Vol. 2, p. 273. Elsevier, Amsterdam.
Rovetta, P. (1956). *Electroencephalog. Clin. Neurophysiol.* **8**:15.
Runge, T. M., Bohls, S. W., Hoerster, S. A., and Thurman, N. (1961). *Diseases Nervous System* **22**:619.
Salomon, K., Gabrio, B. W., and Thale, T. (1949). *J. Pharmacol. Exptl. Therap.* **95**:455.
Sampaio, B. A., and Igert, C. (1961). *Evolution Psychiat.* **26**:287.
Saxena, A., Bhattacharya, B. K., and Mukerji, B. (1962). *Arch. Intern. Pharmacodyn.* **140**:327.
Schopp, R. T., Kreuter, W. F., and Guzak, S. V. (1961). *Am. J. Physiol.* **200**:1226.
Schueler, F. W. (1948). *J. Lab. Clin. Med.* **33**:1297.
Schultes, R. E. (1963a). *Psychedelic Rev.* **1**:145.
Schultes, R. E. (1963b). *Harvard Rev.* **1**:18.
Schwarz, B. E., Bickford, R. G., and Rome, H. P. (1955). *Proc. Staff Meetings Mayo Clin.* **30**:407.
Serko, A. (1913). *Jahrb. Psychiat. Neurol.* **34**:355.
Sharma, J. D., Dandiya, P. C., Baxter, R. M., and Kendel, S. I. (1961). *Nature* **192**:1299.
Shulgin, A. T. (1964). *Nature* **201**:1120.
Shulgin, A. T., Bunnell, S., and Sargent, T. (1961). *Nature* **189**:1011.
Slotta, K. H., and Muller, J. (1936). *Arch. Physiol. Chem.* **238**:14.
Smith, C. M. (1963). *Can. Med. Assoc. J.* **88**:410.
Smith, M. G. (1934). *J. Wash. Acad. Sci.* **24**:10.
Smythies, J. R., and Sykes, E. A. (1966). *Psychopharmacologia* **8**:324.
Smythies, J. R., Benington, F., and Levy, C. K. (1958). *J. Org. Chem.* **23**:1979.
Smythies, J. R., Koella, W. P., and Levy, C. K. (1961). *Biochem. Pharmacol.* **8**:42.
Spath, E. (1919). *Monatsh. Chem.* **40**:129.
Spath, E. (1921a). *Monatsh. Chem.* **42**:97.
Spath, E. (1921b). *Monatsh. Chem.* **42**:263.
Spath, E. (1922). *Monatsh. Chem.* **43**:477.

Spath, E. (1934). *Ber. Deut. Chem. Ges.* **67**:2100.

Spath, E. (1936). *Ber. Deut. Chem. Ges.* **69**:755.

Spath, E. (1938). *Ber. Deut. Chem. Ges.* **71**:1275.

Spath, E., and Becke, F. (1934). *Ber. Deut. Chem. Ges.* **67**:266.

Speck, L. B. (1957). *J. Pharmacol. Exptl. Therap.* **119**:78.

Spector, E. (1961). *Nature* **189**:751.

Steinmetz, E. F. (1960). "Piper Methysticum Kava-Kawa-Yaqona." 347 Keizersgracht, Amsterdam.

Stevenson, I. (1957). *J. Nervous Mental Disease* **125**:438.

Stevenson, I., and Mokrasch, J. C. (1958). *Am. J. Psychiat.* **114**:1038.

Stevenson, I., and Richards, T. W. (1960). *Psychopharmacologia* **1**:241.

Stevenson, I., and Sanchez, A. J. (1957). *Am. J. Psychiat.* **114**:328.

Stockings, G. T. (1940). *J. Mental Sci.* **86**:29.

Swan, H. J. C. (1952). *Brit. Med. J.* **I**:1003.

Szara, S. (1957). *In* "Psychotropic Drugs" (S. Garattini and V. Ghetti, eds.), p. 460. Elsevier, Amsterdam.

Takeyo, Y., and Himwich, H. E. (1965). *Science* **150**:1309.

Thale, T., Gabrio, B. W., and Solomon, K. (1950). *Am. J. Psychiat.* **106**:686.

Tolentino, I. (1957). *In* "Psychotic Reactions and Psychosis Due to B-Phenylisopropylamine and Sympatho-mimetic Drugs" (S. Garattini and V. Ghetti, eds.), p. 585. Elsevier, Amsterdam.

Tripod, J. (1957). *In* "Caraterisation Generale Dis Effects Pharmacoldynameques de Substances Psychotropiques" (S. Garattini and V. Ghetti, eds.), p. 437. Elsevier, Amsterdam.

Truitt, E. B., Callaway, E., Braude, M. C., and Krantz, J. C. (1961). *J. Neuropsychiat.* **2**:205.

Vogel, V. H. (1951). *Am. J. Psychiat.* **107**:611.

Vogt, M. (1935). *Arch. Exptl. Pathol. Pharmakol.* **178**:560.

Wada, J. A. (1962). *Ann. N. Y. Acad. Sci.* **96**:227.

Wada, J. A., Wrinch, J., Hill, D., McGeer, P. L., and McGeer, E. G. (1963). *Arch. Neurol.* **9**:69.

Waud, R. A. (1958). *Can. Fed. Biol. Sci.*

Waud, R. A., and Lam, K. (1959). *Can. Fed. Proc.* **18**.

Wikler, A. (1954). *J. Nervous Mental Disease* **120**:157.

Wolbach, A. B., Isbell, H., and Miner, E. J. (1962). *Psychopharmacologia* **3**:1.

d-Lysergic Acid Diethylamide

Introduction

When Albert Hofmann accidentally experienced what *d*-lysergic acid diethylamide (LSD hereafter) can do to normal human subjects, he began a revolution in psychiatric thought which still has not completed its course. By the end of 1950 only six reports had been published but by the end of 1957 each consecutive year produced 10, 14, 18, 29, 97, 118, and 86 reports and since then about 100 reports per year have been published.

The LSD experience quickly provided ammunition for several major controversies in psychiatry. The first one concerned the experience itself as a model of schizophrenia, the model psychosis concept. The proponents of this newer point of view reasoned that since microgram quantities of LSD could produce such a vivid psychological change it was not improbable that similar quantities of chemicals could be produced within the body and produce schizophrenia. The critics of the model psychosis point of view countered this by denying that LSD could produce something similar to the natural psychosis. They compared it rather to the toxic psychoses.

The second controversy concerned the psychedelic experience used both for exploring facets of the mind and for permanently altering human personality and behavior. These controversies will be discussed in this chapter.

Sources of LSD

Four stereoisomers can be synthesized from lysergic acid but only *d*-lysergic acid diethylamide has the unique psychological properties which we will describe. The synthesis of LSD required over a century of research into the chemistry of ergot alkaloids. A. Stoll (1952) reported that research on ergot began around 1850 A.D. with John Stearn's publication, "Account of the Pulvis Parturiens, a Remedy for Quickening Child-Birth." The first ergot preparation, ergotinine, was crystallized 75 years later. Forty-five years after this it was shown that the strong effect of ergot preparations on uterine muscle was due to these compound ring alkaloids.

Two main sources of LSD are known: ergot from the fungus which contaminates some grasses and some varieties of morning glory plants.

ERGOT

Ergot is the rhizomorph of *Claviceps purpurea,* the fungus which parasitizes the growing kernels in the heads of some members of the grass (Gramineae) family. Rye is the chief grain parasitized but some is also found on wheat and it has worried agriculturists. It destroys the ovaries of the grain and the kernel is replaced by a brown-violet horn-shaped mass which protrudes from the head.

Many years ago appreciable quantities of infested rye appeared in bread or in feed and produced major epidemics of ergotism. The epidemic in France in 994 A.D. killed about 40,000 people and the one in 1129 A.D. in the Cambrai region killed about 1200. No more epidemics appeared when corrective legislation controlled the amount of ergot which contaminated bread grains.

Two clinical kinds of ergotism have been described, the gangrenous and the convulsive. Gangrenous ergotism started with tingling in the fingers, then vomiting and diarrhea, followed within a few days by gangrene in the toes and fingers. Entire limbs were affected by a dry gangrene of the entire limb, followed by its separation. The convulsive form started the same way but was followed by painful spasms of the limb muscles which culminated in epileptic-like convulsions. Many patients became delirious.

Ergotism also assumed two forms in cattle (Simpson and West, 1952). Chronic ergot poisoning produced the gangrenous or classical form characteristized by gangrene affecting the tips of the ears, the end of the tail, and the feet. Pregnant animals often aborted their fetuses. Acute ergotism followed ingestion of large quantities of ergot in a short time. The animals became nervous, excitable, and walked or ran with a swaying incoordinated movement. Farmers have been advised not to feed grain which contains more than 3 ergot sclerotium per thousand kernels but more recently research suggests even this quantity may be toxic (Tremere, 1963). There is no cure for ergotism in livestock.

MORNING GLORY

Involuntary ergotism from contaminated bread is extremely rare but voluntary ergotism may become a problem since it was discovered ergot alkaloids are present in morning glory plants.

Interest in the morning glory arose from Osmond's (1955) self-study with ololiuqui, a Cuban variety, and from the chemical isolation studies by Hofmann (1960), Taber *et al.* (1963a,b), and Genest (1964). These studies began in the Central Americas many centuries ago. Francisco Hernandez first described ololiuqui in 1570 as the narcotic of the Aztecs. In 1954 it was correctly identified as a member of the convovulaceae. This was corroborated by Schultes (1941) and is covered in part B of this chapter.

Ololiuqui [*Rivea corymbosa* or *Ipomoea sidaefolia* (HBK) choisy, or *Turbina corymbosa* (L) Raf] is a large woody vine with broad chordate leaves from 5 to 9 cm long and with many long whitish flowers. The seeds are roundish and woody. It is native to the East Indies, Africa, South and Central America, and the West Indies.

Ololiuqui contains 2 active fractions. One, a glucoside first isolated by Cook and Kieland (1962) is a major component of ololiuqui. Perezamador *et al.* (1964) showed this glucoside is turbicoryn. Preliminary work in Saskatchewan with the pure crystalline glucoside suggests it has interesting antitension properties. The second fractions are ergot alkaloids. Hofmann and Tscherter (1960), Hofmann (1961a,b), and Hofmann and Cerletti (1961) extracted ergot indoles from Mexican *R. corymbosa* seeds and identified ergine (isolysergic acid amide), isoergine (lysergic acid amide), chanoclavine, clymoclavin and lysergol. Of these *d*-lysergic acid amide was the most powerful hallucinogen having one tenth the activity of LSD. The latter is also found in ergot growing on some grasses. Hofmann's controversial findings were completely corroborated by Taber and Heacock (1962) who demonstrated these alkaloids within the ololiuqui seeds were not present because of surface contamination by chemicals or ergot producing spores of fungi. Using the Vining and Taber (1959) method they extracted *R. corymbosa* seeds from the Atkins Garden and Research Laboratory, Cienfuegos, Cuba. Each seed (about 20 mg) contained between 20 and 25 μg of total alkaloid expressed as ergometrine equivalents. The alkaloids were present in the embryo in the hypocotyl and cotyledon portions but not in the coat, in the resinous layer underneath the coat nor in the centrally located membrane. They isolated 52 different fungi from fragmented seeds. They came from the seed coat especially around the hilum. No contaminant fungi were found in the embryo. The *Claviceps* species known to produce alkaloids were not found. Taber and Heacock concluded that the seeds, not the contaminants, were the source of alkaloid.

Ergine and lysergic acid amide were found in the leaf and stem but not in the root of *R. corymbosa* grown in a greenhouse (Taber *et al.*, 1963a,b). The amount increased with maturity until about 0.012% and 0.027% per dry weight of stem and leaf were found at nine months of growth. The seeds did not contain a higher concentration of alkaloid than the rest of the plant tissue until the plant was well beyond the cotyledonous stage. Because there was more leaf and stem than seed, seeds contained only half of the total quantity in the plant. A large number of commercial varieties of morning glory were analyzed. The varieties and their concentration of ergot alkaloids were as follows:

A. 0.04% and higher
   Pearly Gates (California)
   Impomoea rubro–Caerulea praecox
   Rivea corymbosa (Cuba)
B. 0.02–0.039%
   Heavenly Blue (California)
   Convolvulus tricolor Royal Marine
   Ipomoea Pearly Gates
C. 0.01–0.019%
   Convolvulus Royal Blue
   Convolvulus mauritanious
   Ipomoea hybriday Darling
   Convulvulus tricolor Cambridge Blue
   Convulvulus Lavender Rosette
   Ipomoea Scarlet O'Hara

Ergot was not found in any of the following nonconvolvulaceous seeds: mustard, rape, beans, sweet pea, hemp, buckwheat, grapefruit, safflower, marigold, or poppy.

The distribution of ergot between leaf, stem, and root was the same for Pearly Gates grown in a greenhouse as for ololiuqui. However, the chemical composition of the alkaloids varied for different varieties. Ololiuqui contained relatively more lysergic acid amide (the only psychologically active alkaloid) than other varieties. Isoergine and chanoclavine made up 34% of Pearly Gates. Taber *et al.* suggested this could explain the paucity of references in the literature to the psychological properties of morning glory seeds. So many seeds are required to produce an effect that it could be missed more easily, as compared to ololiuqui.

Osmond's (1955) subjective account of ololiuqui's psychological activity is thus explainable since he consumed these ergot alkaloids and substantial quantities of the glucoside. Apparently Central American Indians were good observers and successful in discovering many psychologically active plants.

It is surprising that Isbell (1957) and Kinross-Wright (1959) were unable to corroborate the accounts of Osmond and the Indians. Isbell used drug addicts. Perhaps their addiction had rendered them unfit for these double blind experiments since no significant difference was found. Neither would they be as skillful at introspection as scientists or Indians accustomed to its actions by many centuries of skilled use. Kinross-Wright gave ololiuqui seeds to 8 male volunteers. They received 0.25–2.25 gm (the latter from 125 seeds) of crushed seeds. Two subjects suffered emesis and later mild gastrointestinal discomfort. No subject reported any psychological changes and none were observed.

Kinross-Wright then prepared ethereal and alcoholic extracts of the seeds and found these extracts were inactive even though he consumed an extract from one gram of seeds (50). He concluded that *Rivea corymbosa* had no psychopharmacological activity and that Osmond's findings (and those of the Indians) were due to an overidentification with the ololiuqui legend. His negative results were probably due to the solvent used in making the extraction. These alkaloids were probably present as salts which are relatively insoluble in ether or alcohol. They must first be hydrolyzed. Vining and Taber (1959) first treated ololiuqui seeds with 10% ammonium hydroxide before extracting them with ether. Taber and Heacock (1962) extracted the seeds 3 times with alkaline ether.

Ololiuqui was used extensively as an ingredient of magical ointments and potions, as an anesthetic and analgesic agent. Most of the early writers described these medicinal qualities. It might be very interesting to investigate these properties further. Indeed it may well be that the analgesic effects of ololiuqui made it of particular concern and interest to the Aztecs who used it to stupefy their sacrificial victims. In their ceremonies a willing victim was thought to be more valuable than an unwilling one.

The psychological properties of lysergic acid amide (LA) were compared to LSD and to lysergic acid monoethylamide (LAE) by Solms (1956). About 0.1–1.0 mg of LA given to male subjects, chiefly physicians and chemists, were required to produce a typical LA response. This dose was similar to the dose of LAE required. But LA produced more indifference, a decrease in motor activity and more sleepiness than LAE. The subjects fell asleep after 1 hour and if not aroused they slept about 2 hours. Higher doses caused autonomic changes, emesis, diarrhea and dizziness but no hallucinations. Subjects were sometimes irritable and depressed.

Thus, when the methyl groups were removed and LA produced instead of LSD, the alkaloid had much less hallucinogenic and psychomotor activity and more sedative activity. Perhaps it is the powerful hallucinogenic activity of LSD which overpowers the usual sedative properties of the ergot alkaloids.

Solms' account of LA's activity differs slightly from Osmond's and Schultes' reports. This might be due to the psychopharmacological properties of the other constituents of ololiuqui such as the glucoside.

R. corymbosa is only one of a large number of morning glory varieties. After it was shown that LA and other ergot alkaloids were present, it became apparent to many investigators and to many more curious nonprofessionals that morning glory plants native to North America might also be active. Before long many varieties were sampled and it became generally known that certain varieties aptly named "Heavenly Blue," "Pearly Gates" and "Wedding Bells" were especially active psychologically. According to Cohen (1963) these discoveries initiated a wave of purchases of seeds from feed and seed stores. Federal agents seized many pounds of seeds in single raids. Psychotherapists who had used LSD for psychotherapy turned to the morning glory seeds when cut off from their normal sources. Stories appeared in the daily press and before long it became widely known how to obtain LSD-like experiences cheaply without having to get LSD.

Cohen recommended that large numbers of morning glory seeds should not be consumed since their psychological action was unpredictable and variable and definite adverse effects could result.

A larger proportion of the morning glory alkaloids are not hallucinogenic. In order to obtain the expected psychological effect large quantities of ergot must be consumed. Too enthusiastic use of the seeds could lead to subclinical or clinical ergotism, especially if the seeds were used as abortefaciants.

Chemistry of LSD

d-Lysergic acid diethylamide has the following structure:

Carbons number 5 and 8 are asymmetric so that 4 optically active isomers are possible. These are d-lysergic acid diethylamide, l-lysergic acid diethylamide, d-isolysergic acid diethylamide and l-isolysergic acid diethylamide (A. Stoll, 1952; A. Stoll and Hofmann, 1943).

d-LSD crystallizes in pointed prisms from benzine, has a melting point of 83°C and an optical rotation $D^{20} = 30$°C. The tartrate salt is stable in solution.

Pharmacology

LSD was quickly absorbed into the blood (Rothlin, 1957a,b,c; Hofmann, 1961a,b) in rat blood it was not bound or destroyed. Liver and muscle homogenates destroyed about 50% of its activity in a few minutes. During the next 17 hours little more was destroyed. Brain homogenates reduced LSD activity 58% in 10 minutes and 80% in 17 hours. The same decrease was found at 3° and 38°C.

Both direct assay and radioactive tracer methods have been used to study the distribution of LSD between blood and other organisms in mice and rats. The half life in blood was 7–10 minutes using tracer methods and 35 minutes by direct assay. The maximum level was reached in 10 to 15 minutes in most organs, but in 30 minutes in the liver. In decreasing order LSD was found in gut, liver, kidney, adrenals, lung, spleen, heart, muscle, skin and brain. Axelrod *et al.* (1957) found the same distributions. They found brain contained 0.0003 μg/gm (0.3 μg per human brain).

Gut had 70% of the radioactivity after 12 hours. Only 7–8% of radioactivity was excreted in 12 hours. Only 10 to 20 percent reached rat systemic circulation when it was given IP (Boyd *et al.*, 1955). LSD quickly passed from blood into tissues and brain and was excreted quickly into bile.

Paper chromatographic studies showed most of the LSD was changed. Bile contained 3 different radioactive substances. One of the derivatives was 2-oxy-LSD (Axelrod *et al.*, 1957; Freter *et al.*, 1957). Doses of this derivative of 300 μg had no psychological activity in animals and did not alter spontaneous cortical activity. The half life in cats blood was 130 minutes and in monkeys 100 minutes (Axelrod *et al.*, 1957).

Rothlin (1957a,b,c) reviewed most of the pharmacophysiological effects of LSD. In the periphery it had a direct effect. *In vivo* and *in vitro* it contracted rabbit uterus but was less active than ergometrine. Perfused blood vessels of rat kidney, rabbits ear and spinal cat were constricted. The intact animal suffered a decrease in blood pressure. LSD selectively antagonized serotonin on rat uterus, smooth muscle of guinea pig gut, blood vessels, and bronchial muscles *in vivo*. It expanded female guppy chromatophores. This was inhibited by long pretreatment with serotonin.

On *Venus mercenaria* heart, LSD increased the amplitude without changing sensitivity to acetylcholine and mimicked the serotonin effect but in contrast to the serotonin effect it was not decreased by washing the heart.

LSD produced both sympathetic and parasympathetic activity (Rinkel *et al.*, 1955a). In normal volunteers 1 or ½ μg per kg elevated the pulse rate from 84 to 90 per minute and stabilized the rate. Blood pressure was not altered but a dynamic interview increased blood pressure more in subjects given LSD than it did the comparison controls. The blood pressure response to noradrenaline was not changed but the increase in systolic pressure to adrenaline was less. On the other hand, Sankar *et al.* (1964) found chronic treatment with LSD increased the pressure response to adrenaline. The respiratory rate was more variable and either increased or decreased. In animals, very high doses produced inhibition and paralysis.

The most sensitive and useful measure of LSD activity in subjects was mydriasis. Rinkel *et al.* (1955b) measured increases in pupil size from 3 to 5.25 mm. In subjects the size of the pupil was a very valuable measure of the intensity of the psychological experience. In rabbits the most sensitive test was its pyretogenic effect. Doses as low as ½ to 1 μg per kg elevated rabbit body temperature. This was the only animal measure which was sensitive to doses active in humans. The time sequence of the fever and the psychological response in humans was similar.

In humans LSD produced a prolonged period of analgesia. Kast and Collins (1964) compared the analgesic property of 100 μg of LSD with 2 mg dihydromorphinone. HCl and 100-mg meperidine, HCl in a series of severely ill patients suffering severe pain from terminal carcinoma. After one hour there was no difference between the three compounds. During the second hour Dilaudid was better than meperidine and LSD. LSD was superior to both during the third hour when both Dilaudid and meperidine analgesia began to wane. Meperidine produced 5.7 twenty-minute painfree periods, dilaudid 8.4, and LSD 95.6 (32 hours). These results were very impressive. Even though many subjects were freed of pain for many hours they refused to take LSD a second time.

Biochemistry of LSD

Sankar and Bender (1960) and Sankar *et al.* (1962a) gave rats 500 μg LSD IP per day for two consecutive days. It decreased feed intake, decreased excretion of urea, increased secretion of ammonia, decreased excretion of creatinine, keto acids, sodium, potassium and total amines. The decrease in keto acid and urea excretion was marked.

The diurnal pattern of phosphate excretion in urine was markedly changed. Hoagland *et al.* (1955) compared the excretion of inorganic phosphate in the urine of 12 normal men before and after taking 0.5 to 1.0 μg per kg of LSD. The excretion of inorganic phosphate was reduced substantially for 6 hours after LSD was taken. The injection of ACTH during the reaction increased the excretion of phosphate. LSD produced phosphate excretion patterns which resembled those found in schizophrenics not given LSD. Similar changes in phosphate excretion were produced by adrenolutin (Hoffer and Osmond, 1960). LSD produced similar changes in phosphate excretion in guinea pigs (Bergen and Beisaw, 1956).

Neurophysiological Effects

SPONTANEOUS CEREBRAL ACTIVITY

Evarts (1957a, 1958) reported LSD decreased the amplitude of spontaneous activity in rabbits but did not block the response to activation. In curarized rabbits (Rinaldi and Himwich, 1955a,b,c), small doses (1–5 μg/kg) decreased the amplitude and increased the frequency. Higher doses produced an alert pattern and 20–60 μg produced the reappearance of slow waves. These effects were blocked by frenquel (Rinaldi and Himwich, 1955a,b,c,d). They concluded LSD stimulated the mesodiencephalic activating system.

The electroencephalograms of cats were activated when they were given LSD by mouth or when it was placed in the brain ventricles, (Bradley and Hance, 1956a,b, 1957; Bradley and Elkes, 1953, 1957; Elkes, 1957; Haley and Rutscamann, 1957). Barbiturate spindles were abolished, that is LSD countered barbiturate-induced depression.

Human cortical electrical activity was not altered much by LSD. Rinkel *et al.* (1952) found slight increases in alpha frequency. Gastaut *et al.* (1953) reported 40–60 μg of LSD increased frequency in 9 out of 10 subjects and suppressed alpha activity. In 6 out of 12 cases beta activity was increased. In 7 out of 12 cases occipital evoked potentials were augmented by photic stimulations and in 5 the responses radiated to the frontal region. LSD reduced filtering of impulses through nervous centers by increasing neuron excitability. Schwarz *et al.* (1955) reported 50 μg of LSD produced minimal changes in 13 subjects. In 7 they observed a reduction in alpha rhythm.

A quantitative analysis of changes in EEG was developed by Pfeiffer *et al.* (1959, 1962) and Goldstein *et al.* (1963), which measured the output of electrical activity at the scalp. Normal subjects showed variable but organized activity. When they took LSD both mean energy output and EEG variability were reduced. Amphetamine had similar effects. When chronic schizophrenics were given LSD there was no change in energy output but variability increased until it reached its maximum in 1½ hours.

ON SPONTANEOUS ACTIVITY DEEP IN THE BRAIN

Monroe et al. (1957) using depth electrodes explored the changes in electrical activity caused by schizophrenia and by several hallucinogens. Schizophrenia produced electrical storms in the hippocampal, amygdaloid, and septal areas without changing scalp electroencephalograms. Similar changes were produced by LSD and the intensity of the changes correlated with the increase in psychotic behavior.

Monroe and Heath (1961) compared activity of several LSD analogs in monkeys and cats. LSD was the most active. DAM and LPD (see Table 6) produced moderate EEG activity and about 10% of LSD's psychological activity. MLD-4 and LSM had minimal effects on the EEG and 20–40% of LSD's psychological activity. *l*-LSD, BOL, and UML were inactive. In sharp contrast ALD-52 was as active psychologically as LSD but produced minimal EEG changes. This could be due to the slow release of LSD from its acetyl derivative by hydrolysis in the body.

EFFECT ON SYNAPTIC TRANSMISSION

Marrazzi and Hart (1955a,b,c) studied the effect of LSD on synaptic transmission by injecting it into the carotid artery of cat preparations. LSD reduced the amplitude of the postsynaptic component of the transcallosal response. In an extension of these studies Marrazzi (1957a,b, 1960, 1961, 1962) showed that all the hallucinogens he tested caused some inhibition of this synapse but there was no quantitative relationship. Marrazzi suggested that hallucinations arose from a disturbance in the normal neuronal patterns of activity due to this kind of synaptic inhibition.

LSD also inhibited synaptic transmission in the visual pathways of the cat (Evarts et al., 1955). Intracarotid injection of 30 µg/kg decreased the response of the geniculate postsynaptic response by 80%. Transmission within the retina and between the geniculate radiation fibers and cortical cells was not inhibited (Purpura, 1956a,b, 1957a,b; Purpura et al., 1957). Purpura (1956a,b, 1957a,b) reported LSD facilitated the primary cortical response to visual and auditory stimulation and changed the rate of recovery. Higher doses depressed the auditory evoked-potential but the visual evoked responses were still facilitated. Purpura believed LSD inhibited the synapses of the apical dendrite and this resulted in a cortical aroused pattern.

EFFECT ON ELECTRORETINOGRAMS

According to Apter and Pfeiffer (1956, 1957) LSD initiated spontaneous action potentials in the retina of anesthetized cats. Large spikes developed in the visual cortex of the cats. When the optic nerves were severed they disappeared. They concluded that the hallucinations (visual changes) depended upon these retinal changes as well as upon central changes.

Comparison of Some Ergot Alkaloids for Psychotomimetic Activity

Many derivatives of lysergic acid have been synthesized and examined by Sandoz Laboratories (Rothlin, 1957a,b,c). They are divisible into 5 main groups.

Group 1. These are the 4 isomers of which D-LSD is the one with the greatest activity.

Group 2. The double bond between C-9 and C-10 is saturated to give dihydro-*d*-lysergic acid diethylamide. Both substances are psychologically inert.

Group 3. In this group substitution is made on the indole nucleus. One of them, *dl*-acetyllysergic acid diethylamide is as active psychologically as LSD, probably because the acetyl radical is easily split off to release LSD.

Group 4. These are monosubstitution compounds of the amine nitrogen.

Group 5. These are disubstitution derivatives of the amide nitrogen.

These groups of compounds are compared in Table 6.

See also Abramson (1960a,b), Abramson *et al.* (1958a), Cerletti and Doepfner (1958), Hofmann (1961a,b), and Solms (1956).

Gorodetzky and Isbell (1964) compared the hallucinogenic activity of LSD with a newer derivative 2,3-dihydrolysergic acid diethylamide (2,3-DH-LSD). This newer substance had 4% of the pyretogenic activity of LSD in rabbits. They gave 2,3-DH-LSD to 6 healthy former morphine addicts between the ages of 23 and 33.

2,3-DH-LSD produced similar effects in the subjects. The changes included autonomic symptoms (fewer rapid heart rate, increase in blood pressure and mydriasis) and LSD-like psychological changes. The effect of 2,3-DH-LSD came on more slowly reaching its maximum in 4 to 5 hours. LSD in this experiment reached its peak activity in the usual 2 to 3 hours. For producing psychotomimetic changes they calculated that

TABLE 6

Comparative Activity of Some Lysergic Acid Alkaloids

Full name	Code	Toxicity in rabbits (intravenous)	Pyretogenic effect	Antiserotonin effect	Psychological effect in man	EEG activation
Group 1						
d-Lysergic acid diethylamide	d-LSD-25	100	100	100	100	Marked
l-Lysergic acid diethylamide	l-LSD	1.8	0	0	0	None
d-Isolysergic acid diethylamide	d-iso-LSD	3.7	0	0	0	None
Group 3						
d,l-Methyllysergic acid diethylamide	MLD-41	5.6	5	370	40	Minimal
d,l-Acetyllysergic acid diethylamide	ALD-52	19	13	200	100	None
d-2-Bromlysergic acid diethylamide	BOL-148	5	5	103	0	None
4-l-Methyl-2-bromlysergic acid diethylamide	MBL-61	2	0	533	0	
Group 4						
d-Lysergic acid amide					10	
d-Lysergic acid ethylamide	LAE-32	34	17	12	5	
d-Lysergic acid dimethylamide	DAM-57	78	43	23	10	Moderate
d-Lysergic acid pyrrolidide	LPD-824	73	10	5	10	Moderate
d-Lysergic acid morpholide	LSM-775	43	10	2	20	Minimal
Group 5						
d,l-Methyllysergic acid monoethylamide	MLA-74	3.2	0	835	5	
d,l-Acetyllysergic acid monoethylamide	ALA-10	6	1	39	5	
d,l-Methyllysergic acid pyrrolidide	MPD-75	4	0	130	7	

a dose of 8 μg of 2,3-DH-LSD was equivalent to 1 μg of LSD. It is interesting that hydrogenation at positions 2 and 3 (removal of the double bond) did not eliminate its psychological activity, but saturation of double bond 9–10 did.

Toxicology of LSD

Rothlin and Cerletti (1956) and Rothlin (1957a,b,c) reviewed the toxicology of LSD. The intravenous toxicity (LD-50) varied with the species. For mouse, rat and rabbit it was 46, 16.5 and 0.3 mg/kg. An elephant died after receiving 297 mg of LSD (West *et al.*, 1963), a dose considered 99 times too large by Harwood (1963). The LD-50 cannot be calculated from one dose but one can guess it would be near that level. For an elephant weighing 5000 kg, this would yield an LD-50 for elephants of about 0.15 mg per kg. It appears that the LD-50 decreases as the weight per animal species increases. This suggests the toxicity is related more closely to brain weight than it is to body weight. By interpolation one could assume the LD-50 for man is about 0.2 mg per kg or 14,000 μg per average adult male. Subjects have been given 1.5 without harm but doses any larger than this may be dangerous. In chronic toxicity trials, rats tolerated 2.5 mg per kg IV daily for 30 days. They suffered increased reflex responses, mydriasis, piloerection, and rate of growth was decreased, but there was no cumulative effect. The acute LD-50 for these rats remained the same for untreated animals. No tolerance developed.

LSD is so active in producing psychological changes in man that it can hardly be a toxin in the usual physiological sense. It is a very unusual toxin which selectively affects the psychological functions of the person without altering the other major body systems. It has been given daily to young patients for over a year without there being evidence for any pathological changes.

But the increasing self-use of morning glory seeds will undoubtedly lead to toxic reaction which may be unjustifiably blamed on LSD. These seeds contain LA and other ergot alkaloids. Subjects who take several hundred seeds daily may ingest enough total ergot alkaloid to produce symptoms of ergotism. Two subjects did suffer pronounced vasoconstriction and coldness in their hands after taking several hundred seeds. This could have been a prelude to gangrenous ergotism. The seeds contain other chemicals as well and nothing is known about their toxicity.

Recently we have become aware of one toxic reaction produced by LSD in rats. Lucas (1964) and Lucas and Jaques (1964) found that

LSD was highly hemorrhagic when given to anticoagulant-treated rats. The effect of LSD began 30 minutes after it was given and reached its peak effect in 3 to 4 hours when sympathetic excitation was greatest. Judging the effects by clinical symptoms and time of death, hemorrhage occurred from 4 to 6 days after LSD was given. A dose of 0.1 mg per 200 grams of rat was given. This is of course very much larger than human doses. However, this work suggests that subjects taking anticoagulants should not be given LSD.

Complications When LSD Is Given

Complications arising from the use of LSD must be differentiated from toxic reactions to LSD. It can not be said that LSD is toxic to humans when recommended doses are used because none of the physiological correlates of toxicity are measurable. The complications which arise from the LSD experience are of two kinds; (a) the reaction runs too long, (b) the reaction is too intense. There is a third class of complication which is due solely to the inexperience, thoughtlessness, or incompetence of the therapist and it should be credited to him, not to the LSD. While under the influence of LSD, subjects may have some defect in judgment and carry out decisions which normally they would not do and which they would regret. They may carry out thoughtless acts which endanger themselves or others. Most of these dangers occur when subjects are not observed continuously by therapists.

The most thorough studies of the complications of LSD were reported by Cohen (1960a,b) and Cohen and Ditman (1962, 1963). Cohen (1960a,b) queried 62 investigators about their knowledge of LSD's complications and 44 replied. This group gave 5,000 subjects either LSD or mescaline a total of 25,000 times. Most of them received between 25 and 1500 μg from one to eighty times.

No one reported any serious physical side effects. The most common problem during the LSD experience was unmanageability or panic and severe somatic complaints. According to Cohen, therapists who wished to prove LSD had no therapeutic value gave their subjects an unhappy time. Four psychoanalysts from a small series all had dysphoric reactions.

The most common prolonged reaction was short lived depression. Five out of 5000 subjects (or 25,000 experiences) attempted suicide. Four subjects killed themselves many months after their last LSD experience. This seems to be a very low suicide rate when it is considered that LSD was usually given to the most hopeless cases in psychiatry and the ones least responsive to psychotherapy. The patients included drug addicts, alcoholics, psychopaths, and other personality problems as well as depressions. The suicide rate from these kinds of patients is very high. It might even be argued that 4 suicides out of 5000 subjects is somewhat less than one would expect from this total group.

We have not had any suicides in Saskatchewan since we began the LSD in 1952. During this period about 12 psychiatrists have given LSD over 2000 times to over 1000 subjects. Most of them were alcoholics. These patients were given LSD 1 to 30 times but under carefully controlled conditions which will be described further on. One subject visiting Saskatchewan killed himself 6 months later in another part of Canada. He was a clinical psychologist with a history of 7 years of severe depression. During most of this time he was under psychoanalytic treatment. He attended a meeting in Saskatchewan and requested LSD, not as a treatment, but because he wished to know something about the experience. When he returned home he continued to be depressed and continued to receive psychotherapy. It is impossible to determine whether his suicide was due to his prolonged psychotherapy, to the fact his depression was not lifted by the LSD experience, to a combination of these variables or to other unknown events. Another alcoholic nearly shot himself. During his LSD session his therapists unwisely left him alone, whereupon he walked out of the hospital and was discovered a short time later as he was putting his gun to his head. There have been no serious episodes when therapists have observed the rules established here for using LSD.

Cohen reported several prolonged reactions to LSD. Theoretically these were very important. Two of Cohens respondents (Hoch and Malitz) reported they had given LSD to the normal member of an identical twin pair. The other was schizophrenic. Two days later the reaction recurred and he required treatment in hospital for 5 days. Cohen reported there were 8 prolonged reactions but 7 occurred in patients also undergoing psychotherapy. No cases of addiction to LSD were reported.

Cohen concluded that certain precautions must be observed. These are (a) proper screening of subjects to exclude prepsychotic individuals (b) adequate observation and control during the experience and (c) adequate post-LSD supervision.

In Saskatchewan we have followed the following rules for the past 7 years.

1. Proper screening and diagnosis of subjects. All subjects were first interviewed and diagnosed by psychiatrists. Prepsychotics were not given LSD but recovered patients from depression or from schizophrenia were given LSD if necessary.

2. Every LSD session was elective, that is no hasty decisions to take LSD were made.

3. Every treatment was carried out in the hospital.

4. At no time during the session was the subject left unattended or unobserved.

5. If the subject became panic stricken or unmanageable, the experience was moderated by giving them nicotinic acid (1–2 grams by mouth) or terminated by giving them any of the standard tranquilizers.

6. Subjects were discharged the next day if they were fully recovered. Otherwise they were kept in the hospital for a longer period of time.

7. Prolonged reactions were treated promptly with nicotinic acid and tranquilizers if the latter were required.

8. More recently we have considered malvaria a contraindication. This will be described further on.

Cohen and Ditman (1962) described a series of five cases of prolonged reactions to LSD.

Case 1. He became schizophrenic ten days after a LSD experience for which he required several admissions to the hospital.

Case 2. She took LSD from 200 to 300 times in doses of 25 to 400 μg over a period of 3 years, that she averaged one session every 4 days. She had also taken other hallucinogens.

Case 3. He was a chronically depressed patient who had made a suicide attempt before and had been treated with ECT. He was given LSD 8 times and remained psychotic for 2 years.

Case 4. A boy, age 10, ingested by accident a sugar cube which contained 100 μg of LSD. He was abnormal for 1 month.

Case 5. A hypnotist received 25 sessions of LSD therapy. He remained psychotic for seven months.

The most remarkable fact about LSD complications is their rarity. They have occurred among the emotionally labile, hysterical, and paranoid subjects. In the majority of cases they have gotten LSD from improper or illegal sources. The black market LSD contains other still unidentified ergot compounds which could account for the increased toxicity of these harmful preparations. Many of the subjects have also dabbled with other drugs including peyote, marijuana, amphetamine, barbiturates, narcotics, nutmeg extract, and more recently morning glory seeds.

REASONS FOR COMPLICATIONS

During the Experience

The occurrence of complications during the LSD session was usually due to the inexperience or incompetence of the therapist (physician, psychologist, or nurse). Complications may arise because the experience causes great confusion, deep depression, paranoid thinking, or overwhelming anxiety. The therapist must be so well trained or experienced with LSD's effects that he can anticipate these complications. These reactions do not come on abruptly and in nearly every instance the subject has given many indications that something was going wrong.

Prolonged Experiences

Cohen and Ditman (1962, 1963) recommended that prepsychotic subjects not be given LSD. This is also our recommendation. We have found that many preschizophrenics have the same biochemical pathology as the majority of schizophrenics. The biochemical abnormality apparently is not yet expressed clinically in symptoms and signs. LSD may intensify this biochemical abnormality until it is expressed clinically as a typical schizophrenic reaction and of course it may last anywhere from a few days to a few years.

There are three lines of evidence which suggest schizophrenia is a contraindication.

1. Schizophrenics may have very prolonged reactions to LSD (Cohen and Ditman, 1963). We have had several prolonged reactions. One subject, a clinical psychologist, obtained a small supply of LSD for a small research project on patients. He also took it himself, 3 times over a period of 1 week, without medical supervision. After his last experience he developed insomnia, became suspicious, anxious, and very disturbed and he had to be admitted to the hospital as an emergency patient. He was clearly schizophrenic. He was treated with nicotinic acid, 3 gm per day, and he received a short ECT series. He recovered in a few weeks, at which time it became clear he had been on the verge of schizophrenia for some time before he took LSD. His injudicious use of LSD was merely an illustration of his lack of judgment. He remained well for 12 months while he took nicotinic acid but after being free of medication for 12 months his schizophrenia recurred spontaneously.

Not only do schizophrenics react badly to LSD but patients who are not clearly schizophrenic and who fit the diagnostic term "pseudoneurotic schizophrenia," react in a qualitatively different way. Sedman and Kenna (1965) gave 50–200 µg LSD to 10 patients they considered could be schizophrenic. On reading their case histories there is little doubt many American psychiatrists would consider them either schizophrenic, or pseudoneurotic schizophrenic. The comparison group included 10 patients with depression or personality disorders. Eight of the 10 doubtful schizophrenics had visual experiences compared to 8 out of 10 others. Only one out of 10 doubtful schizophrenics had a disturbance in body image compared to 7 out of 10 from the comparison group. From the 10 doubtful schizophrenics 1 had delusion, 4 hallucinations, 2 thought disorder, 4 bizarre ego changes and one became passive. The numbers suffering these changes from the comparison group were 0, 3, 0, 0, and 1.

Patients with depression and personality disorders are not a normal group and often require much larger quantities of LSD so it may be that Sedman and Kenna (1965) have confused dose response with diagnosis. In our experience, their incidence of perceptual changes in schizophrenics resembles the normal response much more than does their comparison group response. One doubtful schizophrenic became much worse.

The use of LSD for diagnosing doubtful cases remains questionable. A better clinical description and simple tests like the HOD (Hoffer and Osmond, 1961b,c), the EW1 (Osmond and El Meleghi, 1964), or the Malvaria test (Hoffer and Mahon, 1961) would be more helpful. The risk of making them much worse is too great. We know of one case in Canada who was precipitated into a schizophrenic-like psychosis for one year by using LSD in this way.

2. We have referred to the identical twin pair of Hoch and Malitz. A major study by Anastosopoulos and Photiades (1962) corroborated this finding that close relatives of schizophrenics are prone to have prolonged and undesirable reactions to LSD. They gave LSD 97 times to relatives of 21 schizophrenic patients. The relatives included parents, siblings, uncles, and aunts. Each subject was given ½ to 1 μg of LSD per kg. From the 21 families, in only one family were both parents and both siblings normal reactors to LSD. In all the other cases at least one parent of a schizophrenic patient reacted abnormally. These abnormal reactions consisted of paranoid features and ideas of reference, deliria, and strong feelings of unreality which the subject could not delineate from reality and which caused them severe anxiety and severe depression. Visual and auditory hallucinations were common and led to a complete inability to understand what was going on. Reassurance was rarely accepted. The acute phase of the intoxication lasted a few days to 6 weeks. Persistent insomnia was very common. A couple of examples are shown in Fig. 5.

In example 1 the father had an abnormal reaction to LSD but his brother and wife reacted normally. He had four children. The first son reacted normally, the second son reacted abnormally, the first daughter was schizophrenic and the second daughter reacted abnormally to LSD. In example 2, one mother reacted abnormally, but her sister reacted normally. Out of one marriage she had three children of whom one was schizophrenic, one reacted normally, and the third abnormally to LSD. She married a second time to a man who reacted normally to LSD. They had two children of whom one was schizophrenic and the second reacted abnormally to LSD. Her second husband had a son by a previous marriage who reacted normally to LSD.

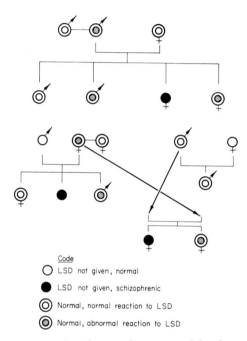

Code
○ LSD not given, normal
● LSD not given, schizophrenic
◎ Normal, normal reaction to LSD
⊘ Normal, abnormal reaction to LSD

FIG. 5. Two examples of unusual reactions of families to LSD.

This frequency of abnormal reactions to LSD in the relatives of schizophrenics is very high and supports the view that close relatives of schizophrenics have a powerful potential for becoming schizophrenic when stimulated by LSD. These authors found that more than one third of their 97 subjects had abnormal reactions which gives an incidence of 0.33, that is a close relative of a schizophrenic given LSD has a ⅓ chance of having an abnormal reaction. This is much higher than for normal subjects. Cohen and Ditman (1962, 1963) found that only 10 out of several thousand subjects had prolonged reactions. In Saskatchewan we have records of about 10 prolonged reactions from about 1000 subjects. Thus the incidence of abnormal reactions in normal subjects is about 0.01 which is close to the expected frequency for developing schizophrenia. A close relative of a schizophrenic therefore is 33 times more likely to have bad and prolonged reactions to LSD.

3. The majority of acute untreated schizophrenics excrete a substance in their urine which stains a mauve color when treated with Ehrlich's reagent on paper chromatograms (Irvine, 1961; Hoffer and Osmond, 1961b,c, 1962a). The frequency with which this substance appeared in various groups of subjects is shown in Table 7.

TABLE 7

PERCENT MALVARIA IN VARIOUS GROUPS OF SUBJECTS

Group	Condition	Number	Percent with malvaria
Normal	(a) Saskatoon	60	0
	(b) Moose Jaw	21	10
Physically ill		over 200	11
Psychiatric patients	(a) Not schizophrenic	over 300	20
	(b) Schizophrenic		
	1. acute, untreated	over 200	70
	2. acute, treated		
	(i) well	over 50	0
	(ii) sick	over 200	50
	(c) After LSD-25	over 60	30
	(d) Adult retarded	20	5
	(e) Children retarded	over 30	30

The presence of this mauve factor cut across all diagnostic groups but it was more clearly related to schizophrenia than to any other group. When the patients recovered the substance was no longer excreted. The subjects who excreted mauve factor resembled each other more than they did subjects who were negative when they were examined clinically, by psychological and EEG tests, and in their response to treatment. Hoffer and Osmond (1963a,b) therefore called them malvarians. A *malvarian* is any human who excretes the mauve factor.

We have examined the relationship between malvaria and prolonged reactions to LSD. Since malvarians (no matter what they are clinically) resemble the majority of schizophrenics biochemically, we hypothesized that they would also react badly to LSD. Only a small number of subjects given LSD were tested for malvaria. So far none of the nonmalvarians have suffered prolonged reactions to LSD but 4 out of 20 malvarians (who were not schizophrenic) had reactions lasting a week or more. The frequency is 20% which is close to the frequency of abnormal reactions among relatives of schizophrenics. A malvarian has a 0.20 probability of reacting badly to LSD. This is 20 times the expected incidence of abnormal reactions for the population at large. By not giving LSD to malvarians the risk of having a bad or prolonged reaction is reduced a great deal. This will be discussed in greater detail further on.

Some subjects develop a transient malvaria after LSD. It was usually present 24 hours after LSD was given but was no longer present after another 24 hours. These subjects also developed bad reactions to LSD on subsequent sessions. One subject diagnosed as having a personality disorder was negative but became positive after LSD. His therapist was advised of this change and cautioned against repeating the LSD treatment. However, a few weeks later he was again given LSD. He remained paranoid and delusional for six days. He was discharged apparently recovered, but a few days later he was readmitted by the emergency service with the diagnosis of schizophrenia.

Dose and Psychological Activity

For many parameters of LSD's activity there is a linear dose response relationship at low doses whereas with higher doses Wilder's Law (1962) begins to operate. Only the relationship of dose to psychological activity will be considered.

MINIMAL RECOGNIZABLE DOSE

The minimal effective dose seems to be about 25 μg per adult. W. A. Stoll (1947, 1949) found that 20–30 μg were active. A few years ago Hoffer completed double blind self-recognition trials in normal volunteers. The subjects could not detect 15 μg doses but most of them were able to detect 25 μg.

OPTIMUM PSYCHOTOMIMETIC OR PSYCHEDELIC DOSES

This varied from 100 to 1000 μg depending upon a large number of variables we will describe. The dose for nonalcoholics varied from 100 to 200 μg but for alcoholics it was higher and ranged from 200 to 500 μg.

RELATION BETWEEN MINIMAL AND OPTIMAL DOSE

Abramson *et al.* (1955b) investigated the dose response of 31 nonpsychotic subjects using doses of 0, 1–25, 26–50, 51–75, 76–100 and 100 μg or more. They classified symptoms as neurotic (nervousness, anxiety, inner trembling, tachycardia, feeling hot or cold) and psychotic (hallucinations, depersonalization, feelings of unreality, confusion, delusions, and uncommunicativeness). The correlation between psychotic and perceptual changes with dose was 0.90 but there was no correlation between dose and neurotic symptoms. This suggested to them neurotic symptoms were more a function of personality and situation. De Marr *et al.* (1960) found that subjects could distinguish between 25, 50 and 100 μg doses. The number of symptoms was related linearly to dose.

There was no relation between dose and the psychedelic experience which had some of the characteristics of an all-or-nothing response. If this experience came with 100 μg in a subject, giving him 200 μg did not improve its quality. Enough LSD was required to overcome the tension which came from smaller doses and this varied markedly. However there was a linear relation between dose and toxic or physiological changes; Hoch (1956) and Klee *et al.* (1961) found that physiological changes were most intense at their highest dose of 1120 μg per 70 kg subject. Some hypertension occurred. The time of onset of symptoms was shorter, perceptual changes were more intense but depression and paranoia were not dose related.

MAXIMUM CLINICAL DOSE

The largest dose reported was 1.5 mg (1500 μg) per adult. This seems to be close to the upper safe limit when given the first time. For subjects who have developed tolerance to it larger doses might be tolerated readily.

Effect of LSD on Normal Subjects

There is no typical LSD experience for it is affected by a large number of variables. This could explain why psychiatrists who have a lot of experience with LSD seem unable to understand each other's work.

VARIABLES WHICH INFLUENCE THE REACTION

Factors in the Subject

PERSONALITY. No generally acceptable definition of personality exists but most of us know what is meant by it. Although personality is not static and is influenced greatly by environmental factors, there is something constant about any human by means of which he is recognized by enemies and friends. This has to do with the body, its rate of reactivity to stimuli, with the manner of speech, with interpersonal reactivity, with reactions to stress, anxiety, misfortune and good fortune, etc. Only a superb novelist can describe personality of people and this may require many years of work and several hundred pages of description. All these intangible factors influence the LSD reaction. Sometimes the reaction is predictable, most often it is not. For example, it can be assumed safely that a quiet, taciturn, reflective person will have an experience which he will not share readily with the observers. A voluble introspective extroverted subject will be more apt to spend many hours and words describing his reaction to his friends. But, these predictions may be completely wrong. The best way of predicting a LSD reaction is to first give it to a subject and then from the response it is possible to guess more accurately what a subsequent response will be.

SOMATOTYPE. Sheldon (1954) described three main types and he presented evidence that there was some correlation between physical type and personality. Dimascio *et al.* (1961) compared a group of athletic types against a group of aesthetic types by giving them LSD, mescaline, and psylocibin. These two types are not comparable to the Sheldonian types since the classification was not based on physical measurements but these authors' athletics might be comparable to Sheldon's somatotypes and their aesthetics might be comparable to Sheldon's cerebrotonics. Most of the athletic types were more anxious and tense under LSD, whereas the other group were less anxious. The effect on clarity of thought was the same in both groups. In general the athletics reacted to the hallucinogens with marked euphoria and physiological discomfort while the aesthetics reacted with mental confusion.

In our large series of subjects it was our impression that the somatotypes were more apt to have psychedelic experiences.

EDUCATION. The level of education plays a decisive role in structuring the LSD experience. A Ph.D. physicist will not react the same way as a ward aid. Not only is the experience different but the ability to describe what has happened is different. Subjects with minimal education have had psychedelic experiences as have scientists but the quality of the account afterward is very different.

VOCATION. A writer accustomed to sharing his impressions and ideas with others will not respond in the same way as a psychiatrist trained to listen and to interpret. Many scientists have failed to grasp the significance of this difference which explains the unhappiness by many psychiatrists of the lyrical accounts and essays of others. There seem to be two main classes of descriptions. The first and most common were those written by research psychiatrists and psychologists. These were descriptions and interpretations of experiences described to them by their patients and experimental subjects and of tests which they had interpreted. These accounts were generally dull, uninteresting, and only partially described what happened to the subject. The second group of essays were written by subjects who were novelists or very literate scientists who were able to describe what had happened. Aldous Huxley's "Doors to Perception" (1954) is the best example of this kind of essay.

Several scientists with the creativity of novelists provided the literature with very vivid detailed and accurate reports of their response to LSD. Havelock Ellis (1897, 1898), Leon (1888), Mitchell Weir (1896), Heinrich Kluver (1928), and Lewin (1931) described reactions to mescaline in this way and Osmond (1953, 1956, 1957a) did the same for LSD. The exciting, fascinating and vivid accounts of LSD reactions were invariably written by this second group. Their experience, true for them, does not necessarily represent the kind of experience the rest of humanity might get. This may lead to disappointment and frustration that they do not have the same reaction as the ones described in the literature.

We have often asked our LSD subjects after they had taken LSD to read these vivid self-accounts to others. Subjects who were unable to let us know what their own experience had been invariably agreed that the descriptions by novelists in many aspects were similar to their own but were described much more effectively.

But one's avocation is no guarantee it will determine the experience. Several philosophers have taken LSD and found nothing in it which quickened or altered their philosophy. There have been Zen mystics who should have had vivid mystical or transcendental reactions who suffered only tension and pain. The LSD experience has been compared to Zen Mysticism (Dusen, 1961). There are several reports in our records of artists who found the visual aspects of their LSD reaction no more vivid or colorful than their normal view of the world.

AGE. The majority of subjects were older than 18 years. But the few young people under 18 who took LSD reacted in the same way as adults and the aged. Recently Hoffer gave LSD to a man aged 88. He had an excellent transcendental experience in which his faith in atheism was revivified. Factors such as education and avocation are probably much more relevant.

HEALTH. The state of health is very important. A subject with a severe cold will not react as well as when he is normal. The presence of psychiatric disease is even more important. As we have already shown schizophrenic patients do not respond to LSD as do normal subjects. Malvarians also react badly, but when they have recovered and have been well for a long time they will react normally. Patients with endogenous depressions, anxiety, neuroses, and epilepsy will also react differently from normal subjects.

REASON FOR TAKING LSD. Set and expectation are very important. The alcoholic who hopes the experience will increase his insight and help him remain sober will not react in the same way as the alcoholic who does not believe he has a problem but is forced by pressure from his wife and family to undergo the experience.

The naive volunteer who takes LSD from a psychologist to earn money will not react in the same way as the learned psychologist forced by a sense of duty or guilt to participate in an LSD program because his colleagues or director expect him to do so.

The preconceptions of the subject, right or wrong, also influence the reaction. If he suspects it is a truth serum he will respond depending upon whether he is prepared to divulge the truth; if he believes early memories will be abreacted he will react differently. The therapist can determine set or expectations by the information and attitudes he conveys to the subject.

THE SUBJECT'S EXPERIENCE WITH HALLUCINOGENS. The first LSD experience is the least typical for anyone even though it may be the most vivid, most startling and most dramatic one of all. For in most cases there is more anxiety, more suspense and more anticipation the first time. It is like opening night in the theater for the players or like the first glimpse of an unknown land, or of the atomic explosion. Thereafter the reaction may be as rewarding or as fearful but is seldom as memorable or as intense. Thereafter each experience has a life of its own and in essence it differs from the one before and from those which will follow.

Tolerance to LSD develops very quickly if the experience is repeated with too short an interval between sessions. The first time it is taken 100 μg of LSD will produce an intense experience in most normal (about 80%) subjects. The same dose taken the next day will produce a much milder reaction and if it is repeated again the third day will produce no reaction. If there is a rest of 3–5 days the experience can regain some or most of its original intensity. We have given subjects 300 μg the first day and thereafter 100 μg per day for several days with no further reaction. After 7 days subjects have noted no unusual reaction and some have been maintained for several months.

Familiarity with other drugs which produce psychological changes affect the LSD experience. Alcoholics and drug addicts are usually sophisticated subjects and are able to cope with the LSD experience better than normal subjects. We have seen more anxiety, fear, tension, and panic from normal subjects than from patients, self-trained by many years of addiction. Perhaps this is why alcoholics need much more LSD than normals in order to achieve the optimum reactions. Our series of over 600 alcoholics suggests that 300 μg given the first time is equivalent to 100 μg for most normal subjects.

PREVIOUS PSYCHIATRIC TREATMENT. Psychiatric treatment prepares a set or state of mind in subjects which depends upon the orientation and skill of the therapist. It is not surprising sophisticated patients re-

spond differently than naive subjects. Patients who have been psycho-
analyzed rarely have a psychedelic experience. Ditman *et al.* (1962)
found that few of these patients were benefited. Their research confirmed our findings. Out of over 1000 subjects given LSD in Saskatchewan only 5 had been analyzed earlier. They all suffered a good deal
of pain and discomfort even though they were treated the same way as
were other patients by therapists with a strong psychological orientation
and interest. Yet well known psychoanalysts such as Professor H. Abramson and Dr. R. Carrier have treated their patients with low and high
doses of LSD very successfully using analytic psychotherapy. Perhaps
the conclusion must be that analyzed subjects should be treated by psychoanalysts.

PREMEDICATION. Many drugs influence the LSD reaction. They will be
described further on. It is important that subjects about to receive LSD
not be heavily dosed with sedatives or tranquilizers for this may prevent
the normal development of the experience.

CIRCADIEN RHYTHM. The time of day may be very important. Our data
suggests that fatigue plays a role and that evening sessions seem different than early morning sessions.

RELATION TO MEALS. For many years we gave our subjects LSD on an
empty stomach in the belief this would reduce the incidence of nausea
and vomiting. But a couple of years ago Dr. R. Laidlaw informed us
that he was giving LSD to his subjects after a full breakfast and that
the induction period seemed much easier. The usual introductory tension, pain and anxiety was much less troublesome. Since then we have
followed his method and the results have been more satisfactory. The
induction period was more pleasant and subjects gradually moved into
their optimum LSD reaction. Nausea was rare and retching and vomiting even rarer. Before this these undesirable reactions were common.

Factors within the Therapist

The key or central person in the LSD reaction is the one in whom
the patient has most confidence. It is usually the therapist but may be a
nurse, social worker, or friend. There should be one person responsible
for the entire treatment session who may delegate some of this responsibility to another. The therapist ought not to take LSD simultaneously
with the subject since his judgment must be unimpaired. Some of the factors within the therapist are:

EXPERIENCE OF THERAPIST WITH HALLUCINOGENIC DRUGS. The most
skillful therapist is one who has himself experienced what LSD can do.
If he has had a psychedelic reaction he will understand a similar reaction in his patients and if he has had a psychotomimetic reaction he will

sympathize with this kind of reaction in his patient. Psychiatrists who have had only psychotomimetic reactions find it hard to believe any other kind is possible much as noncolor-blind people can hardly believe others are color blind.

If the therapist has not taken LSD he can learn nearly as much about it by observing carefully how many patients react to LSD. But this knowledge of LSD's reaction depends also on the therapist's objectives in acquiring his experience. If he has run an experimental program to study LSD as a model psychosis he will not understand it in the same way as a therapist interested in the effect of LSD upon creativity of artists or on performance in psychological tests.

OBJECTIVES OF THERAPIST. The psychologist interested in test performances is determined only that his battery of tests be completed by the subject at the proper time. Early memories or the numerous perceptual changes which subjects find more fascinating are merely a curse to the tester since they interfere with his protocols. On the other hand, the therapist wishing to help his patient will be more interested in those factors which he believes are more relevant and he will dampen other facets of the experience. He may even use compounds such as nicotinic acid to reduce perceptual changes. The psychiatrist who has used LSD to produce a model of delirium tremens will not be surprised if his subjects do develop a condition indistinguishable from delirium tremens and continue to drink thereafter.

OTHER FACTORS. They include personality, avocation, education, and orientation. There is little doubt that a Jungian analyst will find many archtypes nor will Freud's disciples lack early memories of oedipal conflict.

The Setting

As with any drama (and the LSD experience may be included among the great dramas of the world) which has actors and directors there must also be a stage and its setting. The setting is as important to the reaction as are the props and sets of the stage to the performance. It is true that even with badly staged settings the LSD experience may be a good one but this would be unusual. If a psychedelic experience is desired attention must be given to all the factors of space, color, sound, and other environmental matters which increase personal comfort. Noisy, unpleasant, uncomfortable rooms tend to do the reverse to the experience.

PHYSICAL SETTING. Although very little is known about the best physical environment for LSD reactions some investigators have designed spaces which increase the chances that the experience will be a good one. They have provided valuable clues. When architects have become interested in these matters and have studied the space requirements by themselves experiencing what LSD can do, then proper spaces for maximun psychedelic responses will be made.

NUMBER OF PEOPLE PRESENT. The number of other people present has a profound effect on the LSD reaction (Cheek, 1963). No hard and fast rules determine the optimum number. This depends upon the familiarity and trust between subject and observers. The objective is also very important. If the objective is therapy, then an optimum number ranges from two to four. An ideal number is three—patient, nurse, and physician.

If more than four people are present, the LSD subject may easily become confused and disturbed. If the objective is to study group interaction larger groups will be tolerated expecially if the subjects are sophisticated in the self-use of LSD. In any event it is best for all observers to be present in the room with the subject before the LSD experience begins. They may then come and go without disturbing him too much. A stranger coming into the room has a profoundly harmful effect on the experience. The most harmful (to the experience) setting is the one in which strangers, visitors, and other curious people pop in and out.

VISUAL AND AUDITORY AIDS. Photographs, paintings, and colorful objects like drapes and rugs help the subject toward the psychedelic experience. Music also is very helpful. Subjects frozen in a psychotomimetic experience can be transferred within seconds into a psychedelic one when especially meaningful music is played. But these props and aids must not become the end-all or objectives of the reaction. Some subjects find music intolerable and the visual aids repulsive and these aids must not be intruded into the subjects experience. Music may be most distracting and prevent the subject from fully experiencing other components of the reaction. Terrill (1962) pointed out that any attempt to impose a structured test or interview radically altered the experience.

THE EFFECT OF LSD ON NORMAL SUBJECTS

There is no limit to what normal people may experience when they have taken LSD. It would be impossible and inappropriate to describe in detail all the changes which have been reported. The details of changes depend so markedly on the many variables we have already described.

In 1952, Stefaniuk and Osmond gave LSD to 17 normal subjects using usually 100 μg and occasionally 200. One subject took LSD twice.

A verbatim recording was made of each session and in addition detailed subjective retrospective accounts were prepared the following day. These data were analyzed with meticulous detail by Mr. Stefaniuk and classified in a systematic way. We will draw heavily from this massive material which is available for examination. This kind of analysis must necessarily be dull, informative, and descriptive and will not reveal what an LSD experience is to anyone. In order to learn what it is each one will have to experience it for himself. If any subject has been unfortunate and has had schizophrenia or any toxic psychosis he will know roughly what the LSD experience is like—at least the psychotomimetic reaction.

The changes will be described under the major headings; perception, thought, mood, and activity.

Changes in Perception

Perception concerns all the afferent impulses to the brain and includes visual, auditory, touch, taste, smell, kinesthetic, somatic, body image changes, and sense of time passing.

VISUAL CHANGES. For most normal subjects these were the most vivid perceptual changes, especially when LSD was taken the first time. They occurred with eyes open or closed.

Eyes Open. Blurring of vision. This was very common; it was not present all the time and tended to come and go. It was present in 7 out of 18 subjects in the Stefaniuk and Osmond study (hereafter all numbers refer to the number of subjects reporting these changes out of 18). Along with blurring of vision two subjects noted vision was distorted, queer or funny, 4 subjects reported a shifting fluttering vision and 2 complained of difficulty in focusing. The pronounced mydriasis might account for this blurring of vision.

Imagery filling the visual world. Stefaniuk and Osmond ran these experiences in a large, comfortably furnished living room. This determined to a degree the experiences of their subjects. Normal subjects in other rooms or out of doors would also have their experience shaped by their environment in the same way.

Imagery filling the visual world refers to things seen in the three-dimensional space within the subjects field of vision. Eleven (out of 18) subjects noted these. They described the following images—space full of patterns and objects, weird patterns, a lacework pattern over everything, stuff growing all over the room, ribbons streaming all over the room, several layers of patterns superimposed, the air full of little circular things, a rainbow effect, glass balloons filling the air, a grey lacework over everything, fog or smoke filling everything, etc. This imagery usually occurred in front of the subject but could also appear in the periphery of their vision. Two subjects noted that moving objects had a veil which followed closely.

Changes in three-dimensional space. Space was commonly distorted during the LSD experience. It alternately became smaller and larger. Two subjects noted the room changed both in size and in shape. Perspective was altered for 2 more. The floors and walls moved for 7. The rug was particularly mobile and moved for 6, but 4 subjects saw only changes in the rug pattern. Distortion of space also affected the regularity of angles which became too acute or too broad. Some of these changes were very disturbing to some subjects, for example the perception of walls closing in on one.

Many subjects described new dimensions of experience. They should not be confused with spatial coordinates. They were attempting to describe new or different worlds of reality and there was no limit to the number of these new dimensions which were described.

Objective tests confirmed statements that space perception was altered. Weckowicz (1959) studied the effect of 35 μg of LSD on constancy of perception. He used a double blind Latin square crossover design. LSD increased the variability of performance of each individual in judging the size of test objects. Using a larger dose of 125 μg Edwards and Cohen (1961) also found constancy was decreased when the standard object was 30 cm away but not when it was 180 cm distant. The Mueller-Lyer illusion was increased.

Objects appeared to fluctuate in distance from the subject. This was noted by six. Perhaps the normal minor adjustments in distance vision are exaggerated by LSD.

Faces on people and in pictures were altered in unusual ways. Five subjects reported faces were flat (two dimensional) and very frequently two-dimensional pictures in photographs, paintings, and scenes on drapery became three dimensional and alive. When the subjects walked or were driven in a car unusual changes were noted. Objects being passed by enlarged too quickly and the impression created was that these objects exploded into their subject's field of vision.

Long corridors appeared to be interminably long and this was very disconcerting to some. On the contrary, objects in corridors often appeared much too large or too close.

Changes in faces. These were very common and led to many unusual and bizarre associations. Eight subjects described changes in the shape. Three observed changes in shape of eyes which became slanted, oriental, Indian, etc. This gave many faces an Eastern or oriental cast which subjects associated with changes in age or disease. Four noted changes in eyebrows which became animal-like, tufted, etc. Sometimes the face became very young, then it was over corrected and the face appeared very old.

The eyes were commonly seen as piercing and frightening. It was not unusual for subjects to see three eyes as though drawn by the Cubist School of Art. There were two eyes facing to one side in a profile view with one eye facing the viewer directly. Similar drawings have been made by paranoid schizophrenics. Perhaps this was due to a prolonged after image effect as the head was turned.

Shadows and areas of light produced unusual facial changes. The darker areas were accentuated, and shaven beard appeared to grow hair. Colors were altered and often skin developed a marked greenish tint. Very often certain prominent features were accentuated so that faces appeared to be caricatures. Ten subjects at one time or another observed these caricatures of faces which ranged from animal or bird-like faces to old men, old "geizers" resembling W. C. Fields the comedian, a fox, and one face that even appeared to be a snake. The same changes occurred in the subjects' own faces in the mirror and often they saw their faces take on the appearance of their fathers or mothers. This was very valuable for exploring associations and early memories of parents. One patient was able to free himself of his hostility toward his father in a few minutes of examination of his own face in the mirror. He saw his father's face, realized his father was a man like all men, and achieved the insight that his ambivalence, though proper as a boy, was no longer appropriate.

The extremities also changed. Six subjects (out of 18) noted changes in size. To three, their hands seemed to wither away. Seven noted hair or fur growing from their hands. Very often hands and feet pulsated, that is, became alternately larger and smaller, or became alternately closer and further. Rarely subjects saw their limbs float off in space. Many changes in surface, texture, color, shape, etc. also were seen.

Changes in objects. Objects also developed unusual movements as did limbs and faces but the associations were different. They appeared to change shape and size and pulsated. They appeared endowed with life. Wall clocks pulsated and glowed. Parallel lines or patterns became distorted, developed wavelike forms and moved or rippled as if covered with a layer of film or water. Similar changes appeared on pictures. Van Cogh's paintings were especially appropriate for eliciting interesting visual changes, but other artistic works were often just as effective. It was not unusual for subjects to find themselves within the picture which then became their world. Pictures were very useful props for producing psychedelic experiences.

Colors and colored objects. Twelve of the subjects saw changes in shading or in lines, while seven saw one color change to another. Five saw colors of objects project beyond the border of the surface. The unusual appearance of colors on familiar objects made them seem grotesque, for example purple-green hues on faces. Four subjects saw brilliant colors which filled the air.

These subjective reports were supported by objective tests. Edwards and Cohen (1961) found color detection was not altered but Hartman and Hollister (1963) reported LSD increased color experiences for a variety of different stimuli. Hue discrimination was reduced more by psilocybin than by LSD or mescaline but the latter two produced more color imagery. Abramson *et al.* (1955a,b) reported LSD enhanced color perception.

Halos or areas of color or light which were seen to surround living objects, especially heads and shoulders, and sometimes inanimate objects, were seen by some subjects who have taken LSD. Very few normal adults see halos but not infrequently young people do and some schizophrenic patients see halos about people they like. Four subjects saw colored halos around the heads of the observers.

Illusions and hallucinations. Illusions are images based upon visual stimuli coming from real patterns but which are elaborated into formed images. Hallucinations are formed images which are quite independent of external stimuli. Illusions were very common during the LSD experience. Hallucinations were less common but did occur frequently. Usually the subjects knew the hallucinations were due to the LSD even though there was seldom any doubt about their reality. Moments of panic occurred when subjects became so deeply involved in the hallucination they forgot they had taken LSD and thought themselves mad or lost. There is no point in describing the hallucinations. They were the same as those described for mescaline by Ellis, Kluver, Huxley, and many others. These subjects saw animals, explosions, people, Balanese dancers, dancing nymphs, castles, fantastic gardens, visions, infinity, etc. One of our subjects saw a rectangular grid before him. At each intersecting point on the grid he saw a dancing woman, first fully clothed, later nude. Every woman at every intersection danced in rhythm with music being played. This hallucination continued many hours and later that evening while his friends were watching television he found his dancing girls much more interesting.

Changes in intensity of light. Often the first indication of change was sudden awareness that more light was about, or the room or world became darker. Often there was a fluctuation between having too little or too much light.

Visual perseveration. This reaction took place quite often. Eight sub-jects perseverated images, seven noted after-images. The rapid move-ment of objects produced unusual after-images. The moving arm some-times appeared to be a number of arms standing still. A ball flying though the air appeared to be an arc of several balls stopped in flight. Colored after-images also were very common.

Qualitative changes in objects. There were striking changes in the qualitative judgment of objects seen. Objects which normally were free of emotional connotation became unusually distressing or over-whelmingly beautiful and were enveloped by new significance. One subject, a clinical psychologist, was absorbed for 2 hours in a small speck on the wall of the room. He reported he had never seen anything as beautiful or significant. He watched it pulsate and change in shape and color; it developed great significance for him. This property of LSD makes it possible to use visual aids for converting a psychotomimetic experience into a psychedelic one; for example, flowers which were cuplike, for example roses, became alive; the petals seemed to breathe by opening and closing. Many subjects found this very valuable and significant for them as an expression of life in general. There were seldom sexual associations to flowers. On the other hand, the flower sometimes became quite repulsive and was discarded by the subjects.

Kelm *et al.* (1963) found that 200 µg of LSD decreased the magnitude of the figural after-effect in alcoholic subjects. A little earlier, Kelm (1962a) had developed a very accurate and sensitive method for meas-uring the figural after-effect and had found that alcoholics who had taken LSD resembled schizophrenics not given LSD.

Eyes Closed. Even with the eyes closed rich and varied patterns were seen. Seven subjects saw brilliantly colored lights, colors, and objects. Geometrical patterns, formless shapes, colors and forms became visible. Eight subjects saw a succession of formed scenes. Religious scenes were frequent, as were animal scenes, palaces, cathedrals, and jewels.

Blind people do not have vivid visual perceptual changes. Alema (1952) gave 50 µg of LSD to a man blind since his first eye was enucleated. There was only a slight change in colors he was aware of normally. Rinkel (1956a) gave a physicist, blind since birth, LSD twice. He had no visual reaction on either occasion.

Recently, an intelligent student at the University of Saskatchewan, blind since birth, was given 100 µg of LSD. She had overcome her blind-ness handicap very well and she was independent and able to get on without help. During her experience her auditory acuity was increased. She was able to judge herself in relationship to her environment with very little difficulty. Only once during the experience did she have a transient flash of light. However, she had a typical psychedelic reaction to the LSD in the field of sound. The room pulsated, and became larger and smaller. The ceiling came down to her and later she felt that she had floated up to the ceiling. She noted having had the out-of-the-body experience commonly sensed by nonblind people.

In order to simulate blindness, Hoffer and Osmond gave LSD to three normal subjects who were blindfolded. The first subject received 200 μg and he remained blindfolded for 2 hours with no visual changes. But as soon as the blindfold was removed he became violently ill or seasick: He later explained that the violent rush of visual imagery nauseated him. The other two subjects still saw visual changes, even though blindfolded, but they were much less intense (Hoffer, 1956).

Sensory deprivation experiments are in vogue. Early work suggested that subjects isolated for a time, which varied from a few minutes to many hours, experienced changes similar to those produced by hallucinogenic drugs. Recent and better controlled work suggests these conclusions were premature. In any event it seemed likely a combination of sensory deprivation and hallucinogenic drugs would be synergistic. Cohen and Edwards (1964) combined sensory deprivation with the effect of 125 μg of LSD. The sensory deprivation consisted of sitting in a soft armchair in a lightproof, sound-attenuated cubicle for two hours. The experiment was conducted double blind. After the two-hour period the subjects were asked whether they had been given LSD. Of the 10 subjects given LSD without sensory deprivation all concluded correctly they had been given LSD. Of the ten given LSD plus sensory deprivation, six concluded they had been given either placebo or nothing. Another believed he had received a smaller dose of LSD. This research showed that sensory deprivation was antagonistic to the LSD experience. Schizophrenic patients also had fewer symptoms when placed in stimuli-free rooms.

Shortly after deprivation was terminated, all seven subjects soon became aware of the typical LSD visual changes. In one case the reaction came on in the middle of a sentence. The sudden onrush of visual changes was similar to the sudden development of perceptual changes in the blindfolded subject whose blindfold was removed.

The most economical hypothesis which will account for these findings is that LSD alters brain function which is not apparent until there are visual stimuli to be processed. Thus subjects who are blindfolded or placed in isolation will have many fewer stimuli confronting them and will have moderate or minimal changes. When the blindfold is removed or when normal vision is restored the complete reaction becomes possible. A sudden onrush of changes could lead to nausea. But in blind subjects accustomed to using all the nonvisual modes of perception, LSD produces the visual experience within the framework of the sensory field available to them.

AUDITORY CHANGES. To most normal subjects the auditory world is less stimulating than the visual world and the range and quality of sound changes is less. It is not surprising that fewer auditory changes occur under LSD. But when auditory changes become vital as in the blind, then LSD can produce just as vivid alterations as in the field of vision. The example of psychedelic experience in the blind girl demonstrated this.

The auditory changes which did occur were increased sensitivity to sound or decreased sensitivity, inability to localize the source of sound, confusion or inability to understand the sounds, and finally auditory hallucinations. There were also qualitative changes in judging sound.

Increased auditory acuity. This was very common during the LSD experience. Six subjects became aware of background noise not noticeable by the observers. Perhaps this was due to an inability to discriminate between relevant and background sounds.

Decreased auditory acuity. This was uncommon, none of the 18 subjects observed it.

Inability to comprehend sounds. This occurred during LSD confu- and if it did occur did it so at the height of confusion. One subject noted this. It can be very frightening. Some subjects confused their own voices with the observers voice and were surprised when they realized it was their own voice. Five of the subjects reported sound pulsated. This produced an effect as if the speaker was first near, then far. The blind subject heard the room becoming alternately large and small by the echoes of sound in the room.

Inability to Comprehend Sounds. This occurred during LSD confusion. If three or more people were present and conversation was general the subject could become even more confused by a babble (to him) of words.

Hallucinations. These occurred rarely. Auditory hallucinations resembled those heard in delirium tremens or in schizophrenia and included hearing voices, music, laughing and unusual sounds.

Qualitative changes. Very often sounds which normally had no special esthetic appeal were heard in a most unusual manner. Subjects normally indifferent to music often became enthralled by it. One of our subjects, a nuclear physicist, was amazed by the beauty of music being played on an old scratchy record player. After a while he exclaimed "I wish they could play it as beautifully as I now hear it." This enhancement of the auditory experience by LSD was very useful for bringing out the psychedelic reaction. Carefully selected music was very effective in changing the subjects mood and associations to them. One subject, an intellectual, cold, alcoholic physician had no emotional reaction to his LSD after 2½ hours. At this time, "Ave Maria" was played for him. He seemed startled for a moment, then became transfixed with emotion and he began to cry. The song had suddenly taken him to his youth when living with some priests he had been very happy. The music triggered off an emotional catharsis which completely altered a psychotomimetic into a psychedelic experience.

Mixed sensation of sound. Six subjects saw visual objects when certain sounds were made. In one case a telephone rang and the subject saw ripples of waves each time it rang. Another subject saw flashes of light radiating from a glass each time it was struck by a fork.

TASTE CHANGES. Very few changes in taste were reported. For four subjects, foods tasted flat. For some, peculiar new tastes appeared. One subject found coffee had two separate tastes, one sour and the other more like coffee. More important than changes in taste were changes in tactile sensation in the mouth. Foods felt coarse, or gritty and this markedly altered sensation of taste. Some subjects found food tasted bitter and tended to become paranoid and suspected the food had been poisoned.

TACTILE CHANGES. These occurred more frequently than did olfactory and taste changes. Seven subjects reported that cloth changed in texture and became coarse, dry, unreal, different, very fine, very velvety, etc. Hyperacuity to ones own clothing occurred and was sometimes painful. Small pieces of sculpture produced unusual tactile sensations. Occasionally skin felt grimy and dirty and some subjects washed their hands over and over trying to cleanse them. Eight subjects complained of localized anesthesia.

Awareness of temperature was also changed. Six subjects were too warm, one too cool and one alternated between feeling too warm or too cool. Often subjects felt so cold they covered up even on hot days and they became extraordinarily sensitive to slight air currents. Four subjects complained of feeling sweaty.

Edwards and Cohen (1961) found their subjects were less able to discriminate on the two point discrimination test.

KINESTHETIC CHANGES. Under this group we have included changes in awareness of the relationship of the body to gravity. Many changes occurred in sensations of pressure, weight, etc. Subjects felt full up, clogged up, heavy headed, light headed, or empty. Ten subjects felt light headed.

Shaking or vibration phenomena occurred in nine subjects. They occurred independently of other phenomena. Some subjects felt they could not walk, eat or smoke but usually when urged to do so they were surprised to find that they had little difficulty.

Decreased awareness of limb position occurred quite commonly. Subjects sat with one limb limp in an unusual or even dangerous position due to excessive pressure on their limbs. Observers should watch for this and ask the subjects to move about when this happens. The arm of one subject felt so light it floated upward of its own accord and the subject seemed catatonic. Many subjects felt foggy or dizzy. Tingling of the extremities occurred in three subjects.

CHANGES IN BODY IMAGE. Visual changes in one's body have been described. This was an additional peculiar change, the out-of-the-body experience. Many subjects became so unaware of their body they felt free of it and floated off into space. They described themselves as being out of their bodies. They did not stay out very long, but would alternately be within and then outside of their body. This reaction usually occurred with psychedelic reactions, they were usually very pleasant experiences and were used by subjects for exploring the world, for exploring time, etc. The subjects invariably identified their own "real" person, not with their physical bodies, but with what had gone out. Occasionally the person out-of-his-body saw his physical body still in the chair, on the bed, etc. The reverse never occurred.

SOMATIC CHANGES. These are not clearly demarcated from kinesthetic changes but they include bodily sensations which are distinctly unpleasant. They occurred most frequently in the early phases of the LSD reaction. These changes included nausea (8 subjects) and, very rarely, vomiting. Since we have begun to give LSD after a full breakfast instead of on an empty stomach, these undesirable reactions have become rare. Other changes which occurred were tension in the muscles which became tense, rigid, and painful and caused headache, pains in the neck, etc.

SENSE OF TIME PASSING. It is rare for time to remain normal under LSD. Subjective awareness of time passing was altered in most subjects. It stopped, slowed up, or speeded up, and even ran backwards. These changes were very surprising to the subjects probably because the clock has conditioned most people to a steady state of time passing. These time changes were so novel the subjects could find no phrases with which to describe them and used superlatives which may seem like gross exaggerations to naive observers.

Many subjects exclaimed several hours after being given the LSD that only minutes had gone by. More often time was accelerated so that after a few minutes subjects reported it as if thousands of years had passed. Sometimes time stopped for a few seconds. For Hoffer time stopped as he was watching a large electric wall clock. The second hand came to a dead stop and stayed there. Hoffer was stopped in time visually even though he knew intellectually that time was still moving on as before.

Occasionally time had no beginning nor an end. When Hoffer listened to a high note being sung it seemed to last forever with no beginning and no end. In one case time was reversed and the subject who had picked up a cup of tea and drank from it was astonished to find he was sipping from the cup before he picked it up and before the tea was poured, as if a film had been run backward.

Objective time was also altered. Aronson *et al.* (1959) found that 1 to 2 μg of LSD per kg caused subjects to estimate time intervals as having passed sooner than they had. Boardman *et al.* (1957) reported that LSD did not make 4 subjects overestimate 1 second of time but their temporal frame of reference was altered. Kenna and Sedman (1964) found that 8 out of 29 subjects reported changes in the way they experienced time passing with doses ranging from 40 to 200 μg. With higher doses (70–400 μg) an additional 12 noted similar changes. Edwards and Cohen (1961) found reaction time was increased with 125 μg. With lower doses no changes were found (Abramson *et al.*, 1955b), but verbal reaction time was increased as was time required to name colors.

Thought Changes

Process. The authors prefer to describe two main aspects of thinking. These are the process or act of thinking and the content or things being thought about. Process concerns the ability to construct logical sequences of words or phrases to form a coherent account of one's thought. Changes in process include blocking when the mind suddenly seems wiped free of all thought for a moment, skidding, jumping about, erratic responses, over-rapidity and under-rapidity of ideas and finally inability to construct sensible sentences.

The following changes in process were reported: (a) concentration span was shortened (8 subjects), (b) interposed thoughts (2 subjects), (c) mind wandering (3 subjects), (d) wavelike changes in thought (3 subjects), (e) unable to control thought (6 subjects), and (f) memory changes (5 subjects).

Jarvik *et al.* (1955b) reported that 100 μg of LSD significantly impaired performance and arithmetic but 50 μg did not. Jarvik *et al.* (1955a) reported further that LSD decreased performance on tests of attention and concentration. The higher dose impaired recognition and recall of various stimuli. LSD had a deleterious effect upon recall and recognition of various kinds of visual and auditory stimuli.

CONTENT. Content of thought includes the whole subject matter of content. Abnormal content includes ideas of reference, delusions, bizarre ideas and associations, etc. These occurred very frequently during the LSD experience. Thought content was influenced very markedly by variables such as personality, lifes experiences, education, the setting, the particular perceptual changes, etc. Stefaniuk and Osmond's (1952) subjects reported the following changes: feeling of influence (2 subjects), feelings of unusual significance attributed to random events (6 subjects), unusual associations to objects and events (11 subjects), paranoid ideas (10 subjects), and lack of motivation (6 subjects).

Judgment of reality which depends upon normal perception and normal thought, was frequently impaired. Seven subjects felt they had wakened from a different or from an unusual reality. Seven described different forms of reality. Nine subjects were depersonalized. Two felt they were dual beings and two experienced deja vu.

MENTAL TESTING. Stefaniuk tried to have all the subjects under LSD complete a set of psychological tests. It was soon discovered that a basic dilemma faced the research person. When doses were used which gave the subject the greatest number of perceptual changes and which produced the best clinical reaction, they were unable to cooperate and to complete the tests at the time called for in the research protocol. When lower doses were used subjects were able to cooperate but then one tested an experience not typical of LSD. For these reasons reports of psychological tests may be misleading.

General Comprehension Tests. General comprehension as measured by the Wechsler-Bellevue test was impaired. In response to the question about finding a stamped addressed envelope, one subject described what he had done to a letter he had received, another was unable to answer. In response to the "fire in theatre" question, one subject replied "he would head for the door and if it was hot enough he could make it." Another subject replied he would shout. A third stated she wished the observer would not talk about it.

Proverbs. Proverbs aroused associations unrelated to the task. Instead they were drawn from personal elements within the subject. When an attempt was made to explain the proverb it was often concrete. Subjects rephrased the original wording, repeated the qualitative indicators, for example, all that glitters is not gold was responded to by the phrase "nice and shiny."

Problems. The mental solution of problems was difficult under LSD. One subject could not solve the pail-water problem. After awhile he stated the fire was too small for the water and suggested the examiner put out the fire by putting his foot on it. Persistent discussion by the observer finally annoyed the subject and he remarked that the problem was silly as hell. A few minutes later the subject was given one gram of nicotinic acid by mouth and within a few minutes he was able to solve the problem normally.

Comprehension and Similarities. These tests were difficult to score. Replies were inappropriate; for example, when one subject was asked why people require a license to be married he replied there could be no marriage in the experiment. When asked why shoes were made of leather, he replied, because they were down here on the floor and were green. Another replied with the question, should they be made of something else. Bizarre responses were given also to the similarities test.

Digit Span. Silverstein and Klee (1958a) reported 2 μg/kg impaired digit span memory. One of Stefaniuk's subjects, who showed the least response to LSD, was able to recall a sequence of seven digits.

Word Association Test. There was a marked variability of responses in four subjects given this test. One found the test annoying and foolish because it interfered with his perceptual changes. Another subject merely repeated the stimulus word. He was quite confused. A third subject who had no thought disorder answered appropriately. The fourth subject gave slang associations such as seraph to laugh, giraffe to seraph.

When 200 μg of LSD was given, word association tests were seldom completed and merely confirmed the gross impairment noted clinically. Weintraub *et al.* (1959, 1960) using less LSD (2 μg/kg) gave the WAT to 50 subjects. LSD did not produce schizophrenic-like responses but did abolish the differential response between traumatic and nontraumatic stimuli. Their subjects made more errors, fewer popular responses, and reacted more slowly. On retesting, comparison normal subjects were able to correct pathological responses they had made before but when under the influence of LSD they repeated these responses. Grof (1960) and Grof *et al.* (1963) gave the WAT to subjects given LSD. They found that the responses were not much different from responses given to their placebo comparison subjects. The only hallucinogen which produced a high degree of abnormality in the WAT was adrenochrome.

Numerical Test Subtraction. One of the most useful tests was the serial minus seven test. The subject was asked to subtract 7 from 100 and so on. Most subjects were able to cooperate with this test but very few were able to complete the test normally.

Learning. Aronson *et al.* (1962) found LSD impaired learning of paired words when 30 paired words were used but not when 22 were.

Memory, which is basic to learning, was also impaired (Silverstein and Klee, 1958a). Performance on the Dual Pursuit test was also impaired (Silverstein and Klee, 1960).

However LSD may also improve the ability to learn. If this were not so the psychedelic experience would help no one. A large number of subjects (psychopaths, alcoholics, neurotics) have grasped ideas and concepts in a few moments which had eluded them for years. These sudden flashes of insight or inspiration prove new concepts can be acquired very rapidly. One subject, a very intelligent alcoholic physician, prided himself on the fact that he was not a drug addict. Under the influence of LSD he learned very quickly that alcohol was a chemical and by his own older definition a drug. Subjects have learned understanding, compassion, tolerance, the meaning of fear, etc. As a general rule, learning trivial matters would be much impaired. This would include the psychological tests which are looked upon by most LSD subjects as a nuisance which intrude upon their more interesting subjective experiences. However, matters of great importance to the subject such as should he drink or not, should he have faith or not, may be resolved very quickly. Fortunately memory for the newly learned insights remained very good and often they were never forgotten even if they were not always used. This is one of the main advantages of the LSD experience compared to barbiturate abreactions.

Performance Tests. Aronson and Klee (1960) compared performance on the Porteous Maize test of 28 subjects given 75 μg of LSD against 34 comparison subjects. LSD decreased performance by producing a 2 year deficit. It resembled the action of chlorpromazine. LSD also decreased the capability of subjects to carry out well planned and adaptive behavior.

According to Abramson *et al.* (1955d), 100 μg of LSD impaired performance measured by the Thurstone Hand and the Minnesota Paper Form Board tests. Performance on the Bender Gestalt test was poor (Abramson *et al.*, 1955a). Performance on the pursuit rotor test and a modified Dunlap steadiness test was also impaired but on subsequent retesting practice compensated for the mild LSD impairment (Abramson *et al.*, 1955a).

Intellectual Function. Levine *et al.* (1955) concluded that LSD reduced intellectual function. This is undoubtedly true for many aspects of intellectual performance especially for naive subjects. But it is impossible that little impairment would be found if sophisticated subjects who have taken LSD many times were tested. We have spent many hours talking to sophisticated subjects who have taken LSD. They performed so well it would be very difficult to decide whether there was any impairment. Some reported their experiences by writing them on paper while they were observing the reaction and their literary production could not be excelled for clarity, interest, and composition.

Linton *et al.* (1964) tested recall by means of a questionaire. Normal subjects were tested during the LSD reaction and the following day. The retrospective accounts agree with drug day accounts. The correlation coefficient was 0.90. Out of 74 items 26 were stable, 18 were dropped, the following day 8 were added and 6 were added or dropped.

In general, we have found that the vivid parts of the experience were remembered more easily. We have given the HOD test (Hoffer and Osmond, 1961b,c) to subjects a few days after LSD and many years after LSD was given. The scores for both groups of subjects were similar. Our own experiences have remained vivid in our memories up to 12 years after having taken LSD.

Memory for the LSD reaction does not differ from memory for any memorable event. Some will remember details for many years, others only the highlights.

The Rorschach Test. This was one of the least useful tests for LSD subjects. They generally did not like it, were not able to complete all the cards and often preferred their own visual experiences to looking at dull cards. Cards were rejected because they were too dull, too fluid, too alive, or too silly. The cards pulsated, adopted grotesque shapes and colors, and came and went. Subjects saw in them women, bears, puppies, cows, bats, flowers, crabs. Associations of this imagery were often bizarre. Only card number 6 produced one sexual fantasy in one subject. In general when visual changes were minimal subjects found the cards dull, and when visual changes were present the cards were more interesting.

Changes in Mood

The whole spectrum of mood changes may occur.

EUPHORIA. Half the subjects in the Stefaniuk-Osmond series became euphoric during the LSD experience. Often it was the first indication that the LSD was beginning to work. Usually it was uncontrollable. The euphoria ranged in intensity from very slight to a very intense reaction and came in waves. When there were no precipitating events for the euphoria (and this was quite common) subjects felt silly. They could not stop their giggling and laughing. Some rolled on the floor with hilarious laughter.

Euphoria which came during the psychedelic experience was appropriate to what was being seen, heard, or thought.

TRANSCENDENTAL REACTION. This reaction is well known to man, especially to mystics and founders of religions. William James (1902) described it in his classical books on psychology. Many subjects found themselves in this transcendental state. They were thoroughly relaxed, intensely interested in what was happening and supremely happy. Many times the observer was not aware of this in the subjects until the moment had passed and was described to them. Usually these experiences were new to the subjects and they found it difficult or even impossible to describe. Occasionally subjects reported they had experienced similar states of mind before but they had not then had the same intensity or clarity.

FLAT. Six subjects felt flat, that is they felt no emotion whatever. It was very marked in the subject given LSD two days after penicillamine treatment and lasted many days (Hoffer and Callbeck, 1960). This observation led to therapeutic trials with penicillamine-LSD in exceedingly tense alcoholics where a state of flatness might be preferable to a state of severe exaltation or euphoria.

FEAR. Five subjects were very fearful. Fear is not at all uncommon in the psychotomimetic experience. Subjects were anxious and felt alone and cut off from the world.

The intensity of the fear and its consequences depends on the skill of the therapist with LSD therapy. Often subjects became fearful when they forgot temporarily that they had taken LSD and they no longer had a rational explanation for their experience. An effective way of dealing with such fear was to remind the subject repeatedly that they had taken LSD, that the reaction would run for a few hours and that they would be normal after that. The preparation of the subject was also important. They should be assured that they will be given medication to bring them out of the experience if it becomes too intense for them.

Many subjects discovered safety mechanisms which they used to control or moderate their fear. These mechanisms were perceptual or ideational. One subject looked at distant objects which were visually stable for him and this steadied him. Another subject found that looking at the observer's green shirt reduced fear. Several subjects used the corners of the room to reduce fear. These points where lines intersected seldom moved visually in contrast to plane surfaces. One subject discovered a cup held in his hand gave him a sense of security and stability. Often subjects suffering intense fear were helped by holding the nurses or therapists hand. Some subjects found that talking incessantly helped reduce their fear.

Tension without fear was also controlled by similar mechanisms. One subject suffered intense abdominal pain until he discovered that whenever he looked at a small sculptured piece of an animal it became alive and his pain vanished. When he did not look at the figure his pain returned. He repeated this many times over a half-hour period.

DEPRESSION. Depression was present in nearly all the subjects. In the psychotomimetic experience it was present for a long time but in the psychedelic experience it was fleeting. We have seen no instances of depression during the transcendental phase of the reaction. Subjects who suffered prolonged depression were seldom benefited by the experience.

Activity Changes

When the LSD session was directed by a qualified competent therapist there was little motor activity. But when the experience was uncontrolled the patient engaged in restless, impulsive and foolish activity. Some therapists stimulated bizarre behavior. Many years ago one of our therapists caused such behavior in a female subject. At the height of her experience she stated "I am going to take off my clothes." He thoughtlessly responded, "Why don't you?" Whereupon she began to disrobe. The nurse and psychiatrist tried to dissuade her but she became more determined to disrobe and eventually became hostile and violent. The LSD reaction had to be terminated by giving her nicotinic acid. The possibility of impulsive behavior makes it essential subjects must be observed carefully and continually. Recently a schizophrenic patient with malvaria was given LSD for some psychological problem she had. For the first four hours she had a good psychedelic experience but between 1:00 and 2:00 PM she suddenly broke a glass ash tray and before the nurse could stop her had picked up a piece and begun to scratch her wrist.

Creativity

The roots of creativity come from perception, thought, and mood experiences. Because these are altered so strikingly by LSD it has been suggested that creativity might be enhanced. Many artists and authors have been schizophrenic and this apparently was beneficial for their artistic creativity. Van Gogh's paintings have an unusual quality following his psychotic episode, and Blake's work was heavily influenced by his visions. Wasson and Wasson (1957) suggested that early man first saw God after imbibing hallucinogenic mushrooms. Religion would then be considered a by-product of psychedelic reactions.

Creativity may be enhanced only during the experience or it may be permanently improved after the experience is over. In terms of performance it is impossible to test the first proposition, for even if creativity were enhanced during the experience, the profound effect on sensation and on hand–eye coordination would prevent its expression in painting or in other skills requiring motor skill. Verbal creativity could be improved. Berlin *et al.* (1955) treated four nationally known artists with either 50 μg of LSD or 400–700 mg of mescaline. They were expected to paint during the reaction. As would be expected they were reluctant to draw at the height of the reaction. But they did complete some drawings. According to these authors the drawings indicated greater esthetic value when judged by a panel of artists. The published drawings resembled drawings made by schizophrenic patients. But quality in art is as difficult to objectify as improvement in psychiatry.

Tonini and Montanari (1955) gave one artist 60 μg of LSD. At the height of the experience he could not draw but later when he began to recover he could. His productions did not contain any new elements of creativity. They also resembled schizophrenic art. Silverstein and Klee (1958b) had LSD subjects draw for the "draw-a-person" test. Under LSD they, not surprisingly, drew less well.

A more valid test of enduring creativity would be the effect on art for several years after the experience. In Saskatchewan several artists were given LSD about 4 years ago. Since then there have been some major changes in one and his reputation has grown markedly, but this might have occurred even if he had not taken LSD. It will be very difficult to test the hypothesis that LSD permanently enhances creativity.

There is much evidence that LSD improves recognition of art and increases interest in works of art. Many of our subjects who were quite disinterested in music or art, found, to their surprise, that after examining art under LSD the newly created interest remained with them.

Artists may not be good subjects for examining the effect of LSD upon creativity. Many of them normally see the world with the visual richness common to LSD and they are not surprised by what happens to their visual world.

In our opinion LSD does not enhance creativity by putting into a person something which was not present before. A noncreative person will not thereafter become more creative nor will a gifted person become more gifted. The main effect of the experience comes from the alteration of old interests and the production of new ones which then inspire a creative person to enter fields of activity which previously did not interest him. As Savage has stated (1962a,b) the transcendental state may open up avenues of creativity but it is not creativity itself.

Psychotomimetic Reaction to LSD

The first comprehensive clinical reports appeared in the European psychiatric literature. The experience was described as an exogenous or toxic reaction of the Bonhoeffer type (W. A. Stoll, 1947, 1949; Becker, 1949; Condrau, 1949; Rostafinski, 1950; de Giacomio, 1951; Weyl, 1951; Mayer-Gross, 1951; Mayer-Gross et al., 1951; Delay and Pichot, 1951. These clinical reports have not been surpassed. The large number of reports since then merely elaborated what these earlier reports contained. This is another example where no-blind purely subjective studies started by Hofmann in 1943 were confirmed by no-blind studies on subjects by other clinicians. Recently a few double blind studies were made that added nothing to our knowledge of LSD (Linton and Langs, 1962a,b). As we will show later double blind studies of LSD as an hallucinogen against nonhallucinogens are impossible for any sophisticated investigator and nonsophisticated research people ought not to be using LSD.

LSD was first studied as a psychotomimetic in North America by Rinkel in 1949 and reported at the anual meeting of the American Psychiatric Association in 1950 (Rinkel, 1951). These studies as well as those by Hoch (1953) and his colleagues which followed soon after are the classical American studies of LSD (Rinkel et al., 1952; Deshon et al., 1952; Hoch et al., 1952; Osmond, 1953, 1956). They corroborated the earlier European findings but they went much further. They were impressed with the similarity between the LSD experience and if one may call it so, the schizophrenic experience.

This work prepared the way for the valuable concept—the model experimental psychosis. The early American studies suggested LSD psychosis could yield valuable information which would be useful in determining factors which lead to schizophrenia and for developing treatments. The early European reports concentrated primarily on its similarity to toxic psychosis. This latter concept if widely accepted could have led psychiatric research into a dead end. Elements of the controversy still linger on. Recently Hollister (1962) questioned the validity of the model psychosis concept which he felt was misleading. This argument was stimulating intellectually but scientifically was of little value and persuaded few. There are too many ambiguities both in the definitions of schizophrenia and in the production of the LSD experience for it to have much significance. The experience can be made to model (not to ape or to reproduce identically) neurosis, psychopathy, behavioral disorders, depression, schizophrenia, and even toxic psychosis such as delirium tremens. Some will find the differences between the model and the syndrome being modeled as more rewarding, while other investigators will find the similarities more useful. Both aspects of the phenomena are important.

The concept of the model schizophrenia was used by Osmond and Smythies (1952), to develop their toxin M hypothesis of schizophrenia. This in turn led to the first modern specific biochemical hypothesis of schizophrenia—the adrenochrome hypothesis developed by Hoffer and Osmond (1952) and later by Hoffer, Osmond and Smythies (1954).

It is useful to divide the LSD reaction into phases. Deshon *et al.* (1952) gave LSD 17 times to 15 normal subjects. They used between 20 and 90 μg doses. From their experiences they divided the LSD reaction into four periods. These were: (a) the prodromal state which terminated when the experience was fully developed, (b) the height of the experience, (c) the phase from the termination of the height until evening, and (d) the aftermath. We have found this classification a very useful and a natural one which easily accommodated the experience of over 1000 LSD reactions studied in Saskatchewan since 1952. We will call these stages prodromal, experience, recovery, and aftermath. There are no sharp interfaces between these phases.

PRODROMAL PHASE

Generally this phase was unpleasant. It was characterized by the gradual development of sympathetic excitation. The best physiological indicator was the dilatation of the pupil. Nausea, retching, and occasionally vomiting occurred. If subjects were given LSD after breakfast, these prodromal symptoms were much reduced in frequency and intensity. Other prodromal symptoms were severe muscular cramplike pains which came in waves. At the end of the prodromal phase these autonomic changes were less intense and less troublesome in the psychotomimetic experience but they were absent during the psychedelic experience.

The time when LSD symptoms first occurred depended upon the method of administration more than upon the size of the dose. Hoch (1956) found that 100 to 250 μg, given orally, caused symptoms in 30–45 minutes. The intramuscular route of administration produced symptoms in 15–20 minutes. Given intravenously, symptoms appeared in several minutes and the intrathecal route caused symptoms almost immediately. LSD given intrathecally sometimes caused toxic changes and Hoch recommended it not be used.

The time when symptoms first appeared varied a good deal and did not depend on the dose in a linear way except of course when doses were used which were completely ineffective. As a rule 100 μg or more given to normal subjects produced a prodromal phase lasting about 1 hour but it varied from 20 minutes to 2 hours.

THE EXPERIENCE

There is little evidence that the duration of the peak experience is markedly influenced either by the dose or by the method of administration. Whether 100 or 1000 μg was used the experience lasted about one to four hours. It seems as though LSD triggered a series of biochemical and psychological reactions which were programmed to run for a certain number of hours. But the duration of the experience varied with diagnosis between subjects and between classes of subjects. Some alcoholics had an experience for only one-half hour while in normal subjects they lasted up to six hours. Pseudoneurotic schizophrenics or undiagnosed schizophrenic patients had experiences which lasted all day, several days, and in a very few cases over one year. Conversely they may fail to react at all. Because so many variables control the duration of the experience it cannot be predicted accurately. In our studies the psychedelic reaction occurred between 10:00 AM and 12 noon when the LSD was given at 9:00 AM. It is our rule that when the initial quantity of LSD has not taken the subject into stage two by 10:00 AM or so, he is given a booster dose. Thus an alcoholic who has not reached the stage two experience with 300 μg may be given another 300 μg between 10:00 and 10:30 AM.

THE RECOVERY

Recovery begins when symptoms begin to wane. It is certain when the subject experiences the first wave of normality. After that the experience wanes in waves for the rest of the day. With each cycle the waves of normalcy become longer and the waves of experience become shorter. Late in the afternoon (from 2 to 9 hours after taking the drug) residual symptoms are left. During stage 3 the subjects should be kept under observation as in stage 2, for during waves of experience their judgment may be defective. Usually subjects in a controlled hospital setting are well enough by 4:00 PM to be left alone, but they should be checked every 10 minutes until they are asleep. It is a useful precaution to sedate them heavily. Occasionally subjects have wakened and wandered away. Toward evening the experience may be reactivated momentarily by fatigue or by unusual events. It is wise to caution the subject this may occur so they will not be frightened unnecessarily.

THE AFTERMATH

This stage is mild for most subjects and is gone by noon of the following day. Mild fatigue and some tension are common and it may last the whole day. By the second day nearly everyone is normal. Rarely, reactions last much longer, as we have shown especially if the contra-indications discussed earlier are not observed.

Many subjects have been much more relaxed after an LSD session for periods of several days to several months. These subjects found themselves in an unusual state of ease in which it was difficult to become irritable or angry. Invariably they regained their normal state of reactivity or irritability.

The psychedelic experience which we have not described so far arose from the psychotomimetic experience. Busch and Johnson (1950) and Forrer and Goldner (1951) observed psychotomimetic changes in their subjects but they also suggested that the experience could be used for gaining access more readily into the world of the schizophrenic and for shortening psychotherapy.

We have not described typical psychotomimetic experiences because this would merely be repititious of material available in the psychiatric text books. Any experience recorded by schizophrenic patients can be duplicated by experiences described by subjects undergoing the psychotomimetic reaction. Recently Carney Landis' valuable book "Varieties of Psychopathological Experiences" (1964) appeared with descriptions and quotations from autobiographical accounts of patients who suffered from schizophrenia. The psychotomimetic experience may be understood by reading this most valuable book.

The Psychedelic Experience

PSYCHEDELICS
(Hallucinogens)

Give me a button of wild peyote
To munch in my den at night,
That I may set my id afloat
In the country of queer delight.

So ho! it's off to the land of dreams
With never a stop or stay,
Where psychiatrists meet with fairy queens
To sing a roundelay.

Give me a flagon of mescaline
To wash o'er my mundane mind,
That I may feel like a schizophrene
Of the catatonic kind.

So hey! let in the vision of light
To banish banality,
Then will I surely catch a sight
Of the Real Reality.

Give me a chalice of lysergic
To quaff when day is done,
That I may get a perceptual kick
From my diencephalon.

So ho! let all resistance down
For a transcendental glance,
Past the superego's frosty frown
At the cosmic underpants.

Give me a pinch of psilocybin
To sprinkle in my beer,
That my psychopathic next-of-kin
May not seem quite so queer.

So hey! it's off for the visions bizarre
Past the ego boundary,
For a snort at the psychedelic bar
Of the new psychiatry.
                              F. W. Hanley, M.D.

Natural phenomena are usually perceived or known long before they are named but they are seldom given careful study and examination by scientists, philosophers and other interested people until they are dignified by a specific name. For the possession of a name gives the phenomena a kind of reality or solidity they did not have before. Osmond (1957a) showed that many investigators who worked with LSD and mescaline became aware the experience did not always model schizophrenia. On the contrary, many subjects had unusually happy and insightful reactions from which they derived a good deal of understanding about themselves, about others and by their interrelationship. Osmond listed the potential uses of LSD as follows:

1. As an aid to psychotherapy and to its variant psychoanalysis.

2. To educate those who work in psychiatry and psychology to understand the strange ways of the mind.

3. To explore the normal mind under unusual circumstances.

4. To examine the social, religious, and philosophical implications of these agents.

Osmond was aware that none of the potentials had much chance of being realized until the experience which would make them possible was drawn to the attention of the scientific world under a new name. This would then educate those people working with LSD that it was something more than a psychotomimetic, a device for making people mad. Osmond coined the word, psychedelic, which he defined, "A psychedelic compound is one like LSD, or mescaline which enriches the mind and enlarges the vision. It is this kind of experience which provides the greatest possibility for examining those areas most interesting to psychiatry and which has provided men down the ages with experiences they have considered valuable above all others."

Osmond pointed out that this interest in chemically produced new states of mind is not new. It has been sought and studied since before the origin of history and has played a notable part in the evolution of religion, art, philosophy and science. The Wassons make a persuasive case for the origin of all religions in the mental states produced by the hallucinogenic mushrooms. Man has not been deterred by the greatest obstacles in their search for these mystical states. To some these experiences came easily but others had to undergo prolonged and severe mortifications of the spirit and flesh before the desirable visions were achieved. So difficult has it been to achieve these states that man has considered it almost immoral should they come with little effort. In fact, one of the greatest criticisms of the psychedelic experience is that it comes rather too easily as if only what is attainable with extreme difficulty is valuable. The experience is debased, so they say, unless the price is high. An example of this attitude is seen in Dean Peerman's (1962) book review of "The Joyous Cosmology: Adventures in the Chemistry of Consciousness." His title, "Instant Mysticism" is designed to create an atmosphere of hostility and brings to mind the ersatz or instant coffee of many decades ago. Peerman is evidently disturbed by his misconceptions, (a) that hallucinogenic drugs are not natural, that is, are artificial, which is odd since they are synthesized by nature (in fact, starvation and flagellation seem less natural ways of getting instant mysticism); (b) that these instant (chemically induced) experiences will allow men to escape "the world of selves, of time, or moral judgement, of utilitarian considerations—precisely the things with which the Christian who in gratitude seeks to do God's will must be concerned." Peerman represents the immediate thoughtless reaction of the ignorant. For contrary to his fears it is precisely these matters which are brought forcefully to the attention of the individual and society by these psychedelic experiences. They have directly led to some of the most beneficial movements in society, religion, Alcoholics Anonymous and recently Synanon—a new and promising society which may do for the drug addict what A.A. has done for the alcoholic. Osmond anticipated these objections when he wrote, "While we are learning, we may hope that dogmatic religion and authoritarian science will keep away from each others throats. We need not put out the visionary's eyes because we do not share his vision. We need not shout down the voice of the mystic because we cannot hear it, or force our rationalizations on him for our own reassurances. Few of us can accept or understand the mind that emerges from these studies: Kant once said of Swedenborg, 'Philosophy is often much embarrassed when she encounters certain facts she dare not doubt yet will not believe for fear of ridicule."

"In a few years, I expect, the psychedelics will seem as crude as our ways of using them. Whether we employ them for good or ill, whether we use them with skill and deftness or with blundering ineptitude depends not a little on the courage, intelligence and humanity of many of us working in the field today.

"I believe that the psychedelics provide a chance, perhaps only a slender one for homofaber, the cunning, ruthless, foolhardy, pleasure-greedy toolmaker to emerge into that other creature whose presence we have so rashly presumed, homo sapiens, the wise, the understanding, the compassionate, in whose fourfold vision—art, politics, science and religion are one. Surely we must seize the chance."

Since Osmond's delineation of the psychedelic experience there has been an extraordinary development in this field. The subject has been described in poetry, in learned journals, in the lay press and there is the Psychedelic Journal. Even within such a brief period of time there are three stages of psychedelic research. The first consists of Osmond's (1953) early work followed by research we carried out in Saskatchewan, which was largely exploratory but which led to our large therapeutic trials using LSD as a component in their treatment. The second stage was developed by the group at the International Foundation For Advanced Study, Menlo Park, California. Professor Harman with his colleagues has been their ablest advocate. This work expanded the use of psychedelic concept into the broad group of behavioral problems and neuroses. The main catalyst has been A. Hubbard, a pioneer in the use of LSD.

The present stage is typified by the careful studies and researches of Unger (1963a,b, 1964). The first two stages were carried out in relative freedom from harsh criticism since the vast majority of people were unaware these studies were being done. Most psychiatrists were either ignorant of these investigations, or if they had heard of LSD, considered it only a drug used by research psychiatrists for making people mad. But stage three was marked by the tremendous upheaval and turmoil which followed the Harvard University enterprises of R. Alpert and T. Leary in 1962. One result of this massive use of LSD on large numbers of volunteers was a remarkable dissemination of LSD's uses and abuses until it is hardly likely any literate citizen has not heard something about it. The controversy according to Pageant Magazine, "rocked the academic, medical, and psychological professions—as well as the governments of the U.S.A. and Mexico." Feature articles were also published in Confidential, Cosmopolitan, Esquire, Fate, Ladies

Home Journal, Life, Look, MacLeans, Medical Tribune, Medical World, News, Playboy, The Reporter, Saga, Saturday Evening Post, Time, Toronto Star Weekly, and cautionary editorials appeared in the Journal of American Medical Association and in the Archives of General Psychiatry (Grinker, 1963).

As a result of the widespread interest in psychedelic drugs in the mass media, several things predictably followed: (a) there was a public demand supported by professionals for the introduction of strict legal controls. The advice of these professionals fell into two groups: those by research psychiatrists who were very familiar with LSD, its uses and its evils (Cohen, 1960a,b), and our own group in Saskatchewan under Hoffer's direction that recommended controls so that these drugs would be freely available to physicians skillful in the use of LSD, and those professionals (that is, Grinker, 1963), whose criticisms were so severe that if accepted at face value, they would have prevented any one from using these compounds for research or therapy.

The widespread interest in LSD and other drugs used as psychedelics in the mass media resulted in a public demand by physicians for the introduction of strict legal controls. Psychiatrists and psychologists, who were familiar with LSD's psychedelic properties and had used it successfully for psychotherapy, were the first to record the results of abusing these reactions. Cohen (1959, 1960a,b, 1963, 1964a,b) and Cohen and Ditman (1962, 1963) found that the incidence of dangerous and undesirable side effects was low. Cohen recommended that LSD could be used by skillful therapists. Other psychiatrists who had different experiences with the properties of LSD (for example Grinker, 1963) took a harsher view and issued thunderous editorials against the evils of this dangerous drug.

Legal controls were introduced in the United States and, of course, in Canada. For a while it seemed as if LSD would join thalidomide as a banned drug in Canada but fortunately Canadian medical associations advised the Canadian Government not to ban its use. Although the criteria for allowing some physicians to use LSD have not been published, they seem to be available to psychiatrists who have university affiliations and who may be eligible for the Minister of Health's list.

STAGE ONE OF PSYCHEDELIC RESEARCH

Following Osmond's (1957a) review, we began an intensive study of the psychedelic experience. Before this we had used LSD as a treatment in a psychotomimetic way. We hoped that a frightful experience which modeled the worst in natural delirium tremens could persuade our alcoholic patients not to drink anymore and so avoid getting delirium tremens. By 1957 it was apparent that even though many of our patients were helped by LSD, it was not its psychotomimetic activity which was responsible. In spite of our best efforts to produce such an experience some of our subjects escaped into a psychedelic experience. Our psychiatrists were more at ease working with the psychedelic experience because it was possible to establish a therapeutic relationship and to use psychotherapy. By that time, Osmond had studied the claims of A. Hubbard that a number of severe alcoholics treated with high doses of LSD, with a particular frame of reference, had been much benefited. Hubbard's claims were corroborated when Osmond personally interviewed many of the alcoholics after treatment. We, therefore, invited A. Hubbard to demonstrate, under controlled conditions at the University Hospital, some of the techniques he had developed using high doses (200 μg or more). The results of therapy on a group of alcoholics were reported by Chwelos *et al.* (1958, 1959). This study was the first one in which the psychedelic method of treating patients was reported. Chwelos *et al.* classified the subjective psychedelic experience into stages or degrees as follows:

1. *Flight into ideas.* This is characterized by tension, irritability, and a vivid awareness of perceptual changes both internal and external.

2. *Stage of somatic awareness.* The subject remains preoccupied with his somatic discomforts.

3. *Stage of confusion and perceptual distortion.* This is the most schizophrenic-like stage.

4. *Stage of paranoia.*

5. *Stage of dual reality.* Here the subject is aware that the LSD experience compared to the experience of normality is valid experience which can be used to explore many facets of the inner and outer world of experience.

6. *Stage of stabilization.* The experience is accepted as offering a new and richer interpretation of all aspects of reality. This experience was described by William James who said, "They are as convincing to those who have them as any direct sensible experiences can be and they are, as a rule, much more convincing than the results established by mere logic ever are."

These stages or types of experiences are gradations towards the psychedelic experience. Subjects may go through them in this sequence or some may be skipped. Not every one has them all. Subjects who do not reach stages 5 and 6 generally are not benefited. They have few pleasant memories of it and are not anxious to repeat. Subjects who reach stage 5 or 6 have had the psychedelic experience.

As a result of our using LSD as a psychedelic drug, some in our group developed the hypothesis that if a therapist who had had much self-experience with LSD were to take it at the same time as the patient, the patient would be guided more easily and effectively through the unpleasant first stages to stages 5 and 6. The treatment results would therefore be much better. This type of therapy was described by Blewett and Chwelos (1959). The first part of the hypothesis is, of course, very difficult to prove or to disprove. But the expected corollary, that is, better results, remains unproven. A small series of alcoholics were intensively treated by the Blewett and Chwelos technique by these two authors and the recovery rates were not better than those achieved when therapists did not take LSD at the same time.

STAGE TWO OF THE PSYCHEDELIC RESEARCH

In stage one of LSD research no special effort was made to control the environment of the patient undergoing therapy. Hospital rooms or psychiatrist's offices were used and there were many environmental distractions which interfered with the patient's experience. The first group to take these factors into account were Maclean *et al.* (1961) who prepared especially designed settings and aids. They used comfortably furnished rooms free of distractions. Visual aids to comfort and enlarge the experience were used. They included photographs of members of the family, reproductions of works of art, and music. Further modifications were made by the International Foundation for Advanced Study who built treatment rooms which would enhance the psychedelic experience. The results of this research have been reported by J. N. Sherwood *et al.* (1962), Harman (1962, 1963a,b), and Savage *et al.* (1963).

J. N. Sherwood *et al.* (1962) corroborated the psychotherapeutic value of the psychedelic experience. They further described the dynamics of the psychedelic experience. It was divided into three stages. Stage one (the evasive stage) is a condensation of Chwelos *et al.* stages 1 to 4. Stage two (the symbolic stage) comprised Chwelos' stage 5. Sherwood's stage three can be compared to Chwelos' stage six. This is the stage of immediate perception. They described part of it as follows: "He comes to experience himself in a totally new way and finds that the age-old question 'Who am I?' does not have a significant answer. He experiences himself as a far greater being than he had even imagined, with his conscious self a far smaller fraction of the whole than he had realized. Furthermore he sees that his own self is by no means so separate from other selves and the universe about him as he might have thought. Nor is the experience of this newly experienced self so intimately related to his corporeal existence."

"These realizations while not new to mankind, and possibly not new to the subject in an intellectual sense, are very new in an experimental sense. That is they are new in the sense that makes for altered behavior."

The papers by Harman are recommended for those interested in the philosophical aspects of the psychedelic controversy.

STAGE THREE OF PSYCHEDELIC RESEARCH

In stages one and two, double blind comparison studies were not used for evaluating the efficacy of psychedelic therapy. Theoretically, it is impossible to run comparison groups for testing the psychedelic treatment. There is a good deal of evidence which suggests that it is the experience itself and not the drug which is the therapeutic factor provided that the experience is long enough. Mescaline and LSD produce experiences lasting from 6 to 18 hours and both seem equally effective. We preferred LSD because of its shorter duration of activity. There is some evidence that the short experiences induced by psilocybin or dimethyl tryptamine are not as effective, perhaps because that experience is too short and is not so firmly impressed in the memory or in consciousness. Any drug which produces a psychedelic experience should therefore be as effective as LSD. If intravenous amphetamine, for example, were selected as the control drug and if the entire therapeutic session were run as if a psychedelic experience resulted, then there would be no comparison possible. One would merely have a comparison of two sets of psychedelic experiences.

If the comparison drug produced no experience, this would soon become known to both subject and observers and no double blind study would be possible.

Investigators of stage one and two were aware of these matters but these difficulties did not deter them from doing what they could. Those who demand double blind studies are simply ignorant of the nature of these experiences. But investigators of stages one and two investigated a large variety of variables which may more or less be controlled.

Stage three investigators have profited from these studies and have begun large-scale trials particularly at Spring Grove State Hospital.

Comparison of LSD with Some Other Nonergot Hallucinogens

It is generally agreed that the experiences produced by all the known hallucinogens are quite similar. The variability of response to one compound is just as wide as the variability of response between drugs. Mescaline, LSD and psilocybin produce extremely similar experiences

(Hoch *et al.*, 1958; Delay *et al.*, 1959; Hollister, 1961; and others). The most convincing studies were those by Isbell (1959) and Abramson (1960a,b) who reported their subjects could not distinguish between LSD and psilocybin. The general view is that these drugs trigger or activate a process the content of which depends on all the extra drug variables already described. Isbell (1959) hypothesized that some common biochemical mechanism was activated. Cross tolerance between some of these compounds supports this (Balestrieri, 1957; Balestrieri and Fontanari, 1959; Abramson *et al.*, 1960; Isbell *et al.*, 1961).

LSD has also been compared with sodium amytal interviews (Brengelmann *et al.*, 1958a) against Abood's and Biel's (1962) anticholinergic hallucinogens, Lebovits *et al.* (1960), Ostfeld (1961), and Ostfeld *et al.* (1958) against some tryptophane derivatives (Murphree *et al.*, 1960).

Recently, Rosenberg *et al.* (1963) found no direct nor cross tolerance between LSD and *d*-amphetamine in man. Subjects tolerant to 1.5 μg per kg of LSD reacted to 0.6 mg/kg of amphetamine and subjects directly tolerant to amphetamine still reacted to 0.5 μg/kg of LSD.

The LSD experience has become the standard and most compounds which have any activity which resembles LSD are compared against it.

Effect of LSD on Schizophrenic Patients

There is only one disease which so alters men that they do not react to LSD in the normal manner. It is schizophrenia where the range of clinical reactivity is much wider than in normal subjects, both in the effective dose and in the degree of response. Some schizophrenics react to normal doses and they experience a reaction which varies from very slight to the most severe psychotic experience. Others when given very large doses show the same range of reactivity to LSD.

A large number of investigators have studied the effect of LSD on schizophrenic patients: they include W. A. Stoll (1947), Condrau (1949), Forrer and Goldner (1951), de Giacomo (1951), Rinkel *et al.* (1952), Rinkel (1951), Hoch *et al.* (1952, 1953), Belsanti (1952, 1955), Katzenelbogen and Fang (1953), Sloane and Doust (1954), Pennes (1954), Graham and Khalidi (1954a,b), Cholden *et al.* (1955), Sauri and De Onorato (1955), Nunes (1955), Ruiz-Ogara *et al.* (1956), Liebert *et al.* (1957), Clark and Clark (1956), Cline and Freeman (1956), Savage and Cholden (1956), Wapner and Krus (1959, 1960), Machover and Liebert (1960), and Krus *et al.* (1963).

There is hardly any agreement in this large number of studies with respect to the following questions:

1. Do schizophrenics react in the same way as normals?
2. Are they more resistant in terms of dose?
3. Do they develop tolerance more quickly?

The reason for this divergence of opinion probably lies in the numerous variables which influence the LSD effect in normal volunteers plus several new ones unique to schizophrenia.

The observers' conclusions about these matters depends upon the stage of the disease, upon the kind of perceptual changes which develop and the presence of thought disorder. The other variables have already been listed and discussed.

STAGES OF SCHIZOPHRENIA

Malvaria

The malvaria concept was discussed under the heading Complications of LSD (p. 102). There we stated that subjects who are malvarian are more apt to have prolonged reactions. Sometime after we began to test our alcoholics for malvaria it occurred to us that very few of the malvarians had psychedelic experiences. We therefore examined all the records on alcoholics whose urine had been tested and who were given LSD as treatment.

When LSD was given to patients at the University Hospital records were kept of the patients' responses. These were of three kinds: (*a*) the psychiatric nurse, assisting in the observation and therapy, continuously recorded the patients' comments, discussion, etc., every few minutes throughout the day and the report was then placed in the patient's clinical file, (*b*) the psychiatrist also recorded his impressions in the same way but more commonly provided a summary of the experience, and (*c*) the subject reported in his own writing his impressions of his experience. This was done several days after the LSD was given. All files contained the first two records but some subjects were not able to record their own impressions for various reasons. However, the first two records were available for examination in nearly all cases.

In no cases were the nurses or recording psychiatrist aware whether the subjects were malvarian or not. In many this was not known to anyone since urine assays were completed after the experience. The records are, therefore, as free as possible of any prejudice or bias, either for or against malvaria as a factor.

The records were read and the patients' statements describing their own experiences were scored. Any statement which indicated the subject was relaxed, happy, enjoying the experience, or was developing insight was scored as a positive statement. Any statement which indicated tension, pain, restlessness, fear, paranoia, refusal to consider another LSD, etc. were scored as negative statements. A count was made of these positive and negative statements. All subjects had psychotomimetic experiences, that is, they all responded to the LSD The usual minimal dose was 200 μg and many were given 300 μg. In addition some achieved a psychedelic experience. The proof for this was in their records, in the psychiatric assessments and in their own statement the following day. The best evidence was their own description of having reached a psychedelic state as described by Osmond. Finally an assessment was made of the intensity of the perceptual changes. The results are shown in Tables 8 and 9.

When a subject is said to have achieved a psychedelic experience it does not mean he was in that state most of the time. Some subjects had it for a minute, others for several hours. But the one-minute experience may be more vivid and striking than the longer experiences and may have a more permanent impact. Most of the recovered alcoholics came from the group who had psychedelic experiences but not every psychedelic experience was followed by recovery.

The number of positive and negative comments is not as objective as it appears because some statements are not clearly positive or negative. They are listed merely to indicate the relative number of statements. The records are available for inspection. Nor do we claim that other investigators reading these records would come up with exactly the same count. But there is no doubt that an independent count would yield very similar results. These figures are merely an indication of the relative frequency of the positive and negative comments. In a few cases very few of the patients could be classified.

Malvarians made many more negative statements about the experience except for the three who had the psychedelic experience. Only four had psychedelic experiences. The mean number of negative statements recorded per session was 7.0 compared to 2.9 positive statements.

About half of the nonmalvarians reached a psychedelic experience. These patients more often made positive statements than negative statements but this is not surprising since these statements merely confirm that the subject was enjoying the session. For the whole group the mean for positive and negative statements was the same, or 5 each. A few had psychedelic experiences even though most of the statements were negative and a few had many positive statements and enjoyed the experience but did not approach a psychedelic experience. The author's first experience was of this kind. One of the subjects, G. B.,

TABLE 8

NONMALVARIANS RESPONSE TO LSD

Subject	Sex	Psychedelic experience	Number of comments on experience		Intensity of perceptual changes
			Positive	Negative	
J. A.	F	Yes	3	2	Moderate
G. B.	F	Yes	5	8	Marked
H. B.	M	No	0	6	Moderate
K. C.	M	Yes	3	13	Moderate
E. D.	M	No	0	17	Marked
O. E.	M	Yes	21	19	Marked
T. F.	M	Yes	11	6	Marked
M. G.	F	No	1	3	Mild
G. G.	M	Yes	7	2	Mild
J. G.	F	No	9	6	Moderate
E. H.	M	No	5	1	Moderate
O. J.	M	No	0	3	Mild
G. L.	F	No	9	49	Marked
K. M.	F	No	4	4	Moderate
S. N.	F	Yes	6	1	Marked
L. P.	F	Yes	1	5	Moderate
J. R.	M	No	2	0	Moderate
W. R.	M	Yes	16	0	Marked
P. M.	F	No	3	9	Marked
H. M.	M	No	3	0	Moderate
G. M.	M	Yes	9	0	Marked
F. S.	F	Yes	5	11	Marked
S. S.	M	No	2	4	Marked
H. V.	M	No	3	2	Moderate
J. W.	F	No	0	3	Mild
M. C.	F	Yes	8	2	Marked
A. H.	M	No	5	0	Marked
G.	F	Yes	7	0	Marked
S. L.	F	No	6	13	Moderate
Means	N (yes) = 13		5	5[a]	

[a] Omitting G. L.

had been treated successfully and her malvaria vanished. When she was given LSD her urine was negative for mauve factor.

The difference would be much more striking if we had included a very large series of normal subjects. So far no normal adult has had malvaria in our studies and about half of them had psychedelic experiences. If this group were added to the nonmalvarian group the differences between malvaria and nonmalvaria would be significant beyond $P < 0.01$.

TABLE 9

MALVARIANS RESPONSE TO LSD

Subject	Sex	Psychedelic experience	Number of comments on experience		Intensity of perceptual changes
			Positive	Negative	
D. A.	M	Yes	2	1	Moderate
G. B.	F	No	1	13	Moderate
G. B.	M	No	0	2	Moderate
H. D.[a]	M	No	4	15	Mild
I. G.	F	No	1	12	Mild
R. H.	M	No	Not available		Marked
C. I.	M	No	Not available		Marked
A. K.	M	No	10	8	Marked
Z. K.[b]	M	No	0	6	Marked
M. M.	F	Yes	7	0	Marked
E. R.	F	No	2	5	Moderate
C. S.	F	No	3	10	Marked
D. S.	M	No	0	4	Moderate
D. W.	F	No	3	16	Moderate
M. W.	F	No	0	16	Moderate
L. Y.[c]	M	No	0	9	Marked
D. A.	M	Yes	5	1	Marked
A. G.	M	Yes	15	0	Marked
W. C.	F	No	5	20	Moderate
Mean	N (yes) = 4		2.9	7.0	

[a] Prolonged reaction to LSD.
[b] Similar reaction three times.
[c] Later diagnosed schizophrenic.

The malvarians however did not differ in any respect when compared with nonmalvarians who had the usual psychotomimetic experiences, for example, their perceptual changes, changes in thought and in mood were within the normal range. These patients were not schizophrenic and suffered no thought disorder so they had no difficulty in describing their experiences to the observer during the session or after they had recovered from the LSD the following day. Most of the alcoholics were given at least 200 μg of LSD and most often 300 μg. There was no difference in the intensity of the reaction between the malvarians and nonmalvarians.

Malvarians have the same biochemical abnormality as the majority of schizophrenic patients. It is not unreasonable to assume that nonschizophrenic malvarians represent an early or a subclinical form of schizophrenia.

Pseudoneurotic Schizophrenia

This diagnostic term developed by Hoch and Polatin (1949) is a very useful one. It includes a group of patients who are schizophrenic but whose symptoms are primarily neurotic. One could describe them as patients who have the symptoms of a neurosis and the signs of schizophrenia.

Many of these patients have never been typical schizophrenics, many have recovered from the florid symptomatology and remain chronically ill and many have become alcoholic because while drunk the extremely distressing symptoms of schizophrenia are temporarily masked by the intoxication. They often develop typical schizophrenia after they join A.A. We have several patients who have gone through this sequence, some many times. These patients should not be given LSD. In our opinion, this is an absolute contraindication for there is a grave risk that they will be jolted into a florid schizophrenic psychosis in which they may remain for up to several years. Hoch *et al.* (1952) found that with as little as 60 μg of LSD, well-preserved pseudoneurotic schizophrenics showed an intense emotional reaction.

These patients react to normal quantities of LSD, have a reaction which ranges from the usual to a very psychotic reaction, and are apt to have prolonged reactions. Since they do not have a thought-process disorder they are able to describe their experience during or after LSD unless of course an acute schizophrenic reaction is precipitated where a thought-process disorder does develop.

If there are very impelling reasons for giving pseudoneurotic schizophrenics LSD, the therapist should be prepared to treat the prolonged reaction vigorously with nicotinic acid, 3 grams per day and/or tranquilizers. Occasionally a series of ECT will be required. It is hazardous to assume that the patient is suffering merely a prolonged reaction which will subside in a few days.

One young patient developed a pan anxiety phobic state in his last year of his professional training and began to make the rounds of many private psychiatric hospitals desperately seeking help. A review of his history as given us by his father suggested very strongly he was a pseudoneurotic schizophrenic. Finally at one hospital he was given on day one, 100 μg LSD IV. Nothing happened. On day two he was given 200 μg and on day three 400 μg IV. This was considered a diagnostic test. On the third day, he had a florid LSD reaction from which he recovered one year later in another mental hospital. The psychiatrists failed even then to diagnose the schizophrenia and it was said he had an "obsessive compulsive fixation upon LSD."

Sedman and Kenna (1965) gave 50–200 μg of LSD to twenty subjects. Ten were considered doubtful schizophrenics since none had what the authors considered "first rank" symptoms. Some clinicians would call them ambulant or pseudoneurotic schizophrenics according to the mental state which was presented. Ten subjects were a comparison control and consisted of depressions and neurotics. There was a significant difference in three areas: (a) The doubtful schizophrenics had visual disturbances more frequently, (b) they suffered from body disturbances more often, and (c) the group of ten had 18 pathological responses compared to 4 for the comparison group. One doubtful schizophrenic was clinically worse after the LSD. They recommended that LSD could be useful in establishing the diagnosis of schizophrenia, but in our opinion this is a questionable procedure since the risk of making some patients much worse outweighs the slight increase in precision of diagnosis.

Acute Florid Schizophrenia

These patients may or may not react to normal doses of LSD. It may be very difficult to determine this because if thought process disorder is present they will not be able to give a coherent account of their experience. There also may be an accentuation of symptoms already present. If in the waxing and waning of symptoms they have had some just as strong before they may not distinguish the LSD effect. On the other hand, the symptoms may be entirely different and easily distinguishable from those present before LSD was given. A patient having only auditory hallucinations will have no difficulty distinguishing and reporting visual perceptual changes. But a patient hearing voices may not note an increase or decrease in auditory perceptual acuity.

Acute schizophrenics will not have a prolonged reaction to LSD. Since they presumably are already as schizophrenic as they can be, it may not be possible to prolong it, that is, the natural disease will outlast the reaction. But there can be no certainty on this question since it would be impossible to distinguish which reaction is present.

Chronic Schizophrenia

Most studies of LSD effect were carried out on chronic patients. It is geneally agreed that they have an increased tolerance for LSD and require more than do normal subjects in order to have the expected reaction. However, if thought disorder is severe it may not be possible to determine whether LSD changes are present since ability to describe will be impaired.

Recovered Schizophrenics

There are some patients who have completely recovered from their disease. They have no symptoms, no signs can be elicited and the urine test is negative for mauve factor. However, there are personality problems which may be explored under LSD or they are alcoholics who have not yet stopped drinking. It is our policy not to deny them an LSD psychedelic session. But they will have taken nicotinic acid or nicotinamide, 3 grams per day, before and will continue to take it afterwards for several years.

The following case history will illustrate this:

A middle-aged successful businessman came in for treatment of "spells." He was given the usual neurological investigation for epilepsy. A psychiatric history led his psychiatrist to diagnose him as a paranoid personality, because he was punctilious about his business, had a business motto "Do not trust your business competitors" and he was suspicious of his wife. At the diagnostic conference it was reported he had very high blood cholesterol levels; it was suggested that he be started on nicotinic acid to lower his cholesterol and remove his paranoia.

He began to take the vitamin. On the wards he met an alcoholic woman, admitted for LSD treatment, and the couple began to keep company together. After discharge they lived together while each person arranged a divorce from his or her spouse. The woman had been married to a brutal psychopath who left her. The paranoid patient found his wife incompatible. About two years after discharge the patient came for an interview at his request. He wanted to know (a) his diagnosis, and (b) could he get an LSD treatment. He was advised he was a paranoid schizophrenic. He readily agreed and reported that since leaving the hospital he had read a good deal about schizophrenia and had come to the same conclusion. The alcoholic woman had been continuously sober since her LSD treatment and her descriptions of her experience had fired his interest. He was uncomfortable because he still tended to be suspicious of people and he hoped that the LSD session would help him overcome this.

He was admitted to a hospital, given LSD, and had a psychedelic reaction. The following day he told me with some excitement about the spells he had before his first admission. These were apparently very much like the LSD experience but at that time he had no frame of reference which he could use to describe his spells. When asked why he had not told his psychiatrist, he replied that since his psychiatrist had not queried him about them he considered them unimportant.

He made an uneventful recovery. As soon as his own divorce be-

TABLE 10

The Effect of LSD on Various Stages of Schizophrenia

Stage of schizophrenia	Dose range	Perceptual changes	Thought content	Disorder process	Ability to describe	Probability (P) of violent or prolonged reactions
Malvaria	Normal	Yes	Normal	Normal	Normal	0.20
Pseudoneurotic	Normal	Yes	Abnormal	Normal	Normal	0.20
Acute florid	Normal	Yes	Abnormal	Abnormal	Reduced	?
Chronic	Increased tolerance	Reduced	Abnormal	Abnormal	Reduced	?
Recovered	Normal	Yes	Normal	Normal	Normal	0.01

came final, the couple married. Neither his paranoid schizophrenia nor her alcoholism have returned. He has taken nicotinic acid, 3 grams per day, regularly for the past 5 years.

A summary of five stages of schizophrenia and their response to LSD are shown in Table 10.

Use of LSD in Psychotherapy

The field of psychotherapy is broad and complex and unless its limits are defined more narrowly it is impossible to consider how LSD has been used by thousands who believe they are practicing psychotherapy. We will restrict the term "psychotherapy" to that verbal interchange which occurs between a trained therapist, that is, a physician or a psychologist, and a subject who knows he is a patient and hopes the exchange will help him be relieved of certain troublesome symptoms and signs. This definition excludes chemical abreactions used only to obtain information, it excludes use of LSD by other people who are interested in the psychedelic uses of the experience, and of course, it excludes cultic uses by any groups who use LSD as a cult or as a sacrament in their religion. We do not mean to imply these are less desirable, inferior, or evil uses, but simply that in our opinion they do not constitute psychotherapy. In fact, the results as measured by permanent beneficial changes induced in the users may be even better than when psychotherapy, as we have defined it, is practiced.

When a patient receives psychotherapy alone, it is often difficult to determine whether the improvement which may occur is due to the specific action of the verbal exchanges or whether it is due to a host of other variables to which humans are prone, such as physiologic recoveries, changes in marital state, changes in familial relationships, and all the other factors which influence behavior. But when a chemical is used as an integral portion of the therapy another variable is added to the complexity of factors already operating. The chemical may act by a direct chemical effect on the physiological or biochemical reactions of the body and thus initiate a series of corrective biochemical changes which lead to the response. This applies equally well to tranquilizers, amytal interviews, etc., as it does to LSD. The evidence that LSD does influence bodily processes has been reviewed. It is quite likely any one of these or some combination might initiate the changes which lead to recovery.

The only change we will discuss is the effect of LSD on levels of tension. When LSD is given in large doses it produces a state of relaxation in subjects which may vary from a few days to 6 months. We have had one report from a normal subject who stated she was remarkably relaxed for 6 months after one LSD experience. Other subjects have been so free of tension for several months that they were practically unable to become angry. One of our patients was completely relaxed only two days. The permanent changes which some subjects have after LSD may therefore be due to either this tensionfree period, or to the nature of the experience psychologically, or to a combination. The period of freedom from tension following some remarkable experiences and insights allows time in which the newly discovered ways of coping with problems can be practiced. Schmiege (1963) divided the methods of working with LSD into two groups: (a) as a psychoadjuvant, and (b) as a psychedelic. The first method suggested by Busch and Johnson (1950) for LSD was quickly adopted by many therapists including conventional psychotherapists and psychoanalysts such as Abramson (1957, 1956a, 1960a,b). The LSD is used to facilitate therapy and is given frequently in rather small doses beginning with 25 μg, which are generally increased to about 150 μg. The main emphasis is upon a thorough exploration of the psyche repeatedly such as one might use sodium amytal interviews. The second method is quite different. Large doses, that is, 200 μg or more are given a few times or only once and main emphasis is given to the intense psychedelic experience which follows. During the height of the experience which may last several hours there may be no verbal exchanges whatever between subject and therapist. Elsewhere, Hoffer (1960) suggested that in this method psychotherapy is adjuvant to the psychedelic experience. The advantage of this way of looking at it is that it dethrones "psychotherapy" from its position of emperor of all the therapies and places it where it belongs as one of the less-effective therapies used by physicians and psychiatrists.

Psychoadjuvant Use of LSD

Busch and Johnson (1950) found that patients were able to talk about their problems more easily during delirious states. They looked upon LSD as another delirient and so studied LSD's action on various psychiatric conditions. They used what would now be considered very minor doses, 30 μg for women and 40 μg for men. Twenty-one psychotic patients had their psychoses activated but some seemed more interested in their fellow man. Eight more were given these quantities of LSD as a psychoadjuvant. The three schizophrenics were not benefited. Two of the remaining 5 neurotics were improved sufficiently not to require further treatment. They concluded as follows:

1. LSD may offer a method for gaining access to the chronically withdrawn.

2. It may serve as a new tool for shortening psychotherapy.

Guttmann and Maclay (1936) had suggested that the mescaline experience might be a valuable aid to psychotherapy. Since then perhaps 200 reports have appeared which deal with the use of LSD in various groups of psychiatric patients.

The first suggestion that hallucinogenic drugs might be used to facilitate psychotherapy came from Guttmann and Maclay (1936) who had worked with mescaline. By the end of 1954, the groundwork for using LSD as an adjuvant to psychotherapy had been completed. The pioneers in this research include Busch and Johnson (1950), Forrer and Goldner (1951), Weyl (1951), Savage (1952), Benedetti (1951), Katzenelbogen and Fang (1953), Frederking (1953), Sandison *et al.* (1954), Sandison (1954, 1955, 1956), Anderson and Rawnsley (1954). These authors established LSD's use as an aid to psychotherapy. Their findings have been enlarged and expanded until LSD has achieved a definite role in psychotherapy.

Abramson (1955, 1956a,b, 1960a,b) in an interesting series of studies demonstrated how LSD can be used as an aid to psychoanalytic psychotherapy. He started with small doses of LSD and in subsequent sessions increased the dose gradually. Abramson found it very effective in removing blocks in the analysis and in increasing tolerance to anxiety in intensifying the transference phenomenon.

Anderson and Rawnsley (1954) treated 19 patients with 10–600 μg of LSD. Of this group, 6 were improved. The authors did not draw any conclusions about LSD's effectiveness.

Chandler and Hartman (1960) treated 110 patients with LSD. The group included 44 neurotics, 36 personality disorders, 22 sociopaths and 8 others. Each patient had an average of 6.2 (1–26) or 30 hours psychoanalytic therapy each. The patients were prepared by several sessions of psychotherapy beforehand. The interval between LSD sessions was 2 weeks. They routinely started with 50 μg and increased it by 25 μg each session until they reached 150 μg. After 4–5 hours the sessions were terminated. If the subjects remained anxious they were given chlorpromazine, if depressed methylphenidate.

Out of this group 24 were markedly improved, 26 were considerably improved and the rest were not improved. Only 2 subjects withdrew from therapy and subsequently made good life adjustments. In only 3 cases was there no facilitation of psychotherapy. In most cases there was a profound penetration and accelerated psychotherapeutic effect.

Cohen (1959, 1960a,b), Cohen and Ditman (1962, 1963), Cohen and Eisner (1959), Cohen *et al.* (1958) and Eisner and Cohen (1958) studied not only the therapeutic potential of LSD but its complications and side effects. The side effects have been discussed earlier. Eisner and Cohen treated 22 subjects. The initial dose was 25 μg and it was increased from 25 μg to 125 μg over a follow-up period of 6–17 months. Sixteen of the group were improved.

Feld *et al.* (1958) gave 18 cases 52 treatments with LSD (range 1–8 sessions). LSD brought into focus the patients repressed emotional attitudes, conflicts, etc., and activated them so they could be used in psychotherapy. An intense transference developed.

Fontana (1961) found LSD most effective for facilitation of individual psychotherapy after the patient had been in psychotherapy up to 6 months. Frederking (1955) based his conclusions on 200 treatments with LSD or mescaline. He recommended doses lower than 100 μg. He used an analytic approach and sought a psychocathartic effect. The LSD was given when it was desirable to shorten therapy, to reactivate a stalled treatment, and to dissolve affect or memory blocks. Hoch (1957) also believed LSD could be used as an adjunct to psychotherapy.

Sandison's group have been particularly active in developing the therapeutic uses of LSD. Sandison (1954) and Sandison *et al.* (1954) described in some detail their results with 36 neurotic patients. Their approach was Jungian psychotherapy. Out of the 36, only one did not complete therapy. All had failed to respond to earlier treatments. They suffered extreme tension of the kind where leucotomy was indicated. The duration of illness was 9 for 0–2 years, 7 for 3–5 years, 12 for 6–10 years and 8 for over 10 years. The dose varied from 25 to 400 μg. The number of sessions varied with the individual case. Of the total group 14 recovered, 1 was much improved, 6 were moderately improved and 2 not at all. The rest were still under treatment.

Sandison and Whitelaw (1957) reported what had happened to the original 36 patients two years later. The results were 4 recovered, 8 greatly improved, 7 moderately improved, 11 did not improve, and 6 were unknown. For a group of intractable neurotics, these results are very good. In 1954, 21 were improved and two years later 19 still remained improved.

Before treatment with LSD, 27 out of 36 had required treatment in mental hospitals. They reported an enlarged series of 94. Of these, 21 recovered, 20 were greatly improved, 20 were moderately improved, and 65% were improved. None had responded to earlier therapies.

Sandison (1963) defined psychotherapy with LSD as follows: "A psychotherapeutic relationship between the patient and the therapists during which LSD is administered to the patient. The immediate result of giving the LSD is to produce a deepening of the patient's emotional tone, a change of thinking, sometimes regression to an earlier emotional and intellectual period and the relieving of emotionally charged memories."

Savage (1952) treated 15 patients with LSD. Of these 2 involutional psychotics recovered and 4 schizophrenic depressions were not benefited, but 5 schizoid depressions were improved. He used 20–100 μg LSD per day for one month. Savage (1957, 1962a,b) discussed some of the problems involved in using LSD. Savage *et al.* (1962a,b) described therapeutic effects of LSD. Finally Savage *et al.* (1964) reported results of treatment on patients treated between March 1961 and November 1963. Their results are given in Table 11.

TABLE 11

RESULTS OF TREATMENT WITH LSD[a]

Group	Number	Better	No change	Worse
Neurotics	62	53	8	1
Psychotics	15	6	7	2
Personality disorders	137	118	18	1
Alcoholics	24	17	6	1

[a] Savage, Hughes and Mogar (1964).

Whitaker (1964) treated one hundred successive cases of nonpsychotics with LSD as an adjuvant. They used 100–250 μg LSD and routinely gave their subjects 200 mg nicotinic acid orally to reduce perceptual changes and so facilitate psychotherapy. Each patient averaged 3.28 treatments. Out of the 100 subjects, 47 were recovered, 18 improved, and 35 failed. A group of neurotics treated by other methods before LSD was started showed that 12 recovered, 30 improved, and 59 failed.

The recovery rate was closely related to chronicity as Table 12 shows: The majority of patients who were improved did not relapse.

Leuner (1963), using methods developed by Sandison, treated 54 subjects. Previously 22 had been treated unsuccessfully with ECT psychoanalysis and continuous narcosis. Of this group 19 recovered or were much improved, 17 were improved. The best results were found with character neuroses of whom 10 out of 12 were in the recovered or much improved group.

In his discussion Leuner referred to 500 cases reported at the European Symposium on Psychotherapy and LSD held at Gottingen, November 1960.

TABLE 12

RELATION OF DURATION OF ILLNESS AND RESPONSE TO LSD[a]

Duration of illness (years)	Number	Recovery (%)
0–2	8	75
3–5	32	50
6–10	25	40
11–20	24	45
Over 21	11	37

[a] Whitaker (1964).

PSYCHEDELIC USE OF LSD

This has been developed primarily for the treatment of personality problems, addicts, alcoholics, etc. A complete description of LSD therapy of alcoholics will give the reader a good account of the psychedelic use of LSD. The Native American Church of North America used peyote, which contains mescaline, in a similar way (Slotkin, 1956).

Alcoholics

Sometime in 1952 we began to study LSD as an hallucinogenic substance. We planned to use it for producing model psychoses, of schizophrenia and delirium tremens (toxic psychoses). It soon became evident that LSD changed the state of mind of the subject, but the kind of experience which occurred depended very much on the therapists and their objectives. With normal subjects who volunteered to take LSD, there was no therapeutic intent. The experimenters stayed continuously with them, but played a passive roll in shaping the experience. The subjects were encouraged to see, hear, taste, and feel everything during the experience and attention was drawn to objects, sounds, smells, etc., in order to draw the subjects' attention to them. Attempts were made to have the subjects tested using various physiological and psychological tests, but we were not obsessive about this and if the subjects showed any reluctance to do these tests they were allowed the privilege of experiencing their own private new world with little distraction.

Very few of our subjects were terrified or fearful during LSD for more than a few moments and most of them volunteered to take it again. At no time were we short of volunteers. In fact, we were forced to accept only special cases in order to dissuade the student body from coming en masse for LSD.

We restricted its use to subjects who had special skills or special interests. These included scientists, ministers, workers with alcoholics, psychiatrists, psychologists, and psychiatric nurses.

Sometime in 1953, while discussing LSD and its uses, in an Ottawa, Ontario hotel at 4:00 o'clock in the morning, we hit upon the idea that perhaps the LSD experience could be made a model of delirium tremens and could therefore be developed into a treatment for alcoholism. It is believed by Alcoholics Anonymous and by many alcoholics that alcoholics began to recover after they have reached a state of existence called "hitting bottom." Hitting bottom has not been defined for it is a personal matter to most subjects. From the accounts we have gotten from alcoholics and from the alcoholic literature, it may vary from being told "you are an alcoholic" to a state of degradation, from a successful happy person to a person bereft of all financial resources, continuously psychotic from alcohol, and excluded from all family and community ties. For some it has meant a remarkable psychological experience during delirium tremens or sometime after this.

Delirium tremens in 1953 carried with it a high mortality, estimated by some to be about 10%. But, we reasoned, because the LSD experience in a controlled setting was completely safe, it could be used to give our subjects something like a delirium tremens experience from which they might draw benefit with none of the risks attending clinical delirium tremens.

We were aware then that models are not identities, that we would not be giving them delirium tremens. Models are similar to natural or manmade phenomena only in those aspects which man desires to study. In other ways they are different. It is inherent in the formation of models that these major differences must exist, for if one created an identity it could be studied no more readily than the natural state being modeled.

Many alcoholics have one or more episodes of delirium tremens without either hitting bottom or changing their ways. We considered this and concluded that the differences between delirium tremens in its natural habitat and the LSD experience in a therapeutic setting were sufficiently great that we could reduce to a minimum the undesirable features of the experience and increase to an optimum the therapeutic aspects.

Delirium tremens occurs in an alcoholic at the end of a series of continuous or interrupted bouts of drinking. Usually the subject is physically ill, suffering from malnutrition (including avitaminosis especially nicotinic acid), he is toxic and suffering from poisoning with alcohol. He is physically extremely tense as his body is flooded with his own adrenaline and he lives in a state of fluctuating consciousness. Because of this

his memory, after recovery of his experiences, is rather vague. Finally delirium tremens occurs at inappropriate times and places so that the experience and recovery from it occur in settings such as general hospitals, etc., where there is no psychiatric therapeutic atmosphere and no therapeutic intent. It is odd that in spite of these contrary factors, so many alcoholics do look upon their delirium tremens as a turning point in their battle for sobriety, the peak experience described by Maslow (1959). It is likely they have had their experience under less favorable conditions, at the end of their delirium tremens, etc., Bill W., the co-founder of A.A., had his peak experience after having recovered from a severe bout of heavy drinking to the point of severe exhaustion.

We hoped that by using LSD we could avoid all the undesirable features of the natural delirium tremens experience and that alcoholics having once seen what the experience was, would be in a better position thereafter to avoid attaining a natural delirium tremens, that is, they would be fearful of developing delirium tremens and so would not drink anymore.

We had, as we later learned, merely hit upon a solution to alcoholism which the Native American Church of North America, or its antecedent groups, had used long before. According to Slotkin (1956) the Indians believed peyote took away the desire for strong drink and claimed that hundreds of drunkards had been "dragged from their downward way." The small band of Indians in Saskatchewan who allowed us to observe their ceremonies one night, explained that their religion based upon God and the use of peyote to reach Him included three important principles: (a) The member must be a good man, (b) he must educate himself, and (c) he must not drink. Thus we can only conclude that the peyote religion is the chief variable. Several Indians related to us how they had achieved sobriety only after joining this church.

The first two alcoholics were given 200 μg of LSD as a treatment in 1953, at the Saskatchewan Hospital at Weyburn. One, a male patient, remained sober for several months after discharge. The other, a female, continued to drink with the same intensity for six months as she had before certification. Then, as she reported many years later, she stopped drinking as she no longer got the same kick out of it. As far as we know, she has remained sober. Later, we became aware that Benedetti (1951) had given 100 μg to an alcoholic. He had a marked emotional reaction and apparently was much benefited. These results were sufficiently encouraging for larger trials to begin.

This project was then turned over to Dr. C. Smith who had recently joined the research group. At that time, it was impossible to conduct double blind studies because of the dramatic nature of the experience.

It would have been a trivial procedure to use placebo since both subject and therapists of any experience with LSD would know the difference. An attempt was made to compensate for this by selecting the most difficult alcoholics available, that is alcoholics who had already failed every other treatment and who, in the opinion of their own therapists, had a very bad prognosis.

From the beginning, LSD was not considered a chemical that could produce a major change in the alcoholic on its own. It was always looked upon rather as an essential factor in an overall treatment program in which were included other important therapeutic variables already described in the introductory section under LSD.

In 1958, Dr. Smith released the first report. A series of 24 of the most difficult alcoholics we could obtain had been treated and followed up from 2 months to 3 years (mean—1 year). All but 4 had tried and failed A.A. Eight had experienced delirium tremens at least once. Only two cases had not had complications of alcoholism. The diagnoses were psychopathy—12 cases, character disorder—8 cases, borderline or actual psychoses—4 cases. The average period of uncontrolled drinking was 12.1 years. Smith described the treatment as follows:

> In the present study, an attempt was made to enter into a psychotherapeutic relationship with the patient and to delineate the main problems. This phase lasted 2 to 4 weeks. As might be expected, the building up of adequate rapport was of critical importance during this period and on it largely depended the success or failure of the next phase. The patients were next given a single dose of LSD or mescaline orally while in hospital. Early in the study it was noted that alcoholics tend to be resistant to these drugs and doses of 200 to 400 μg of LSD or 0.5 gm of mescaline were used. A prolonged interview was carried out with the patient, who was never left alone while under the influence of the drug. In addition to discussing with the patient, problems leading to and arising out of his drinking, strong suggestions were made to the effect that he discontinue the use of alcohol. No attempt was made to arouse fear. The material which emerged was discussed during the next few days and the patient was discharged. In some cases, follow-up psychotherapy was possible; in most, however, further contact was made through A.A., which provided much valuable and objective information. Dissulfiram was not employed in the study, nor were tranquilizers.

The results of treatment were evaluated as follows:

> *Much improved,* that is, completely abstinent since treatment or drinking only very small quantities
> *Improved,* that is, definite reduction in alcohol intake
> *Unchanged*

None of the patients could have gotten worse and of course none did. The results of this treatment are given in Table 13.

Since this was an exploratory study, the criteria for selecting patients for treatment were not known. Four psychotic, or near psychotic patients, were given LSD. Of these none were *much improved* and only one was *improved*. As a result of this study, these diagnostic categories were not included for LSD treatment thereafter unless they had first been treated for and recovered from their psychoses. Excluding these 4 patients *improved* the results because 11 out of 20 would be classed as *improved* or *much improved*. The development of the mauve factor test (Irvine, 1961; Hoffer and Osmond, 1961b,c) and the clinical description of malvaria (Hoffer and Osmond, 1962a,b, 1963a,b) has simplified our task. Our rule now is not to give LSD treatment to alcoholic malvarians unless they have previously been treated with nicotinic acid or nicotinamide and have become nonmalvarian, or unless they would begin this treatment immediately after having received LSD.

TABLE 13

RESULTS OF TREATMENT WITH LSD

Group	Number	Much improved	Improved	No change
Character disorder	8	4	3	1
Psychopathy	12	2	2	8
Borderline and actual psychosis	4	0	1	3
Total	24	6	6	12

We have shown (Hoffer and Osmond, 1963a,b) that alcoholic malvarians treated with either nicotinic acid or nicotinamide at a dose of 3 grams per day, as a rule are able to remain sober for as long as they take the medication regularly.

Smith reported that, contrary to our expectations, patients with definite evidence for liver damage did not react in any way differently from patients with no evidence for liver damage. Our earlier reluctance to give LSD to patients with liver damage had been based on reports by R. Fischer *et al.* (1951). In addition, Smith could not confirm the observation of Mayer-Gross *et al.* (1952) that elevation of blood glucose over 200 mg percent would ameliorate the LSD reaction. One of the alcoholics was a diabetic. At the height of his experience he was given 100 gm of glucose. His blood sugar level reached 278 mg percent, but no observable psychological change occurred. Smith in his discussion concluded:

In general, those patients who had an intense reaction did better than those having a mild one, but this statement requires some qualification. In cases where severe anxiety was aroused and communication blocked, the result was seldom good. Cases 4, 16, and 17 were of this type. No attempt was made to produce fear during the interviews; instead an attempt was made to promote a more vivid awareness of interpersonal difficulties and their bases.

That attitude of the therapist is another important variable in the treatment. This method as described, probably lends itself best to a technique of exhortation, persuasion, and suggestion which may not come easily to all therapists (as it certainly did not to the present one). It must be admitted, however, that therapies which avoid these techniques and concentrate on providing insight have not been brilliantly successful in alcoholism. Moreover, many of these patients did, in fact, seem to gain an enhanced self-understanding as a result of the experience and this appeared to influence their subsequent behavior.

I believe that contact between the therapist and the patient can be improved if the therapist has taken the drug himself. Unfortunately, I did not do this until the present series was completed. Since then, I believe that my capacity to empathize with these patients has been much enhanced. In view of the refractory nature of the group, the results appear sufficiently encouraging to merit more extensive and preferably controlled trials. Modifications of the technique might also produce improvements, for example giving the subjects some alcohol during the experience or using small dosages of the drugs as an adjunct to psychotherapy.

A final observation of some interest is the fact that the group tended to be remarkably resistant to these drugs. In normal subjects 100 gamma of LSD is sufficient to provoke a profound reaction in 80% of cases, 200 gamma in all cases;[1] in these patients, 200–400 gamma of LSD were used to obtain comparable results.

Hubbard, as we have said earlier, was invited to spend two weeks with us in Saskatoon and to demonstrate to us the details of his method. Three of our most difficult alcoholics were selected and after Hoffer had given them 200 μg or more of LSD, Hubbard sat by the patient and conducted the session while three psychiatrists (A. Hoffer, C. Smith, and N. Chwelos) observed him and the patient. It turned out that his method was designed to create a situation most apt to lead to a transcendental or psychedelic experience. In this aspect of the treatment, it was not radically different from the methods we had at that time developed as a result of our own experiences and observations. But, he did demonstrate the value of visual and auditory aids, such as paintings, works of art, and music. He showed great skill and sensitivity in his discussions with the patients under LSD. In general, it appeared to us that his method would be more apt to give alcoholic patients the psychedelic experience we considered they should have.

Chwelos *et al.* (1959) reported the results of our revised technique on an additional 16 alcoholics. The newer technique was described as follows:

Following this original series, our research group was in contact with

[1] Hoffer (1958).

Hubbard (1957), who had demonstrated a somewhat different approach. We have adopted some of his modifications and have introduced others.

We had noted before from our studies of the psychotomimetic properties of this drug that the environment and particularly the attitude of the people around the person undergoing the LSD experience seemed to influence his reaction profoundly. Staff members who have had an insightful LSD experience or who have participated in many sessions as observers are more able to aid the subject during his experience. On the other hand, unsympathetic, hostile, and unfeeling personnel bring about fear and hostility with a marked increase in the psychotic aspect of the experience. Allowing staff members an LSD experience automatically changed attitudes by greatly increasing empathy with the person undergoing the experience.

The modifications used since January 1958 are as follows. The environment surrounding the patient taking LSD was changed by the addition of auditory stimuli, visual stimuli, emotional stimuli, and a change in the attitude of the people in contact with the patient.

The auditory stimuli consisted mainly of music supplied by a record player. Usually classical, semiclassical, and relaxing music was played. The person was encouraged to lie down, relax, and listen closely. Visual stimuli consisted of various pictures which the patient examined and concentrated on intently. Other visual stimuli such as cut flowers were sometimes used. The auditory and visual stimuli served to show the person the great enhancement of perception, but, what appears to be more important, they aided him in getting his mind off himself. He was reassured that it was not unusual to have visual imagery in the experience. For emotional stimuli, photographs of relatives were often used. The subject was encouraged to study these closely for long periods. The suggestion was made that he could become markedly aware of unhealthy attitudes toward the people in the photographs and he was assured that his thinking in the area would be clear and free of rationalizations and thus more useful to him later on. He was also asked to concentrate on a list of questions that he had previously compiled about his problems.

We believe that it is absolutely necessary for every therapist to undergo the LSD experience; we feel that doing so substantially increases understanding of the patient's experience and that the therapist's attitude becomes much more accepting, thereby making him more effective not only during the experience but in terms of after-care. The patient was encouraged to accept himself during this period while his thinking was more emotionally charged and he was less likely either to rationalize or to have guilt feelings. The therapist avoided all forms of reproach, but at the same time he stressed the patient's own responsibility for the perpetuation of his difficulties and for the removal of the unhealthy attitudes from which these difficulties arose.

Optimism is important and it was emphasized that the subject, by becoming aware of his pathological attitudes, could modify them.

No psychotic patients were included in our newer series. The results did seem to be superior (see Table 11) but the series was a small one and the follow-up period was shorter than was Smith's (1958).

Maclean *et al.* (1961) had further developed the method and used it to treat 61 alcoholics. They described it as follows:

"Once the autobiography and history are completed the therapist has **several preparatory** sessions with the patient during the 2 days prior to the special treatment day. The emphasis here is on those aspects of the self which could emerge as barriers to a constructive or integrated LSD-25 experience. A half hour is spent with the patient shortly before he goes to the treatment room.

THE GROUP TECHNIQUE. "Our method employs a professional therapeutic group which acts as a stabilizing influence on the patient, providing him with support. Each group member contributes a unique pattern of temperament and personality. We suggest that it may be possible for the patient to see reflections of the different facets of his own personality in each of these individuals. We think a group of 4 is best. Generally this includes the psychiatrist (as therapist), a psychologist (co-therapist), a psychiatric nurse, and a music therapist. Ideally the group would be made up of two men and two women. Unless all of these have firsthand knowledge of a successful psychedelic experience, they tend to become bored or confused during the session and are unable to offer support to the patient under circumstances they do not understand. This tends to upset and confuse the patient.

"In our technique the group is usually somewhat larger and participates without taking the drug. The advantages in our method are threefold.

"First, the patient who takes the drug alone is less distracted from intense self-scrutiny and self-evaluation than the subject who is one of a group all directly participating in the experience.

"Second, we consider it important that the therapist refrain from projecting his views upon the subject, and in a group session where all participants have taken the drug it is impossible to avoid this.

"Third, the function of the therapist is enhanced when he is free to act at times as an objective observer and so modify his approach to the patient. Such objective assessment for therapy or research purposes is only possible when the therapist is not taking LSD-25 himself.

SETTING AND EQUIPMENT. "The environment in which treatment is given is a significant factor, for just as the presence of a select group lends support to the patient, so do his physical surroundings. A quiet room is needed to prevent distraction. The appointments of the room—drapes, floor coverings, and furnishings—should be tastefully combined with floral arrangements and pictures to create a harmonious atmosphere. The dominant theme of the decor should be composed of various universal symbols. The patient will go through a good part of the experience laying down, consequently comfortable facilities are required. Technical equipment should not intrude upon the atmosphere of the room. Adequate measures should be prearranged to avoid the disruptive influence of interruptions during the session.

DOSAGE. "We use doses varying from 400 to 1500 gamma given by mouth. The initial dose depends on the psychiatric appraisal of the subject's defense mechanisms. We think that the closer a person is to self-acceptance the less the dosage required, and we use this as a working guide. We usually start with a dose of 400 gamma; experience as the session progresses is used to decide whether and when more is required. If after 1 or 2 hours the patient shows signs of anxiety because he is holding on desperately to his reality ties, more LSD-25 is needed to induce the psychedelic experience.

"Some therapists have suggested gradually increasing doses over a number of treatment sessions, believing that this reduces the patient's fear. We have found, however, that small-doses techniques are less effective as they do not lead to a full realization of the therapeutic potential of the experience. Small doses do not alter the habitual frames of reference which may initially have induced the patient's problems, and often reinforce those same unfavorable patterns of thinking and feeling which constitute his problems.

ADMINISTRATION. "LSD-25 can be obtained as a clear, tasteless, odorless liquid. In our procedure the dose is measured into a glass of water and taken orally. The drug may also be obtained in the form of an oral tablet or intravenous solution.

PROCEDURE. "The patient comes to the treatment room at 8:00 AM where he finds the group convened and ready to receive him. Rapport is established through general conversation over coffee. At 8:20 AM the drug is administered and the therapist explains to the patient the functions of the group, the setting, and the symbols. The patient's questions are discussed by the group. Variation in the psychiatric problem and the individual's tolerance for the drug make each experience somewhat unique. The first symptoms may appear within 15 minutes to an hour.

Mild physical discomforts may be experienced during the first hour or two. The height of the experience is reached between 10:30 and 12 o'clock.

"A complete time-indexed record or transcript is kept by one of the attending therapists. From about 10:30 AM to 2:00 PM most subjects are quietly engaged in intense self-scrutiny. At about 2:00 PM or 3:00 PM the subject will begin trying to conceptualize his experience and at this time the therapist can aid him greatly by nondirective methods. At about 4 PM the patient returns to his room. A counselor trained in psychedelic therapy remains with him until bedtime. This can be one of the most valuable portions of the session. The process of applying what he has learned begins in the treatment room and is further expanded in his relationship with the counselor. It is important not to shut down the integrative process, while it remains active, by the use of chlorpromazine or the like. Before discharge the next day he is interviewed by the therapist and is asked to give a written account and an assessment of his experience."

Jensen began one of the best controlled comparison experiments at the Saskatchewan Hospital at Weyburn under one of us (H. O.). This was reported at the Third International Congress of Psychiatry, Montreal in 1961 and later published (1962).

Treatment was carried out on a male admission ward where 10 alcoholic patients comprised part of a group of 40 psychotic patients. The alcoholics had their own dormitory. After physical examination and treatment of the complications of alcoholism, the patients were started on a series of three A.A. meetings per week. These were not compulsory, but strong encouragement was given them to attend. They also were given two hours of group psychotherapy. The alcoholics were encouraged to form a group which they did. Toward the end of the period of hospitalization (mean—two months) the patients were given the LSD treatment. They received 200 μg. During the session the therapist remained 7 to 8 hours with the patient. Patients were encouraged to bring their own records and family photographs. The therapist then worked with the patient using psychotherapy to bring out repressed memories, abreactions, new insights, and new understanding.

Another group received the same therapy, but for several reasons they were not given LSD and left the hospital early. They were considered unfit to take LSD because of physical reasons or because they refused to have LSD.

A third comparison group consisted of alcoholic patients admitted during the same period and they received individual therapy from other psychiatrists. The results are shown in Table 14.

TABLE 14

RESULTS OF TREATING ALCOHOLICS WITH LSD AS A MAIN TREATMENT VARIABLE

Investigators	Number	Follow-up period (months)	Results Much improved	Improved	No change
Osmond (1953)	2	9	1	—	1
Smith (1958)	24	2–36	6	6	12
Chwelos *et al.* (1959)	16	2–9	10	5	1
Maclean *et al.* (1961)	61	3–18	30	16	15
Jensen (1962)	58	6–18	34	7	17
O'Reilly and Reich (1962)	33	2–22	7	10	16
Sherwood *et. al.* (1962)	3	5	3	—	—
Eisner and Cohen (1958)	2	—	1	—	1
Savage (1962a)	20	—	10	—	10
Savage *et al.* (1964)	24	4–36	17	—	7
O'Reilly (1963)	68	2–34	26	—	—
Total LSD			145	44	80
Comparison Controls—LSD					
Jensen (1962b)	80	6–18	11	7	62

Jensen's criteria for *much improved* were complete abstinence after discharge or after a brief drinking bout shortly following discharge. Jensen was given a very difficult group of alcoholics. The Bureau of Alcoholism sent alcoholics only after they had exhausted every possibility of treatment. These results are therefore particularly striking.

O'Reilly and Reich (1962) treated a fairly large number of difficult alcoholic patients with LSD. They described the treatment as follows:

The treatment team included the patient, his nurse and the therapist. The environment in which the treatment is given is considered important. A special single room was designated as the treatment room. This room was tastefully furnished. Visual stimuli such as paintings and cut flowers were introduced to show the person the great enchantment of perception. Auditory stimuli consisting mainly of music supplied by a record player were utilized. The patient was encouraged to lie down, relax, and listen to music which was usually classical or semiclassical and relaxing. He was given his choice of music. The patient was encouraged to go through a good part of the experience lying down

PROCEDURE. The patient came to the treatment room with his special nurse at 8:30 AM. He was given a dose of 200 μg of LSD in a glass of water and asked to lie down and relax on the bed. An initial discussion occurred between the therapist and the patient. A prolonged interview was carried out at the height of the experience about two hours after ingestion. The interview was conducted along psychodynamic principles and the therapist led the patient to ventilate these particular areas. The patient was never left alone, his special nurse remaining with him throughout the treatment period. During the treatment the patient was encouraged to verbalize the experience and to think about it and discuss his problems. If the patient needed more LSD-25 to induce a psychedelic experience (characterized by development of useful insight in contrast to a psychotomimetic one in which psychoses were merely mimiced), an additional 100 μg is given. When the therapist decided that an adequate experience and abreaction had occurred, the session was terminated by giving 100 mg of niacin intravenously and 1 gram orally. At 9:00 PM on the night of the experience the patient was given six grains of Tuinal orally to ensure that the subject would have a good night's sleep. Each subject was asked to write an account of his experience on the day following the treatment. Providing the patient was over his experience, he was discharged on the second day following this session.

Recently O'Reilly and Funk (1964) completed a community follow-up study of 68 alcoholics who had been treated from December 1959 to August 1962 in O'Reilly's Psychiatric Department with LSD. About two thirds had been alcoholics for more than ten years. None were psychotic when they were given the LSD treatment.

All alcoholics who were totally abstinent for 2 months before being seen on follow-up were classed as abstainers. Of the group, 26 or 38% were abstainers at follow-up. The rest were not, but the group did include many whose drinking had become less pathological. Many variables were examined which could affect the outcome. These were age, marital state, educational level, membership in Alcoholics Anonymous, or in Church groups, number of years of alcoholism, diagnoses, number of previous treatment sessions, and the treating psychiatrists. None of these were related or predicted outcome. The only factor which correlated significantly with abstinence, that is, at the $P < .01$ level, was the kind of experience the subject had. The outcome in patients experiencing depression and/or claiming a transcendental experience without signs of physical distress, or of post-treatment disturbance, was much better. Using this criterion, the authors identified 46% of the abstainers. Only 6% of the nonabstainers had this kind of experience. Only one patient (out of 68) subsequently developed paranoid symptoms.

J. N. Sherwood *et al.* (1962) used similar psychedelic techniques for treating three alcoholics amongst a group of 25 psychiatric patients. All 3 remained much improved after treatment.

Eisner and Cohen (1958) reported a series of 22 psychiatric patients had been treated with LSD. Two of them were alcoholics. It is interesting that one was improved and the other unimproved. The one who improved had received LSD 6 times culminating with a dose of 500 μg. The subject who failed to improve was given LSD 4 times, with the last and highest dose being 100 μg.

Terrill (1962) used a similar method. They tried to provide a relatively permissive, comfortable atmosphere.

All drug sessions were conducted in a small soundproofed room that was very comfortably furnished with a couch, carpet, pictures on the wall, and a stereo record player. Subjects were usually provided with an opportunity to listen to music or look at visual stimuli. An attempt was made to reduce the amount of stress to a minimum. Someone was with the subject during most of the day. He therefore had the opportunity to talk with someone if he wished, although it was made clear to each subject that he need not talk if he did not feel like it.

Volunteer subjects and patients were treated in much the same manner, except that the patients entered the sessions with a very different set.

According to Savage (1962a,b), out of a group of twenty hospitalized alcoholics given 150 to 500 μg, 50% had stopped drinking at follow-up.

Recently Savage *et al.* (1964) reported that out of 24 alcoholics followed up, 17 were better, 6 were not altered, and 1 was made worse.

These 11 studies are all remarkably alike. The philosophy and method of treatments were based on the psychedelic experiences. The settings were comfortable and relaxed and the subjects were allowed to think, feel and meditate on the insights they learned. The results were similar (see Table 14).

The only comparison study was reported by Jensen. Out of 80 patients who were not given LSD, 18 were improved or much improved; out of 219 patients, 146 were improved or much improved (Chi Square is over 50).

The Bureau on Alcoholism (Calder, 1962) prepared an interim report on 150 alcoholics treated in various units of the Psychiatric Services Branch, Department of Public Health, Saskatchewan. The period reviewed spanned 5 years from October 31, 1957. The length of time from the last treatment varied from 5 years to 2 months, most cases having had the last treatment from 2 to 4 years before the follow-up survey was made.

They used the following categories of improvement:

Dry—subjects totally dry, that is, no relapses since last treatment.

Improved—subjects still have occasional relapses, but continue to seek sobriety. In some the periods between bouts were becoming longer; gainfully employed as compared to former chronic unemployment.

Unimproved

The results of this survey are shown in Table 15.

None of the 4 treatment centers were aware that this study was underway until the final report was completed.

In Table 15, Group A represented patients treated by a two-man team

TABLE 15

COMPARISON OF TREATMENT OF ALCOHOLICS WITH LSD AT FOUR CENTERS IN SASKATCHEWAN

| | Special group with therapists taking LSD during treatment | Treatment centers | | | Total |
		Saskatchewan Hospital, Weyburn (Jensen, Osmond)	University Hospital, Saskatoon (Hoffer, Smith)	Moose Jaw Union Hospital (O'Reilly)	
Number	24	65	32	29	150
Dry	5	22	13	10	50
Improved	0	9	7	3	19
Unimproved	18	31	11	16	76
Unknown	1	3	1	0	5
Percent improved and dry	22	50	64	45	47

whose techniques represented the most variations from those of other groups, for example the Group A therapists experimented considerably with the hypothesis that for optimum results the therapists should take the drug along with the patient. From an attempt to assess results thus far, recovery rates do not appear to indicate that this approach resulted in as many recoveries as the other methods. However, there are indications that this method resulted in findings of some importance in determining the general nature of the LSD experience, not the least of which was that further studies should be made on the significance of the LSD group experience. The patients treated in this experimental group were administered the drug in a variety of settings. The length of stay varied. They were usually out-patients, day patients or overnight patients in a clinic. There was 22% recovery.

Group B were treated in a ten-bed alcoholism pavilion for males which was operated for approximately 20 months, 1961–1962, at Saskatchewan Hospital, Weyburn. The LSD experience constituted the common element of a treatment program which generally included A.A. meetings, individual and group therapy, and informal discussions among patients. Alcoholics Anonymous members and the staff of the Bureau on Alcoholism worked in close relationship with the hospital treatment staff. The Bureau screened cases for treatment and did follow-up work following discharge.

The patients in this group included a higher average of "difficult cases" with poor prognoses and previously treated patients than any other group. The length of stay was from 6 to 8 weeks and the recovery rate was 50%.

Group C were treated in psychiatric ward, University Hospital, Saskatoon, on a short-stay basis that generally varied from 4 days to 2 weeks, and very occasionally longer. Usually very little psychotherapy was given, the main emphasis being on the LSD experience for physical and emotional complications where these were acute. This unit had a good working relationship with Alcoholics Anonymous. The recovery rate was 64%.

Group D were treated at Psychiatric Wing, Union Hospital, Moose Jaw. Some psychotherapy was involved. There was a cooperative arrangement with Alcoholics Anonymous in some cases. The length of stay was 4 or 5 days, occasionally longer. The recovery rate was 45%.

In addition to the 150 alcoholics referred by the Bureau and reported here, the psychiatric units involved treated additional cases referred from other sources. Surveys are now underway to determine overall results. In cases referred by the Bureau, an endeavor was made to follow the policy of preliminary screening and counseling by Bureau, contact with patients by the Bureau staff during in-patient stay, and follow-up therapy which included counseling and help with the rehabilitation problems. Occasionally, the Bureau was able to provide follow-up assistance to expatients who had been referred for treatment by other agencies, and who had no previous Bureau contact.

It should be noted that as this experimental treatment program developed the investigators gradually evolved new treatment theories based on accumulative experience in this heretofore unknown area. There was continuing comparison of experiences of the general guidelines on treatment techniques. A system of precautions was worked into the method and certain protective measures were introduced to ensure against possible adverse reactions and to avoid any chance of harm coming to the patient.

In presenting statistical material, Mr. Angus Campbell, senior counselor at the Regina Counselling and Referral Centre, advised: "It should be pointed out that we purposely were conservative in making our counts. In cases of doubt, we made it a rule to mark the results negatively. We therefore feel that a careful re-check might indicate somewhat higher rates of recovery than our tables show."

Calder concluded that for an accurate and more satisfactory appraisal of results to date of such referrals to LSD treatment to Saskatchewan, further study and follow-up is required. Much of this is now underway and in varying stages of completion. A many times larger sample should reinforce the abovementioned evidence. Since this report covers referrals by the Bureau only, and referrals were made by many other agencies, the final count will be several times higher.

Interim indications are that the LSD experience, usually involved with other forms of treatment and supportive measures, results in marked improvement in the recovery rates that would be otherwise obtained.

It is felt that further investigation will establish the fact that the LSD experience is an important and unique new form of therapy in the alcoholism field. Such excellent results have been noted by the Bureau staff in individual cases, usually with records of resistance to other forms of therapy, that LSD treatment, which was originally regarded by the Bureau as experimental, became a standard form of treatment to be used where indicated.

Many alcoholism treatment centers are investigating LSD and other psychedelic drugs as a treatment. Their publications are just beginning to appear. In a recent report Locke (1963) interviewed Dr. Florence Nichols of the Bell Clinic, Toronto, who stated she had treated about 100 alcoholics. The large majority of these confirmed alcoholics of 20 years' standing had attained sobriety and most of the others were progressing toward contented sobriety. In a personal communication, Dr. Nichols (1963) corroborated the statements published by Locke.

Studies by Belden and Hitchen (1962, 1963) using similar methods, corroborated these results. Belden *et al.* used about 300 μg of LSD. They found that the treatment was unusually effective for psychopathic or character disorder alcoholics. Schizo-affective patients were not benefited. They estimated their results conservatively as follows: One third total—abstinence over prolonged periods with improvement in socio-economic mobility, one third—failures, and one third—no longer heard from. Our experience suggests that a small proportion of those not heard of move to other places to start life again and do very well.

Other studies underway have not been reported yet. Working with Dr. H. Osmond in New Jersey, F. Cheek found that LSD produced significant improvement in alcoholics. The pilot study at Spring Grove State Hospital, described by Unger, suggests that they will obtain similar results. Out of about 45 alcoholics treated and followed up for 3–6 months, about two thirds were much improved.

LSD Pretreated with Penicillamine

A few years ago, one of our experiments resulted in a totally unexpected conclusion and this eventually led to a way of developing an adequate comparison experiment using LSD.

We were following the hypothesis that one of the ways LSD acted in the body was by increasing the concentration of adrenochrome. Penicillamine reacts with adrenochrome *in vitro* to produce indole derivatives which we have found are nontoxic for man. We developed the idea that pretreating a normal subject with penicillamine for a couple of days would protect the subject against a normal dose of LSD, that the adrenochrome would be removed by the penicillamine as quickly as it would be formed. To our great surprise the subject experienced the usual perceptual and thought changes, but she was completely without affect. This was reported by Hoffer and Callbeck (1960). Her own account of the penicillamine—LSD combination experience follows:

Towards the end of the hour I became restless and more sickened by the horrible odor. During the second hour I began feeling quite cold and I think I remained cold until about noon. When I closed my eyes I envisioned mounds of ulcerative decaying flesh. I felt it strange that this imagery should not be repulsive to me or frighten me—I merely noted and reported it. This imagery came in waves for a short time and seemed to me to relate to the odor. Following this, I noted very slight visual changes, mainly in lighting and depth perception within the room. Music was playing and I was aware of it, but not responsive to it. I remember remarking that when some Mexican music was playing I would expect to imagine fat paunchy little people, but this was not the case now. It became a bit difficult for me to think clearly, but there was no over-all time distortion. About one and a half hours after I took LSD-25, I began having marked visual distortions which I associated with former experiences.

The striking differences were that (a) they were not preceded by the usual shimmering effect, (b) they were clear-cut distortions of pattern and depth rather than an effect superimposed on a surface, (c) the distortions did not take the form of human beings and that (d) they elicited no emotional response from me. As these changes became more marked, I became unaware of the odor and of my body. During the next hour this visual flow was very striking and fast moving. Music was played throughout and I was quite aware of it but not involved in it in any way. When I looked at the record player I was very sensitive to the sight of the record turning around and the spots of dust jumping up and down. I was asked to try to leave my body but this I could not do. I was entirely unaware of my body, I could neither feel nor imagine, so (to me) actually there was no "me"; I did not exist. During this time the experience consisted of one area where visual changes were occurring and one area where music was being played. There was no relation one to the other and I was merely an instrument noting these facts like a camera making an impression on a negative.

Shortly after noon I could make out an animal from a distortion of the drapes so I commented on this, saying I was coming out of it. Soon after this I could make out two people leading a horse and for the first time I had a fleeting surge of feeling (interest) and thought my emotions would return. I said I was definitely coming out of the experience and waited for a flood of emotions. The visual flow slowed down. I became aware of my body and aware that I was now warm. (I had wrapped myself in a blanket in a most uncomfortable position, so I now removed it and made myself comfortable). During the next half hour the two areas became three areas—that is, visual, sound and body—but there was no harmony between them and each existed as a separate entity. One of the visual effects that was most marked now was a distinct stroboscopic effect of movement. I had never seen it to this degree before. I commented upon it as a neutral observer would. Also there was marked afterimage seen peripherally.

Between 1 PM and 2 PM I became aware, once more, of the unpleasant odor but it did not overpower me as earlier. I noticed it mainly when I voided. The visual flow subsided but detail stood out very clearly still. I was given 1 gm of nicotinic acid by mouth which I took automatically—I had protested vehemently on previous occasions when I had had LSD-25. The flush that followed was not unpleasant. In fact, I was unaware of it unless my attention was drawn to it. It lasted an unusually long time and I remember when I got ready for bed at about 6 PM I noted my body was still flushed. (My normal flush from nicotinic acid lasts about one hour). During this period I knew my emotional tone had not returned. I tried to visualize the faces of my friends, as I normally can when I think of them, and have always been able to do in previous LSD-25 experiences, but was totally unable to do this.

Following this, I began to have a feeling of uncertainty as to whether or not I had been the one who had the experience. The visual changes had lessened considerably, but I was still without feeling. This did not worry me at all, I merely reported it as unusual. It became necessary for me to produce another specimen of urine for the laboratory but I was unable to do this, and this too I found strange. I was given a cup of coffee which tasted like coffee and an egg sandwich which I could identify as egg but otherwise was not tasty. I consumed this lunch automatically. I still found it hard to comprehend conversation directed toward me, but followed short orders like an automat. I began to feel chilly again and this continued until I went to sleep that night. At no time did I recognize myself as feeling tired, which is quite unusual for me following a long LSD-25 experience.

I was taken to a friend's home for supper—part of which I consumed. While there, I could correctly identify the feelings of those around me, but was not able to respond to them. I felt confused by so many people and so much activity, so I quickly gave up eating and asked to be taken home.

Many years before she had taken only LSD and the experience was much different. She then described it as follows:

During this period, I experienced some anxiety, irritability and slight euphoria. Some nausea of a butterfly type was noted but it did not remain very long.

During the next two hours, I was subjected to a variety of nursing approaches. When I felt comfortable with the nurse, the room seemed very bright and at times there seemed to be a lovely orange halo around the nurse's head. When I felt rejected and threatened, the room would appear cell-like with very drab colors. On one occasion the nurse assumed the appearance of an animal, then on looking away from her and at my knees, I too seemed to turn into another animal with whiskers growing out of my mouth. This terrified me and I seemed to be wandering around lost in a long tunnel through which the wind was howling. I felt this lasted an eternity when in reality (according to the tape recording) it lasted under a minute. My mood changed quickly but was appropriate to the situation as I experienced it.

The lighting in the room was changing constantly as well as the dimensions. My perception of depth shifted fluidly. Flat surfaces often changed so that I saw what looked like the basic structure of the material. At times a fly which was actually in the room would become a swarm of them in flight. This occurred in the third hour and eventually I came to realize there must be a fly present because a single one would light on an object but none of the others ever did.

My concept of time was disturbed; the day seemed to cover years. My thinking was very concrete and quite paranoid at times. Blocking was apparent during the height of the experience. I was disoriented as to place and person on only one occasion as mentioned above. My emotions were highly responsive. I communicated very little verbally with the observers present—perhaps for two reasons, (a) things changed too rapidly to give a coherent account, and (b) the unpleasant nature of much of the experience.

During the fifth hour the experience receded in waves. It was suggested that I take nicotinic acid, 1 gm by mouth to terminate it more quickly, but I refused. I had a tingling sensation over my body and felt the effects of the nicotinic acid would heighten this even more. I was still slightly paranoid on occasions and my mood tended toward mild depression.

Again when this subject took LSD, 2 years later, she responded with a typical positive psychedelic experience. She then had recorded her experience as follows:

During this period music was playing which I found interesting and enjoyable. I felt no anxiety and was quite relaxed, no nausea was present.

Fifty minutes after I took LSD-25, my right hand appeared to change in size and texture. When I looked at reproductions of oil paintings—flowers seemed to be sculptured in clear harsh surfaces. I could see no beauty or life in them. The lighting effect in the room was heightened but there was very little disturbance of depth perception. My mood remained pleasant and I found the experience interesting.

About one-and-one-half hours after the start, I was really into the experience and it remained intense for the next two hours. I was asked to look into a mirror and I saw my image change gradually to that of an older and older 'me,' until eventually I seemed to get right into the mirror and look out from there. When I looked at paintings of people, they got older, then younger. Occasionally I was completely engulfed in the portrait. I found the paintings fascinating, and landscapes as well were beautiful beyond description, very much alive and produced a tremendous amount of emotion in me.

When I looked at the people in the room with me, changes occurred in them. One person's face became older, then changed into an Egyptian—later a mosaic pattern formed over his entire face except for one cheek which bore a shield. Sometimes a further change occurred and he resembled a Zulu warrior.

I was able to travel back in time and saw myself at different ages in my family setting and was quite surprised by some events I saw taking place.

I traveled in space to various parts of the world, to other planets, and to the bottom of the sea, I found this most interesting and enjoyable. I was tremendously impressed by the comprehensiveness of the universe and the insignificance of the human being with his petty problems.

During these two hours, time had no meaning for me—I was bound by neither time nor space.

Parts of a tape recording of the chanting and drumming by Indians of the Native American Church of Canada performing a peyote ceremony were played for me during the fourth to fifth hour. While I listened, symbolic pictures formed (it made no difference if my eyes were open or closed) by which I felt I could interpret the messages of the drums and the prayers. My emotions corresponded to my interpretation and I was tremendously moved by the whole ceremony.

Time was unimportant to me. I seemed to live a lifetime in seconds. My thinking was very clear. I was never disoriented as to place or person. At no time did I lose sight of the fact that I had taken a drug which had induced this 'amazing' experience. I was able to communicate freely to those present what I saw and felt.

During the fifth hour the experience receded in waves. I was somewhat introspective, but at the same time could readily relate to those around me. I felt bathed in a warm glow. I was tired but happy. Music was playing most of the time and I was very responsive to it.

I went to a friend's house for supper and enjoyed the company. I ate only a small meal because I was not really hungry. I told my friends about the experience and we were all very gay.

The chief difference between the experience induced by LSD only and the penicillamine–LSD experience was the complete absence of affect in the second. The first LSD experience was characterized by irritation, fear, depression, and warm affection. The second in an altogether different setting and with a different objective was characterized by relaxation, warmth, friendliness—an abundance of warm affection was present. The penicillamine–LSD experience had all the visual and thought changes, but was without affect.

After Hoffer had recovered from the shock of seeing a senior research worker become psychotic for 2 weeks, it became important to develop further the possibility of applying this combination of drugs to patients for the purpose of producing an affectless state. This would be highly undesirable for normal people who are accustomed to normal changes in mood from mild depression to mild euphoria and to occasional appropriate violent excursions into deep depression or intense euphoria. But for some people already suffering from violent prolonged states of depression or tension, it might be valuable for them to dampen their mood swings to some flatter level.

Many alcoholics have violent mood swings from which they seek relief in alcohol. We have known several alcoholics who relapsed when very depressed or again when very euphoric. A research project was therefore begun to test the hypothesis that alcoholics treated with penicillamine–LSD would respond better than alcoholics given a Methedrine intravenous abreaction. It was predicted that the penicillamine–LSD group would show a better response than our usual LSD-only treatment, that is it would produce about 75% recovery, whereas the Methedrine experience would benefit a very small proportion and would be considered our comparison group. Patients were admitted to University Hospital in the usual way. They were given a complete physical examination and if drunk or sick on admission, were treated until they were well. After a detailed psychiatric examination and diagnosis, LSD was offered to them as a treatment. During this phase of our alcoholic treatment program, LSD was well known to our community of alcoholics from which our sample was drawn. Schizophrenics, malvarians and endogenous depressives were excluded. As soon as a patient was ready he was then given either 30 mg of Methedrine IV or penicillamine for two days followed by 200 μg of LSD. The selection was from a set of random numbers laid out before the study began. The patient in each case thought he was getting LSD. There was usually only one patient at a time on this project on the ward and there did not appear to be any contamination. The therapist was Dr. J. Groenendijk, Research Psychiatrist, who carried out the therapy and followed up the patients. He, of course, knew which drugs were given, that is it was a single blind treatment. (As we have already pointed out, no double blind was possible.)

The results of this project were surprising and are shown in Table 16. There was no significant difference between both groups and the results with both groups were markedly inferior to the results of our previous and present studies by Smith, Jensen, Chwelos, O'Reilly, and so on. In 2 years the 14 subjects having had methedrine required 11 readmissions. Of thirteen penicillamine–LSD patients 11 required readmissions. These are shown in Table 16.

It was clear that the combination penicillamine–LSD was not more therapeutic than methedrine abreactions for the treatment of these alcoholics and it is likely these results would not be significantly better than chance. This was a surprising result and much at variance with our previous penicillamine–LSD work on alcoholics.

TABLE 16

COMPARISON OF METHEDRINE AND PENICILLAMINE–LSD TREATMENT OF ALCOHOLICS

Treatment	Number	Much improved	Improved	Unimproved
Methedrine	14	3	1	10
Penicillamine–LSD	13	2	0	11

Before this study was started we had used penicillamine–LSD only for severely tense alcoholics who had already had LSD at least once, usually several times, but had not responded. They had already experienced the psychological benefits to be gained from the LSD but they were still alcoholic. Their level of tension was so enormous that insight alone seemed useless. As a group they responded very well to the combination. The present group had not had LSD alone and included tense and less tense alcoholics. The major differences were (a) none of the present group had had a psychedelic experience with LSD, (b) penicillamine prevented them from having a proper affective response to LSD, and (c) the previous group had experienced an insightful LSD.

This suggested that the LSD experience without affect is of little value therapeutically for alcoholics. O'Reilly and Funks' (1964) observations support this conclusion. Penicillamine–LSD should be reserved for alcoholics who have already had the LSD experience preferably several times and who are not able to tolerate sobriety because of excessive tension. Methedrine has been used for many years as a chemical way of mobilizing affect and in many subjects prodcues marked abreactions. But, the results with methedrine were not good. LSD combines in its experience the proper relationship of perceptual and affective change. Methedrine mobilizes affect but produces an inadequate perceptual change. Penicillamine–LSD produces an adequate perceptual change, but with the absence of affect.

The following case represents in our view the proper way of using first LSD, later penicillamine–LSD as a treatment of alcoholism.

Mr. W. H. This patient, age 38, was committed to a mental hospital in November 1958 as an alcoholic. He had started to drink at age 18, continued throughout his Air Force career and noted it had become uncontrollable about five years before admission. Since then he consumed daily about 25 ounces of whiskey, had suffered innumerable blackouts and bouts of tremor and had been fired from five jobs because of drinking. He believed severe tension was his chief reason for drinking.

On examination his mental state was found normal. He was very tense. He was given his first LSD experience and discharged.

In April of 1959 he was again given LSD, 300 μg in a joint session with two therapists who had also taken it. The subject believed he had gotten more out of this second session.

He remained sober until his second admission in June 1959 for two weeks. He was severely inebriated with marked tremor. After he recovered he received a third experience with 200 μg of LSD. This time he achieved a transcendental experience and had a feeling of oneness with God and man. On July 4, 1959 he received his fourth experience with 100 μg of LSD. This was an elective treatment. He had remained sober after the third one but had been very tense. During this session he experienced several hours of remorse and depression. On July 9, 1959, he took it together with his wife. He received 200 μg and his wife 300 μg. The joint session did not go well.

By July 23, 1959, he had been drunk one day and his relationship with his wife had not improved. He was again admitted in drunken state in November 1959 for three weeks. He was given his sixth experience in the hospital, 600 μg followed in one-and-one-half hours by 300 μg. He had an intense, insightful experience.

A few months later he was again committed to a mental hospital. He was discharged in March 1960 and came to Saskatoon where, in April, he was discovered very ill and nearly unconscious in a hotel. He had consumed a huge quantity of alcohol in a few days. He was treated vigorously with nicotinic acid until he recovered. Then he was given penicillamine, 4 grams per day, for 2 days and then 300 μg of LSD. He had an LSD experience which was similar visually to his earlier ones. He received no therapy. Most of the time he found the experience very flat. He was discharged April 18, 1960.

A few days later he found another job. For 2 months he remained sober. This was the first time in many years he had been sober and free of tension. He was involved in the problem of reestablishing his family life. His wife and children had been living on Social Aid in a room in another city and he would commute there every weekend. His wife had not accepted his sobriety nor believed it would last. On June 26, 1960 he became extremely tense and drank 13 ounces of liquor. He then became frightened and called Dr. Hoffer who started him on nicotinic acid for a few days. One month later he had a second one-day relapse after which he has remained continuously sober for over 4 years. At present he is a partner in a successful business and is reunited and getting on reasonably well with his wife. He is a very active and dedicated member of A.A.

On a recent visit he described his last LSD as an experience which left him emotionally flat for several months. Previously he had been subject to violent swings in mood from intense tension to intense euphoria. Both states he found most unpleasant and he used alcohol to dampen these feelings.

It is now possible to run double blind comparison experiments with LSD. We would suggest this could be done by pretreating one sample with penicillamine, another sample with placebo and then giving them both LSD.

So far there have been no therapeutic studies in which LSD has been used as a psychedelic agent where similar success rates were not found. It is rather odd that there have been no negative papers. But no negative report can be accepted as valid when it does appear, unless methods similar to the ones described here are used. Psychiatric scientists must learn to repeat other peoples work using methods which if not identical must be as close to them as possible and where there are differences in methodology the onus of proof is on them to show that the difference in technique was unimportant.

PSYCHOPATHS AND BEHAVIORAL PROBLEMS

The treatments already outlined in detail have been used successfully for treating many of these patients.

DRUG ADDICTS. Isbell *et al.* (1956) found addicts reacted normally to LSD. We have given LSD to two addicts. They reacted in much the same way as alcoholics. A direct result of LSD therapy was the development of Synanon, the new self-help organization developed by addicts for addicts. It seems to be as effective for addicts as A.A. for alcoholics.

HOMOSEXUALITY. Ball and Armstrong (1961) treated ten homosexual patients with LSD. Two were much improved. Martin (1963) treated one homosexual with 8 LSD sessions. Six years later he was still normal. We have treated 3 homosexual men with LSD. One was also schizophrenic and alcoholic. He was treated with nicotinamide for his schizo-phrenia and later with LSD for his alcoholism and homosexuality. He is now well, three months later. Of the other two, one is well.

ADOLESCENT BEHAVIORAL PROBLEMS IN BOYS. Cameron (1963) treated 8 severely disturbed boys age 14 to 18 with LSD. Four were much improved. We have treated two boys with behavioral problems. Of these one has been well 5 years since treatment.

CRIMINAL PSYCHOPATHS. Arendsen-Hein (1963) treated twenty-one severe criminal psychopaths with LSD. They were all considered hope-less cases. They had a history of 5–20 court sentences each. Treatment consisted of sessions with LSD (50–450 μg) every week or two for 10–20 weeks. Between LSD sessions they were given group therapy. Of the 21 psychopaths, 12 were clinically improved and 2 much improved. One was a chronic alcoholic who remained sober after treatment. The advantages of using LSD for these different cases were:

1. There was no fear of the procedure
2. Motivation was activated
3. Past experiences were relived
4. Much therapy time was saved
5. The internalizing of conflicts was promoted

These few studies with these behavioral problems are very encouraging. Well-conceived large clinical studies are essential so that the indications and uses of LSD may be worked out.

GROUP PSYCHOTHERAPY AND LSD

A good deal of skill and much experience is required to run LSD groups. Over the past 8 years we have run many groups. In our opinion they are no better for the patient than are individual sessions. The main advantage is for the therapist who can give the experience to two or more subjects and so conserve time. There are many disadvantages, the chief being it is difficult to observe more than one patient accurately and subtle clues to change which are so valuable in individual sessions are missed.

However groups may be very advantageous for studying group interactions. It is advisable for every member of the group who will take LSD to have had one or more individual sessions so that the severe disorganization of the first experience is avoided. As a rule there should be one nonlysergized observer for each two subjects who have taken LSD. We have not had any experience with groups larger than four. It is probable they would break down into several smaller groups.

Slater *et al.* (1957) studied the effect of group interaction on the LSD reaction. Subjects who took LSD in groups had more manic or schizo-affective reactions. The group did not reduce symptoms such as unreality, indifference, changes in body image, or the other severe psychotic symptoms. But anxiety, depression, inappropriate behavior, underactivity, hallucinations, and thinking and speech disturbances were reduced.

Several times we have observed groups of 2 which had to be separated. One would develop great anxiety or panic and this would often induce panic in the others. There was a kind of reverberation of affect which was not controlled until the subjects were taken to separate rooms when anxiety in each quickly subsided.

Spencer (1963) combined permissive group therapy with LSD. They found its chief value was it mobilized repressed experiences. A group of 10 very different patients with hopeless prognoses comprised the group. They had failed every previous treatment. The group included psychopaths, hysterics, phobics, and recurrent depressions. Of 10, 3 were so improved that they no longer needed therapy, 4 were helped, and 3 were not helped.

Recently Cheek (1963) used the Bales technique for measuring the effect of LSD on group interactions. The LSD was given to a four-person group of reformatory inmates. At times only one group member was given LSD, at times all four. LSD had a marked effect on group interactions. Total interaction rates, signs of tension, tension release, overt hostility, and in some cases marked behavioral changes were detected by the interaction technique even when subjective accounts showed little change.

Autistic Children and LSD

A. M. Freedman *et al.* (1962) gave 12 autistic children 100 μg of LSD. Their ages varied from 6–12 years. The results were very similar to those of adult schizophrenics. None were improved.

Bender *et al.* (1962, 1963) used LSD for treating autistic children using an entirely new concept in LSD therapy. A group of 50 autistic children were given daily doses of LSD starting with 25 μg and increasing it until daily doses of 150 μg were given. Treatment continued from 2 months to 12 months. No previous treatment had helped any of them. UML was also used as another treatment.

Autistic Children

There were no serious side effects. All showed some response. They became "gay, happy, laughing frequently." Nearly all were more alert, interested in other people. Some showed appropriate facial emotion for the first time; many were able to understand. and follow directions more readily. Some of the quieter aggressive children became quieter and more normal. There were no sleeping problems. The vocabularies of several improved.

Verbal Children

These were schizophrenic children, ages 6–12 years, their illness had been less chronic and they had attended public school. All could talk. All of them were improved. None was a management problem on the ward. Their interpersonal relationships improved, they developed insight, lost their hallucinations and generally were much better. Psychological tests before and during therapy confirmed the clinical evaluations.

When half the children were taken off medication for four weeks there was evidence of regression within a short time. Reserpine or Imipramine administered for 4 weeks had no beneficial effect. When LSD was resumed the children again responded.

It is likely that these striking results are not due to the LSD experience for UML which does produce an experience was just about as good.

Both LSD and UML increased uptake of inorganic phosphate by red blood corpuscles, thus normalizing phosphate metabolism (see section on phosphates, p. 91).

Malvaria, LSD, and Alcoholism

The disease "alcoholism" is defined as the act of drinking excessively. This may be due to a variety of reasons or even diseases which underly this action. Clinicians have been fully aware of this and they have made many serious attempts to classify alcoholism according to these other factors or diseases. This has been and still is difficult because clinical methods for diagnosis are inherently imprecise; subjective methods do not have the same precision (reliability and validity) as do laboratory tests. The natural history of the disease concept in medicine shows clearly that there has been a steady subdivision of broad heterogenous groups (for example, fevers) into smaller more homogeneous groups. In each case it became possible to divide the larger groups because laboratory tests were developed. Many homogeneous groups were then diagnosed operationally and there was a steady refinement of signs and symptoms to syndromes to precise diseases. Thus the syndrome cough, pain in the chest, and fever became tuberculosis or pneumonia of a particular sort depending upon the results of some specific laboratory tests.

In effect, syndromes are used primarily to indicate which laboratory tests should be used, and frequently the laboratory tests alone are adequate to establish diagnosis even when no syndrome is present.

Alcoholism unfortunately is still a syndrome since no laboratory tests are known which subdivide the syndrome into more homogeneous groups. The subdivision into depressions, neuroses, psychopathies, and schizophrenia is a slight improvement but since these diagnoses are themselves clinical impressions (skillful guesses, for to diagnose is to guess) there is little gain in accuracy or precision.

The Disease Malvaria

Many different chemical substances are present in urine from normal subjects or from subjects either physically or mentally ill. But few biochemists are prepared to examine large numbers of urines for any particular substance (or even family of substances) in the hope one will be present less frequently or in smaller concentration in normal subjects compared to other diagnostic groups. What is required is a reason for examining for a specific group of substances. This was the line of reasoning which led to the isolation by Irvine (1961) of substances rarely present in normal subjects, from schizophrenic urine. It was postulated that d-lysergic acid diethylamide produced not only a clinical but also a biochemical model of schizophrenia, in short that LSD would lead to the excretion of the same abnormal substances in normal subjects which were assumed to be present in schizophrenics' urine. Urines were, therefore, obtained before and after giving alcoholic patients LSD treatment.

The urines were analyzed chromatographically with techniques less apt to destroy unstable or reactive substances by oxidation, etc. Very soon it was found that the systems developed by Irvine demonstrated certain mauve-colored spots in the high R_f region after LSD administration. When it was clear this was not LSD or its direct decomposition product the same procedures were applied to urines from various psychiatric groups. Irvine (1961) found that this mauve staining substance was present more frequently in schizophrenic patients than in any other group. His detailed examination of the substance led him to believe it was a pyrrole but it still remains unidentified. Using a slightly different method which seems to pick up fewer substances, Hoffer and Mahon (1961) found that similar mauve staining compounds were also present more frequently in schizophrenic urine than in any other group. Irvine's (1961) substance extracted from schizophrenic urine was used as the standard reference compound.

The Hoffer-Mahon method was taught to a laboratory technician who then installed in a laboratory at the Saskatchewan Hospital, Weyburn, under the supervision of Dr. H. Osmond, then medical superintendent. The results obtained were similar to those found in University Hospital. Since the technique at these two laboratories was identical we have pooled all the results. The following groups of psychiatric patients were examined and of these a certain proportion had these substances in their urine (see Table 7).

At the same time Hoffer and Osmond (1961a,b,c) developed a simple and crude card sort test for assisting in the diagnosis of schizophrenia. This test (hereafter HOD test) consists of a set of 145 cards—each card contained a question which the patient stated was true or false by placing it in a box marked "true" or "false." Scores were obtained by recording the cards placed in the "true" box. The questions were so framed that schizophrenic patients would declare many more of them to be true than would any other group except the toxic psychoses. Questions dealt with perceptual changes, changes in thought and changes in mood. It was found that the HOD scores did relate in a significant and very high degree to the diagnostic groups. Hoffer and Osmond (1961c) then found that all subjects who had the mauve staining factor in their urine had much higher HOD scores than had similar diagnostic groups who did not have it. The relationship of HOD scores to the presence of the chemical substances in urine, was in fact, much better than was the relationship of either one to diagnosis (Hoffer and Osmond, 1962a).

Thus two objective tests, one a chemical assay and the other a clinical psychological test, were highly associated. This increased confidence in the hypothesis that different facets of the same disease process were being examined.

Since all subjects who had these chemicals in urine resembled each other more than any other group it seemed appropriate to drop the clinical criteria for diagnosing and to use the simple objective test. Hoffer and Osmond (1962a) proposed the term "malvaria" as a diagnosis for this group. Malvaria is present in any subject who has the mauve staining factor in his urine. Thus, referring to Table 5, 75% of the acute untreated schizophrenics had malvaria, etc. Of the alcoholics tested, 20% also had malvaria. Hoffer and Osmond (1963a,b) gave a comprehensive description of malvaria.

Comparison of Malvarian and Nonmalvarian Alcoholics

Over a 3-year period 42 alcoholic patients were examined for the presence of malvaria. In every case first morning samples were taken a few days after admission and the samples were then analyzed. The results were recorded before the clinical assessment was completed. The HOD test was given by the nursing staff within a few days after admission. Tests were used if given a few days after admission, or if it seemed certain that the patients were not intoxicated on the day of admission.

A comparison of the 2 groups of patients is given in Table 17.

Of the 14 malvarians, 3 were schizophrenic using the usual clinical criteria. They were so diagnosed at other mental hospitals. Two alcoholics developed malvaria after being given LSD treatment and one had malvaria the morning after he had withdrawal convulsions. Of the 28 nonmalvarian alcoholics, only 2 were diagnosed schizophrenic by any psychiatrist.

TABLE 17

COMPARISON OF MALVARIAN AND NONMALVARIAN ALCOHOLICS

Group	Number	Number male	Mean HOD scores[a]			
			DS	Per S	PS	TS
Malvaria	9	7	13.4	14.0	5.7	76.0
Malvaria only after LSD and rum fits	3	3	0.7	0	0	2
Nonmalvarians	28	26	5.5	2.2	2.3	22
Alcoholics (nontoxic)	95	89	5.3	2.4	1.5	20.4
Alcoholics (toxic)	29	26	8.8	11.3	4.1	60.0

[a] DS, depression score; Per S, perception score; PS, paranoid score; TS, total score.

There were major differences in HOD scores, malvarians scored higher on depression, on perceptual disturbances and on thought disorder. The three alcoholics who were transiently malvarian had very low scores and so resembled the larger group of nonmalvarian alcoholics. This group did not differ significantly in any of the HOD scores from a much larger group of alcoholics tested who were not examined for malvaria.

A smaller group (29) of alcoholics were toxic from alcohol when admitted and tested, that is they were either drunk or had delirium tremens. Their urine was not examined. Their HOD scores were extremely high as one would expect since in toxic states there are major perceptual disturbances. Their scores were similar to schizophrenic scores.

HOD admission scores can be used to assess the degree of toxicity. High scores on admission which go down very quickly in a few days suggest the patient had been drinking heavily before admission (very common) or is either developing into or coming out of delirium tremens. Daily HODs give one a good measure of the effectiveness of detoxifying measures. If, however, HOD scores remain high when the patient is sober and not suffering delirium tremens, then schizophrenia should be considered in the differential diagnosis.

All the subjects in Table 17 fell into 3 groups (a) normals with very low scores (b) nonschizophrenics (neurotics, depressions, etc.), nonmalvarians including nonmalvarian schizophrenics, and nonmalvarian alcoholics; these have intermediate scores, (c) schizophrenics, malvarians (which includes schizophrenics and nonschizophrenics) and alcoholic malvarians.

The malvarian alcoholics had the highest scores, even higher than schizophrenic scores. However, there were only nine in the group. Those alcoholics malvarian after LSD are somewhat different. Larger groups will be examined to settle this point. In contrast nonmalvarian alcoholics did not differ from other nonmalvarian groups.

Results of Treatment with LSD and Nicotinic Acid

If the excretion of mauve factor signifies similar biochemical dysfunction then chemical treatment should be equally effective. About 75% of any group of malvarians are schizophrenic. Therefore, malvarians should respond as well to treatment given schizophrenics as do schizophrenics.

For 10 years we have used massive doses of either nicotinic acid or nicotinamide as an important adjunct in the treatment of schizophrenic patients (Hoffer *et al.*, 1957; Hoffer and Osmond, 1962a,b; Denson, 1962; Osmond and Hoffer, 1962; Hoffer, 1962, 1963). When this vitamin was included in a treatment program with other drugs and ECT, 75% of the patients remained well for 10 years. A comparison group yielded a 35% ten-year cure rate. Schizophrenics not given nicotinic acid had the same prognosis as schizophrenics anywhere else, that is many killed themselves, they tended to remain chronically ill, were repeatedly re-admitted to psychiatric wards or mental hospitals and a large proportion became chronically ill in mental hospitals. The patients treated with nicotinic acid, however, did not commit suicides, had very few read-missions, and a much smaller proportion became chronic. Out of a hundred or more acute schizophrenics there have been hardly any failures. The treatment failures have come from the group who had already been treated previously over a period of years and had not recovered.

We, therefore, began to treat all malvarians with nicotinic acid and other therapies that we used for schizophrenia to test the hypothesis that alcoholic malvarians would respond better to such treatment than they would if treated simply as alcoholics.

Fourteen of the alcoholics had malvaria, eleven before receiving LSD and three only after LSD or during withdrawal after rum fits. Some of this group were treated with nicotinic acid. Others were not given the advantage of this treatment because they had been discharged before we decided to treat alcoholic malvarians as if they were schizophrenic. The group of malvarian alcoholics who were treated with nicotinic acid will be compared with those who were not. All members of the group except H. M. were given one or more treatments with LSD. The much larger nonmalvarian group will not be discussed.

Alcoholic Malvarians Not Given an Adequate Treatment Trial

Several reports have been published where the method of using nicotinic acid is described. Patients are classified into treatment phases where phase 1 treatment is simpler than phase 3.

Phase 1 treatment consists of a treatment trial of either nicotinic acid or nicotinamide, 3 grams per day for one month. This is carried out on an out-patient basis. If alcoholics continue to drink there is usually no response. If the patient responds he is continued on medication for 1 year. Those patients who are not improved, or who are not able to co-operate because they are too ill, or because they cannot stop drinking, enter phase two of the treatment program. The vitamin is continued at the same dose but in addition they are given a series of 5–8 ECT. It is possible that some of the newer antipsychotic drugs such as Triperidol (Tobin *et al.*, 1966) might be combined with nicotinic acid to replace ECT. This possibility is now being examined in clinical trials.

Patients who fail to recover with this treatment are classed as phase three patients. They are continued on nicotinic acid and given an additional short series of ECT and penicillamine by mouth, 2 grams per day for up to 12 days, or until they develop a rash and high fever. For the purpose of discussing treatment results we will consider no treatment adequate until phase three is completed, if it is needed—that is if a patient responds to phase one he will not need the more intensive phases of treatment but if he fails to respond he will be classified in the not-adequate-treatment class. The reason for not completing the treatment was usually unavailability of beds for further readmission and treatment.

Between March 1, 1960 and March 1, 1961, 40 schizophrenic patients were treated. Sixteen required phase one treatment only; 3 were completely cured, while 11 were much improved, that is, able to function well in the community but some symptoms still were present. Two remained ill at home. Nineteen patients failed phase one and were given phase two treatment. Of these 10 were cured, 6 were much improved, and 3 were unimproved. Five who failed phase two were given phase three treatment. Of these, 3 were thereafter much improved; the remaining 2 were not. Of the entire group of 40, 13 (32.5%) were cured, twenty (50%) were much improved, and 7 failed to respond. Thus 82.5% achieved a clinical state which was compatible with nearly normal life in the community. The 7 failures were all patients who had been ill many years in the community before they were treated.

Malvarians Treated Only with LSD

The first 6 patients to be described in this section had not received an adequate treatment trial and none are doing well (that is, are sober). The seventh had adequate treatment only for several years. After this he discontinued his vitamin and after half a year began to drink heavily.

Mr. D. A., Age 48, Married. Mr. D. A. began to drink at age 13 and two years later he was a regular weekend drinker. At age 23 he was jailed two years for theft while drunk. He had several other sentences for offences committed while drunk. He was treated in a mental hospital for nine months in 1950–1951 and thereafter was sober 18 months. He had four more admissions to the same mental hospital by 1955. He remained sober while in A.A. for three years until his last admission there. Again he joined A.A. and remained sober for two years. After that he never lasted for more than 6–8 months of abstinence. In December 1961, he developed severe bleeding from his stomach with a recurrence a year later. In the spring of 1963 he required two more admissions to a mental hospital. Finally, in May 30, 1963, he was admitted to University Hospital Saskatoon for seven days. His mental state was normal and he was diagnosed as a chronic alcoholic. He received 300 μg of LSD as a treatment. The next morning his urine had mauve factor. He was started on nicotinamide (3 grams per day) and discharged. However, he continued to drink, did not take the medication, and a few months later was sentenced to jail for offences committed while drunk.

Mr. H. D., Age 36. This patient joined the armed services at age 17. When discharged in 1946 he was a very heavy drinker. He was continually in trouble with his family over his drunken behavior. He continued to get drunk at least once each week. In 1949 he again enlisted and married on discharge in 1953. He continued to drink heavily until 1958 when he joined A.A. and remained sober for two years. In mid 1960, while driving, he had a head-on collision with another car. This resulted in the death of his mother. He began to drink heavily again and when he was admitted January 2, 1963, he was consuming 26 ounces of liquor daily.

Upon admission, no changes in perception were found. His thinking was somewhat odd. He blamed himself for his mother's death and believed that had he continued to drink the accident would not have occurred. He felt his neighbors also held him responsible and he would have liked a public hearing at which he could have been absolved. He was also very depressed. The diagnosis made was reactive depression in a chronic alcoholic. His urine had the mauve factor.

Two weeks after admission he was given 200 μg of LSD but he had a very moderate experience. He afterward felt he had gained some insight from it. For the following week he remained deeply depressed. To help him recover he was given nicotinic acid (3 grams per day) for six days. On discharge, February 4, 1963, he was cheerful, relaxed and optimistic. He was given 10 mg Dexamyl each day for out-patient treatment.

After discharge he remained sober for two-and-a-half months but then his tension and depression began to increase until four months after discharge he began to drink. He was admitted as an emergency but discharged himself the same day. He has continued to drink very heavily until this time.

Miss M. M., Age 37. This patient began drinking at about age 27. She had completed her university degree in social work. Her drinking gradually increased in intensity and in 1960 she was involved in a car accident for which she was fined. Early in 1961 she came to Saskatoon for an LSD treatment. She received such a treatment which helped her for a few months only. Then she was admitted to a state mental hospital because of intoxication. She left against advice, continued to drink, and was in another car accident. She was readmitted to the same state hospital after a suicide attempt while drunk. She then returned to Saskatchewan for another treatment with LSD. After discharge she again began to drink. Hoffer saw her in December 1961, and found her to be schizophrenic. She refused to be admitted so she was started on nicotinamide, 3 grams per day. However, she continued to drink. Much of her schizophrenic symptomatology cleared but she remained severely depressed. She was admitted May 31st until June 26th, 1962, for second phase treatment. On admission there were no perceptual changes, some paranoia was present but she was primarily severely depressed, dejected, and suicidal.

She was treated with nicotinic acid, 3 grams per day and received six ECT. Her depression lifted but she remained paranoid, bitter, hostile, and discharged herself too soon. Phase three treatment could not be given.

Mr. D. U., Age 31. This patient completed high school, took a course in business administration, and while carrying on a responsible administrative job began to drink excessively; with the repeated urging of his superior, he stated. In 1957 he began to drink very heavily with repeated blackouts and bouts of delirium tremens. He was treated several times in a general hospital. His behavior became quite unpredictable and he was committed to a mental hospital for 2 months late in 1960, as an alcoholic and drug addict. There he received 200 μg of LSD. He derived little benefit from the experience which was very frightening. After discharge there was no let up in his uncontrolled drinking and he was admitted a second time to a psychiatric ward, February 22 to April 11, 1961. Here he received one treatment with psilocybin, 15 mg, and two weeks later a second LSD treatment. He developed some insight about the relationship of his feelings to his drinking and he appeared improved. Nevertheless, he continued to drink and to take large quantities of barbiturates. He was admitted for the third time to University Hospital, August 7–16, 1961. The second day after admission he was exceedingly tense, complained that he was going into delirium and that evening had one grand mal convulsion. The next day he had a second convulsion.

After that he slowly recovered with no more seizures. He was treated with small quantities of sodium amytal and 3 grams of nicotinic acid per day. His urine contained mauve factor. He refused to take LSD again and he was discharged. Since then he has required admissions in a psychiatric ward (November 3–4, 1961), and in a mental hospital (November 12 to January 22, 1961) where he again suffered from convulsions followed by severe delirium tremens with violent hallucinations and delusions (he did not receive nicotinic acid this time). He showed a great deal of organic brain damage. He was admitted for the sixth time to a psychiatric ward December 29 to January 25, 1963, in much the same state. At no time had he been benefited by this repeated series of treatments.

Mr. F. K., Age 45. F. K. was first admitted to University Hospital April 20 to June 18, 1960. There had been a change in his personality going back about 8 years. He was very irritable, short tempered, and easily exploded into violent temper outbursts. He drank very heavily. When drunk he was aggressive and violent. One year before admission his drinking became excessive. He was admitted because he was threatening to kill himself. The urine test showed he had malvaria.

On September 26, 1960, he was committed to a mental hospital with the same clinical condition and stayed there until October 15, 1960.

After discharge he was quite depressed for several months but then he slowly began to improve. At follow-up he was working, felt much improved, and continued to drink but not as severely as before. His wife was quite content with his present stage. His depression was lifted but he remained alcoholic.

Mr. A. D., Age 41. This case illustrates the response of one alcoholic to LSD and subsequently to nicotinic acid. Within 2 years after nicotinic acid was discontinued he was readmitted once and again two years later. A. D. was first admitted to a psychiatric ward in March 1955, for two weeks. He had then been drinking very heavily for three years. During this period he felt continually tired, bored and tense, and did not derive any pleasure from his work. He was discharged on nicotinic acid, one gram per day, which he took regularly until September 1956, when he decided he no longer needed it.

Two months later his drinking was becoming severe again and he was unhappy over this. He was again nervous and tense. At the end of November, he was again started on nicotinic acid (3 grams per day). In March 1957, he was still well. He had occasionally taken a drink but he found that it did not taste as good when he took nicotinic acid. During the spring of 1957 he drank occasionally. He had not accepted the idea that he was an alcoholic and he had a few bouts for several weeks. His wife was concerned because he at times seemed queer, and when drunk, became very aggressive.

He was seen in September 1957, and treated with Dexamyl, one tablet per day, and continued on nicotinic acid. In January 1958, he was well and had been sober for four months. In May 1958 he was still well. However follow-up was then discontinued and it was left to him to ask for more supplies of nicotinic acid. He did not take any more.

In July 1959, he developed a peptic ulcer and was investigated in the hospital. When discharged he was very aggressive toward his wife and appeared to be intoxicated when, in fact, he had not been drinking. In December 1959, he began to drink heavily again and was admitted to University Hospital, April 28 to May 9, 1960. Here it was discovered he had malvaria. His depression was treated with adrenaline methyl ether, a mild central stimulant (J. A. Page and Hoffer, 1964), and with psychotherapy. He was improved on discharge. A few months later he was very irritable. In March 1961, he had a subtotal gastrectomy. In January 1962, he was admitted to a general hospital with generalized edema due to low plasma proteins. He continued to drink very heavily. He was admitted again May 24 to June 1, 1962, for another treatment with LSD. But he has continued to drink excessively and on August 26, 1963, again was seen at the Alcoholic Counselling Centre.

Mrs. G. B., Age 39. G. B. was a shy lonely person who began to drink very heavily about 1956. Her husband discovered this much later and then persuaded her to seek treatment. She did not have blackouts or delirium tremens. She was admitted August 28 to September 2, 1961. There were no perceptual changes, her thought content was paranoid, and she was very tense. When drunk she often thought about suicide. Upon examination she was found to have malvaria. She was treated with 200 μg of LSD but had a very mild emotional reaction. On discharge she was started on nicotinamide (3 grams per day), which she took for two months. But she continued to drink and did not take any more medication. At follow-up she was following her pretreatment pattern of drinking.

Alcoholics Treated as Malvarians

The next two patients stopped drinking, one in A.A. and the other in jail before they were given treatment, but since then phase one treatment only has been very helpful to them.

Mr. C. I., Age 31. This patient was a chronic alcoholic for many years. When drunk he would write bad checks but usually his father made these good. He was first admitted to a psychiatric ward in July and August 1959 for LSD treatment. He was admitted to a mental hospital November 24, 1959 for about 1 month for another treatment with LSD. He had an insightful experience but after discharge continued to drink and he was admitted to the mental hospital again January 9, 1961, for two weeks. In between he had been in jail for 6 months for writing bad checks. Upon discharge from jail he immediately resumed drinking. During this admission to the mental hospital he received another LSD treatment. There was no change in his drinking habit.

He was given several more LSD treatments. After one session at the end of May 1961, he remained under the influence of LSD for 1 week when we saw him for the first time. He was very disturbed and described in detail the perceptual changes which were still present.

We started him on nicotinic acid (3 grams per day), to bring him out of the experience and diagnosed him a pseudoneurotic schizophrenic. Two weeks later his LSD-like experience was gone. He discontinued his nicotinic acid but he began to drink again and was again admitted to a mental hospital in August 1961. He discharged himself voluntarily and was admitted to University Hospital from August 29 to September 2, 1961. His urine was positive for mauve factor. It was discovered that a brother had been treated for schizophrenia. Because he was malvarian and because of his prolonged reaction to LSD, he was advised no longer to take LSD, and on discharge he was started on nicotinamide, 3 grams per day. But he continued to drink. On January 12, 1962, he was sentenced to jail for 2 more months for writing bad checks. He took the tablets for a brief period but after discharge began to drink again and in August 1962, he was again sentenced to jail for two years. For over 16 months, while in jail, he has regularly taken the nicotinamide. This with the enforced sobriety has apparently produced a marked change in him as evidenced in his letters. On July 11, 1963, he wrote "I never thought that it could be possible to have the feeling of 'really belonging' and to have a purpose in life. It is like a jig-saw puzzle suddenly falling into place." He then informed me that he was applying for parole and that he would seek psychiatric treatment during parole to help him stay sober and to achieve maturity and independence. He was discharged May, 1964, and is still able to maintain his sobriety.

Mr. S. H., Age 45. This patient began to drink socially at age 20. During his army service between 1939 and 1945 it increased in frequency and intensity. He drank to the limit of his financial resources. After discharge he drank less until 1952 when it was discovered that his wife had cancer. From that point on his drinking began to increase. Between 1958 and 1960, he drank at least 13 ounces of liquor each day for up to one month and then remained sober one month. He at no time had blackouts or delirium tremens. In 1949 he was committed to a mental hospital where he stayed a short time.

He was admitted to University Hospital, April 18 to 27, 1960, where he received LSD therapy modified by penicillamine (Hoffer, 1962). His urine contained mauve factor the next day. On discharge he began to drink heavily again and he was admitted as a voluntary patient to the mental hospital, May, 1960, for 7 weeks. He was given a second treatment with LSD. He remained sober for several months only and he was readmitted for the third time to the mental hospital in February, 1961, for 1 month, at which time he received a third treatment with LSD. But he continued to drink heavily for the rest of 1961. However, when he was demoted in his job, December, 1961, he stopped drinking and thereafter remained sober.

At this time I contacted him, not knowing what had happened, and interviewed him in January, 1962. He was still sober but he was becoming exceedingly tense. He was quite disturbed and feared he would start drinking. Because of his malvaria I started him on nicotinamide, 3 grams per day. Three months later he reported his emotions had leveled out, he no longer had extremes of being either too euphoric or too depressed, he was sleeping better, his personality was improved and the temptation to drink had decreased. December, 1963, he still remained well and sober.

The last group of five patients were all treated adequately. Of these 4 eventually responded to treatment. The first two required phase one treatment only. The second required phase two while the last two required phase three treatment plus additional treatment elsewhere.

PHASE ONE TREATMENT

Mr. H. M., Age 67. Mr. H. M. became a heavy drinker during the First World War while serving overseas. From that time on he drank very heavily the rest of his life but he was able to consume large quantities and not show much effect from it. In 1952 he joined A.A. and remained sober for about nine months. After that he again drank very heavily. For 3 years before admission he continued to drink as before but his tolerance for alcohol had gone down markedly. He suffered many blackouts, many bouts of irritability and when intoxicated he became very delusional and paranoid.

He was treated at University Hospital, August 2 to 11, 1960. He was found to have malvaria. Mentally he showed much evidence of senile deterioration. Because of both these findings he was not given an LSD treatment but started on nicotinic acid, 3 grams per day. He was told the nature of his illness and advised not to drink any more. From discharge until April, 1963, when he died because of a coronary, he took the vitamin regularly, remained sober and mentally was normal and able to continue his job.

Mr. H. W., Age 44. Mr. H. W. drank excessively while overseas in the service during the last war but it was more or less controlled until 1950. At that time he injured his back. This resulted in severe pain for 1 year and he consumed very much alcohol and barbiturates for pain. After an operation on his back the pain was reduced but he continued to drink excessively. In 1959 he joined A.A. and remained sober. However, the pain in his back troubled him and toward the end of 1961 he began to use analgesics excessively. In the spring of 1961 he received one LSD treatment from which he derived a good deal of benefit. But he remained very tense with constant pain in his back from which he was nearly incapacited. He became very irritable and depressed and in danger of losing his job. When seen in the fall of 1961 he was diagnosed as a pseudoneurotic schizophrenic and he was started on nicotinic acid, 3 grams per day. But there was little improvement and it was essential to admit him February, 1962, for 1 month. He was continued on the vitamin and given 4 ECT. He was slightly improved on discharge.

For one month after discharge he seemed unchanged although he took his medication regularly. Then over a period of a few weeks he recovered, lost most of the pain in his back, and became secure and happy in his job. In the spring of 1963 he requested and received another LSD treatment from which he derived more benefit, he believed, than from any of the previous sessions. He is still well.

PHASE TWO TREATMENT

Mr. D. S., Age 31. D. S. began to drink heavily at age 16 and came into repeated conflict with his father. His father later developed paranoid schizophrenia which was cured by putting him on nicotinic acid, 3 grams per day. Until age 30 he drifted about a good deal, then got a job in spite of his severe drinking. He also became involved with prostitutes and psychopathic women, one of whom he married. He was admitted to University Hospital, April 21 to 26, 1960. He had perceptual changes, with visual and auditory hallucinations, thought blocking with paranoid ideation and he was very anxious and tense. His activities were inappropriate. He was diagnosed as a pseudoneurotic schizophrenic. He was given 300 μg of LSD as a treatment. On discharge he was given nicotinic acid, 3 grams per day. This he took regularly for 1 year.

He remained sober but very tense and irritable for about four months then he began to drink again. He was admitted for a second time April 25 to May 13, 1961 and he was given a series of ECT.

He continued to take the vitamin regularly until now (27 months after second admission). During this time he remained sober but he was plagued by a series of illnesses and misfortunes, most of them a result of his previous decisions made while drinking. He continued slowly to improve and seemed better than he had been for many years. Late in 1963 he was very depressed and sought psychiatric treatment in order to have another LSD treatment. He had not started to drink again.

PHASE THREE TREATMENT

Mr. G. B., Age 36. Mr. G. B. complained of great tension, anorexia, and insomnia for 6 to 7 years. We first saw him on September 29, 1959, when he had major perceptual changes, thought disorder, and was depressed. He was diagnosed as having schizophrenia and was treated with nicotinamide for 2 months with no improvement. He was, therefore, given 5,6-dihydroxy-*N*-methyl indole, 15 mg per day, for severe tension. Within 3 days he was well and remained so for 4 months, at which time his depression returned. He developed severe abdominal pain. On laparotomy nothing was found wrong. On discharge he continued to drink very heavily and was admitted April 15 to May 21, 1960. He was then quite psychotic and received a series of eight ECT. He seemed well on discharge and remained well for about 1 month when he again became very disturbed. He went to a mental hospital July 5 to 12, 1960 as a voluntary patient. He was readmitted July 15 to 24, 1960. There was no recurrence of his schizophrenia (he still remained mauve positive) and he was given a penicillamine–LSD treatment for his alcoholism which was now well entrenched. But a few days later he was drunk and seemed to go berserk. He threatened his family and was admitted as an emergency. He was given 12 ECT continued on nicotinic acid and given 2 grams penicillamine daily (Phase III). When sober he appeared quite well but after discharge he continued to drink and a few days later he was committed to a mental hospital in September 1960 (his second admission there). He was diagnosed as a paranoid schizophrenic and given long-term care and treated with tranquilizers. Until April 7, 1962, he required 3 more admissions but since his discharge on May 11, 1962, he has remained sober and is now doing well at his work and is beginning to rehabilitate himself.

Mr. R. H., Age 41. R. H. began to drink at age 16. His behavior was unpredictable and aggressive. He continued to drink freely until 1958 when he first realized he was an alcoholic. He joined A.A. for 9 months. He then began to drink again and did so until about one year ago. In the meantime he had become a very successful author. In June 1962, his alcoholism became much worse, he developed deep depression. His wife could not tolerate his behavior and left him. For the next eight months he continued to have repeated attacks of severe fear and panic. He maintained he could carry on only by using alcohol. During this period he was in mental hospital three times, once after a serious suicidal attempt.

He arrived unexpectedly early in 1963, drunk, broke and alone. He was diagnosed as a pseudoneurotic schizophrenic and started on nicotinic acid, but he could not stop drinking. He was admitted to University Hospital, February 25 to May 4, 1963, where he was treated with penicillamine–LSD.

After discharge he began to drink again and became deeply depressed and suicidal. He was still malvarian. He was admitted April 2 to 27, 1963, and was given 5 ECT. The medication with nicotinic acid was continued. On discharge his depression lifted but a few days later he drank again and he was committed to a mental hospital July 6 to 18, 1963. Since then, he has continued to drink very heavily in spite of 2 more admissions to University Hospital for further treatment.

A comparison of the two classes of malvarian alcoholics is shown in Table 18.

TABLE 18

RESULTS OF TREATMENT OF ALCOHOLIC MALVARIANS

Patient	Treatment phase	Age	Months since first seen	Number admissions	Number treatments with LSD	Months sober to 12/31/63
D. A.	I	48	21	8	1	0
H. D.	0	36	27	2	1	0
M. M.	II	37	39	5	3	0
D. U.	0	31	42	6	3	0
F. K.	0	46	58	2	0	0
G. B.	I	39	42	1	1	0
Mean		39.5	38.2	4	1.5	0
C. I.	I	31	55	5	5	30
S. H.	I	45	57	4	3	39
H. M.	I	67	50	1	0	50
H. W.	I	44	39	2	2	39
D. S.	II	31	58	2	1	45
G. B.	III	36	66	9	1	33
R. H.	III	41	27	8	2	0
Mean		42.1	49	4.4	2.0	35.4

The six who had not received adequate treatment had been followed 38.2 months. They each had 4 admissions and 1.5 LSD sessions. None were sober at follow-up. The seven who received adequate treatment had a mean 49 month follow-up. They required 4.4 admissions (for a period 1½ times as long as the first group) but they have been sober nearly 72% of the time, that is, the proportion of the follow-up time from achieving sobriety until December 31, 1964.

One patient not included in the table was much improved (sober most of the time) between 1955 and the fall of 1959. During this period he regularly took nicotinic acid, 3 grams per day. Then he discontinued medication. He was soon drinking heavily again and required two admissions in a general hospital and 2 admissions in a psychiatric ward between 1959 and 1962. We have not included him in this table because his treatment was adequate at first and then became inadequate in contrast to the other patients who continued with adequate treatment as needed. Had he been given nicotinic acid again in 1959 he might have been spared much difficulty.

We have included C. I. and S. H. although it is clear they were different. C. I. became sober only in jail where he had little access to alcohol (it is possible to get alcohol occasionally in jail and several have continued to drink in jail) and S. H. was already sober when treatment was started. If they are removed from the calculation of means then the remaining group of five were sober the last 33.4 months out of a follow-up period of 48 months, that is 69% of the follow-up period. The most striking difference was in the way the group achieved sobriety. None of the first group and 6 out of 7 of the second group were sober at follow-up. No statistical test is required to demonstrate the significance of this difference [Chi Square (Yates Correction) = 6.0, $P < 0.01$].

Of the entire group of 14 malvarians, 12 received the kind of LSD therapy described by Chwelos *et al.* (1959). Only one of these, S. H., remained sober after his last treatment.

Had the malvaria diagnostic test not been available this could have been very discouraging: The improvement rate is certainly much less than would be expected from all the clinical reports from Saskatchewan. It can be concluded that malvarian alcoholics should not be treated with LSD alone. Assuming that 30% of any group of alcoholics are malvarian, then the theoretical maximum recovery rate after LSD therapy alone is about 70%. It is interesting that Jensen (1962) has, in fact, reported this recovery rate on a group of intractable alcoholics.

Smith (1958) in his original series of 24 alcoholics included four psychotic patients. Only 1 of these was improved after treatment. In contrast of the remaining 20, 6 were much improved after treatment and 5 were improved. The present finding with malvaria corroborates Smith's earlier clinical observations.

When the alcoholic malvarians were given the treatment program devised for schizophrenics (Hoffer *et al.*, 1957) the statistics became reversed and eventually nearly all the failures after LSD become successes. This further suggests that malvaria is the more basic pathology in malvarian alcoholics but, of course, both conditions must be controlled. Malvarians who drink do not respond nearly as well to the treatment and the drinking must be controlled by treatment in hospital. Occasionally alcoholics who take nicotinic acid regularly while drinking are able to reduce their drinking very slowly.

Although malvarians do not respond to treatment with LSD unless the malvaria is adequately treated, it may be useful to give them the LSD treatment once the biochemical lesion has been controlled, for the insight has been beneficial for nearly all of the alcoholics so treated. It is advisable to start them on nicotinic acid the day after LSD. Nicotinic acid reduces the perceptual experiences of LSD (Agnew and Hoffer, 1955; Hoffer, 1962). When given after LSD it prevents prolonged reactions which are more common in malvarians than in other alcoholics. Thus H. D. and C. L. had very prolonged reactions. This is most uncommon for alcoholics, in general, who seem able to experience LSD with very little panic or anxiety. In fact they seem to react to LSD in a more mature manner than do neurotic patients. Perhaps their frequent experiences with alcohol, another psychotomimetic, has prepared them for the LSD experience.

Rapid Personality Change and LSD

Three techniques have been used for demonstrating permanent personality changes. These are (a) clinical descriptions which include subjective statements by patients and clinical evaluation by their therapist and have already been discussed in this review, (b) more objective questionnaires, and (c) psychological tests.

McGlothlin *et al.* (1964) used questionnaires which subjects completed some time after they had experienced the LSD reaction. In the first study McGlothlin was given access to a large volume of Janiger's (1959) unpublished data. The therapy groups claimed more lasting benefit than nontherapy groups. From the latter, artists claimed the best response. Of the four nontherapy groups the physicians–psychologists groups claimed the fewest benefits but the interval between the session and testing was longest for them. Increasing this interval tends to decrease claims of benefit.

In the second study McGlothlin *et al.* gave 15 subjects 200 μg of LSD. There were 14 comparison subjects. They were again tested 1 week later with Cattell's anxiety measures. There was no change in their comparison group but the treated subjects showed a drop in dogmatism and an increase in constructive responses. A comparison was made of claims or expression of opinion about the experience between subjects reported by Ditman *et al.* (1962), by Janiger and by their own subjects. These are given in Table 19.

Mogar *et al.* (1963) tested a large series of patients treated with LSD as described by J. N. Sherwood *et al.* (1962). One month before the treatment each subject was tested with the Minnesota Multiphasic Per-

TABLE 19

COMPARISON OF PERSONALITY CHANGES[a]

	Group		
	Ditman N = 74	Janiger N = 194	McGlothlin N = 15
Experience described as			
1. Pleasant	72	66	60
2. Upsetting	18	—	20
3. Would like to repeat	66	74	87
4. An experience of great beauty	66		67
5. Greatest thing that ever happened to me	49		60
After-effects			
1. Enhanced understanding	54	61	67
2. Reduced anxiety and tension	34	—	53
3. Better relations with others	37	41	40

[a] Values represent percentage of changes in each group.

sonality Inventory (MMPI), the Interpersonal Check List (ICL), and the Value-Belief Q-sort. They were retested 3 days later, after 2 months, and again after 6 months.

After two months there was a decrease in all MMPI scores except on the manic scale. The most notable decrease occurred in depression, psychesthenia, schizophrenia, social introversion, anxiety, neurotic overcontrol, and evaluation of improvement. At 6 months, there was a trend for scores to drift back to pretreatment levels but the scores were still much lower than pretreatment scores. In clinical language as a result of treatment with LSD, subjects were less depressed, had a greater sense of well-being, were less compulsive and anxious, had more adequate ego resources, and were friendlier. Patients who were most severely ill showed the greatest changes afterwards.

Criticisms of LSD Therapy and Rebuttal

Within a few months after LSD was introduced into North America the ideas generated by the LSD experience produced a good deal of criticism. The unhappy Harvard affair brought this situation to a boil and it spilled over into the popluar press. Critics have been very effective in creating a climate of opinion hostile to the use of LSD. There is an inverse square law which states that the degree of hostile criticism varies inversely with the square of the distance from any first-hand experience and knowledge of the drug.

Thus, in Canada the greatest resistance against LSD came from the professors who were least familiar with it. Our criterion of familiarity is the number of research papers published in scientific journals.

This criticism seems entirely based on factors described by Barber (1961). These include (a) substantive concepts and theories held by scientists at any given time, (b) an antitheoretical bias, (c) religious ideas, (d) professional standing, (e) professional specialization, and (f) societies, schools, and seniority. The criticism has sometimes taken on a cultic attitude and there has been private circulation of papers which have been unavailable to the general reader (Tyhurst, 1964b). In addition, critics have issued public pronouncements to the press, radio, and television which have not been based upon published data. It is therefore important to list the criticisms and then examine them carefully in order to determine whether they need be taken seriously or not. Before doing so we will quote Michael Polanyi (1956) because he makes the case so well. If we are to convince our opponents of the potential value of LSD therapy they must be converted by exposing them to careful data, reasoned argument, and a firm determination to do our work as we see fit and not to become their laboratory technician trying to disprove every will of the wisp they may conjure up.

Scientists—that is creative scientists—spend their lives in trying to guess right. They are sustained and guided therein by their heuristic passion. We call their work creative because it changes the world as we see it, by deepening our understanding of it. The change is irrevocable. A problem that I have once solved can no longer puzzle me; I cannot guess what I already know. Having made a discovery, I shall never see the world again as before. My eyes have become different; I have made myself into a person seeing and thinking differently. I have crossed a gap, the heuristic gap which lies between problem and discovery.

To the extent to which discovery changes our interpretive framework, it is logically impossible to arrive at it by the continued application of our previous interpretative framework. In other words, discovery is creative also in the sense that it is not to be achieved by the diligent application of any previously known and specifiable procedure. Its production requires originality. The application of existing rules can produce valuable surveys, but they can as little advance the principles of science as a poem can be written according to rule. We have to cross the logical gap between a problem and its solution by relying on the unspecifiable impulse of our heuristic passion, and must undergo as we do so a change of our intellectual personality. Like all ventures in which we comprehensively dispose of ourselves, such an intentional change of our personality requires a passionate motive to accomplish it. Originality must be passionate.

But this passionate quest seeks no personal possession. Intellectual passions are not like appetites; they do not reach out to grab, but set out to enrich the world. Yet such a move is also an attack. It raises a claim and makes a tremendous demand on other men; first it asks that its gift—its gift of humanity—be accepted by all. In order to be satisfied, our intellectual passions must find response. This universal intent creates a tension. We suffer when a vision of reality to which we have committed ourselves is contemptuously ignored by others. For a general unbelief threatens to evoke a similar response in us which would imperil our own convictions. Our vision must conquer or die.

Like the heuristic passion from which it flows, the persuasive passion too finds itself facing a logical gap. To the extent to which a discoverer has committed himself to a new vision of reality, he has separated himself from others who still think on the old lines. His persuasive passion spurs him now to cross this gap by converting everybody to his way of seeing things, even as his heuristic passion has spurred him to cross the heuristic gap which separated him from discovery.

We can now see the great difficulty that may arise in the attempt to persuade others to accept a new idea in science. To the extent to which it represents a new way of reasoning, we cannot convince others of it by formal argument, for so long as we argue within their framework we can never induce them to abandon it. Demonstration must be supplemented therefore by forms of persuasion which can induce a conversion. The refusal to enter on the opponent's way of arguing must be justified by making it appear altogether unreasonable.

Such comprehensive rejection cannot fail to discredit the opponent. He will be made to appear as thoroughly deluded, which in the heat of the battle will easily come to imply that he was a fool, a crank, or a fraud. And once we are out to establish such charges we shall readily go on to expose our opponent as a metaphysician, a Jesuit, a Jew, or a Bolshevik, as the case may be or—speaking from the other side of the Iron Curtain—as an 'objectivist,' and 'idealist,' and a 'cosmopolitan.' In a clash of intellectual passions each side must inevitably attack the opponent's person.

Here are the current claims made by critics:

1. LSD is a dangerous drug
2. Long-term personality changes cannot be produced by LSD
3. No good can come from a chemically induced delirium or psychoses
4. It "has not been proved to be effective or safe for any psychiatric condition" (Cole and Katz, 1964)

    (a) because there are no detailed, carefully controlled studies designed to be free from possible distortions due to bias or enthusiasm,

    (b) because explanations given are often formulations not common either to medicine in general or psychiatry in particular,

    (c) because explanations have a mystical or philosophical sound which appeals to enthusiasts—but are likely to produce doubt or even violent disbelief and concern in physicians used to a more pragmatic approach,

    (d) because components of the therapeutic process described may often have a bizarre—almost schizophrenic—component which tends to make serious investigators discount this whole area as a delusional belief shared by a group of unstable clinicians

Please read Polanyi's argument again. The rebuttal to these criticisms is not difficult.

1. Is LSD a dangerous drug? Of course it is, so is salt, sugar, water, and even air. There is no chemical which is wholly safe nor any human activity which is completely free of risk. The degree of toxicity or danger associated with any activity depends on its use. Just as a scalpel may be used to cure, it may also kill. Yet we hear no strong condemnatory statements against scalpels, etc. When LSD is used as treatment by competent physicians who are trained in its use it is no more dangerous than psychotherapy. It certainly is less dangerous than ECT insulin subcoma, and the use of tranquilizers and antidepression compounds. Statements that LSD is dangerous really are meaningless as they stand. Every clinician working with LSD who has published his data uniformly agrees it must be used by physicians with proper safeguards for the safety of the patient. There are no known physical contraindications.

2. Long-term personality changes cannot be produced. There is a curious quality about these criticisms for while it is generally denied that patients who experience LSD can be permanently changed it is, on the contrary, assumed that psychiatrists very readily suffer permanent deformations of their personality, and it is claimed that they are now overly enthusiastic and even delusional and no longer competent to honestly judge their own therapeutic efforts. It has been stated that only claims made by therapists who have not themselves taken LSD are valid (see Cole and Katz, 1964). If this argument were generally accepted in medicine no surgeon who had recovered from an acute appendicitis by surgery would be competent to judge results of his surgery on patients.

The claims of many authors that the psychedelic experience could produce a permanent change in patients have been rejected by many psychiatrists whose orientation is psychoanalytic. It is basic to their belief to assume that each person has a stable personality which is altered with great difficulty. People become sick because their personality has been warped or not allowed to develop due to pathological relationships with their parents. The only sure way of changing these twisted personalities is by a thoroughgoing analysis of many years duration during which all the roots of the pathological personality are uncovered and treated. Any other treatment, psychotherapy, or drug therapy is considered merely symptomatic treatment which leaves the patient superficially better. Obviously these psychiatrists cannot accept rapid permanent personality changes. Another group are psychologists who have accepted the hypothesis that personality is a stable attribute to man.

This reluctance to believe that people can be permanently altered in a short time seems strange. History is replete with these sudden transformations. Religions and mass self-help movements, for example Alcoholics Anonymous, originated from these changes. William James described many of them in "The Varieties of Religious Experience" (1902). Unger (1963a) has given a particularly lucid account of the issue of rapid personality change. Maslow (1959) has described this phenomena as "peak" experience and Sargant (1957) tried to abstract those factors which make man susceptible to these rapid changes. According to Sargant two factors are essential, (a) a state of increased excitation in the subject, (b) persuasion. He included psychoanalysis as one of the conversion techniques together with religious conversions, etc.

We have already referred to research reports where permanent personality changes were demonstrated (McGlothlin, 1962, 1964; McGlothlin *et al.*, 1964; Mogar *et al.*, 1963, Mogar and Savage, 1964).

3. No good can come from a chemically induced delirium or psychosis. This criticism so contradicts man's experience with drugs that it requires no answer.

4. LSD has not been proved to be effective or safe for any psychiatric condition (Cole and Katz, 1964). These critics assume that no therapy is "proved" unless a double blind comparison experiment is conducted. The word "proved" is a strange one in clinical science. Usually clinical scientists define the level of confidence or proof by a probability. That is, they will if they are statistically inclined, accept a 5% level of confidence. They will accept as proof a finding if there is only 5% chance the claims are wrong. Others may demand much stronger evidence and some may be satisfied merely with an indication. In general no statement demanding proof has any scientific meaning unless the author indicates which level of proof he would accept. Using a puristic point of view one could claim no psychiatric therapy has been "proven" to be effective for any psychiatric condition.

Criticism 4(a) really is a demand for double blind studies of LSD. The answer consists of two parts, (a) are double blind studies really superior to classical methods in proving drug efficiency and (b) is it possible to double blind LSD.

The majority of clinicians have not accepted the oft-repeated claim that double blind techniques are superior to classical clinical methods. As an example Baird (1964) stated "The insistence in recent years on 'blindness' or 'double blindness' in evaluating the effect of therapy is an insult to the intelligence of the average clinician." In addition a large number of scientists who have worked with double blind procedures have become increasingly disenchanted with it. It has been a clumsy expensive method which has not convinced anyone of its value and which is readily dispensed with when decisive action is required. The toxicity of thalidomide was not proven by double blind studies nor have the many new drugs removed from the market been proven toxic by double blind studies. It appears that when firm action is indicated classical clinical methods are adequate, but when matters of efficiency are involved these methods suddenly become much too crude.

If Baird were unsupported one could ignore him, but when in fact he is supported by (a) eminent statisticians such as Hogben (1957), R. A. Fischer (1963), Chassan (1961, 1963, 1964), Bellak and Chassan (1964), and by others we have reported (Hoffer and Osmond, 1961a, 1962a,b), and by (b) eminent clinicians including S. Cohen, H. Lehmann, and many others, and also (c) eminent psychologists like H. Kluver, then we must ask the proponents of double blind methodology to prove at the usual 5% level of confidence that their methods are more apt to show which chemicals are effective for certain conditions and which are not effective. Until this is done no clinician need feel guilty about using the old-fashioned clinical methods including single case studies, for these were the methods which introduced into psychiatry ECT, tranquilizers, antidepression drugs, open wards, eradication of pellagra psychosis and of general pareses of the insane, and a host of other minor treatments. Better methods will and must be found and double blind methods are indeed useful in mopping up studies. They do serve a useful function as large-scale human toxicity trials and they are more convincing to inspectorial physicians concerned about global efficacy. However they have hung a millstone around our necks which is steadily becoming more burdensome. It is ironic that one man's observation (Lehmann on chlorpromazine) recently required one million dollars to be confirmed—see million dollar fizzle (Margolis, 1964).

Some critics (see inverse square law, p. 197) have suggested that a placebo be used to double blind LSD. This betrays an extraordinary lack of experience with LSD. No experienced therapist would be in any doubt within one hour about determining whether distilled water or 200 μg of LSD had been given even if he were blind and could not see the pupillary dilatation produced by LSD. Every scientist who has worked with LSD agrees with this. Only a person completely unfamiliar with psychiatry and with LSD could mistake situational anxiety for the LSD reaction in a nonpsychotic subject. It has been suggested further that a new compound should be developed which would produce the same (or similar) visual changes as LSD. But this is not helpful, since no such compound is known, and if it were, would not prove anything, for it is possible these visual changes are responsible for the therapeutic results. There is no valid reason to suppose LSD is more effective than psilocybin or mescaline. It is the experience not the compound which induces it which is responsible.

However if double blind studies were possible investigators would use them, not because they are better, but because they are more fashionable. Perhaps pretreatment with penicillamine would provide such a design. Statistically identical groups could be pretreated with penicillamine and with placebo. Then all would be given LSD in the usual way. The penicillamine would not interfere with the perceptual component of the experience but would dampen its emotional component. It would be very difficult for therapists to decide which patients had received placebo or penicillamine. One could then conclude that the normal LSD experience was or was not superior to penicillamine–LSD. Our data suggests that the improvement rates would be 10% after penicillamine–LSD and 50% after LSD. However, even such a controlled double blind experiment would not persuade the critics for by then they could have produced newer unverified suggestions.

Criticism 4(b) means little. Any new explanation if it is to be new must be uncommon in medicine or in psychiatry. Commonality of ideas is usually not appealed to by scientists. It applies more to legal and ethical requirements in a court of law. However we find Cole and Katz' (1964) statement most surprising. Presumably they are unfamiliar with the enormous range of theoretical formulations from conservative Freudism to radical biochemical reasoning. We find it difficult to understand how modern psychiatry which bases so much on random events, dreams, ideas, and lapsae linguae can find any formulation uncommon.

Criticism 4(c) is very like 4(b). It is an inevitable consequence of any new idea that it should produce violent disbelief and concern in physicians. We should remember that many novel ideas of our past are commonplace today. Just a few examples will demonstrate how science has reversed itself at times. Mendelian theory was resisted from 1865 until about 1900 because Mendel's conceptions ran counter to predominant conceptions of inheritance (were not common to medicine in general). Mendel's peers condescendingly considered his work insignificantly provincial (not common to medicine).

The application of mathematics to biology was seriously questioned for many years. In his biography of Galton, Pearson reported that he sent a paper to the Royal Society in 1900 which used statistics. Before it was published the Council of the Royal Society passed a resolution "that in future papers mathematics should be kept apart from biological applications." Galton founded a new journal and in its first issue wrote "a new science cannot depend on a welcome from the followers of the older one." Harvey, Pasteur, Magendie, Lister, Funk and Fleming all found their ideas severely tested by unreasoning hostile criticism because their ideas were uncommon. It seems new ideas rarely are accepted with an open mind.

Criticism 4(d) is another variant of 4(b) and 4(c). Any new explanation, however sound it may eventually prove to be, seems bizarre, almost schizophrenic, to the defenders of the faith. But it goes a bit further by the adhominem diagnosis of scientists who use LSD for therapy as having states of paranoia (that is sharing a delusional belief). This is, of course, a redundant non sequitur for the definition of delusion is an uncommon idea from which its possessor will not part when confronted with common ideas. This is what these authors have already said in 4(b) and 4(c).

Many factors have been suggested which could account for the therapeutic results claimed by LSD therapists. The usual ones include faith, bad samples, bias in observors, etc. These are possible factors but are they merely possible or are they likely? Before they can be seriously accepted it must be shown that these variables do improve a proportion of alcoholics. Where are the double blinds which prove that faith, bias, etc. can produce equivalent results? We suggest that proponents of these variables should provide data for their favorite hypothesis before they expect others to work them into their clinical studies. The critics of LSD therapy would enormously strengthen their position if they would demonstrate a double blind study of placebo or faith.

The scientific literature [excluding editorials (Grinker, 1963, 1964) and review articles] is singularly affirmative. Every worker who has studied LSD's use for treating alcoholism is in unusual agreement. The only study recorded where there is some disagreement is the study of Ditman *et al.* (1962). They examined the duration of claims for improvement made by subjects who had been given LSD. The authors stated "the subjects had originally been given 100 μg of LSD-25 orally in a permissive but *non-treatment*[1] setting in order to compare the LSD experience with that of delirium tremens." Ditman and Whittlesey (1959) again stated "our subjects received no intended psychotherapy during the LSD experience." Questionnaires were sent to their subjects about ½ to 1½ years after their last LSD experience and of those who responded, 27 were alcoholics. Of this group of 27, 18 subjects claimed they were better, that they were in more comfortable circumstances, earning more money, and had decreased or stopped drinking.

In as much as this group had not been given LSD as therapy or in a therapeutic setting and had only received 100 μg of LSD, which we

[1] Emphasis is ours, not the authors.

have found is relatively ineffectual for most alcoholics, this is indeed a surprising result.

However, a second questionnaire two years later was answered by only 16. Of the other 11, 4 had died, 3 from drinking. Of this group of 16, 11 still claimed periods of abstinence ranging from 1 to $1\frac{1}{2}$ years and twelve claimed lasting benefit. These authors state that this indicated fewer claims but a chi square analysis of their own reported data does not support this contention. Thus, in their first questionnaire, 18 out of 27 claimed improvement; in their second questionnaire, 11 out of 16. Chi Square is less than 0.5. These results are practically identical. However, none had maintained their sobriety. We interpret this to mean that although nearly $\frac{2}{3}$ of the group maintained they were improved at the time of the second questionnaire, three-and-one-half years after having had received an ineffectual dose of LSD, none had been continuously sober that entire period.

We mention this report in some detail because other people have made claims based on this report not made by Ditman *et al.*, that is, that LSD was not an effective *therapy* for alcoholism. Their concluding statement merely stated "Three and one-half years after *exposure* to LSD there remained only claims of slight improvement and none of the alcoholic subjects had maintained their sobriety." Had they given 200 μg or more with a therapeutic objective in a therapeutic setting by therapists interested in the therapeutic experience and had they used the community resources including A.A., perhaps at three and one-half years about 50% of their subjects or better would have been sober.

Modifiers of the LSD Experience

The LSD experience may be decreased in intensity or it may be intensified by the use of other chemical or physiological techniques. In this section we will discuss only chemical modifiers.

REDUCERS

Sedatives and Tranquilizers

As a class these compounds antagonize the LSD effect. Sodium amytal was the first one used before tranquilizes came into general use. Hoch (1956) found that it decreased the intensity of the experience very effectively when it was given by mouth or by vein. We have routinely given our patients about 500 mg of sodium amytal at 8 o'clock each evening by injection, to ensure deep uninterrupted sleep. Occasionally much larger doses are needed. One subject did not fall asleep until he had been given 1.2 grams but then he slept for about 30 hours.

The nonstimulant tranquilizers have been used most frequently. Chlorpromazine works very well. Pretreatment with chlorpromazine for several days will protect subjects against the effect of LSD (Cooper, 1955; Hoch, 1956; Giberti and Gregoretti, 1955; Schwarz *et al.*, 1955; Cholden *et al.*, 1955; Isbell, 1956; MacDonald and Galvin, 1956; Isbell and Logan, 1957; Sandison and Whitelaw, 1957). The minimum dose intramuscularly is 50 mg. There is no reason why other phenothiazines should not work just as well.

Murphree (1962) investigated the effect of chlorpromazine on the ability of normal subjects to detect small doses of LSD. He gave 18 subjects 0, 5, 10, 15, and 20 μg doses. Doses below 20 μg were not recognized. When the subjects were given 25 mg of chlorpromazine at the same time recognition was not blocked but when they were given 50 mg, 30 minutes before the LSD, recognition and mydriasis were blocked.

The results were not as clear for reserpine. Giberti and Gregoretti (1955) pretreated several subjects with 10 mg of reserpine for several days. They did not react to the LSD but Isbell (1956), Isbell and Logan (1957), and Elder *et al.* (1957) reported that pretreatment with reserpine potentiated the effect of the LSD.

Frenquel (α-C-4-piperidylbenzhydrol-HCl) a mild antipsychotic substance later displaced by the tranquilizers, controlled the LSD reaction according to Fabing (1955a,b,c, 1956). Double blind studies with 10 to 30 mg per day for one week blocked the LSD reaction nearly completely in 5 out of 6 normal subjects when they were given 100 μg. In addition Brown *et al.* (1955, 1956) found that 100 mg of Frenquel given IV at the height of the experience promptly relieved the symptoms in 4 out of 5 subjects and Rinaldi and Himwich (1955a,b) found Frenquel corrected the EEG abnormalities produced in rabbits with LSD. The antagonism was specific for these EEG changes and mydriasis was not altered. On the other hand, Isbell (1956), Clark (1956), and Isbell and Logan (1957) found Frenquel was no better than placebo. Chronologically the last word is with the negative side but perhaps a reinvestigation would show why these investigations found different results. Much more is known about using LSD many years after this minor controversy.

Substances Which Modify Glucose Metabolism

GLUCOSE. Mayer-Gross *et al.* (1952) reported that the breakdown of hexose monophosphate was inhibited by LSD. They believed LSD produced its psychological effect by interfering with glucose utilization. Bain (1957) could not corroborate these findings. Following this line of thought Mayer-Gross *et al.* fed subjects glucose during an LSD experience and noted a slight amelioration in the symptoms. Smith (1958) repeated this experiment using an alcoholic diabetic subject who was treated with LSD. At noon during the height of the experience he was given 100 grams of glucose by mouth. His blood sugar level rose to over 200 mg percent but there was no significant effect on the symptomatology. One case does not disprove an hypothesis but it seems certain that this quantity of glucose is less effective than any of the tranquilizers or nicotinic acid in modifying LSD symptoms.

GLUTAMIC ACID AND SUCCINIC ACID. Hoff and Arnold (1954), Arnold and Hofmann (1955), and Arnold *et al.* (1958) found that 20 grams of glutamic acid given by vein or 100 grams given by mouth and 10 grams of succinic acid given by vein interrupted or retarded the LSD reaction for from 3 to 5 hours. This reaction may be similar to the antidotal action of succinic acid on the mescaline experience.

NICOTINIC ACID. Agnew and Hoffer (1955) tested the antagonistic effect of nicotinic acid against the LSD experience in two ways. A series of normal volunteers were pretreated with 3 grams of nicotinic acid each day for 3 days. Then they were given 100 μg of LSD. The LSD reaction was much different than it had been for the same volunteers who had been given LSD unmodified. Difficulties in power of expression were mild while with LSD alone they were unable to describe their experiences as well. Visual disturbances were rare and when they did occur they were mild. Only one out of five subjects had pronounced visual changes. As a group there was a marked increase in feelings of unreality and in uncertainty about their own identity. Nicotinic acid used this way did not prevent LSD from acting but it so altered the type of reaction that a new kind of model psychosis was produced. This seemed more schizophrenic-like than did the usual LSD reactions.

A second group of 5 volunteers were first given 100 μg of LSD. At the height of the reaction they were injected intravenously with 200 mg of nicotinic acid. There was an immediate and striking reduction in all the disturbances except mood and this was maintained the rest of the day. Since then we have used nicotinic acid as required during LSD therapy to decrease confusion and perceptual changes. This allowed psychedelic experiences to appear without the need to terminate the reaction. O'Reilly and Reich (1962) terminated each LSD session later in the day by giving their patients nicotinic acid. Ruiz-Ogara *et al.* (1956) corroborated these studies. Whitaker (1964) routinely gave his subjects nicotinic acid to reduce the perceptual components of the experience. This facilitated and improved the psychotherapeutic exchange.

Miller *et al.* (1957) and Bertino *et al.* (1959) also found that nicotinic acid modified the LSD experience. They saw a reduction of anxiety in their subjects. The latter group reported that out of 8 subjects given nicotinic acid, 3 reported lasting and substantial improvement. Out of 44 other subjects given saline, nicotinamide, histamine (a vasodilator even more powerful than nicotinic acid) thiamine and pyridoxine not one subject reported similar changes (Chi Square, -10 $0.05 > P$ > 0.001). The remarkable conclusion of these authors was that nicotinic acid did not have any effect but did have a nonspecific action (whatever that is) due to the flush. Yet their histamine subjects who probably flushed just as severely reported no subjective improvement whatever. When we gave nicotinic acid to LSD subjects they did not become physically more comfortable while they flushed. On the contrary, they did not like nor appreciate the discomfort produced by the vasodilation nor by the burning sensation which was often accentuated by the perceptual disturbances. It is very likely that the Bertino *et al.* subjects became less anxious because they were having fewer perceptual disturbances and not that there was a nonspecific reduction in anxiety which then made them feel better.

LSD Congeners

The best antagonist against LSD, according to Abramson, is LSD itself. Subjects who take LSD every day quickly become tolerant to it and are no longer capable of reacting in the same way. However, if LSD is given to a subject already reacting to LSD the experience will not be reduced but will be either intensified or prolonged in time or both. Isbell *et al.* (1956) Abramson *et al.* (1956), and Abramson (1956a,b) found that subjects quickly developed tolerance to LSD. This also occurred in chronic schizophrenic patients. A free period of 4–6 days was required before the complete LSD experience recurred.

Other LSD congeners developed cross tolerance to LSD. Abramson *et al.* (1958b) reported that MLD-41 and BOL-148 developed cross tolerance to LSD but BOL-148 was only one third as effective. Ginzel and Mayer-Gross (1956) treated 6 volunteers with 2–3 mg of BOL-148 for 1 to 2 days, then gave them LSD. One day's pretreatment reduced the effect. Two days' pretreatment protected the subjects against the LSD. Given IV at the height of the experience BOL-148 had no effect.

Apparently ergotamine also modifies the LSD reaction. Matussek and Halbach (1964) pretreated 7 normal subjects with 2–4 mg of ergotamine for 3–5 days. They were given 1.5 μg of LSD per kg of body weight. Some time later the same subjects were given LSD only. They reported that the pretreatment with ergotamine decreased central sympathetic activity and prolonged or intensified the psychological symptoms. However they did not randomize the order of their experiments. It is common for first experiences to be more intense and more prolonged with no pretreatment whatever and they may have been seen an order effect and not a reduction of symptoms.

Other Substances

CERULOPLASMIN. Melander (1957) discovered that when animals were pretreated with ceruloplasmin they did not react to LSD. This protective effect will be described further on in this section.

PENICILLAMINE. Pretreatment with penicillamine removed the affective component of the LSD reaction (Hoffer and Callbeck, 1960). This reaction has been described earlier in this chapter.

ASCORBIC ACID. Hoffer (1959) pretreated a few subjects with 4 grams of ascorbic acid each day for several days, then gave them LSD. Other subjects were given ascorbic acid at the height of the experience. This vitamin did not change the intensity of the experience but it did alter its quality. There was no decrease in the intensity of perceptual changes. The subjects were able to concentrate better and developed less paranoia. Twenty-four hours later subjects who had been given ascorbic acid were not as tired as the controls.

HISTAMINE. Histamine infusions caused a marked but transient decrease in the LSD reaction in 7 out of 9 subjects, according to Yamada and Takumi (1956), but Bertino et al. (1959) found that histamine given subcutaneously did not moderate the experience.

SEROTONIN. Serotonin does alter the LSD experience but is not clearly an activator or reducer. Poloni (1955) found that 5 mg of serotonin injected intravenously accelerated the onset of the experience when 50 μg of LSD was given. At the height of the experience it accentuated the reaction and shortened the time of the reaction. Brengelmann et al. (1958b) pretreated subjects with 35 mg of DL-hydroxytryptophan, the precursor of serotonin. Then they gave them 60 μg of LSD intravenously. They saw no clinical effect on the LSD reaction but some of the psychological tests suggested there was a reduction in the intensity of the reaction.

DIBENZYLIN. Elder et al. (1957) found that dibenzylin decreased the intensity of the reaction in cats. It also blocked mydriasis and other peripheral effects but not the psychological response, according to Bertino et al. (1960).

STEROID HORMONES. Some of the steroid hormones suppressed the effect of LSD on rats (Bergen and Pincus, 1960; Bergen et al., 1960). Abramson and Sklarofsky (1960) treated five sophisticated subjects many times with 25 to 50 μg of LSD after they had been pretreated with 40 to 165 mg of prednisone a day for 3 to 7 days. This reduced or eliminated their anxiety but did not change any other part of the experience. Krus *et al.* (1961) using a double blind study gave 12 subjects 600 mg of progesterone one hour after they had been given 75 μg of LSD. There was a slight decrease in the reaction.

Activators

The main activators of the LSD reaction are the sympathomimetic amines, sympatholytics, and adrenochrome and adrenolutin. It is well known to many workers that the amphetamines potentiate the effect of LSD. The intensity of the reaction is increased and the duration of the experience is extended. They are used frequently in this way during LSD thearpy when more psychotherapy is indicated. Bradley and Elkes (1953) found that *dl*-amphetamine produced an alerting response in the cat. The EEG developed low amplitude, diffuse, fast waves. LSD produced a similar reaction. Thus it is not surprising that they potentiate each other. LSD also has marked sympathomimetic properties. Benadryl given before LSD also increased the reaction in cats (Elder *et al.*, 1957).

LSD potentiated the psychological effect of adrenochrome and adrenolutin in animals and in man. Melander and Martens (1958) found that animals pretreated with clinically inactive doses of LSD were much more reactive to very low doses of adrenolutin. Hoffer (1959) found a similar potentiation with adrenochrome. The potentiation seems independent of order. When alcoholic subjects failed to have a psychedelic experience after an adequate quantity of LSD, the IV injection of 10 mg of adrenochrome immediately produced the usual experience and a quick dissolution of the tension. One could then consider that LSD potentiated adrenochrome or vice versa.

Substances Which Have No Effect on LSD

A number of substances seem to have no effect on the LSD reaction but few studies have been reported with them. Additional investigation may show that some of these compounds do have activity. The inactive substances are:

1. Phenoxybenzamine (Murphree, 1962)
2. Cortisone (Clark and Clark, 1956)
3. Atropine and scopolamine (Elder *et al.*, 1957; Miller *et al.*, 1957)
4. Saline (Bertino *et al.*, 1959)
5. Nicotinamide, thiamine, and pyridoxine (Bertino *et al.*, 1959)

6. Methylene blue and Diparcol. R. Fischer (1954) while working in our laboratory reported that one subject pretreated with methylene blue which was given intramuscularly reduced the intensity of the reaction by 40%. Hoffer was the only psychiatric observer present and concluded that the methylene blue did not produce any significant change in the subject except intense pain at the injection site. Due to a combination of unfortunate errors, Fischer's statement appeared in the literature. Neither was there any evidence that Diparcol modified the reaction.

How Does LSD Work

BIOCHEMICAL

The LSD experience is one about which there can be no argument about priorities between chemical and psychological factors. For there is no doubt whatever the chemical is given first and must cause the biochemical changes which later find expression in the psychological experience. This as we have shown is shaped by the host of variables which shape human reactions. But the trigger is biochemical and after that the reaction runs on as long as the biochemical process continues. Perhaps these inescapable facts have so aroused opponents of the model psychosis hypothesis who preferred to believe that every human reaction, normal or abnormal, is a result of psychological forces only.

It is not correct to say that the biochemical reaction of LSD in the body is unknown. A good deal is known about its phenomenal reactivity. What is not known is which one of its many biochemical reactions is the most relevant in producing the psychological changes. LSD has an effect on a large number of reactions and influences the cells, tissues, and organs of the entire body. Not one of these reactions has been accepted as the primary one and everyone of them is shared to a degree with other chemicals, but of them all LSD is the most powerful relative to dose. It seems likely LSD owes its unique activity to its interference in many places in the biochemistry of the body. Very few other substances share these properties and minor changes in the molecule would remove the molecule from participation in some reactions and so inactivate the original compound.

There is little doubt that LSD must interfere in the transmission of stimuli from one cell to another in the nervous system either at the synapse or by altering cellular activity. Either change could lead to a marked change in brain function. For in a system so complex as the brain, a slight change at the synapses repeated in sequence would produce a major change in the final circuit.

LSD could influence the cell by blocking energy production, by altering cell membrane permeability, by reducing the blood supply to local or general areas of the brain, or by increasing permeability of the blood–brain barrier. Substances nontoxic in the blood could become toxic if allowed to enter the brain. It could alter synaptic transmission by competitive inhibition or by facilitating the direct action of some neurohormones such as serotonin, noradrenaline, adrenaline, or histamine. These we will consider direct effects of LSD.

An indirect effect is one where LSD produces a major change in another biochemical system which increases or decreases the concentration of other normally nontoxic metabolites beyond normal limits. At least two systems could be changed in this way, the acetylcholine system which controls the parasympathetic nervous system and the noradrenaline, adrenaline, adrenochrome system which forms part of the sympathetic nervous system.

Direct Action of LSD

Effect on Brain Cells. Woolley (1958a,b), Woolley and Shaw (1957), and Miura *et al.* (1957) reported that the normal rhythmic activity of oligodendroglia in pure culture was altered by LSD. Five μg per ml in the culture medium caused first a relaxation and vacuolization of the cells which eventually subsided and second, a strong contraction. The contraction was augmented by serotonin. The initial relaxation and vacuolization was prevented by serotonin. The reaction was much stronger when 100 μg of LSD was used.

Woolley and Shaw discussed the fact that brain is poorly vascularized compared to other tissues. They suggested that this defect in structure and function was compensated by the slow pulsations of the oligodendroglia which would thus act as small stirrers or pumps. They could accelerate exchange of chemicals between blood cells. If LSD interfered with this rhythmic pumping action it would change metabolism of the cells by impeding uptake of oxygen and other essential nutrients and by decreasing the removal of the end products of metabolism from the cell.

Geiger (1957, 1960) found that neurons grown in pure culture were also changed by LSD. She observed and photographed mixed cultures and subcultures of neurons and glia using time-lapse phase-contrast microcinemaphotography. Concentrations of 0.0002–0.001 μg per ml produced definite changes in 15–20 minutes. Granules which were concentrated about the nucleus dispersed through the cytoplasm. The body of the neurons contracted and the processes of the axonal ends and dendrites frequently retracted. The normal movement of the terminal boutons upon the surface of the cell body slowed. The nucleus moved about more quickly and more randomly. Similar changes were seen when the cells were stimulated by metrazole, electric current, etc. LSD also decreased the Nissl substance in the nucleus. When cells were exposed to 0.001 μg per ml of LSD for a long time chromatolysis occurred. Oligodendroglia contracted, then expanded slowly, and remained in an expanded condition several hours. A lower concentration of 0.0002 μg per ml produced similar changes. When the LSD was washed out the observed changes were reversed in one-half hour.

Not every neuron reacted the same way and neurons from different parts of the brain reacted differently. Nissl substance from cerebellar cortex, for example, reacted more quickly to LSD than did neurons derived from cerebral cortex.

Geiger often saw the extrusion of cellular material into the environment from contracted oligodendroglia. She also suggested the rhythmic contractions of the neurons could control the transfer of nutrients and metabolites into the cell. Serotonin, adrenaline, and noradrenaline also altered neuron behavior. But the most toxic substance of all was adrenochrome. At a concentration of 0.0001 μg per ml it produced much more rapid and drastic changes in the neuron than did adrenaline or noradrenaline. The neurons died within 24 hours.

The concentration of LSD which affected activity of neurones and oligodendroglia was very low, that is, 0.2 μg to 1 μg per liter. If we assume that there is an equal and homogeneous distribution of LSD in the one liter or so of brain, then 1 μg of LSD entering the brain could produce major changes. This is the quantity which apparently does cross into the brain.

The changes in the physical activity of the cells must arise from major biochemical changes inside the cell. These changes have been reviewed by Bain (1957). Mayer-Gross *et al.* (1952, 1953) found that 4×10^{-9} M of LSD stimulated oxidation of glucose 30% and inhibited utilization of hexose monophosphate 40% Lewis and McIlwain (1954), Bain (1957) and Clark *et al.* (1954) could not corroborate these findings but Geronimus *et al.* (1956) did find that guinea pig brain homogenates were inhibited from using oxygen by LSD, BOL-148, L-LSD-25, *d*-iso-LSD-25 and *d*-LAE-32 even in the absence of electrical stimulation. Lewis and McIlwain (1954) did find that 5×10^{-5} M LSD inhibited glucose oxidation 40% when guinea pig brain slices were stimulated electrically. This seems to be a better model of normal brain activity wherein neurons are firing or being stimulated all the time.

Clark *et al.* reported that succinic acid dehydrogenase from brain was inhibited 23% by 1 millimole of LSD while cytochrome oxidase was stimulated. Rudolph and Olsen (1957) studied the effect of LSD on the metabolism of glucose using tracer methods. Glucose-1-^{14}C and glucose-6-^{14}C were added to dog prostate slices. The total radioactivity in the carbon dioxide from glucose-1-^{14}C was considerably higher than from the glucose-6-^{14}C. When 5×10^{-4} M LSD was added, the labeled carbon dioxide was markedly increased from the glucose-6-^{14}C and not from glucose-1-^{14}C.

Sankar and Bender (1960) reported that LSD enhanced glucose oxidation by cerebral homogenates but depressed oxidation by cerebellar homogenates. The oxidation of γ-aminobutyric acid, citrate, and succinate was increased by both but the oxidation of serotonin and noradrenaline was inhibited. LSD activated glutamic acid decarboxylase in cerebral tissue and inhibited it in cerebellar tissue.

Greig and Gibbons (1959) reported that LSD decreased the penetration of radioactive glucose-^{14}C into mouse brain. They suggested that this arose from the inhibition of cholinesterase which caused a relative deficiency of glucose. The major disturbance in phosphate excretion, already described, adds more support to the suggestions that LSD changes glucose metabolism.

The number 4 position of the indole nucleus seems to be closely involved in psychotomimetic activity. Molecules where this carbon is combined with more atoms are more active psychologically. Mescaline which can be indolized *in vitro* and might be indolized in the body cannot form these 4-substituted indole derivatives (Cerletti, 1963). Psilocybin has a phosphate group on the indole at position 4. LSD has this position incorporated into two rings and thus forms the most stable linkages for this carbon atom. The respective comparable doses are 500 mg, 10 to 20 mg and 0.1 mg. Apparently the body has no enzymes which can split this group and so detoxify these substances quickly. Supporting this view are the findings of Heacock *et al.* (1964) using the method developed by Heacock and Mahon (1964) for assaying all four isomers of the hydroxyskatoles. They found that the 5, 6, and 7 isomers were present in the body in most subjects but no evidence was found for the presence of the 4-hydroxy derivatives. The 5-hydroxyskatoles were present in patients and control subjects to the same degree. The 6- and 7-hydroxy derivatives were present more often in psychiatric patients than in the comparison normal controls.

EFFECT ON BRAIN CIRCULATION. LSD has no effect on blood circulation through the brain. Sokoloff *et al.* (1957) reported that LSD did not affect blood flow, vascular resistance, oxygen and glucose utilization, or the respiratory quotient when given to subjects. Since their methods of necessity are crude it does not provide any information about localized changes in the brain. It is quite possible that localized contractions and relaxations of blood vessels might produce a redistribution of the blood flow through the brain but it is so far not possible to test this hypothesis. Perhaps very high doses would decrease total blood flow in the brain but since these doses are not used clinically the results of such an experiment would not be helpful in deciding how LSD works.

EFFECT ON BLOOD–BRAIN BARRIER. LSD could change brain function by increasing the permeability of the blood–brain barrier. This would allow blood constituents which are not toxic in the blood to enter the brain where they could be very toxic. It is known that some blood constituents must not get into the brain. One of these is adrenaline: When adrenaline is injected parenterally blood pressure and blood sugar levels are changed but there is little effect on brain function. When adrenaline is placed directly into the ventricles of the brain there is very little change in either blood pressure or blood sugar but there is a marked change in brain function. Profound changes in consciousness lead to surgical anesthesia.

Melander and Martens (1959) and Martens *et al.* (1959a,b) found that taraxein and LSD markedly potentiated the psychotomimetic action of adrenolutin on monkeys and on cats. Hoffer (1959) and Hoffer and Osmond (1960) found that LSD potentiated the effect of adrenochrome in the same way in human subjects. Perhaps the LSD is potentiated by the adrenochrome. In our research we have given alcoholic subjects adrenochrome by injections intravenously when they failed to react properly to LSD. One female alcoholic was given 300 μg of LSD. For the following 2 hours she remained extremely uncomfortable and tense with no visual changes. At 11:00 AM she was given 10 mg of adrenochrome. Within one minute her tension subsided and the usual LSD reaction developed. Melander and Martens proposed the hypothesis that LSD increased permeability of the brain at certain sites so that some substances in blood penetrated. Support for this idea also came from their discovery that ceruloplasmin, which bound adrenolutin irreversibly, protected their animals against the effect of both taraxein and LSD. We have also found that adrenolutin was bound irreversibly by ceruloplasmin. Taraxein in small doses also potentiated the effect of adrenolutin.

According to their hypothesis, ceruloplasmin bound toxic metabolites which might be present in blood and prevented them from entering the brain even though the blood-brain barrier was breached to some degree by LSD. Ceruloplasmin was also found to be a good treatment for schizophrenia.

LSD could also facilitate the transfer of normal constituents into brain by changing the permeability of the red blood cells. There is some evidence that adrenochrome is stored in the red blood cells where its antimitotic properties would do no harm. LSD appears to lower the red cell permeability and as a result adrenochrome is absorbed less effectively. Thus a combination of increased permeability of the red cells releasing adrenochrome and increased permeability of the blood–brain barrier which would enhance penetration would account for some of LSD's unique activity.

EFFECT OF LSD ON TRANSMISSION OF STIMULI. Marrazzi and his colleagues in an extensive series of papers studied the effect of hallucinogens upon synaptic transmission. They formulated the hypothesis that the visual changes produced by the hallucinogens came from some interference at the synapse. The present theory of synaptic function holds that when a stimulus reaches the synapse it causes the release of acetylcholine. This diffuses across the synaptic gap to the receptor site which is in turn stimulated and closes the electrical circuit. It is obvious this sequence of chemical activity must not be inhibited. An acceleration or inhibition could throw the entire reaction out of phase. If this occurred along a series of synapses a minor change at one repeated several times would produce a major disruption of cerebral function. Marrazzi measured the effect of psychoactive compounds on synapses in the transcallosal pathway of lightly anesthetized cats. A test message was initiated using a weak electrical stimulus on the visual cortex on one side. He recorded the electrical changes of the evoked response at a symmetrical point on the contralateral cortex. The compounds were injected directly into the cerebral blood system by means of the common carotid artery. This increased the concentration on the ipsilateral side of the recording electrodes. After passing through the brain the drug was diluted into the general blood circulation and so did not cause any peripheral stimulation. As a result an uncomplicated central synaptic response was measured. Marrazzi found that the potency of these compounds varied from 1 to 10,000 in terms of concentration. Three classes of activities were found: (a) mescaline noradrenaline, and adrenochrome had low activity, (b) γ-aminobutyric acid, adrenaline, and LSD had medium activity and (c) serotonin and bufotenine has the highest activity.

ANTAGONISM OF SEROTONIN. Woolley (1952, 1955, 1957) and Woolley and Shaw (1954a,b, 1957) first involved serotonin in brain function. Since then a voluminous literature has grown (Gaddum, 1953; Erspamer, 1954, 1961; I. H. Page, 1958; Brodie and Costa, 1962. Woolley marshaled the evidence which links serotonin activity to mental disease and to the psychological effects of LSD. Their evidence and some additional evidence we have gathered is as follows: (a) there is a firm relationship between mental disease and the excretion of indoles in the urine (Sprince, 1961, 1962; Sprince *et al.*, 1963); (b) most of the known psychotomimetics or hallucinogens are indoles (Hoffer and Osmond, 1952; Hoffer *et al.*, 1954). These compounds include the ergot compounds, adrenochrome and adrenolutin, harmine, tryptamine and its derivatives, dimethyl and diethyltryptamine, bufotenine and psilocybin, ibogaine and mitrogynine. (c) Indoles have definite neurophysiological and biochemical effects on the brain. They depress synaptic transmission, reduce spontaneous electrical activity of the brain, inhibit amine oxidase, cholinesterases, glutamic acid decarboxylase, and decrease the production of hexose monophosphate. (d) Nicotinic acid, sedatives, and tranquilizers which are therapeutic for schizophrenia and for toxic psychosis antagonize many of the effects of indole hallucinogens, (e) stress increases the excretion of some indoles (Mandell, 1963; Brune and Pscheidt, 1961), (f) actively psychotic patients excrete larger quantities of indoles than patients whose psychosis is quiescent (Brune and Pscheidt, 1961).

When Woolley and his colleagues observed that many of the psychoactive indoles were active stimulants of uterine muscle *in vitro* and that this was antagonized by LSD they suggested that LSD acted in the brain by interfering in the central activity of serotonin. It could do so by producing too little or too much serotonin at active receptor sites. Following Woolley's proposals Brodie (1957), Brodie *et al.* (1955, 1956a,b), and Brodie and Shore (1957) developed the hypothesis serotonin was a neurohormone. The evidence linking LSD directly to serotonin activity is that (a) serotonin is present in the brain and is distributed in a highly specific manner. It is especially rich in the same areas of the brain which carry most of the noradrenaline and adrenaline. Monoamine oxidase which destroys serotonin is present wherever serotonin is found, (b) serotonin is protected from enzyme inactivation until it has served its function, and (c) increasing serotonin levels in the brain of dogs produced gross behavioral changes (Himwich and Costa, 1960). This was done by pretreating the animals with amine oxidase inhibitors which would protect serotonin from destruction and then giving them the precursor of serotonin, 5-hydroxytryptophan, (d) LSD causes small increases in brain serotonin levels in dogs

(D. X. Freedman and Giarman, 1962). Serotonin levels were normal in 24 hours. If the rats were pretreated with reserpine the effect of LSD on brain serotonin was much more pronounced. Two inactive ergot compounds 1-methyl-d-lysergic acid butanolamine (UML) and 1-LSD did not increase serotonin concentrations even though UML was the most potent ergot antiserotonin peripherally. BOL-148 increased serotonin levels only slightly and less than either LSD or ALD. In reserpine treated animals psychotomimetic activity correlated well with the ability to elevate serotonin levels. According to D. X. Freedman (1963), LSD elevated serotonin levels 117% in the rat brain 30 to 120 minutes after treatment but noradrenaline was decreased 21%. Similar changes were found in rabbit brain. ALD, MLD, and psilocybin cause similar changes. The serotonin levels became elevated in the particulate fraction of the brain tissue. (e) Pretreatment of rats and man for 2–3 days with reserpine changes the LSD reaction, produced more toxicity and prolonged the reaction in man. The majority of subjects experienced marked tremor and akathesia and in each case the experience was less pleasant than in the comparison controls (D. X. Freedman and Giarman, 1962); (f) LSD increased metabolism of serotonin and increased serotonin concentration in all parts of the body except the cerebrum (Sankar et al., 1961). Sankar et al. (1962b) treated rabbits with radioactive 5-hydroxytryptophan, followed 45 minutes later by LSD, BOL-148 or chlorpromazine. LSD increased total radioactivity in every region of the brain except the cerebrum. BOL-148 and chlorpromazine did not increase serotonin in these areas to the same degree. LSD had a specific effect on serotonin levels in the brain stem and in all the brain excluding the cerebrum and the cerebellum. (g) Reserpine depleted serotonin from its storage sites without blocking its formation. Reserpine was one of the first tranquilizers and probably would still be in general use if it had not been displaced by the more predictable phenothiazines. The depletion of brain serotonin and the sedative effect of reserpine persisted for about the same length of time; (h) barbiturate narcosis was potentiated by serotonin and this was inhibited by LSD; (i) LSD was a powerful antagonist to serotonin in many tissues. Bunag and Walaszek (1962) reported lysergic acid derivatives blocked the arterial pressure response to serotonin, to histamine and to adrenaline. LSD was more active than BOL-148 and UML was less active than either one. LSD and BOL-148 antagonized the pressor-depressor responses to serotonin irregularly and slightly, and in dogs BOL-148 was a weak inhibitor (Salmoiraghi et al., 1956, 1957); (j) serotonin placed in the brain ventricles of cats produced a state of lethargy from which they were aroused by large quantities of LSD; (k) d-amphetamine and LSD rapidly reversed reserpine induced depression in mice. *dl*-amphetamine and LAE were less active antagonists and acetylcholine and adrenaline were inactive (Burton, 1957).

There is thus a substantial amount of data which support the serotonin hypothesis of LSD's activity but some facts are not yet accounted for. Brom lysergic acid diethylamide (BOL-148) is just as powerful an antiserotonin as LSD but in doses 200 times as large it has hardly any psychological activity. LSD is primarily sympathomimetic in its activity while BOL-148 is primarily parasympathomimetic. But both inhibit the potentiation of barbiturate sedation in mice produced by serotonin. In addition Haley (1957) found that when both serotonin and LSD were placed in the brain ventricles of mice the LSD reaction predominated, i.e. there was no antagonism in the brain. Neither did serotonin antagonize the effect of LSD in ventricles of cats (Bradley and Hance, 1956a,b).

These and other observations led Costa *et al.* (1962) to conclude that more attention should be given to the fact that structurally LSD is a phenylethylamine and that its main action is a stimulation of the central adrenergic receptors. They suggested that LSD's psychological activity may be unrelated to its antiserotonin action.

ANTAGONISM TO HISTAMINE. There is no definite relationship between histamine and brain function. But here is some evidence it may have something to do with the transfer of electrical stimuli. McGeer *et al.* (1963) found that the hypothalamus had much more histamine than any other part of the brain. The next most concentrated areas were the hypothalamic regions which had little more than the cortical areas. Somewhat earlier Harris *et al.* (1952) and Harris (1955) had found that the basal areas of the brain were the most concentrated in histamine. The highest quantities were found in the median eminence of the hypothalamus and in the anterior portion of the pituitary gland. He suggested that histamine was secreted from the brain and moved down the stalk into the pituitary gland, thereby initiating stress activity. The recent work by Selye *et al.* (1964) shows that histamine does have marked activity in certain portions of the nervous system. When animals were sensitized with certain vitamin D compounds and then treated with histamine there was a remarkable calcification of the entire peripheral autonomic nervous system. It was possible to produce an animal completely bereft of any autonomic activity by chemical techniques alone.

Sawyer (1955) found that histamine placed in the third ventricle of rabbits produced high amplitude spindling from the septal region. The injection of histamine produced no electrical disturbance if a lesion was first created in the septal region. According to Heath (1961) the injection of large amounts of histamine into the septal region produced marked behavioral changes in animals who became catatonic. Slow waves and spikes were seen in the electroencephalograms. Heath suggested histamine might play a significant role in controlling behavior and could act by stimulating specific parts of the limbic system of the brain. Marrazzi *et al.* (1961) also found that histamine was a synaptic inhibitor about as strong as serotonin. An antihistamine tripennamine, counteracted this inhibition. They suggested that histamine might have a role to play in the production of some psychoses. Another report by Trendelenburg (1956) showed that histamine had a direct action on the central ganglionic cells of the sympathetic nervous system. Histamine could also play a role in arterial pressor responses. Bunag and Walaszek (1962) suggested that lysergic acid derivatives blocked arterial pressor responses to serotonin by preventing the release of histamine.

Theories about the activity of LSD will therefore need to consider what part histamine plays.

ANTAGONISM TO SYMPATHOMIMETIC AMINES. LSD antagonizes noradrenaline and adrenaline. The evidence parallels the evidence that LSD antagonizes serotonin. This is to say:

1. Adrenaline is more clearly implicated in mental disease, in anxiety and stress, than is serotonin.

2. Adrenaline is converted *in vitro* and *in vivo* into adrenochrome and other psychoactive indoles which may be either psychotomimetic or antitension.

3. Adrenochrome has a powerful effect on the electrical activity of the brain *in vivo* and interferes with synaptic transmission.

4. Substances which antagonize the psychological and EEG effects of adrenochrome also antagonize the psychological effects of LSD.

5. The amines are neurohormones and so readily available to the brain.

6. High levels of the amines placed in the brain ventricles produced surgical anesthesia.

7. Noradrenaline and adrenaline are localized in the same areas of the brain as serotonin.

8. The same enzyme, monoamine oxidase, metabolizes noradrenaline, adrenaline and serotonin.

9. Recent work in our laboratory (Mattok *et al.*, 1965) showed that LSD had a pronounced effect upon the relative concentrations of dopamine, noradrenaline, adrenaline, normetanephrine and metanephrine in the first morning specimens of urine taken 24 hours after the LSD was given. There was a major decrease in dopamine and in metanephrine and an increase in the other constituents in a subject who became malvarian after taking LSD.

LSD could block transmission of stimuli in the brain by any one of the following mechanisms:

1. by mimicking the amines, most likely noradrenaline or adrenaline
2. by blocking the action of the amine, most likely serotonin
3. preventing destruction of amines by enzymes (this is not likely)
4. by depleting amines from nerve endings, most likely noradrenaline and adrenaline
5. by interfering with their synthesis; there is no evidence for this
6. by interfering with liberation of histamine or serotonin

Sankar *et al.* (1964) were among the first to correlate LSD's activities with all these three substances. Using radioactive tracers they found that in rabbits LSD increased serotonin levels in all tissues but cerebrum and decreased levels of histamine and noradrenaline. Higher levels of serotonin could release noradrenaline and increase sympathetic excitation. This could be followed by increased enzymatic destruction and decreased levels of noradrenaline. LSD also decreased excretion of the methylated derivatives of noradrenaline. Sankar *et al.* suggested that LSD increased bound serotonin, released noradrenaline, and prevented its conversion into normetanephrine. LSD also increased blood serotonin levels by 170% and decreased histamine levels by 26%.

To complicate matters even more it is possible that noradrenaline is not methylated to normetanephrine. It may be oxidized into noradrenochrome. Adrenaline would be oxidized into adrenochrome even more readily.

Indirect Activity to LSD

PARASYMPATHETIC NERVOUS SYSTEM. The parasympathetic changes in subjects given LSD are clear enough. They included salivation, lacrimation, nausea, retching and vomiting (Rothlin, 1957a,b,c). Doses of 50–100 μg/kg in anesthetized cats caused bradycardia. This came from central stimulation of the vagus nerve and a fall in blood pressure. The usual clinical doses have only a slight effect on blood pressure. LSD is parasympathetic probably because it blocks the activity of the cholinesterases. Thompson *et al.* (1954, 1955) found that 10^{-6} M inhibited human plasma cholinesterase 50%. True cholinesterase was not inhibited by ten times this concentration. Human esterase was inhibited more powerfully than esterase from any other animal species including the monkey. With this degree of inhibition one would expect an increase in acetylcholine levels in brain (Poloni and Maffezzoni, 1952).

Very small concentrations of LSD potentiated cholinesterase activity is rat brains (Tonini, 1955; Fried and Antopol, 1956, 1957; Zsigmond *et al.*, 1960, 1961a,b,c) found that LSD inhibited plasma cholinesterase more than it did red cell or gray matter (true) cholinesterase. Rabbit enzyme was inhibited less than human enzyme. Low concentrations of LSD did not accelerate hydrolysis of acetylcholine, according to these investigators. LSD was a true competitive inhibitor of both true and pseudocholinesterase.

LSD is the most powerful esterase inhibitor of the ergot alkaloids (Nandy and Bourne, 1964). It approaches eserine in activity. Goldenberg and Goldenberg (1956) found that the order of activity was eserine, followed by LSD, BOL-148 and LAE. Zender and Cerletti (1956) also found BOL was less active than LSD. Both BOL-148 and LSD were quite selective in their action on various cholinesterases from different animal mammalian species. Tabachnick and Grelis (1958) found LSD and BOL did not inhibit cat, dog, and guinea pig esterases but did inhibit mouse and human esterases. They concluded that LSD and BOL inhibited only enzymes which could hydrolyze imidazole propionylcholine (dihydromurexine).

The inhibition of these esterases by both BOL-148 which is psychologically inactive and LSD removes any correlation between the central activity of these substances and esterase inhibition. It would have been theoretically interesting if LSD only was an inhibitor. Perhaps further study will yet show that this does occur, for *in vitro* enzyme studies are still far from *in vivo* reactions. Goldberger (1961) using histochemical methods measured the effect of LSD on esterase activity in rat brain sections. LSD did not inhibit pseudocholinesterase but did inhibit markedly true cholinesterase in brain sections. There was no inhibition in the noncortical areas. Cell bodies positive for esterase in the control sections were negative after the LSD. Unfortunately they did not examine the activity of BOL-148. Goldberger (1961) suggested that LSD psychosis could result in part from an uncontrolled diffuse stimulation of the cells of the brain due to a buildup of acetylcholine levels.

SYMPATHETIC NERVOUS SYSTEM. The sympathetic nervous changes produced by LSD have been described several times. They include mydriasis, increases in body temperature in some animals, piloerection, and increases in blood sugar. These changes are blocked by ganglionic blocking agents or sympatholytics.

Hoagland *et al.* (1955) first suggested that LSD owed its activity to an interference in adrenaline metabolism. The evidence they listed then and which has accrued since is substantial. It is as follows: (a) After LSD was given to some subjects adrenaline plasma levels were elevated, they later decreased below the original levels, and then became normal (Liddell and Weil-Malherbe, 1953). Preliminary studies in our own laboratories supported these earlier findings as already mentioned. (b) LSD activated the adrenal gland. The medulla became more active as measured by the increase in uptake of radioactive phosphorus. The cortex also was activated. Ganong *et al.* (1961) found that LSD given to anesthetized dogs increased the excretion of 17-hydroxycorticosteroids. Similar increases were found by Sackler *et al.* (1963) in rats. The 17-ketosteroid excretion was also increased. (c) LSD potentiated the psychological action of adrenolutin in some animals (Melander and Martens, 1958) and adrenochrome in man (Hoffer, 1959). (d) Adrenolutin was irreversibly bound by ceruloplasmin *in vitro* (Melander, 1957). Pretreatment with ceruloplasmin protected animals against the psychological action of both adrenolutin and LSD. Ceruloplasmin could protect against the action of LSD if it bound and so removed any adrenolutin formed from receptor sites. (e) When adrenochrome was injected intravenously, blood levels immediately became very high. Hoffer (1959) and Hoffer and Osmond (1960) found that in normal subjects injected with adrenochrome, base line levels were reached in about 30 minutes. In sharp contrast, the same quantity of adrenochrome given to schizophrenic patients was not cleared in one hour and sometimes up to two hours. When a normal subject who cleared the adrenochrome within one half hour was pretreated two hours before with 35 μg of LSD, the injected adrenochrome was not removed in one hour. When 100 μg of LSD was used for pretreatment, the adrenochrome was not cleared in two hours and blood levels were still much above normal levels. BOL-148 had no effect on these adrenochrome tolerance curves. It was apparent LSD interfered in some major way with the clearance of adrenochrome from plasma, (f) substances which reacted strongly with adrenochrome *in vitro* markedly altered the LSD experience. These compounds included ascorbic acid which bleached adrenochrome solutions and penicillamine. Both substances converted adrenochrome into several types of psychoactive indoles. (g) Substances which antagonized the effect of adrenochrome and adrenolutin in human subjects also modified the LSD reaction. Szatmari *et al.* (1955) found that adrenochrome injected intravenously into some epileptic subjects produced an intensification of EEG abnormalities. When the same subjects were later injected intravenously with nicotinic acid at the height of the electrical disturbance, the EEG became normal in a few minutes and remained normal for the rest of the day. Nicotinic acid also counteracted the adrenochrome and adrenolutin reaction in some subjects and modified the LSD reaction (Agnew and Hoffer, 1955; Hoffer, 1962). (h) LSD increased the conversion of adrenaline into adrenolutin in plasma (Heath and Leach, 1956). Sankar *et al.* (1964) found LSD inhibited the conversion of noradrenaline into normetanephrine. In addition they found the effect of adrenaline on the blood pressure of children treated with LSD was markedly increased. A small dose of adrenaline increased the systolic blood pressure 12.5 mm and decreased diastolic pressure 8.9 mm before LSD was given. After being treated with LSD each day for 6–8 weeks the increase in systolic pressure was 28.4 mm and the decrease in diastolic pressure was 12.9 mm. (i) LSD increased the ascorbic acid depletion from the adrenal gland which followed adrenaline injections (Costa and Zetler, 1958). LSD, 10 μg per kg given intraperitoneally, increased this ascorbic acid depletion. LSD alone had no effect nor did BOL-148 potentiate the effect.

Indirect Action Hypothesis

The autonomic nervous system may be involved in the activity of LSD. It is likely that the unique psychotomimetic activity of LSD depends upon a combination of direct and indirect factors already discussed. LSD by blocking acetylcholinesterase would interfere with parasympathetic activity and elevate acetylcholine levels. The increased secretion of acetylcholine would lead to an increase in the output of sympathomimetic amines from the adrenal medulla and from other storage sites in the brain and in the chromaffin ganglia present in other parts of the body. LSD by blocking methyl transferases could increase the conversion of adrenaline into adrenochrome. The combination of high acetylcholine levels, increased secretion of adrenaline and the increased production of adrenochrome and its indole derivatives could account for the changes which follow the administration of LSD. This hypothesis would account for the following:

1. the known changes in acetylcholine and adrenaline levels
2. activation of the adrenal gland
3. potentiation of adrenochrome by LSD
4. protective action of ceruloplasmin
5. increased stability of adrenochrome in blood of LSD-treated subjects
6. effect of adrenochrome antagonizers on the LSD reaction
7. decreased formation of normetanephrine
8. the development of LSD tolerance

The last point needs further clarification. The effect of LSD on adrenochrome tolerance curves may be due to the effect of LSD on red cell permeability. It could increase membrane permeability as in the blood–brain barrier. In this way adrenochrome present in red cells would be released into plasma. Red cells probably are storage sites. Adrenaline has long been known to be stored there and freshly prepared hemoglobin absorbs large quantities of adrenochrome. Few tissues could store adrenochrome safely since it is a very powerful mitotic poison. But red cells do not have a nucleus and do not divide. The administration of LSD could increase red cell membrane permeability and allow adrenochrome to leak out into plasma. A further dose of LSD would therefore have much less effect since insufficient adrenochrome would be present in the cells. A rest of from 5 to 7 days would allow these storage sites to be replenished and an additional quantity of LSD would have its usual effect. The psychological effect of LSD given on consecutive days would then simply be the effect of LSD alone (without adrenochrome). Its action is very similar to that of BOL-148 given for the first time, that is there is no psychological effect of LSD. BOL-148 did not change adrenochrome tolerance curves.

Nandy and Bourne (1964) proposed a similar mechanism. LSD could act, they suggested, by inhibiting enzymes which control transfer of synaptic impulses and allow a buildup of acetylcholine, adrenaline and adrenochrome.

With this hypothesis in mind we have treated chronic intractable schizophrenic patients who were also malvarian (Hoffer and Osmond, 1962a,b, 1963a,b) with LSD. The LSD was given to reduce the quantity of adrenochrome within the red cells while protecting the subjects against the undesirable effect of the adrenochrome by treating them with large quantities of nicotinic acid.

The mauve factor was discovered for the first time when LSD was given to alcoholics being treated for their alcoholism (Irvine, 1961). About one fifth of the nonmalvarian alcoholics secreted the mauve factor in their urine 24 hours after being given LSD.

The schizophrenic patients so treated with LSD began to show encouraging improvement and many of them are now well. They also became mauve negative. Perhaps this is the biochemical rationale for the treatment of autistic children with LSD (Bender *et al.,* 1963).

PSYCHOLOGICAL THEORIES

The LSD experience provides a model of schizophrenia with striking similarities and, of course, striking differences. It has thrown a good deal of understanding on the phenomenology of schizophrenia. It is only fair that the schizophrenic experience should be used in a parallel way to model the LSD reaction. In this way we have found it possible to offer some explanations for the thinking and feeling (and of course activity) changes which may occur in subjects.

In a series of papers (Hoffer and Osmond, 1963a, 1966) we offered what we considered a comprehensive hypothesis of schizophrenia. According to our hypothesis the biochemical changes led to an interference in brain metabolism due to the production of adrenochrome derivatives, the aminochromes, such as adrenolutin. The brain mechanisms which deal with sensory perception and its integration and stabilization were chiefly affected, we suggested. As a result, the subject received erroneous or misleading information about the environment and about his own body. But being unaware the changes are false he would react as if the external world had altered. To the rational observer his behavior would therefore be abnormal and he would react in a way he (the normal observer) considered inappropriate. But the subjects would consider the observers behavior odd or inappropriate. In other words both the schizophrenic subject and the normal observer would live in different environments. To each the other's behavior would appear abnormal.

The subject's thinking would therefore be dependent upon the specific perceptual changes present and his reaction to the people about him would depend upon the variables which shaped him, that is his intelligence, his education, his station in life, his interests, and his culture.

Within this comprehensive hypothesis it is possible to account for the clinical syndromes seen in schizophrenic patients in a economical way. Our hypothesis did not originate with us. It was first described in a simple way by Sir Thomas Willis who stated over 300 years ago that psychotic patients seemed to see the world through a distorted looking glass. It was later amplified by John Connolly who stated over 100 years ago that many patients rolled on the floor because their skin was too warm and that many other patients believed their food was poisoned because it had a coppery taste.

The extensive evidence is as follows:

1. Schizophrenic patients have described their world when ill, how it affected them and how they responded to it. There is a very large literature. The descriptions have been compiled into an excellent book by Carney Landis (1964), who provided accurate descriptions of the phenomenonology of schizophrenia as seen by those best able to make these descriptions, that is, the patients themselves. There is no textbook of psychiatry which has done it as well. Patients described in elaborate detail that they did respond to their misperceptions until they became aware they were misperceptions. The well-known phrase "reality testing" should refer to this need for judging whether perceptions are real or not.

2. Objective tests of schizophrenics have demonstrated that perception is disordered (Weckowicz, 1957, 1960; Weckowicz and Hall, 1960;

Weckowicz and Blewett, 1959; Weckowicz and Sommer, 1960; Weckowicz *et al.*, 1958; Hoffer and Osmond, 1963a,b; Kelm, 1962a,b).

3. Schizophrenic patients reported a large number of perceptual abnormalities when tested by a specially designed card sort test (Hoffer and Osmond, 1961b,c; Kelm *et al.*, 1965a,b). This test consisted of a set of 145 cards. Each card contained a question on one side and a number on the other. The questions dealt with aspects of mental function normally covered by the examination of the mental state of the patient. The patients placed the cards one by one in boxes marked true or false and in this way described their real world in which they found themselves. A perceptual score was developed which in one figure indicated the degree of perceptual disturbance. High scores were abnormal. The vast majority of normal adults scored between 0 and 4. The mean score for over 100 normal subjects, over age 21, was 0.5. The mean perceptual score for various diagnostic groups of patients is shown in the following tabulation.

Group	Number	Mean score
1. Normal	100	0.5
2. Psychiatric patients not schizophrenic and not malvarian	121	2.0
3. Psychiatric patients not schizophrenic but malvarian	18	9.0
4. Schizophrenic	158	11.9
5. Subjects under LSD	17	17.2
6. Organic psychoses	13	14.7

Schizophrenic patients, patients with malvaria (Hoffer and Osmond, 1963a,b) and toxic psychoses and subjects undergoing the LSD experience all had very high perceptual scores. Other subjects who were normal or who fell into other psychiatric categories scored very much lower.

4. The production of perceptual abnormalities by hypnosis led to a series of model psychotic reactions in normal subjects (Fogel and Hoffer, 1962a,b; Aaronsen, 1964). It was possible to produce models of typical schizophrenic reactions which lasted from a few minutes to many hours. Experienced subjects were used who were able to achieve a deep trance and who could carry suggestions which were given to them over into the post-trance state. As soon as the suggested perceptual changes were removed the subjects became normal. The model reactions which appeared were uniform for any one subject and could be repeated as frequently as necessary but in each experiment the subject reacted in a way which depended upon the setting, the people there, etc. The re-

action was in essence the same for all subjects and the differences were explainable by the differences in personality and reactivity. We will list a few examples of model psychosis which were produced by this newer technique.

Visual Perception

The subjects were taken into their trance and then told in the post-trance state they would find that people were watching. Invariably (three subjects), they became paranoid, suspicious, hostile, irritable, nasty, and in many ways caricatured or highlighted pure paranoid schizophrenia. One subject while in the post-trance state was referred to a competent psychiatrist for a consultation about her diagnosis. He was not informed she was an experimental subject. After about 20 minutes he had diagnosed her as a paranoid schizophrenic who required immediate certification to a mental hospital.

It was possible to produce a grandiose form of paranoia by altering the emotional reaction of the subject. If they were told they liked being watched they developed delusions they were famous singers, queens, etc., but if no instructions were given about their mood, they were always angry, hostile, and belligerent.

When subjects were told faces would be funny, they developed a type of hebephrenic reaction, giggled continually, and appeared very silly and inappropriate.

Auditory Perception

If patients hear voices and believe they come from a real source they will respond to them either verbally or by taking some action. Often, the first step in recovery of patients occurred when they were able to judge the voices as unreal. When normal subjects were told they would not be able to locate the sources of sound they became confused, disturbed, silent, and then mute.

Other Changes

A change in any of the remaining perceptual modalities including time perception resulted in marked changes in the subjects personality for as long as the change in perception was allowed to act.

Changes in thought were easily produced by interfering with time or with memory. This was done by removing the past or the future or by speeding up or slowing down the tempo of thought. Changes in mood were easily produced by altering the brightness or colorfulness of the environment and/or by accelerating or decreasing the sensing of time passing.

One subject, a good hypnotic subject, was given LSD (Fogel and Hoffer, 1962a). At the height of her experience she was hypnotized and the entire LSD reaction was suppressed. She came out of her hypnotic state normal. However LSD was still acting physiologically for her pupils remained widely dilated. When rehypnotized and allowed to come out of her trance, with no suggestion whatever, she came out into a typical LSD experience. Since she could not voluntarily prevent the biochemical effect of LSD from operating she must have suppressed the major perceptual changes. The powerful suggestion given to her plus her own stabilizing function overcame the effect of the LSD.

We have therefore hypothesized that normal or patient subjects who are reacting to LSD will have their experience shaped by their new perceptions of the world, of themselves and, of course, by the new associations which they develop in response to these newer perceptions. In simple terms they will react to what they see, hear, smell, etc., as they normally do.

CLINICAL

Clinical factors refer to psychodynamic matters and to changes in personality which endure after the experience is over. These factors have been studied very little but there is no reason why dynamic factors which operate in normal and abnormal conditions should cease to operate when subjects are given LSD.

In our large experience with alcoholics and normal subjects we have not seen any uniform responses which could account for the changes which occurred later on. The subjects themselves often did not know why they had changed and when asked "Why were you able to keep away from alcohol?", they replied "I don't know" or "I had no further desire to drink" or "I realized what my drinking was doing to my wife" or "I realized I was not as bad as I thought" or "I now understand the A.A. program" or "I saw God" etc., etc.

Objectively there was a wide variety of responses. Some patients abreacted early life experiences, others saw only into the future. Some patients talked throughout the entire session, others said hardly a word. But psychedelic states were more often associated with recovery or change than were psychotomimetic reactions. Smith (1958, 1959) and O'Reilly and Reich (1962) observed as did we that patients who had good emotional responses had better therapeutic results.

The penicillamine–LSD reaction, already described, was nearly devoid of affective changes but the perceptual changes were unimpaired. Yet the recoveries were only 10% which was much less than recoveries found with LSD alone. The affective component was very important. Methedrine injections produced emotional abreactions which were very intense but there were very slight perceptual changes. It appears that the combination of perceptual changes and a normal degree of emotional reactivity was essential.

All the variables known to affect the LSD experience are vitally important but of these the therapist is one of the most important. He should be eclectic, knowledgeable about LSD, and continually alert to any clue produced by the patient which can be used for keeping the patients main problems before him. Sargant (1957) believed conversion reactions or striking personality changes resulted from at least two main variables: (a) a high degree of excitation or emotional involvement, and (b) a powerfully persuasive atmosphere.

In the LSD experience, the LSD produces the powerful emotional reaction and the therapist and setting provide the persuasive elements. In our opinion any research with LSD therapy where either factor is neglected or abused will fail. So-called controlled experiments which do not take these factors into account have no bearing on psychedelic psychotherapy.

Every therapist who is familiar with the psychoadjuvent use of psychedelics explained LSD's clinical action within the framework of his own clinical orientation. Thus, Abramson used LSD to facilitate his psychoanalysis of his patients. LSD helped release material quickly which might have required several months to appear. Barrios (1965) developed an hypothesis of stimulus hierarchies. According to this idea, a highly vivid image will occur when a cognitive stimulus rises to a dominant position in the stimulus preference hierarchy. The evidence used to make this hypothesis was as follows:

1. Increasing cognitive stimulation produced hallucinations, for example, by electrical stimulation of certain areas of the brain.
2. Reduction of competing stimuli allowed perceptual changes to appear, for example, sensory deprivation.
3. LSD alerted the brain by acting on the brain stem.
4. LSD suppressed sensory stimuli competing with cognitive stimuli and elevated the latter to the level of hallucinations.

According to Barrios, LSD also produced a state of hypersuggestibility where vivid imagery could be invoked. The suggestibility led to personality changes by a process of conditioning-cognitive conditioning.

By suppressing stimuli higher in the hierarchy (especially negative images such as patients self-concept) LSD facilitated formation of newer healthier self-images and the patient came to experience himself in a totally new way. He saw himself as a new and better person. Once these new images were accepted new conditioned associations were formed which in turn resulted in newer patterns of behavior.

Belden and Hitchen (1962) called upon the dreamlike quality of the LSD experience when they explained its action. In retrospect many subjects do consider that their LSD experience had many dreamlike qualities. They claimed that alcoholics had two psychopathological problems, an early encapsulated deprivation syndrome and a power syndrome. They interpreted situations including the LSD experience as a power struggle due to their early damaging life experiences. The LSD experience being more powerful that any alcoholic intoxication overpowered and was corrective in the presence of a benign authoritative person, the therapist, who interpreted and brought into consciousness the patients power orientation. Factors which enhanced the probability of success in therapy were total involvement in an inescapable situation, the powerful conscious-changing quality of LSD and the nonpunitive attitude of the therapist together with his traditional interpretative function.

Jackson (1962) considered the LSD experience a new beginning in those who later changed. Those who did not change were unable to let go; they clung desperately to their old familiar terminology and maintained a death grip on their cathexis and repressions. Clinging to the old they were unable to let go and be intrigued by the new.

Klee (1963) believed LSD released the bonds which contained the inhibited person. Ego functions were released from these repressive influences and allowed the ego to function better. The LSD experience allowed the subject to regress to a more primitive ego state which was welcome for the well-integrated person and useful, but did not represent a genuine enhancement of ego function. Klee's hypothesis seems incompatible with the data derived from the majority of clinical therapeutic studies with LSD. In our experience, which extends over 12 years, we found that well-integrated individuals changed least after LSD. That is not surprising since normal people need to change least. They had good experiences which were enjoyable and informative but their lives flowed on afterwards with very little obvious change in their personality. They were not touched by it. The changes were in the area of increased information. On the other hand, we have seen the most pronounced changes in subjects who had the poorest integrated egos: addicts, alcoholics, psychopathic personalities, and neurotics. We have seen psychopathic liars and alcoholics become honest, truthful, normal people. Jackson splits hairs by claiming ego enhancement was apparent only. It is merely his affirmation of his belief that only prolonged psychoanalysis can really enhance ego. Since ego is in essence, ill-defined, and measured with great difficulty, arguments about enhancement of ego function seem a bit futile.

Sandison (1963) described the therapeutic response to LSD more simply. He stated that the immediate result of giving LSD was a deepening of the patient's emotional tone, a change in his drinking, sometimes regression to an earlier emotional and intellectual period, and reliving of charged memories.

Savage (1962a,b) believed LSD cured patients by producing a mystical state or a conversion experience. The transcendental state opened up avenues to creativity but did not produce creativity.

Savage (1957) also believed LSD caused the reliving of earlier experiences, brought out repressed and painful feelings, liberated unconscious material, and allowed the production of dramatic insights.

Stevenson (1957) stated that LSD experiences increased one's appreciation of beauty and of the external world, that their normal percepts were unstable and only partially true.

In our view, LSD produced the same changes in subjects as Sargant's conversion reactions. It allowed subjects to extricate themselves quickly from inhibiting attitudes, ideas, complexes, and conditioned habits. It may well be that beyond these limits each subject's recovery will require an individual hypothesis and for many years each therapist will develop his own.

Schmiege (1963) summarized LSD's action clinically as follows:

1. It helped patients remember and to abreact both recent and childhood traumatic experiences.
2. It increased the transference reaction.
3. It activated the conscious to bring up fantasies and emotional phenomena which could be handled by the therapist.
4. It intensified affectivity and reduced the use of excessive intellectualization.
5. It allowed the patient to see his customary defenses better and so alter them.

Some Consequences of LSD's Introduction to Psychiatry

Mescaline was described many years ago but it had very little impact on psychiatry. Perhaps it would have had an eventual impact since many scientific discoveries have long induction periods. However, the accidental discovery by Hofmann about 20 years ago produced a remarkable upsurge in psychiatric interest in the psychotomimetics. As a result there has been a major revolution in psychiatry but like most revolutions in scientific thought, contemporary scientists seem unaware of it. The end of the revolution is not visible and the impact has already stirred society at large. Its uses and abuses have been discussed freely in the public press, on radio, and on television. University campuses from Saskatchewan to Boston have witnessed students engaging in self-experimentation with peyote, morning glory seeds, and other natural hallucinogens, much as they once studied laughing gas many years ago.

Last year, according to Heard (1964), Dr. Glen T. Seaborg, chairman of the U.S. Atomic Energy Commission, included the psychomimetics among the 15 most revolutionary discoveries of our present era. He was referring particularly to mescaline, psilocybin and especially LSD. Seaborg suggested governments might have to establish new legal and moral codes to govern the use of these compounds.

The psychomimetics and psychedelics have already resulted in the following developments.

Model Psychosis

PSYCHOLOGICAL. This has increased greatly understanding of the inner world of the psychotic and the impact upon it of disordered perceptions. It also led to the development of our HOD test (Hoffer and Osmond, 1961b,c).

BIOCHEMICAL. 1. As a result of our LSD model Irvine (1961) and Hoffer and Mahon (1961) isolated a mauve staining factor from schizophrenic urine and from patients given LSD. This led to the development of the malvaria concept (Hoffer and Osmond, 1961b,c, 1962a,b, 1963a,b).

2. The biochemical model also led the first clear difference between schizophrenics and normal subjects (Hoagland *et al.*, 1955).

3. The adrenochrome metabolite hypothesis of schizophrenia (Hoffer and Osmond, 1952).

4. The serotonin hypothesis of mental disease.

5. The serotonin neurohormone hypothesis.

TREATMENT. 1. Schizophrenia. (a) Nicotinic acid (Hoffer *et al.*, 1957; Hoffer, 1962; Hoffer and Osmond, 1962a,b). (b) Penicillamine (Hoffer, 1962). (c) LSD for autism (Bender *et al.*, 1962).

2. Alcoholism—with or without LSD.

3. Other conditions.

Teaching

PSYCHIATRISTS. The inner world of the psychotic may be explored by working very closely with patients, by recovering from schizophrenia, or preferably by taking LSD or any one of the psychomimetics.

NURSES. They can learn much from the experience, and generally profit from it. A large number of psychiatric nurses have taken LSD in Saskatchewan. In our opinion, and they have also believed this, they became more sympathetic and better nurses (see Bolton, 1961).

Architecture

Perceptual studies by Osmond (1957b) led directly to the construction of several new types of hospitals which have been called Osmond-Izumi or Izumi-Osmond hospitals. Osmond wrote, "In my own clinical experience changes in spatial perception are often accompanied by changes in perception of the body, which is only a special but very important aspect of general perception. So the huge corridors and unnecessarily enlarged spaces so often found in mental hospitals are liable to enhance one of the most harmful and distressing of schizophrenic experiences— uncertainty about the integrity of the self."

"An appreciation of the nature of the mentally ill person's disease and the sort of experience which he may be enduring allows an imaginative architect to evolve certain simple rules which can then be applied. Luckily today we can depend less on imagination and more on experience because, thanks to psychiatric tools such as LSD-25 and mescaline changes in perception resembling those found in some schizophrenic people can be produced experimentally" (see also Weckowicz, 1957; Izumi, 1957).

Religion

Wasson and Wasson presented a persuasive case for their thesis that religion originated from the use of hallucinogenic mushrooms many centuries ago. Certainly, many of the great religions of man are known to have come from powerful transcendental experiences. Men who have experienced God do not need witnesses thereafter to reinforce their faith and they were able to convey their faith very persuasively to their followers.

These compounds have been used in two main ways.

1. To reinforce faith and to increase conviction. A large number of clergy in Canada and England have taken LSD to learn more about psychodynamics, and to revive their own feelings for their own religion. Ministers have become better preachers. Jarman (1961) for example

used his experience of being in heaven or in hell as the subject for some of his sermons. He found that his preaching afterwards was more effective than it had been for many years. His audience was more interested and had many more questions. Many of his congregation felt they would never be the same again.

2. As sacraments. No religion has yet incorporated LSD into its ceremonies and rituals. Peyote (containing mescaline) is a sacrament of the Native American Church of North America. Psilocybin is used by Indians in the Central Americas.

Philosophy

We are not aware of any major changes in current philosophy as a result of the use of these compounds. Perhaps this will yet occur when some unknown person in the near future, having taken LSD as a student at some university or high school, produces a new direction in philosophy.

Group Dynamics

LSD has been used to facilitate and to study group interactions and it may prove very valuable in highlighting group processes.

New Psychological Frontiers

1. A reexamination of the popular concept personality is a stable attribute of man (Fogel and Hoffer, 1962a,b; Aaronsen, 1964).
2. Examination of personal space.
3. Creativity.
4. Parapsychology.

Synanon (for Drug Addicts)

Several years ago a small number of alcoholics were given LSD in California to model delirium tremens. As a result one of them developed the concept of Synanon. This is a new self-help group which has already helped many drug addicts learn to live without drugs (Cherkas, 1963; Manas, 1963).

Easing the Terror and the Pain of Death

"I was sorry," he mumbled, "to hear she was so ill." "It's a matter of a few days now," said Dr. Robert. "Four or five at the most. But she is still perfectly lucid, perfectly conscious of what is happening to her. Yesterday she asked me if we could take the moksha medicine together— the moksha medicine, the dope as you prefer to call it, hardly upset her at all. All that happened to her was the mental transformation."

In Aldous Huxley's "Island" (1962), psychedelic drugs were used very carefully, not only to learn about the present world but to investigate the hereafter. Pain was relieved at the same time.

"Is the pain bad?", she asked. "It would be bad" Lakshimi (Mrs. Robert) explained, "if it were really my pain, but somehow it isn't. The pain is here, but I'm somewhere else. It's like what you discover with the moksha medicine. Nothing really belongs to you, not even your pain."

LSD was used not only in "Island," but in Chicago to relieve pain. It has powerful analgesic properties. Kast and Collins (1964) gave LSD to a group of patients many of whom knew they were dying of terminal cancer. In addition to their relief from pain some of the patients developed a peculiar disregard for the gravity of their situation. They spoke freely of their impending death with much less depression than they had had previously. The newer attitude to death lasted much longer than the analgesic action. It is likely those who have a visionary, psychedelic or transcendental reaction may equate this with life after death. This would account for the new more beneficial frame of mind for those patients who were dying.

One of our subjects recently told us that since his psychedelic experience several years ago, he no longer feared death.

Chapter II B

Ololiuqui: The Ancient Aztec Narcotic

History and Identification

Ololiuqui is another of the amazing varieties of hallucinogenic plants discovered and used by the Indians of Meso America. It was ignored for a long time because of an error in botanical classification which was not finally corrected until Schultes published his classic monograph in 1941. Most of this section is abstracted from his paper.

As a result of extensive research from 1570 to 1575, Francisco Hernandez, first described ololiuqui. Sahagun described 3 ololiuqui plants but stated that only 1 was a narcotic (medically these plants scarcely qualify as narcotics but Schultes listed them as such and we shall use his classification). In 1629, Alarcon repeated in some detail how the Indians used ololiuqui. He stated that "ololiuqui is a kind of lentil which is produced by a species of ivy of this land; when it is drunk, this seed deprives of his senses him who has taken it, for it is very powerful." Schultes gave the following translation of Hernandez's account of ololiuqui:

Oliliuhqui, which some call coaxihuitl, or snakeplant, is a twining herb with thin, green cordate leaves; slender, green, terete stems; and long, white flowers. The seed is round and very much like coriander whence the name (in Nahuatl, the term 'ololiuqui' means 'round thing') of the plant. The roots are fibrous and slender. The plant is hot in the fourth degree. . . . The seed has some medicinal use. If pulverized or taken in a decoction or used as a poultice on the head or forehead, with milk and chili, it is said to cure eye troubles. When drunk, it acts as an aphrodisiac. It has a sharp taste and is very hot. Formerly when the priests wanted to commune with their gods and to receive a message from them, they ate this plant to induce a delirium. A thousand visions and satanic hallucinations appeared to them. In its manner of action, this plant can be compared with Solanum Maniacum of Dioscorides.

Oliva (1854) correctly placed ololiuqui amongst the *Convolvulaceae*. This identification was accepted later by Leon (1888) and Urbina (1897) who correctly identified ololiuqui as *Rivea corymbosa*. But Hartwich (1911) wrongly placed ololiuqui with the *Solanaceae*. Safford

(1915) disagreed with Urbina's identification, not because the facts were against this but because "it is not known that any of the *Convolvulaceae* are narcotic, though many of the *Solanaceae* are." Furthermore, Safford doubted the early Mexican accounts of their plants and their properties. He identified ololiuqui as *Datura meteloides* and repeated this assertion so dogmatically and so frequently that it eventually became generally accepted.

Louis Lewin also believed ololiuqui belonged to the *Datura*. But in Mexico it was generally accepted that ololiuqui was *Rivea corymbosa*. Reko provided the first field evidence that Urbina had been correct and Safford wrong. In 1919 he defined ololuc as the round, lentil-like seeds of *R. corymbosa* and stated that medicine-men used them to produce intoxication resembling somnambulism. In 1934, Reko reviewed the ololiuqui literature and again stated that it must be *Rivea corymbosa*. He even collected the narcotic seeds which Safford identified as the seeds of *Rivea corymbosa*.

The argument was finally settled by Schultes when he identified ololiuqui as *Rivea corymbosa*. But it is curious that this same argument continued until Hofmann recently isolated lysergic acid derivatives from ololiuqui. Safford refused to believe that ololiuqui was a member of the *Convolvulaceae* because everyone "knew" they did not contain narcotics, whereas *Datura* did, and he gave no credit whatever to early Mexican accounts.

When Osmond (1955) reported the results of the first psychiatric self-experiment with ololiuqui, psychiatrists could not believe he was correct for similar reasons and in addition for a more modern reason—because it was a self-experiment and not done in what has since become the fashion in psychiatric research—the double blind experiment. In fact some have considered a self account no more and no less than a self deception (see Kinross-Wright). When Hofmann first reported that he had extracted lysergic acid amide as well as other lysergic acid derivatives from ololiuqui his announcement was greeted with disbelief. Botanical chemists would not believe him because hitherto ergot compounds had been found only in fungii. It was suggested that these compounds were not rightfully extracted from ololiuqui seeds but had gotten there because of contamination with spores or given less charitably with lysergic acid derivatives presumed to be floating about in Hofmann's laboratory. The history of ololiuqui has been bedeviled by a good deal of a priori reasoning. But the corroboration of Hofmann's (1960, 1961a,b) findings by Taber and Heacock (1962), Taber *et al.* (1963a), and Genest (1964) has finally established the presence of ergot alkaloids in ololiuqui and in other species of Convolvulaceae (morning glory) and

d-lysergic acid amide

isolysergic acid amide

chanoclavin

lysergol

clymoclavin

Fɪɢ. 6. Some lysergic acid derivatives in ololiuqui.

these can partially account for the psychological effects which follow the ingestion of ololiuqui.

Taxonomy of Convolvulaceae Containing Ergot Alkaloids

Rivea corymbosa [*Ipomoea sidaefolia* (HBK) Choisy, *Turbina corymbosa* (L) *Raf.*] was described as follows (Schultes, 1941):

The plant is a large, scandent, woody vine. The leaves are 5–9 cm long, 2.5–4 cm wide, broadly cordate or ovate cordate, entire, glabrous or very sparingly pubescent, long petiolate. Peduncles axillary, usually many-flowered. Flowers born in congested cymes. Corolla gamopetalouse, infundibuliform of hypocraterimorphous, 2–4 cm long white or whitish, the lobes entire, glabrous. Stigmas two. Stamens included. Ovary glabrous, 2-celled. Sepals ovate to ovate-lanceolate, enlarged in fruit, scarious, somewhat ligneous, about 1 cm long. Fruit ellipsoidal, baccate, indehiscent, 1-celled, 1-seeded. Seed roundish minutely puberulent, rather woody.

Rivea may be confused with the genus *Ipomoea*. But *Rivea* has sepals which are ligneous whereas *Ipomoea* usually has membranous, often herbaceous sepals. In *Rivea* the flower is usually hypocraterimorphous, a shape uncommon in *Ipomoea*. The fruit of *Rivea* is baccate, dry and indehiscent with one seed while fruit of *Ipomoea* is a dehiscent capsule with 2 or more seeds.

Rivea is found in the East Indies, Africa, South and Middle America and the West Indies. *Rivea corymbosa* is the only species native to the new world where it is widely distributed in Central America, in Mexico, Guatemala, Honduras, Costa Rica, and Nicaragua; in South America in Venezuela, Peru, and Bolivia, and in North America in Florida.

Ipomoea arborescens (Humb. and Bonpl) S. Don, found in Morelos Mexico is believed to cause insanity and cerebral disorders if taken internally.

Chemistry

Urbina pointed out that ololiuqui was rich in glucosides. Santesson (1937) isolated narcotic substances from ololiuqui, and he suspected that some of the activity was due to an alkaloid set free when the glucoside was split. Thus Santesson's work foreshadowed the two chief chemical constituents present in ololiuqui.

Glucosides

Cook and Kieland (1962) isolated a glucoside from the ethanolic extract of the defatted pulverized seed. The white crystalline glucoside had a melting point of 241. The formula was $C_{28}H_{46}O_{12}$. The infrared spectrum indicated only hydroxyl and ether functional groups. They postulated that the carbon skeleton of the aglucone was a hydrogenated pyranonaphthalene which contained 4 hydroxyls and 3 bridged ether groups.

The glucoside was 5 times as potent a central nervous system stimulant as the initial ethanolic extracts of *Rivea corymbosa.* Doses over 31.6 mg/kg were fatal to test animals in 5–10 minutes.

LYSERGIC ACID ALKALOIDS

These alkaloids have been described in the LSD section.

Psychological Properties

THE OLOLIUQUI SEEDS

From the earliest records of the 16th century to the present time the Indians of Southern Mexico used *Rivea corymbosa* chiefly for divination. Schultes translated Alarcon as follows:

It is remarkable how much faith these natives have in the seed, for when they drink it, they consult it as an oracle in order to learn many things . . . especially those things which are beyond the power of the human mind to penetrate. . . . The doctor appoints the day and hour when the drink must be taken. . . . Finally, the one drinking the ololiuqui must seclude himself in his room alone. . . . He who is consulting the seeds believes that ololiuqui . . . is revealing what he wants to know . . .

It happens that he who drinks ololiuqui to excess loses his mind because of the great potency of the seeds . . . the senses are distorted . . . and these unfortunate people believe the utterances attributing everything to ololiuqui.

Serva as translated by Schultes wrote as follows:

They venerate these plants as though they were divine. When they drink these herbs, they consult them like oracles. . . . They consult these herbs about all things which cannot be fathomed by the human mind . . . consulting these plants . . . all their doubts and uncertainties are dispelled.

These seeds . . . are held in great veneration. . . . They place offerings to the seeds . . . in secret places so that the offerings cannot be found if a search be made. They also place these seeds among the idols of their ancestors.

According to Schultes the dose of ololiuqui varied but thirteen seeds were used. The intoxication began soon after and rapidly resulted in the appearance of visual hallucinations. Often there was an intervening stage of dizziness followed by a feeling of general ease and well-being, then lassitude and drowsiness. Usually the drowsiness advanced into a stupor. The visions were described as similar to the ones seen when peyote or the psilocybe mushrooms were consumed. The intoxication lasted about 3 hours and was followed by few unpleasant aftereffects.

This was the background against which Osmond (1955) began his self-experiments. This was how it then appeared to him:

Schultes has drawn his information on the psycho-physiological effects of ololiuqui from many sources, starting with Spanish conquistadors and ending with modern investigators and reports of Indian ololiuqui users. This is the least satisfactory aspect of his fine monograph, and it is hardly fair to blame him for shortcomings which arise because his interest centered in botanical and not in psychological matters.

Schultes discusses only two experiments on human subjects, and since neither of these was in any way affected no further clues became available from their work. A Dr. Marsh of the U. S. Agricultural Service 'obtained negative results when he experimented with the seeds of *Rivea corymbosa,* and Reko although he had been warned that five or six seeds would produce an intoxication, ate a handful without noticeable effect.' Santesson was much puzzled by this immunity and indulged in some speculation about 'racial differences in susceptibility to intoxica-tion' to account for it. Where there are differences in susceptibility to all sorts of intoxication, and doubtless racial characteristics play some part in this, there seems to be a simpler explanation for Reko's immunity. The impetuous man had a whole handful to get down and unless I am much mistaken he swallowed them whole. The seeds are small, round and very hard-skinned. It requires a determined crunching to smash them with the teeth and unless they are broken up I believe they pass unchanged through the gut. Clement (1) has suggested that the narcotic content of different plants can vary greatly.

Schultes was not able to witness a ceremony in which ololiuqui was being used, nor could he, in the field, partake of the narcotic. Nevertheless it was being used by the Mazatecs as late as 1939 for medicinal and divinatory purposes. I found that the gravest shortcoming was that I was never quite certain whether human or animal experiments were being described. Schultes refers to Santesson's descrip-tion of what he calls 'halbnarcose' and Reko's (16) term 'hypnotischsomnambuli-stisch.' Schultes (17) opines that Santesson's work refers solely to frogs and mice, and tells me that Reko informed him that his account of the intoxication was based chiefly on Indian reports.

However, it seems fairly clear that the Indians, apart from the curative properties which they ascribed to it, also valued it for its use in divination and magic which resembled that of peyote (even though the two drugs are not found in contiguous areas). There seems to have been one interesting difference, for while the peyotist enjoys his transcendental experience in company the ololiuqui-taker is said to prefer to be alone. A further difference is that most accounts seem to agree that the effects of ololiuqui last only about three hours, which is less than those of peyote. The Spaniards are full of references to witchcraft and deviltry, but much of their evidence is colored by prejudice. Hallucinations and visions are mentioned often but without very much precise description.

Dr. Clement (1) in a personal communication tells me that he has been unable to discover any evidence that it has ever been used as a narcotic in Cuba. Like many other plants, it has a reputation as an abortifacient, though there is no information about its efficiency in this respect. There is some evidence that ololiuqui honey, which is of a very excellent quality, has a somnorific effect.

Since this was the first controlled[1] self-experiment by any psychiatrist, one skillful in introspection and who had experienced the effects of mescaline, LSD, adrenochrome, and adrenolutin, we will reproduce verbatim this first scientific account.

[1] The word "control" has been preempted by many statisticians, psychologists, and psychiatrists to mean a double blind experiment using a placebo comparison group. We wish to restore the correct meaning as used in the physical sciences that is, a controlled experiment is one wherein major variables are set at constant levels.

Dosage

The investigator of any new drug is always glad to have some hint about the amount needed to produce its characteristic effect; the more precise this information, the better. When investigating something whose characteristic effects are said to be psychological, and in which therefore, the value of experimental animals is small, it is very hard to determine a suitable dose. The synthetic hallucinogens are easier to work with than the naturally occurring ones, because we know fairly accurately the amount of mescaline or lysergic acid required to produce a model psychosis. We also know that only one substance is responsible. With peyote, we are dealing not only with a mixture of alkaloids, but in addition, the relative concentrations of the eight alkaloids can vary. The directions for taking the comparatively well-known peyote show great differences, so that it is hardly surprising that the information about ololiuqui is likewise deficient.

The natural unwillingness of the Indians to disclose their religious secrets to strangers has been greatly increased by the zeal of generations of Spanish busybodies. Serna (19) gives us a vivid description of the reticence of the Indians and the attitude of the Spaniards. 'These seeds . . . are held in great veneration. . . . They place offerings to the seeds . . . in secret places so that the offerings cannot be found if a search be made. They also place these seeds among the idols of their ancestors . . . the natives do these things with so much respect that when some transgressor of the law who has the seeds in his possession is arrested and is asked for the paraphernalia which are used in taking ololiuqi . . . or for the seeds themselves, he denies vehemently that he knows anything about the practices. The natives do this not so much because of fear of the law as because of the veneration in which they hold the seed ololiuqui. They do not wish to offend ololiuqui with demonstrations before the judges of the use of the seeds and with public destruction of the seed by burning.'

According to Schultes it seems that at least three groups of Indians told investigators that they commonly took thirteen seeds. One of these groups claimed that their reason for doing this is because thirteen was the sacred number that represents Jesus Christ and his apostles at the Last Supper. The seeds are taken in water or with an alcoholic drink such as pulque, mescal (a drink not to be confused with the alkaloid of the peyote), aquadiente, or tepache.

I, therefore, expected, that, if anything happened, thirteen seeds would be enough to produce in a short time dizziness or giddiness followed by lassitude, increasing drowsiness and finally a stuporous state in which visual hallucinations would occur, and I would be only dimly aware of what was going on around me. The evidence suggested that this would last about three hours, but I was not at all clear how I might expect to feel after the stage which has been so oddly termed 'somnambulistic narcosis' had worn off.

I had a little information from Mr. L. LeCron and Mr. Aldous Huxley, who took six seeds in February, 1954, without any very clear effect. I later discovered that Mrs. Huxley, on a similar dose, had some delightful visions depicting some new adventure in the life of Wu-Cheng-Ens (23) heroic and archetypal ape, Monkey. I did not, however, know of this until after I had taken ololiuqui myself.

The Experimenter, His Surroundings, and the Seeds

I weigh about 170 pounds and am 5 feet 9.5 inches. I am aged 36 and enjoy good health. I have never suffered from jaundice (4). I am experienced in the model psychoses, having taken mescaline on one occasion and watched others take it. I have taken part in many lysergic acid experiments, although I have not yet ingested it myself. I have taken adrenochrome on three occasions. I can, therefore claim some sophistication in these matters. This has the advantage that such a trained observer may be alert to subtle changes which others might ignore and the disadvantage that he might be suggestible and report shall changes attributable simply to heightened expectation. There is no easy way out of this dilemma, but in a preliminary trial it is not very important, although in a larger experiment it would have to be guarded against. A full evaluation of a new hallucinogen is, as I have pointed out elsewhere (10), a major enterprise calling for the co-operation and co-ordination of many disciplines. Stefaniuk (20) has shown how complex are the experiential and behavioral changes with which we have to be prepared to deal. I know of no satisfactory study of such an evaluation, or even any discussion of the methods that would be most helpful.

The seeds of *Rivea corymbosa* are about the size, hardness, and color of a small sweet pea. Technically they are described thus, 'being bacchate, dry, and indehiscent with only one seed.' They are hard enough to need grinding with the molar teeth. Those with dentures should use a hammer or a pestle and mortar. With the help of Mr. D. Sheldon and Mr. Doisey, of the Saskatchewan Hospital, Weyburn, I have devised a tubular steel pestle and mortar with a detachable base which reduces the effort required to smash the seeds and eliminates danger to teeth and dentures. I would be glad to describe it to other experimenters.

The seeds have a bitter taste like lupin or wild bean seed. My sample was not in the least peppery and could not possibly be described in Hernandez's (3) words of 1951 as having a 'sharp taste and is very hot.' It does not in the least resemble the burning taste of chili, with which, as a curry eater, I am familiar, although Reko states that its Mixtec name 'vucu-vaha,' meaning chili plant, refers to its hot taste. Chewing large numbers of seeds is tedious and they leave a slightly nauseating after-taste in the mouth.

The first and second experiments were done in my own home, alone except for my little daughter who was going to bed when the seeds were taken. My excuse for this slovenly procedure was scepticism about the potency of ololiuqui fostered by reading Dr. Marsh's experiment. My wife, who has done a good deal of work in this field, and my sister, who is a registered nurse, were present during the third experiment I had no verbal means of recording for two of the first three experiments, and when I had a dictaphone, for reasons that are not clear, I did not use it. I did, however, take notes with a greater or lesser degree of assiduity.

In the fourth experiment, which was again conducted in my home, my psychologist colleague Mr. Ben Stefaniuk was present. He took down most of our conversation on tape, and also made a series of notes such as he has used in our lysergic acid experiments, indicating changes in behavior and the time at which these occurred. The number of seeds taken were 14, 20, 26, 60, and 100 in that order. For the first three experiments, they were chewed and washed down with iced water. In the fourth they were smashed with a hammer and then ground to a fine flour in a glass pestle and mortar. This fine flour was placed on the tongue with a teaspoon and swallowed with iced water.

THE EXPERIMENTS

One

At 6:15 PM on Friday, 20th February, 1954, I chewed up fourteen of the seeds. I felt that this number was less of a challenge to the fates than the thirteen favored by the Indians. I noted 'I am alone with little H. A definitely unexperimental atmosphere—am strongly of the opinion that nothing will happen.'

6:30 PM One of those curious things that might be suggestion: an extraordinary clarity of objects. 'The tennis ball, white and furry on the tomato colored carpet and a little cluster of glass marbles some eighteen inches away from it. All seem to related to one another and each seems to have special significance' . . . 'Irritability is noticeable especially when disturbed'. . . . 'My gaze is caught by the polish on the willow shoots, the greenness of a leaf, the furriness of a cactus. This could be heightened awareness due to heightened expectation.'

6:45 PM I ate a fair supper although not keen to do so. Nothing more happened. I read quietly all evening. I did not record another note although I had meant do do so.

Two

Exactly a week later I took 26 seeds in similar circumstances and had a very similar experience. Although I had a dictaphone with me and had brought it a considerable distance for this express purpose, I failed to record or keep notes of any sort. This could be ascribed either to incompetence or to the affects of ololiuqui, I prefer the latter explanation, because I am quite aware of the requirements of this sort of research and am usually a fluent writer.

Three

March 7, 1954. At 12:30 PM I chewed sixty seeds and washed them down with water. I took notes most of the time. At 1:00 PM I had lunch, which was tasteless, though I ate some of the same food later with enjoyment. At 1:30 PM I noted this—'A slight headache, vague, unlocalized. A great effort to write, easier just to sit. People irritate; things fascinate; the texture of wood; the almost metallic gold center of an African violet. Mildly nauseated. The little warm dog on my lap the only contact.'

2:00 PM Very indolent and irritable, curious sense of distance—noise uncomfortable—pup consolingly real. Children coming in a very real threat. (H) my 4 year old daughter, wants to come close to me and the dog. Find this most disturbing, say 'Go away, go away.' Lethargic, irritable, scarcely bother to write.

2:10 PM On closing my eyes hypnagogic phenomena, much vivider than usual at this time of day. [Normally on eye closing I do not have hypnagogic phenomena unless they are tired.] I have no wish to explain or communicate. The little dog alone remains in contact, demanding nothing not even understanding.

2:20 PM Eyes closed. Curious patterns. First patterns. First blackness so deep that my hair stood on end. Then a beige-grey ceramic design, with silver stippled patterns, an abstract design of an ibex. Do I mean ibex—a horned deer—yes ibex, not ibis the bird.

2:40 PM 'A very difficult state to describe. Every action seems discreet and uncertain. Very difficult to make up one's mind to do anything' J, my wife, read my notes. 'J. is reading this and I am conscious of this in an entirely detached way, as if she were reading my diaries post-mortem. Also feel rather silly as I write this down, though I know it will worry her and she is worried.' 'Objects seemed to have an extraordinary solidity and dimensionality.' 'That scarlet piece of wood on the brown carpet, it is so intensely bright that the color seems to sink into the carpet.' 'A curious idea that I am writing and wasn't getting any forrader or anything down—a sort of nightmare self-erasing writing.' 'One is bewildered by the wonder of each single object.'

3:30 PM 'Irritable apathy is the keynote. Too apathetic to call out. Too irritable to dare to do so. On and on and on.' 'Eyeball pressure does change the hypnagogic images temporarily but they return when the pressure is released. How bright the light—how shadowy people, even H. Even their voices seem dull and meaningless. The little dog is deliciously alive. N.B., shouldn't psychotic people have pets? Wouldn't they be more helpful than humans? Probably. Why? Because they are not self-conscious, hardly selves at all. Maybe this is why we can't help each other because we are literally selfish. Self gets in the way, even with H. but not with the dog. A cat too is so completely cattish that no self, no human self intervenes. Animals are alive but undemanding.'[2] 'Bodily sensations less than mescaline, some epigastric burning, some tingling in face and hands, slight headache, not much else.' 'This is a waking dream.[3] So little changed, but enough. The cat might be artificial, a mechanical cat, but little Mesca (dog) is clearly alive.' 'Looking at one's self in the mirror. How can I be sure that it is me; perhaps it isn't.' 'Once I start writing I keep going automatically, my attention is fixed on the writing. It is the same with everything. I stick in a groove. If I got angry would I stick in it? I don't know, I'd better not try.'

6:00 PM 'This is very curious stuff. I have been lying on my bed asleep, but not really asleep for the last 2½ hours. I have slept a bit and have been profoundly tired, yet acutely aware of everything that was going on. A sort of paralysis of the will; it is an immense effort to do anything yet when I do it, I can.' . . . 'Although not keen to be near people I feel it when they go away.' . . . 'In this dose this is not a hallucinogen to any great extent. In larger doses it may be so. It produces stupefaction without disorientation or the motor effects of alcohol. One is irritable, stuporous, apathetic, but not very uninhibited.'

7:00 PM Within an hour of eating a sugary meal and drinking tea I note 'Now very much more normal, very alert, and very aware of what is going on. It looks as if this stuff acts on different centers at different times.'

8:00 PM I eat a hearty meal. 'It seems to have worn off leaving elation and clarity without tension. It is the reverse way round from Benzedrine.'

That night I went to bed about midnight and slept fairly well, though I had some hypnagogic phenomena before falling off to sleep. When I awoke next day I was slightly tense and had a mild frontal headache—nothing like a hangover—my tongue was clean and moist.

[2] As Walt Whitman put it in "Song of Myself":
> I think I could turn and live with animals, they are so placid and self contained,
> I stand and look at them sometimes half the day long.
> They do not sweat and whine about their condition.
> They do not lie awake in the dark and weep for their sins,
> They do not make me sick discussing their duty to God,
> Not one is dissatisfied, not one is demented with the mania of owning things,
> Not one kneels to another, nor to his kind that lived thousands of years ago.
> Not one is respectable and industrious over the whole earth,
> So they show their relations to me, and I accept them.
> They bring me tokens of myself, they evince them plainly in their possession.

[3] Somnambulistic narcosis although a clumsy term would not be an entirely inappropriate description.

Four

This experiment was again conducted in my home on the March 21, 1954. It was fully recorded on tape and where I quote it is from a transcript of this record or from the few notes which I made. My colleague Mr. Ben Stefaniuk was present as an observer. At 12:10 PM I took 100 seeds reduced to a powder as I have already described. The symptoms, which started within twenty minutes of swallowing the powder, followed the same general pattern as the third experiment, and consisted of apathy, anergia, withdrawal, some sharpening of visual perception, and an increase in hypnagogic visions when the eyes were closed.

The apathy extended to the experiment, showing itself in a lack of interest. For instance when I was pressed to talk more I said, 'Yes, this is an experiment but I don't attach much importance to it.' My interest in people lessened, 'It is difficult to be interested in them, they shift around so much.' I had feelings of weakness and doubted when I could hold the microphone, but this weakness was not accompanied by clumsiness as in alcoholic excess. 'I feel extremely steady but very weak.'

At 1:34 PM a curious thing happened. I raised my hand above my head and couldn't get it down. No urging or verbal pressure by my colleague made any difference, neither did voluntary effort on my part. 'I can't. It's stuck. That is strange, an unpleasant feeling.' Eventually I pulled it down with the other hand.

I had no slurring of speech and at about 2:30 PM repeated 'Popocatepetl' several times and very clearly. It was not easy to judge time and I had to work it out. 'I'm not disorientated in time but it is extremely difficult to tell where in time I am.' I referred frequently to my tiredness. Towards 3:30 PM I began to feel hungry, having had no inclination for food before that, but I was too lethargic to do anything about it. 'It is quite strange how I fluctuate from feeling full of energy to feeling completely done in.' About this time my companion asked 'What about the seriousness of the experiment?' I replied, 'It is there intellectually but I don't feel about it—intellectually I am well aware that this is an interesting thing, but the fact is I don't feel interested in it. I really don't feel that I have the energy to be interested you know. And this doesn't quite fit into anything. It's not derealization or depersonalization. Those are almost meaningless words for certain states certain people believe they have observed in other people. But these things are not exactly applicable to me. It's something you can apply to someone else but not to yourself. This is not the feeling of being it at all. It is simply a feeling of complete detachment from the situation and being an observer; not being a thing.'

Pressed to explain myself by Mr. Stefaniuk I continued, 'I was feeling that I really hadn't the energy either intellectual or physical to discuss what was happening, and though there were these perceptual changes which were not unlike the early stages of mescal or adrenochrome, the main thing was this extraordinary lack of energy[4]—an extreme unwillingness to do anything at all.' This apathy and anergic could, most of the time, be overcome by an intense effort, but at the height of the experience voluntary effort made little difference.

From 4:00 4:30 PM I found that it was increasingly possible to exert sufficient effort to dispel the lethargy. 'You can overcome apathy if it lasts a short time, but if it lasts a long time you just can't do anything.'

About 5:00 PM I went for a drive and was interested to discover that I had

[4] In an experiment with adrenochrome (4) I had the curious experience that I was a thing, not a person.

none of the time and distance disturbances that I had had with adrenochrome. I ate a substantial meal.

By 6:00 PM I felt recovered and was active and interested and continued in this state for many hours, I noted, 'Apathy, lack of energy, seems to be the keynote with only a little disturbance of perception. . . . Apathy (no mood) is clearly differentiated from depression (low mood). . . . The lack of angst differentiates this from LSD or mescal.'

11:15 PM After driving my friend home—'Still a depth and brightness in things such as they have on a May morning when you are twenty-one. A newness, freshness as if everything had had a shower.' . . . 'Silence seems deeper, noises seem crisper. Oddly this was present in the apathy and is still present in this pleasant alertness without tension and without foreboding. It is very different from the touch-me-not feeling after mescaline or the bruised blunting after alcohol.'

I went to bed about midnight but did not go to sleep immediately but lay relaxed and wakeful, letting associations come and making notes in the dark which weeks later are legible and seem quite sensible. At about 1:00 AM our little daughter awoke with a cough. Normally I would have found this irritating and would have been disgruntled. I noted, 'I was cheerful, relaxed and alert. The lack of caffeine or benzedrine tension is remarkable.'

Next day I awoke at 7:00 AM. I had a slight dryness of the mouth—no hangover. I was, it seemed, hypo-irritable yet hyper-alert. Doors banging, etc. did not in the least disturb me even though it was Monday morning. During the day's work, I think I was more active and less touchy than I would expect after such exertion and a poor night's sleep.

Psychologist's Comments

Mr. Ben Stefaniuk was kind enough to make the following comment on the fourth experiment:

The most apparent and constant element in the experiment was that Dr. Osmond, who usually is a very energetic and talkative person, became extremely lethargic and uncommunicative. I tried to interest him in the importance of the experiment at various intervals, but, very much to my surprise, he claimed that it wasn't too important and the recording of the experiment could wait. This is an amazing reaction because, from previous discussion, I knew him to be extremely interested in the outcome of this experiment. There was nothing bizarre in either his behavior or his verbal productions; it was not similar to most LSD reactions. His type of uncommunicativeness was displayed in many qualifying instances by one of my female volunteers for LSD. The main changes, I feel, were lethargy, alternating with periods of restlessness, a similar type of loss in interests and the extreme slowing down of verbalization.

Discussion

I believe that this is the first series of experiments with ololiuqui, said by Safford (4) to be 'the chief narcotic of the Aztecs,' conducted solely for the purpose of psychological investigation. Previously, apart from Marsh and Reko (16), who heroically swallowed a 'handful' of the seeds, all accounts of the effect of ololiuqui seem to have been obtained from the Indians. The descriptions recorded by the conquistadors and their descendants were distorted by the hatred which they felt for the defeated. Later enquiries by scientists were impeded by lack of psychological knowledge which would have enabled them to make the most of their informants, who were no doubt becoming increasingly wary of divulging their secrets. In support of my contention that neither Marsh nor Reko chewed the seeds which they swallowed is the fact that Reko, in 1934, still repeats Hernandez's (13) assertions of 1651 that ololiuqui 'has a sharp taste and is very hot.' Reko sta.es that the Mixtecs give it the same name as the chili plant, yuca-yaha.

My sample of ololiuqui had only a slightly bitter taste, and bore not the slightest resemblance to chili, whose pungency could not possibly be overlooked when placed in powdered form on the tongue. Can it be that a reputation for such pepperiness would discourage the curious? Or could it be that the seeds were gathered unripe or less ripe in one case than the other?

Nevertheless, apart from this and the number of seeds needed, the information gathered from the Indians seems to have been accurate, although incomplete. Thirteen seeds, in spite of their sacred significance, had very little effect on me. There may be more subtle explanations, but I suggest that red men, from bitter experience, have found it prudent to mislead white men, lest they once more prohibit the sacred seed and persecute its devotees.

This preliminary exploration suggests that ololiuqui differs from mescaline lysergic acid, and adrenochrome. In doses of 60–100 seeds it produces marked anergia and irritable apathy, combined with alert thought processes and increased hypnagogic phenomena. This is odd; even odder is the rapid onset, short duration, and lack of hangover, followed by alert wakefulness without tension. This alert wakefulness is noteworthy for an unusual placidity combined with a capacity for constructive action when required. I could drive a car so that a critical passenger was not disturbed.

The 'paralysis of the will,' which occurred with the apathy and anergia, is not unlike the complaints of some people who are labeled schizophrenic. These unlucky folk complain about their lack of energy and are looked upon as being 'bizarrely hypochondriacal.' They get very little understanding or attention, usually. When they are forced to overcome their anergia, they often become irritable and sometimes their behavior seems to be impulsive. I know that in one experiment I made what was intended to be a gentle push at my little daughter to fend her away and knocked her flat. The effort once made resulted in action that did not seem to be fully controlled. At the height of the experience so much effort was needed to do even the smallest thing that there was a temptation to remain totally immobile. Even in this immobility I was alert and aware what was going on most of the time. Most psychiatrists have seen patients who could be described in this way.

Most writers agree that the Indians revere ololiuqui for its use in magic, divination, and as a vision maker. Taylor (22) quoting an old authority writes: 'They consult it as an oracle in order to learn many things . . . especially those things which are beyond the power of the mind to penetrate.' May it not be that the Indians take it as much for the astonishing, detached, serene well-being and mental clarity combined with a capacity for action without anxiety which follows the apathy as for the visions, etc.? Surely this remarkable state would be an excellent jumping-off place for starting that 'active contemplation' so much sought by explorers of the soul, and so hard to achieve?

Like most writers whose special province is not psychology, Schultes is vague about 'hallucinations.' I did not experience any, though I had some heightening of visual perception with the eyes open and some increase of hypnagogic visions when they were closed.

My response to ololiuqui is almost the reverse of that to amphetamine, which causes me to have a short period of tense elation and over-activity, followed by black depression. If other experimenters also find this happens, there would be a very strong case for isolating the active principle and comparing its spatial formula and effect on cerebral enzyme systems with amphetamine.

The comfort which I derived from the close presence of the little dog requires some thought. While we have made a cult of pet animals in the West, there seem to have been few studies of the relationships which develop between animals and humans. This is often dismissed as being a substitute for another relationship— a human one. In my view this is superficial and misleading. The relationship between man and dog has developed over tens of thousands of years and seems to be based on a deeper level of understanding than words. Perhaps then, when words fail us this is why dogs can be so comforting.

A few experiments on one subject can tell us very little, but this seems to be another instrument which may allow us to ask questions which will help us towards a greater understanding of ourselves.

Many questions spring to mind. What is the active principle of the elusive ololiuqui? How and where does it act? In what other ways will people respond to it? But future investigators would be glad if a few quite mundane questions were answered first. What exactly are the local anaesthetic properties that Schultes mentions? A full pharmacological investigation would be very welcome.

In view of the literature reviewed by Schultes it is not surprising that Osmond found activity in the ololiuqui seeds. There is not much evidence that the Indians were poorer than White men at introspection and at discovering plants which contained hallucinogenic substances. What was surprising were the failures by Isbell (1957) and by Kinross-Wright (1959) to find any activity. Presumably Isbell used addicts who perhaps are physiologically different and would not be expected to respond in the same way. In the same way we have found that alcoholics require more than twice as much LSD in order to achieve a psychedelic experience. They were probably also not adept at introspection. We believe that, in general, such subjects are not the best type of volunteers to use.

OLOLIUQUI GLUCOSIDE

A glucoside was extracted from *Rivea corymbosa* seeds in our laboratory by Ahmed, Abramovitch, and Heacock in 1961. No comparative studies were completed to relate this to Cook and Kieland's preparations, but it is likely that it is the same or a similar glucoside.

Because ololiuqui has been used so extensively with hardly any reports of acute toxicity, we conducted a series of self-experiments without testing its pharmacological and behavioral action on animals. The glucoside was a white crystalline material.

September 12, 1961 (2 mg sublingually)

Hoffer (weighing 190 pounds and being 6 feet tall) placed 2 mg under his tongue. It had a bitter, but not unpleasant taste which lingered on for about 7 minutes. No change was noted. Thereafter, the following findings were recorded.

September 13, 1961 (5 mg sublingually)

I took 5 mg of the ololiuqui glucoside sublingually. It was quite bitter. After thirty minutes there was a slight suggestion of more light in my office. At 1 hour I still had this sensation of slightly increased brilliance. At 1¾ hours, while walking up some stairs I noted a queer dragging sensation in my legs, a reluctance to move. I felt somewhat unsteady. A little later while drinking coffee my mood, which had been good, became elevated. The sensation of greater brilliance about me was present again. I was normal at 2¼ hours and I then concluded there had been a very slight reaction. There had been no reaction reminiscent of adrenochrome, adrenolutin, LSD or mescaline.

September 20, 1961 (10 mg sublingually)

At 50 minutes I observed a feeling of lassitude and a slight motor incoordination of my legs. I noted no change in mood but again there was the slight sensation of more light. After 2 hours I was normal.

February 28, 1962 (20 mg oral)

At the end of thirty minutes, I had become aware of a facial flush which lasted for nearly 2½ hours. At two hours I felt more energetic and active than I had been before and was talking more freely. By three hours I felt normal.

However, there was an interesting residual change. It was a very cold February day (25 degrees below zero) and I was curling on an indoor artificial ice rink. Normally I would be either comfortable or slightly cold. This evening I became very warm after starting the game and had to remove my heavy woolen vest which I wore beneath my heavy curling sweater. On leaving my office at 5:15 PM I had no impact from the cold as I normally have. The striking thing was I had no sense of irritation at the continual cold weather which I had before this experiment. We had one of the coldest Februarys on record. It seemed I had been unusually indifferent to cold and my irritation had been lifted.

March 9, 1962 (30 mg glucoside oral)

After 25 minutes I developed a strong sense of boredom with some psychiatric histories I was abstracting. They seemed to be interminable and I put them away relieved to be rid of them. I was irritable and jumpy. To an observer my movements appeared drowsy, but I noted no change. I was aware of perspiration on my forehead, and I felt warm. There were no changes in perception.

After 40 minutes I became aware that I was more awkward in my movements. This was noticeable when I attempted to open my mail. At 50 minutes I could think clearly but I had trouble articulating my words. I was still warm and in good humor. I compared my reactions to having taken one ounce of alcohol.

At the end of 1¼ hours I noted no further change. An observer stated that I seemed depressed and I spoke in a monotone. However, I did not feel depressed or sad. At 1¼ hours I was still flushed and unsteady, and my face felt rigid but my mood had not changed. After 1 hour and 50 minutes my face felt less flushed and less stiff. The observer reported that my face seemed masklike and felt I had changed more than I had felt I had. I was quite relaxed.

After 2 hours I felt I was recovering from the reaction. I now agreed I had been somewhat depressed, at least in the motor area but I had not felt in the least bit low spirited or dejected. At 2⅓ hours I still had a slight flush. I felt much more alert and cheerful. At 2 hours and 40 minutes my face became slightly blanched. At 3 hours I was relaxed and although I completed writing a letter to an organization about a matter that should have irritated me, I was not annoyed or angry.

That evening I was normal but apparently less susceptible to pain. For an unknown reason I had severe pain in my right lower jaw but this did not prevent me from chewing on it. This was unusual for me as I am not normally that insensitive to pain. I slept well.

I concluded that the glucoside had had some psychological effects of an inhibitory nature. Thirty milligrams was too much, and 20 mg not quite enough. About 25 mg would be about right for me. Summarizing the effect, I noted facial flushing, increased awareness of light at lower doses, a feeling of relaxation and ease and decreased awareness of cold and pain. The highest dose sedated me a bit. These are not conclusive experiments, but they do suggest the glucoside is active centrally and should be further investigated. The narcotic-like properties described by the early writers would appear to be corroborated.

Perezamador *et al.* (1964) extracted a glucoside from *Turbina corymbosa* (Roth) Rasin. After extracting the seeds with hexane to remove the oils they prepared turbicaryn, a new glucoside from the alcoholic extract. Its formula was $C_{27}H_{46}O_{11}$. After hydrolysis with glucosidase, glucose was identified and a new agylcone turbicorytan was isolated. The authors gave no pharmacological properties for their compound.

CONVOLVULACEOUS RESINS

Shellard (1961) found that Vera Cruz jalap contained the following compounds: tiglic acid, some fatty acids, and a complex oligosaccharidic acid which had two compounds (a) ipurolic 3,11-dihydroxymyristic acid and (b) other substances still unidentified. Brazilian jalap is probably contained in hydroxymyristic acid. If some of these compounds were present in other convolvulaceous resin as in *Rivea corymbosa* they might influence the reaction.

REFERENCES

Aaronsen, B. S. (1964). *Perceptual Motor Skills* 18:30.
Abood, L. G., and Biel, J. H. (1962). *Intern. Rev. Neurobiol.* 4:217.
Abramson, H. A. (1955). *J. Psychol.* 39:127.
Abramson, H. A. (1956a). *J. Psychol.* 41:199.
Abramson, H. A. (1956b). *J. Psychol.* 41:51.

Abramson, H. A. (1957). *J. Nervous Mental Disease* **125**:444.

Abramson, H. A., ed. (1960a). "The Use of L.S.D. in Psychotherapy." Josiah Macy, Jr. Found., New York.

Abramson, H. A. (1960b). *J. Mental Sci.* **106**:1120.

Abramson, H. A., and Sklarofsky, A. B. (1960). *Arch. Gen. Psychiat.* **2**:89.

Abramson, H. A., Waxenberg, S. E., Levine, A., Kaufman, M. R., and Kornetsky, C. (1955a). *J. Psychol.* **40**:341.

Abramson, H. A., Jarvik, M. E., and Hirsch, M. W. (1955b). *J. Psychol.* **39**:455.

Abramson, H. A., Jarvik, M. E., and Hirsch, M. W. (1955c). *J. Psychol.* **40**:39.

Abramson, H. A., Jarvik, M. E., Hirsch, M. W., and Ewald, A. T. (1955d). *J. Psychol.* **39**:435.

Abramson, H. A., Jarvik, M. E., Kaufman, M. R., Kornetsky, C., Levine, A., and Wagner, M. (1955e). *J. Psychol.* **39**:3.

Abramson, H. A., Kornetsky, C., Jarvik, M. E., Kaufman, M. R., and Ferguson, M. W. (1955f). *J. Psychol.* **40**:53.

Abramson, H. A., Jarvik, M. E., Gorin, M. H., and Hirsch, M. W. (1956). *J. Psychol.* **41**:81.

Abramson, H. A., Hewitt, M. P., Lennard, H., Turner, W. J., O'Neill, F. J., and Merlis, S. (1958a). *J. Psychol.* **45**:75.

Abramson, H. A., Sklarofsky, B., Baron, M. O., and Fremont-Smith, F. (1958b). *A.M.A. Arch. Neurol. Psychiat.* **79**:201.

Abramson, H. A., Rolo, A., Sklarofsky, B., and Stache, J. (1960). *J. Psychol.* **49**:151.

Agnew, N., and Hoffer, A. (1955). *J. Mental Sci.* **101**:12.

Alema, G. (1952). *Riv. Neurol.* **22**:720.

Anastasopoulos, G., and Photiades, H. (1962). *J. Mental Sci.* **108**:95.

Anderson, E. W., and Rawnsley, K. (1954). *Monatsschr. Psychiat. Neurol.* **128**:38.

Apter, J. T., and Pfeiffer, C. C. (1956). *Am. J. Opthalmol.* [3] **42**:206.

Apter, T., and Pfeiffer, C. (1957). *Ann. N.Y. Acad. Sci.* **66**:508.

Arendsen-Hein, G. W. (1963). *In* "Hallucinogenic Drugs and Their Psychotherapeutic Use" (R. Crocket, R. A. Sandison, and A. Walk, eds.), p. 101. Lewis, London.

Arnold, O. H., and Hofmann, G. (1955). *Wien. Z. Nervenheilk. Grenzg.* **11**:92.

Arnold, O. H., Hofmann, G., and Leupold-Lowenthal, H. (1958). *Strahlentherapie, Sonderbaende* **38**:66.

Aronson, H., and Klee, G. D. (1960). *J. Nervous Mental Disease* **131**:536.

Aronson, H., Silverstein, A. B., and Klee, G. D. (1959). *A.M.A. Arch. Gen. Psychiat.* **1**:469.

Aronson, H., Watermann, C. E., and Klee, G. D. (1962). *J. Clin. Exptl. Psychopathol. & Quart. Rev. Psychiat. Neurol.* **23**:17.

Axelrod, J., Brady, O., Witkop, B., and Evarts, E. V. (1957). *Ann. N.Y. Acad. Sci.* **66**:435.

Bain, J. A. (1957). *Ann. N.Y. Acad. Sci.* **66**:459.

Baird, K. A. (1964). *Can. Med. Assoc. J.* **90**:1279.

Balestrieri, A. (1957). *In* "Psychotropic Drugs" (S. Garattini and V. Ghetti, eds.), p. 581. Elsevier, Amsterdam.

Balestrieri, A., and Fontanari, D. (1959). *A.M.A. Arch. Gen. Psychiat.* **1**:279.

Ball, J. R., and Armstrong, J. J. (1961). *Can. Psychiat. Assoc. J.* **6**:231.

Barber, B. (1961). *Science* **134**:596.

Barrios, A. A. (1965). *Intern. J. Neuropsychiat.* **1**:574.

Becker, A. M. (1949). *Wien. Z. Nervenheilk. Grenzg.* **2**:403.

Belden, E., and Hitchen, R. (1962). Prepublished copies. Calif. Dept. Mental Hygiene, Sacramento, Calif.

Belden, E., and Hitchen, R. (1963). *Am. J. Psychiat.* **119**:985.

Bellak, L., and Chassan, J. B. (1964). *J. Nervous Mental Disease* **139**:20.

Belsanti, R. (1952). *Acta Neurol.* (Naples) **7**:340.

Belsanti, R. (1955). *Acta Neurol.* (Naples) **10**:460.

Benedetti, G. (1951). *Z. Psychotherapie Med. Psychol.* **1**:176.

Bender, L., Goldschmidt, L., and Sankar, D. V. S. (1962). *In* "Recent Advances in Biological Psychiatry" (J. Wortis, ed.), Vol. 4, p. 170. Plenum Press, New York.

Bender, L., Faretra, G., and Cobrinik, L. (1963). *In* "Recent Advances in Biological Psychiatry" (J. Wortis, ed.), Vol. 5, p. 84. Plenum Press, New York.

Bergen, J. R., and Beisaw, N. E. (1956). *Am. Physiol. Soc.* **15**:15.

Bergen, J. R., and Pincus, G. G. (1960). *Federation Proc.* **19**:20.

Bergen, J. R., Krus, D. M., and Pincus, G. G. (1960). *Proc. Soc. Exptl. Biol. Med.* **105**:254.

Berlin, L., Guthrie, T., Weider, A., Goodell, H., and Wolff, H. G. (1955). *J. Nervous Mental Disease* **122**:487.

Bertino, J. R., Klee, G. D., and Weintraub, W. (1959). *J. Mental Sci.* **105**:1095.

Bertino, J. R., Klee, G. D., Collier, D., and Weintraub, W. (1960). *J. Clin. Exptl. Psychopathol. & Quart. Rev. Psychiat. Neurol.* **21**:293.

Blewett, D. B., and Chwelos, N. (1959). Handbook for the Therapeutic Use of LSD-25. Individual and Group Procedures. Mimeographed.

Boardman, W. K., Goldstone, S., and Lhamon, W. T. (1957). *A.M.A. Arch. Neurol. Psychiat.* **78**:321.

Bolton, W. B. (1961). *Can. J. Occupational Therapy* **281**:55.

Boyd, E. S., Rothlin, E., Bonner, J. F., Slater, I. H., and Hodge, H. C. (1955). *J. Nervous Mental Disease* **122**:470.

Bradley, P. B., and Elkes, J. (1953). *J. Physiol.* (*London*) **120**:13P.

Bradley, P. B., and Elkes, J. (1957). *Brain* **80**:77.

Bradley, P. B., and Hance, A. J. (1956a). *J. Physiol.* (*London*) **132**:50.

Bradley, P. B., and Hance, A. J. (1956b). *Electroencephalog. Clin. Neurophysiol.* **8**:699.

Bradley, P. B., and Hance, A. J. (1957). *Electroencephalog. Clin. Neurophysiol.* **9**:191.

Brengelmann, J. C., Laverty, S. G., and Lewis, D. (1958a). *J. Mental Sci.* **104**:144.

Brengelmann, J. C., Care, C. M., and Sandler, M. (1958b). *J. Mental Sci.* **104**:1237.

Brodie, B. B. (1957). *Neuropharmacol. Trans. 3rd Conf.* p. 323. Josiah Macy, Jr. Found., New York.

Brodie, B. B., and Costa, E. (1962). *Psychopharmacol. Serv. Center Bull.* **2**:1.

Brodie, B. B., and Shore, P. A. (1957). *Hormones, Brain Function, Behavior, Proc. Conf. Neuroendocrinol., Harriman, N.Y. 1956* p. 161. Academic Press, New York.

Brodie, B. B., Pletscher, A., and Shore, P. A. (1955). *Science* **122**:968.

Brodie, B. B., Pletscher, A., and Shore, P. A. (1956a). *J. Pharmacol. Exptl. Therap.* **116**:9.

Brodie, B. A., Shore, P. A., and Pletscher, A. (1956b). *Science* **123**:992.

Brown, B. B., Feldman, R. G., and Braun, D. L. (1955). *Federation Proc.* **14**:322.

Brown, B. B., Braun, D. L., and Feldman, R. G. (1956). *J. Pharmacol. Exptl. Therap.* **118**:153.

Brune, G. G., and Pscheidt, G. R. (1961). *Federation Proc.* **20**:889.

Bunag, R. D., and Walaszek, E. J. (1962). *Arch. Intern. Pharmacodyn.* **135**:142.

Burton, R. M. (1957). *Ann. N. Y. Acad. Sci.* **66**:695.

Busch, A. K., and Johnson, C. (1950). *Diseases Nervous System* **11**:241.

Calder, J. (1962). "Apparent Results of Referrals of Alcoholics for L.S.D. Therapy." Bureau on Alcoholism, Regina.

Cameron, K. (1963). *In* "Hallucinogenic Drugs and Their Psychotherapeutic Use" (R. Crocket, R. A. Sandison, and A. Walk, eds.), p. 107. Lewis, London.

Cerletti, A. (1963). *In* "Hallucinogenic Drugs and Their Psychotherapeutic Use" (R. Crocket, R. A. Sandison, and A. Walk, eds.), p. 1. Lewis, London.

Cerletti, A., and Doepfner, W. (1958). *J. Pharmacol. Exptl. Therap.* **122**:124.

Chandler, A. L., and Hartman, M. A. (1960). *Arch. Gen. Psychiat.* **2**:286.

Chassan, J. B. (1961). *Behavioral Sci.* **6**:42.

Chassan, J. B. (1963). *Psychopharmacologia* **4**:78.

Chassan, J. B. (1964). *2nd Ann. Meeting Am. Coll. Neuropsychopharmacol.*

Cheek, F. E. (1963). *Arch. Gen. Psychiat.* **9**:566.

Cherkas, M. S. (1963). *Mind* **1**:113.

Cholden, L. S., Kurland, A., and Savage, C. (1955). *J. Nervous Mental Disease* **122**:211.

Chwelos, N., Blewett, D., Hoffer, A., and Smith, C. (1958). "Use of d-Lysergic Acid Diethylamide in the Treatment of Chronic Alcoholism." NAAAP Meeting, Washington, D.C.

Chwelos, N., Blewett, D. B., Smith, C. M., and Hoffer, A. (1959). *Quart. J. Studies Alc.* **20**:577.

Clark, L. D. (1956). *J. Nervous Mental Disease* **123**:557.

Clark, L. D., and Clark, L. S. (1956). *J. Nervous Mental Disease* **123**:561.

Clark, L. D., Fox, R. P., Benington, F., Morin, R. (1954). *Federation Proc.* **13**:27.

Cline, H. S., and Freeman, H. (1956). *Psychiat. Quart.* **30**:676.

Cohen, S. (1959). *J. Wadsworth Gen. Hosp.* **3**:79.

Cohen, S. (1960a). *Intern. Rec. Med.* **173**:380.

Cohen, S. (1960b). *J. Nervous Mental Disease* **130**:30.

Cohen, S. (1963). *Mind* **1**:228.

Cohen, S. (1964a). *Am. J. Psychiat.* **120**:1024.

Cohen, S. (1964b). *Mind* **2**:217.

Cohen, S., and Ditman, K. S. (1962). *J. Am. Med. Assoc.* **181**:161.

Cohen, S., and Ditman, K. S. (1963). *Arch. Gen. Psychiat.* **8**:475.

Cohen, S., and Edwards, A. E. (1964). *In* "Recent Advances in Biological Psychiatry" (J. Wortis, ed.), Vol. 6, p. 139. Plenum Press, New York.

Cohen, S., and Eisner, B. (1959). *A.M.A. Arch. Neurol. Psychiat.* **81**:615.

Cohen, S., Fichman, L., Eisner, B., and Grover, B. (1958). *Am. J. Psychiat.* **115**:30.

Cole, J. O., and Katz, M. M. (1964). *J. Am. Med. Assoc.* **187**:758.

Condrau, G. (1949). *Clin. Acta Psychiat. Neurol. Neurol.* **24**:9.

Cook, W. B., and Kieland, W. E. (1962). *J. Org. Chem.* **27**:1061.

Cooper, H. A. (1955). "Hallucinogenic Drugs." Lancet, London.

Costa, E., and Zetler, G. (1958). *Proc. Soc. Exptl. Biol. Med.* **98**:249.

Costa, E., Gessa, G. L., Hirsch, C., Kuntzman, R., and Brodie, B. B. (1962). *Ann. N.Y. Acad. Sci.* **96**:118.

de Giacomo, U. (1951). *Acta. Neurol.* (*Milano*) **6**:5.

Delay, J., and Pichot, P. (1951). *Compt. Rend. Soc. Biol.* **145**:1609.

Delay, J., Pichot, P., Lemperiere, T. Nicolas-Charles, P., and Quetin, A. M. (1959). *Ann. Med.-Psychol.* **117**:899.

De Maar, E. W. J., Williams, H. L., Miller, A. I., and Pfeiffer, C. C. (1960). *Clin. Pharmacol. Therap.* **1**:23.

Denson, R. (1962). *Diseases Nervous System* **23**:167.

Deshon, H. J., Rinkel, M., and Solomon, H. C. (1952). *Psychiat. Quart.* **26**:33.

Dimascio, A., Rinkell, M., and Leiberman, J. (1961). *Proc. 3rd Congr. Psychiat., 1961, Montreal,* Vol. 2, p. 933. Montreal.

Ditman, K. S., and Whittlesey, R. B. (1959). *A.M.A. Arch. Gen. Psychiat.* **1**:47.

Ditman, K. S., Hayman, M., and Whittlesey, J. R. B. (1962). *J. Nervous Mental Disease* **134**:346.

Dusen, W. V. (1961). *Psychologia* **4**:11.

Edwards, A. E., and Cohen, S. (1961). *Psychopharmacologia* **2**:297.

Eisner, B., and Cohen, S. (1958). *J. Nervous Mental Disease* **127**:528.

Elder, J. T., Gogerty, J. H., and Dille, J. M. (1957). *Federation Proc.* **16**:293.

Elkes, J. (1957). *Neuropharmacol., Trans. 3rd Conf.* p. 205. Josiah Macy, Jr. Found., New York.

Ellis, H. (1897). *Smithsonian Inst., Ann. Rept.* p. 537.

Ellis, H. (1898). *Contemp. Rev.* **73**:130.

Ellis, H. (1902). *Popular Sci. Monthly* **61**:52.

Erspamer, V. (1954). *Pharmacol. Rev.* **6**:425.

Erspamer, V. (1961). In "Progress in Drug Research" (E. Jucker, ed.), p. 151. Wiley (Interscience), New York.

Evarts, E. V. (1957). *Ann. N.Y. Acad. Med.* **66**:479.

Evarts, E. V. (1958). In "Chemical Concepts of Psychosis" (M. Rinkel and H. C. B. Denber, eds.), p. 41. McDowell, Obolensky, New York.

Evarts, E. V., Landau, W., Freygang, E., and Marshall, W. H. (1955). *Am. J. Physiol.* **182**:594.

Fabing, H. D. (1955a). *Psychiat. Res. Rept.* **1**:140.

Fabing, H. D. (1955b). *Science* **121**:208.

Fabing, H. D. (1955c). *Neurology* **5**:603.

Fabing, H. D. (1956). *Intern. Rec. Med.* **169**:177.

Feld, M., Goodman, J. R., and Guido, J. A. (1958). *J. Nervous Mental Disease* **126**:176.

Fischer, R. (1954). *J. Mental Sci.* **100**:623.

Fischer, R., Georgi, F., and Weber, R. (1951). *Schweiz. Med. Wochschr.* **81**:817.

Fischer, R. A. (1963). Personal communication to L. Goldstein as told to us in Princeton.

Fogel, S., and Hoffer, A. (1962a). *J. Clin. Exptl. Psychopathol. & Quart. Rev. Psychiat. Neurol.* **23**:11.

Fogel, S., and Hoffer, A. (1962b). *J. Clin. Exptl. Psychopathol. & Quart. Rev. Psychiat. Neurol.* **23**:24.

Fontana, A. E. (1961). *Acta. Neuropsiquiat. Arg.* **7**:94.

Forrer, G. R., and Goldner, R. D. (1951). *Arch. Neurol. Psychiat.* **65**:581.

Frederking, W. (1953–1954). *Psyche (Stuttgart)* **7**:342.

Frederking, W. (1955). *J. Nervous Mental Disease* **121**:262.

Freedman, A. M., Ebin, E. V., and Wilson, E. A. (1962). *Arch. Gen. Psychiat.* **6**:203.

Freedman, D. X. (1963). *Am. J. Psychiat.* **119**:843.

Freedman, D. X., and Giarman, N. J. (1962). *Ann. N.Y. Acad. Sci.* **96**:98.

Freter, K., Axelrod, J., and Witkop, B. (1957). *J. Am. Chem. Soc.* **79**:3111.

Fried, G. H., and Antopol, W. (1956). *Anat. Record* **125**:610.
Fried, G. H., and Antopol, W. (1957). *J. Appl. Physiol.* **11**:25.
Gaddum, J. H. (1953). *J. Physiol. (London)* **121**:15P.
Ganong, W. F., Goldfeen, A., Halevy, A., Davidson, J. M., and Boryczka, A. (1961). *Acta Endocrinol.* **37**:583.
Gastaut, H., Ferrer, S., Castells, C., Leserre, N., and Lushnat, K. (1953). *Confinia Neurol.* **13**:102.
Geiger, R. S. (1957). *Federation Proc.* **16**:44.
Geiger, R. S. (1960). *J. Neuropsychiat.* **1**:185.
Genest, K. (1964). *Proc. 13th Ann. Conf. Supt. Lab. Food Drug Directorate, Ottawa, 1964.*
Geronimus, L. H., Abramson, H. A., and Ingraham, L. J. (1956). *J. Psychol.* **42**:157.
Giberti, F., and Gregoretti, L. (1955). *Sistema Nervoso* **7**:301.
Ginzel, K. H., and Mayer-Gross, W. (1956). *Nature* **178**:210.
Goldberger, M. (1961). *Acta Anat.* **46**:185.
Goldenberg, H., and Goldenberg, V. (1956). *J. Hillside Hosp.* **5**:246.
Goldstein, L., Murphie, H. B., and Pfeiffer, C. C. (1963). *Ann. N.Y. Acad. Sci.* **107**:1045.
Gorodetzky, G. W., and Isbell, H. (1964). *Psychopharmacologia* **6**:229.
Graham, J. D. P., and Khalidi, A. I. (1954a). *J. Fac. Med. Baghdad, Iraq* **18**:1.
Graham, J. D. P., and Khalidi, A. I. (1954b). *J. Fac. Med. Baghdad, Iraq* **18**:35.
Greig, M. E., and Gibbons, A. J. (1959). *Am. J. Physiol.* **196**:803.
Grinker, R. R. (1963). *Arch. Gen. Psychiat.* **8**:425.
Grinker, R. R. (1964). *J. Am. Med. Assoc.* **187**:768.
Grof, S. (1960). *Activitas Nervosa Super.* **2**:426.
Grof, S., Vojtechovsky, M., Vitek, V., and Prankova, S. (1963). *J. Neuropsychiat.* **5**:33.
Guttmann, E., and Maclay, W. S. (1936). *J. Neurol. Psychopathol.* **16**:193.
Haley, T. J. (1957). *J. Am. Pharm. Assoc.* **46**:428.
Haley, T. J., and Rutscamann, J. (1957). *Experientia* **13**:199.
Harman, W. W. (1962). *Main Currents Mod. Thought* **18**:75.
Harman, W. W. (1963a). *Main Currents Mod. Thought* **20**:5.
Harman, W. W. (1963b). *J. Humanist. Psychol.* **3**:93.
Harris, G. W. (1955). *In* "CIBA Foundation Colloquia Endocrinology" (G. E. W. Wolstenholme, ed.), Vol. 4, p. 106. McGraw-Hill (Blakiston), New York.
Harris, G. W., Jacobsohn, D., and Kablson, G. (1952). *In* "CIBA Foundation Colloquia Endocrinology" (G. E. W. Wolstenholme, ed.), p. 186. McGraw-Hill (Blakiston), New York.
Hartman, A. M., and Hollister, L. E. (1963). *Psychopharmacologia* **4**:441.
Hartwich, C. (1911). "Die Menschlichen Genusermittel." Leipzig.
Harwood, P. D. (1963). *Science* **139**:684.
Heacock, R. A., and Mahon, M. (1964). *Can. J. Bicohem.* **42**:813.
Heacock, R. A., Mahon, M. E., and Hoffer, A. (1964). *Am. J. Psychiat.* **121**:172.
Heard, G. (1964). *Can. Dimensions* **1**:11.
Heath, R. G. (1954). "Studies in Schizophrenia." Harvard Univ. Press, Cambridge, Massachusetts.
Heath, R. G. (1961). *In* "Recent Advances in Biological Psychiatry" (J. Wortis, ed.), p. 164. Grune & Stratton, New York.
Heath, R. G., and Leach, B. E. (1956). "Multidisciplinary Research in Schizophrenia Changing Concepts of Psychoanalytic Medicine." Grune & Stratton, New York.
Himwich, W. A., and Costa, E. (1960). *Federation Proc.* **19**:838.

Hoagland, H., Rinkel, M., and Hyde, R. W. (1955). *A.M.A. Arch. Neurol. Psychiat.* 73:100.

Hoch, P. H. (1953). *Res. Publ., Assoc. Res. Nervous Mental Disease* 32:287.

Hoch, P. H. (1956). *In* "Lysergic Acid Diethylamide and Mescaline in Experimental Psychiatry" (L. Cholden, ed.), p. 8. Grune & Stratton, New York.

Hoch, P. H. (1957). *J. Nervous Mental Disease* 125:442.

Hoch, P. H., and Polatin, P. (1949). *Psychiat. Quart.* 23:248.

Hoch, P. H., Cattell, J. P., and Pennes, H. H. (1952). *Am. J. Psychiat.* 108:585.

Hoch, P. H., Pennes, H. H., and Cattell, J. P. (1953). *Res. Publ. Assoc. Res. Nervous Mental Disease* 32:287.

Hoch, P. H., Pennes, H. H., and Cattell, J. P. (1958a). *In* "Chemical Concepts of Psychosis" (M. Rinkel and H. C. B. Denber, eds.), p. 141. McDowell, Obolensky, New York.

Hoff, H., and Arnold, O. H. (1954). *Wien. Klin. Wochschr.* 66:345.

Hoffer, A. (1956). *In* "Lysergic Acid Diethylamide and Mescaline in Experimental Psychiatry" (L. Cholden, ed.), p. 77. Grune & Stratton, New York.

Hoffer, A. (1958). Personal Communication.

Hoffer, A. (1959). *In* "Molecules and Mental Health" (F. A. Gibbs, ed.), p. 44. Lippincott, Philadelphia, Pennsylvania.

Hoffer, A. (1960). *In* "The Use of L.S.D. in Psychotherapy" (H. A. Abramson, ed.). Josiah Macy, Jr. Found., New York.

Hoffer, A. (1962). "Niacin Therapy in Psychiatry." Thomas, Springfield, Illinois.

Hoffer, A. (1963). *Am. J. Psychiat.* 120:171.

Hoffer, A., and Mahon, M. (1961). *J. Neuropsychiat.* 2:331.

Hoffer, A., and Osmond, H. (1952). Paper delivered to Dementia Praecox Committee, Scottich Rites Masons, New York.

Hoffer, A., and Osmond, H. (1960). *The Chemical Bases of Clinical Psychiatry.* Thomas, Springfield, Illinois.

Hoffer, A., and Osmond, H. (1961a). *J. Neuropsychiat.* 2:221.

Hoffer, A., and Osmond, H. (1961b). *J. Neuropsychiat.* 2:306.

Hoffer, A., and Osmond, H. (1961c). *J. Neuropsychiat.* 2:363.

Hoffer, A., and Callbeck, M. J. (1960). *J. Mental Sci.* 106:138.

Hoffer, A., and Osmond, H. (1962a). *Can. Med. Assoc. J.* 87:641.

Hoffer, A., and Osmond, H. (1962b). *Diseases Nervous System* 23:204.

Hoffer, A., and Osmond, H. (1963a). *Acta Psychiat. Scand.* 39:335.

Hoffer, A., and Osmond, H. (1963b). *J. Neuropsychiat.* 5:97.

Hoffer, A., and Osmond, H. (1966). *Intern. J. Neuropsychiat.* 2:1.

Hoffer, A., Osmond, H., and Smythies, J. (1954). *J. Mental Sci.* 100:29.

Hoffer, A., Osmond, H., Callbeck, M. J., and Kahan, I. (1957). *J. Clin. Exptl. Psychopathol. & Quart. Rev. Psychiat. Neurol.* 18:131.

Hofmann, A. (1960). *Abstr. Papers, I.U.P.A.C. Symp., Australia, 1960.*

Hofmann, A. (1961a). *Indian Pract.* 14:195.

Hofmann, A. (1961b). *Planta Med.* 9:354.

Hofmann, A., and Cerletti, A. (1961). *Deut. Med. Wochsch.* 18:885.

Hofmann, A., and Tscherter, H. (1960). *Experientia* 16:414.

Hogben, L. (1957). "Statistical Theory: The Relationship of Probability, Credibility and Error." Allen & Unwin, London.

Hollister, L. E. (1961). *Arch. Intern. Pharmacodyn.* 130:42.

Hollister, L. E. (1962). *Ann. N. Y. Acad. Sci.* 96:80.

Hubbard, A. M. (1957). Personal communication.

Huxley, A. (1962). "Island." Clarke, Irwin, Toronto.

Irvine, D. (1961). *J. Neuropsychiat.* **2**:292.

Isbell, H. (1956). *Federation Proc.* **15**:442.

Isbell, H. (1957). Personal communication to H. Osmond.

Isbell, H. (1959). *Psychopharmacologia* **1**:29.

Isbell, H., Belleville, R. E., Fraser, H. F., Wikler, A., and Logan, C. R. (1956). *A.M.A. Arch. Neurol. Psychiat.* **76**:468.

Isbell, H., and Logan, C. R. (1957). *A.M.A. Arch. Neurol. Psychiat.* **77**:350.

Isbell, H., Wolback, A. B., Wikler, A., and Miner, E. J. (1961). *Psychopharmacologia* **2**:147.

Izumi, K. (1957). *Mental Hosp.* **8**:31.

Jackson, D. D. (1962). *J. Nervous Mental Disease* **135**:435.

James, W. (1902). "Varieties of Religious Experience." Longmans, Green, New York.

Janiger, O. (1959). *Calif. Clinician* **55**:251.

Jarman, R. C. (1961). The Most Astounding Experience of My Life. A sermon published in Chapel Bells South Gate, California.

Jarvik, M. E., Abramson, H. A., and Hirsch, M. W. (1955a). *J. Psychol.* **39**:373.

Jarvik, M. E., Abramson, H. A., Hirsch, M. W., and Ewald, A. T. (1955b). *J. Psychol.* **39**:465.

Jensen, S. E. (1961). *Proc. 3rd World Congr. Psychiat., Montreal, 1961* Vol. 1, p. 428. Univ. Montreal, Montreal.

Jensen, S. E. (1962). *Quart. J. Studies Alc.* **23**:315.

Kast, E. C., and Collins, V. J. (1964). *J. Intern. Anesthet. Res. Soc.* **43**:285.

Katzenelbogen, S., and Fang, Ai Ding (1953). *Diseases Nervous System* **14**:85.

Kelm, H. (1962a). *Perceptual Motor Skills* **15**:216.

Kelm, H. (1962b). *J. Nervous Mental Disease* **135**:338.

Kelm, H., Jensen, S. E., and Ramsay, R. W. (1963). *J. Nervous Mental Disease* **137**:557.

Kelm, H., Grunberg, F., and Hall, R. W. (1965a). *Diseases Nervous System* **26**:790.

Kelm, H., Grunberg, F., and Hall, R. W. (1965b). *Intern. J. Neuropsychiat.* **1**:307.

Kenna, J. C., and Sedman, G. (1964). *Psychopharmacologia* **5**:280.

Kinross-Wright, V. J. (1959). *Proc. 1st Intern. Congr., Neuropsychopharm., Amsterdam*, p. 453.

Klee, G. D. (1963). *Arch. Gen. Psychiat.* **8**:461.

Klee, G. D., Bertino, J., Weintraub, W., and Callaway, E. (1961). *J. Nervous Mental Disease* **132**:404.

Kluver, H. (1928). "Mescal. The Divine Plant and Its Psychological Effects." Kegan Paul, Trench Trubner & Co. Ltd.

Krus, D. M., Wapner, S., Bergen, S., and Freeman, H. (1961). *Psychopharmacologia* **2**:177.

Krus, D. M., Wapner, S., Freeman, H., and Casey, T. M. (1963). *Arch. Gen. Psychiat.* **8**:557.

Landis, C. (1904). *In* "Varieties of Psychopathological Experience" (F. A. Mettler, ed.). Holt, New York.

Lebovits, B. Z., Visotsky, H. M., and Ostfeld, A. M. (1960). *Arch. Gen. Psychiat.* **2**:390.

Leon, N. (1888). *Morelia* **14**:113.

Leuner, H. (1963). *In* "Hallucinogenic Drugs and Their Psychotherapeutic Use" (R. Crocket, R. A. Sandison, and A. Walk, eds.), p. 67. Lewis, London.

Levine, A., Abramson, H. A., Kaufman, M. R., and Markham, S. (1955). *J. Psychol.* **40**:385.

Lewin, L. (1931). "Phantastica, Narcotic and Stimulating Drugs." Routledge & Kegan Paul, London.

Lewis, J. L., McIlwain, H. (1954). *Biochem. J.* **57**:680.

Liddell, D. S., and Weil-Malherbe, H. (1953). *J. Neurol., Neurosurg., Psychiat.* [N.S.] **16**:7.

Liebert, R. S., Wapner, S., and Werner, H. (1957). *A.M.A. Arch. Neurol. Psychiat.* **77**:193.

Linton, H. B., and Langs, R. J. (1962a). *Arch. Gen. Psychiat.* **6**:369.

Linton, H. B., and Langs, R. J. (1962b). *Arch. Gen. Psychiat.* **6**:352.

Linton, H. B., Langs, R. J., and Paul, I. H. (1964). *J. Nervous Mental Disease* **138**:409.

Locke, J. (1963). Star. Weekly Magazine, Toronto.

Lucas, O. N. (1964). Ph.D. Thesis, University of Saskatchewan, Saskatoon, Saskatchewan.

Lucas, O. N., and Jacques, L. B. (1964). *Can. J. Physiol. Pharmacol.* **42**:803.

MacDonald, J. M., and Galvin, J. A. V. (1956). *Am. J. Psychiat.* **112**:970.

McGeer, P. L., Wada, J. A., and McGeer, E. G. (1963). *Recent Advan. Biol. Psychiat.* **5**:228.

McGlothlin, W. H. (1962). Report No. P-2575. Rand Corporation, Los Angeles, California.

McGlothlin, W. H. (1964). Report No. P-2937. Rand Corporation, Los Angeles, California.

McGlothlin, W. H., Cohen, S., and McGlothlin, M. S. (1964). *J. Nervous Mental Disease* **139**:266.

Machover, K., and Liebert, R. (1960). *Arch. Gen. Psychiat.* **3**:139.

Maclean, J. R., MacDonald, D. C., Byrne, V. P., and Hubbard, A. M. (1961). *Quart. J. Studies Alc.* **22**:34.

MANAS, eds. (1963). "Synanon." A Manas Pamphlet.

Mandell, A. J. (1963). *Recent Advan. Biol. Psychiat.* **5**:237.

Margolis, L. H. (1964). *2nd Ann. Meeting, Washington, D.C.*

Marrazzi, A. S. (1953). *Science* **118**:367.

Marrazzi, A. (1957a). *Ann. N.Y. Acad. Sci.* **66**:496.

Marrazzi, A. S. (1957b). *In* "American College Neuropsychopharmacology. Brain Mechanisms and Drug Action" (W. S. Fields, ed.), p. 45. Thomas, Springfield, Illinois.

Marrazzi, A. S. (1960). *Recent Adv. Biol. Psychiat.* **2**:333.

Marrazzi, A. S. (1961). *Ann. N.Y. Acad. Sci.* **92**:990.

Marrazzi, A. S. (1962). *Ann. N.Y. Acad. Sci.* **96**:211.

Marrazzi, A. S., and Hart, E. R. (1955a). *Science* **121**:365.

Marrazzi, A. S., and Hart, E. R. (1955b). *J. Nervous Mental Disease* **122**:453.

Marrazzi, A. S., and Hart, E. R. (1955c). *Electroencephalog. Clin. Neurophysiol.* **7**:146.

Marrazzi, A. S., Hart, E. R., and Gilfoil, T. M. (1961). *In* "Recent Advances in Biological Psychiatry" (J. Wortis, ed.), p. 164. Grune & Stratton, New York.

Martens, S., Vallbo, S., and Melander, B. (1959a). *Acta Psychiat. Neurol. Scand.* **34**:349.

Martens, S., Vallbo, S., and Melander, B. (1959b). *In* "Biological Psychiatry" (J. H. Masserman, ed.), p. 273. Grune & Stratton, New York.

Martens, S., Vallbo, S., Andersen, K., and Melander, B. (1959c). *Acta Psychiat. Neurol. Scand.* 34:361.

Martin, J. (1963). *In* "Hallucinogenic Drugs and Their Psychotherapeutic Use" (R. Crocket, R. A. Sandison, and A. Walk, eds.), p. 112. Lewis, London.

Maslow, A. H. (1959). *J. Genet. Psychol.* 94:43.

Maslow, A. H. (1962).

Mattok, G., Wilson, D., and Hoffer, A. (1965). Personal observations.

Matussek, N., and Halbach, A. (1964). *Psychopharmacologia* 15:158.

Mayer-Gross, W. (1951). *Brit. Med. J.* II:317.

Mayer-Gross, W., McAdam, W., and Walker, J. W. (1951). *Nature* 168:827.

Mayer-Gross, W., McAdam, W., and Walker, J. (1952). *Nervenarzt.* 23:30.

Mayer-Gross, W., McAdam, W., and Walker, J. W. (1953). *J. Mental Sci.* 99:804.

Melander, B. (1957). Personal communication.

Melander, B., and Martens, S. (1958). *Diseases Nervous System* 19:478.

Melander, B., and Martens, S. (1959). *Acta Psychiat. Neurol. Scand.* 34:344.

Miller, A. I., Williams, H. L., and Murphree, H. B. (1957). *Federation Proc.* 16:169.

Miura, T., Tsujiyama, Y., Makita, K., Nakazwa, T., Sato, K., and Nakahara, A. (1957). *In* "Psychotropic Drugs" (S. Garattini and V. Ghetti, eds.), p. 478. Elsevier, Amsterdam.

Mogar, R., and Savage, C. (1964). *Psychotherapy* 1:154.

Mogar, R., Fadiman, J., and Savage, C. (1963). Personal communications.

Monroe, R. R., and Heath, R. G. (1961). *J. Neuropsychiat.* 3:75.

Monroe, R. R., Heath, R. G., Mickle, W. A., and Llewellyn, R. C. (1957). *Electroencephalog. Clin. Neurophysiol.* 9:623.

Murphree, H. B. (1962). *Clin. Pharmacol. Therap.* 3:314.

Murphree, H. B., Jenney, E. H., and Pfeiffer, C. C. (1960). *Pharmacologist* 2:64.

Nandy, K., and Bourne, G. H. (1964). *J. Neurol., Neurosurg., Psychiat.* [N.S.] 27:259.

Nichols, F. (1963). Personal communication.

Nunes, E. P. (1955). *J. Brasil. Psiquiat.* 4:407.

Oliva, L. (1854). *Lecciones, Farmacol.* 2:392.

O'Reilly, P. O., and Funk, A. (1964). *Can. Psychiat. Assoc. J.* 9:258.

O'Reilly, P. O., and Reich, G. (1962). *Diseases Nervous System* 23:331.

Osmond, H. (1953). *Saskatchewan Psychiat. Serv. J.* 1:168.

Osmond, H. (1955). *J. Mental Sci.* 101:526.

Osmond, H. (1956). *Neuropharmacol., Trans. 2nd Conf.* p. 183. Josiah Macy, Jr. Found., New York.

Osmond, H. (1957a). *Ann. N.Y. Acad. Sci.* 66:418.

Osmond, H. (1957b). *Mental Hosp.* 8:23.

Osmond, H., and El-Meleghi, M. (1964). Personal communication.

Osmond, M., and Hoffer, A. (1962). *Lancet* I:316.

Osmond, H., and Smythies, J. (1952). *J.M.S.* 98:309.

Ostfeld, A. M. (1901). *Federation Proc.* 20:876.

Ostfeld, A. M., Visotsky, H. M., and Lebovits, B. Z. (1958). *Clin. Res.* 6:416.

Page, I. H. (1958). *Physiol. Rev.* 38:277.

Page, J. A., and Hoffer, A. (1964). *Diseases Nervous System* 25:558.

Peerman, D. (1962). "The Christian Century." The Christian Century Foundation. Chicago.

Pennes, H. H. (1954). *J. Nervous Mental Disease* 119:95.

Perezamador, M. C., Jimenez, F. G., Herran, J., and Flores, S. E. (1964). *Tetrahedron* **20**:2999.

Pfeiffer, C. C., Murphree, H. B., Jenney, E. H., Robertson, M. G., Randall, A. H., and Bryan, L. (1959). *Neurology* **9**:249.

Pfeiffer, C. C., Jenney, E. H., Murphree, H. B., and Goldstein, L. (1962). *Pharmacologist* **4**:166B.

Polanyi, M. (1956). *Lancet* **I**:921.

Poloni, A. (1955). *Cervello* **31**:271 and 355.

Poloni, A., and Maffezzoni, G. (1952). *Sistema Nervoso* **4**:578.

Purpura, D. P. (1956a). *Arch. Neurol. Psychiat.* **75**:122.

Purpura, D. P. (1956b). *Arch. Neurol. Psychiat.* **75**:132.

Purpura, P. (1957a). *Ann. N.Y. Acad. Sci.* **66**:515.

Purpura, D. P. (1957b). *Ann. N.Y. Acad. Sci.* **66**:417.

Purpura, D. P., Pool, J. L., Ransohoff, J., Frumin, M. J., and Housepian, E. M. (1957). *Electroencephalog. Clin. Neurophysiol.* **9**:453.

Rinaldi, F., and Himwich, H. E. (1955a). *Science* **122**:198.

Rinaldi, F., and Himwich, H. E. (1955b). *Diseases Nervous System* **16**:133.

Rinaldi, F., and Himwich, H. E. (1955c). *J. Nervous Mental Disease* **122**:424.

Rinkel, M. (1951). *J. Clin. Exptl. Psychopathol.* **12**:42.

Rinkel, M. (1956a). *Neuropharmacol., Trans. 2nd Conf.* p. 235. Josiah Macy, Jr. Found., New York.

Rinkel, M. (1956b). *In* "Lysergic Acid Diethylamide and Mescaline in Experimental Psychiatry" (L. Cholden, ed.), p. 13. Grune & Stratton, New York.

Rinkel, M., Deshon, H. J., Hyde, R. W., and Solomon, H. C. (1952). *Am. J. Psychiat.* **108**:572.

Rinkel, M., Hyde, R., Solomon, H. C., and Hoagland, H. (1955a). *Am. J. Psychiat.* **111**:881.

Rinkel, M., Hyde, R., and Solomon, H. C. (1955b). *Diseases Nervous System* **16**:229.

Rosenberg, D. E., Wolbach, A. B., Miner, E. J., and Isbell, H. (1963). *Psychopharmacologia* **5**:1.

Rostafinski, M. (1950). *Rocznik Psychiat.* **38**:109.

Rothlin, E. (1957a). *J. Pharm. Pharmacol.* **9**:569.

Rothlin, E. (1957b). *Ann. N.Y. Acad. Sci.* **66**:668.

Rothlin, E. (1957c). *In* "Psychotropic Drugs" (S. Garattini and V. Ghetti, eds.), p. 36. Elsevier, Amsterdam.

Rothlin, E., and Cerletti, A. (1956). *In* "Lysergic Acid Diethylamide and Mescaline in Experimental Psychiatry" (L. Cholden, ed.), p. 1. Grune & Stratton, New York.

Rudolph, G. G., and Olsen, N. W. (1957). *Federation Proc.* **16**:110.

Ruiz-Ogara, C., Marti-Tusquets, J. L., and Gonzales-Monclus, E. (1956). *Rev. Psiquiat. Psicol. Med.* **2**:566.

Sackler, A. M., Weltman, A. S., and Owens, H. (1963). *Nature* **198**:1119.

Safford, W. E. (1915). *J. Heredity* **6**:291.

Salmoiraghi, G. C., Sollero, L., and Page, I. H. (1956). *J. Pharmacol. Exptl. Therap.* **117**:166.

Salmoiraghi, G. C., McCubbin, J. W., and Page, I. H. (1957). *J. Pharmacol. Exptl. Therap.* **119**:240.

Sandison, R. A. (1954). *J. Mental Sci.* **100**:508.

Sandison, R. A. (1955). *Nursing Mirror* **100**:1529.

Sandison, R. A. (1956). *In* "Lysergic Acid Diethylamide and Mescaline in Experimental Psychiatry" (L. Cholden, ed.), p. 27. Grune & Stratton, New York.

Sandison, R. A. (1963). *In* "Hallucinogenic Drugs and Their Psychotherapeutic Use" (R. Crocket, R. A. Sandison, and A. Walk, eds.), p. 33. Lewis, London.

Sandison, R. A., and Whitelaw, J. D. A. (1957). *J. Mental Sci.* **103**:332.

Sandison, R. A., Spencer, A. M., and Whitelaw, J. D. A. (1954). *J. Mental Sci.* **100**:491.

Sankar, D. V. S., and Bender, L. (1960). *Recent Adv. Biol. Psychiat.* **2**:363.

Sankar, D. V. S., Sankar, D. B., Phipps, E., and Gold, E. (1961). *Nature* **191**:499.

Sankar, D. V. S., Gold, E., and Sankar, D. B. (1962a). *Recent Advan. Biol. Psychiat.* **4**:247.

Sankar, D. V. S., Phipps, E., Gold, E., and Sankar, D. B. (1962b). *Science* **96**:93.

Sankar, D. V. S., Broer, H. H., Cates, N., and Sankar, D. B. (1964). *Trans. N.Y. Acad. Sci.* [2] **26**:369.

Santesson, C. G. (1937). *Ethnolog. Studies* **4**:1.

Sargant, W. (1957). "Battle for the Mind: A Psychology of Conversion and Brain Washing." Doubleday, New York.

Sauri, J. J., and De Onorato, A. C. (1955). *Acta Neuropsiquiat. Arg.* **1**:469.

Savage, C. (1952). *Am. J. Psychiat.* **108**:896.

Savage, C. (1957). *J. Nervous Mental Disease* **125**:434.

Savage, C. (1962a). *J. Nervous Mental Disease* **135**:425.

Savage, C. (1962b). *J. Nervous Mental Disease* **135**:429.

Savage, C., and Cholden, L. (1956). *J. Clin. Exptl. Psychopathol. & Quart. Rev. Psychiat. Neurol.* **17**:405.

Savage, C., Harman, W. W., Fadiman, J., and Savage, E. (1963). *Ann. Meeting Am. Psychiat. Assoc., St. Louis, 1963.*

Savage, C., Hughes, M. A., and Mogar, R. E. (1964). Personal communication.

Sawyer, C. H. (1955). *Am. J. Physiol.* **180**:37.

Schmiege, G. R. (1963). *J. Med. Soc. New Jersey* **60**:203.

Schultes, R. E. (1941). Botanical Museum of Harvard University, Cambridge, Massachusetts.

Schwarz, B. E., Bickford, R. G., and Rome, H. P. (1955). *Proc. Staff Meetings Mayo Clinic* **30**:407.

Sedman, G., and Kenna, J. C. (1965). *Brit. J. Psychiat.* **111**:96.

Selye, H., Tuchweber, B., and Caruso, P. L. (1964). *J. Pharmacol. Exptl. Therap.* **146**:252.

Sheldon, W. (1954). "Atlas of Men." Harper, New York.

Shellard, E. J. (1961). *Planta Med.* **9**:102, 141, and 146.

Shelton, J. (1963). *Mind* **1**:339.

Sherwood, J. N., Stolaroff, M. J., and Harman, W. W. (1962). *J. Neuropsychiat.* **3**:370.

Sherwood, S. L. (1956). *In* "Neuropharmacology," *Trans. 2nd Cent.* p. 85. Josiah Macy, Jr. Found., New York.

Silverstein, A. B., and Klee, G. D. (1958a). *A.M.A. Arch. Neurol. Psychiat.* **80**:477.

Silverstein, A. B., and Klee, G. D. (1958b). *J. Nervous Mental Disease* **127**:323.

Silverstein, A. B., and Klee, G. D. (1960). *J. Clin. Exptl. Psychopathol. & Quart. Rev. Psychiat. Neurol.* **21**:300.

Simpson, C. R., and West, E. (1952). *Florida Univ., Agr. Expt. Sta. (Gainesville), Circ.* **543**:1.

Slater, P. E., Morimoto, K., and Hyde, R. W. (1957). *J. Nervous Mental Disease* **125**:312.

Sloane, B., and Doust, J. W. L. (1954). *J. Mental Sci.* **100**:129.

Slotkin, J. S. (1956). "The Peyote Religion." Free Press, Glenco, Illinois.

Smith, C. M. (1958). *Quart. J. Studies Alc.* **19**:406.

Smith, C. M. (1959). *Quart. J. Studies Alc.* **20**:292.

Sokoloff, L., Perlin, S., Kornetsky, C., and Kety, S. S. (1957). *Ann. N.Y. Acad. Sci.* **66**:468.

Solms, H. (1956). *J. Clin. Exptl. Psychopathol. & Quart. Rev. Psychiat. Neurol.* **17**:429.

Spencer, A. M. (1963). *Brit. J. Psychiat.* **109**:37.

Sprince, H. (1961). *Clin. Chem.* 7:203.

Sprince, H. (1962). *Ann. N.Y. Acad. Sci.* **96**:399.

Sprince, H., Parker, C. M., Jameson, D., and Alexander, F. (1963). *J. Nervous Mental Disease* **137**:246.

Stefaniuk, B., and Osmond, H. (1952). Unpublished observations.

Stevenson, I. (1957). *J. Nervous Mental Disease* **125**:438.

Stoll, A. (1952). *Progr. Allergy* 3:388.

Stoll, A., and Hofmann, A. (1943). *Helv. Chim. Acta* **26**:944.

Stoll, A., and Hofmann, A. (1965). *Helv. Chim. Acta* **26**:944.

Stoll, W. A. (1947). *A.M.A. Arch. Neurol. Psychiat.* **60**:279.

Stoll, W. A. (1948). *Schweiz. Med. Wochschr.* **79**:110.

Stoll, W. A. (1949). *Schweiz. Arch. Neurol. Psychiat.* **64**:483.

Szatmari, A., Hoffer, A., and Schneider, R. (1955). *Am. J. Psychiat.* **111**:603.

Tabachnick, I. I., and Grelis, M. E. (1958). *Nature* **182**:935.

Taber, W. A., and Heacock, R. A. (1962). *Can. J. Microbiol.* **81**:137.

Taber, W. A., Heacock, R. A., and Mahon, M. E. (1963a). *Phytochemistry* 2:99.

Taber, W. A., Vining, L. C., and Heacock, R. A. (1963b). *Phytochemistry* 2:65.

Terrill, J. (1962). *J. Nervous Mental Disease* **135**:425.

Thompson, R. H. S., Tickner, A., and Webster, G. R. (1954). *Biochem. J.* **58**:19.

Thompson, R. H. S., Tickner, A., and Webster, G. R. (1955). *Brit. J. Pharmacol.* **10**:61.

Tobin, J. M., Brousseau, E. R., Lorenz, A. A., Hoffer, A., and Conner, W. R. (1966). In press.

Tonini, G. (1955). *Boll. Soc. Ital. Biol. Sper.* **31**:768.

Tonini, G., and Montanari, G. (1955). *Confinia Neurol.* **15**:225.

Tremere, A. W. (1963). Ergot Seminar, University of Saskatchewan College of Agriculture.

Trendelenburg, V. (1956). *In* "Histamine" (G. E. W. Wolstenholme and C. M. O'Connor, eds.), p. 278. Churchill, London.

Tyhurst, J. S. (1964a). *Quart. J. Studies Alc.* **25**:333.

Tyhurst, J. S. (1964b). *Report on LSD to Council, College Physicians and Surgeons.* British Columbia, Canada.

Unger, S. M. (1963a). *J. Study Interpersonal Processes* **26**:111.

Unger, S. M. (1963b). *Psychiatry* **26**:111.

Unger, S. M. (1964). *Conf. Methods Phil. Sci.,* New York.

Urbina, M. (1897). "Catalugo de Plantas Mexicanas (Fanerogamas)," p. 243.

Vining, L. C., and Taber, W. A. (1959). *Can. J. Microbiol.* **5**:441.

Wapner, S., and Krus, D. M. (1959). *Arch. Gen. Psychiat.* **1**:417.

Wapner, S., and Krus, D. M. (1960). *J. Neuropsychiat.* **2**:76.

Wasson, V. P., and Wasson, R. G. (1957). "Mushrooms Russia and History." Pantheon Books, New York.

Weckowicz, T. E. (1957). *Mental Hosp.* **81**:25.

Weckowicz, T. E. (1959). *Can. Psychiat. Assoc. J.* **4**:255.

Weckowicz, T. E. (1960). *Arch. Gen. Psychiat.* **2**:521.

Weckowicz, T. E., and Blewett, D. B. (1959). *J. Mental Sci.* **105**:909.

Weckowicz, T. E., and Hall, R. W. (1960). *J. Clin. Psychol.* **16**:272.

Weckowicz, T. E., and Sommer, R. (1960). *J. Mental Sci.* **106**:17.

Weckowicz, T. E., Sommer, R., and Hall, R. W. (1958). *J. Mental Sci.* **104**:1174.

Weintraub, W., Silverstein, A. B., and Klee, G. D. (1959). *J. Nervous Mental Disease* **128**:409.

Weintraub, W., Silverstein, A., and Klee, G. D. (1960). *Arch. Gen. Psychiat.* **3**:17.

Weir, Mitchell, S. (1896). *Brit. Med. J.* **II**:1625.

West, L. J., Pierce, C. M., and Thomas, W. D. (1963). *Science* **138**:1100.

Weyl, B. (1951). Diss. Freiburg. i. Br., Munchen.

Whitaker, L. H. (1964). *Med. J. Australia* **1**:5 and 36.

Wilder, J. (1962). *Proc. 3rd World Congr. Psychiat., Montreal, 1961* Vol. 1, p. 341.

Woolley, D. W. (1952). "A Study of AntiMetabolites." Wiley, New York.

Woolley, D. W. (1955). *Proc. Natl. Acad. Sci. U.S.* **41**:338.

Woolley, D. W. (1957). *Science* **125**:752.

Woolley, D. W. (1958a). *Res. Publ., Assoc. Res. Nervous Mental Disease* **33**:381.

Woolley, D. W. (1958b). *In* "Chemical Concepts of Psychosis" (M. Rinkel and H. C. B. Denber, eds.), p. 176. McDowell, Obolensky, New York.

Woolley, D. W., and Shaw, E. (1954a). *Proc. Natl. Acad. Sci. U.S.* **40**:228.

Woolley, D. W., and Shaw, E. (1954b). *Brit. Med. J.* **II**:122.

Woolley, D. W., and Shaw, E. N. (1957). *Ann. N.Y. Acad. Sci.* **66**:649.

Yamada, T., and Takumi, A. (1956). *Folia Psychiat. Neurol. Japon.* **10**:163.

Zender, K., and Cerletti, A. (1956). *Physiol. Pharmacol. Acta* **14**:264.

Zsigmond, E. K., Foldes, F. F., and Foldes, V. (1960). *Federation Proc.* **19**:266.

Zsigmond, E. K., Foldes, F. M., and Foldes, F. F. (1961a). *Pharmacologist* **3**:70.

Zsigmond, E. K., Foldes, F. F., and Foldes, V. M. (1961b). *J. Neurochem.* **8**:72.

Zsigmond, E. K., Foldes, F. F., and Foldes, V. M. (1961c). *Federation Proc.* **20**:393.

Chapter III

Adrenochrome and Some of Its Derivatives

Introduction

Adrenochrome, adrenolutin, and 5,6-dihydroxy-*N*-methylindole are derivatives of adrenaline which have not yet been isolated and crystallized from natural sources. In this, they resemble several other hallucinogens including LSD which is a synthetic derivative of lysergic acid. But in contrast to LSD, these adrenaline derivatives have a special relationship to pharmacology, medicine, and psychiatry because they could be formed *in vivo* and, in fact, the evidence that they are formed naturally is strong enough for most investigators in this field.

The presence in the human body of substances which are hallucinogenic when present in excessive concentration, is of vital importance because they play a part in many of the psychiatric conditions in man. For this reason, substances like adrenochrome and its derivatives, noradrenochrome, dopachrome and their derivatives, and the indoles from tryptophan, are inherently more important than hallucinogens such as LSD which are less likely to be formed in the mammalian organism.

In the 15 years which have followed its first crystallization in 1937, adrenochrome has been embroiled in 4 major controversies. Passions were so high at one time that some of the scientists involved have had their scientific careers permanently altered as a result of this embittered debate. For a while it was considered unwise to write the word "adrenochrome" into applications for research money and we know of attempts to dissuade reputable investigators from undertaking research with adrenochrome. Adrenochrome, at one time, became a dirty word.

The first controversy concerned adrenochrome's role as a metabolite of adrenaline. There were two schools of thought—one led by Bacq (1949) who suggested that adrenochrome was a derivative of adrenaline and had an important biological role; the other believed adrenochrome was not an important derivative of adrenaline. This controversy was fought in the field of pharmacology. The adjective "important" here

267

referred to the amount which was formed in the body and the physiological effects of the adrenochrome. At this time no one suggested that it had any psychological effects. The hemostatic and antimitotic properties were discovered at this time. As we will show later, it is likely that the extensive use of adrenochrome semicarbazide by surgeons may derive, in part at least, from its euphorient properties and not simply because it is a major hemostatic chemical, as they think.

The second controversy arose from the adrenochrome hypothesis of schizophrenia which we first discussed in 1952 at a meeting of the Dementia Praecox Committee of the Scottish Rite Masons, at the Canada Club of the Waldorf Astoria Hotel in New York City. After the report by Hoffer *et al.* (1954) and Osmond and Hoffer (1959) that adrenochrome was an hallucinogen—the now common word that we coined at that time—early attempts to corroborate our work failed for several reasons. Early workers used adrenochrome semicarbazide, or poor preparations of commercial adrenochrome that contained large quantities of many impurities including some of the silver used to catalyze the oxidation of adrenaline to adrenochrome. The commercial preparations were very unstable because of these impurities. Some preparations tested by Heacock *et al.* (1963) contained as much as 50% of impurity. Even the best commercial preparation was only 82% pure. We would like to refer to these noncorroborative studies in detail but they have not been published. Investigators reported at meetings that they had been unable to corroborate but no description was given of the adrenochrome used, the quantity or means of administration, the subjects involved or anything else. This second controversy must be one of the unusual ones in science since every paper published, so far, on adrenochrome showed that it was psychologically active and changed the behavior of man and animals. A curious situation resulted in which many who had worked with adrenochrome provided data that showed it was hallucinogenic while several who had not studied adrenochrome insisted that it was not.

The third controversy centered on whether adrenochrome was a major or minor metabolite of adrenaline. The terms "major" or "minor" were never clearly defined and while pharmacologists used a quantitative definition, that is, whether a large or small portion of the adrenaline was converted into adrenochrome, psychiatrists misinterpreted their meaning and supposed that if a small amount of adrenaline were converted into adrenochrome this must mean that it could only play a minor part. The evidence available does, indeed, suggest that if adrenochrome is formed from adrenaline in the body; usually only a small fraction of the adrenaline is used. However, even a small but continuous conversion of adrenaline into adrenochrome could, over a period of time, create a very serious problem by overloading the biochemical mechanisms available for its disposition. Indeed, the body would most probably be less equipped to dispose of minor toxic metabolites which became too abundant than to deal with more common substances. The exact proportion of adrenaline converted into adrenochrome will not be known until accurate assays are available.

The fourth controversy has developed as the adherents of a variety of psychodynamic and psychosocial schools of psychiatry marshal their arguments in support of their numerous hypotheses. The point at issue is whether adrenochrome metabolism has much to do with the disease, schizophrenia. In order to establish schizophrenia as an adrenochrome disease, it is necessary to prove that (a) adrenochrome is an hallucinogen, (b) adrenochrome is formed *in vivo* from adrenaline or from some other substrate and (c) the production of adrenochrome and its toxic derivatives wax and wane as the disease schizophrenia waxes and wanes. It also follows that treatments which normalize the abnormal metabolism of adrenochrome should be curative for schizophrenia. It may also be a taraxein disease. The taraxein and adrenochrome hypothesis developed together and have run a close and parallel path. They seem to be closer than ever since it has been shown that the small molecular component of taraxein may be noradrenaline derivatives, perhaps something like noradrenochrome.

Chemistry

According to Heacock (1959), Vulpian, in 1856, reported that adrenal gland extracts became rose-carmine in color upon standing in air, and that certain oxidizing agents facilitated this reaction. He seems to have been the first man to notice adrenochrome. But it was not until 1935 that Weinstein and Manning at the University of Saskatchewan in Saskatoon obtained a red crystalline product by oxidizing adrenaline with silver oxide. They believed that they had isolated adrenaline-quinone but D. E. Green and Richter (1937) correctly identified the red substance and called it adrenochrome. Before that, the oxidation product had been known as omega.

Green and Richter's preparations were unstable red powders which quickly deteriorated both in the solid state or in solution. When we began our studies in 1952, the adrenochrome was made by Hutcheon *et al.* (1956). This preparation was a bright red powder which we stored under nitrogen at $-40°C$. Even under these conditions it turned black, that is, developed surface melanization of the particles within a few weeks. We allowed for this unusual reactivity by using it within a few days after it was synthesized.

Heacock *et al.* (1958) reported that the samples of adrenochrome then available were contaminated by varying amounts of adrenolutin and black water insoluble melaninlike compounds. It was possible that the extraordinary instability of the preparation was due to contamination with silver either in a colloidal form or as metallic ions. In order to reduce the degree of contamination the adrenaline-silver oxide reaction mixture in methanol was filtered through an anion exchange resin bed in the chloride form. The adrenochrome then crystallized readily at −20°C and contained less than 0.01% silver.

This preparation was a stable crystalline material which, in the solid state, did not decompose even after many months at room temperature. Dilute solutions of adrenochrome were stable for many hours in pure water, but very concentrated solutions formed amorphous percipitates. The deep violet crystals began to decompose at about 112°C. Ultraviolet and visible absorption spectra in aqueous solution were λ max: 301,487 mμ; λ min: 262,361 mμ.

Adrenolutin (3,5,6-trihydroxy-N-methylindole) is the substance chiefly responsible for the intense yellow-green fluorescence which develops in adrenaline solutions oxidized in alkaline medium. It was first isolated and identified by Lund (1949b). Adrenolutin made from impure adrenochrome was also unstable. The yellowish crystals slowly turned greenish black. Our first preparation of adrenolutin was synthesized in the laboratory of Professor Harley-Mason (1954). It was a bright golden color with a slightly green tinge which was stable and did not deteriorate even when stored at room temperature. However, later preparations from the same laboratory were greenish powders which quickly turned dark. Later we used adrenolutin made by Dr. D. Hutcheon (courtesy of Charles Pfizer and Company, New York). This material was shipped to us by air packed in dry ice. It was stable enough for our experiments since it required over 3 months for it to deteriorate when stored at low temperature.

When purified stable adrenochrome was used for synthesizing adrenolutin, Heacock and Mahon (1958) consistently obtained good yields of the monohydrate of adrenolutin. When the water of crystallization was removed an amorphous brownish green powder was left. High vacuum sublimation of the hydrate yielded an anhydrous preparation; M.P. 245°C with decomposition. Adrenolutin is not very soluble in water whereas adrenochrome is. The structures of these compounds are shown in Fig. 7.

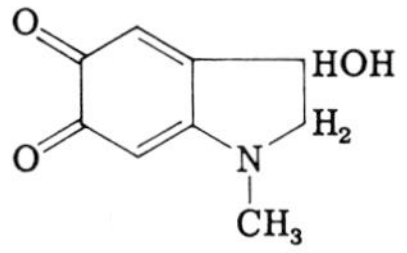

Adrenochrome

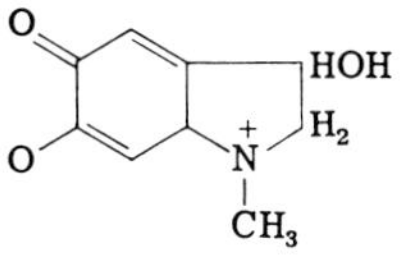

Zwitterion form of adrenochrome

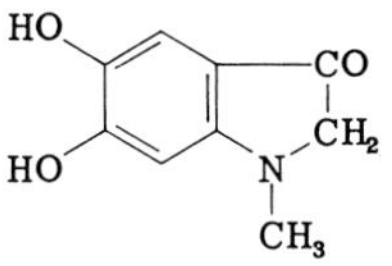

Adrenolutin

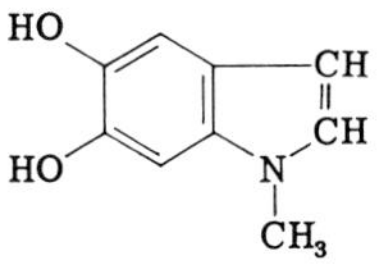

5,6-Dihydroxy-*N*-methylindole

FIG. 7. Structure of adrenochrome and some of its derivatives.

Chemical Properties

As Heacock (1959, 1965) has shown in his comprehensive review adrenochrome is extremely reactive in biological systems. We shall make use of his article here.

REARRANGEMENTS

The rearrangement of aminochromes to colorless or yellowish solutions is one of the most characteristic reactions. Adrenochrome rearranges to adrenolutin and other substances. Dopachrome formed from dopa rearranges to 5,6-dihydroxyindole or into 2-carboxy-5,6-dihydroxyindole; with alkali or with zinc or aluminum cations, adrenochrome is converted into adrenolutin. Zinc and aluminum salts catalyze the rearrangement of aminochromes to 5,6-dihydroxyindoles. During zinc-catalyzed rearrangement of dopa carbon dioxide is lost. Alumina columns would not, therefore, be suitable for assaying adrenochrome solutions.

REDUCTION

Sodium hydrosulfite is a common reducing agent for adrenochrome. There are two primary reduction products—5,6-dihydroxy-*N*-methylindole and an adrenochrome-sodium bisulfite complex which is converted into adrenolutin by alkali. Other reducing substances are ascorbic acid, cysteine, glutathione, glycine, dihydroxymaleic acid, dihydroxyfumaric acid, sodium bisulfite, and pencillamine. Adrenochrome released into blood would be quickly reduced by one or more of these substances usually found in blood.

Before adrenochrome was prepared in a crystalline stable form, many workers studied deteriorated adrenaline solutions. These solutions were pink, port wine, yellow, or brown and also contained black insoluble melanins as well as unchanged adrenaline. The solutions would contain adrenochrome (pink), adrenolutin (yellow and fluorescent), dihydroxy-N-methylindole, and probably indolequinone oxadrenochrome, dimeric indigo-type molecules, and other uncharacterized substances. Commercial adrenaline solutions which are stabilized by ascorbic acid or sodium bisulfite do not usually become pink or red, since the red adrenochrome color would be discharged by the stabilizer. But adrenochrome could be present briefly in the ascorbic acid or bound as the adrenochrome bisulfite complex. The absence of pink color is, therefore, no guarantee that adrenaline solutions have not deteriorated.

OXIDATION

Further oxidation of adrenochrome leads to the formation of brown or black insoluble polymeric pigments (melanins) of unknown structure. Noradrenochrome is oxidized to melanotic pigments more readily than adrenochrome.

Acid solutions of adrenolutin take up oxygen slowly in the cold to form a dimeric oxidation product.

Biochemical Properties

One of our objectives in this chapter on adrenochrome is to relate the known biochemical properties of adrenochrome and of adrenolutin to similar changes which have been reported to occur in schizophrenia.

There is still much disagreement about the biochemical findings in schizophrenia, but having noted this, and having reminded the reader that our adrenochrome hypothesis, although highly suggestive and intriguing, is still a hypothesis, we shall continue to review adrenochrome in this context. Some of the findings reported here are our investigations and their use of comparison groups meet the standards required by the most exacting critics. However, not all do so. Nevertheless, since many valuable discoveries have been made in medicine in which comparison groups have been small, deficient, or even absent, we shall not omit studies solely because of this shortcoming—experience shows that this would be unwise.

CARBOHYDRATE METABOLISM

D. E. Green and Richter (1937) found that adrenochrome was a hydrogen carrier in the lactic and maleic dehydrogenase system at 6×10^{-7} M concentration. Randall (1946) reported that adrenochrome inhibited anaerobic glycolysis in brain tissue. Glutathione inactivated adrenochrome. Meyerhoff and Randall (1948) believed that adrenochrome inhibited hexokinase and phosphohexokinase. Adrenochrome also inhibited the uptake of oxygen by chopped rat brain tissue under aerobic conditions when glucose, pyruvate, succinate, and malate were substrates. Reduced glutathione, adenosine triphosphate, nicotinic acid, and ferrous sulfate did not reverse this inhibition. Radsma and Golterman (1954) used a hydrogen transport system involving ascorbic acid. Adrenochrome stimulated oxidation of ascorbic acid (10^{-6} M) and inhibited oxidation of lactate (10^{-4} M).

Park *et al.* (1956a) found that 5×10^{-4} M adrenochrome completely uncoupled oxidative phosphorylation in hamster liver mitochondria. This was not reversed by magnesium and was activated by small quantities of thyroxine. Park *et al.* (1956b) later found that glutathione and ethylenediaminetetraacetate prevented phosphorylation uncoupling. Krall *et al.* (1964) reported 10^{-4} M adrenochrome inhibited pyruvate oxidation and its associated phosphorylation in brain mitochondria 50%. It did so by binding free sulfhydril groups on the enzymes.

Adrenochrome is also a powerful inhibitor of adenosinetriphosphatase activity of uterine muscle preparations. Inchiosa and Van Demark (1958) and Inchiosa and Freedberg (1961) found that 10^{-6} to 10^{-7} M concentrations inhibited ATPase activity. Adrenaline alone in concentrations of 6×10^{-5} to 6×10^{-6} M produced no inhibition. Inchiosa (1959) reported 3×10^{-6} M adrenochrome inhibited ATPase 20%.

Adrenochrome by interfering in phosphorylation could readily produce those alterations that have been found in schizophrenic tissues.

Boszormenyi-Nagy and Gerty (1955) found that with normal erythrocytes, insulin pretreatment decreased the formation of adenosine triphosphate by hemolyzed cells. They suggested this may be due to an increased rate of consumption of high-energy phosphate. Insulin did not interfere with this process in the red cells of schizophrenics, which appear to be resistant to insulin in this regard. They further suggested that the insulin disrupted some energy transfer in the citric acid cycle.

Streifler and Kornblueth (1958) used rat retina in a biological test for the presence of toxins in serum by measuring its consumption of oxygen. They found that serum from schizophrenic patients decreased the consumption of glucose by rat retina. The decrease was less than that produced by serum from patients suffering from organic nervous system disease.

Walaas *et al.* (1954) found that rat diaphragm utilized less glucose in the presence of schizophrenic serum. Bullough (1952) showed that adrenochrome inhibited mitosis in mouse epidermis both *in vitro* and *in vivo.* He suggested that the inhibition of mitosis in mice observed during stress was due to the endogenous conversion of epinephrine into adrenochrome.

Henneman *et al.* (1955) found disturbances in carbohydrate metabolism of psychotic patients. Most of these patients were probably schizophrenic.

This evidence suggests that cell multiplication ought to be inhibited, at least in severe illnesses. One would expect that more rapidly growing tissues would be more noticeably inhibited. We suggest that there would be a reduction in the growth rate of the following tissues, (a) hair, (b) nails, (c) epidermis, (d) fibrous tissue; as well as in the following processes, (e) spermatogenesis and (f) erythropoiesis. There is evidence which suggests such an interference with growth. Brodny (1955) found a high incidence of spermatic abnormalities in the semen of schizophrenics. He suggested that schizophrenics produced an X substance which both decreased spermatogenesis and encouraged abnormal spermatozoa.

We have seen no studies of hair growth rates in schizophrenics compared to comparison controls. It is our impression schizophrenics do not require haircuts as frequently but when they recover seem to have normal growth. In the past ten years we have treated two patients for schizophrenia whose hair growth markedly accelerated as they recovered. One was a female patient who was bald and wore a wig. She was much better after 6 months of medication with nicotinic acid. When we suggested she discontinue the tablets she refused to do so stating her hair was coming back and she was worried she would become bald again. The second case was a man in his early thirties beginning to lose his hair. After three months of medication with nicotinic acid his hair returned. However, in two bald normal men, nicotinic acid had no effect whatever.

The relationship of nail growth to schizophrenia has not been examined although it would be very easy to do.

If antimitosis is a factor, it should be more pathological in children before puberty. It follows from this that any general interference with growth would only be observed in people whose growth was not completed. As with diabetes mellitus and with tuberculosis, the order in which the event occurs is vital. Those who look for an effect of schizophrenia on body build will, therefore, find it in those patients where the illness has first expressed itself at an age before growth was complete. Two lines of evidence support this proposition: (a) Schizophrenic children, in general, according to the work of Bender are slightly more deformed or asymmetrical than normal children and (b) schizophrenics in whom the illness has been present a long time are more ectomorphic than those in whom the illness came on late. Rees (1957) reviewed the evidence which shows a relationship between physical type and schizophrenia. In general, schizophrenics are smaller and have shorter antero-posterior diameters. There is still much controversy about this. Perhaps if the data were reexamined and the patients classified according to age of onset this controversy might be resolved. Rees states, "the work of (various authors) suggests that schizophrenics with a leptomorphic body build tend to have an early age of onset, show a greater degree of withdrawal, apathy and scattered thinking, whereas schizophrenics of eurymorphic body build tend to have a later age of onset and to show a better preservation of personality and better affective relations with the environment." This could be rewritten "suggests that schizophrenics with an early age of onset tend to have a leptomorphic body build, etc." Wittman (1948) compared a group of shut-in personality schizophrenics, ill since childhood with an early and insidious onset, against a group where onset was acute in response to some situational stress. The first group was largely ectomorphic. The second group was less ectomorphic with more mesomorphy. There was a high association between schizophrenia and tuberculosis, according to Appel *et al.* (1958). The mortality from tuberculosis among schizophrenics and their relatives is higher than average. A main variable for the control of pulmonary tuberculosis is the ability to enclose a lesion with fibrous tissue. If the rate of fibrosis (growth or mitosis) is defective one would expect some defect in dealing with tuberculosis. This means that in the presence of schizophrenia, tuberculosis is more malignant, that is, more schizophrenics will have more severe tuberculosis. However, the converse need not apply. The presence of tuberculosis does not imply adrenochrome is present in excess. One must not disregard the order in which two diseases develop when they coexist. Bleuler and Zurgilgen (1949) found no increase in prevalence of schizophrenia among tuberculotic patients and therefore concluded that the increased incidence of tuberculosis was due to greater exposure to infection only. They assumed that a coexistence should be present in both illnesses. Ordered events are common in medicine and in life. Thus, all pregnancies occur in women but not all women are pregnant. Similarly schizophrenics are unusually susceptible to tuberculosis but tuberculotics are not unusually susceptible to schizophrenia. This is easily accounted for by the adreno-chrome hypothesis.

Schizophrenic patients have abnormal phosphate excretion patterns, perhaps as a result of the disturbance of carbohydrate metabolism. Normal subjects given adrenolutin have similar diurnal changes (Hoffer and Osmond, 1960). These results are shown in Table 20.

TABLE 20

PHOSPHATE EXCRETION (IN MILLIGRAMS PER MINUTE)

	4:00–6:00 PM	6:00–8:00 PM	8:00–10:00 PM	Night sample	AM sample
Schizophrenics		0.83	0.83	0.52	0.21
Adrenolutin (50 mg)	0.81	0.76	0.61	0.51	0.41
Adrenolutin (25 mg)		0.78	0.68	0.63	0.58
Placebo	0.79	0.70	0.70	0.68	0.66
Control	0.82	0.91	0.84	0.70	0.56

There was no significant variance at each time period for the various groups. However, schizophrenics and subjects given 50 mg of adrenolutin retained more during the night. The values found for the night sample are mean values of the entire sleeping period. Values at 10 PM are different. It is therefore possible to calculate the excretion per minute toward the end of the collection period using the 10:00 PM value as representative of the rate for the first part of this collection period and the mean value for the entire period. These are shown in Table 21. Calculated schizophrenic excretions for the last interval are much lower than for all other groups followed by the normals receiving the most adrenolutin (Hoffer and Osmond, 1959).

TABLE 21

PHOSPHATE EXCRETION (MILLIGRAM PER MILLIGRAM CREATININE)

	6:00–10:00 PM Mean	Night	Change %
Schizophrenic	0.90	0.82	− 9
Adrenolutin (50 mg)	0.49	0.43	−12
Adrenolutin (25 mg)	0.59	0.56	− 5
Placebo	0.47	0.60	+28
Control	0.59	0.64	+ 8

In order to check the validity of this calculation, urines were collected between 7:00 and 10:00 AM for 28 schizophrenic patients and 13 mentally ill nonschizophrenic patients residing in the same hospital. The mean phosphate excretion in mg per minute was 0.32 for schizophrenics and 0.53 for the other group. This difference in means is statistically significant ($k = 2.10$, $p = 0.03$).

Using the 6:00 or 8:00 PM values or their mean when both are available as a baseline, the following retention of phosphate was found:

Schizophrenics	37%
Adrenolutin (50 mg)	35%
Adrenolutin (25 mg)	19%
Placebo	9%
Control	20%

The excretion of phosphorus per unit of creatinine for the period from 6:00 to 10:00 PM is compared with the night excretion.

The adrenolutin effect of phosphate excretion is quite different from any placebo (anxiety) effect and adrenolutinized subjects show changes in phosphate excretion very similar to those seen in schizophrenia.

Phosphate retention was not affected by anxiety. However, retention of phosphate was greater for schizophrenics and for adrenolutin at 50 mg level. The other adrenolutin group showed little displacement from controls. Comparing the evening rate and morning rate it is seen that the excretion of phosphate per unit of creatinine is quite different separating placebo and controls on one hand from the other 3 groups.

The retention of phosphate following administration of adrenolutin resembles the similar retention induced by LSD in humans (Hoagland *et al.*, 1955) and in animals (Bergen and Beisaw, 1956). Similarly, the calculated morning excretion rates for schizophrenics which are about 40% of normal for the calculated late night rates (see Table 21) and 60% for the collection period from 7:00 to 10:00 AM are similar to those reported by Hoagland *et al.*

Inhibition of Acetylcholinesterase

Adrenochrome is an inhibitor of acetylcholinesterase. Waelsch and Rachow (1942) first discovered this property of adrenochrome and in their paper suggested that this could set up an *in vivo* positive feedback system which would disrupt the parasympathetic sympathetic biochemical cycles. Inhibiting esterase would elevate acetylcholine levels. This in turn would increase the secretion of adrenaline and noradrenaline which would increase adrenochrome levels. This would inhibit esterase even more.

Many indoles are inhibitors of these esterases and most of the indole hallucinogens already described such as LSD, bufotenine, etc., are very active. Greig and Gibbons (1959) reported that adrenochrome decreased penetration of glucose, labeled with ^{14}C, into mouse brain, as did bulbocapnine, bufotenine, and mescaline. The effect of LSD was variable but adrenolutin had no effect. Human serum pseudocholinesterase was inhibited up to 50% by the following concentrations of LSD, bulbocapnine, bufotenine, adrenolutin, and adrenochrome, respectively: 9×10^{-7}, 2×10^{-5}, 4×10^{-4}, 3.8×10^{-3}, and 3.3×10^{-3} M. They suggested that the hallucinogens could act by reducing the transfer of glucose into the brain.

ADRENOCHROME AND BRAIN INHIBITOR FACTOR

Factor I appears to be a transmitter of inhibitor neurons. It is present in an inactive form and is released by heat and chemical treatment. Much of its activity is apparently produced by γ-aminobutyric acid (GABA). Lack of GABA would increase nervous activity. Woodbury and Vernadakis (1958) found that brain excitability varied inversely with GABA concentrations in brain. The correlation coefficient was 0.66. According to Holtz and Westermann (1956) adrenochrome was a powerful inhibitor of glutamic acid decarboxylase in brain tissue. Too much adrenochrome would decrease production of GABA from glutamic acid and so increase the excitability of the brain. This could account for the pronounced activation of the encephalograms in epileptic subjects (Szatmari et al., 1955). We will discuss this further in the section on oxygen toxicity.

ADRENOCHROME AND AMINO ACIDS

Greig and Gibbons (1957) reported that adrenochrome stimulated the oxidation of glycine to carbon dioxide, ammonia, and formic acid. In rat kidney tissue oxidation of glycine to glycolic acid was accelerated. Other amino acids, including glutamic acid, phenylalanine, and tryptophan, were also oxidized. They suggested that this reaction of adrenochrome accounted for the apparent deficiency of glycine and the increased formation of phosphoglycolic acid in the erythrocytes of schizophrenic patients. The increased oxidation of glutamic acid combined with the inhibition of its decarboxylase would further decrease GABA formation even more.

The reduction of adrenochrome by cysteine and glutathione has already been described.

Heacock and Mattok (1963) and Mattok and Heacock (1965) conducted a careful study of the reaction of adrenochrome with glutathione,

one of the simplest amino acids. Adrenochrome combined with glutathione to form a pale yellow aqueous solution. The solution contained 3 compounds (I) 5,6-dihydroxy-*N*-methylindole, (II) 7-*S*-glutathionyl-5,6-dihydroxy-*N*-methylindole and (III) 9-*S*-glutathionyl-2,3,6,9-tetrahydro-3,5-dihydroxy-6-oxo-*N*-methylindole. The 5,6-dihydroxy-*N*-methylindole was a minor component in the reaction and probably resulted from the reduction of adrenochrome by the glutathione adrenochrome addition complex. Compound II was similar to one of the substances formed from the reaction of dopachrome with glutathione. The adrenochrome was easily regenerated from the glutathione complex by treatment with mild alkali. Roston (1965) found adrenaline also reacted with glutathione.

Mattok and Heacock referred to the significance of this reaction in biological processes. Melanins could be bound to proteins by a sulfide linkage formed by an interaction of one of the third group of the glutathione adrenochrome compounds with one of the indole-5,6-quinone units in melanin. These interactions could occur with the aminochrome units present in melanin. Mattok and Heacock concluded that the formation of aminochrome-thiol addition products offers the intriguing possibility that some thiols, such as glutathione, could react with adrenochrome (or other aminochromes such as dopachrome) resulting either in their complete elimination as the 7-indole derivative, or in the formation of the 3-substituted compound which could act as an aminochrome carrier and so could readily regenerate the aminochromes under appropriate conditions.

Many workers have found that adrenochrome is bound to protein by the sulfhydril groups. Denisoff (1964) reported that heart muscle myosin ATPase activity was lowered by adrenochrome and adrenoxyl. This, he believed, was due to the binding of these compounds on SH groups and their subsequent oxidation to —S—S— groups. Roston (1963) found that coenzyme A combined with adrenochrome and noradrenochrome at the active sulfhydril (SH) site. He suggested coenzyme A–catecholamine compounds could represent an important stage in intermediary metabolism since their breakdown could lead to the regeneration of coenzyme A and the formation of physiologically active catecholamine derivatives.

The other reports suggest that adrenochrome can be bound to proteins *in vivo*. Braines *et al.* (1959) examined serum proteins by fluorescent spectral analysis. When serum proteins were irradiated with very short ultraviolet light there was a peak fluorescence at 280 Å and another one at 243 Å. The peak at 243 Å was absent in hydrolyzed or denatured protein. The authors suggested it was due to the energy transfer along the long polypeptide chains which was discharged as fluorescence from tryptophan molecules within the chain. The ratio of the intensity of fluorescence at 280 Å over the intensity at 243 Å was defined as a K ratio. The mean K value for 19 normal subjects was 2.26, for 9 alcoholics was 2.25, and for 35 schizophrenics was 3.19. Only 6 schizophrenic patients had K values within the normal range, of these 3 had received treatment before blood was drawn for assay. Dog serum protein had a normal fluorescence spectrum but when dogs were injected with 0.1% solution of adrenochrome (0.4 mg per kg) the K values went up into the schizophrenic range as long as the animals were catatonic. When they recovered the K values dropped again to normal values. The 343 Å peak became scarcely visible in schizophrenic serum and in adrenochrome-treated dogs. The absorption of adrenochrome onto the protein chain by mechanisms suggested by Mattok and Heacock could interfere with the transfer of energy along the polypeptide chain and so decrease emission at the tryptophan molecules at 243 Å.

The other report is by Runge *et al.* (1961) who examined lyophilized serum in the infrared spectrophotometer. Normal serum had two absorption minima between 6 and 7 microns but many schizophrenic patients had serum wherein the maximum absorption between these two minima disappeared. When 20 mg of mescaline or 20 mg of adrenochrome were added to 3 ml of serum, the infrared curve resembled that found for schizophrenic untreated serum.

ADRENOCHROME AND MELANIN PIGMENTATION

Adrenochrome readily polymerizes *in vitro* to form melaninlike pigments. In the presence of the phenolase complex (Mason, 1955), it may react with amino acids to form red pigments. This accounts for the conversion of adrenaline solutions in the absence of stabilizers into adrenochrome, and later to melanotic pigments (Szepesey, 1962).

Adrenaline may affect pigmentation either by acting upon the pineal gland and its hormone melatonin, or by being itself a source of this pigment. It is not unusual for patients who have anxiety neuroses to deposit brown pigment in the skin of the face, which disappears as they improve. Anxiety states are associated with increased levels of adrenaline production, so one would expect a decrease in melanin formation unless it came from adrenaline. In 1952 when Hoffer was injected subcutaneously in the forearm with adrenochrome, a brown pigmented area about 1 cm across remained there for about 3 months. It looked very much like a tanned spot or a freckle. Meirowsky (1940) found that adrenochrome increased the production of pigment in human skin. Nicolaus (1962) classes adrenaline among the melanogens, that is precursors of natural melanin. Perhaps the first demonstration of the *in vivo* conversion of adrenaline into adrenochrome was made by Rigdon (1940a,b). Rabbit skin was shaved clean. Twenty-four hours later adrenaline was injected intradermally. The skin blanched for several hours. If xylol was placed on the skin either before, or after, the injection the skin became reddish brown in color 15–30 minutes after xylol application. Hoffer (1962a) injected 1 mg of adrenochrome intradermally into shaved rabbit skin. A faint brownish red color formed and remained in the skin for many hours. Apparently epidermis can convert adrenaline into adrenochrome *in vivo*. Salivary gland tissue, another ectodermal structure, also can oxidize adrenaline into adrenochrome (Axelrod, 1964). The reactive adrenochrome was trapped by β-phenylisopropylphenylhydrazine. Ascorbic acid and glutathione inhibited this reaction.

The melanin pigments in skin are generally assumed to derive from dopachrome and not from noradrenochrome or adrenochrome. The weight of evidence (Mason, 1955) supports this view. When tyrosinase is absent as in albinism no dopachrome can be formed and these subjects lack melanin pigment in their skin, eyes, hair, etc. It is believed that in Addison's disease the dopamine is not used in the formation of adrenaline by the defective adrenal medulla. This causes the unconsumed dopamine to be converted into dopachrome and skin melanins. This would account for the characteristic skin pigmentation in this condition, but there are other possible explanations. Rangier (1962) showed that melanins derived from adrenochrome resembled the structure of normal melanins more closely than those deriving from dopa. He combined orthoquinone with adrenochrome in water. A compound was obtained which corresponded to 8 indole molecules and 16 benzoquinone molecules. The amount of ammonia nitrogen corresponded to a terminal hydrogen peroxide group. The infrared spectrum confirmed the postulated structure. He also prepared dopachrome melanin which was insoluble in methyl alcohol, formic acid, or any other acid. Dopa melanin was prepared by oxidizing dopa in alkali and precipitating it in HCl, but this compound had a different infrared spectrum and did not resemble melanin.

Hair melanin was extracted by alkaline hydrolysis of hair followed by washing it with water, acetone, benzene and petroleum ether. In this extracted melanin the nitrogen quantity was consistent with the 8-adrenochrome model. It had the same infrared spectrum and migrated the same way electrophoretically.

Rangier also prepared melanin from urine. Urine was adjusted to pH 5.0 with acetic acid and hydrolyzed for 10 minutes with 5% HCl. After cooling the melanin sediment was dissolved in ammonia, filtered, precipitated with HCl, and washed. The amount of nitrogen was 7.7% — not far from 7.4% expected from the adrenochrome melanin model.

The electrophoretic migration of dopa melanin was different from melanin prepared from hair or urine. The latter two melanins resembled each other and adrenochrome melanin with respect to electrophoretic movement and infrared spectra.

If these results are corroborated new light will be thrown on the role of adrenochrome in pigment formation and on the role of pigment formation in removing toxic adrenaline metabolites. It is possible that epidermis with its growth of hair provides a mechanism for converting toxic chromes into inert materials which are then discarded in dead epithelial cells and hair.

Lea (1955) deduced that if there were, indeed, an overproduction of adrenochrome in schizophrenia, then more melaninlike pigments should be deposed in schizophrenia. Melanin pigments come from tyrosine either by way of dihydroxyphenylalanine (dopa) leading to dark brown or black pigments, or by way of epinephrine and adrenochrome leading to yellow or yellow-brown pigments. Langemann and Koelle (1958) reported that cells of the intestinal mucosa polymerize adrenaline and adrenochrome *in vitro* into these brownish pigments. The increase in adrenochrome in the body would therefore lead to an increase in brown coloration rather than of black pigmentation. Lea compared the eye and hair colors of 1008 schizophrenics against 5127 cases of injury. Eye color did not discriminate between these groups. But in the age group from 15 to 19 years old there were 241 dark haired subjects and 58 fair haired subjects whereas in the injury group there were 1066 dark and 246 fair, that is, 80% of the schizophrenics and 71% of the controls had dark hair (Chi Square—over 10.58). There was no significant difference in the 20–24 age group.

We have made a similar study of 1182 patients admitted to a psychiatric ward of a General Hospital over a 3-year period (Munroe Wing). The hair and eye color was recorded by the receiving psychiatric nurse, for a routine data admission sheet. The evaluation of hair

TABLE 22

PERCENTAGE OF GROUP HAVING DARK HAIR

	Age			
Group	15–19	20–29	30–49	Over 49
Schizophrenic	80	73	71	58
Others	71	72	70	15

color was subjective but probably sufficiently accurate. It corresponds to the data reported by Lea. The distribution of eye color was the same for both groups. The distribution of hair color for the two younger age groups was also similar. However, in the age group 50 and over, a greater proportion of schizophrenic patients retained their hair color, that is, did not turn gray. Unfortunately there were very few schizophrenics in the group. We therefore examined the hair color of 200 schizophrenics in our mental hospitals, many of whom have grown old there. Of this group, 56% still had dark hair.

The lack of differentiation in the age groups reported here confirms Lea's finding. Too few patients in our group fall into this 15–19 age group. Combining the data gathered by Lea and reported here, it is apparent that schizophrenic patients develop darker hair more quickly and retain it longer than nonschizophrenics. This is shown in Table 23. The 15–19 age group data is from Lea.

This data may be explained on the basis of two assumptions: (a) that every person has a genetic potential for his maximum hair darkening, and (b) that the rate of pigment deposition is increased in people who become schizophrenic. Thus the differences would show up in the

TABLE 23

RELATIONSHIP OF SCHIZOPHRENIA TO HAIR COLOR

		Hair color (%)				
	N	Blond	Gray	Brown	Black	Brown and black
Age 10–29						
Schizophrenia	123	33	0	66	24	73
All others	217	60	1	110	46	72
Age 30–49						
Schizophrenia	175	25	26	81	43	71
All others	339	37	74	156	72	70
Age 50 and over						
Schizophrenia						
Munroe Wing Sask. Hospital[a]	21	2	12	5	2	34
North Battleford Sask. Hospital[b]	100	8	24	56	12	68
Weyburn	100	1	51	32	16	48
Total	221	11	87	93	30	58
All others[c]	307	6	246	32	23	15

[a] Mean age 56.

[b] Mean age 61.

[c] Mean age 61.

younger age group and would not be altered in the middle age group but be maintained longer since the extra pigmentation would compensate the factors leading to graying. That is to say, schizophrenia can be considered as a catalyst which hastens the rate of maximum color development but not the final endpoint. It also counteracts natural graying processes. The schizophrenic group over age 49 have proportionately more brown than black haired subjects (Chi Square = 5.0). This suggests that the black haired subjects have suffered more depigmentation. Perhaps the black melanin pigments are removed whereas the brownish adrenochrome pigments which continue to be formed maintain the brown color.

The pronounced difference in graying of the nonschizophrenic population is not due to the greater age. The mean age of the nonschizophrenic group was only 5 years more than the mean age of the schizophrenic group. If all nonschizophrenic patients older than 60 are excluded from the nonschizophrenic group, the proportion gray remains about the same. It may be said that life in a mental hospital is less stressful for schizophrenics than it is for other types of mental disease. Those who suggest this must prove this is so. In our opinion there is no evidence for this concept. On the contrary our observations lead up to believe that modern mental hospitals are more stressful on their patients. Furthermore, there is no clear association between stress (whatever that is) and rate of graying.

Pigmentation in skin has not been studied as thoroughly. Harris (1942) described a schizophrenic-like psychosis associated with generalized brownish yellow pigmentation (adrenochrome pigments) of skin, much deeper in the areola and nipples which were nearly black. We have observed many chronic patients whose skin was brown as if they had been tanned by sun but had not been in the sun for months.

The hypothesis that adrenochrome forms melanin pigments is compatible with the chemistry of albinism since a lack of tyrosinase could also lead to a reduction in the formation of dopa noradrenaline and adrenaline. But it appears to be incompatible with the increased pigmentation found in Addison's disease. At one time it was not known that chromaffin tissue regenerated very quickly. Even after total medullectomy some adrenaline is produced in animals within 6 months from other chromaffin tissue. So that there is, after recovery, no essential deficiency in noradrenaline and adrenaline. The pigmentation of Addison's disease may be due, therefore, to another mechanism.

The combination of adrenochrome with ascorbic acid has already been touched on. Hoffer and Osmond (1963) discussed the relationship between ascorbic acid, adrenochrome, and schizophrenia.

Beauvillain and Sarradin (1948) showed that ascorbic acid reduced adrenochrome, that is, was oxidized by the adrenochrome which was decolorized. Early in 1952 we tested the psychological effect of adreno-chrome solutions decolorized with ascorbic acid. Later on Heacock and Laidlaw (1958a,b), Heacock and Scott (1959), and Heacock (1959) examined this reaction in greater detail. The reaction solution contained 5,6-dihydroxy-*N*-methylindole and at least two other indoles. Ascorbic acid is also an inhibitor of tyrosinase and decreases melanin pigmentation in man by two mechanisms (Fitzpatrick and Lerner, 1954): (a) by preventing further oxidation of dopa quinone (tyrosinase cannot act on tyrosine until all the ascorbic acid is oxidized); and (b) ascorbic acid reduces melanin in skin to a relatively light-colored substance. Large doses of ascorbic acid decrease pigmentation in patients who have Addison's disease (Rothman, 1942).

One of the peculiarities of ascorbic acid is its peculiar distribution in the body. The highest concentration of ascorbic acid is found in the adrenal cortex which surrounds the medulla, the great source of adrenaline, and in the brain where adrenochrome could do most harm. In the brain, the highest concentrations are present in the intermediate and anterior lobe of the pituitary gland. The adrenal cortex has nearly 10 times as much as brain. Roston (1962) pointed out that the 400–500 mg of ascorbic acid in 100 gm of fresh adrenal tissue was not there by accident. He reported that a great excess of ascorbic acid was required to decolorize adrenochrome, noradrenochrome, and dopachrome, the implication being that this could be the function of ascorbic acid in the adrenal gland.

Since the medullary adrenaline and noradrenaline filters through cortex before entering the blood, it seems reasonable to suppose that it picks up some ascorbic acid during its passage and that this alters the metabolism of adrenaline. One of the classic tests for stress consists of measuring the amount of ascorbic acid in rat adrenal gland.

This suggests that in Addison's disease the fault may be an insufficiency of ascorbic acid rather than too little adrenaline. If this happened, the formation of adrenochrome and adrenolutin melanins might well be increased and deposited in the skin and other pigmented areas of the body. This would account for the fact that very large doses of ascorbic acid decrease pigmentation in Addison's disease.

The relationship of schizophrenia to ascorbic acid, adrenochrome, and copper metabolism was discussed by Hoffer and Osmond (1963). This can be summarized as follows: (a) The blood of schizophrenics was generally low in ascorbic acid even when they had taken adequate quantities, that is, they were using too much ascorbic acid which might be a result of making too much adrenochrome. (b) Schizophrenia predisposes to scurvy but the converse is apparently not the case. (c) The literature was reviewed showing that ascorbic acid was helpful in the treatment of schizophrenia.

There is a more direct relationship between ascorbic acid, adrenochrome, and schizophrenia. Briggs (1962b) and Briggs and Harvey (1962) showed that there was an excessive breakdown of ascorbic acid in schizophrenia. They suggested that since ascorbic acid was an activator of p-hydroxyphenylpyruvate oxidase, its deficiency would lead to the excretion of unusual metabolites of phenylalanine and tyrosine. They examined urine from 15 schizophrenic patients, 18 normal subjects, and 12 other psychiatric patients. The normal and other psychiatric subjects were very similar and we will add them together. Of 15 schizophrenic subjects, 15 had p-hydroxyphenylpyruvate in their urine while of 30 others only 9 were positive ($X^2 = 20$ $P < 0.01$). Of 15 schizophrenics, 12 had p-hydroxyphenyllacetate and only 7 out of 30 others had it ($X^2 = 13$ $P < 0.01$). Briggs *et al.* (1962a) then reported "The most likely explanation of the metabolic abnormality in schizophrenics is a partial inhibition of p-hydroxyphenylpyruvate oxidase due to suboptimum amounts of ascorbate. The mental defect could be caused by a toxic effect of the circulating aromatic metabolites or by an imbalance in aromatic transformations. Thus an increased synthesis of adrenaline from dihydroxyphenylalanine would be a likely result of impaired oxidation of tyrosine. There is known to be increased adrenaline metabolism in schizophrenics. Excess adrenaline could be metabolized to some compound having psychotomimetic properties, such as adrenochrome, adrenolutin, or other metabolite bearing a structural resemblance to mescaline or related hallucinogens."

In 1962, we sent some pure adrenochrome to Dr. M. H. Briggs (1962a), who injected 10 mg into adult male guinea pigs. Using paper chromatography, he found there was a definite intensification of the spots due to the two substances found in excess in schizophrenics. In his opinion, adrenochrome could do this by accelerating ascorbic acid breakdown.

Cells of intestinal mucosa (endodermal tissue) can also produce melaninlike pigments from adrenaline and from adrenochrome (Langemann and Koelle, 1958). Yellow or yellow-brown pigments are formed.

Finally, brain tissue contains red pigments which apparently do not derive from dopa. Foley and Baxter (1958) examined the brains of two albino human subjects. In both cases the intensity and pigmentation in the cells of the locus caerulus and substantia nigra appeared normal. One patient had in addition several pigmented cells in the dorsal motor nucleus of the vagus. In marked contrast neither brain contained any melanin in the pial melanophores. They concluded that melanins of the brain stem must differ fundamentally from melanin of skin, choroid, and pia since they were not formed by the tyrosinase complex. The other most likely source would be noradrenaline and adrenaline by means of their chromes. Fellman (1958) found that the substantia migra contained enzymes which rapidly oxidized adrenaline. He observed that it contains argentophilic granules not unlike those seen in the adrenal medulla and in other chromaffin tissue.

The ability of these indoles to form melanins may determine their biochemical reactions in the body. According to Nicolaus (1962), Mason (1959), and others, dopachrome and 5,6-dihydroxyindole form the long chain disorderly polymers (melanins) by linkages which involve position 4 and 7. The indoles may have a 4 to 4, a 7 to 7, or a 4 to 7 combination. Position 3 may be involved in cross linkage formation. Since epidermis, one of the largest organs in the body, is capable of forming large quantities of melanin quickly, compounds which can be incorporated into melanin may be metabolized very quickly and, therefore, have a short active life in the body. Indoles which have position 4 or 7 blocked could be incorporated into melanins less quickly and should be more active. This may be an explanation for the psychological activity of psilocybin, a 4-substituted indole. We would expect all 4 substituted indoles to be more active than 5- and 6-substituted indoles. For the same reason 7-substituted indoles like 7-iodoadrenochrome should be very active, as indeed they are. The most active substance should be indoles with both position 4 and 7 occupied by other substituents. We would also suspect that dopachrome which is converted into melanins *in vivo* so quickly would be less active psychologically than adrenochrome.

Tyrosinase, the enzyme which oxidizes tyrosine, has the curious property of combining dopa quinone (the precursor of dopachrome) with 3-hydroxykynurenine to form ommochromes (Fitzpatrick and Kukita, 1959). These substances are very similar in structure to the phenothiazines, nonmonoamine oxidase antidepressants, and the azepines. Ehrensvard *et al.* (1960) and Heath and Leach (1962) found that schizophrenic serum oxidized 3-hydroxyanthranilic acid enzymatically more slowly than did normal serum. This suggests schizophrenic serum contains less of the enzyme which converts 3-hydroxyanthranilic acid into nicotinic acid. The result would be an increase in 3-hydroxyanthranilic acid, an increase in 3-hydroxykynurenine, an increase in ommochromes formation, and a deficiency of nicotinic acid. If adrenaline oxidases were also increased it would not be surprising if tyrosinase was more active. This too would increase the formation of ommochromes. Perhaps this is why phenothiazines are effective in treating some schizophrenics. They might saturate the enzymes forming ommochromes and decrease their formation. The relative deficiency of nicotinic acid could account for the beneficial effect of high doses of niacin in schizophrenia.

Adrenochrome and Oxygen Toxicity (OHP)

Oxygen is essential for the conversion of adrenaline to adrenochrome. Too much oxygen would accelerate the rate of conversion of adrenaline into adrenochrome, increase its production, and overwhelm the detoxifying systems for adrenochrome. As adrenochrome is harmful to most cells, excessive quantities of oxygen should be harmful for this and for other reasons. Within the past ten years, the factors leading to oxygen toxicity have clarified somewhat. It is remarkable how the facts agree with the hypothesis that it is this conversion of adrenaline into adrenochrome that is one of the main factors. The evidence is as follows:

1. Under the impact of OHP, adrenaline is lost and adrenochrome concentrations increase in brain. Gershenovich *et al.* (1955) showed that the transformation of adrenaline into adrenochrome in brain is accelerated at high oxygen tension. They placed rabbits in chambers filled with oxygen at pressures of 3.5 and 6 atmospheres. At the higher pressure the animals went through the following phases (a) a period of stimulation with motor restlessness 10–13 minutes after the beginning of the experiment. Brain adrenaline decreased 60%, adrenal medulla adrenaline increased 234%. Brain and medulla adrenochrome increased 15 and 34%. (b) A period of convulsions 20–25 minutes after the beginning. Brain adrenaline increased slightly but medulla adrenaline decreased 42%. In both areas adrenochrome levels decreased slightly. (c) A terminal period characterized by coma, disturbed respiration, and terminal convulsions. Brain adrenaline increased slightly but medulla had no more adrenaline. Brain adrenochrome increased 33% and medulla adrenochrome was still elevated.

High oxygen tension then caused a massive discharge of adrenaline from the adrenal medulla until at death it was depleted. Adrenochrome levels were elevated. In the brain there was an initial decrease in adrenaline followed by a slight increase. The massive discharge from the medulla could have been an attempt to replace the great loss of brain adrenaline in the first phase of the reaction. It is evident that the massive conversion of adrenaline to adrenochrome in brain and medulla must upset the brain-medulla adrenaline cycle. It is interesting that convulsions which were not terminal reduced adrenochrome levels. Perhaps this is a rationale for electroconvulsive therapy. Under 3.5

atmospheres of oxygen similar changes were measured but they occurred more slowly. Laborit *et al.* (1957a,b) found that adrenochrome slightly increased the tendency for mice to have convulsions in pure oxygen. Adrenochrome monosemicarbazone (adrenoxyl) also increased convulsions.

2. When adrenaline is not available toxicity to OHP is decreased. As we would expect the removal of the main adrenaline depot by adrenalectomy protected animals against oxygen toxicity. Bean and Johnson (1955) reported that, in contrast to most stresses, high oxygen tension was less toxic to animals after adrenal medullation. In the absence of the corticosteroids, adrenaline injection increased the toxicity of oxygen. This also occurred in normal animals. Gerschman *et al.* (1955) made similar observations. Taylor (1958) reported that adrenalectomy protected animals against the convulsant effect of 6 atmospheres of oxygen. Bean (1956) found that reserpine offered some protection in rats against OHP. But chlorpromazine was much better. Bean suggested this was due to an inhibition of sympathetic outflow and a decrease in release of adrenaline. Chlorpromazine also has some anti-adrenaline properties. According to Bean the sympathetic nervous system and the sympathomimetic substances contributed in very large measure to the augmentation of the OHP toxicity. This could be partially nullified by peripheral sympathetic blockage.

Chlorpromazine produces many biochemical changes in the body, which suggested to Ban and Lehmann (1965) that it decreased the production of noradrenaline and adrenaline and so forced the increased formation of dopa melanin pigments. Greiner and Berry (1964), Greiner and Nicolson (1964), Satanove (1965), and Ban and Lehmann (1965) found that some schizophrenic patients who had been on high doses of chlorpromazine for many years, developed an unusual form of increased melanin pigmentation. This was controlled by the use of a copper chelating agent—penicillamine (Greiner *et al.*, 1964). This increased pigmentation plus orthostatic hypotension, and extrapyramidal symptoms support the view of Ban *et al.* that dopa was shunted into melanin because of a decrease in sympathomimetic amine production.

It is, therefore, not surprising that chlorpromazine has a protective effect against oxygen toxicity.

3. Adrenochrome is a powerful inhibitor of glutamic acid decarboxylase (Holtz and Westerman, 1956). In the presence of excessive adrenochrome there should be a deficiency of GABA due to the inhibition of glutamic acid decarboxylase. Wood and Watson (1963, 1964a,b) and Wood *et al.* (1963) found that when rats were exposed to 6 atmospheres of oxygen the concentration in the brain of glutamic acid, aspartic acid,

and total α-amino acids were not altered even after convulsions. But the concentration of GABA was decreased significantly. When the animals convulsed severely, GABA decreased 35%, with mild convulsions it decreased 27%, but when the animals did not convulse GABA went down 19%. The intraperitoneal injection of GABA in the rats, prior to breathing OHP, provided some protection against the toxicity. A brief exposure also lowered GABA. High-pressure air on 8 minutes of 100% oxygen at 1 atmosphere did not alter GABA. The GABA values were nearly normal after 1 hour. They suggested the toxicity of OHP was due to an impairment of oxidative metabolism in the brain due to an inhibition of α-ketoglutamic dehydrogenase and to a shortage of GABA.

The injected GABA protected the animals only as long as GABA values were elevated. This then allowed the GABA shunt to operate normally. Wood and Watson (1964a,b) reported that oxygen decreased glutamic acid decarboxylase activity in rat brain homogenates 35%. There was no effect on the transaminase which metabolizes GABA. Haugaard (1965) also found that OHP decreased glutamic acid decarboxylase in rats and GABA was decreased with 4–6 atmospheres oxygen.

4. Catalysts which increase oxidation of adrenaline to adrenochrome increased OHP toxicity. Conversely, reducing catalytic action would decrease toxicity. Haugaard (1965) reported that EDTA protected brain tissue against 1 atmosphere oxygen. In brain tissue, toxicity appeared rather quickly. In heart homogenates poisoning came on slowly. This suggests again that brain is more sensitive to adrenochrome, or that it is formed more quickly. EDTA would bind copper and so reduce oxidation of adrenaline. The addition of trace amounts of copper increased toxicity, as did ferrous ion, another metallic catalyst.

5. Many of the toxic responses to OHP are neurological and psychiatric. The current interest in hyperbaric oxygenation, in scuba diving, and in space travel, has forced serious examination of the toxic effects of OHP. An excellent series of reports is available in the *Annals of the New York Academy of Sciences* (1965). The psychiatric changes include nausea, vertigo, visual difficulties, loss of judgment, and finally convulsions (Mollaret *et al.*, 1965). The most serious change which could interfere in hyperbaric oxygen chambers is lack of judgment and difficulty in altering a set of instructions. Physicians who have to treat emergency conditions under OHP are themselves liable to errors of judgment and in the U.S. Navy they are controlled by physicians outside the pressure area. Very few subjects develop convulsions at 2.8 atmospheres of oxygen for 30 minutes, but at 3.4 atmospheres 80% of normal subjects will develop convulsions in 2 hours.

Adrenochrome placed in the lateral ventricles of cats produced convulsions (Hoffer, 1962b) when 1 mg was injected clear behavioral changes were seen. When 2 mg were placed therein, two cats went into status epilepticus. One died, but at autopsy no pathological changes were seen in the brain. The other cat was kept alive by heavy doses of sodium pentothal but continued to have tremors for several days. The injection of 1 mg of heparin with the adrenochrome protected the cats completely against the toxic and convulsive effect of the adrenochrome.

It is likely that the *folie des profondeurs* (Cousteau and Dumas, 1953) is due to the synergistic effect of increased oxygen pressure and nitrogen narcosis. Fenn (1965) reported that both argon and nitrogen were synergistic with oxygen. At 30 atmospheres nitrogen pressure and 0.21 atmospheres oxygen, fruit flies remained alive for 1–14 days. But when 1 atmosphere of oxygen was combined with 30 atmospheres nitrogen the 50% survival rate was 5 hours. Fenn suggested that keeping oxygen tension low or normal, would avoid the narcotic effect of nitrogen at great depths. Few cases of nitrogen narcosis have been reported when oxygen tension was kept normal. In addition, performance tests in humans showed that oxygen and nitrogen were synergistic. Fenn (1965) reported that nitrogen added to oxygen in diving operations led to the onset of convulsions at toxic pressures when oxygen itself was not toxic.

Although argon, an inert gas, is synergistic with oxygen, it is possible that the high pressures of argon and nitrogen merely act as methods of increasing the pressure of the oxygen and thus as methods to increase the oxidation of adrenaline and other easily oxidized metabolites.

Pure oxygen at one atmosphere may also be psychotomimetic. Donald Campbell (1965) holder of several speed records on land and water recently described one of his early races as follows:

I had accelerated up to 250 mph when I felt the car beginning to weave away from the black center line I was watching carefully. But I had her under control and was feeling as confident as ever.

I was half-way down the track and approaching 300 mph when I saw what seemed to be a large lorry moving straight across the track less than a mile away.

It couldn't be a lorry. But something was there on the course and getting bigger every instant. Instinctively I cut the power and braced myself to drive off the track rather than risk a collision.

I was just about to turn the wheel when the lorry changed shape and I realized it was nothing more than a big track marker which the mirage effect of the sun on the salt had distorted until it looked exactly like a moving lorry. I took a very deep breath and let Bluebird coast on to the end of the track, not realizing quite how keyed up I was.

There was half an hour's wait while the team turned Bluebird around for the return run.

'How do you feel, Skipper?' said Leo.

'On top of the world. Never felt better,' I replied.

'It's vital to find out how fast Bluebird will accelerate,' Leo said. 'So make this run an acceleration test. Three hundred by the second mile marker and then ease her off, and we'll all be happy.'

But I was happy already. As I left I noticed a film crew driving beside the track filming the car.

'I'll give those boys something to film,' I said and put my foot down as hard as it would go. The effect was phenomenal. With a turbine you have no gear changes to worry about and that smooth thrust forward was one of the most exciting things I have ever felt. I was overwhelmed with it and quite unconcerned with steering trouble we had been having. Already I must have been keeping her on course by instinct as I have no memory at all of how she was handling.

I didn't know what I was doing at all. All I could think of was that second mile marker. And something in my brain was telling me that all that mattered was to pass it as fast as I could. There was no sense of logic. No sense of fear. Nothing except intense elation and an obsession to put on every scrap of power we had.

The steering began to go, but I was past worrying about that by now. I felt the rear wheels slip as they lost adhesion on the salt, but not even this could worry me. All that mattered was that second marker and getting past it as fast as Bluebird could carry me.

I had almost reached it when Bluebird passed out of control. I knew she was going. Yet all I could think was: 'Oh, well. It looks as if we're going into the rough. Don't worry.'

I noticed that the speedometer reading was 365 and then lost interest. The car rocketed off the track.

My survival was a miracle. But it turned out that the crash had fractured the base of the skull, bruising the thalamus area of the brain. My eardrums were broken, my eyes were black and blue, and for 12 days I lay in a darkened room with cerebral spinal fluid trickling steadily from my left ear.

As I lay there during those dreadful days I was tormented with the thought of what I had done. Why had the crash occurred? Why had I behaved so abnormally on the morning of the run?

Sir Arnold Hall, head of Bristol Aircraft and the scientist who had solved the mystery of the early Comet crashes, helped me find the solution.

'You were breathing pure oxygen,' he said. 'During the war I carried out experiments putting night fighter pilots on pure oxygen to improve their vision. Some of them reacted exactly as you did. They got a sort of oxygen poisoning. It was rather as if they were drunk. They were light-headed, with no sense of judgment or fear. Does that tie in with your reactions?'

It did. As I discovered later, I was one of a minority who are subject to this 'oxygen poisoning,' and if I had been breathing the compressed air at Utah that I have relied on since, the crash would never have occurred.

Apparently there was a high incidence of "gremlins" in the RAF during the war, especially in night fighters and night bombers. The resulting conditions were common anxiety, fatigue, reduced environmental input, low pressure, and increased oxygen. These are not unlike conditions in deep sea diving. It is important to study these matters further in space pilots who will be subjected to even greater stresses.

Recently, a man knowledgeable about schizophrenia and the perceptual changes produced in subjects compared his reaction to the inhalation of oxygen while a pilot during the last war and similar reactions experienced as a skin diver. At a depth of about 135 feet this man experienced euphoria and loss of judgment which often led to a desire to remove his oxygen mask and swim free. For this reason he dived only in the company of another diver so they could watch each other. This euphoric zone was quite constant for him. When he dived deeper than that it went away partially. After returning to land, a feeling of euphoria remained for several hours. The experience was nearly identical with the one he used to experience when, as a pilot, he inhaled pure oxygen.

Among his skin diving friends were 18 who dived only occasionally, none of whom were in any way abnormal. However, 2 others were professional divers. Of these, one was undoubtedly very bizarre and queer, or as our informant stated "punchy" and the other was mildly bizarre. These data suggest that prolonged deep sea diving can lead to permanent psychological changes but does not prove it since the two men might have been strange before they began to dive as professionals. A study of personality changes in professional skin divers is indicated.

These reactions are remarkably like those experienced by Osmond after taking adrenolutin and then driving in a car (Hoffer *et al.*, 1954).

6. Compounds which are known to be antihallucinogenic compounds also protect animals against nitrogen toxicity. Bennett (1963) found that Frenquel at a dose of 70–410 mg/kg in rats protected them against nitrogen narcosis. The maximum protection came 48 hours after the last dose and lasted about 3 days. In humans 1200 mg Frenquel protected them against nitrogen narcosis. We have already referred to the protective action of reserpine and chlorpromazine against oxygen toxicity. Bennett concluded that drugs which accelerated oxygen poisoning also accelerated nitrogen narcosis. Methedrine megimide and leptazol enhanced nitrogen narcosis and shortened the time for convulsions to appear in OHP.

7. Oxygen toxicity comes on relatively slowly. This means that increase of oxygen toxicity which follows injection of adrenaline can not be due to unchanged adrenaline. The time required for convulsions to develop suggests there is a gradual conversion of adrenaline into adrenochrome which overwhelms the systems available for its removal or destruction.

We can summarize these reactions as follows:

$$\text{adrenaline} + O_2 \xrightarrow[\text{(adrenaline oxidase)}]{} \text{adrenochrome} \tag{1}$$

$$\text{glutamic acid} \xrightarrow[\text{(glutamic acid decarboxylase)}]{} GABA + CO_2 \tag{2}$$

Therefore, convulsants are—

a. adrenaline
b. adrenergic compounds

c. oxygen
d. adrenaline oxidase activators (Cu^+, Fe^{2+})

and anticonvulsants (OHP) are—

a. medullectomy
b. sympathetic blocking substances
c. chelating compounds

d. GABA
e. low copper diets

We would expect that carbon dioxide would inhibit the action of glutamic acid decarboxylase according to the law of mass action. Bean (1965) reported that lower concentrations of CO_2 augmented oxygen toxicity. Higher concentrations eliminated the convulsions but not death. The effect of higher CO_2 doses was considered to be a form of CO_2 depression or CO_2 narcosis. But both augmentation and inhibition of CO_2 for oxygen toxicity are in part mediated through the effect on cerebral vessels and brain blood flow, so the effect on decarboxylase would be difficult to sort out. Foster and Churchill-Davidson (1963) also found increased CO_2 levels complicated the reaction to oxygen.

High oxygen pressure blocked peripheral nerve conduction (Perot and Stein, 1956). This may be related to Marrazzi and Hart's (1956) observation that adrenochrome blocked synaptic transmission.

These reactions suggest methods for reducing oxygen toxicity. These are ways for decreasing the oxidation of adrenaline to adrenochrome and for neutralizing any adrenochrome which may be formed. Protective chemicals should, therefore, be those substances which are useful in treating schizophrenia. They are as follows:

1. Ascorbic acid—for decreasing conversion of adrenaline to adrenochrome.
2. Glutathione—also for decreasing oxidation.
3. Pencillamine—for binding copper and removing adrenochrome which is formed.
4. Nicotinic acid—for antagonizing the psychological and EEG changes of adrenochrome.
5. Ceruloplasmin—for binding adrenolutin.
6. Low copper diets for decreasing oxidation of adrenaline.

7. Antipsychotic drugs.
8. Adrenaline oxidase inhibitors.

ALLERGIES AND ADRENOCHROME

Hutcheon *et al.* (1956) found that adrenochrome had weak antihistaminic properties. A concentration of $2–10 \times 10^{-6}$ M adrenochrome inhibited histamine and induced contraction of isolated guinea pig ileum. It had about 4% of the activity of pyrilamine. Synthetic antihistamines are given intermittently. A weak natural antihistamine continuously present might be more effective than its apparent activity suggests. Alberty and Takkunen (1956) reported that adrenochrome monosemicarbazone prevented the increase in vascular permeability which followed intradermal injections of histamine. It was just as active an antihistamine in suppressing the skin reaction to 48/80, one of the most powerful histamine releasers. When given intraperitoneally it had the same order of activity as the current synthetic antihistamines. J. Noval (1965) also found that adrenochrome monosemicarbazone had antihistamine properties.

Adrenochrome had antihistamine properties *in vivo*. Halpern *et al.* (1952) found that adrenalectomized rats were more sensitive to histamine. Adrenaline restored normal histamine tolerance while corticosteroid hormones did not do so.

One would expect that people who have large amounts of adrenochrome either in tissues or fluids would show a tolerance toward histamine. R. R. Sackler *et al.* (1951) and M. D. Sackler *et al.* (1951) found that schizophrenic patients could tolerate increased quantities of histamine. This was confirmed by Lucy (1954) who showed that the histamine tolerance increased with the chronicity of the illness. Weckowicz and Hall (1957) further found that the wheal produced by schizophrenic patients after intradermal injection of histamine came on more slowly than in normals. This simple test satisfactorily differentiated blind between a chronic group of schizophrenic patients and nonschizophrenic subjects. Finally, Doust *et al.* (1956) found that a series of schizophrenic patients had 106 μg/liter histamine in their blood compared with 88 μg/liter for normals. This difference was significant and indicates again that schizophrenics can tolerate more histamine.

Since antihistaminics are useful in the treatment of allergies thought to be mediated by the presence of too much histamine, one would expect that if schizophrenics have more adrenochrome available than other people then they would be less likely to develop allergies. It has been observed by Lea (1955), A. M. Sackler *et al.* (1956), as well as others that allergic states do seem to be rare among schizophrenic patients. Recently LeBlanc and Lemieux (1961) and Donovan and Osmond (1963) again confirmed these observations. Lea found 1 allergic condition in a carefully studied series of 500 schizophrenics. There were 22 cases in 500 head injury controls. This finding is most significant. That this is not simply a characteristic of those who become schizophrenic, but of schizophrenia itself, is suggested by the fact that they develop allergies when freed of schizophrenia. Funkenstein (1950) reported a small series of psychotic patients who had alternately asthma or psychosis (most frequently schizophrenia) but never both together. He also reviewed the literature showing the scarcity of allergies in psychotic patients. Rheumatoid arthritis is also very rare (Trevathan and Tatum, 1954).

Using the adrenochrome hypothesis, it is possible to understand these apparently unrelated findings. During period of mental health, there would be normal adrenochrome production and therefor a normal probability for allergy reactions. During schizophrenic episodes, the increased production of adrenochrome would prevent the allergy. Since adrenaline is a standard treatment for asthma, it is possible that asthmatics who take large quantities of adrenaline may develop schizophrenic states (Hoffer, 1957c), as has occurred after inhalation of discolored adrenaline (Osmond and Hoffer, 1958).

ADRENOCHROME AND HYPOTHERMIA

Eade (1954) and Hutcheon *et al.* (1956) discovered that both adrenochrome and adrenolutin, when injected intraperitoneally, lowered the body temperature of rats markedly. A dose of 2.5 mg per rat lowered the temperature $1°C$ after one-half hour and this did not return to normal for 4 hours. A dose of 5 mg lowered the temperature $2\frac{1}{2}°C$. Normal temperature was restored in 6 hours. Since there was no decrease in oxygen consumption these authors suggested the hypothermia must be due to a central effect on the temperature regulating mechanism of the hypothalamus. According to Cerletti (1956), LSD and other ergot alkaloids also lowered body temperature of rats. The most active was LSD and the least effective BOL. Rabbits, on the other hand, responded with an increase in temperature when given LSD. Rinkel (discussion after Cerletti, 1956) reported that the skin temperatures of human subjects decreased after LSD, probably due to the vasoconstriction stimulated by the increased secretion of adrenaline.

Recently Miller (1964) referred to work of Feldberg and Myers (1965) who showed that small quantities of serotonin placed in the anterior hypothalamus caused shivering and an increase in temperature.

But noradrenaline and adrenaline inhibited shivering and reduced temperature. They also decreased temperature in normal cats. Injection in any other area of the brain was ineffective. Miller reported that 22 μg of noradrenaline in the lateral hypothalamus of rats decreased body temperature 0.5°C. The same dose given intravenously also lowered temperature.

There is a parallel relationship between diurnal temperature variations and secretion of noradrenaline and adrenaline. Buck *et al.* (1950) reported that in normal subjects body temperature (rectal) began to rise after awakening in the morning and increased until it reached its peak value at 4:00 PM. It then decreased regularly until the minimum was reached at 4:00 in the morning. For normal subjects this diurnal cycle was fairly regular and reproducible. Sundin (1958) reported that the excretion of noradrenaline and adrenaline during the day was materially higher than during the night. He measured excretion in urine of both amines, when normal subjects were recumbent, tilted to 25°, 50° and 75°. The excretion of adrenaline increased 2.0, 4.8 and 7.6 mμg/minute, and noradrenaline excretion increased 12.5, 11.7, and 24.3 mμg/minute. Using a 100% correction factor since about 1% of the total adrenaline secreted in the body would appear in urine, tilting a recumbent subject to 75° increased adrenaline and noradrenaline secretion by roughly 1 mg and 3 mg per day.

Ellis (1956) reviewed the metabolic effects of adrenaline. He reported that although adrenaline regularly increased overall utilization of oxygen when given *in vivo* it did not regularly directly stimulate use of oxygen by tissues. Many of the observed effects, he stated, were attributable to adrenochrome. As we have noted earlier, adrenochrome did not alter total consumption of oxygen by rats. Adrenaline in low doses decreased heat loss because it constricted skin vessels and reduced blood flow. As a result, body temperatures were elevated. But at high doses it caused hypothermia even though the vasoconstriction in skin was more intense than before.

It seems likely that the increasing body temperature until 4:00 PM is due to the increased secretion of noradrenaline and adrenaline and that the decrease in temperature after that is due to the increased formation of adrenochrome which is hypothermic. This explanation is consistent with the effect of large doses of adrenaline which should elevate body temperature even more than lower doses but which, in fact, lower it.

If schizophrenics have a derangement of adrenochrome metabolism it would not be surprising if they also suffered abnormalities in their daily control of temperature. This has been observed many times, but the most recent studies were reported by Buck *et al.* (1950, 1951). Excessive production of adrenochrome would lower body temperature and since the regular conversion of adrenaline to adrenochrome would be interrupted, many irregularities in diurnal temperature control should occur. Buck *et al.* found (a) the day–night mean range of temperature variation from high to low was 1.1°F for normal subjects, and 0.5°F for 40 schizophrenic subjects, (b) the mean rectal temperature was 98.7°F for normal subjects and 98.5° for schizophrenics. Schizophrenic diurnal curves were very seldom regular as were normal curves. They had either very flat curves or very variable curves with sharp temperature changes. When placed in a hot bath at 102°F schizophrenics and normal subjects were the same—their temperature went up. Since the total body was immersed up to the neck, no counter measures would be helpful and rate of temperature gain would be mechanical. When placed in cold baths schizophrenics were very different. Normal subjects decreased body temperature slowly in the bath and more quickly after they were removed from the bath. Patients seldom had these predictable responses. Again the temperature curve was either too flat or too marked and erratic. Patients sick for four years or less, were more abnormal than more chronic patients. Lobotomy made the diurnal temperature rhythm of patients more normal. Their response to cold baths also improved.

Two years ago the oral temperatures of 183 patients admitted consecutively to the University Hospital (Saskatoon) were measured and recorded by a senior psychiatric nurse.[1] When the patients were discharged their final diagnosis was used as recorded in the discharge note.[2] Temperatures were taken between 8 and 9 AM for the AM reading, and 4 and 5 PM for the PM reading.

The following results were obtained—

	Number	Mean temperature		
		AM	PM	Difference
Schizophrenic	51	97.50	97.68	0.18
Nonschizophrenic	132	97.70	98.05	0.35

These results are not directly comparable to those of Buck *et al.* since only 2 points were used—the AM on the ascending part of the diurnal curve and the PM one at the expected maximum portion, but they support their general conclusions. Schizophrenics had lower body

[1] Miss E. Helfrich, R.N.
[2] By Miss M. J. Callbeck, R.N., Chief Psychiatric Research Nurse.

temperatures and the AM–PM differential was less. Schizophrenic patients also had lower skin temperatures when exposed to cold (Shattock, 1950).

The fact that temperature control is defective in schizophrenic patients is thus additional indirect evidence for an abnormality of adrenochrome metabolism and for the *in vivo* conversion of adrenaline into adrenochrome.

ANTITHYROID PROPERTIES OF ADRENOCHROME

Quinones in general have antithyroid properties. It is not surprising that adrenochrome also is antithyroid. Pastan *et al.* (1962) found that adrenochrome stimulated the pentose phosphate cycle of a thyroid mitochondrial microsomal preparation more than did adrenaline. It accelerated the oxidation of TPNH and DPNH. Another site of activity is at the hexose monophosphate shunt. Dumont and Hupka (1963) found that adrenaline stimulated hexose monophosphate shunt of thyroid tissue. This was due primarily to its oxidation to adrenochrome. The evidence was (a) preincubation with adrenaline increased the activation of oxidation but preincubation with adrenochrome did not increase it. (b) Bisulfite (which combines with adrenochrome to form a stable complex) inhibited the action of adrenochrome but ascorbic acid did not. (c) Both bisulfite and ascorbic acid considerably decreased the action of adrenaline. (d) Adrenochrome was demonstrated by spectrophotometric examination.

Schizophrenic patients can tolerate large quantities of thyroid even though less than 10% of any schizophrenic population seem to be hypothyroid. One of the more curious facts of modern psychiatry is the selectivity of many psychiatrists who accept pragmatic treatments for which there is, as yet, no rationale and reject other treatments for which there is powerful evidence; while on the other hand huge schools of therapy are in existence which have no basis in data but are recommended by those who write textbooks and create fashions. Careful scientists, including psychologists like Eysenck, who might be biased in favor of psychotherapy, have shown repeatedly that cure rates following psychotherapy are not significantly different from natural remission rates. But psychotherapy is considered the prime therapy in psychiatry.

In sharp contrast a large number of workers have shown that thyroid hormone either in the form of dried gland or as the pure hormone, triiodothyronine does improve cure rates much above the natural untreated rates and other standard treatments used, including the tranquilizers.

Recently Lochner *et al.* (1963) published an excellent literature review of this field. A large number of authors including Asher (1949), Claude and Bernard (124), L. H. Cohen (1939), Danziger (1958), Danziger and Kendwall (1953, 1954), Hoskins (1932, 1946), Hoskins and Sleeper (1929, 1931), R. Gjessing (1938, 1953), Gornall *et al.* (1953, 1958), Mall (1960), L. R. Gjessing (1964), and Wakoh (1959) found that many more schizophrenic patients were rendered completely free of symptoms and signs when treatment with thyroid was maintained. This included not only periodic catatonics but other schizophrenics who had no regular periodicity but seemed to have the usual more or less random fluctuations seen in most patients.

Danziger (1958) reported some astonishingly successful results which have never been repeated by other workers using conventional treatments. He selected a series of 120 schizophrenics between the years 1946 and 1956. Many of them had not responded to any other therapy including ECT, psychotherapy, or psychoanalysis. Of this group 45% recovered, that is became normal in every respect. Thyroid medication was continued for at least 100 days since recovery was slow for many. Of the 80 patients who were given thyroid medication for at least 100 days and who had been ill 6 months or less, *all* recovered. Relapses occurred only if patients discontinued medication while at home. The proper dose of thyroid would be considered excessively high by many physicians. We have found that some of our patients were taken off thyroid by family physicians as they were beginning to recover from their schizophrenia. The range of dose was 2–20 grains (128–1280 mg) of USP thyroid extract, or 1–9 mg of thyroxine. Only 10 subjects needed more than 10 grains.

Recently a sixteen-year-old girl from the United States was admitted for treatment of her schizophrenia. She had been severely ill for nearly 2 years and had not responded to prolonged psychoanalytic therapy for many months. She had failed to respond to treatment in a university psychiatric ward in Texas, in a large well-known psychiatric clinic on the west coast, to 6 months of continuous high doses of tranquilizers in another hospital, or to a combination of nicotinic acid (3 gm per day), penicillamine (2 gm per day for 10 days), and ECT in a fourth hospital. When she was admitted to University Hospital she was a classical adolescent schizophrenic with changes in perception, gross thought disorder, inappropriate affect, and activity. She was filled with hatred for her parents, something we rarely see in our patients not exposed to psychoanalysis. She also had malvaria. She was immediately started on a second series of ECT plus nicotinic acid (Hoffer *et al.*, 1957) plus pencillamine and within 2 weeks had recovered clinically, but her HOD scores remained very high. After 1 week she suddenly relapsed within a period of 24 hours and became catatonic. About this time Dr. L. Gjessing, son of Dr. R. Gjessing, visited our research at Saskatoon and brought us up to date on periodic catatonia. A review of her illness then showed that although she had not once recovered spontaneously from schizophrenia, she had several times been very much improved after a series of ECT. She did not fit into the Gjessing syndrome but she had a periodicity imposed on her by treatment.

At this time she was started on dessicated thyroid and the dose was increased until her pulse rate hovered between 110 and 120 per minutes. She was maintained on nicotinic acid and given small doses of haloperidol to control agitation. The thyroid was begun as her clinical condition was rapidly worsening into a catatonic stupor. Within a day her condition steadied and she slowly began to improve. When she was discharged in December, 1964, after 2 months in hospital, she was very much better but her HOD scores were too high and the stigmata of schizophrenia were still present. Six months later she was nearly well. Her scores had become normal, she was being tutored at home in preparation for her return to high school and she was able to relate to her parents and friends in her normal manner. She had quickly lost her hostility to her parents as she recovered and she was assured they had not made her ill. It was explained to her that ambivalence and hostility were merely symptoms of schizophrenia to be ignored, if possible, and controlled. She is still on 7 grains thyroid per day. With this dramatic result before us a series of 12 schizophrenics were started on a similar program. All had been treated with nicotinic acid. All were at home and getting on reasonably well, but none were completely free of symptoms. From this group of 12 only 3 were not benefited but of these, one discontinued it before it could become effective on the advice of her family physician. Of the remaining 9, 6 were very much better and seem to be moving rapidly toward recovery and the other 3 are improving as the doses of thyroid are being increased. One of the 6 with a history of 16 admissions to University Hospital (Saskatoon) because he was constantly plagued by auditory hallucinations, is now nearly well and has been free of voices over 2 months. The usual maintenance dose is 5 grains of dessicated thyroid. All are, of course, still taking nicotinic acid.

Lochner et al. (1963) conducted a double blind controlled comparison study on 30 schizophrenic patients who had been in the hospital for 4 years or more, with a chronic history running 8 years or more. Of this group, half were given 200 μg of l-triiodothyronine each day and the other half, placebo. Of the drug group 12 were improved and, of the placebo group, 2 were improved. $P < 0.01$. Out of 12 drug patients who changed, 7 increased motor activity, sociability, interest in their environment and performed better at work. They became more spontaneous, their thinking became more logical and relevant and they felt better. One subject who had not responded to any medication in many years improved enough to work in the hospital kitchen. The remaining 5 who changed because overly active but revealed for the first time, a good deal of pathology they had suppressed. Of the placebo group, none improved but 2 became more active.

It is clear from Lochner *et al.*'s (1963) review that thyroid medication has not come into general use simply because there is no acceptable rationale. The majority of schizophrenic patients had normally functioning thyroid glands. Reiss and Haigh (1954) using radioactive tracer methods found that of 1539 subjects in a mental hospital in England, 17% were underactive and 17% were overactive.

But there is a peripheral insensitivity to thyroid hormone. Large doses of hormone did not increase oxygen consumption. It has been known for a long time that schizophrenic patients could tolerate large doses of thyroid and not show any evidence of hyperthyroidism. Hoskins (1932) reported that schizophrenic patients were resistant to large doses of thyroid. We have found that 5 grains must usually be given before the pulse rate is elevated to 100 or more. This is nearly twice the normal endogenous production of thyroid. Brody and Man (1950) found that the concentrated serum precipitable iodine for 57 schizophrenic patients was normal. They also suggested that the low basal metabolic rate of these patients was a function of a defective response to the circulating hormone.

If tissues do not respond to normal levels of hormone this must be due to a metabolic block on the tissue receptors. The report of Brody *et al.* rules out excessive destruction of hormone. The metabolic block might be due to a toxin as was suggested by L. Gjessing (1964) who believed that such a toxin could accumulate gradually until a critical level was reached. At this time the hypothalamus would be affected which would, in turn, stimulate discharge of large amounts of amines, increase thyroid activity slightly, and precipitate the psychosis. The adrenergically altered metabolism would gradually break down the toxin and allow the patient to enter a quiet phase. The administration of thyroid and the elevation of oxygen consumption would increase the detoxification process and so prevent a buildup of toxin and so abort a relapse.

Quinones are antithyroid. It is not surprising that adrenochrome which has a quinoid structure, can also interfere in thyroid function. It is likely the accumulation of substances like adrenochrome and adrenolutin is responsible for these curious relationships between schizophrenia and thyroid function. Rawson *et al.* (1957) stated that adrenochrome prevented metamorphosis of tadpoles. This is a property shared with other indoles and provides direct evidence that thyroid hormone and adrenochrome are antagonists.

It is curious that both thyroxine and adrenochrome are uncouplers of oxidative phosphorylation. J. Bain (1957) reported that a subeffective dose of thyroxin (5×10^{-5} M) and a subeffective dose of adrenochrome (2×10^{-5} M) added together produced 50% uncoupling of oxidative phosphorylation.

ANTI-INSULINASE ACTIVITY OF ADRENOLUTIN

Schizophrenia and diabetes mellitus seem to be relatively incompatible one with the other. Bellak (1948) in his first review referred to published accounts of this relationship. Between 1930 and 1939 the death rate from diabetes in schizophrenia was 11.9 per 100,000 compared to the death rate of other patients by diabetes of 89.8 in New York general hospitals. Many others have noted this unusual occurrence of diabetes in mental hospitals. Both Saskatchewan Hospitals (population of 3300) have less than 5 diabetics. Dynamic psychiatrists have explained this by stating that one defense mechanism removes the need for a second. But is this any more enlightening than merely noting that they are seen together infrequently?

Insulinase, the enzyme which destroys insulin, is believed to play a part in the genesis of diabetes. Substances which inhibit insulinase decrease demand on the pancreas and help control some mild diabetes. With this in mind, we sent Dr. B. Witkop at the National Institutes of Health some adrenolutin in mid-1956. This was our best preparation but not as good as crystalline adrenolutin. Dr. M. Vaughan of the National Heart Institute found adrenolutin at a concentration of 3×10^{-4} M caused 40% inhibition of insulinase. It was 10 times stronger than 5-hydroxyindole. This inhibition is not far from those oral insulinase inhibitors used clinically. If then adrenolutin plays some part in schizophrenia, it would act as an antidiabetic substance, and one would expect that once schizophrenia is established diabetes should be seen only infrequently if at all. In addition, mild diabetes should become less troublesome if the patient should become schizophrenic. Well-established diabetes can be followed by schizophrenia. Once again, then, it is important when establishing coincidence between two conditions, one of which is schizophrenia, to know which came first. Where the two are associated, we would predict that the diabetes was present first. Naturally diabetes not due to primary insufficiency of insulin must be excluded from this prediction.

Recently, Herjanic (1965) reported that 2 chronic schizophrenics kept on heavy doses of chlorpromazine suddenly developed diabetes mellitus. This was a very unusual occurrence. But if Ban and Lehmann (1965) are correct in supposing that chlorpromazine prevented the formation of adrenaline this could be expected. There would now be too little adrenochrome and adrenolutin and the protective action excreted by schizophrenia against diabetus mellitus would be removed. Amdison (1965) found 40% of the subjects on chlorpromazine had abnormal glucose tolerance curves and diabetic patients became worse.

The Relation of Adrenochrome to Erythrocyte Metabolism

Because adrenochrome is a very potent antimitotic substance there are only a few tissues in the body where it could be stored safely. These are tissues whose cells do not need to divide and grow. Erythrocytes which have no nucleus and do not divide would form excellent storage tissue. Erythrocytes absorb large quantities of adrenaline. W. A. Bain *et al.* (1937) and G. Cohen (1959) demonstrated that erythrocytes absorbed adrenaline very quickly. Another tissue which does not divide is myocardial tissue which also absorbs large quantities of adrenaline. Once adrenaline is absorbed in the erythrocytes some of it could be oxidized into adrenochrome and there stored in some adrenochrome glutathione complex. Hemoglobin markedly catalyzes the oxidation of adrenaline to adrenochrome *in vitro*.

One of the more interesting relationships is that which occurs between adrenochrome, primaquin-sensitive erythrocytes, and glucose-6-phosphate dehydrogenase deficiency (G6PD) known originally as primaquin sensitivity.

According to Hsia (1964), this disease is one of the metabolic disturbances in carbohydrate metabolism effecting the pentose phosphate cycle especially.

Primaquin sensitivity (hereafter G6PD) is a disease transmitted by a sex-linked gene with partial penetrance. Males either have it or are free of the disease, but females fall into three groups (a) normal (b) affected, and (c) partially affected—there is 75% penetrance. G6PD is found most often in Negroes, and about 10% of them have it. Where malaria is prevalent there is some biological advantage in having G6PD because the parasite requires reduced glutathione (GSH) and an oxidative pathway. In G6PD, the erythrocytes are deficient in GSH and have a diminished activity of the pentose phosphate pathway. This makes it more difficult for the parasite to grow. But when these people are given antimalarials they develop intravascular hemolysis.

In normal erythrocytes, triphosphopyridine nucleotide (TPN$^+$) is the factor which limits the rate of oxidation. The rate can be increased by adding electron carriers such as methylene blue. In G6PD disease it is the limiting factor and electron carriers are of no use. The cells are also low in GSH and in catalase. When incubated with acetylphenyl-hydrazine there is a marked fall in GSH. This also occurs at the beginning of drug hemolysis.

According to Pon (1964), the pentose phosphate cycle is influenced by methylene blue, age, thiamine, cysteine, ascorbic acid, pyruvate, hydrazines, and primaquin. In G6PD the erythrocytes cannot maintain GSH levels in the presence of low levels of hydrogen peroxide (H_2O_2). Adrenaline has no effect on the pentose phosphate cycle (Pastan *et al.,* 1962), but adrenaline which has turned pink or adrenochrome had a marked effect in accelerating oxidation of TPNH and DPNH by thyroid mitochondrial microsomal preparations.

Apparently similar reactions occur in brain tissue. G. Cohen and Hochstein (1963) pointed out that quinoid substances which can readily undergo reversible oxidation and reduction, like adrenochrome, and noradrenochrome, are potent inhibitors of aerobic glycolysis in brain. Amines like adrenaline noradrenaline, and dopamine, which must first be oxidized to become quinoid substances, are moderate inhibitors.

In the presence of glucose normal erythrocytes were not sensitive to small quantities of peroxide. In the absence of glucose, the cells were sensitive. The GSH was oxidized, methemoglobin was formed and cells became progressively less resistant to osmotic stress until they lysed. Quinones also generated H_2O_2 and so replaced it as toxic agents. In their presence the cells lost GSH, formed methemoglobin and suffered increased osmotic fragility. Glucose protected the cells against these toxic effects.

But G6PD erythrocytes were sensitive to peroxide even in the presence of glucose. Glutathione peroxidase linked to glucose metabolism through G6PD has been established as a major cellular pathway of peroxide detoxication. These reactions are shown below:

Glucose → 6PG ... G6P ... TPN / TPNH ... 2GSH / GSSG ... H_2O_2 / $2H_2O$

Hexokinase   Dehydrogenase   Reductase   Peroxidase

This illustrates how glucose protects erythrocytes against peroxides as long as G6P is present in normal concentrations.

But this protective chain of reactions fails in brain tissue because, according to G. Cohen and Hochstein (1963), brain tissue does not contain GSH peroxidase. They, therefore, suggested that peroxide generating compounds could affect brain metabolism if they could penetrate the blood brain barrier and produce fine to gross impairment of brain function.

We would expect that in primaquin sensitivity the erythrocytes would be much more sensitive to substances like adrenochrome since the detoxifying mechanism operates much less efficiently. Primaquin-sensitive Negroes ought, therefore, to be very sensitive to adrenochrome, noradrenochrome, or dopachrome and even to LSD, if LSD does operate via an adrenochrome mechanism.

In addition, primaquin-sensitive subjects should be more sensitive to schizophrenia if adrenochrome plays a role here, as we believe it does. It was, therefore, very interesting for us to study the findings of Dern *et al.* (1963) who found that male and female negro schizophrenics fell into widely divergent groups. The catatonic patients group had over 20% primaquin-sensitive subjects, while the paranoids had fewer than 10% sensitives. They suggested that G6PD patients were more vulnerable to schizophrenia if it did occur. Few will argue with the widespread belief that catatonic schizophrenics are physically and mentally much sicker than are the paranoids. Therefore, it seems logical that G6PD does decrease the tolerance for schizophrenia as one would expect if adrenochrome and similar substances were heavily involved. Schizophrenic erythrocytes are somewhat lower in glutathione and more fragile in hypotonic saline solutions (see Hoffer and Osmond, 1960).

There is other evidence that the red cells of schizophrenics are peculiar. Ansley *et al.* (1957) found that they were more variable in diameter compared to normal erythrocytes. The standard deviation of diameter distribution was 1.023 for schizophrenics and 0.546 for others. There was little overlap. Hoffer (1959a) found that schizophrenic erythrocytes were more fragile to hypotonic solutions of saline and appeared to be more readily ruptured by mechanical activity. In addition, the fresh hemoglobin was optically more dense per unit of iron between 410 and 420 mμ on the DU spectrophotometer. This might be due to the presence of substances in the red cells of schizophrenics which absorb light at this wavelength. Hoffer (1957d) also reported that the addition of adrenochrome or adrenaline to plasma increased the optical density at this absorption frequency.

Boszormenyi-Nagy and Gerty's observation that schizophrenic red cells have unusual metabolism may be accounted for by their relationship to adrenaline and adrenochrome. Thus (a) adrenaline and adrenochrome are bound in the cell, (b) adrenochrome interferes in the citric acid cycle of carbohydrate metabolism and uncouples phosphorylation. This would also be an explanation for the increased optical density of hemoglobin at 410 μ/mg iron, the increased fragility of hypotonic saline, and the increased variability of cell size.

Sjovall (1947) reported that mice which had been injected with serum from schizophrenics showed marked hemoglobin uria 1 hour after the injection. He did not find this result with serum from normal controls.

There is a good deal of data which show that schizophrenic erythrocytes do not metabolize glucose in the same way as normal erythrocytes. Boszormenyi-Nagy and Gerty (1955) found that insulin pretreatment of normal erythrocytes inhibited the accumulation of adenosine triphosphate (ATP) by hemolysates incubated with pyruvate and hexose diphosphate. This inhibition of ATP buildup was not observed with schizophrenic erythrocytes. Since adrenochrome is a very powerful inhibitor of ATPase while adrenaline alone has no effect it is likely this differential effect of erythrocytes is due to an accumulation of oxidized adrenaline derivatives. That is with normal erythrocytes insulin would increase utilization of ATP but with ATPase inhibited by adrenochrome this could not occur in schizophrenic cells. Orstrum and Skaug (1950) also found a decreased turnover of ATP in schizophrenics. Randall (1946) and Meyerhoff, and Randall (1948) found that adrenochrome inhibited hexokinase and phosphohexokinase. A concentration of 4×10^{-5} M inhibited these enzymes 50%. The degree of inhibition was inversely related to the amount of ATP present.

These earlier findings have some relevance to recent work on toxic protein fractions in schizophrenics. Frohman *et al.* (1960) found that schizophrenic red cells under basal conditions took up much more labeled ^{32}P than did normal subjects. There was an inability to utilize ATP. When insulin was injected into the patients a differential response occurred. In normal subjects the incorporation of ^{32}P was greatly increased. Insulin is known to increase secretion of adrenaline by its marked hypoglycemic action. An increased oxidation of adrenaline into adrenochrome would promote a buildup of ATP by inhibiting ATPase, but the same quantity of insulin (10 units of regular insulin) would have much less effect in lowering glucose of chronic schizophrenics so that the insulin could allow an increase in utilization of ATP so reducing it. Perhaps this is a rationale for the use of insulin in treating schizophrenics.

Using chicken erythrocytes Frohman *et al.* (1960) reported that schizophrenic serum inhibited glucose oxidation as measured by the lactic acid pyruvic acid ratios. When adrenaline and noradrenaline were incubated in normal serum with the chicken erythrocytes oxidation was promoted. Adrenochrome and adrenolutin were inactive. Doses were not given. These data suggest that adrenochrome alone is not the active inhibitor in this system but it may be that it is formed from adrenaline within the cell where it would be combined with sulfhydril amino acids.

The administration of noradrenaline, adrenaline, metanephrine and normetanephrine activated oxidation (Frohman *et al.*, 1965). These amines were injected intramuscularly into chickens. Cold stress, by releasing endogenous adrenaline, was also effective. Erythrocytes from cold stressed chickens were not inhibited in oxidation of glucose by schizophrenic serum. To account for these interesting findings we need only to assume the adrenaline–adrenochrome (or noradrenaline–noradrenochrome) systems are important in erythrocyte metabolism of glucose. Schizophrenics with excess adrenochrome would accumulate ATP. Adrenaline would restore the ratio but at an elevated level. Insulin in normals would increase both adrenaline and adrenochrome and accumulate ATP, but not in schizophrenics where there would be only a slight effect of 10 units of insulin.

ADRENOCHROME, IRON, AND COPPER METABOLISM

S. Green *et al.* (1956) reported that Fenton's reagent, ferrous iron plus H_2O_2, oxidized adrenaline to adrenochrome at pH 4.5. Ferritin also oxidized adrenaline in the presence of H_2O_2 at pH 7.4, the oxidation of adrenaline to melanin was accelerated tenfold by iron chelating agents. Adrenochrome is a vaso constrictor of the smooth muscles of capillaries but melanin is not. This, they suggested, was the reason why ferritin inhibited the constriction of muscle capillaries by adrenaline.

Ovshinsky (1957) suggested that adrenaline, as an iron binding substance, removed it from ferritin stored in liver and spleen and in the process was oxidized to adrenochrome. As a result adrenaline would be removed continuously resulting in the steady generation of adrenochrome while transferrin levels would be decreased. In a small series of cases Ovshinsky (1958) did find that schizophrenic patients had 16% less transferrin than normal controls.

Any reaction involving iron cannot avoid being related to the erythrocytes. Scheid (1938) reported changes in hemoglobin metabolism during febrile episodes in schizophrenic patients. Urobilinogen in the urine increased and red blood cells were destroyed.

Scheid and Baumer (1937) noted that some schizophrenic reactions were related to febrile episodes. Their patients were usually catatonic. Before the febrile episode, hemolysis increased and hemoglobin values fell. They suggested that the increased lysis of cells led to the intoxication.

Copper and Schizophrenia

The relationship of copper plasma levels to schizophrenia is about as equivocal as is the relationship of ceruloplasmin and/or glutathione to schizophrenia. It may be that a geographical variable has been overlooked here and has resulted in different results in different places. It is well known that glaciated soils (areas which were covered by the glaciers and which are covered with material carried down from the north) are richer in minerals such as lead, zinc, copper, etc., than nonglaciated soils. In North America, these soils cover most of Canada and the northern part of the United States and similarly in Europe and Asia, the areas down to 45° latitude are more often glaciated than not. People living on these soils are more apt to have slightly more of these trace elements in their body. Thus, patients from New Orleans, Louisiana, where soils were not glaciated, would not be comparable with patients from Saskatoon. An elevation of copper levels might obscure slight differences. In addition, it might accentuate the tendency for predisposed subjects to develop schizophrenia so that schizophrenics living on glaciated copper-rich soils would have no more copper than controls. We would, therefore, expect significant differences to be found only in those patients living off glaciated soils with the exception of those high in copper for reasons of nutritional idiosyncrasies. Studies conducted in the northern hemisphere, south of 50° latitude, should then show there is a significant difference whereas studies on glacial till soils will show there is no difference.

These predictions will apply only to baseline nonstressed levels of copper. Abood (1957) found that blood copper levels can fluctuate very widely in response to stress, anxiety, hallucinations, etc. It is likely that people with higher copper baseline stores can suffer more violent fluctuations in copper. So our prediction would be that schizophrenics living on copper-free soils will have higher baseline levels but a smaller coefficient of variability of copper fluctuation. Schizophrenics living on high copper soils will have similar baseline levels (although, of course, higher than those found in subjects from low copper soils), but will have a greater coefficient of variability.

The results of some oxidation studies and the geographical locations are shown in Table 24.

Most of the studies were carried out on glaciated soils.

A series of comparative studies between states below latitude 40°
north and 40° using identical methods for measuring copper and ceruloplasmin would settle this issue. Diagnostic criteria would have to be
similar and other factors such as muscular activity controlled.

TABLE 24

RELATION OF GEOGRAPHY TO DIFFERENCES IN COPPER[a] BETWEEN SCHIZOPHRENIC AND
CONTROL SUBJECTS

References	Location	Glaciated	Differences oxidation	Found copper levels different
Abood *et al.* (1957)	Illinois	+	+	
Akerfeldt (1957a)	Scandinavia	+	+	
Angel *et al.* (1957)	New Orleans	−	+	
Bischoff (1952)	Germany	+		+
Bonasera and Criscuoli (1961)	Italy	−	+	+
Brenner and Breier (1949)	Germany	+		+
Friedhoff *et al.* (1959)	New York	+	+	
Frohman *et al.* (1958)	Michigan	+	−	−
Gussion *et al.* (1958)	New York	+	−	
Horwitt *et al.* (1957)	Illinois	+	−	+
Leach *et al.* (1956)	New Orleans	−	+	
Maas *et al.* (1961)	Ohio	+	+	−
Ozek (1957)	Germany	+		−
Saunders and Chipkiewicz (1959)	New York	+	+	−
Scheinberg *et al.* (1957)	New York	+	+	−
Stennett and Callowhill (1960)	Ontario	+	−	
Yuwiler *et al.* (1961)	Michigan	+	−	

[a] Measured as copper ion or as ceruloplasmin. + = Yes; − = No.

Another reason why a clear relationship to copper metabolism might
not be found is the marked variation in copper values in some patients.
Mefferd *et al.* (1960) reported a longitudinal study on 1 patient over
a period of 240 days. Copper levels were assayed every second day.
Clinical evaluation and psychological tests were recorded frequently.
For the first 60 days, the patient received placebo. There was little
clinical change and copper values fluctuated between about 118 μg
per 100 ml to about 108 μg per ml. For the second 60-day period
chlorpromazine was given. A few days after it had been started, copper
levels fell rapidly and the patient showed some improvement. Then
copper levels stayed around 95 μg per 100 ml.

The third 60-day period the patient continued to take chlorpromazine and in addition was given a electroconvulsive therapy series. His condition rapidly worsened and his blood copper levels quickly increased to about 120 μg per 100 ml. The fourth 60-day period he was again treated with placebo, his condition clinically returned to its prechlorpromazine state and his copper values decreased below 100. During chlorpromazine therapy there was a high negative correlation between copper levels and the results of the word association test ($r = -0.72$).

In contrast, Rice (1962) reported copper variations in 7 healthy adults. All copper levels were within the normal range and did not have the variations reported in the schizophrenic.

The clearest association between copper levels, ceruloplasmin, and psychosis occurs in hepatolenticular degeneration where ceruloplasmin levels are low and excessive deposits of copper are found in certain areas of brain and liver. According to Beard (1959) patients who have this condition do not have schizophrenia but have toxic psychosis. The association between Wilson's disease and psychiatric and neurological changes, is very high. The best treatments are chelating agents which pick up the excessive copper and excrete it in the urine. British antilewisite was used originally but it has been replaced by penicillamine.

Hoffer and Osmond (1960) used penicillamine combined with nicotinic acid and ECT for schizophrenics who had failed to respond to the combination of ECT plus nicotinic acid. Half the failures recovered when penicillamine was added. The rationale behind penicillamine consisted of two parts: (a) to bind copper and remove it and so decrease oxidation of adrenaline to adrenochrome and (b) to combine with adrenochrome and convert most of it into the nontoxic 5,6-dihydroxy-*N*-methylindole, as it does *in vitro*.

Greiner (1965) and Nicolson *et al.* (1966) sought for a way of reversing the hypermelanization found in some schizophrenic patients treated with high doses of tranquilizers. They treated a small group of chronic schizophrenics with penicillamine and low copper diets. The majority of patients who were blue (due to increased melanin deposition) lost their blueness. To their amazement, most of this small group also improved mentally. Greiner then completed a double blind study on 10 middle-aged chronic schizophrenics. One group received the low copper regimen. Both groups were retained on their previous tranquilizer medication. The low copper group improved mentally. One patient remained much improved until he broke his diet and consumed normal quantities of copper.

In the absence of copper, melanogenesis ceases in some animals (Nicolaus, 1962).

Harman (1960, 1961, 1962, 1965) found a relationship between age in human subjects and the presence of free radicals. Serum mercaptan levels decreased with age, ascorbic acid levels in females decreased with age. Copper levels increased linearly by the following reaction:

$$\text{Cu } (\mu g/100 \text{ ml}) = 113.2 + 0.523 \text{ age}$$

and in mice antioxidants prolonged life span significantly.

Schizophrenic patients suffer a higher mortality rate than the normal population even when they are not residing in the hospital, Niswander *et al.* (1963). The increased copper levels and increased free radicals which could come from the aminochromes might account for this increase in death rate.

Friedman *et al.* (1965) reported a most unusual finding. They found a significant relationship between cosmic radiation and psychiatric disturbances as measured by admission rates to 8 psychiatric hospitals between July 1, 1957 and October 31, 1961. They also found a significant relationship between the degree of psychiatric disturbances in schizophrenic patients and cosmic radiation. Tracks left in living tissue by cosmic radiation would contain increased quantities of free radicals. In a normal person this would be relatively unimportant, but if these levels were already high as in schizophrenia, or in old age, the additional burden might be enough to increase these abnormalities of behavior.

Travelers in space will undoubtedly be exposed to increased radiation. Unless adequate chemotherapeutic measures are taken the consequences may be very serious.

Effect of Adrenochrome on Electrograms

Slocombe (1956) and Slocombe *et al.* (1956) measured the changes produced in spontaneous and evoked electrical potentials in albino rats by serotonin, LSD, adrenaline, noradrenaline, and adrenochrome. All the compounds flattened spontaneous activity at the cortical and subcortical sites. The most effective was serotonin. The rest were effective in decreasing order of activity as listed. The changes were profound with thiopental anesthesia, but there was no change when ether was used. These authors believed the action was nonspecific on lower centers which have cortical and subcortical projections.

Krupp and Monnier (1960) injected adrenochrome into rabbits. There was a change in the EEG right after the injection. The amplitude of the spontaneous activity of the neocortex decreased, and slow wave activity disappeared. Simultaneously, there was an increase in synchronicity in the hippocampus and thalamus. There was thus a typical arousal pattern. After intercollicular decerebration, adrenochrome produced neocortical desynchronization with a slight increase in hippocampal synchronicity. After adrenochrome, there was an increase in the arousal reaction to sensory stimulation. The excitability of the hippocampus and its connections to the neocortex was increased. These authors concluded that LSD, mescaline, and psilocybin altered spontaneous electrical activity in a similar way to adrenochrome. All produced a sharp arousal pattern of activity. LSD caused desynchronization of the subcortex but the other three substances intensified subcortical synchronicity. LSD had no action on the "encéphale isolé" or the "cerveau isole" but adrenochrome had a slight effect and the other two compounds a marked effect. Both adrenochrome and mescaline activated the hippocampus but did not release spontaneous discharges. LSD released spontaneous discharge and psilocybin decreased hippocampal activity.

Schwarz *et al.* (1956b), using the ventricular cannula technique of Feldberg and Sherwood (1954) found that after the injection of 1 mg adrenochrome the cats were drowsy for 24 hours. The deep EEG showed occipital 4 cycles/sec slow waves with low-voltage spike components spreading to the frontal region and then diffusely over the brain. Painful stimulation caused inconsistent arousal. An arousal pattern appeared when the animal was drinking milk. These authors described the EEG changes as a trance pattern.

Heath *et al.* (1959) observed no change in the EEG pattern of monkeys. However, one monkey pretreated with taraxein was sensitized to adrenolutin and died after 100 mg. EEG changes then were present.

Hoffer *et al.* (1954) reported that adrenochrome produced pathological changes in the electrogram of some epileptic patients. A detailed report was presented by Szatmari *et al.* (1955). A few volunteers with normal electrograms were given 10–25 mg by vein. There was no change in the electrograms. Epileptic patients were given 10, 25, or 50 mg of adrenochrome. Five patients had a high-voltage, diffuse, paroxysmal abnormality with bilateral hypersynchrony, and diffuse high-voltage 5 per second activity. Adrenochrome produced a marked increase of the dysrhythmia and an increased sensitivity to hyperventilation. In two cases, the threshold for convulsions was lowered.

Another group of 15 patients had focal activity showing spike, sharp wave, and irregular delta activity in all cases, and diffuse bilateral slow activity in 10 of them. After adrenochrome, there was an increase of dysrhythmia, an increase in voltage and decrease in frequency, a marked increase in all cases of focal activity during hyperventilation along with a spread of pathological activity in the opposite homologous cortical area, and in 4 cases a spontaneous increase in irritability of the focus.

Schwarz *et al.* (1956a) measured changes in depth electrogram induced by adrenochrome. Patient 1, a chronic paranoid schizophrenic, on 3 occasions was given 50, 60, and 75 mg of adrenochrome by vein. There was a moderate increase in bitemporal paroxysmal discharge of 2–7 cycles/sec, and increased persistence and amplitude of the focal temporal sharp wave discharge from the depths, in all three instances. Subject 2 was given 50 and 60 mg on 2 occasions. There was a moderate increase in paroxysmal activity. Patient 5, who had psychosis with epilepsy, was given 50 mg of adrenochrome. This produced high-voltage waves 2 to 3 cycles/sec, associated with drowsiness. The depth electrograms of patient number 1 resembled that reported for a schizophrenic by Sem-Jacobsen *et al.* (1955), but after adrenochrome, the focal sharp wave activity of maximum amplitude from the temporal region was persistent. The authors concluded that "administration of mescaline, LSD, and adrenochrome can cause striking changes in the depth electrogram."

Grof *et al.* (1961a,b) gave 6 subjects 20 mg of adrenochrome sublingually. In 5, there were marked changes between 30 and 90 minutes. Alpha activity was slightly disintegrated. Theta waves appeared with spikes and the EEG became hypersensitive to hyperventilation. There was no correlation between the EEG changes and the intensity of the psychological changes.

CERULOPLASMIN

Ceruloplasmin, a copper protein enzyme, normally present in serum oxidizes catechol, adrenaline, serotonin, and other amines. Leach *et al.* (1956) believed it was the catalyst in the oxidation of adrenaline to adrenochrome. Akerfeldt (1957a,b) found that N,N-diethyl-p-phenylenediamine was a useful substrate for measuring ceruloplasmin levels. Akerfeldt reported that schizophrenic patients generally were higher in ceruloplasmin thus supporting the suggestion of Angel *et al.* (1957) that schizophrenic serum converted more adrenaline into adrenolutin. Since then conflicting reports have appeared regarding the relationship of ceruloplasmin concentration and schizophrenia. However, it now appears that schizophrenics as a group do have higher levels of ceruloplasmin although there is considerable overlap with other types of patients (Abood *et al.*, 1957; Scheinberg *et al.*, 1957). Abood (1957) and Ostfeld *et al.* (1958) reported that a new series of atropinelike compounds (for example N-ethyl-3-piperidyl benzilate) are psychotomimetic and also elevate ceruloplasmin levels. Ceruloplasmin levels were also elevated in psychiatric patients who were excited compared to patients not excited.

The adrenaline oxidase activity of ceruloplasmin and its increase in schizophrenia as well as in other physical illnesses apparently provides support for the adrenochrome hypothesis. However, other findings throw doubt on ceruloplasmin as a major pathological factor: (a) Payza and Zaleschuk (1959) and Payza and Hoffer (1959) compared the enzymatic properties of the enzyme oxidizing adrenaline and p-phenylenediamine. The properties were so markedly different that it was unlikely they were the same. They suggested that adrenaline oxidase in tissues is not ceruloplasmin although it may play a role. (b) Ceruloplasmin is elevated in physical illnesses and during excitement without the production of schizophrenia. (c) Ceruloplasmin has been used in the treatment of schizophrenia. (d) Schizophrenics with increased ceruloplasmin levels have a better prognosis (Heath *et al.*, 1958). They suggested that the ceruloplasmin response might be an important part of the mechanism or counteracting the psychotic process.

Martens *et al.* (1959) support this hypothesis, that is that ceruloplasmin is part of a protective mechanism which may be faulty in schizophrenia. Heath *et al.* (1958) showed that injected ceruloplasmin has a half life of 5 days. In 4 patients, they doubled serum ceruloplasmin. There were indications that their adrenaline metabolism had become more normal and these patients responded clinically to subcutaneous adrenaline more like normal subjects.

Martens *et al.* (1959) administered ceruloplasmin to 22 schizophrenic patients. Nineteen were improved. Usually clinical improvement occurred ¾ to 2 hours after the injection and sometimes was very dramatic. Of the 19 patients, 9 remitted completely, and 6 have remained well. In all cases, serum copper levels increased and remained high for 1 week after last treatment. Adrenaline oxidation by serum also increased. Ascorbic acid levels were decreased. Administration of ascorbic acid decreased adrenaline oxidation but copper levels remained high. Since clinical improvement did occur, they suggested maintenance of high copper is more important than maintaining a high rate of adrenaline oxidation.

The ability of ceruloplasmin to protect against schizophrenia may account for the interesting relationship between pregnancy and schizophrenia. During pregnancy, especially in the last trimester, ceruloplasmin levels are markedly elevated. Two weeks after parturition, serum ceruloplasmin levels have decreased appreciably. During pregnancy, some schizophrenic patients became clinically improved. Recently we have seen a young schizophrenic patient become normal during pregnancy and at present this has been maintained for 2½ years. She had been treated with nicotinic acid and electroconvulsive therapy over a year before pregnancy with moderate improvement. However, her adjustment to the community was most tenuous. During the third trimester, a dramatic change in the schizophrenic occurred.

Wiedorn (1954) and Wiedorn and Ervin (1954) found that the incidence of toxemia is greater in schizophrenic women than in controls. Before term, adrenaline levels are elevated and very quickly decrease during labor (Ritzel *et al.*, 1957). Puerperal psychosis occurs following birth, at a time when ceruloplasmin levels are falling quickly.

Melander (1957) found that ceruloplasmin absorbs adrenolutin. Adrenolutin readily dialyzes through a semipermeable membrane. When ceruloplasmin is added, no further dialysis occurs. Other globulins do not bind adrenolutin. Payza and Zaleschuk (1959) showed that adrenolutin strongly inhibits ceruloplasmin activity on *p*-phenylenediamine. Adrenochrome does not. Ceruloplasmin also protects animals against catatonic dosages of adrenolutin. Perhaps it is the role of ceruloplasmin to bind adrenolutin and thus protect against excessive quantities. Under stress, adrenaline and adrenochrome production may increase. Ceruloplasmin would also increase and the ratio of adrenaline metabolites to ceruloplasmin remain normal. Pathological changes could occur when this ratio is unbalanced by excessive production of adrenaline metabolites or by defective formation of ceruloplasmin. With this hypothesis, it will follow that:

1. Ceruloplasmin will increase in conditions of stress and excitement.

2. Deficiency in ceruloplasmin will be harmful and may be responsible for some toxemias of pregnancy and for puerperal psychosis.

3. Ceruloplasmin will be therapeutic. If not available, transfusions from pregnant women in third trimester may be therapeutic.

4. Schizophrenics, lacking ceruloplasmin, will not bind adrenolutin and thus by some chemical mass action may decrease oxidation of hypodermically administered adrenaline. Administration of ceruloplasmin will thus allow more rapid metabolism of adrenaline.

ADRENOCHROME AND MITOSIS

Adrenochrome markedly inhibits mitotic rate of cells, probably by interfering in the glucolytic cycles (Lettre and Albrecht, 1941). Bullough (1952) found that when mice were stressed by overcrowding, the adrenal medulla increased in size 80%. At the same time the epidermal mitotic rate fell 60%. *In vitro* adrenaline had no antimitotic effect on epidermis but when it was injected it did. In contrast adrenochrome was antimitotic both *in vitro* and *in vivo*. Bullough suggested that during stress the increased quantity of adrenaline was converted into adrenochrome which produced the antimitosis.

Bullough and Rytomaa (1965) recently reviewed mitotic homeostasis. They showed that chalones, substances which depress mitotic activity, are tissue specific, are water soluble, nondialyzable and unstable, and control the rate of mitosis. Similar diurnal cycles were described for 15 other tissues. After adrenalectomy the epidermal mitotic rate increased threefold.

In this report Bullough and Rytomaa did not refer to adrenochrome, but it is likely that adrenaline-chalone would not long remain that way but would be converted into an adrenochrome sulfhydril complex. There are no known adrenaline protein or amino acid complexes which do not undergo this change. The hypothesis that an adrenochrome-chalone complex is found is compatible with the same data which support the adrenaline-chalone complex hypothesis. It will be difficult to determine which is the correct hypothesis. However, we would expect that schizophrenics would have less clear diurnal rhythm of mitosis if they really do have increased concentrations of adrenochrome. Increased quantities of adrenochrome-chalone would suppress mitosis and promote cell survival. Schizophrenics would be expected to have better cell survival rates and, indeed, many schizophrenics do appear to be remarkably youthful in appearance.

The erythrocyte system also contains a chalone. In the presence of reduced oxygen tension there is a rapid increase in production of new erythrocytes. This depends upon the secretion of erythropoietin but with decreased oxygen less adrenaline would be converted into adrenochrome, depleting the chalone complex and this could also allow an increase in the production of erythrocytes.

If animals are placed in high oxygen tension chambers there should be no major effect on mitosis rates if the chalone complex requires unchanged adrenaline only but, if it must first be converted into adrenochrome high oxygen tension would shorten the lag between increased adrenaline secretion and a drop in the rate of mitosis.

AFFINITY OF ADRENOCHROME FOR MUCOPOLYSACCHARIDES

Kato *et al.* (1962) found that antipsychotic drugs reacted *in vivo*, with the edema-provoking and edema-inhibiting reactive sites of dextran. This was shown by inhibition or provocation of the dextran response. This is the edema which follows injection of dextran into rats. For example, trifluoperazine at a dose of 150 μg per 100 gm was active.

The dose of phenobarbital was 1600 μg/100 gm. These authors suggested that this peculiar effect of some compounds on the dextran edema reaction could be used as a screening test for psychoactive drugs.

According to Tokusawa *et al.* (1957) a sulfite soluble form of adrenochrome monosemicarbazone inhibited the appearance of dextran-induced edema in guinea pigs and rats. It is, therefore, very likely that adrenochrome itself would also inhibit dextran edema. This experiment has not been carried out.

ADRENOCHROME AND THE CARDIOVASCULAR SYSTEM

Adrenochrome has some effect on cardiac muscle, according to Raab and Lepeschkin (1950). It was an oxidation catalyst in heart muscle, but did not increase oxygen consumption. It augmented the coronary blood flow in dogs longer than it elevated their blood pressure. It produced bradycardia both in the frog and in the atropinized mammalian heart, but rabbits occasionally responded with tachydardia. In frog heart, a heart alternation was seen with prolonged A-V conduction. In the hypodynamic amphibian, heart perfusion with adrenochrome reestablished reactivity to stimulation. In dogs, the heart output was increased.

In atropinized cats adrenochrome injected into the femoral vein produced a moderate elevation of blood pressure. In one animal, 6 mg of adrenochrome raised the blood pressure from 110 mm to 150 mm reaching this maximum in 20 seconds. The shape of the blood pressure curves resembled those caused by small doses of adrenaline and noradrenaline.

Doses of 1 mg or less slowed heart rate slightly but doses of 1–15 mg accelerated the rate. Adrenochrome produced an inversion of the T-wave over the right ventricle in lead CRI but less marked than that produced by adrenaline. Adrenochrome also caused a slight increase in serum potassium at 30 and 60 seconds after injection. In general, all these effects were similar to those produced by smaller quantities of adrenaline with 1 major difference, extrasystoles, which frequently appeared when 50 μg of adrenaline or noradrenaline was given, did not appear even after 15 mg of adrenochrome was injected. Since the adrenochrome used was not as pure as present preparations are, it would be worthwhile to repeat these interesting experiments.

Adrenochrome had little effect on pulse rate and blood pressure in human subjects. Early in our experiments, we measured these variables routinely, but when no effect was seen this was discontinued. Neither has adrenochrome monosemicarbazide an effect on blood pressure.

Recent research by Barsel (1964) suggests that adrenochrome may play an important part in blood pressure control. Noradrenaline is a powerful pressor agent, adrenaline, its methylated derivative is less active. It is likely that these amines adsorbed on the receptor sites which control muscle tone in the blood vessels are oxidized to their respective chromes. The reaction

$$\text{adrenaline} + O_2 = \text{adrenochrome}$$

may be of vital significance. If insufficient adrenochrome was present on these active sites, pressure would be lowered. It would be most difficult to have too much adrenochrome continuously present since it is so reactive and is quickly metabolized. However, an unnatural derivative might be adsorbed and could then be markedly hypotensive since no enzymes would be present to destroy it. Barsel (1964) synthesized halogenated adrenochrome derivatives and was awarded a patent in these compounds. He claimed that they were very potent hypotensive compounds. A solution of 5 mg of 7 iodoadrenochrome semicarbazone in 80 mg of the sodium salt of 3-hydroxy-2-naphthoic acid per ml was injected intravenously into rats. The decrease in pressure was related to dose. An injection of 0.05 mg produced a pressure drop of 90 seconds. At a dose of 0.1, 0.5 mg per kilo was hypotensive. These compounds were nontoxic. A dose of 0.05 mg given to a hypertensive rat whose initial pressure was 180 mm lowered it to 100 ml for 12 hours. In the standard test animal LD-50 was 15–20 mg per kg while the effective dose was 0.01 to 0.1 mg for keeping the pressure at about 55% of its previous value for 12 hours. If fluorine was used to make the 7-fluoro derivative, the compound was too toxic. When the 7-iodo compound was given orally the effective dose was 0.1–0.5 mg for rats.

Another situation in which there might be excessive adrenochrome or some of its derivatives is schizophrenia. As we stated earlier, adrenochrome is metabolized very quickly so we would not expect any significant difference in base line blood pressure. But a defect in the adrenaline–adrenochrome system could lead to defective homeostasis. Hoskins (1946) postulated that schizophrenics had a rigid vascular system because they had a very high correlation between systolic and diastolic pressure. Hoffer (1954) also found a very high correlation in acute schizophrenic patients which decreased after treatment. In addition Hoffer (1954) found that in 70% of acute and chronic schizophrenics 3 mg of atropine decreased systolic blood pressure after thirty minutes, while in other groups including normals, it was decreased in about 25%. Systolic pressure for 178 schizophrenics decreased from 129 to 126 mm and for 142 other subjects increased from 118 to 124 mm. This was confirmed on a different group of patients in a different hospital by

Hoffer and Callbeck (1959). Out of 161 schizophrenics 49 showed increases in systolic blood pressure and 61 showed decreases. Out of 161 comparison controls 73 showed an increase and 10 a decrease. For this 2- to 3-fold distribution $X^2 = 40.61$, $P < 0.0001$. Peck (1963) validated this atropine work. Using a more accurate device for measuring blood pressure he reported that the blood pressure response to atropine differentiated schizophrenic patients from others. In 14 schizophrenic patients, systolic pressure decreased 9.0 mm and only 2 showed an increase. Out of 31 nonschizophrenic subjects the mean increase was 5.0 mm and only 5 showed a decrease in pressure ($X^2 = 11.28$, $P < 0.001$). Peck believed this would be a valuable diagnostic test for doubtful cases.

We have referred to the remarkable histamine tolerance shown by schizophrenic patients. This is shown by their ability to absorb large quantities of histamine while maintaining normal blood pressure and by the reduced flare reaction to histamine.

Lucy (1954) tried to reduce the blood pressure of chronic schizophrenic patients by giving them increasing quantities of histamine by subcutaneous injection. A group of 10 acute schizophrenics required a mean of 4.8 mg histamine base to lower their systolic blood pressure to 60 mm. A group of 10 patients ill from 5 to 10 years required an average of 11.1 mg. Ten patients ill from 10 to 15 years required 12.0 mg and 10 ill from 20 to 25 years required 15.4 mg. For comparison, a group of 10 nonschizophrenic patients in the same hospital 10 years and more, only required 6.4 mg (mean for 20 schizophrenics in hospital over 10 years was 13.7 mg). One schizophrenic was able to tolerate 28 mg with some blood pressure decrease and no side effects. It is quite clear these patients were so unreactive to histamine either because their blood pressure was no longer capable of decreasing which seems highly unlikely or because they were protected by the presence of large quantities of some powerful antihistamine. Adrenochrome and its indolic derivatives are perhaps the substances which protected them.

LeBlanc et al. (1963) and LeBlanc and Lemieux (1961) reported that phenothiazine treatment partially restored histamine responsivity in schizophrenic patients. If the suggestion put forward by Ban and Lehmann (1965) that phenothiazines prevent formation of adrenaline is correct this would account for the restoration of normal histamine reactivity. The decrease in the production of adrenaline would decrease adrenochrome etc., and remove the natural antihistamine.

The cold pressor test was also abnormal (LeBlanc et al., 1963). With normal subjects systolic blood pressure increased 16 mm after 1 minute immersion of the hand in cold water. Schizophrenics, however, had a very slight increase of 4 mm. Epileptic and other psychiatric patients have a normal response. After 1 to 2 weeks of treatment with pheno-thiazines schizophrenics had systolic pressure increases up to 10 mm.

ADRENALINE, ADRENOCHROME, AND PULMONARY FUNCTION

There is some connection between the psychological activity of adrenochrome and pulmonary function. Perhaps this accounts for the high frequency of mental changes in patients suffering from major lung pathology, e.g., asthma, tuberculosis, and bronchiogenic carcinoma.

The original observation that discolored adrenaline was psychologi-cally active was made by a person who was forced to inhale large quantities of adrenaline for his asthma (Hoffer *et al.*, 1954). He de-scribed the changes as if he had taken mescaline. We have since ob-served that these changes are not infrequent and, in fact, have been observed by many internists who have insisted that their patients not be given discolored adrenaline. Mr. Kovish (Hoffer and Osmond, 1958) became psychotic a few hours after he began to inhale a port wine-colored adrenaline solution and remained so for one month while he continued to inhale it. Vencovsky and Peterova (1963) reported that a 57-year-old woman with asthma was made psychotic by inhalation of adrenaline. When the patient was admitted and given no more adren-aline she recovered but when, as a test, more adrenaline was given she once more became psychotic. The authors suggested the anoxia in asthma had something to do with an abnormal conversion of adrenaline to adrenochrome. It could then quickly be swept into the brain from the left side of the heart. In 1954, Wiedorn and Ervin reported a high in-cidence of schizophrenic-like reactions following administration of isoniazid or iproniazid for treatment of tuberculosis. Incidents of psy-chosis following treatment with amine oxidase inhibitors still produce psychotic reactions but they seem to be infrequent or perhaps they are now infrequently reported.

We have found a possible connection between lung pathology and psychiatric changes. Nine patients with terminal bronchiogenic carci-noma were tested for malvaria. Out of 6 tested before treatment was given, 5 had malvaria. Out of the 3 tested after treatment, none were positive on this urine test. One of the 5 positives was grossly psychotic (see Hoffer, 1965). Lung tissue is fairly rich in adrenaline oxidase (Payza and Hoffer, 1959). It has half as much as brain but twice as much as liver. Under certain conditions lung tissue in the presence of oxygen, adrenaline oxidase and adrenaline already containing traces of adrenochrome, which acts as a catalyst for further oxidation, may con-vert too much adrenaline into adrenochrome. This would be rapidly carried to the brain and so interfere with brain function.

Formation and Metabolism of Adrenochrome

SOURCE

There are several substances known to be present in the body which can be converted into quinoneindoles and then into indoles. These are dihydroxyphenylalanine (dopa) and dopamine which form dopachrome, noradrenaline which is converted into noradrenochrome, and adrenaline into adrenochrome. Isopropylnoradrenaline would not be changed into isopropylnoradrenochrome unless it was first converted into another substance. There has been practically universal acceptance of the conversion of dopa into dopachrome and then into various melanins (Mason, 1955). The natural conversion of noradrenaline into noradrenochrome and adrenaline into adrenochrome has not received this same kind of acceptance, especially in English-speaking laboratories. Other scientists no longer argue about this, for example, Banshikoff and Stolaroff (1963) who report that Soviet workers accept 3 main metabolic routes for adrenaline, (a) via monoamine oxidase, (b) via adrenochrome, and (c) via esters of sulfuric acid. Serotonin may be another source of adrenochrome or similar aminochromes. Ling and Blum (1958) reported that when serotonin was incubated with whole blood, washed erythrocytes or hemolyzed erythrocytes or hemoglobin, it lost its fluorescence rapidly and formed dihydroindoles. Porter *et al.* (1957) suggested that ceruloplasmin catalyzed the conversion of serotonin to paraquinone amines which on further oxidation would be converted into aminochromes. G. Martin *et al.* (1958) also found that serum oxidized serotonin to colored compounds. They believed the enzyme was ceruloplasmin. It was inhibited 80% by 0.003 M iproniazid.

Since there is no doubt that these substrates could be converted *in vivo* into their aminochromes, an examination was made to decide whether enough substrate was available to account for the theoretical quantity of aminochrome one would expect to be active in the body. The earliest attack objectors to the adrenochrome hypothesis of schizophrenia made was that the body did not make enough adrenaline. This has always puzzled us since there is no firm evidence which shows how much adrenaline is formed in an average day, nor is there much information to suggest how much *in vivo* production of toxic aminochromes would produce pathological changes.

We have examined this question (Hoffer and Osmond, 1960) and an analysis of 8 reports showed that estimates of the daily production of noradrenaline plus adrenaline probably varied from 0.3 to 23.1 mg per day. Our best estimate suggested that about 5 mg per day was produced. Under stress, and when ill with certain diseases such as schizophrenia or manic depressive psychosis much larger quantities would be secreted. It is, therefore, clear that the question revolves around the quantity formed, the quantity converted into aminochromes, the quantity stored in various tissues for future release and the quantity immediately removed by destruction or secretion. There are no answers to these questions at present.

An estimate of the quantity of adrenaline produced in the body can be seen in patients who have Addison's disease. When the adrenal glands are destroyed a quantity of tyrosine and dopa which would be converted into noradrenaline and adrenaline goes instead into other metabolic pools. One of the results is a remarkable accumulation of pigment in the skin, one of the heaviest organs in the body. The intact adrenal medullae must, therefore, divert enough dopa away from melanin pigment to prevent us all from becoming bronzed like the Addisonian patient. This is striking visual proof that substantial quantities of adrenaline and noradrenaline are formed.

The fact that the aminochromes from adrenaline and noradrenaline could be formed does not, of course, prove they are formed. But this is another issue which we will discuss later.

ENZYMES WHICH METABOLIZE ADRENALINE

We will not review in great detail the biochemistry of the enzymes which can metabolize adrenaline. This information is available in current textbooks of biochemistry. But in order to consider the possible formation of adrenochrome we must at least list some of the enzymes and, of course, the metabolic pathways so controlled.

Adrenaline is distributed to all tissues of the body by the arterial blood system after it has diffused through the adrenal cortex and through other chromaffin tissue. It does not penetrate brain tissue very readily but since it is present in all tissue, it may be formed *in situ*. Liver and muscle tissue appear to be major sites for inactivation.

Since adrenaline is a molecule which has many reactive sites many possible reactions for inactivation are possible. The main toxic reaction against which we must be protected is its great pressor quality. Any reaction which will bind or remove one of the 3 hydroxyl groups will detoxify adrenaline. The removal of the terminal nitrogen will do the same thing. Adrenaline may be considered a detoxified derivative of noradrenaline, and isopropyl noradrenaline, a detoxified derivative of adrenaline, since the addition of methyl groups reduces the pressor effects.

Excretion of Adrenaline in Urine, Sweat, Saliva, and Feces

Only the urine has been studied in detail but since most urine assays are inaccurate and cumbersome they have not been very helpful. It is apparent, however, that only a very small fraction of the natural adrenaline is excreted into urine. When adrenaline is transfused about 1% appears in the urine. When large quantities are transfused perhaps 2 or 3% will be excreted, indicating an overload on the metabolizing enzyme systems. Under natural conditions with small steady releases much less than 1% will be secreted. Some of the adrenaline appears unchanged and some is excreted as the glucuronic acid conjugate from which the adrenaline can be released by enzymatic hydrolysis.

Storage

Adrenaline may be termed a tissuephilic substance since it is so readily taken up by many tissues in the body. When adrenaline is injected intravenously it rapidly leaves the body fluids. When added to whole blood *in vitro* it is quickly taken up by the red cells where it may remain active for as long as 10 hours. When the red cells are lysed about 80% of the adrenaline is recovered. What happens to the rest is unknown. Adrenaline is also stored in myocardial and skeletal muscle and in platelets.

When adrenaline is injected intravenously it soon disappears from the serum but the additional adrenaline will appear in the urine in small quantities for a long time showing that after it is absorbed it can be slowly released and excreted.

Monoamine Oxidase

This enzyme removes the amine group and leaves behind an aromatic aldehyde, 3,4-dihydroxyphenylhydroxyacetaldehyde which apparently has slight sympathomimetic properties but has no known psychologic properties. Amine oxidase is present chiefly in liver, intestinal tract, and in the central nervous system.

According to Burn (1952) amine oxidase plays a role in the sympathetic nervous system compared to that of acetylcholinesterase in the parasympathetic system. The enzyme is present in sympathetic nerve endings in blood vessels, in the nictitating membrane and in the iris of the cat. In denervated vessels, amine oxidase levels fall and sensitivity to noradrenaline increases. Inhibitors of amine oxidase include cocaine, ephedrine, histamine, adrenochrome, caffeine, amphetamine, and nicotine.

Monoamine oxidase seems to be relatively more active in heart and brain than in liver. Croot, *et al.* (1961) found the ratio of activity of monoamine oxidase is not accurately reflected in urine studies which pick up chiefly substances metabolized in the liver.

Esterification of the Phenolic Hydroxyls

For a long time it was assumed that adrenaline was detoxified by addition of sulfate to the phenolic hydroxyls. When large quantities of adrenaline were given parenterally, substantial quantities of conjugates were found in the urine.

Osmond and Smythies (1952) suggested that methoxylated derivatives of adrenaline might be formed in the body. This suggestion was confirmed by Armstrong *et al.* (1957) who showed that substantial quantities of methoxylated derivatives were found in urine. The enzyme which is active is known as *O*-methyltransferase. Noradrenaline is converted into normetanephrine, then into 3-methoxy-4-hydroxymandelic aldehyde and other derivatives. Adrenaline is converted into metanephrine, then into other derivatives. It is believed that about 70% of the adrenaline is converted into metanephrine.

O-Methyltransferase can also demethylate metanephrine back into adrenaline.

Adrenaline Oxidase, Ceruloplasmin, and Schizophrenia

Akerfeldt's (1957a,b) demonstration that ceruloplasmin levels (as measured by the oxidation of *N,N*-dimethylparaphenylenediamine) were elevated in some schizophrenic patients' blood serum initiated a series of studies and arguments which still remain unsettled. Leach and Heath's (1956) observation that adrenaline was oxidized more rapidly in schizophrenics' plasma to adrenochrome and eventually into adrenolutin gave some urgency to these problems for it was then believed that ceruloplasmin was the oxidase which oxidized both adrenaline and DPP. The critical comments published by Kety (1959) have had two consequences: (a) There was a marked drop in interest in pursuing these studies and few papers have appeared since 1959, while before they were coming along frequently; (b) most psychiatrists were convinced the matter was finally settled in the negative, e.g., that oxidative rates in schizophrenic blood (plasma and serum) were in fact no different from those found in nonschizophrenic but physically normal comparison groups. A review of this literature by Hoffer and Osmond (1963) suggested the contrary, that the great weight of evidence strongly favors Akerfeldt's early views and that, in fact, schizophrenics' blood does oxidize adrenaline and DPP more rapidly than do comparison groups blood. Recently we read a paper by Osaki *et al.* (1964) which completely alters the picture. Indeed, it now seems likely that the whole question must be reopened. In the light of our present knowledge most of the earlier studies were inadequate, not because they were poorly done, but because Osaki's findings were not then known.

Some workers have not distinguished clearly between serum and plasma—as if they were biochemically identical. Yet plasma contains substantial quantities of fibrinogen and serum does not. This may alter oxidation rates. Another major difference is that plasma contains anticoagulants. These are heparin, citrates, oxalates and EDTA. Osaki *et al.*, showed that citrates are powerful inhibitors of ceruloplasmin and that the quantities normally present in blood will inhibit ceruloplasmin 95%. They showed that this substance is the natural blood dialyzable inhibitor of ceruloplasmin.

These authors concluded that tests for ceruloplasmin activity in either serum or plasma are not valid unless the dialyzable inhibitors are removed. Obviously anticoagulants such as citrates oxalates or EDTA must be avoided. Since dialyzable inhibitors have not been removed in most of the studies previously published it seems that the entire question of ceruloplasmin oxidation and schizophrenia must be reinvestigated. We have reexamined the published reports. In 10, serum was used, presumably with no anticoagulant. Six groups of investigators reported real (significant) differences between their schizophrenic populations and the comparison groups: Abood *et al.* (1957), Akerfeldt (1957a,b), Bonasera and Criscuoli (1961), Friedhoff *et al.* (1959), Saunders *et al.* (1959), and Scheinberg *et al.* (1957). Four groups found no significant differences, that is, Frohman *et al.* (1958), Gussion *et al.* (1958), Horwitt *et al.* (1957), and Stennett and Callowhill (1960). The evidence on serum thus favors the view there is increased oxidation in schizophrenic serum.

There were only 2 reports on plasma. Both found significant differences, that is, Maas *et al.* (1961) and Goldschmidt and Whittier (1958). An additional report by Yuwiler *et al.* (1961) cannot be accurately evaluated because it is not clear whether serum or plasma was used. Even then, Yuwiler's data show there is a trend for their schizophrenics to have more ceruloplasmin activity.

Eight studies showed there were real differences; 4 failed to do so. The weight of evidence is clearly on the side of those who find increased levels in schizophrenics.

The whole matter should be reopened using wherever possible plasma with heparin as the anticoagulant. In our research group Payza and Zaleschuk (1959) found that heparin is not an inhibitor of ceruloplasmin. Citrate should be removed by dialyzing against aqueous solutions so that this complicating factor is removed.

The question of adrenaline oxidases must be considered separately from that of ceruloplasmin. Only 3 groups have investigated rates of adrenaline oxidation using optimum conditions for measuring rates of change. Leach and Heath (1956) established a method for measuring oxidation of adrenaline. Fortunately they used heparinized plasma. Schizophrenics' plasma oxidized adrenaline more rapidly than did non-schizophrenic, nonphysically ill comparison groups. Physically ill subjects also had higher rates of oxidation. This is proof in a way that schizophrenics are also physically ill, and that other factors play a role. These factors could be changes in protein levels such as increased erythrocyte sedimentation rates, increased hemolysis of blood red cells, increased consumption of ascorbic acid due to infections, fevers, and wastage of tissue, etc.

Payza and Hoffer (1959) and Payza and Zaleschuk (1959) studied and compared the properties of adrenaline oxidase and ceruloplasmin. They concluded that they were not the same enzymes. Payza and Hoffer (1959) used fresh heparinized blood or acetone powders of various tissues as their source of enzyme. Activity was measured by allowing 1 ml of plasma to react with 1 ml of adrenaline (75 μmoles) at 37°C in the presence of semicarbazide and buffers at pH 6.8. The formation of adrenochrome monosemicarbazone was followed by an increase in optical density at 360 mμ in a model DU Beckman Spectrophotometer.

Acetone powders of tissues were made by homogenizing 1 part of fresh tissue with 20 parts of acetone at −20°C. The homogenate was suction filtered and dried in air. The powder was stored at −20°C. One-hundred milligrams of this dry powder was treated with 5 ml 0.02 M buffer (pH 5) for 1 hour at 0°C and adjusted to the required pH before use.

The amount of adrenochrome formed increased with time until at 3 hours a 25% yield was found. Both d- and l-adrenaline were oxidized but noradrenaline was not converted into noradrenochrome. The optimal pH was 6.8. The enzyme was inactivated completely by heating at 80°C for 15 minutes. The conversion of adrenaline into adrenochrome was related linearly to the quantity of enzyme used. The dried powder was as active as intact plasma for equivalent protein content. The enzyme was most active at low salt concentrations.

The major activators of adrenaline enzyme were semicarbazide, copper ion and fresh hemoglobin. Semicarbazide increased enzyme activity fivefold, it trapped the adrenochrome and prevented its conversion to adrenolutin. Zinc ions at higher concentrations were as active as copper ions. Dialysis against EDTA and then distilled water overnight at 0°C removed all activity which was restored when copper ion was replaced.

Adding 5–100 mg μg/ml of fresh hemoglobin increased enzyme activity threefold. Autoxidation was not increased so there was no direct oxidation of adrenaline by the hemoglobin. Iproniazid (0.05 to 3 μg/ml) activated adrenaline oxidase.

Sodium cyanide, sodium diethyldithiocarbamate, tris buffer, ascorbic acid, and EDTA were inhibitors. Ephedrine, adrenochrome, monosemicarbazone, heparin, nicotinic acid, LSD, and mescaline neither activated nor inhibited the enzyme.

Pig plasma was fractionated for ceruloplasmin. Adrenaline oxidase activity was decreased in these fractions. Adrenaline oxidase was present in all the tissues examined with the greatest activity being found in brain. Liver and spleen had the least and plasma kidney and lung were in between.

A comparison between adrenaline oxidase and p-phenylenediamine oxidase (Payza and Zaleschuk, 1959) is shown in Table 25.

It is apparent that these enzymes are not the same. PPD oxidase is probably ceruloplasmin because it was inhibited strongly by the usual amine oxidase inhibitors—iproniazid, semicarbazide and hydroquinone—whereas adrenaline oxidase were not inhibited by these substances. Adrenaline was a substrate for adrenaline oxidase and a powerful inhibitor of PPD oxidase (ceruloplasmin). Adrenochrome had no effect as activator or inhibitor. But adrenolutin which had no effect on adrenaline oxidase was a powerful inhibitor of ceruloplasmin. The irreversible adsorption of adrenolutin by ceruloplasmin is consistent with this powerful inhibition.

D-Penicillamine (or its DL-preparation) is an amino acid derived from penicillin. It is an excellent metal chelator which has a high affinity for copper. It is, in fact, able to remove copper from ceruloplasmin and this decreases its oxidase activity. It would also decrease adrenaline oxidase activity. This reduction of adrenaline oxidase activity plus the increased conversion of adrenochrome into 5,6-dihydroxy-N-methylindole *in vivo* comprise our rationale for treating schizophrenia with penicillamine (Hoffer and Osmond, 1960).

RELATIONSHIP OF DIAGNOSIS TO ADRENALINE OXIDASE ACTIVITY. Hoffer *et al.* (1959) measured adrenaline oxidase in plasma using the technique developed by Leach and Heath (1956) and Hoffer and Kenyon (1957). Heparinized blood only was used since heparin did not alter adrenaline oxidase or ceruloplasmin activity. The amount of adrenolutin formed was measured by the optical activity at 395 in a spectrophotometer. A comparison of several groups of subjects is shown in Table 26.

Normal (and nonschizophrenic psychiatric cases) subjects had the least adrenaline oxidase, followed by schizophrenics, alcoholics expect-

TABLE 25

Comparison of Adrenaline Oxidase and p-Phenylenediamine Oxidase

Function	Adrenaline oxidase	PPD oxidase
Optimum pH	6.8	5.0
Effect of heat	Inactivated	Inactivated
Effect of enzyme Cmc.	Linear increase in adrenochrome	Linear increase in adrenochrome
Optimum salt molarity	Low	Low
Effect of dialysis	Inactivated	No effect
Activators	Semicarbazide	
	Copper ion	Copper ion
	Zinc ion	Zinc ion
	Hemoglobin	Hemoglobin
	Oxygen	Oxygen
	Iproniazid	
		Sulfanilamide
Inhibitors	Sodium cyanide	Sodium cyanide
	EDTA	EDTA
	Tris buffer	
	Ascorbic acid	Ascorbic acid
		Hydroquinone
		Semicarbazide
		Iproniazid
		Adrenaline[a]
		Adrenolutin[a]
		Cysteine
		Glutathione
Inert substances	Ephedrine	
	{Adrenochrome	
	{Monosemicarbazone	Adrenochrome
	Heparin	Heparin
	Nicotinic acid	Nicotinamide
	LSD	LSD
	Mescaline	Mescaline
		GABA
Effect of ammonium sulfate fractionation	Less enzyme present	More enzyme present

[a] Powerful inhibitors.

ing LSD and physically ill patients expecting surgery. Schizophrenic patients had increased adrenaline oxidase levels before and after treatment. Patients awaiting LSD therapy and surgery are apprehensive and probably secreting increased quantities of adrenaline. Billewicz-Stankiewicz *et al.* (1964) showed that adrenaline, noradrenaline, histamine, and iproniazid produced an increase in the adrenaline oxidase in plasma. They also found that adrenaline oxidase was not ceruloplasmin ferritin or catalase. Since adrenaline oxidase must, therefore, be an adaptive enzyme this would account for increased levels in stressed and anxious subjects. The highest values were found in bloods drawn from patients during surgical operation. These values must be spuriously high. It is well known that surgery traumatizes tissue and releases hemoglobin. This freshly liberated hemoglobin would increase oxidation of adrenaline without any increase in enzyme levels.

TABLE 26

EFFECT OF LSD AND OF VARIOUS DIAGNOSTIC GROUPS ON A
CONVERSION OF ADRENALINE INTO ADRENOLUTIN

| Subjects | Number | Optical density (at 395) | |
		Mean	Range
Alcoholics			
Before LSD (hours)	5	0.36	0.24–0.62
2	5	0.48	0.21–0.94
5	5	0.40	0.39–0.62
7	5	0.36	0.25–0.49
Normal	18	0.30	0.17–0.45
Nonschizophrenic	15	0.31	0.15–0.42
Schizophrenic			
Before treatment	13	0.35	0.08–0.54
After treatment	11	0.35	0.17–0.49
Surgical			
Before operation	28	0.36	0.24–0.69
During operation	12	0.43	0.26–0.61

EFFECT OF LSD, LAE, AND BOL. The LSD experience in 5 alcoholic subjects greatly increased adrenaline oxidase at 2 hours when the LSD experience is usually reaching its highest intensity. Adrenaline oxidase activity was even greater than that found during surgical operation and increased 30%. This could not be due to hemolysis since LSD in the doses used, in the absence of anticoagulants, would not do this. Neither can it be ascribed to stress since most of the alcoholic subjects enjoyed their experience and could not be considered to be gravely stressed; indeed, they were usually quite relaxed. It must, therefore, be a unique effect of the LSD. At 5 hours adrenaline oxidase levels were returning to normal and after 7 hours were at the pre-LSD values.

Fifty micrograms of LSD added to the system *in vitro* increased conversion of adrenaline to adrenolutin 27%, 50 μg of LAE increased it 37% while 50 μg of BOL had no effect. Other enzyme systems are present in natural tissues which can oxidize adrenaline into adrenochrome. They include a catechol oxidase prepared from mushroom (D. E. Green and Richter, 1937), a cytochrome–indophenol–oxidase system present in all cells (D. E. Green and Richter, 1937), and an adrenaline adrenochrome system in mammalian skeletal muscle (Wajzer, 1947). These enzymes have been variously referred to as tyrosinases, phenolasis catechol oxidase. Ferritin also oxidizes adrenaline. Recently Axelrod (1964) has shown that salivary tissue can also oxidize adrenaline into adrenochrome.

Is Adrenochrome Formed in the Body

Dopachrome is an intermediate between tyrosine and melanin. In the past 10 years, we have seen no scientific criticism of the hypothesis that dopa is oxidized into dopachrome, yet dopachrome has never been crystallized from body tissues, nor has any stable derivative known to come from dopachrome, been isolated. There are no assay methods for measuring dopachrome in fluids. There can be no reasonable doubt that dopachrome is formed and whenever one sees the color of one's skin and hair this is considered proof. No one has shown what proportion of dopa is converted into dopachrome, into noradrenaline and into other substances. Yet adrenochrome which is very similar in structure to dopachrome, is still not considered to be a natural derivative by some critics. Nevertheless the evidence for its presence is just as powerful and a lot more is known about the chemistry of adrenochrome and its metabolism than about the chemistry of dopachrome. This double set of standards has puzzled us. It is, undoubtedly, due to the reluctance of many to accept the adrenochrome hypothesis of schizophrenia. If we had developed a dopachrome hypothesis, which can be done with some plausibility, they might have denied the presence of dopachrome in the body. Our adrenochrome hypothesis was a model hypothesis which related the indole derivatives of the sympathomimetic amines to schizophrenia. We have considered dopachrome, noradrenochrome, and even *N*-isopropylnoradrenochrome, more or less interchangeable with adrenochrome in our theoretical formulations. Other investigators have made the same analogies. Thus Van Der Wende and Spoerlein (1962) found that 3,4-dihydroxyphenylalanine (dopa) in slightly alkaline solution produced catatonic stupor in mice, that these animals also became very vicious and bit each other or those who handled them. From 0.4–0.5 gm/kg was effective.

They suggested that oxidized intermediates such as dopachrome were the active psychotomimetic agents. Ascorbic acid would not prevent indole formation although it would react with dopachrome; in the same way that ascorbic acid does not prevent adrenochrome's psychotomimetic activity.

The presence of substrates, and of enzymes which can convert them into their aminochromes, provides some evidence this oxidation does indeed occur. But it is still possible that adrenaline is not converted into adrenochrome. There are two lines of evidence that this reaction does occur *in vivo*. The first line of evidence is indirect. This again divides into two types: (a) evidence which depends upon biochemical properties of adrenaline which are accountable only if one assumed it is first converted into adrenochrome, and (b) evidence which orders a large number of apparently random physiological changes in schizophrenia into a simple unified system. The second line of evidence consists of analytic studies by many investigators who reported they were able to measure fluorescent derivatives of adrenaline, adrenochrome, adrenolutin, or their derivatives.

First Line of Evidence

EVIDENCE FROM PROPERTIES OF ADRENALINE. Long before a chemical is isolated from natural tissue it becomes evident that there is something which is there to be isolated. Thus thiamine was hunted in cereal grain because this food cured beriberi and serotonin was for some time merely a vasoconstrictor blood factor. This is the kind of evidence which was presented by (1) Anguiano *et al.* (1958); (2) Bacq (1949); (3) Blaschko and Schlossmann (1940); (4) Bullough (1952, 1955); (5) Fellman (1958); (6) Foley and Baxter (1958); (7) Gamburg (1962); (8) S. Green *et al.* (1956); (9) Greig and Gibbons (1957, 1959); (10) Iordanis and Kuchino (1959); (11) Kaliman (1961); (12) Kisch (1947); (13) Korzoff and Kuchino (1959); (14) Kuchino (1959); (15) Langemann and Koelle (1958); (16) Meirowsky (1940); (17) Pastan *et al.* (1962); (18) Derovaux and Roskam (1949); (19) Roston (1960, 1963); (20) Sweat and Bryson (1965); and (21) Takahashi and Akabane (1960).

Anguiana *et al.* (1958) studied the potentiation of sympathetic excitation upon the submaximal responses of the pupillary sphincter to cholinergic stimulation from ciliary nerves in cats. This potentiation was maximal after 20–30 seconds after sympathetic stimulation ceased and lasted 2–3 minutes. Adrenaline, noradrenaline, and adrenochrome had the same effect. Homogenized frozen iris in Ringers solution quickly converted adrenaline into adrenolutin. These authors believed that the effect of sympathetic stimulation was due to the conversion of adrenaline into adrenochrome and adrenolutin which accounted for the lag of 20–30 seconds.

Bacq (1949) summarized several lines of evidence which suggested that adrenaline was oxidized into adrenochrome. Adrenochrome exerted hemostatic activity much earlier than did adrenaline.

Bullough (1952, 1955) found that *in vivo* both adrenaline and adreno-chrome were antimitotic for mouse epidermis, but *in vitro* only adreno-chrome was active.

Fellman (1958) found that red pigmented areas of the brain were rich in enzymes which oxidized adrenaline. Foley and Baxter (1958) reported that in albinos where dopachrome melanin was not formed, the brain still contained normal pigment. This suggests that another sub-strate was being converted into these reddish pigments.

S. Green *et al.* (1956) considered that the inhibition of capillary con-striction by ferritin was due to its oxidizing adrenaline into adreno-chrome.

Greig and Gibbons (1957, 1959) suggested hallucinogens acted on brain by decreasing transfer of glucose into brain. Adrenochrome in-hibited glucose transfer. They also suggested that adrenochrome in erythrocytes accounted for the deficiency of glycine and the excess phosphoglycolic acid in schizophrenics.

Iordanis' work (Iordanis and Kuchino, 1959) indicated that adreno-chrome was formed and inhibited ATPase in muscle; he suggests that this accounts for the relaxing effect of adrenaline on uterine muscle.

Apparently mydriatics are more effective in light than in dark eyes (Angenent and Koelle, 1952). Homogenates of the irides and ciliary bodies of pigmented and albino rabbits had the same quantity of mono-amine oxidase, cytochrome oxidase, succinic dehydrogenase, cholin-esterase or reducing substances. Dopa was oxidized by pigmented but not by albino homogenates. When adrenaline was used as a substrate, pigmented tissue regularly consumed more oxygen. When both adren-aline and dopa were added, the oxygen uptake of pigmented homog-enates was much greater than the sum of the individual oxygen con-sumption. Adrenaline was used up. Albino homogenates did not consume any oxygen and 0.001 M α-naphthothiourea, an inhibitor of tyrosinase, reduced oxygen uptake 50% in pigmented homogenates. There was no deamination nor decarboxylation. With mixtures of dopa and adrenaline this inhibitor prevented any augmentation of oxygen uptake. The solu-tions in pigmented homogenates developed a reddish orange color. These data suggested that *in vivo* darkly pigmented eyes converted adrenaline to adrenochrome more rapidly and thus decreased its mydriatic effect.

Langemann and Koelle (1958) found intestinal mucosa produced brownish pigments from adrenaline. Meirowsky (1940) reported adreno-chrome increased skin pigmentation. In 1952 Hoffer noted a brown pigmented area in the site over the injection of adrenochrome. The pig-mented area was present several months. Rigdon (1940a,b) found that adrenaline in rabbit skin produced reddish pigment areas after xylol. Hoffer (1962a) found adrenochrome injections did the same.

Roston suggested coenzyme A–adrenochrome combinations could be important in intermediary metabolism.

EVIDENCE FROM ENZYME INHIBITORS. There are 4 main enzymes which metabolize noradrenaline and adrenaline. These are (a) *O*-methyltransferase which produces normetanephrine and metanephrine; (b) monoamine oxidase which deaminates noradrenaline, adrenaline, normetanephrine, and metanephrine; (c) a sulfate esterase which sulfates these amines; and (d) adrenaline oxidase.

Only two enzyme systems inactivate noradrenaline and adrenaline in such a way that adrenochrome cannot be formed. These are monoamine oxidase and sulfoesterase. *O*-Methyltransferase produces methoxylated derivatives which are just as easily oxidized to adrenochrome and noradrenochrome as the original amines. Being more lipid soluble they are probably more readily transferred into brain tissue. The enzyme works both ways and can demethylate the methoxylated derivatives. *O*-Methyltransferase is, therefore, an enzyme which produces derivatives of adrenaline which are much less potent pressors but which can be converted further into deaminated products or adrenochrome. It is also possible that metanephrine is stored in the body and can be called upon as a reliable source of adrenaline when required. If this is the case phenylethylamine derivatives could displace metanephrine from its storage depots. Perhaps the amphetamines act by releasing metanephrine. Mescaline could release a large quantity of metanephrine and so increase the formation of adrenochrome. We are now examining these possibilities with the simple method of Mattok *et al.* (1966) which measures dopamine, adrenaline, noradrenaline, normetanephrine, and metanephrine on 1 sample of urine.

According to the adrenochrome hypothesis any inhibitor which forces adrenaline to be converted into adrenochrome will tend to produce psychotic reactions. Inhibitors of monoamine oxidase and of sulfoesterase should, therefore, be toxic. *O*-Methyltransferase inhibitors will have an unpredictable effect since this enzyme is not within the main path of final inactivation. If metanephrine does cross the blood–brain barrier more easily, inhibitors of this enzyme should increase blood pressure by preventing inactivation of adrenaline's pressor properties and should increase tension and anxiety by increasing penetration into brain. These are conjectures. We have seen no psychological studies of *O*-methyltransferase inhibitors.

In sharp contrast inhibitors of adrenaline oxidase should not produce toxic changes. They should be therapeutic for schizophrenics. We would also expect that enzyme inhibitors which force adrenaline into the adrenochrome pathway should increase melanization (yellow and brown nondopa melanins) and all the other biochemical and physiological changes frequently observed in schizophrenic patients. On the contrary, adrenaline oxidase inhibitors should decrease melanization and these other schizophrenic changes.

Monoamine Oxidase Inhibitors. Pscheidt (1964) recently reviewed the known monoamine oxidase inhibitors. They include the well-known antidepressants or euphorients such as iproniazid, isocarboxazid, nialamide, phenelgine, catron, tranylcypromine, etryptamine, harmine, amphetamine, etc.

These compounds are euphorients, stimulants, and hallucinogens. Even the usually nontoxic inhibitors such as iproniazid have produced schizophrenic-like reactions (Wiedorn and Ervin, 1954). Harmine is a well-known hallucinogen as are some of the tryptamine derivatives. We have described them earlier in this book. None of these compounds have much therapeutic effect for schizophrenic subjects although their mood may be improved. The toxic responses to amphetamine have been so similar to schizophrenia that these patients were given insulin coma, even when a high concentration dose of amphetamine had been found in their urine (Connell, 1957).

The semicarbazide inhibitors may be doubly toxic since they are also activators of adrenaline oxidase. Billewicz-Stankiewicz *et al.* (1964) showed that iproniazid increased the activity of adrenaline oxidase *in vivo*. It was an adaptive enzyme. Payza and Hoffer (1959) found that iproniazid activated adrenaline oxidase *in vitro*.

Heath *et al.* (1965) found that tetraethylthiuram disulfide (Antabuse) decreased excretion of vanilmandelic acid from about 4.5 mg per day to 1.0 mg per day in about 20 days. It appears to be a very active inhibitor of monoamine oxidase. At the same time definite behavioral changes were seen in all 18 subjects. They became evident 2–3 days after the dose was increased to 1.0 grams daily.

Schizophrenic patients were far more seriously impaired than control subjects. All schizophrenic symptoms, especially secondary ones, were augmented. Auditory hallucinations became much more pronounced. Of the 9 schizophrenic subjects, 8 had not reported hallucinations before this. Delusions, autism, and depersonalization became more prominent. Ideation became bizarre, association defects worsened, and affect became inappropriate. Four of the 9 became disoriented. In contrast, 8 of the normal controls developed no psychotic changes. One of the controls who had a temporal lobe abnormality became psychotic.

Heath *et al.* (1965) concluded that these data supported the hypothesis that catecholamine metabolism differed in schizophrenic patients and that Antabuse accentuated these differences. Ward (1965) observed that one alcoholic who reacted strongly to alcohol when he took Antabuse, reacted very mildly when he also took 4.5 grams of nicotinic acid per day. Nicotinic acid would likely reduce the violent reactions of schizophrenics to Antabuse.

Methylene blue is an inhibitor of monoamine oxidase (Lund, 1951). It decreased the loss of adrenaline in liver to from 20 to 30% of the original rate. Potassium cyanide, in addition, decreased destruction to zero. This suggests that little adrenaline would be converted to adrenochrome in liver.

There is another way in which adrenaline could be forced into adrenochrome. This is to administer large doses of monoamine oxidase substrates. These would saturate the enzyme and so decrease the quantity of adrenaline which could be metabolized. These compounds include the tryptamines, serotonin, bufotenine, etc. Perhaps this saturation effect accounts for some of the psychotomimetic properties of the hallucinogenic substances.

Sulfoesterase Inhibitors. The only inhibitor we have read about is cocaine which is the well-known narcotic euphorient and delirient. But cocaine is also an monoamine oxidase inhibitor. In the presence of large quantities of it, only the adrenochrome pathway would be available for removing adrenaline. Perhaps this is why cocaine is such a toxic narcotic. Cocaine psychosis has frequently been described.

Adrenaline Oxidase Inhibitors. Payza and Hoffer (1959) found only 4 inhibitors of this enzyme, sodium cyanide, ethylenediaminetetraacetate (EDTA) tris buffer and ascorbic acid. Sodium cyanide could not be tested as an hallucinogen. In nontoxic doses it has produced lucid episodes in some schizophrenic patients. EDTA has not been used clinically and its toxic properties are not known. We would expect it to be nontoxic and, in fact, therapeutic for schizophrenics as is penicillamine. Both are copper chelating agents and by removing copper would inhibit adrenaline oxidase. G. J. Martin *et al.* (1942) found that *p*-aminobenzoic acid inhibited oxidation of adrenaline to adrenochrome by tryosinase. We have not heard of any psychotic reactions following the use of heavy doses of PABA. In its absence convulsions may develop. PABA should be therapeutic for schizophrenia.

Inhibitors of tryosinase also include cysteine, thioureas, glycine, and histidine (Hirsch, 1959), and monohydroxybenzoic acid isomers (Yasunobu, 1959). Benzoic acid itself is a good inhibitor. These compounds may be valuable therapeutic chemicals for some schizophrenics. *d*-Phenylalanine is another inhibitor and is believed responsible for the deficiency of melanization in phenylpyruvic oligophrenia.

Potassium cyanide is a powerful inhibitor of catechol oxidases and caused complete inhibition of adrenaline destruction in muscle. Methylene blue inhibited loss of adrenaline in muscle only slightly. Lund (1951) concluded "there is thus much evidence to suggest that most of the adrenaline destruction in the liver is due to deamination and that only a small proportion is oxidized to adrenochrome, and reverse seems to be true of cardiac muscle." Muscle removed adrenaline quickly but it was then oxidized slowly to adrenochrome.

As we would expect, activators of adrenaline oxidase are euphorients, antidepressive compounds, and hallucinogens. They include semicarbazides, iproniazid, copper ion, high oxygen tension, and LSD. BOL, which is inactive, is not an adrenaline oxidase activator.

Dopa may also be an activator of adrenaline oxidase (Angenent and Koelle, 1952). The combination of dopa and adrenaline was consumed much more oxygen than the same quantities of each substrate incubated separately. These ideas are shown schematically in Fig. 8.

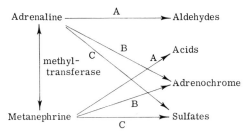

FIG. 8. A scheme relating adrenaline destroying enzymes to psychotomimetic activity. A = monoamine oxidase, B = adrenaline oxidase, C = sulfoesterase.
Psychotomimetic: monoamine oxidase inhibitors and adrenaline oxidase activators.
Antipsychotic: monoamine oxidase activators and adrenaline oxidase inhibitors.

MALVARIA. Irvine (1961) and Hoffer and Mahon (1961) found that the majority of schizophrenic patients excreted high R_f substances which developed a mauve color when treated with Ehrlichs reagent. Irvine (1961) believed that these were pyrroles although no final identification was possible.

According to Nicolaus (1962) and Mason (1959) the oxidation of natural melanin by alkaline H_2O_2 leads to the formation of pyrrole carboxylic acids. Apparently these pyrroles form a part of the basic structure of natural melanin. Melanogenesis consists, in part, of the rupture of the benzene portion of indoles like dopachrome to form carboxylic acid pyrroles.

The excretion of pyrroles in increased quantities in urine of schizophrenics would be consistent with the presence of too much adrenochrome or adrenolutin or similar indoles.

EVIDENCE FROM SCHIZOPHRENIA. From the known properties of adrenochrome plus its metabolite adrenolutin it is possible to predict what might happen to a subject who continually produced too much adrenochrome and adrenolutin. This is what we have done in Table 27.

TABLE 27

A COMPARISON OF SOME PROPERTIES OF ADRENOCHROME AND SOME CHANGES FOUND IN
SCHIZOPHRENIA[a]

Property	Adrenochrome	Clinical changes in schizophrenia
Psychological	Perceptual changes Thought changes Mood changes	Changes in perception Changes in thought Changes in mood
Antihistamine	Weak antihistamine	Increased tolerance of histamine Decreased incidence of allergies
Pigmentation	Melanin formation	Increased pigmentation of hair and skin Decreased incidence of graying of hair
Antithyroid	Increased oxidation	Thyroid disturbances Increased tolerance to thyroid
Mitosis	Antimitotic Rejection mechanism	Decreased resistance to tuberculosis Decreased incidence of arthritis Decreased rejection mechanism Deviations in growth
Temperature control	Hypothermic	Low temperature Defective diurnal rhythm
Glutamic acid decarboxylase	Inhibitor	Increased incidence of EEG arrhythmia
Insulinase	Inhibitor	Decreased incidence of diabetes mellitus
Phosphorylation in intermediary metabolism	Inhibitor hexokinase Pentose shunt inhibitor Other phosphorylation changes Disturbance in phosphate excretion	Disturbed carbohydrate metabolism Increased erythrocyte fragility Disturbed secretion of phosphates
Ascorbic acid	Oxidation	Deficiency (over-utilization)
Glutathione	Oxidation	Deficiency
Oxidation-reduction	Oxidizer	Abnormal adrenochrome tolerance curves

TABLE 27 (*Continued*)

Property	Adrenochrome	Clinical changes in schizophrenia
Diurnal rhythm	Increased secretion of adrenaline and adreno- chrome during day	Better in morning, worse in evening
Serum proteins	Abnormal fluorescence Braines *et al.* (1959) Abnormal infrared spectrum Runge *et al.* (1961)	Abnormal fluorescence as for adrenochrome Abnormal infrared spectrum as for adrenochrome
Treatment (based on need to prevent for- mation of, remove, or neutralize forma- tion of adrenochrome and/or adrenolutin)	Decrease formation of adrenochrome Decrease formation of adrenolutin Antidote to adrenochrome and adrenolutin Removal of adrenochrome Removal of adrenolutin	Decrease anxiety, nicotinic acid, penicillamine, ascorbic acid glutathione, chlorpromazine Penicillamine pineal extract Nicotinic acid Artificial kidney Artificial kidney ceruloplasmin
Inhibition of mono- amine oxidase	Diversion of adrenaline into other pathways including adrenochrome	Schizophrenic-like reactions

* These are tied together by the adrenochrome hypothesis.

In the right-hand half of this table we have listed those clinical changes which occur in schizophrenic patients more often than in any normal comparison group. In addition we have listed those therapies which should help schizophrenics by decreasing the toxic effect of adreno- chrome or adrenolutin. These reactions are related schematically in Fig. 9.

We know of no other chemical in the body which could account so well for the amazing variety of unusual clinical changes found in schizophrenia.

Second Line of Evidence

This kind of evidence is more powerful and consists of a large number of reports by investigators who have found fluorescent derivatives of adrenaline in body fluids or in tissues. These reports include (1) Alt- schule (1960, 1962a,b); (2) Fischer *et al.* (1950), Fischer and Landtsheer (1950), Fischer and Lecomte (1951); (3) Gershenovich *et al.* (1955); (4) Goldenberg *et al.* (1950); (5) S. Green *et al.* (1956); (6) Kaliman

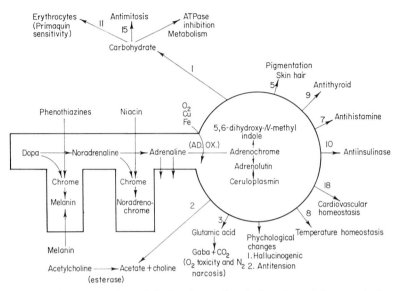

Fɪɢ. 9. A schematic outline of the biochemical and physiological factors which may be involved in schizophrenia.

(1961); (7) Kaufmann and Koch (1959a,b), Koch (1966); (8) Lecomte and Fischer (1951); (9) Maslova (1959); (10) Osinskaya (1957); (11) Payza and Mahon (1959, 1960); (12) Reio (1964); (13) Rigdon (1940a,b); (14) Rangier (1962); (15) Sulkovitch (1956); (16) Sulkovitch and Altschule (1958); (17) Sulkovitch *et al.* (1957); (18) Utevskii (1963a,b); (19) Utevskii (1957, 1964, 1965); and (20) Veech *et al.* (1960, 1961).

What is lacking is the final proof which could be (a) the isolation of crystalline adrenochrome or adrenolutin from tissues or (b) the demonstration of radioactive tracer substances in chromatograms or in other analytical systems which could only come from adrenochrome. (c) It could be the isolation of adrenochrome or adrenolutin derivatives from urine, blood, or hair. It may seem that if adrenochrome was really present in tissue or body fluids, its presence would already have been demonstrated. The fact that this has not yet proved has been used by some to deny all the evidence presented so far. There are several valid explanations for this lack of proof. (a) The chemistry of adrenochrome has only recently been carefully investigated using crystalline-pure adrenochrome (Heacock, 1959). (b) Relatively few investigators have searched body tissues and fluids diligently. (c) Adrenochrome is highly reactive. (d) The reduced form of the aminochromes rather than the oxidized form may be present in biological tissue (Harrison, 1963).

Since everyone has looked for the oxidized form, this could explain why it has not been isolated. (e) Adrenochrome may have a transient life in biological tissue. (f) Few attempts have been made to corroborate those investigators who claim to have found adrenochrome. Each report seems to remain untested by other investigators.

The storage sites may have special properties which make it difficult to remove the adrenochrome. Lemberg and Legge (1949) reported that mild denaturation of globins of oxyhemoglobin and oxymyoglobin in the presence of acid transformed oxyferroprotoporphyrin complexes into rather strong oxidizing agents which rapidly consumed ascorbic acid or adrenaline. Since it would be very difficult to disrupt erythrocytes without denaturing the hemoglobin special techniques will need to be developed for extracting adrenochrome unchanged.

The reports by Altschule and his collaborators are particularly interesting because they have found that schizophrenic blood is sufficiently richer in aminochromes (they suggest adrenolutin) to be of diagnostic value. Altschule (1962a–b) uses blood adrenolutin values for characterizing what he has termed hyperaminochromia. He has used paper chromatograms to characterize the adrenolutin.

Koch (1962) (see Kaufmann and Koch, 1959a,b) has found evidence for adrenochrome in the urine of human subjects. Adrenochrome was found in increased concentration in conditions marked by great stress, for example, in long distance bicycle rides in France. When Hoffer visited her laboratory in Prague recently she was further developing her assays. Utevskii (1963b) reported he had data from his laboratory which supported the conclusion that adrenochrome was formed. His most convincing evidence was the detection of substances in animal tissues with properties characteristic of adrenochrome.

Payza and Mahon found evidence for aminochrome in blood, cerebrospinal fluid, and urine. But Feldstein (1959) suggested that the fluorescence was an artifact due to the presence of ascorbic acid. It does not seem likely that this occurs in plasma even though it might occur in aqueous solution. Nevertheless, a further modification was made but the newer method has not been tested by other laboratories. These methods share the disadvantage of all fluorescent methods.

Lund (1951) found that adrenaline injected into veins of rabbits and dogs was removed within 8 minutes but it was not destroyed in the blood. This would be expected since adrenaline could not be an effective chemical mediator of the sympathetic nervous system if it did not arrive at its destination. But destruction in liver was very rapid. Blood containing 400 μg per 100 ml was cleared in one passage. The rate of destruction in muscle was much less.

When blood containing muscle and the erythrocytes centrifuged down, the plasma was pink. When alkali was added, the solution developed a transient green fluorescence. It is evident muscle tissue converted adrenaline into adrenochrome which was pink and which was converted by alkali into the fluorescent adrenolutin.

The evidence for the formation of adrenochrome is very powerful and it is likely the final proof by isolation, by radioactive tracer studies or by other techniques, is not far off.

METABOLISM OF ADRENOCHROME

Fischer and Lecomte (1951) found that the major portion of the adrenochrome injected into some animals was converted into adrenolutin. Fischer and Landtscheer (1950) reported that adrenochrome disappeared rapidly from blood and was found in liver and kidney where it was changed to adrenolutin and excreted. Leach and Heath (1956) and Hoffer and Kenyon (1957) showed adrenaline was converted in plasma via adrenochrome into adrenolutin. Later, Noval showed that radioactive adrenochrome was converted in rats into 5,6-dihydroxy-N-methylindole and adrenolutin.

Adrenochrome Tolerance Curves

Using the Payza and Mahon (1959, 1960) method for measuring adrenochrome in blood, Hoffer (1959a) developed an adrenochrome tolerance curve. The basis of the method was the rate of removal of injected adrenochrome from plasma. A sample of blood was taken. Then 10 mg of crystalline adrenochrome in water was injected. Additional samples of blood were taken at 15, 30, and 60 minutes. All the samples were then analyzed for adrenochrome. Whether or not this method measures the adrenochrome naturally present in blood has been questioned on the basis of which was the proper blank. But no one has questioned the value of this method for measuring injected adrenochrome. The adrenochrome tolerance curve provides a measure of the ability of the body to remove plasma adrenochrome. The results of a few tolerance curves are shown in Table 28. Because of the doubt regarding the initial values these will not be shown. Only changes at 15, 30, and 60 minutes will be shown.

In subjects who were neither schizophrenic nor depressed 10 mg of adrenochrome increased baseline values 170% at 15 minutes but they were normal by 30 minutes. In subjects suffering from depression the 15-minute increase was only 117% and after 2 days of treatment with iproniazid the increase was even less and a nearly flat adrenochrome tolerance curve was found. Schizophrenic subjects showed the greatest increases and the adrenochrome levels had not reached baseline levels in 1 hour. A small quantity of LSD (35 μg) given by mouth to 6 normal subjects produced a schizophrenic-like adrenochrome tolerance curve and in 2 cases 100 μg of LSD resulted in values 170% above the baseline even after 1 hour.

When schizophrenic patients were given iproniazid for 2 days, the adrenochrome tolerance curve were the same as those found in depressions treated with iproniazid.

The only other report we have seen on adrenochrome conversions in serum was Jantz' (1956) report that serum from alcoholics metabolized adrenochrome to adrenolutin more quickly than did normal serum.

TABLE 28

ADRENOCHROME TOLERANCE CURVES

Group	Number	Treatment	15 (minutes)	30 (minutes)	60 (minutes)
Nonschizophrenic	9	None	+170	−45	−22
Schizophrenic	6	None	+280	+75	+107
Nonschizophrenic	6	LSD (35 μg)	+260	+100	+67
Nonschizophrenic	2	LSD (100 μg)	—	—	+170
Schizophrenic	3	No iproniazid	+200	−10	+60
Same schizophrenic	3	Iproniazid	+33	+12	−16
Depressions	3	No iproniazid	+117	−22	−17
Same schizophrenic	3	Iproniazid	+54	−3	−32

Psychological Properties of Adrenochrome

ADRENOCHROME FROM *l*-ADRENALINE

Adrenochrome may be made from *l*-adrenaline, the natural form, from *d*-adrenaline and, of course, from *dl*-adrenaline. The early studies were conducted with adrenochrome made from *l*-adrenaline.

We and our wives were the first human subjects to receive adrenochrome. The preparation was made by Professors D. E. Hutcheon and N. R. Eade (1952; personal communication, 1954). The LD-50 for rats was 137 mg/kg and we were reasonably certain that it would not kill us. Since these were the first psychological experiments we will reproduce our first published statement of the changes we noted (Hoffer et al., 1954).

The first subject (A. Hoffer) received what we supposed was 1 mg in 1 ml of water subcutaneously. This makes a fine port-wine colored liquid. The injection was accompanied by a sharp and persistent pain at the site of injection. There were no recognizable psychological changes.

Blood pressure and pulse readings taken every 5 minutes for half an hour showed no change.

The second subject (H. Osmond) was given what we believed was 0.5 mg. Again there were no pressor effects but there were marked psychological changes (see below).

Further experiments on our wives and one of us (A. Hoffer), using 1 mg subcutaneously, produced some minor results, but by this time it seemed that our adrenochrome, which is very unstable, was beginning to deteriorate. Five milligrams of this deteriorating solution was given to H. Osmond and produced a response which was unpleasantly prolonged.

Since the subcutaneous injections were so painful, the first intravenous injection was given to a volunteer, Mr. C. R. Jillings, M.A., clinical psychologist. It was believed that adrenochrome given by this route would be much less painful. Therefore, 1.0 mg of adrenochrome was diluted with 2 ml of sterile physiological saline and injected into the left antecubital vein. Almost immediately after the injection, Jillings experienced a very severe pain which traveled up his left arm to the praecordium. This lasted about 10 minutes and was accompanied by pallor and sweating. There were no obvious psychological effects apart from alarm and dismay in the experimenters. It was later discovered that, if the adrenochrome solution is mixed with blood from the patient's vein, pain can usually be completely avoided.

Later, Hoffer and his wife each took 10-mg doses intravenously and had marked changes, particularly in effect and behavior. Hoffer became overactive, showed poor judgment, and lack of insight. Hoffer's wife became deeply depressed for 4 days and endured a condition which was indistinguishable from an endogenous depression. This unpleasant experience was aggravated by lack of insight, for she was unable to relate her depression to the injection of adrenochrome, although her change of mood came on immediately after it.

To those who are familiar with mescaline and lysergic acid we would emphasize that judging from the little experience which we have, it does seem that adrenochrome is more insidious than these two hallucinogens, its effects last longer and possibly in consequence of this its administration is accompanied by a loss of insight. Since this may have serious results experimenters should guard their subjects very carefully.

Summary of an Account of an Adrenochrome Trial (September, 1952), 20–30 Hours Approximately [condensed from notes made at the time by the subject (Osmond)]

After the purple red liquid was injected into my right forearm I had a good deal of pain. I did not expect that we would get any results from a preliminary trial and so was not, as far as I can judge, in a state of heightened expectancy. The fact that my blood pressure did not rise suggests that I was not unduly tense. After about 10 minutes, while I was lying on a couch looking up at the ceiling, I found that it had changed color. It seemed that the lighting had become brighter. I asked Abe and Neil if they had noticed anything, but they had not. I looked across the room and it seemed to have changed in some not easily definable way. I wondered if I could have suggested these things to myself. I closed my eyes and a brightly colored pattern of dots appeared. The colors were not as brilliant as those which I have seen under mescal, but were of the same type. The patterns of dots gradually resolved themselves into fish-like shapes. I felt that I was at the bottom of the sea or in an aquarium among a shoal of brilliant fishes. At one moment I concluded that I was a sea anemone in this pool. Abe and Neil kept pestering me to tell them what was happening, which annoyed me. They brought me a Van Gogh self-portrait to look at. I have never seen a picture so plastic and alive. Van Gogh gazed at me from the paper, crop headed, with hurt, mad eyes and seemed to be three dimensional. I felt that I could stroke the cloth of his coat and that he might turn around in his frame. Neil showed me the Rorschach cards. Their texture, their bas relief appearance, and the strange and amusing shapes which I had never before seen in the cards were extraordinary.

My experiences in the laboratory were, on the whole, pleasant but when I left I found the corridors outside sinister and unfriendly. I wondered what the cracks in the floor meant and why there were so many of them. Once we got out of doors the hospital buildings, which I know well, seemed sharp and unfamiliar. As we drove through the streets the houses appeared to have some special meaning, but I couldn't tell what it was. In one window I saw a lamp burning and I was astonished by its grace and brilliance. I drew my friends' attention to it, but they were unimpressed.

We reached Abe's home where I felt cut off from people but not unhappy. I knew that I should be discussing the experience with Abe and his wife but could not be bothered to do so. I felt no special interest in our experiment and had no satisfaction at our success, although I told myself that it was very important. Before I got to sleep I noticed that the colored visions returned when I shut my eyes. (Normally I have hypnogogic visions after several minutes in a darkened room when I am tired.) I slept well.

Next morning, although I had only slept a few hours, life seemed good. Colors were bright and my appetite keen. I was completely aware of the possibilities arising from the experiment. Color had extra meaning for me. Voices, typewriting, any sound was very clear. With those whom I felt did not appreciate the importance of the new discovery I could have easily become irritable, but I was able to control myself.

H. *Osmond's Second Adrenochrome Experience* (1953) (PM)

I had 5 mg of adrenochrome this time because we thought that it was probably deteriorating.

I saw only a few visual patterns with my eyes closed. I had the feeling that there was something wonderful waiting to be seen, but somehow I couldn't see it. However, in the outside world everything seemed sharper and the Van Gogh was three dimensional. I began to feel that I was losing touch with everything. My sister telephoned and, although I am usually glad to hear her voice, I couldn't feel any warmth or happiness. I watched a group of patients dancing and, although I enjoy watching dancing with the envious interest of one who is clumsy on his feet, I didn't have a flicker of feeling.

As we drove back to Abe's house a pedestrian walked across the road in front of us. I thought we might run him down, and watched with detached curiosity. I had no concern for the victim. We did not knock him down.

I began to wonder whether I was a person any more and to think that I might be a plant or a stone. As my feeling for these inanimate objects increased my feeling for and my interest in humans diminished. I felt indifferent towards humans and had to curb myself from making unpleasant personal remarks about them. I had no inclination to say more or less than I observed. If I was asked if I liked a picture I said what I felt and disregarded the owner's feeling.

I did not wish to talk and found it most comfortable to gaze at the floor or a lamp. Time seemed to be of no importance. I slept well that night and awoke feeling lively, but although I had to attend a meeting that morning, I did not hurry myself. Eventually I had to be more or less dragged out of the house by Abe. I had to get my car from a garage where it was being repaired. There was some trouble about finding it in the garage when at last I was seated in the driver's seat I realized that I couldn't drive it through traffic, although quite able to do so usually. I did not, however, feel anxious or distressed by this but persuaded the garage proprietor to drive me to my destination. I would, I believe, have normally found this a humiliating situation. I did not feel humiliated.

I attended the scientific meeting, and during it I wrote this note: "Dear Abe, this damn stuff is still working. The odd thing is that stress brings it on, after about 15 minutes. I have this 'glass wall other side of the barrier' feeling. It is fluctuant, almost intangible, but I know it is there. It wasn't there three quarters of an hour ago; the stress was the minor one of getting the car. I have a feeling that I don't know anyone here; absurd but unpleasant. Also some slight ideas of reference arising from my sensation of oddness. I have just begun to wonder if my hands are writing this, crazy of course."

I fluctuated for the rest of the day. While being driven home by my psychologist colleague, Mr. B. Stefaniuk, I discovered that I could not relate distance and time. I would see a vehicle far away on the long, straight prairie roads, but would be uncertain whether we might not be about to collide with it. We had coffee at a wayside halt and here I became disturbed by the covert glances of a sinister looking man. I could not be sure whether he was "really" doing this or not. I went out to look at two wrecked cars which had been brought in to a nearby garage. I became deeply preoccupied with them and the fate of their occupants. I could only tear myself away from them with an effort. I seemed in some way to be involved in them.

Later in the day when I reached home the telephone rang. I took no notice of it and allowed it to ring itself out. Normally, no matter how tired I am, I respond to it.

By the morning I felt that I was my usual self again.

Subject's Comment

I shall make no attempt to elaborate or discuss these two experiences. I am satisfied that they represent a model psychosis, but each reader must decide for himself on the evidence of what I have written and what my colleagues report.

Observations by Hoffer and N. A. on Subject H. Osmond's Reaction to Adrenochrome

Within 15 to 25 minutes of receiving the adrenochrome injection Osmond was preoccupied with the distasteful color of the laboratory.

He had never before made any comment concerning this. After he had described some of his experiences to us we showed him a reproduction of a Van Gogh painting which he observed very carefully for a long time. It was difficult to divert his attention toward some Rorschach cards we wished him to see. He stated they were not nearly as interesting. But when he did consent to examine these cards he refused to change cards until ordered to do so. Continual persuasion was needed to get a response. For this reason no complete evaluation of the protocol was obtained. However, in response to upper center D section of Card No. 10 he gave the response "these are shrimps, no they are statesmen—they are shrimp statesmen." This tendency toward contamination or the process of loosely combining two associations is not typical of Osmond who normally tends toward high F plus percent. On the other hand, in word association tests under normal conditions, Osmond does give above-average distant responses but is able to report the path of the associative process with no difficulty.

The change in Osmond, marked by strong preoccupation with inanimate objects, by a marked refusal to communicate with us, and by strong resistance to our requests, was in striking contrast with Osmond's normal social behavior.

On the occasion of Osmond's second trial the most noticeable objective change was his withdrawal from people. After the laboratory session, we drove to the home of A. Hoffer. Osmond entered, found a chair where he sat for approximately one hour intently examining the rug. He did not greet the group of people who were at the house nor enter into the discussion.

Osmond was anxious and fearful on retiring and once was found wandering about. In the morning he was easily distracted. He required two hours to dress.

Briefly, the changes noted were preoccupation with inanimate objects, negativism, loosening of the associative process, anxiety and distractability.

In that paper we listed 10 variables which were involved in any reaction to hallucinogenic (psychotomimetic) drugs or to schizophrenia. These were (1) the cultural setting, (2) the personality of the patient, (3) the age of onset, (4) the rate of production of M substance, (5) the quantity produced, (6) the exact substance produced, (7) the specific cerebral enzymes altered, (8) the capacity of the body for storing M substance, (9) the capacity of the body for detoxifying it, and (10) the success of the sick person in dealing with the psychological disturbances. Cultural factors were considered here. A discussion of these factors has been given in the LSD section and need not be repeated here.

At the time we carried out these experiments in 1952 we expected either that adrenochrome would be inactive or that it would affect us as had LSD. We were, in fact, hoping for an LSD-like reaction. But these first experiments first disappointed us since the changes although clear and definite were so subtle. Many criticisms were later made of these pilot trials, the chief one being that they were subjective anecdotal accounts. No one ever told us how one could carry out preliminary experiments in any other way. Fortunately, both of us are experienced in taking psychologically active compounds and we are not placebo reactors. On the contrary, we tend to underreact to active compounds. We have detected psychological activity in ololiuqui, in deteriorated adrenaline solutions, and in several indoles derived from adrenaline and sympathomimetic amines using simple self-observational techniques, when so-called controlled experiments showed no activity. It is likely that double blind experiments on new drugs would be worse than useless since one would not know what activity to look for.

For the next three years, there was a good deal of discussion in the literature about the psychological activity of adrenochrome with most commentators agreeing that it must be inactive. But no scientific reports appeared, probably because investigators were unable to synthesize pure adrenochrome, or were not inclined to take it themselves, or give it to their subjects.

Schwarz *et al.* (1956b) were the first investigators to corroborate our findings. Using adrenochrome which we sent them, they found similar changes in their subjects. They gave it by intravenous injection and reported—"It was difficult to evaluate the effects of adrenochrome on the psyche. The epileptic appeared to be relaxed and became drowsy. One schizophrenic appeared to show loosening of associations and increase in disturbance of body image; for instance, he raised his hand, gazed at it and said 'my arm wiggles and waves, ha, ha.' The other schizophrenic who received adrenochrome experienced cataplexy on 2 occasions which persisted for more than 30 minutes. At these times his upper extremities were held in unnatural positions which volunteers who served as controls could not maintain for long and was not his usual reaction and a similar state did not develop with either mescaline or LSD-25," and in the meantime Taubmann and Jantz (1957) at the instigation of Mayer-Gross (1959) made a careful study of adrenochrome and confirmed its psychotomimetic effect. They believed that it produces a toxic psychosis but this is a matter of interpretation and definition (Hoffer and Osmond, 1959; Osmond and Hoffer, 1959).

Taubmann and Jantz reasoned that if adrenochrome was given under the tongue it would reach the brain with less destruction than by vein.

They believed that it would get to the brain directly through the sublingual venous anastomosis, just as novocaine is believed to reach the brain more readily by this route. Many euphorients are commonly absorbed through the buccal mucosa, for example coca, betal nut, hashish. They, therefore, administered 3 mg adrenochrome as a powder under the tongue. The adrenochrome produced a biting sensation. After 10 minutes, the subject noted a slight feeling of facial warmth and tingling in the fingers. They often complained of mild pain about the heart region. All somatic feelings were gone within 30 minutes. Psychic changes occurred within 10 minutes. They varied from person to person and even from time to time in the same person. Depression was more frequent than euphoria.

Marked visual perceptual changes occurred. Colors of objects changed in quality and appeared peculiar or strange and disproportionate. Their perceptions of their own bodies were distorted. Distant objects appeared to be too close. Movement was observed in stationary objects. No disorders of thought or of consciousness were observed. All changes ceased after one-half hour. They suggest that an active substance resembling adrenochrome is the psychotoxic agent and that activity apparently depended upon the type of chemical syntheses. Their adrenochrome crystallized very rapidly at the temperature of liquid carbon dioxide was less active than adrenochrome precipitated at higher temperatures.

However, the best psychological human studies were completed by Grof *et al.* (1963). The adrenochrome was synthesized by Dr. V. Vitek according to Feldstein (1958) or purchased from L. Light and Company. They carried out double blind studies on 15 volunteers using subjects very similar to those used in our studies in Saskatchewan, that is, intelligent, educated, normal subjects as well as some psychiatric patients. Many of their subjects were sophisticated in psychological experiments, having taken LSD, mescaline, or psilocybin. The placebo was a red dye; the dose of adrenochrome varied between 15 and 30 mg sublingually. In the double blind design, out of 15 subjects given placebo, only one thought he had received an active compound. Out of 15 subjects given adrenochrome, only 4 believed they had received placebo. [Chi Square for 1 d.f. is over 11 ($P < 0.001$).]

CLINICAL CHANGES. *Perception.* There were no perceptual changes in 8 subjects. Changes in body image including depersonalization and derealization occurred in 4 subjects. Of these one had a disorder of body image and derealization and felt his legs were short. Visual perceptual changes occurred in 5 subjects and ranged from increased sensitivity to color, to illusions, pseudohallucinations of mysterious messages in telegraphic code coming from the universe. Tactile hallucinations occurred in 3 subjects. Taste and olfactory hallucinations were not reported. Eight had alterations in perception and estimation of time. Very few and vague changes were reported by 3 placebo subjects. They included transitory derealization, and minor undulations in the visual field.

Thought. There were no clinical changes in thought in 5 subjects. Some of these showed marked changes on association tests. Paranoid and other delusions were present in 7 subjects. Changes in tempo of thinking such as flight of ideas, difficulty in concentrating, blocking, and speech alterations occurred in 5. One showed negativism, ambivalence, and splitting of personality. Another developed inappropriate behavior such as sitting in a wastebasket or creeping along the floor. Two subjects had no insight into the fact that their condition had been changed. None of the placebo subjects showed any pathological changes in thinking.

The most sensitive method for demonstrating the central effects of adrenochrome was the word-association experiment. There was a high frequency of disturbed associations compared to the placebo experiments. It was significantly different, at the 1% level at 30 minutes, 2–5% level at 60 minutes, and at the 5% level at 120 minutes. The latency period, that is, the time between stimulus word and response, was prolonged significantly by adrenochrome at the 5% level at 2 hours. In 11 subjects given 330 verbal stimulus words, there were 81 disturbed associations (25%). The most frequent were clang associations. There were only 6 to 7% disturbed associations with placebo. The quantity of disturbed associations is about the same as for schizophrenic patients. The authors concluded that in many cases the subjects formed answers before they understood the meaning of the stimulus word. But for other cases, the origin of the disturbed association was not known. In a few subjects disturbed associations carried on until the next placebo experiment although they had been normal before. This they had never observed with LSD, mescaline, or psilocybin. They finally concluded that the changes in thinking induced by adrenochrome were similar to those observed in schizophrenia. Adrenochrome caused an elective inhibition of the process which determines the content of associative thinking. This occurred in doses which did not heighten lability of basic processes, did not reduce excitation, and did not loosen temporary connections as was the case with LSD.

Sommer and Osmond (1960) used the Kent-Rosanoff word-association test for testing the hypothesis that schizophrenics had a specific language which had been suggested by some psychoanalytic writers. They found that a group of 49 schizophrenic patients gave about 15% uncommon responses. This degree of unusual responses is very similar to 25% disturbed associations found by Grof *et al.* (1963). The non-schizophrenic group of 69 subjects gave only 7% uncommon responses. Furthermore, schizophrenics were less stable on repetition of the test ($P < 0.02$) and fewer patients "thought alike" ($P < 0.0001$).

Mood. Eight subjects reported or demonstrated no changes in affect. Euphoria and silly laughter or giggling occurred in 6. Three subjects had anxiety, 1 was fearful and 1 became hostile and depressed. Very often early tension or anxiety was replaced by euphoria and relaxation.

Comparison to Other Psychotomimetic Experiences. Most of the subjects had not taken other hallucinogens and so had no basis for comparison. Of the group that did, two compared it to mild psilocybine experiments and three to mild LSD reactions but in each instance without the autonomic changes.

General. The other tests used were in agreement with the clinical observations. The changes in 3 subjects varied from no reaction to severe schizophrenic-like states. Nine subjects received doses of 30 mg sublingually. Four suffered endogenous Bonhoeffer-type psychosis, 3 schizophrenic-like psychosis, and in one the reaction was doubtful. One failed to react. There were thus 7 out of 9 reactors, or nearly 80%. When 15 mg was given, there were 6 definite reactions (1 toxic, 1 schizophrenic-like, and 4 neurotic), that is, nearly 40%. Five subjects had uncertain reactions and 5 were without reaction.

We have reviewed this work in some detail because of its importance. It is the first double blind study with adrenochrome on humans and fully corroborates the Saskatchewan findings.

Several years ago we sent these investigators pure crystalline adrenochrome and on repeating their experiments, they found the same kind of activity as before. Apparently their preparations were pure enough so that there was enough adrenochrome present to produce its characteristic effect.

One experiment which we have not yet reported is included because it occurred during a large research demonstration, was unusually well documented and happened to a very skillful clinician, well-trained in psychodynamic theory.

Dr. A. B. was a senior member of a well-known psychiatric research unit. The adrenochrome hypothesis had appealed to him since it incorporated elements of internal medicine, depth psychology, psychiatry, and biochemistry. He had had many years of experience in research in medicine and in psychiatry, and he had been mainly instrumental in the United States in selecting several new psychoactive drugs which are now in common use.

He determined to take adrenochrome himself at the first opportunity and for this reason he had refused to read any of the adrenochrome accounts which had been published lest they later bias his own judgment. However, there was no doubt that he hoped that something would happen to him. In spite of this, he remained intellectually skeptical.

On October 29, 1959, he decided to start the experiment. Hoffer had arrived to demonstrate a treatment for alcoholism and Dr. A. B. wished to take advantage of my presence as an observer. Hoffer reluctantly agreed, chiefly because Dr. A. B. stated he would take it whether he agreed or not, and because another physician, Dr. J. P., was present and agreed to act as the main observer. Hoffer had to work with an alcoholic patient that day. A closed circuit TV had been set up so the large staff of a mental hospital could, at their leisure observe the proceedings. The reaction to adrenochrome was recorded by Hoffer.

9:32 A.M. 10-mg adrenochrome placed sublingually, then observed him in his office with J. P.

9:37 A.M. Rest of adrenochrome swallowed. He reports it has a bittersweet taste and he had a momentary slight feeling of nausea. This is his usual adrenergic reaction to drugs. Pupils—$\frac{1}{3}$. The taste persisted for several minutes.

9:40 A.M. He noted slight nausea when he took off his glasses. He is more irritable than he was earlier. I asked him to assess his afterimage and asked him "Do you know what I mean?" He was quite sharp in his retort that he well knew what I meant as he had studied this phenomenon before. He then examined his reactions after examining a bright light bulb.

9:42 A.M. He reports it is hard to focus and that there is a marked halo effect. Nausea is present. With his eyes closed, he reported scotomata and a bright afterimage with the edge indented and purple, like a planet. The afterimage pulsated—alternately enlarging and constricting. The corona became larger and brighter. Nausea was coming in waves. There were no geometric patterns.

9:44 A.M. The afterimage is still there, swinging and pulsing. This has never happened to him before. At this point, the corona disappeared. He estimated 30 seconds as 20 seconds.

9:45 A.M. Blood taken.

9:47 A.M. No nausea now. I told him he had underestimated the time which greatly surprised him and I asked him to try it again. Called out 31, 30, and 37. Immediately he was startled and stated he had seen the ceiling pulsating and found this very unpleasant. This occurred between the 2nd and 3rd estimate. He estimates it as between 25 and 30 minutes since he took the compound.

9:53 AM. He has pain over the left frontal region which is quite severe. J. P. tested his visual fields and reported they were wider than he would have expected.

10:00 AM. I gave him a page to read. He reported there was difficulty in focusing. The words were sharp but they jiggled laterally. The lines along the right-hand border were running together. He does not like seeing the words move about. He estimated the distance to the end of his secretary's room as 40–45 feet. I stepped it off and it was 30 feet. When I told him this he refused to believe me and I challenged him to measure it for himself which he did.

There is no change in mood. On 100–7, performed badly as follows: 100 93 86 79 73 86 66 59 59 52, talks 45 38 24 17 24 17 10 3. Took 100 seconds. He estimates it took 60 seconds. He was very surprised it took so long.

10:07 AM. I asked him to repeat which he did after urging. 100 93 86 79 72 80 65—talking. Then he refused to continue—took 83 seconds. He refused to perform mechanical tasks because he feels uncertain.

J. P. asked him to estimate distance to the fire plug outside. Reported it was 300 yards. It was well under 200 yards. I estimated 150 yards and J. P. 170 yards. He was again surprised at this for he was a keen golfer accustomed to judging these distances accurately. I gave him some similarities and thinking tests which he did very well.

10:12 AM. He refuses to do 30-second test. I swung my arm in front of him in an arc from the elbow. He thought I wanted to Indian wrestle with him. My arm formed a blurred area before him.

He then told us he had an impulse to smash his fist through the door panel but restrained himself.

10:15 AM. We drove to B building for the treatment. On the way he did not like the sensation of the trees coming at him. They appeared to explode in his field of vision. He is disappointed in the reaction and feels nothing has happened.

I have so far observed perceptual distortions, changes in estimation of space and time, marked irritability and lack of concern for others which is abnormal for him. There is no insight for these changes. He is somewhat depressed.

After we arrived at B building I left Dr. A. B. for my LSD session, but I had asked Dr. J. P. to observe him very carefully and not leave him out of his sight until I could again join him at noon. Dr. J. P. wrote the following account a few days later.

On entering the TV viewing room of the LSD experiments being carried out, Dr. A. B. appeared for all intents and purposes, normal.

After sitting alone a few minutes, it became obvious that his eyes were troubling him as he was taking his glasses off and on, holding his forehead and was slightly restless. He was conversing with people quite normally and telling them he had taken adrenochrome.

After about 15 minutes, he left the room to make a telephone call. I was not present at this time but, on going out some 20 minutes later, he was still on the telephone and repeatedly saying, yes; he was all right. It would appear that the person to whom he was speaking on the phone detected some alteration in his manner and speech.

He gave a fairly erudite account of depression and seemed to be perfectly in control of his recall functions in relation to his specialty.

He called Doctor A of X drug company ostensibly to inquire whether he could obtain admission for me to a meeting in Texas. During the course of this discussion, he divulged the fact that we were undertaking extract studies in cooperation with X. This is the first time, to my knowledge that A. B. has ever divulged the confidence of one company to another.

From general observation, he was somewhat more abrupt than usual although his thoughts and verbalization appeared to be within normal limits. Rather than be friendly, he would either walk in front or behind you, and seemed to drift away from whomever he was talking with.

During the course of writing on the blackboard, he found difficulty in forming certain letters, particularly the letter D.

Throughout this entire period, his distance perception was way off and he said that he was frankly scared to make any attempt at judgments. During the whole period, he claimed that he was getting no effects whatsoever from the adrenochrome and was quite irritable when you suggested that he was not behaving exactly normally.

In talking to him, one got the impression that his judgment was way off and he was inclined to make all sorts of promises without having carefully assessed the significance of doing so.

This report takes us from 10:45 to 12:30 PM.

12:00 noon. I went to lunch with him and several others. Joe was distinctly irritable and was very flushed. He reported his thinking was slow. J. P. reported Joe was abrupt, showed decreased judgment and was didactic. He read a lecture to J. on the depression study.

1:00 PM. He returned to the TV room to observe. According to Mrs. C. he walked in and was unusual. She did not know he had taken anything. He placed his hand heavily on her shoulder. Her reaction was, what have I done—why does he support me this way. He seemed irritable and aloof. He sat down in a corner of the room alone and watched for a few minutes. Then he walked out. She had seldom seen him this way and never when there had been no provocation.

2:30 PM. A. T. reported trouble lighting a match and sluggishness in thinking. Gave him 1 gram nicotinic acid by mouth.

3:00 PM. Flushed

3:30 PM. Marked flush. He reports his vision has cleared up and his thinking is clearer.

4:00 PM. Mrs. C. reports he is much more like himself but is slower than usual.

4:30 PM. Still flushed but feels nearly normal.

He reported the following:

1. After 10:00 AM he was quite suspicious of J. and myself, and felt we had given him placebo. After ten o'clock he phoned J. N. to check on whether he really had received adrenochrome.
2. Slight feeling of unreality.
3. Was surprised at some of the things I told him about himself.
4. Stopwatch on table pulsated (10:00 AM).
5. He is perceptually normal.
6. His secretaries reported he was irritable and slow in the morning.
7. He is surprised he was not aware of change because he is normally so aware of his own mechanisms of thought.
8. Believes his judgment was defective.
9. Was very uncomfortable riding in car.

Explanatory Notes. 9:40 AM. We had known Dr. A. B. for about 2 years and had never known him to be discourteous, rude, or acid. His response to my question was very surprising and indicated a distinct change in his personality.

10:15 AM. By now his irritability was very obvious and he overreacted to my comments and those of Dr. J. P. as we prepared to leave, Dr. A. B. suddenly disappeared. Dr. J. P. and I concluded he had gone into his secretary's office to clear a few administrative matters. Apart from his irritability he seemed well in control of himself. But a few minutes later when he failed to return we went to search for him and we found him purposefully striding toward our car without letting us know he was going. There was an element of rudeness in this which I had never seen before, or since, in over 5 years of steady friendship. We chased him and all entered the car together. As we started away he was perturbed by the apparent explosion of a tree into his field of vision as we drove by.

12:00 noon. During lunch Dr. A. B. was morose and irritable. When I asked him how he felt he responded that he was very sorry that the adrenochrome was a dud and had produced no change in him whatever. Dr. J. P. was still shaken by Dr. A. B.'s major break in confidence over their joint drug study, and told me that had this sort of thing happened on any other occasion his company would have immediately ceased all further cooperation with him. But as he had seen A. B. take the adrenochrome and seen the reaction develop, he could not take any action.

2:30 PM. I was very concerned that A. B. had not begun to recover from his reaction. I knew he faced a heavy afternoon and evening and he seemed to be in no condition to face his patients who were scheduled for that afternoon. I gave him 1 gram of nicotinic acid in order to hasten his recovery. Before 2:30 he had refused to take any since he had decided nothing had happened to him. But at 2:30 his insight had returned partially.

On October 30, 1959 A. B. became convinced that he was markedly altered by the adrenochrome and now realizes it is a dangerous drug to be dispensed carefully. He felt well yesterday evening. His last patient at about midnight remarked that A. B. did not seem to be himself. This morning in retrospect he is aware of the changes. This is very surprising to him as he had before been so confident he would be aware of his own psychological changes.

Dr. B. B. observed some changes in A. B. In the TV viewing room A. B. came in and sat on the radiator cover and did not seem to be himself. Once when he looked up at Dr. B. B. he seemed very startled. Today A. B. reported he was very startled by seeing B. B.'s face suddenly become twice as large. B. B. noted that A. B. fumbled around trying to light a cigarette and he had more than his usual trouble with tremor in getting it lit.

A. B. reported that the first reaction to adrenochrome occurred within 1 minute with nausea. About half an hour later he toyed with the idea of fooling us by making believe that he really was reacting, but did not do so. Then he became negativistic and felt like doing the reverse of what we asked him. He did report during the 100–7 test that he felt like going up rather than down.

He was particularly annoyed by the sensation of the trees suddenly exploding before him as he drove toward them. He was also nauseated and felt he would vomit.

In the afternoon, his administrative assistant in jest asked him, "Well, how is the adrenochrome kid?" He appeared to have a daydream or reverie about this and upon awakening fired him—until he was fully awake.

This morning he is as usual. There seems to be no residual effect.

A. B. reported that after he began to flush from the nicotinic acid he felt nearly normal and he was able to work in his usual manner, with a succession of patients who had come for psychotherapy. However, he became very disturbed late in the evening when his last patient asked him if he was all right. He then realized he must still be abnormal.

On October 31, 1959 when I left for home A. B. drove me to the train. He reported he was now normal but had not been on the previous day. Many months later he told me he did not fully recover for about two weeks but his wife felt it took several months.

This experiment was well controlled and well observed by many scientists, many of whom did not know A. B. had taken adrenochrome. But it was not double blind. It was along the lines of the classic experiments of James, Mitchell, and Kluver with mescaline, Hofmann with LSD, and Osmond with LSD, adrenochrome, adrenolutin, and ololiuqui. In general, these self-experiments by skillful introspective observers have been much more successful in selecting active hallucinogens than have double blind experiments.

Account by A. B. After the Experiment. Attitude toward experiment. I tried to maintain as objective an attitude as possible by not reading any descriptions of the effects of the drug on human volunteers. However, several factors must be considered as possible determinants: (a) my respect for the work of Dr. Hoffer and (b) our commitments to the investigation of the adrenochrome hypothesis. There is little doubt that I was biased in wanting the experiment to work and that the effective component was positive in spite of the apparent intellectual skepticism.

General health and mental status. My general health was good. I was somewhat underweight (147 lb) and quite fatigued. There was some tension but little or no perceptive anxiety and no depression. I was quite convinced that I would be able to accurately record my experiences.

My first experience, that is, after taking the adrenochrome sublingually, was taste. This was slightly bitter and aromatic but not unpleasant. I did not notice anything else for the first few minutes until I happened to look at the ceiling. It seemed to move down toward me although I did not have the sensation that it was falling. It was unpleasant but not frightening. During the testing period I was interested in the persistence of the halo in the afterimage and somewhat annoyed by the tests of counting and distance. The affect accompanying my failure in these tests remained one of annoyance at my colleagues rather than concern for my inability to perform routine tasks. I felt slightly impatient to see the demonstration.

Riding over to the other building in the car, it was difficult to focus on trees as they seemed to grow suddenly bigger. Again this was unpleasant but not frightening. By this time I was convinced that the adrenochrome was having no effect in spite of the perceptual changes and my prevailing feeling was one of disappointment. It was difficult to watch the TV screen because of the shift in image size. On one occasion Dr. B. turned suddenly toward me to light my cigarette. His face seemed extraordinarily large and I drew back involuntarily. Again, this was not a frightening experience but was somewhat startling. My suspicions that I had been given a placebo continued to mount. I decided to go out and telephone Dr. N. and observed that Dr. P. got up to follow me out. I resented this and decided to elude him. During the rest of the morning I made some improvident telephone calls, although at the time I did not feel that there was any contraindication to making these calls. I had promised Dr. P. that I would discuss the differential diagnosis of depression with him and felt quite confident while doing so. The only subjective experience I had was one of slight impatience. At noon time, riding in the car again was unpleasant because of the change in image size of the trees but otherwise I did not notice anything out of the ordinary.

During the afternoon prior to taking nicotinic acid the only change that I observed was a slight tendency to withdraw from people around me. I did not feel depressed or truly apathetic. I was aware of an associated impatience and some irritation. During the afternoon and evening while at practice, I felt somewhat tired but until my 11 o'clock patient, I was not aware of any other changes. During my 11 o'clock hour I again felt somewhat withdrawn and impatient although my patient was one who I had worked with for several years and normally find quite enjoyable. He observed something different and asked me if I was well. I slept well that night and felt my usual self in the morning, although a friend who has known me well for several years, felt that there was some change in my personality. She later described this as not being myself, somehow or other, apart from the group.

The most disturbing aspect of this experience from my point of view was the apparent lack of insight into the changes that were noted by others around me. My peculiar indifference to the perceptual changes is in keeping with what now appears to me to have been a form of dissociative effect. I have not as yet seen the reports of my behavior but have been told that the major changes in terms of my relationship to other people were characterized by unusual abruptness, curtness and apparent desire to be left alone. In retrospect, this is exactly how I felt, although I was not aware of the degree to which it was manifest. Changes in spelling would be no indication since I cannot spell anyway. The same is true for problems in arithmetic. However, I have administered the 100–1 test a thousand times.

In summary, I am sure that there were some changes in personality. They appeared to be primarily in the area of affect. I am not sure what role suggestion may have played. The total lack of insight would be difficult to account for on this basis.

Observations by Dr. B. B., Chief Psychiatrist of the Mental Hospital. In response to your recent letter, kindly be advised that A. B. told me on Tuesday, October 27th, that the next morning he was going to take some adrenochrome, and was taking advantage of your being here to take it to see what the affect would be.

On Wednesday, I was in the conference room in the B basement watching the second patient get his treatment, and was sitting in an armchair next to the windows, in front of which was a covered radiator. About 10 AM I was surprised to see A. B. coming in the walk with you and, I believe, a third person. I was surprised as I had anticipated that, if he took adrenochrome, he wouldn't be traveling around very much.

About ten minutes later A. B. came in and sat on the edge of the radiator cover right alongside me. The first thing he said was that J. N. had 'goofed' because the so-and-so adrenochrome hadn't worked. I commiserated with him on this fact inasmuch as we had all been so delighted that Dr. N. had been able to produce adrenochrome, and here it appeared that it didn't have any effect. The patient under treatment at this time recounted how he had seen some lights. A. B. mentioned that this was about the only effect it had on him, that for a short period he had seen different colored lights. That was all.

I would estimate that A. B. had been in the conference room about ten minutes when I noticed that he seemed to be somewhat on the tremulous side, moving about and changing his sitting position rather frequently. He got out a cigarette and I noticed that when he got out his matches, he seemed to be unable to get the match head to strike the abrasive on the paper matches. With A. B. sitting on the radiator cover, his head was 12 to 18 inches higher than mine. He was to my left and a little bit in front of me. Noting his difficulty, and without thinking, I whipped out my matches, struck one and reached right up to the end of A. B.'s cigarette. I was immediately aware that I had startled him and he looked at me in a very strange way. I can best describe it as a combination of apprehension, startled reaction, and fear. He stared at me for a fraction of a second, then took the light and said nothing.

It flashed through my mind at the time that possibly his reaction was the same as I have heard schizophrenics described. How, when you reach out to pat them on the shoulder, for instance, it appears to them that you are going to strike them and the movement seems rapid and precipitous. I made a mental note not to frighten A. B. like this again. He puffed on his cigarette, squirmed, and about 5 minutes later I noticed that his eyelids were all wrinkled, forming slits, and he seemed to be gazing intently at the center of the ceiling. I sat and watched him, and I would estimate that he gazed intently at that one spot for at least a full minute.

He looked then at the television. He sat and watched and listened to what was going on. He made some comment that he was having difficulty with his depth perception; that the television set seemed to move further away and then come closer. He again got out a cigarette and again had difficulty striking the match. Not wishing to repeat what had happened previously, I said to him, 'A. B. how about my lighting the match for you.' He agreed, saying that he was having trouble with his depth perception. I told him that I would strike the match and hold it up to his cigarette, which I did, moving my hand rather slowly. He didn't appear to be apprehensive or frightened by this motion.

He just about finished the cigarette when all of a sudden he said, 'I'm going out for awhile.' He left and in my own mind I had the distinct impression that the adrenochrome was having considerably more effect on A. B. than he appreciated, as within the course of the approximate 25 minutes he was there, he mentioned on several occasions that he was getting very minimal affect from the adrenochrome and was quite disgusted about the whole thing. In about 10 minutes he popped back into the conference room and stayed for awhile. I don't know just how long he stayed as I got interested watching the LSD treatment, and later on when I looked around he was gone.

It seems to run in my memory that when you broke for luncheon that day, you said you were going over to have lunch with A. B. Either I mentioned something to you about A. B.'s reaction or felt that when you saw him you would be in a position to gauge how much reaction he was having, and do anything that might be indicated.

I promptly proceeded to forget about the whole thing until the next day when we got talking with A. B. about it. As you will recall, he mentioned that the first time I lit the cigarette for him, the thing that startled him was, all of a sudden my face seemed to get so large.

Trusting this information will be of assistance to you.

Report from Dr. J. N., the Chemist Who Had Made the Adrenochrome. Concerning Dr. A. B.'s reaction to adrenochrome, there is no doubt in my mind that he behaved abnormally after taking it. This conclusion is based, in part, on the visual disturbances, and to do the simple 100–7 routine, but especially on his attitudes and behavior towards us. I was very amazed that Dr. A. B. became so abrupt and uncooperative with us. I have never seen him react so unreasonably; he is normally very friendly, considerate, and gracious to you, J. P., the secretaries, and myself.

SUMMARY. Dr. A. B. hoped he would have an adrenochrome reaction but since he had not read any of the previous accounts, did not really know what to expect. He had not taken any hallucinogen before. His reaction came on in about 10 minutes which is typical when it is given sublingually, and he remained under its influence until 1 gram of nicotinic acid partially restored his personality to normal, but he did not really become normal for several weeks or months.

His experience was characterized by the following changes.

Perception. Changes in afterimage, in lighting, in judging distance, in far vision and some feelings of unreality. Objects pulsated and the normal smooth relationship of size and distance was distorted. There were no hallucinations. Time became inconstant.

Thought–Content. He was irritable, abrupt, showed lack of judgment and no insight that he was different. He had, in fact, concluded he had been given placebo even though he saw his chemist weigh out the adrenochrome from her stock. The most striking changes were his absolute lack of insight and his poor judgment.

Process. He could not perform the simple serial sevens test.

Mood. He was irritable, slightly hostile and abrupt. It was apparent to every one who had any contact with him that they had never seen him this way before. During the five years following he has had some serious physical illness, but even when severely ill his personality was never altered in the same way and he remained recognizable. Only after adrenochrome was his personality so changed he might not have been recognized by his colleagues and friends.

We have examined adrenochrome made from the dextro isomer of adrenaline that is, *d*-adrenaline. It was synthesized in 1958 by Dr. R. A. Heacock. Three milligrams given sublingually produced the following changes in 2 subjects.

Subject one observed some difficulty in reading and focusing at 7 minutes. At 10 minutes, he was lightheaded. At 12 minutes, far objects seemed very far away. At 24 minutes, he was euphoric and could not estimate time. At 35 minutes, time had seemed almost stationary. At 45 minutes, colors were very bright and vivid. At 80 minutes, he was very active in speech and movements and abrupt with people. At 5½ hours, he felt normal. However, for the next 24 hours, people's faces and other objects would become alternately small and large in size. In one instance, a speaker's face appeared to move away and towards him. Objects moving toward him increased in size too quickly.

Subject two also received 3 mg. At 4 minutes, the print on a page became blurred and he had difficulty grasping the meaning of words. At 9 minutes, he became tired and his vision was blurred. At 30 minutes, his thinking was fuzzy. He was apathetic and could not concentrate. The outline of his hand seemed blurred. At 39 minutes, curtains in the room appeared to shimmer. At 52 minutes, he was withdrawn. For the next 30 hours, he was depressed, withdrawn, and disinterested.

ADRENOCHROME FROM *dl*-ADRENALINE

The same subject who had taken 3 mg *d*-adrenochrome (from *l*-adrenaline) took 3 mg *dl*-adrenochrome sublingually.

Slight changes in perception (dizziness, lightheadedness, increased brightness of room, changes in size of far objects) occurred. There was no change in thought and there was slight euphoria. After 2 hours, he found the experience unpleasant and took 1 gm of nicotinic acid by mouth. That evening, he was irritable, restless, and without ambition. He was bothered by the odor of new wax on the floor, and later by insomnia.

The following subjects received 6 mg of *dl*-adrenochrome sublingually.

Subject one took his adrenochrome at 4:00 PM. Ten minutes later, he had an anesthetized area over both cheeks and he had difficulty in focusing. At 4:15 PM he was very quiet and appeared sad, but denied this. He underestimated the size of objects about 20%. Three minutes later, he was dizzy as if he would faint. At 4:25, he could no longer estimate the passage of time. He thought he had been in all afternoon. His limbs became very light. His hands changed in size as he looked at them and the observer's face changed in size. The rest of the hour, he found paintings unusually vivid. At the end of the hour, he had a headache in the occipital area and felt indifferent. Because of his discomfort, he was given 1 gm of nicotinic acid. In 10 minutes as he began to flush, the perceptual changes vanished and he felt normal. That night, he slept lightly and was not sure whether he had been awake or asleep (twilight sleep). The next morning, he was very tired and considered not coming to work. At work, he was irritable all day.

Subject two had had much experience with LSD and was skilled at introspective observation. At 2:00 PM, he received the adrenochrome. In 5 minutes, he became aware that colors and detail were more distinct. People in pictures seemed more lifelike and larger. In 10 minutes, he had a marked frontal headache. He was able to read but could not make sense out of what he read. At 20 minutes, the visual changes were very clear. He estimated 30 seconds as 45 seconds (mean of 3 trials). At 25 minutes, he looked older in the mirror. He was relaxed and disinterested. His headache was almost gone but he felt clumsy when moving. One hour after starting he was depressed and irritable. His face was flushed. He was withdrawn and indifferent. While lined up in a cafeteria for coffee, the other people appeared to be puppets. When he drank his coffee, he complained about the noisiness. He felt the people around him were puppetlike, lacked understanding. They annoyed him but he stated he was superior to them. They seemed empty people. At 3:15 PM his facial flush was gone. The white uniforms of nurses in the cafeteria annoyed him. At 3:40 he thought 2 hours had elapsed since taking adrenochrome. He markedly overestimated the size of objects (12 trials). At 2 hours, he felt music was being played at half speed. He liked the experience to the initial symptoms of LSD. It seemed like 3½ hours since taking it. His headache was now gone. He reported that the most pleasant part of the experience was that it was wearing off. The next hour, he was easily confused and still could not estimate time correctly. After that he was normal.

POTENTIATION OF THE ACTION OF ADRENOCHROME

Melander and Martens (1958) found that lysergic acid diethylamide (15–30 μg/kg) and taraxein when given ahead of adrenolutin markedly potentiated its effect. Thus 20–25 mg/kg when given by vein produced only slight changes in cats. But pretreated cats showed a marked response of drowsiness and muscle relaxation after 2–3 mg/kg. Acetyl-LSD also was a potentiator but bromo-LSD was not. Martens *et al.* (1959) reported that LSD and taraxein sensitized cats to acetylcholine, adrenaline, atropine, chlorpromazine, histamine, mescaline, and serotonin. They, therefore, made the sensible suggestion that taraxein, LSD, and *dl*-acetyllysergic acid diethylamide (ALD) increase the permeability of these substances through the blood–brain barrier, that is, they "have the property of enabling certain intravenously injected drugs to act on selected brain centers not normally accessible to them."

Hoffer (1959) and Hoffer and Osmond (1960) found that humans reacted to the combination of LSD followed by adrenochrome or adrenolutin in the same way. There was a marked potentiation of the adrenochrome effect. This was especially notable in human subjects who reacted to LSD primarily by the production of severe tension and anxiety. Visual and psychedelic changes were minimal, if present at all. In these subjects, the injection of 10 mg adrenochrome or adrenolutin produced a certain relaxation from tension and the usual LSD experience of marked visual and other changes. Adrenochrome can be used in this way to help break across the tension barrier into the psychedelic experience, which is helpful in treating alcoholics.

Heath *et al.* (1958) postulated that ceruloplasmin formed part of a protective system. Its function would be to protect the body against amines or their metabolites liberated during stress. Martens *et al.* (1959) provided powerful evidence in support of this idea. Ceruloplasmin irreversibly binds adrenolutin (Melander, 1957) and histamine (Martens *et al.*, 1959). When animals were pretreated with ceruloplasmin, they were protected against the psychotomimetic properties of LSD alone or LSD followed by other compounds listed by these authors above. It also decreased the toxicity of histamine. Further support for the protective role of ceruloplasmin were the interesting therapeutic responses of schizophrenic patients to ceruloplasmin, reported by Martens *et al.* (1959).

The psychotomimetic experience induced by adrenochrome and adrenolutin does not resemble the usual LSD or mescaline experience. The changes occur primarily in thought and mood. Perceptual changes are subtle and not obvious. These are in sharp contrast with visual changes often found after consuming LSD.

Since pretreatment with LSD stabilized adrenochrome when injected into normal subjects, it is not surprising that pretreatment with LSD markedly potentiates the effect of adrenochrome (J. S. Noval *et al.*, 1959), and adrenolutin (Melander and Martens, 1958). The potentiation of the adrenochrome experience by LSD was examined by giving normal volunteers 35 μg of LSD orally, followed one or more weeks later by 10 mg of adrenochrome intravenously and 1 or more weeks later by a combination of both, that is the adrenochrome was administered 1½–2 hours after the LSD. The same sequence was not used in all the experiments.

Subject One—First Experiment. After 35 μg of LSD, no change was noted in the first hour. During the second hour, the subject became nervous and complained of feeling jumpy similar to the feeling he had during examinations but more intense. During the injection with adrenochrome, 2 hours later, he blanched, began to breathe deeply and complained of air hunger and of feeling intensely nervous. There was no change in the pulse rate. Five minutes later, his normal color reappeared. After 20 minutes he was very nervous and felt quite chilly. He was markedly restless and irritable. He now noted some blurring of vision when looking at book titles a couple of yards from him. He was able to read but had difficulty comprehending what he read. He now reported he had completely lost any sensation of time and he could not estimate how long he had been in the experimental setting. On suggestion, he looked at his hands and noted momentarily that one was smaller. His movements were clumsy and fumbling. Fast moving objects appeared blurred. He was not as nervous now. On walking, his knees had a tendency to knock. Two hours later while walking down stairs he realized how weak his legs were. Driving him home, he was less aware of surroundings and had difficulty in telling his driver how to get to his home. The next day he reported "I experienced very slight nervousness with LSD. For a short time after the adrenochrome injection I had difficulty getting enough air and could also feel my heart pounding quite hard. After the injection, I was intensely jumpy and could not move smoothly. With the picture tests in which I had to lay out the pictures myself, I experienced some confusion. I could have gone through them much faster normally. When I got home I had a letter waiting from a company. I had some trouble getting the drift of the letter. I could not remember what I had read before at times. Also, had a headache for approximately two hours during the evening after the experiment."

Subject One—Second Experiment. Two weeks later, he received the same quantity of LSD without adrenochrome. There was no change until 1½ hours when there was an increase in nervousness. There was no change in perception of passage of time. At 2 hours, he was a "bit jumpy." Dots tended to look smaller. Book titles at no time appeared blurred. On his way home, he noted no weakness and no other unusual changes. Two days later, he reported that since so little had happened he had no written report to submit. The experience was more pleasant than the first one.

Subject One—Third Experiment. Two weeks later, he was given 20 mg of adrenochrome intravenously. During the injection he blanched, became very pale and complained of marked air hunger and felt his heart pounding in his throat. He also developed a slight frontal headache. Ten minutes later, he felt physically normal and very relaxed. This was the first time during the 3 experiments that he noted this relaxation. He remarked he was less interested in the situation. There were no visual changes. Time sense was changed and he estimated time since injection as 10 minutes when it was 20 minutes. Thirty minutes later he was not able to estimate closely to 30 seconds as his mind wandered. One hour later, he felt entirely normal with normal awareness of the passage of time. He was relaxed more so than during previous experiments.

Subject Two. Subject two received LSD followed by adrenochrome as above, followed 1 week later by 0.5 mg from LSD 2 hours before 10 mg of adrenochrome, and finally 2 weeks later 35 μg LSD followed 3 hours later by adrenolutin. His written report for the experiences follows:

LSD and adrenochrome. I reported at 9:00 AM, am in good spirits. Following the ingestion of LSD, I tried to find changes in my mental and physical state but was hard pressed to do so. Eventually about an hour after I thought I detected a very slight increase in intracranial pressure in the frontal region and a slight feeling of warmth in my abdomen. Looking back on this, I am suspicious that these findings may have been only because I wanted to be able to report something. I know that my general mental and physical state was well within the range of my own normal.

At about 10:30 I was injected with the adrenochrome and within a minute I felt a marked tightness about the midsternal region of my chest which passed off very shortly and increased difficulty in sufficiently ventilating my lungs which diminished as time passed but did not completely abate until after the ingestion of nicotinic acid about 3:30.

Within half an hour I had an increasing feeling that there was little or nothing in the world for which I would profitably live. Nothing interested me and though I ordinarily have a very good appetite I was completely apathetic toward the mention of food. However, during the experiment the extreme lowness of spirit and physical lethargy which came in waves abated and allowed me to eat when food was brought in. Shortly after I was asked to do a short test. I didn't want to do so, not because I didn't want to cooperate but because I felt so physically and mentally weak and exhausted that I actually felt that I could hardly do it. With extreme effort I was able to do as I was told.

During my time of depression I felt they were watching me (the investigators) quite keenly and I felt much more apart from them than I had at the beginning of the experiment. During the midafternoon coffee break (6 hours after taking LSD), I felt that people were watching me and would think I was acting a bit odd but I did not mind because I was with the investigators and I thought that people would realize that I was a psychiatric research 'guinea pig.' Although people were laughing and singing carols and I ordinarily enjoy trying to sing, I had absolutely no desire to join in the festivities. I think my feeling during my periods of depression could best be described by saying that I couldn't care less about anything that happened as long as it entailed no physical and mental effort. During the period 10:30 to 3:30 while I had brief periods in which I felt normal or close to normal my characteristic feeling was one of depression, flatness, and lethargy. During the day time passed very quickly and looking back on it, it seems remarkable that I put in a whole 8-hour day. One other thing I should mention is my judgement of size. Often small things looked very large to me and relatively large things generally looked larger and what to me was the most important observation was that I was perfectly confident that I could judge size without difficulty. I was completely astonished when I found out how bad my judgment was.

LSD alone. I reported for the experiment shortly after 4:30 PM in good spirits although a wee bit apprehensive that the combination of drugs would produce the same effect in me that LSD and adrenochrome had about 3 weeks ago. That experience was invaluable to me but nevertheless something that I have no desire to repeat. Shortly after taking the LSD I noted a very odd feeling in the parietal region of my cranium. I felt quite dizzy and yet neither the room nor I seemed to be going round in circles. I have felt slightly similar things before but never in the same intensity. It did not bother me but after it continued for some time became annoying. I was very surprised at this since the previous time I had taken LSD there had been virtually no effect. This and some difficulty in visual judgment were my only findings until after the injection of adrenolutin.

Subject Three. This female alcoholic subject was given 200 μg of LSD by mouth. She became extremely tense with a minimal visual reaction to the drug. Her adrenochrome levels 4 hours after were much lower than the baseline sample. This has happened only to her out of 12 subjects. Five hours after she was still very tense and had not experienced visual changes of note. She was then given 10 mg of adrenochrome by vein. Within 5 minutes she lost her tension and for the next 2 hours had a normal LSD reaction. One hour after the injection, the adrenochrome level was 144 μg/liter compared to 44 before the injection.

The psychological experience induced by adrenochrome following LSD is similar to changes we have reported before for adrenochrome alone but more clearly demonstrated and in each instance were clearly known to the subject. The combination of these two substances produced more pronounced changes than that of either compound alone.

Adrenolutin

Our first trials with adrenolutin in 1954 suggested it was as active as adrenochrome but here were fewer perceptual changes and it took much longer for our subjects to recover. A double blind controlled experiment was, therefore, completed in 1956.

Selection of Volunteers

Volunteers from the university were obtained by advertisement. They were over the age of 21 with no history of severe physical and mental disorders. Subjects wih a history of jaundice were excluded. Only students with A and B averages were selected. For the day of the experiment, the volunteer must have been in good health, have had a reasonably normal day, and be in the intermenstrual period. Each volunteer was seen for a brief interview, and if schizophrenia, psychopathy, or hysteria were suspected, the subject was excluded. The volunteers were asked to determine the effectiveness of 2 compounds as euphoriants. They were advised that there would be no hallucinations and that the changes would be minimal. They were told that the compounds were not mescaline or LSD; they were not informed that one of them would be a placebo.

STATISTICAL DESIGN

It is clear that the effect of a drug upon a person depends upon the personality of the subject. Some compounds impose a pattern of reaction which is characteristic of the drug and readily recognized, whereas other compounds impose a disintegration of the person's thought processes and permit a wide variety of response. Earlier trials with adrenolutin placed it in the latter group of compounds. Therefore, since the volunteers are relatively unknown to the research group, the ability to detect whether or not the subject had received placebo or adrenolutin might be little better than chance. However, after having studied a single response to either drug or placebo, the predictions of the second experiment would be better than chance. Each subject was used twice and received either treatment each time. The administration of placebo or drug was laid out from random tables and the code was kept by someone who did not participate in the evaluation. The original group was designed for a total of 52 subjects, which provided the following 4 groups: (a) 13 subjects to receive placebo twice, (b) 13 subjects to receive first placebo and then adrenolutin, (c) 13 subjects to receive first adrenolutin and then placebo, and (d) 13 subjects to receive adrenolutin twice. The placebo consisted of 5 mg of riboflavin made up in distilled water. The adrenolutin was also made up with 5 mg of riboflavin in order to equalize taste.

The volunteer arrived at the laboratory at 5:30 PM without dinner. Between 5:30 and 6:00 PM, his frequency flicker fusion (FFF) was tested and he was evaluated for the presence of anxiety, insight, etc. At 6:00 PM, he was administered the compound. Between 6:00 and 7:00 PM, he was again tested for FFF every 15 minutes and engaged in discussion with the research team, consisting of one psychiatrist and one psychologist. At 7:00, he was taken to the EEG laboratory. Between 7:00 and 8:00 PM, while the electrodes were applied, he was engaged in discussion, in argument, and was asked to define proverbs and tested with similarities and comprehensive subtests of Wechsler Bellevue. Memory and ability to calculate were examined. Between 8:00 and 9:00 PM, various EEG runs were made and the visual and

EEG response to the stroboscope determined, starting with a frequency of thirty and decreasing by 2 until 6 per second was reached. At each frequency, the lamp was left on for 60 seconds. At the end of 30 seconds, the subject described into a tape recorder his impression for the next 30 seconds. At 9:00, the subject returned to the research laboratory, repeated the FFF, the stipple test, and the Watson-Glazer Critical Thinking Test. The subject was then driven home. The next morning, he described his experiences of the previous night and was interviewed by the psychiatrist. A week later, the same procedure was repeated exactly but with the drug as laid down in the design. After the double experiment, the volunteer was asked to describe which drug was more effective as a euphoriant and in producing psychological change.

At the end of the evening's experiment, the psychologist and psychiatrist completed a prediction scale and recorded their predictions, that is, whether the volunteer had placebo or adrenolutin, with a description of reasons. The next morning, the psychologist rated the psychological tests objectively and in addition, the psychiatrist interviewed the subject and decided on his final clinical prediction, which theoretically might be different than the prediction he made the previous night depending upon the experiences of the volunteer during the night. After all the predictions were in, the psychologist and psychiatrist discussed the evening's research in great detail. The drug was decoded. The team now knew how the subject had reacted to either placebo or adrenolutin.

Clinical

The clinical observations include changes in all areas of personality and follow the procedure of mental status examination.

THOUGHT. Changes in thought were determined by asking the subject to define proverbs, to perform calculations, to engage in reasoned argument. Usually the subject was engaged in conversation by the research team regarding matters in which the subject had become most recently proficient; for example, a student in physics was asked to discuss problems in physics or a graduate nurse who had been trained in the avoirdupois system of dosages and now was converting to the metric system was asked to make conversions. The research team pushed the subject very strongly and attempted to irritate them by their persistence and stubbornness. These are experiences that bring into sharper focus the presence of thought disorder. The subject was also tested for abstraction using discussions, proverbs, and the similarities part of Wechsler Bellevue. He was also encouraged to discuss subjectively whether there had been any change.

Mood. This was observed during the evening objectively and the subject was asked to described changes subjectively.

Insight. This is the ability of the subject to recognize that a change in intellectual ability has occurred when this is apparent to the investigator.

Sociability. This includes the reaction of the volunteer to the investigator during the evening. If the subject appears disinhibited as evidenced by comments about the experiment or critical comments about the investigator or comments that appear inappropriate, he was said to be disinhibited or showing decreased sociability.

Anxiety. This was measured objectively by using clinical criteria for the presence of anxiety. The volunteer's subjective statements were also recorded.

Somatic Changes. This includes any change in the motor or sensory areas, for example, headache and tremor.

Other Changes. The subject was asked to describe any change that he had noted irrespective of whether he had had similar feelings before. Some volunteers noticed changes but explained it to themselves as due to the situation and failed to report important changes.

Psychological Testing

It was planned to start with a preliminary series of tests and as the experiment continued to discard those that failed to discriminate, maintain the tests that did discriminate, and add new tests, depending on the time available. The original tests included the Bender-Gestalt test, the Maze test, a Stipple test, and a Watson-Glazer critical thinking test. In addition, in a few instances, the Rorschach was used. The Bender-Gestalt and the Maze tests did not discriminate and were discarded. The Stipple test showed a high degree of discrimination and has been retained. The Watson-Glazer test in retrospect tends to indicate which experiment is the drug, provided it is known that a subject has received both placebo and drug.

The stipple test (Palthe *et al.*, 1954) was developed in the Netherlands in order to differentiate between hysteria and epilepsy and has recently been used by the Dutch Air Force to bring to light cases of latent epilepsy. It consists of a long sheet of paper containing groups of dots with 3, 4, or 5 dots per group. There are 50 lines. The subject is instructed to cross out each group of 4 dots. The time required to complete each line is recorded. The test is analyzed by counting the number of errors and by determining the standard error of the mean time required to complete 1 line for the first 25 lines compared to the standard error of the mean for the second 25 lines. One thus obtains a measure of variability of the first half of the test compared to the second half. The test requires about 10 minutes.

The Watson-Glazer (Watson and Glazer, 1952) is a test designed to measure logical inference and thinking and consists of parts A and B, both matched. Thus test A can be given one time and test B the second time. The score is obtained by determining the number of correct responses.

Physiological Tests

Flicker Fusion Frequency (Simonson and Brozek, 1952). The Flicker Fusion Frequency is a function of occipital cortical activity and for any individual is relatively constant. It is not affected by fatigue. The FFF depends upon the intensity of the light stimulus. The lower the intensity of the light source, the lower is the FFF. Benzedrine (amphetamine) and Pervitin (dl-α-phenyl-β-methylaminopropane) elevate the FFF, whereas it is depressed by alcohol.

If adrenolutin, which appears to produce some perceptual changes, had an effect on cortical function, it might show up in the FFF.

EEG. Standard EEG was determined by using an 8-channel Grass machine with hyperventilation and stroboscopic analyses. It has recently been reported that 3,4,5-trimethoxyphenyl-β-aminopropane is an hallucinogen especially when the person is stimulated with a stroboscope (Peretz *et al.*, 1955). For this reason, the stroboscopic analyses was made in each case for 1 minute with a starting frequency of 30 per second and working down by 2 to 6. During the first 30 seconds, the recordings were made, and during the second 30 seconds, the subject described his visual impressions.

At the beginning of the experiments, clinical changes which had earlier appeared highly selective for adrenolutin became relatively less important; some occurred during placebo reactions. However, other findings became relatively more important. With one exception, none of the subjects who had taken adrenolutin were called placebo. The one subject who was miscalled appeared to be a nonreactor. On the other hand, a larger number of placebo experiments were miscalled adrenolutin at the beginning of the project.

The following changes were characteristic of adrenolutin. Obviously they will not all occur in every subject, but a certain proportion of them must be present. From our knowledge of the person before the experiment, it was impossible to predict the type of reaction to either placebo or adrenolutin.

Thought Disorder. It is extremely difficult to measure thought disorder clinically or by the use of psychological tests. Even when a thought disorder is suspected, the investigator may find it difficult to justify his suspicions. Our experience with adrenolutin has been that the clinical hunch is a bit more reliable than the psychological tests so far used. This was also found in a sleep-deprivation study (Tyler, 1955) where it was shown that after 40 hours deprivation, all normal subjects developed psychotic-like changes but even after 120 hours, no psychological tests reliably detected thought disorder. This became apparent away from the experimental situation, for example during dinner or during marches when the soldiers were not in a test situation, and was most noticeable in the evenings.

Thought disorder was measured by engaging the volunteer in a severe and critical discussion about subjects pertaining to his own field of interest. The investigators were deliberately hostile, difficult, and antagonistic. As the subjects became hostile, they were able to participate in the argument less effectively. In addition, the EEG technician was simultaneously attaching the EEG electrodes and this was quite distracting to the subjects. During placebo runs, the subjects did well during debate. During adrenolutin, the subjects became irritable or hostile and they found it difficult to present adequate arguments. Some withdrew from the situation by becoming giggly or silly or by questioning the motives and good faith of the investigators, or brought in circumstantial evidence. With one subject, a graduate nurse, the merits of an increase in salary were discussed. The investigator pointed out that nurses were already earning too much and that they were using nursing as a stop gap until marriage shortly after graduation. This subject was quite euphoric and giggly although she was normally a reserved shy rather quiet girl. After some thought, she remarked, "We were told by a speaker recently that all nurses are frigid and therefore do not get married." This was clearly out of character for her. The next day, she was unable to account for this statement. During placebo, she was able to defend her point of view quite well using appropriate arguments. Other subjects thought the investigators were silly and were irritated by them. One subject was bored and fatigued by the argument. A week later under placebo, she relished the argument, found it most enjoyable and interesting, and found the intellectual challenge very stimulating.

With some subjects, discussions around areas with which they were very familiar produced no evidence of thought disorder. This made it especially difficult for the investigator, especially since some subjects were more sophisticated in certain areas than the investigators were.

The use of proverbs was very useful for the detection of thought disorder in that most subjects on adrenolutin failed to comprehend the meanings of proverbs or if they did comprehend the meanings, were unable to explain them. Some subjects refused to define or defined the proverb by quoting back another proverb. One subject felt she understood the meaning of the proverb but disagreed with its meaning. Under placebo, the subjects had little difficulty with proverbs and no bizarre responses were obtained. The subject who disagreed with the meanings of proverbs under adrenolutin, did not disagree with the proverbs under placebo. Matched but different proverbs were used for each experiment.

Under adrenolutin, some unusual responses were obtained, for example, a graduate student in physics felt that the proverb "A stitch in time saves nine" referred to some unit of time; that is "stitch" was a unit of time. He was unable to explain this proverb until it was read to him, "A stitch in time saves nine stitches," after which he was able to understand it. The proverb "Many hands make light work" caused him to burst into laughter and reply that it reminded him of his children's handprints on the wall.

Proverbs were also useful in that one could pounce upon any unusual response and, by encouraging the subject to elaborate, bring out more clearly thought disorder.

Problems in calculation were also used, for example, the serial seven test. With adrenolutin, subjects made more errors until it was brought to their attention, after which they were able to do this correctly. One subject was unable to do this correctly, which surprised her as she enjoyed mathematics. The following week on a placebo run, she was able very rapidly to perform the serial six and seven test without any difficulty. On adrenolutin, she was unable to work out medical dosage problems in grains but was able to do so in milligrams. Her basic training had been in the avoirdupois but she was now teaching undergraduates to make conversions daily; for example, after it had been established that 30 mg is equivalent to half a grain, on questioning, she replied that she would hesitate to give a patient half a grain of morphine because it appeared excessive and in the same breath reported that she would not hesitate to give a patient 30 mg of morphine because "This was not very much." A week later, on placebo, the subject was extremely fluent in all conversions and it was impossible to confuse her.

The comprehensive and similarity items of the Wechsler Bellevue intelligence scale are most useful in picking up thought disorder. For example, one subject, under adrenolutin, reported on the similarities test that an orange and a banana were similar because they had skins and they contained material inside the skins. When asked how a wagon and bicycle were similar, she reported that they had wheels. The same subject under placebo was able to grasp the similarities quite readily.

The next day after adrenolutin, she did not understand why she had been unable to detect the similarities since she now knew what they were. A physician reported that the eye and the ear were similar because they were both on the head, and that a lion and dog were similar because they both had fur. On adrenolutin, subjects were less voluble and more quiet and conversation became more of a question–answer type. On placebo, this tendency was not as great, the subjects were more spontaneous in their comments and asked more questions about the purpose of the experiment. It was more difficult for the subjects to describe their feelings and to describe the visual patterns while under the impact of the stroboscope. Many complained of thought disturbance and thought slowing and felt they were not doing as well as they should do but this was also found in some placebo experiments.

Memory, orientation, and consciousness were normal. The next day most subjects were able to recall the experience with 2 exceptions. One felt as if the experience had occurred 3 months ago and the other subject who can normally reconstruct an evening's conversation was unable to do so for the experimental evening. This did not occur after placebo when she was able to reconstruct the evening. The third subject, during the second experiment (placebo) ascribed an error to the investigator which she herself had made during the first experiment (adrenolutin).

Many adrenolutin subjects became suspicious and showed referential thinking. This has occurred with 1 placebo subject. Many become sensitive to experimental scrutiny and were aware of the fact that they were being closely observed. This feeling is much less intense or nonexistent with placebo.

In two cases, adrenolutin has produced disturbances in sleep. In one instance, the subject had a most unusual dream with a nightmarish quality. She dreamt that there were furry animals nestling against her neck.

ANXIETY. Anxiety is very difficult to quantify, but this has been done by noting the subjective reports and by clinical observations, looking for the usual physiological concomitants of anxiety. The entire experimental situation was suitable for the production of anxiety. Before the experiment, the subjects had been informed that changes would be minimal and that perceptual changes would be nonexistent. However, all volunteers knew they were participating in a schizophrenia research program that employed drugs which might reproduce some of the phases of schizophrenia. They were called a few days before the experiment and given printed instructions as well as bottles for urine collections. By the time they arrived at the laboratory, especially for the first experiment, most of the subjects were anxious, this they felt subjectively and it was evident to the investigators. After the administration of placebo, the anxiety decreased or increased, but at no time disappeared. In some instances the anxiety was so intense that after 3 hours the subjects became quite fatigued. With adrenolutin, there was a remarkable reduction of anxiety in all subjects within one-half hour after the administration of adrenolutin. In some cases, the subjects appeared quite flat whereas previously they had been very anxious. The decrease in anxiety was manifest by feelings of relaxation, by spontaneous comments that they felt very much at ease, and by the calm relaxed attitude of the subject. When the anxiety was very high at the beginning of the experiment, the change was most dramatic. When anxiety was low at the start, it was difficult to detect change.

An interesting dissociation occurred between clinical anxiety, on the one hand, and intellectual performance and EEG anxiety on the other hand. Some placebo subjects showed great anxiety, throughout the experiment, but on the EEG run were relaxed and in general showed great interest and no intellectual impairment. The same subjects on adrenolutin showed no anxiety at all, but intellectual performance was deteriorated and on the EEG they showed an anxious type of pattern, that is a low amplitude, high frequency pattern quite different from the previous placebo pattern. This has been observed in many subjects. There does appear to be a dissociation as if the anxiety is still present but no longer noticeable to the subject. It is possible that adrenolutin destroys insight for the presence of anxiety which is still present and seen on the EEG tracings. Of course, this may be an EEG pattern specific for adrenolutin.

Mood. Mild but clear changes in mood were produced by adrenolutin. Usually these were depressive in character accompanied by increased irritation. This occurred within the first 2 hours of the experiment and was always present during the second half of the experiment. In a few subjects, the first half was marked by silliness and euphoria later replaced by depression. One subject showed euphoria the first 2 hours, depression the second 2 hours, and when she arrived home that evening, again showed marked euphoria, silliness, and hypomanic behavior. After completing both experiments, most subjects selected the placebo as the most effective euphoriant.

Level of Interest. This was determined by the spontaneity of the subject and the number of questions asked regarding the experiment, the willingness of the subject to elaborate on his experiences and to participate in the various tests. Under placebo, the level of interest usually remained very high although in a few instances, it began to decrease after about 3 hours. In this case, where the level of interest was markedly down during the performance of any particular test, it was easily reawakened by conversation. With adrenolutin, most subjects became disinterested by 7 o'clock and more often found the tests boring. The level of interest with them did not reawaken as readily, although in a few cases by 10 o'clock, they were once again becoming more interested in the experiment. Some subjects stated that they were quite disinterested in the whole experiment. Many stated that they were interested but appeared quite withdrawn from the situation. Under placebo, the subjects were anxious to perform well and quite critical of their performance. Under drug, the subjects were less critical of their performance and performed many of their tests with an increased number of errors.

SOCIABILITY. In an experimental situation where the subject does not know the investigators, certain patterns of behavior are accepted. Under placebo, no incongruity was determined but under adrenolutin quite often the subjects were critical of the experiment or found the experiment silly or could find no reason why certain tests were being done or came out with inappropriate sexual comments. This was used as evidence of social disinhibition and in one instance, this continued in a subject for 2 or 3 days. It was noted by her friends that she showed little empathy and most unusual behavior.

VISUAL CHANGES. Visual changes were mild and were not reported spontaneously except by one placebo subject. As a standard test, the subject is asked to look at a spinning Archimedes wheel in which the lines appear to move outward, During the afterimage, the lines appear to move inward. One subject under adrenolutin saw the disk moving toward her when it was spinning, and during the afterimage, the disk moved away from her. Under placebo, she saw it in the normal way. Other subjects have noticed difficulty in seeing lines.

When the subjects were exposed to the stroboscope, they saw vivid colors and geometric patterns with placebo and with adrenolutin. However, with adrenolutin, the colors were more vivid, the patterns less geometrical, and much more disorganized. In a couple of instances, clear-cut images were seen. For example, one subject saw pairs of eyes of different sizes but perfectly matched with the eyelids but without eyebrow and face, moving across the field in a clockwise direction. The eyes were very bright, pleasant, and very real. Under placebo, she did not see these eyes. Another subject saw the redwood trees of the Pacific Coast with the sun glinting on them. In many cases, the stroboscope produced strong feelings of unreality. One subject under adrenolutin felt that he had just seen a nightmare in technicolor. Very often, the flashing light interfered with thought processes and made it difficult to describe the visual pattern. This, however, has occurred with some placebo subjects. The subjects usually found the stroboscopic experience more exciting when they have taken adrenolutin.

OTHER CHANGES. Feelings of unreality have occurred; for example, one subject said he felt dizzy and added, "It is like being dizzy but suffering from none of its effects." Another subject complained that she had a fuzzy feeling in her head and found it difficult to focus on things. Another subject felt numbness in his right leg as if it were going to sleep but after walking around on it for some time noticed no change. When looking at the stroboscope, he felt as if he had 2 independent eyes looking at the visual field. Another subject complained that his head felt dull. Another subject reported that he felt quite strange and had a similar feeling only once during the war when he had been on guard duty for 36 hours without sleep. Some subjects compared the adrenolutin reaction to having taken a couple of alcoholic drinks. They did not notice any of the other effects that they had noticed with alcohol.

INSIGHT. When volunteers are given hallucinogenic drugs, for example, mescaline or lysergic acid, they observe vivid visual phenomena and usually have no difficulty in being aware of marked change. With mescaline or LSD, the subjective experiences are more striking than the objective changes. Other drugs which do not produce vivid perceptual changes may produce a change in the volunteer which is not recognized by him. Very few of the volunteers were able to detect whether or not they had been given adrenolutin. Many of them felt that placebo was a more active drug, probably because they remained anxious throughout the evening and ascribed the anxiety to the drug rather than the situation. It was impossible to predict from the subjective statements whether or not the volunteer had taken adrenolutin. The most common reply to the question, "Has anything happened" was that nothing had happened with adrenolutin but something had happened with placebo. It became, therefore, important to disregard subjective statements of change and to use as much as possible objective criteria for change.

It is interesting that where the subjects were aware of a change, they readily found explanations and excluded the possibility that this was due to the drug; for example, one subject did become quite free of anxiety 1 hour after taking adrenolutin and explained it as due to his familiarity with the situation and with the experimenters. Most subjects felt that the placebo was the most active euphoriant.

In order to assist in the evaluation of response, a rating scale was developed and is shown in Table 29. Although it is difficult to place the various items into subjective or objective factors, items 1, 4, 6, 13, 14, and 15 are primarily subjective and the other items are objective factors.

The scales are completed by the investigator crossing out the appropriate boxes by using the numbers on the right-hand side. The mean scores for placebo and adrenolutin are shown in Table 30. In this table, the ratings are divided into objective ratings (6 items) and subjective ratings (9 items). The scale is so designed that the items on the right are normal and the items on the left are abnormal; high values for any item indicate abnormality.

The items which discriminated well between placebo and adrenolutin are shown in Table 31. Objective ratings showed a wider difference between placebo and adrenolutin than did subjective ratings. The ratio of the values for adrenolutin over placebo was 1.6 whereas for subjective ratings, it was 1.1.

The mean rating using the items that discriminate well is 1.4 for placebo and 2.7 for adrenolutin with a ratio of 1.9. For the item of thought disorder, objective, the ratio went up to 2.5 whereas for subjective, the ratio went down to 0.6. The subjects under placebo were more aware of thought difficulty, although this was not evident to the investigator, whereas in performance, the subjects, under adrenolutin, were much less aware of change, although it was quite apparent to the investigator.

Psychological Changes

The stipple test was analyzed by counting the number of errors and by dividing the total test into 2 portions, the first 25 lines compared to the second 25 lines. The standard error of the mean time required to complete 1 line was determined for each subject. The results obtained are shown in Table 32. It will be seen that when the subjects were given adrenolutin, the standard deviation of the second half was in every case but one lower than the standard deviation of the first half. The means are significantly different. With placebo, the opposite occurred. The stipple test was able to predict correctly 21 out of 26 experiments. The group variation was similar for the first half of the stipple test for adrenolutin and for the two halves of the placebo run. It was significantly less for the second half of the adrenolutin run.

With placebo, the subjects did well on the first half of the stipple test and then fell off in accuracy perhaps due to increasing disinterest in the rather tiresome test. On the other hand, with adrenolutin, the subjects had more difficulty getting down to the task but once they got going, they were able to continue the test much better and with less distraction.

The Watson-Glazer test was also predictive where it was known that one subject had had both placebo and adrenolutin. With adrenolutin,

TABLE 29

NAME	DATE		ASSESSOR		
1. Perception abnormality	Reported voluntarily	Evident on questioning	Evident on testing	Not evident	4,3,2,1
2. Level of interest (first 2 hours)	Disinterested withdrawn bored	Disinterested	Cooperative few spontaneous questions	High level sustained	4,3,2,1
3. Level of interest (second 2 hours)	Disinterested withdrawn bored	Disinterested	Cooperative few spontaneous questions	High level sustained	4,3,2,1
4. Fatigue	Very marked sleepy	Marked	Slight	No change	4,3,2,1
5. Speech	Unable to speak clearly	Clear but hesitant	Slight change	No change	4,3,2,1
6. Thought (subjective)	Complains of confusion bizarreness	Complains of difficulty	Complains of slowing	No complaint	4,3,2,1
7. Thought (objective)	Referential unable to solve problems	Unable to match argument in subjective field	Any mild change	No change	4,3,2,1
8. Mood (first 2 hours)	Depressed or euphoric	Slightly depressed or giggly	Quiet	No change	4,3,2,1
9. Mood (second 2 hours)	Depressed or euphoric	Slightly depressed or giggly	Quiet	No change	4,3,2,1

		From first to second 2-hour period	From 6 to 10 PM		
10. Mood (fluctuation)	Marked, more than once per hour			No change	4,3,2,1
11. Anxiety	Flat, apathetic	No anxiety	Less anxious	Normal anxiety for situation	4,3,2,1
12. Social inhibition	Disinhibited (comments about investigators, sex, appearance)	Decreased	Mild change	Normal	4,3,2,1
13. Strobe (color)	Most unusual never seen before	Vivid	Marked	Moderate	4,3,2,1
14. Strobe (pattern)	Disorganized hallucinations	Organized geom., assym.	Organized rapid move, some assym.	Normal	4,3,2,1
15. Feeling of being different	Marked unreality never had before	Feels different can't define	Sedated dreamy	No change	4,3,2,1

TABLE 30

	N	Objective (9 items)		Subjective (6 items)		Ratio O/S
		Mean	Range	Mean	Range	
Placebo	13	1.4	1.1–1.6	1.7	1.3–2.1	0.8
Adrenolutin	9	2.3	1.3–3.3	1.9	0.8–2.6	1.2
Ratio A/P		1.6		1.1		

TABLE 31

Effect of Adrenolutin on Level of Interest, Thought Disorder, Anxiety, Social Disinhibition, and Stroboscopic Visual Patterns; Mean Ratings

Factor	Placebo	Adrenolutin	Ratio Ad/Pl
Level of interest			
First 2 hours	1.4	1.9	1.4
Second 2 hours	1.5	2.9	1.9
Thought disorder			
Subjective	1.3	0.8	0.6
Objective	1.3	3.3	2.5
Anxiety	1.1	2.9	2.6
Social disinhibition	1.1	2.3	2.1
Stroboscope	2.0	2.8	1.4
Mean (omitting subjective thought			
disorder)	1.4	2.7	1.9

in most cases, there was no change in total score, that is they did as well as with placebo. There was, however, an increased scatter of response among the 5 items so that they did extremely well on a few items and very poorly on others. The standard deviation of the five items is usually greater for adrenolutin. In two instances, there was a marked decrease in the total score with adrenolutin. It thus appears that where the total score is not changed the increased variability will detect adrenolutin. If there is a marked decrease in score, it is due to adrenolutin.

Physiological Changes

The results of the flicker fusion experiments are shown in Table 33. With placebo, the flicker fusion decreased for 30 minutes and then remained constant the rest of the evening. With adrenolutin, there was no effect at 15 minutes, but at 30 minutes it began to rise and at the end of the experiment was back to its original baseline. It thus appears

TABLE 32

SPLIT HALF STANDARD DEVIATIONS OF MEAN TIME OF STIPPLE TEST PRODUCED BY PLACEBO AND ADRENOLUTIN

Subject	Placebo			Adrenolutin		
	SD 1	SD 2	Prediction[a]	SD 1	SD 2	Prediction[a]
1	1.16	0.91	X	1.34	1.13	C
2	1.36	1.53	C	1.86	1.15	C
3	1.31	1.44	C	1.16	1.03	C
4	1.87	2.25	C	2.86	1.74	C
5	1.44	1.64	C	1.29	1.20	C
6	1.50	2.71	C	2.84	1.35	C
7	1.17	1.10	X	1.27	0.90	C
8	1.30	1.33	C	1.11	1.41	X
9	—	—	—	1.65	1.34	C
9	—	—	—	1.76	1.61	C
10	—	—	—	1.41	0.66	C
11	1.20	1.51	C	—	—	—
11	1.15	2.28	C	—	—	—
12	2.87	2.62	X	—	—	—
12	1.54	1.57	C	—	—	—
13	2.04	1.18	X	—	—	—
14	0.98	1.28	C	—	—	—
14	0.90	1.00	C	—	—	—
Mean	1.45	1.62		1.69	1.23	
S.E.	0.13	0.15		0.17	0.09	
Limits	1.20–1.70	1.33–1.86		1.52–1.86	1.14–1.32	
C.V.	33%	34%		35%	24%	

[a] X = wrong prediction, C = correct prediction, C.V. = coefficient of variation.

that adrenolutin prevents the fatigue produced by repeated visual stimuli. It will be noted that between 2 and 2½ hours, the subject is exposed to intermittent stroposcope frequency from 30 down to 6 for about 20 minutes. In spite of this, the FFF with adrenolutin was back to its baseline. With placebo, there was a mean decrease of 6% in the FFF at the end of 3 hours. With adrenolutin, the FFF was back to its original value. If a decrease greater than 2.5% of the initial value is used as a criterion of a placebo reaction, the FFF predicted correctly 18 out of 20 experiments, beyond the 1% level of probability.

TABLE 33

Effect of Adrenolutin and Placebo on Flicker Fusion Frequency Per Second

Subject	Adrenolutin					Placebo				
	0	15	30	45	180	0	15	30	45	180
1	20.3	19.5	19.2	19.5	20.5	17.1	15.4	16.3	16.6	16.2
2	19.1	18.9	19.0	18.5	19.1	19.7	19.5	19.2	18.7	19.0
3	20.5	19.9	20.3	20.6	21.0	20.4	19.1	19.3	19.5	20.8
4	16.6	16.1	15.8	15.8	16.2	17.5	16.7	16.2	15.3	15.0
5	20.6	19.9	19.8	20.8	20.1	22.2	20.4	21.0	20.9	19.4
6	18.4	17.8	18.4	18.3	19.1	20.1	20.1	19.7	19.6	19.5
7	21.0	16.8	17.3	16.8	17.3	18.0	—	15.3	15.3	15.3
8	18.9	17.7	17.8	17.6	19.5	19.2	19.0	17.6	—	18.7
9	18.5	—	18.0	18.9	18.2					
9	18.5	—	19.2	19.0	18.9					
10	18.9	18.9	19.1	18.4	19.1					
12						18.0	17.8	16.3	15.7	15.9
12						16.9	16.9	16.9	17.1	16.9
13						22.1	19.4	19.4	19.5	19.9
14						20.4	18.7	18.5	20.0	19.2
14						20.6	19.3	19.6	19.9	19.6
Means	19.2	18.4	18.5	18.6	19.0	19.4	18.5	18.1	18.2	18.1

The number of correct and incorrect predictions made by the research group (two predictions for each experiment—one by the psychiatrist and one by the psychologist) are shown in Table 33. The predictions were made by means of the stipple test (SD2 < SD1 = adrenolutin) and by the FFF (frequency at 180 minutes less than original by 2.5% = placebo) are shown in Table 34. The predictions may be scored by assigning the value two to each stipple and to each FFF prediction for adrenolutin. The mean scores are given in Tables 34 and 35.

Thought disorder is the chief characteristic of schizophrenia and when present in combination with normal memory, orientation, and consciousness distinguishes it from other mental diseases. Unfortunately, thought

TABLE 34

RESULTS OF DOUBLE BLIND PREDICTION FOR THIRTEEN SUBJECTS[a]

	Placebo		Adrenolutin		Total	
	Right	Wrong	Right	Wrong	Right	Wrong
First experiment	7	7	8	4	15	11
Second experiment	14	4	6	2	20	6
Total	21	11	14	6	35	17

[a] One quarter of series.

TABLE 35

STIPPLE TEST AND FREQUENCY FLICKER FUSION PREDICTIONS[a]

	Placebo		Adrenolutin	
Subject	Stipple	Flicker	Stipple	Flicker
1	X	C	C	C
2	C	C	C	C
3	C	X	C	C
4	C	C	C	C
5	C	C	C	C
6	C	C	C	C
7	X	C	C	X
8	C	C	X	C
9	—	—	C	C
9	—	—	C	C
10	—	—	C	C
11	C	—	—	—
11	C	—	—	—
12	X	C	—	—
12	C	X	—	—
13	X	X	—	—
14	C	C	—	—
14	C	C	—	—
Means score	0.5	0.4	1.8	1.8
Total	0.9		3.6	

[a] X = wrong prediction, C = correct prediction.

disorder alone, unless it is very pronounced, does not often bring the afflicted person to psychiatric examination. More often, secondary phenomena such as depression, somatic complaints, hallucinations, and delusions force recognition of the illness.

Psychotic-like changes induced in normal subjects by mescaline and LSD most clearly reproduce the secondary aspects. Thought disorder may be present, but is often completely masked by the vivid perceptual changes that consume the entire attention of the subject. Many subjects show no evidence of basic thought disorder and some have shown heightened levels of abstraction and productivity.

For many years, the difference between the mescaline psychosis and schizophrenia were emphasized by research scientists and if similarities were noted, this was done apologetically. This attitude has been replaced by one of scientific curiosity willing to consider similarities as well as differences. A real difficulty has been the reproduction of schizophrenic-like thought disorder without marked perceptual changes. Adrenolutin appears to have this property. It can induce in volunteer subjects clear evidence of thought disorder clinically and by objective psychological testing, with decreased anxiety, with decreased insight that change has occurred, with some affective disharmony and with other subtle somatic and psychological changes that are described with great difficulty. These are distinguished from anxiety or situational (placebo) changes at 5% level during double blind experimentation.

Thought becomes more concrete after adrenolutin, in some instances strikingly in subjects who, with placebo, were quite normal. Some subjects with much superior intellectual endowment scored at normal or below normal levels on tests of abstraction.

The FFF changes indicate that adrenolutin induces some cortical change. The prevention of fatigue resembles the action of amphetamine (Benzedrine) and Pervitin, both stimulants. In several instances, this effect was noted within fifteen minutes after the administration by mouth of adrenolutin. This might be evidence for a direct action of adrenolutin. This action may be due to the effect of adrenolutin on sympathetic nerves. Adrenochrome (Derouaux and Roskam, 1949) prevents fatigue of stimulated sympathetic vasoconstrictor nerves in rabbit ear preparation. Adrenolutin might be formed from adrenochrome in the body. More likely, it has a similar activity.

It is possible that amine oxidase inhibitors (amphetamine, etc.) may produce the increase in FFF by stimulating the endogenous production of adrenolutinlike compounds.

The effect of adrenolutin on split half stipple test performance is totally unexpected and difficult to interpret. It more accurately predicted adrenolutin than did errors and omissions and mean time to complete the test. A possible explanation is that with placebo, subjects start out highly motivated and interested but begin to feel fatigue and boredom by the second half of the test. With adrenolutin, there is more difficulty getting started. The mean SD 1 for adrenolutin is greater than for placebo. However, once started on the task, there is perhaps less visual fatigue (as in FFF) and this they do much better. In the second half, the mean SD 2 for adrenolutin is 1.23 compared to mean of 1.62 for placebo. The ability of catatonic schizophrenics to maintain unusual attitudes and postures for periods of time which would markedly fatigue nonschizophrenics may be related to the presence of a similar antifatigue factor. Perhaps also the tenacity and devotion to delusional paranoid ideas is also related to such an antifatigue mental factor. Whether schizophrenics show the same reaction on the stipple test as adrenolutin subjects is not known.

The Watson-Glazer test measures the ability to think logically and is not primarily a measure of intelligence. When one subject has had both placebo and adrenolutin, this test will select which has been given by (a) the greater variability of subtest response of the 5 items, or (b) a marked decrease in overall performance. The first factor is more frequent. A marked decrease in total score occurred in 1 out of 9 subjects.

Adrenolutin has a remarkable effect on anxiety within 30 minutes after oral administration. This raises an interesting theoretic problem of the role of both adrenaline and its oxidized derivative in the maintenance of homeostasis. According to Cannon, adrenaline plays an emergency role in preparing animals for flight or fight. But with an overproduction of adrenaline, the ability to meet the stress of the situation may be decreased. When the response must be motoric, an overproduction of adrenaline is improbable, but with human material, often the response cannot be muscular. Therefore an overproduction of adrenaline is quite injurious in the production of marked anxiety and its concomitants. The conversion to adrenolutin will decrease the self-appreciation of anxiety to tolerable levels. In addition, it seems likely that in emergency situations, the ability to think in abstract terms is detrimental. The ability to perform in acute situations may be improved by concrete thinking. Thus the conversion of adrenaline to adrenolutin will help the emergency situation by (a) the reduction in the self-awareness of anxiety and (b) by the decrease in the level of abstraction. For the mathematicians, one can postulate that the quantity of subjective anxiety is proportional to the concentration of adrenolutin and adrenaline or

$$\text{Subjective anxiety} = \text{adrenaline/adrenolutin}$$

It follows that in the presence of large quantities of adrenolutin, the subject can not feel anxiety. This is testible by determining (a) whether adrenaline produces anxiety in subjects given adrenolutin, or (b) whether adrenolutin will materially alleviate anxiety in an extremely anxious person (the price may be schizophrenia).

The schizophrenic person has solved the problem of anxiety by not being aware of it and by loss of ability to use abstract reasoning. This combination must remain an impossible one in any society.

Adrenolutin produces thought disorder, marked by decreased ability toward abstraction, by inability to solve problems and proverbs, combined with changes in mood, reduction of anxiety, and loss of insight into intellectual performance. These changes are clear and enable the prediction of adrenolutin over placebo in a double blind experiment at 5% level of probability. In addition, one psychological test, the stipple test, and one physiological test, that is, the effect of repeated stimulation of flickering light on FFF, were able to predict 18 out of 23 experiments correctly or better than the 5% level. Adrenolutin prevented flicker fatigue indicating some occipital cortical activity and in this, it resembles Benzedrine and Pervitin.

We hoped that the observers would record their observations free of bias. Second, they attempted to predict after the 2 experiments were completed whether the subject had received placebo (riboflavin) or adrenolutin. In testing the predictions of the observers against what the subjects had really taken, a very harsh criterion was used. The assumption was made that all subjects given adrenolutin would react in a clear and noticeable manner and that no subjects given placebo would react. Even with well-known hallucinogens like LSD, this would not be true. We have seen many subjects have no reaction to 100 μg of LSD and a few have failed to react to 500 μg with anything but increased tension. Anxiety will induce some volunteers to have some LSD-like reactions. But inasmuch as there was no way of knowing what proportion of subjects would react, there was no other way of testing this. The first 13 subjects were tested between October 4 and December 19, 1955, using fresh adrenolutin which had been synthesized by Pfizer and Company, New York. The second series of 12 subjects was tested between January 9 and April 13, 1956. By this time, the adrenolutin, which when fresh had been yellow-green, was dark green in color. There was no doubt that it had deteriorated. The observers were able to predict the drug given to the first series at the 5% level of confidence. But this was not possible with the second series. This provides some evidence that autooxidized derivatives of adrenolutin are less active psychotomimetics than is pure adrenolutin. It might be argued that the series should have been discontinued as soon as it was noticed the chemical was changing. But this would have biased our data in favor of a positive result. Furthermore, it was then impossible to get any more. Each sample sent to us by various manufacturers was as dark and deteriorated on arrival as our own stock had become.

Another way of examining the data statistically is to examine the recorded data for certain changes. These as recorded by Hoffer (1957c,d) were summarized from records made by the observers and by the subjects before the compound given was known. The code was not broken for each subject until all the written material which forms the raw data were complete. I have reexamined the reports and from data published there (Hoffer, 1957c) scored each subject for the presence or absence of definite changes. This is shown in Table 36. In all categories but anxiety, the evidence of abnormality was much greater in the subjects given adrenolutin, but they were singularly free from anxiety.

TABLE 36

EFFECT OF ADRENOLUTIN AND RIBOFLAVIN ON MENTAL STATUS
OF VOLUNTEERS IN A DOUBLE BLIND STUDY[a]

Type of change	Number of subjects showing this change	
	Receiving adrenolutin	Receiving placebo
Perception	12	1
Thought	14	1
Mood	3	1
Anxiety	1	7
Personality	3	1
Carryover, next day	8	1
Total number subjects	20	14

[a] From Hoffer (1957c).

This kind of report provides merely the dry bones of a study. For this reason, we will now give in clinical detail a few typical cases which were recorded many years ago. It might be argued that rather than report data obtained with adrenolutin now known to be less pure than it could have been, it would be desirable to repeat the study with stable crystalline adrenolutin. The reasons we have not done so involve economics of research, priorities, and faith. It is doubtful whether several repetitions of similar experiments would be any more convincing than the original ones. Skeptics are not convinced by overselling one's point of view. What would be more convincing would be reproduction of similar work by other investigators. One independent corroboration is worth several repetitions by the same worker. Fortunately several research groups have begun to provide some corroboration as will be shown later.

The following accounts include 2 subjects who had received both riboflavin (placebo) and adrenolutin, 1 subject who had received placebo twice, and 2 who had received adrenolutin twice.

SUBJECTS RECEIVING ADRENOLUTIN AND PLACEBO. *Miss B. X.* (*Riboflavin*). Miss B. X., a graduate nurse, was tense for the first half hour and felt her speech and thinking were slow. At the end of the first hour, no change was seen. Two hours after starting, no changes had occurred. She remained alert and interested, and felt stimulated by the questions hurled at her to test her thinking. At 10:00 PM, she was sleepy and very tired. For a moment, the printed word appeared altered. She slept well. The next morning, she was normal.

One week later, she received adrenolutin. There was no change the first half hour. Then she noted she was much less anxious than she had been the previous week at this time. At 7:00 PM, she was relaxed and cheerful and felt it was amusing she did not do as well on the tests While doing the Bender Gestalt test, she could hardly keep from laughing. She was not able to do the 100-minus-7 test correctly nor make simple conversions of grains to milligrams. These are routine for nurses and she had done very well the previous week. The investigator seemed much funnier to her. Her conversation was flippant and for her inappropriate. At 8:00, she was indifferent to pain and the proceedings and found everything amusing.

When the stroboscope was flashing before her closed eyes at 12 per second, she saw a bright white light rimmed with red. This turned into a large moss rose. At 9:30, she was depressed but not tired. The experience of the testing, etc., appeared very silly to her and she could not understand why she had been so free in her conversation. Later, she had a frontal headache.

That evening, she arrived home elated and very talkative. She was amused by the research and remained hilarious to an unusual degree. The next day, she was normal. She reported that she had felt unusually disinhibited socially and had made remarks she would have made only to a close friend or sister and not to strangers. She had been much more relaxed with the second EEG run. There was less fatigue during the first experiment and the whole evening had passed more quickly.

Dr. L. J. (*Adrenolutin*). Dr. L. J., a very intelligent intern, wrote the following account after his first session:

From the period of 5:30 to 6:00, I had a vague feeling of apprehension and some very very slight anxiety not knowing quite what to expect but knowing that the experiment, generally speaking, was considered boring by several of my friends who had taken the test. At 6:00 I took the drug and from 6:00 to 7:00, I noticed several interesting features. The first thing I noticed was that I was mildly to moderately anxious of what was happening in spite of the fact that I was in fairly familiar surroundings and knew the psychiatric personnel who were examining me. I was made particularly anxious by some of the questions that were asked by the psychiatrist. I found that I was completely unable to answer fairly simple questions. I felt a definite frustration and some humility and also a quite marked antagonism towards the psychiatrist because he insisted on asking questions I was unable to handle. I felt that I was definitely putting on a very poor performance to begin with and I assumed that if I had had a drug, that in the first hour it would probably have little effect, and that most of my slowness in performing these questions was either due to anxiety or to sheer stupidity. I was quite apologetic about not answering the questions smartly. I had definite symptoms of moderate anxiety—my hands were very cold and extremely sweaty. I felt upset, I had marked tachycardia and a feeling of discomfort in the epigastrium which is extremely uncommon for me. From the period 6:30 to 7:00, I noticed an increasing inability to perform the questions. I could remember the facts presented to me quite quickly in these mathematical questions, but I lacked the energy, the initiative to carry the solution through to a final answer. I was almost incapable of setting up the equations in any manner. Towards the latter part of the questioning, drawing close to 7:00 I believe, I could hardly even entertain the questions and this I attributed to my marked anxiety. I found this most frustrating and upsetting experience for I seemed to lack ability to localize my thoughts in a forward direction in handling these relatively simple arithmetic problems which I should imagine would be at grade eight level. I, towards 7:00, also began to feel a tremendous lethargy and apathy towards things in general and this I attributed to the fact that I was overtired when the experiment began which, on looking back, is probably not exactly true. Some time after 7:00, I found it extremely difficult to concentrate on the questions being asked me because during the application of the electrodes portions of my hair were being snipped off and also acetone and compressed air were used during this procedure, all of which I found fairly distracting. At about this time, which I would imagine would be 7:30, although I could not be sure, my attitude seemed to be changing somewhat and I had lost much of my initial anxiety and this was being rapidly replaced by a type of apathy which seemed to be increasing to tremendous fatigue. Accompanying these feelings, I began to lose my feeling of initial humility and also much of my initial hostility. These feelings were being replaced by a feeling of disinterestedness. Also a feeling that I was rather above these frivolous questions that were being asked of me. My examiners no longer seemed quite as friendly as they had formerly and

I felt rather like they were young schoolboys wasting the government's money asking rather stupid and superfluous questions. At one point, during this procedure, I was asked to interpret some proverbs. Because of the distractions going on around my head I adopted a policy of answering the questions as quickly as possible and with as much dispatch as possible and sloughed off the answers in an effort to get them behind me as quickly as possible. Although the questions did not irritate me, I felt them rather frivolous and somewhat senseless and my main object was to get that part of the questioning over with as quickly as possible and likewise get the evening over with as quickly as possible because the whole thing by this time had become rather boring. I thought my questions to the proverbs being asked were sometimes rather clever. Likewise when I was asked such questions as 'why are people taxed' and 'what is the function of government' etc., I thought my answers to these were quite concise and astute and at least would be sufficiently good to satisfy this young group of upstarts that were attempting to question me. Towards 8:00, I found the results of the stroboscopic examination were not too disagreeable although rather tiresome. The flicker fusion test following the stroboscopic examination required a good deal more concentration for at this time I felt very fatigued, very apathetic and very often during the flicker fusion test, I would just take a rough stab at what I estimated was the fusion point. I had lost my enthusiasm completely for the experiment but considered that I would play the game and continue with the experiment just to please my examiners who I felt were carrying on in a rather frivolous manner.

The culmination of the tests came when I was given the critical thinking test which I found extremely difficult. It seemed to never end and I must have taken well over an hour to perform it. Not only did I find the questions difficult but I found the instructions difficult to understand and I believe most of my time was spent trying to figure out what was required of me in the test rather than getting on and doing the actual questions. I found that I had to read over the questions perhaps two or three times and even then was not entirely clear as to what was intended. I was fairly discouraged and rather depressed, and thoroughly fatigued, and yet I had a supreme apathy much as a lotus eater must have had. I was very thankful when the test was finally finished. Following the experiment I returned to my ward where I had several duties to carry out. Although I felt very very tired and certainly ready to go to bed, I felt that I was in my right mind actually. I had to start an intravenous injection and to my chagrin I had great difficulty, making four or five attempts. However, this did not particularly upset me although it must have upset the patient somewhat and I continued to attempt to start this intravenous with some abandon. Later that night at 4:00 in the morning, I was required to get up to give another intravenous injection on the ward on which I worked. For this duty which was to be carried out on a ward some considerable distance from where I sleep, I decided I would get out my bicycle which was kept in a cupboard close by my room and ride down to the ward which I felt was a very practical thing to do at that hour. I had not done this before, although that evening I thought it would be a very sensible thing to do. On reaching the ward, I again experienced considerable difficulty giving an intravenous injection but again this did not worry me very much. This is perhaps unusual for me for when I miss intravenous injections, I normally become quite disturbed when I miss them for the second time. However, at that hour I didn't think it mattered if it took three or four or five trys which I again carried out with the same abandon as previously. The next morning I awoke and I was quite tired, still very very apathetic, and with a rather dull headache. I was unable to pick up any speed in my work throughout the morning and even into the early afternoon and although I had a fairly heavy schedule of work ahead of me, I was unable to muster the necessary energy and initiative to carry out these various duties. The fact that I couldn't seem to carry out these duties didn't really worry me too much at any time. By the following evening, however, I felt I had considerably more energy, I was more awake and more able and willing to carry out the necessary daily tasks. The following day I felt completely normal in all respects. On looking back over the whole evening, I might say that I had received a depressant drug which made me very apathetic, rather depressed and did not seem to completely abolish my anxiety. Although I felt anxious I didn't seem to be really able to do much about it because of this tremendous sense of fatigue. Generally speaking, I felt I had done only moderately well or rather poorly on the tests, particularly on the first few and especially on the critical thinking test. I regarded the evening as rather unpleasant and one which placed a considerable strain on me. As a result, I was not particularly looking forward to the next week's experiment, which I was afraid might have a somewhat similar effect.

One week later, D. L. J. was given riboflavin. At 6:30, there was no change. At 6:45, he was able to do calculations better than the previous week. At 7:00, he did pretty well but failing to find a correct answer to a problem made him upset and anxious. At 7:45, he seemed more relaxed, somewhat elated, and full of good humor. This he described as his normal personality. The rest of the evening, there were no changes. The following day, he was sure he had placebo the second time because he had been wide awake, more attentive, and much more alert. The questions had been easier, there had been no headache, no fatigue, and the memory for the evening had remained clear. He concluded that the second drug was either a placebo or an euphorient. His own account follows:

"On this Monday, in spite of the fact that I had again stayed out rather late Sunday evening, the day before the test, I was in moderately good spirits when I embarked upon the test. I felt somewhat more confident about what was going to happen. I knew that the test would be somewhat similar and, therefore, I had no particular apprehension. At 5:30 to 6:00, I had the usual flicker test which I did with some enthusiasm as before, knowing that they would be rather boring but that it could be well tolerated. From 6:00 to 7:00 my reactions were considerably different from the previous week and I didn't feel nearly the anxiety that I'd had. My hands remained warm and dry, I was attentive and relaxed. The psychiatrist fired a similar type of question at me involving the rather simple arithmetic questions. Unlike the previous week, I did not have a certain sense of panic and confusion but was able to make at least an effort at working out an equation. I was making a sincere and somewhat enthusiastic effort to at least make a good stab at the question even though I might not be able to get the answer. The fact that I couldn't get the answer didn't particularly worry me as it had the week before. I seemed generally able to give more answers this week in a quick and more accurate manner. I did not feel the humility nor was I as apologetic when I made mistakes on this occasion. My examiners did not arouse the antagonism and hostility in me as they had done previously. I felt in a quite good humor from the hours of 6:00 to 7:00. I seemed to be able to muster the necessary energy and initiative and enthusiasm to tackle the questions even though I probably would not get the right answer. I was not particularly discouraged or depressed at all and was in an exceptionally good mood when we moved on to the second part of the experiment which again consisted of the EEG and stroboscopic examination. . . . I think I did a better job on the proverbs although there were one or two which I seemed to have a mental block in explaining. On the questions of abstract thinking . . . my performance was better than the week before. On the EEG and stroboscopic examination, I think the results were markedly different from the previous week. At no time was I really aware of geometry and symmetry to the field that I saw; there were no definite centers of light particularly and no straight radiating lines coming off the center of light. . . . The critical thinking test, I noticed a very marked subjective difference. I was able to understand the instructions immediately on reading them over. I found the questions quite difficult and still not clear today, but I was able to make what I thought was an astute try at the questions and on the whole, I felt much better about the test when I finished than the week before. I felt that I was clearer in my mind, my judgment was better, and I had definitely done the test in a more precise and much more rapid manner. I believe that I had bettered my time by perhaps twenty minutes to half an hour. I felt no particular sensations other than one of extremely well being. I was much more awake at that hour than I usually am.

". . . In retrospect, looking back over the evening, I felt the whole experience was much more pleasant the second evening and I think that I actually enjoyed it. I was able to maintain my interest throughout it and I seemed able to bring my powers of concentration to bear on all the questions so that I could give them all a good try. I didn't feel any anxiety and was in extremely good spirits throughout the evening. I felt quite kindly towards my psychiatrists who I felt were my colleagues and generally felt that the experiment on the second evening was well worthwhile and that the tests were astute ones. As a final conclusion therefore I think that on the first evening I was given a depressant drug, which made a very unpleasant evening for me. On the second evening, I was given an euphorient drug, a stimulant type of drug and the evening was quite passable. However, the drugs are of such a subtle nature that following the first evening, I would not be sure that I had had anything and even following the second evening, taken by itself, I could not be sure that I had had anything. However, in comparing the two evenings, there was a very very marked difference in the way I felt and therefore I must have had contradictory types of drugs on these occasions."

After the two sessions had been completed the subject was very concerned. For most of the week after having had adrenolutin he was very disturbed because of his unusual paranoid ideation during the first experimental night, which he had not disclosed to the investigators. On the second day after the first experience he reported to Hoffer that he had not told the two investigators everything that had occurred as he had been instructed to do. What had happened was now worrying him since he was quite certain he had had placebo. Hoffer asked him to come for an interview after he had finished the second half of the experiment because Hoffer then did not know what he had had.

After the experiments were over, he reported what he had neglected to tell the two observers. During the first experiment he was asked his opinion of socialized medicine. He immediately felt very strongly that the two observers were both communists and were trying to draw him out. He thought he would play along with their little game and tried to draw them out in order to obtain evidence that they really were communists. This he proceeded to do by agreeing with everything they said about socialized medicine. He watched them carefully for evidence. He felt B. was a very sinister person although he had known him before. Finally he saw B. pick up a pencil marked "Government of Saskatchewan." This immediately confirmed his suspicions, for who but a communist would get a pencil from the Government of Saskatchewan? He then became preoccupied with the EEG procedure. The next morning, he could not understand how he could have had these ridiculous ideas. He felt so guilty over this he did not wish to tell anyone. For the next few days, he was very quiet and subdued on the wards, quite unusual for him.

SUBJECT RECEIVING ADRENOLUTIN TWICE. *Miss H. G.* This graduate nurse was given 50 mg adrenolutin. Before taking the chemical, she was exceedingly tense and her hands were wet with perspiration. At 6:30, she suddenly noted a marked sense of relaxation and some lightheadedness. At 6:40, her head felt funny and she felt that her thinking was fuzzy. She had difficulty following conversation. The observers' faces seemed distant from her and she became suspicious of one. She was strongly aware of being watched. At 7:00, she seemed to be small and the two observers towered over her and looked down at her. She considered these visual changes foolish. Words hopped up and down on a page and she had difficulty concentrating. Her thinking was very sluggish and she could not solve elementary nursing arithmetical conversions. At 7:40, there was no more fuzziness and she was relaxed. Words still moved up and down on the page. At 8:00, her hands were dry and this surprised her as she felt she should have been anxious and was not. At 9:00 after the EEG test, she was uneasy and felt oppressed by the stroboscopic light and thought things were closing in on her. At 9:35, she was relaxed again and there were no more visual changes.

After the third test, it appeared to me that perhaps I was being looked down upon and the letters of a psychology book had a dancing movement up and down. It was difficult to convince myself that the words were moving when I knew they should not be.

I was quite disturbed at not being able to try to do my calculations and thought Dr. H. would think I was very incompetent as a nurse. During the EEG, I was very disturbed at the technician who was just talking too much and not paying attention to his work. My head hurt and I could have screamed out but I told Dr. H. I was all right. The flashing light gave me a suffocating feeling and I felt like running away or telling them to stop, but couldn't. Later, I went to the bathroom and felt like getting away from the experiment. There were some people in the hall. I thought they were looking at me and thinking I was foolish.

The next three tests seemed very foolish but I still maintained I was interested. I did not care how I had done. Before going home I believed nothing had happened and that I had been normal.

At home I decided not to tell my friends anything. I slept well. The next morning I was tired but my head was clear. I was able to figure out the math problem in my head easily (the one she could not solve the previous night). I realized I had been uncommunicative last night but was able to talk freely now. I realized that I had not reacted normally last night but today I'm thinking more clearly and critically.

Two weeks later, she was again given 50 mg adrenolutin. She was more relaxed this time. The first half hour, she discussed the 3 things which had impressed her about the first experience. These were (a) her feeling she must not communicate; (b) her feeling of suspiciousness; and (c) her difficulty in thinking. At 6:30, she again felt she must not talk, became suspicious, and felt again that we were looking down at her. She also felt quiet. She described one observer's face as having cruel eyes, an accentuated mouth and eyebrows. At 6:45, she again saw words move but less than the first experiment, and they were blurred. At 6:50, these visual changes were gone. At 7:00, she felt more relaxed and was more sure of herself. She tried the serial seven test 4 times and failed each one but it did not disturb her. On proverbs and on the Wechsler Bellevue test, she was somewhat better. At 8:00, there was no tension. She felt quiet. There was less paranoid feeling about the observers this time. At 10:00, she was relaxed and felt she had done much better this evening. There was actually very little difference on the scores.

The next day she reported as follows:

At 5:15 PM I was not apprehensive, and was looking forward to the evening. I was curious to know what would happen. After the first test, I took the drug. After a few minutes, we went back to the first room-repeating the first test to which I felt I responded fairly well. After this, Dr. Hoffer gave me a book and asked me if I saw the same thing as last week (movement in page)—I did not. I then experienced the feeling of being looked down upon by A. more than Dr. H. A's eyes appeared somewhat cruel, his eyebrows were pronounced as was his mouth; just Dr. H.'s eyes and eyebrows were pronounced. This lasted only momentarily and was not as intense as last week. After this we went out to do the 'distance test.' At this time I realized that my mood was definitely calm, that I was not suspicious as on the previous test and that I would probably be more truthful in my comments but still not too talkative. My reaction towards the resident psychiatrist was friendly and not critical realizing he knew his work. The test passed quickly; I was sure of my measurement and did not feel as though I was underestimating myself. Interest did not seem to fade during the test. I believe at this time I was somewhat relieved to think I was not having the same reactions. Dr. Hoffer began his math quiz again. I thought I could do better than I did, however. I did have several different answers to the 93–7 test; felt I did better on the math but the fact that I had made some errors did not greatly concern me. I felt that Dr. H. and A. were friendly and kindly towards me; also was not as worried about not being able to answer questions but felt perhaps I could still do better. During the EEG, I felt very relaxed and calm—could easily have gone to sleep. The time of the test did not annoy me, the hyperventilation part of the test—had some headache, but not as severe as last week. I was finding the evening more interesting even though the tests were the same—perhaps I enjoyed the calm, relaxed feeling I was experiencing in contrast to the previous evening. The Rorschach test also was more enjoyable—I still saw some bats and crawling animals although not as sinister or frightening; and I was able to see more pleasant things—clouds, melting snow, rock and tree reflections in water, just modern art painting for my imagination could not see anything but color. The colors were softer, warmer blue.

February 25. This morning I was still tired—somewhat more than usual. Talked to the Director—was not the least bit annoyed with her this morning either—a feeling which is different from the annoyance I have felt towards her (P.S., this is a feeling that is experienced not only by myself, but also by my fellow workers). I still feel relaxed and calmer I believe than what I normally am.

February 26. I believe the calming effect lasted well into Saturday evening. I was going out Saturday evening and had none of my usual apprehensive manifestations— an excessive perspiration in axilla and palms of the hands. I am still somewhat tired this morning but I am unable to be definitely certain that this is a result of the medication. The experience still remains enjoyable and is beginning to repress the first evening from my mind.

SUBJECTS RECEIVING PLACEBO TWICE. *Miss B. C.* This subject received riboflavin twice. There was no change evident during either experiment; this was typical of the placebo runs. The following account was submitted by the subject on the day following the first session:

I can remember everything that happened last night quite clearly. I think I was at ease all evening and not exceptionally nervous. I recall that my eyes seemed to be jumping with the lights flashing on and off and flickering, but I had no head-ache. While walking to the EEG lab, I did feel slightly unsteady and not too sure of how I was walking. When I was being asked questions at EEG, I felt a little slow in my thinking, partly because of the work being done on my head. It didn't annoy me much but did distract me some. I felt quite relaxed and sleepy after the questioning and when the EEG first started. With the light flashing in my eyes, I saw various colors and designs—all symmetrical and moving but no images of any kind. For a while I was dizzy, with my eyes closed. The bed seemed to be turning under me and I was turning around in the opposite direction—similar to a ride at the exhibition. But it did not last too long, cleared some when I opened my eyes. It stopped without leaving any different feeling—no headache or nausea. After the EEG and the lights, I felt rather tired and not interested in any more problems. But on walking back to the office, I wakened up again and felt quite normal. However, I was beginning to get hungry. I think I did and said the same things on the tests then as I would have without any drug. After I returned home, I felt quite normal, ate, and went to bed and to sleep right away.

SUMMARY. A summary of the 14 subjects who received adrenolutin and placebo is shown in Table 37. A score was derived by giving the subject 1 point for an abnormality and 0 for normality under the headings shown in the table. Thus the presence of changes in thought is scored as 1. We consider it normal for the subject to have had anxiety during these experiments. Its absence is scored as 1. The mean score of 14 adrenolutin runs was 4.43, with a range of from 1 to 7. For placebo, it was 0.93 with a range of 0 to 3. In 11 pairs of results the scores for placebo were less.

The subjective accounts were then examined for the presence of residual changes in the days following the experiments. Out of 18 subjects given adrenolutin, there were 9 prolonged reactions. Out of 32 placebo experiments, only 4 were prolonged (Chi Square $= 6.4$, $P < 0.01$).

The subjects were not asked regularly what they thought they had received. But several spontaneously remarked that they had had something active or inactive. Of 9 subjects each of whom received both adrenolutin and a placebo, only 1 subject erred by calling adrenolutin inactive; in all instances the placebo was termed inactive. (For this distribution, with one d.f., the value of Chi Square is 10; therefore $P < 0.001$.)

This sample of series is of course biased in that people guessing what they had may have been different, and it is possible that if all subjects had been asked to make these predictions, the results would have been different. The work reported by Grof *et al.* (1961a,b) makes this suggestion quite unlikely. Their subjects were able to detect adrenochrome very well.

Prolonged Reactions to Adrenochrome and Adrenolutin

ADRENOCHROME

Some of the changes produced by adrenochrome may persist several days, and in some cases the effects nearly led to disastrous results. Two cases of prolonged reactions will be discussed. These experiences with adrenochrome have made us quite cautious with this drug which seems to be so mild in its action but which can be so dangerous because of the lack of insight it induces in some subjects.

Miss F. M. This young female, age 16, had been well until age 8. For the next 2 years, she had unusual sensations in her chest and nose every night. A few weeks before this investigation, she developed changes in perception (her mother's face seemed strange and altered as she watched; the visual field was covered with a checkerboard pattern, her body image was different, time moved very slowly, and houses looked like cornflake boxes). There was no thought disorder but she was very apprehensive. For several years, she had been given Dilantin and phenobarbital for mixed petit and grand mal epilepsy. At the time of investigation, she was normal. The EEG showed a very marked left anterior temporal focus characterized by high voltage, slow waves, and an occasional saw-tooth wave with single spikes (Szatmari *et al.*, 1955, p. 607). The left temporal focus increased with hyperventilation.

At the beginning of the EEG test, she was happy, cheerful and friendly. She was given 50 mg of adrenochrome by vein. After 10 minutes, she developed a feeling of estrangement and fear and her nose itched. The pathological activity of the temporal focus increased and dysrhythmia became generalized. She was now morose, quiet, and depressed. When she was urged to describe how she felt she cried. Then she reported that the strange feelings and disturbances in body image which had been present 2 weeks before had returned. She was given 500 mg of nicotinic acid by vein. Within 15 minutes, the focus was less intense, the dysrhythmia had disappeared, and she was mentally normal.

That evening at home, she was moody and quiet. One week later, she was very disturbed and 2 weeks after the treatment required committal to a mental hospital.

On admission, she suffered from perceptual changes (all faces were strange, there were marked *deja vu*, feelings of estrangement and unreality, and visual hallucinations). She had thought disorder (her present life was merely show and a replay of a previous period in her life; she was confused, rambling, and almost incoherent) and referential ideas with delusions of guilt, and she was paranoid. Her mood was flat. The staff were not aware she had received adrenochrome. On admission, the diagnosis of schizophrenia was entertained but with her history of epilepsy, she was finally diagnosed as having an epileptic psychosis.

A few days after admission, her psychosis cleared and a few weeks later, she had typical grand mal convulsions. These were controlled by anticonvulsant medication. She was in the hospital about 6 months. Over the next 6½ years, she has shown no schizophrenic-like symptoms.

Mr. D. S. This patient, age 18, was first treated June 7 to September 29, 1957. He was diagnosed as having a neurotic hysterical reaction with marked depression. Schizophrenic features were present. He was given regular psychotherapy and 20 ECT and was discharged much improved. Two weeks later, he remained well. He was readmitted on February 21 until March 21, 1958, in the same condition as on his first admission. A better history was taken and he was found to have had perceptual changes. He felt people were staring at him, thought his nose was getting bigger; he felt small in stature compared to others, and he had visual hallucinations of shadows and people. He had thought disorder and paranoid delusions, and was extremely tense. He restlessly paced up and down in his room for many hours. He was diagnosed as an early schizophrenic. Three days after admission, he was given 10 mg of *d*-adrenochrome by vein. Almost immediately he became more relaxed but developed vivid hallucinations. He could see his hands growing larger and smaller, he could no longer estimate the distance of people from himself, and pictures appeared very vivid. One hour later, while looking in a mirror, he saw his face divided into 2 halves, one white and one black. For the next 6 days, this recurred whenever he became very tense.

ADRENOLUTIN

There have been many prolonged reactions to adrenolutin; some of these changes have already been described in the case histories. Other reactions lasted more than 1 day after a single administration of adrenolutin, and reactions up to 1 week have occurred.

Mr. I. K. Mr. I. K. was given 25 mg of adrenolutin at 6:00 PM on January 27, 1955. Over the next few hours, a few visual changes were present; he was relaxed and felt his mind was clear but his thinking was altered. He had difficulty in following conversation and felt other people about him were unimportant to him. Between 8:30 and 10:00 PM voices seemed unnaturally loud. The next day he suffered from a slight headache all morning, and he was listless and tired.

On March 3, 1965, he was given 50 mg of adrenolutin at 6:00 PM. There was little change in him. Two hours later he was quieter and spoke with difficulty. Later, he developed an irritating headache over his left eye. We concluded that there had been no reaction and he was allowed to go home at 10:00 PM. His wife reported that he looked drawn and tired. He was unusually unresponsive and did not tell his wife anything about the evening. That night he slept fitfully and he was less responsive to the fussing of his two young children. The next morning he was irritable and seemed disinterested in his mail. Episodes which normally did not bother him were causes for irritation. That night, he was angry about his car being stuck in the snow near his house.

The second morning, he seemed more normal. When he could not start his car, he came rushing in and shouted at his wife that he could not start the car and that it was her fault, he stated "if she had not wakened him yesterday, he wouldn't have been able to help her sister get her car out and therefore she wouldn't have had to drive home again and so get stuck in the same hole and that therefore he wouldn't have had to drive his car around to the front and leave it there to freeze on the road and ruin the starter."

That evening, when Mrs. I. K. was feeding a young child, he suddenly without warning shouted her name in a violent manner and then said she was harming the child by her concern over the feeding. When Mrs. K. asked him why he shouted instead of just quietly telling her, he glowered and muttered something. That evening, he appeared haggard and ill. He was unreasonable and uncommunicative. The third day, he awoke cheerful and normal until late in the afternoon when his irritability, restlessness, and peevishness returned. The rest of the day he was alternately normal and withdrawn and irritable.

Much has been made of placebo reactions, and they are indeed very powerful. But the incidence of prolonged reactions was very unusual with our placebo subjects. Most of them stated that they were normal on the day following the experiment. The records of 25 subjects were re-examined and only their subjective accounts used. In these accounts they described how they felt the following day. Thirty-two subjects had placebo. Four stated there was some residual effect which consisted of some dizziness in 3 and euphoria in 1. Most subjects received Tuinal, 200 mg at bedtime. Eighteen subjects received adrenolutin. Of these, 9 had prolonged reactions. Chi Square for this is about 6.4. There is less than 2% chance that this difference is due only to chance. Furthermore, not a single placebo subject had any residual reaction lasting more than one-half day. Yet many adrenolutin subjects were not normal by noon and some were clearly abnormal for several days; there was one reaction that lasted 2 weeks.

REVERSAL OF THE ADRENOCHROME REACTION

The psychological action of adrenochrome has been recently described by Hoffer and Osmond (1960). A substantial number of volunteers who were given adrenochrome and also adrenolutin had prolonged reactions. These are disturbing to the subject but even more so to the experimenter for the subject very often has no insight although some are acutely aware of the defect. Here are excerpts from a volunteer who received adrenolutin and later nicotinamide because the adrenolutin reaction had not disappeared the next day. The description of the adrenolutin experience is given in some detail in order to show more clearly how the experience was altered by nicotinamide. (See Hoffer *et al.*, 1957.)

"September 15 at 11 o'clock. This is an attempt to record impressions of taking 50 mg of adrenolutin by mouth starting at 6 o'clock yester-

day evening. This is a difficult kind of experience to record because it
is really typified by not much happening. I took LSD about two years
ago and that was an experience in which there were great changes in
ideational spheres mainly. There was a feeling of becoming four entities
at once, very powerful feeling of emotion, of emotional experience of
subjective color. It was an experience that kept me excited for days
afterwards. The adrenolutin, on the other hand, was a very mild kind of
experience and yet I can realize that it did have a rather large effect
on me. Yet there were no immediate dramatic changs. There was
only a change in mood and in general approach to things. I took the drug
at 6 and about forty-five minutes later, I was conscious of a headache.
I called it a headache; it was a sensation of pressure almost from the
outside in across the forehead particularly on the temples. About that
same time, I began to be very slightly euphoric. So slightly, that I
wasn't sure really that I had been talking louder, faster, but I think
I was interacting with Dr. Hoffer at a higher rate than usual. A little
bit after that, the euphoria began to slip away and I began to get a
bit depressed. At that time, I couldn't call it depression, I reacted against
the word depression because it seemed to me that depression was a kind
of dynamic thing and when a person is depressed, he wants to keep
other things away from him, other people, other ideas, he wants to
keep by himself. I did not want to be by myself. I did not want to keep
interesting talk from coming in on me. I just did not care. I became
passive, the edge on spirit went off and I became a little bit more depressed in this passive manner, disinterested. Then after about an hour,
the depression began to lift and it never did come back up to normal.
During this time, a number of tasks were set for me and I thought that
I was doing them quite well and yet I made a great many errors. I was
asked what is the square of twenty-five and I insisted that it was five
hundred seventy-five. Mental arithmetic was very difficult and I went
through it several times and discovered it was six hundred twenty-five.
Other mental tasks, mental arithmetic tasks were set for me, and I
found that I could solve them but it took a very conscious effort. I
felt I had to push myself to do it, and this was a little unpleasant.
I would much rather not have done it. I would much rather have sat
in doubt about things I couldn't handle without stretching myself, without exerting myself with conscious effort. Talking about Chi Square was
easy because Chi Square I know very well. I figured a couple of Chi
Squares in my head and stated whether they were significant or not,
even there I had a little bit of difficulty. I believe if I had gotten off
into fields in which I had very little experience in which I would have
had to do creative highly original kind of work that I would have been

quite confused. At any rate, it was an effort to carry on this kind of work.

"Throughout the experience, I was struck by the parallel between the reaction to adrenolutin and the reaction to alcohol. I felt a little bit of euphoria. Almost as though I had had one drink, perhaps two, not more than that. And then, almost immediately, came the depression, the kind of depression that I feel personally after having taken some alcohol and not being in a social situation which facilitates and keeps one active and away from depression. I became depressed, indifferent; I did not want to exert myself to take part in what was going on and I became more irritable. I was not really aware of this until it was pointed out and then looking back in that respect I could see that I had become more irritable. Dr. Hoffer's daughter came into the room and asked a question and I recognized that had it been my own child breaking in on something that I was very intensely interested in, I would probably have yelled at him or in some way shown emotion that I normally would not show.

"In several of the answers to questions that were put to me, particularly when contradictions were pointed out, I was inflexible. I did not want to yield or take the other person's point of view. I think that I could have been made angry quite easily had I been pushed. I think that it would have been a slightly different kind of anger from what I might call normal anger. I think that I would have defended an idea without becoming personally too angry at the two investigators. However, I don't know. No one pushed me that far. When one takes alcohol, and goes into a state where the effects are marked, either euphoria or depression, there is kind of a piecemeal progression effect. One's vision is affected, then one's cutaneous sensations; there is a feeling of floating perhaps but all these things come singly. The thing that was striking about the adrenolutin is that it sneaked up on me. All distortions such as they were seemed to come at once and I was not aware of anything having happened really until I began to come out of it. This was about 10:30 or 11:00.

"After a nice steak which I ate with a good deal of enjoyment I began to realize that my vision was a little bit clearer. I could see things as though I were a little closer to them. I realized then that I had felt a little detached, perhaps this would account for my feelings of unreality. However, they were so slight that I had not recognized them before. There were several cues that seemed to be sharpened up for me as I came out of it and then I became aware of the real parallel between adrenolutin and alcohol. The coming out in alcohol seems to be very much like the adrenolutin, some functions come back and one becomes aware that he is becoming more sober by changes back to normal behavior from a kind of behavior to which he has become almost accommodated and which he intended to accept. I went back to the hotel about midnight and went right to sleep. This morning I got up at about eight o'clock and I felt fairly normal, I felt a little bit depressed, I felt fatigued.

"There is still a trace of a headache, a diffused kind of a headache, not an ordinary headache, but not very severe. There was a great deal of difficulty in making decisions. I had to pack my bag and check out of the hotel and it took me a matter of about twenty minutes to go through the motions that I would ordinarily handle in four or five. Because I had to decide each thing as a separate problem. Creative thinking or nonroutine thinking problem solving was a definite effort and I did not want to do it, I did not want to solve problems, and would have been much more content to merely sit down on the bed, lie down or forget about the whole thing, but I did go through the process-packed, checked out and everything was all right. I was a little irritated when I ate breakfast. The fellow who sat next to me had a bowl of porridge and he had his elbow stuck way out. He bumped me only once, ordinarily this wouldn't bother me a bit and yet I felt a flicker of irritation at it. As I walked from the hotel to the hospital, the cars seemed to be coming at me in a slightly different way, they seemed to curve in towards me and then go past. I could not put my finger on what was different except that things did seem a little unreal. I don't know if that is the proper word, certainly a little bit changed. Last night at about 9:30, I was asked about color contrast in the room about me and I became very much aware of brilliance and saturation, I called it saturation in reds. There were a number of reds in the bookcase in red-backed books, in a picture over the fireplace, it was a picture with a good deal of red in it and the reds seemed to be in a class by themselves, they seemed to have almost a fluorescent quality. I was very curious about this and I was unable to say whether this was a change or not although they seem to be different, because I hadn't paid much attention to either the pictures or the books before taking the drug.

"When I went back to the hotel I was much struck by the color in the carpet, a deep red, and the drapes hanging in the room. These seemed to be very much richer in color than I previously experienced them. I looked out the window, neon signs were tremendously rich, almost a blood red. The headlights of cars coming up the street were not white as I normally see them but an almost red, a very warm color, they looked as though the batteries had run down, a yellowish color and yet I know that it was a change in my way of seeing color rather than a change in the light itself. When I turned off the bedlamp, I realized that I didn't have an afterimage so I turned it on and off a number of times, stared at it and did what I could to pick up afterimages. I got afterimages all right but it was much more difficult than usual. Then I began to play around in color with afterimages and subjective color was very much washed out, it was very difficult to get any kind of afterimage color response. I turned on the bedlamp and looked directly into it and then produced a flicker with my fingers passing between the lamp and my eyes. Normally, I can see color and patterning in this manner. I got practically nothing, a kind of cold gray, bluish gray light and very little patterning. I am quite certain that it was a reduction in the amount of afterimage and the color components in afterimage as a result of the drug.

"When I finally dressed at the hotel and left to come up here to the hospital, I felt that I was changed in some way and when I tied my necktie I looked into the mirror and I was quite startled, I didn't look like I normally look. I looked as though I had been beaten in some way, I looked as though I were not nearly as self-confident, as though I were a different kind of a person. I didn't stop to analyze it or to find out really what the difference was and I wished now that I had. I was quite conscious of the fact that I looked different, in addition, of course, I felt different. I felt perhaps less sure of myself. I felt that I could do things but that it would be a good deal of effort and that I wouldn't know how well I had done it. There are very few parallels between the adrenolutin experience and the LSD. The LSD experience was one of tremendous change, particularly in ideation and there was no question as to what the change was, as to what the effect of the drug had been. In the adrenolutin experience, it was characterized by just the opposite, the change was so minute or perhaps so subtle that one wasn't really sure the change had taken place. In an overall view, one could say I feel about the way I normally do, but when one then attended to particular behavior, he found that he didn't really feel that way, that there were changes. This morning when I woke up, thought back over the night before and the experience of the drug, it seemed to have a slightly unreal quality, the outstanding experience seemed to have leveled off and I could almost accept it as not being any experience at all, until I went back and thought over particular aspects of the experience, I realized of course it had been a major experience but of which I had only a minor awareness. My way of thinking about it is in terms of a kind of frame of reference theory and this leads to the comparison with alcohol. I think that a great many things did change in response to the drug. I think that they all changed together and in proportion. I made a simile the night before in terms of a camera. An illumination within a scene can be changed by changing the amount of light that falls on different parts of it or the total amount of light can be changed by something like an iris diaphragm which may cut down the amount of light to one fourth and yet each part of the scene is getting the same proportional amount of light so there is no change except that it is dimmer.

"I didn't feel when I woke up this morning as though I were a six-cylinder car running on four cylinders but I felt like I was a six-cylinder car running on low test gasoline. I was operating all right only I wasn't operating at a very high level. It was almost like plugging an electric razor into a 60 cycle current and then having the cycle go down to 40 or 45. The whole thing runs but it runs less well. It doesn't run as fast. I feel today that the adrenolutin experience was something like that, everything changed at once and because everything changed at once, I wasn't aware of change at all; but could only be aware of change as one thing changing in relation to other things and everything changed at once. I didn't know that I had changed until the behaviors were pointed out to me, such as aggressiveness, lack of clarity and so forth. When I began to come out of it, or felt that I was coming out at 10:30 to 11:00, I came out a little unevenly and I could see that there were differences. Right now, twenty minutes past eleven, I feel that I am not myself and yet I don't know exactly how I'm different, except that I have less energy, I feel fatigued, I feel that I can do anything that I would normally do but I wouldn't do it as well, or it would be more effort in order to do it. Again, back to the camera analogy, I feel that everything in the way of faculties, abilities, have been affected about equally. I think that I can do creative work, that I have been somewhat organized dictating this, only stopping one or two times and yet I know that I am not operating at a very high level of efficiency. During the war, I came to know what intense fatigue felt like and what intense pain felt like and I think that there is a similarity here in that one can go on and on until he absolutely collapses but there is a point at which it becomes more and more effort to keep going. I know and I am quite certain that I am correct that I could go on feeling like this and do quite well but I wouldn't want to. It wouldn't be any fun, it would be a great deal of effort and if I could relax my super ego enough, I would say to hell with it and not do it. There is only one other parallel that I can give from my experience concerning the ad-

TABLE 37

COMPARISON OF SUBJECTS RECEIVING ADRENOLUTIN (A) AND PLACEBO (P)

Subject and treatment		Headache	Perception	Thought	Mood	Anxiety	Personality change	Residual	Score
A	A	yes	yes	yes	yes[a]	no	yes	yes	7
	P	no	no	no	no	yes	no	no	0
B	A	no	no	no	no	no	yes	no	2
	P	no	no	no	no	no	no	no	1
C	A	no	yes	yes	no	no	no	no	3
	P	no	no	yes	no	yes	no	no	1
D	A	yes	yes	yes	yes[a]	no	no	yes	6
	P	no	no	yes	yes[b]	yes	no	no	2
E	A	no	no	no	no	no	yes	no	2
	P	no	yes	yes	no	yes	no	no	2
F	A	yes	yes	yes	yes[b]	no	yes	no	6
	P	no	no	no	no	yes	no	no	0
G	A	no	no	no	no	no	no	yes	2
	P	no	yes	no	no	yes	no	no	1
H	A	no	yes	yes	no	no	yes	no	4
	P	no	no	no	no	no	no	no	1

I	A	yes	yes	yes	yes	yes[a]	no	yes	no	6
	P	no	no	no	no	no	yes	no	no	0
J	A	yes	yes	no	yes	yes[a]	no	yes	yes	6
	P	no	no	no	no	no	yes	no	no	0
K	A	yes	yes	no	yes	yes[a]	yes	yes	yes	6
	P	no	no	no	no	no	yes	no	no	0
L	A	yes	yes	no	yes	yes[a]	no	yes	yes	6
	P	no	no	no	no	yes[b]	yes	no	no	1
M	A	no	yes	no	yes	no	yes	no	no	1
	P	no	yes	no	no	no	no	no	no	1
N	A	yes	yes	yes	yes	no	no	no	yes	5
	P	no	yes	yes	no	no	no	yes	yes	3

[a] Depressed.   [b] Euphoric.

renolutin, and that is in relation to anoxia. The adrenolutin experience I said came on without my actually knowing there was an experience.

"During the war, while I was at Pensacola, Florida, I had some training in low pressure chambers. You go into a large tank, the air is partially evacuated to a pressure equivalent to say 45,000-foot altitude and then one finds out what it is like without the oxygen equipment. I volunteered for some guinea pig work and was taken to simulated altitudes, forty to fifty thousand feet. I took off my oxygen mask and breathed the air, very very rare, which of course, could not support life for very long. I remember that a task was set for me to write my name and the phrase, fifty-four forty or fight. So I wrote my name, fifty-four forty or fight and then my name, fifty-four forty or fight over and over. If I remember correctly, I wrote it eleven times feeling absolutely in control of the situation and when I came to, somebody was fooling with the oxygen mask on my face. What had happened of course was that anoxia had set in, and I became less and less able to carry on and passed out. They put the mask back on with under-forced feed and I immediately came back. The thing that is striking is that I felt fine all the time that I was going under from lack of oxygen. I remember thinking as I wrote—gosh there is nothing to this, I don't see what has everyone so excited. There was a medic on each side of me, waiting to catch me as I went down.

"When I examined the paper afterwards, I found the last two lines were run together and garbled, instead of fight I have chigt, a combination of my name and the word fight and finally the pencil went off in a tangent off the edge of the paper, as I folded up completely. This seems to be somewhat like the adrenolutin experience in that there is no warning, there seemed to be no perceptual knowledge that an experience or a change is coming on. It is only after the change had taken place and behavior was pointed out—why did you answer this way, what did you mean and so forth—that I became aware of the fact that I was reacting in a different manner. I wasn't anxious, I don't believe I was frightened at any point during the proceedings. The one major kind of mood which I remember was only that of being passive, of not particularly caring of being a little separated from the world around me.

"At 3:15, I feel a little bit clearer than I did this morning, although there is still a trace of headache and a kind of a feeling of being a little out of touch. I am not absolutely sharp on creative thinking, I tried a Chi Square computation and made a couple of mistakes in it, mistakes that I don't think I would normally make. I am going to take nicotinamide dissolved in water in just a few moments and see if this will clear up the remaining effects of the adrenolutin.

3:21 PM. "I took 1000 mg of nicotinamide dissolved in water. Twelve minutes after taking the nicotinamide, the headache which had been very slight was gone. At sixteen minutes, I felt more sure of myself, I felt that I was able to think clearly, without any difficulty at all. The headache is completely gone. There were no great changes, I felt fairly normal before, I felt a little bit out of contact, but I have been able to see no change other than the loss of the headache and feeling a little bit more sure of myself.

3:27 PM. "I feel much more sure of myself and think that my conceptual processes are more clear. There has been no dramatic change but I feel somehow better and different.

4:15 PM. "I leave the hospital to go south with my family. I feel a little better but am a bit dissapointed since I had expected a more radical change than this. We drive downtown to the hotel to pick up my bags and I described my experience to wife and kids. Feel pretty good about it. We start driving for Regina.

5:00 PM. "I feel quite happy. All symptoms have vanished and I am laughing and joking with the kids. I feel less tired and am very satisfied with the summer's work. Break into spontaneous song.

6:00 PM. "I feel very happy and exhilarated, way up in the air. This is a very wonderful euphoria, almost like six drinks although there is none of the indisposition to activity that commonly goes with a good deal of alcohol. I am all ready to drive all night if necessary. I am aware of being tired but of not *feeling* the way I would if I were this tired. I feel wonderful, all aglow, at peace with the world and with myself. I can think and plan and can interact with the kids in a very relaxed and enjoyable manner.

7:00 PM. "Still gay and relaxed. Just plain feel wonderful.

8:30 PM. "Suddenly find that euphoria has gone. I feel a bit irritable and the headache is back in a low-intensity way. Just outside of Regina.

8:45 PM. "Entering Regina. Notice that the neon lights are getting more vivid. Am decidedly depressed and mean. Feel very tired, my face is tight and wooden, my legs ache. I feel fatigued, depressed, and bleak. I wonder if I can make it the next ten minutes to an auto court. I marvel at the speed with which the good euphoric mood went to hell and I fell into nastiness and disagreeableness. I warn the kids that I am going back into the experience and they leave me alone in glowering silence for the last leg of the trip.

9:00 PM. "Arrive at the motor court and obtain a room. Decide to let the 'psychosis' come back a little more before taking pill. Notice that the reds are extremely vivid, almost produce shock when looked at intently. I am almost afraid to look directly at them. My stomach feels on the edge of nausea. I am very irritated at the kids roaring around the auto court. I feel passive and detached, very blue and sad.

9:05 PM. "Mood deepens, decide I can't stick it out much longer. Motivation to engage in pure scientific research has all gone to pot and I want to be rescued from this feeling of depression. I am afraid that I might not be able to control myself if pushed too far, as if I might become physically violent if I let it go much longer.

9:10 PM. "Take one gram of nicotinamide. Chew up pills and swallow with water. Want the effect to start fast and last long. Slight cutaneous prickle on face, forehead.

9:19 PM. "Feel a sudden easing of the situation. My headache faded out a good deal, depression lifting. Feel a wave of lighter spirits, almost of hope (the situation really felt desperate there for a while). Color is still more intense than normal. I feel more in control of myself but am still irritable when the situation touches me directly.

9:23 PM. "Stomach unease is gone. I feel better but still a little dissociated.

9:29 PM. "Feel very sleepy. Yawn. Still have a trace of a headache but the depression is less bitter than before.

9:45 PM. "Depression lifting gradually but still not gone. I am tired and my head still aches a little. My face is slightly stiff and wooden. I am not happy but I am not depressed to any great degree.

10:00 PM. "In bed and ready to go to sleep. I have occasional intestinal cramps from the amide and I think that I am going to have a hell of a night but shortly drop off to sleep and experience no more trouble. Sleep is broken by periodic wakings and some headache persists for a while.

Day 3—8:00 AM. "Wake up and feel wonderful. There is no trace of depression left. I lie in bed and tell stories to the kids for a half hour, outrageous lies about Feebold Feeboldson. Have a good time of it. This is not the usual waking routine.

8:45 AM. "Slight headache coming back, spirits fall off a little, so take 750 mg of an acid-amide composition, go directly out to breakfast. Fairly strong flush reaction with sense of shock—cold hands, little nausea, feel shaky. There was definite feeling of malaise from the acid-amide composition and I decided not to take any more. Shock reaction persists.

9:45 A.M. "Shock going away although still a trace of nausea sensation.

11:30 A.M. "Have felt better and busy packing the car for trip south. Now feel quite fatigued, legs almost shaky and weak, hands cold and numb-feeling and lacking in coordination so that tying knots is difficult. Take 750 mg nicotinamide. Feel a little short of breath, tired, physically inadequate. I feel O.K. psychologically.

12:30 P.M. "I feel much better and take off on errands I have to run in town before leaving. Shop and take car to garage for repair to wheels. Feel very good, euphoria, no trace of depression.

2:45 P.M. "Suddenly feel tired and a bit depressed. Colors are bright once again, particularly reds. Notice this in Kresge's store and know that I must take some more amide. Decide to take small dosage and see what effect it has on the symptoms. Face feels strained and legs wobbly and shaky. Take 0.5 gm of amide with ginger ale.

3:00 P.M. "Mechanic gave me a seemingly foolish answer and I cracked back at him quite sharply. Just plain irritated. Not depressed but not myself.

3:15 P.M. "The strained feeling in my face is almost gone and I feel a lot happier. I have felt anxious and a little afraid at time before the last pill. Cars seemed to curve in toward me as they went along the street and seemed to be going very fast. I felt inadequate to deal with them, not sure of myself. Depression is coming back a little.

4:00 P.M. "Depression coming back and I realize that 0.5 gram of the stuff is not enough so take another 0.5 gram.

4:15 P.M. "Feel decidedly better, depression is gone and the strain is almost gone. I had felt as though I were on the edge of the drug effect from 2:45 on and have concluded that this effect requires an awful lot of the amide to combat it; half-way measures are more threatening than none, almost; and I resolve to take plenty from here on out.

4:45 P.M. "Feel euphoric again, quite happy although a little tired. We have packed, prepared lunch, and are almost ready to take off for the States. A. D., who knows me fairly well, says that I look different even though I feel quite O.K. as though I were very tired and should rest a while.

8:45 P.M. "It is now almost fifty-one hours since first taking the drug. I have been going at top speed all day and have been alternately very high and very low but have finally learned how to juggle mood with pill. Euphoria begins to go while visiting friends under the stress of arguing with the kids. They are nervous and excited about leaving for home. Take 1 gram of amide. My legs tingle a bit, I feel dissociated a little, and know that I am going into depression again.

11:00 PM. "Finally break away from our friends and start the trip home.[1] I am physically a little tired but otherwise quite alert and clear, feel happy and relaxed. Very interested in getting back to the University. Drive about 100 miles and then take a nap while L drives.

Day 4—3:25 AM. "Wake from nap (about forty minutes) and pull in for coffee. Feel very clear and happy. L is sleepy so my turn to drive, take one gram amide on general principles. I feel now that I am ahead of my physical demand for an antidote to the drug and want to stay that way for the balance of the trip.

9:10 AM. "Get about two hours' sleep between Winnipeg and the border. I feel very happy and relaxed and tell the kids a story about how the Lone Ranger fell off his horse. Feel quite gay, in fact, and not fatigued and listless although I know that I am physically tired.

12:15 PM. "I began to feel a bit depressed, the mood change coming on very gradually but unmistakably. There is a touch of headache, I feel a little fatigued and stale. We are in Minnesota now and I have been driving quite steadily. Take one gram amide with water.

12:27 PM. "The headache is gone and I feel a lot better.

5:00 PM. "Now feel very tired and sleepy, begin to feel depressed. Take one gram and shortly feel revived.

12:00 PM. "Midnight and I am sleepy and feeling a bit depressed. Euphoria has come and gone again. Take 0.5 gram and L drives for a while.

1:30 AM. "Day 5—Driving conditions are not very good, many road repairs and both of us sleepy enough to be dangerous. Pull off to side of road and get some rest. Am not depressed but merely damned tired.

8:00 AM. "Wake up, now in Michigan on the Upper Peninsula. I feel quite good, alert, no longer tired or fatigued.

9:00 AM. "I get a feeling of depression coming on, slight headache develops, feel tired. Take 1 gram of amide.

11:00 AM. "Feel fine again and enjoy scenery on a beautiful day. No depression, no fatigue, some physical tiredness but no irritability.

1:30 PM. "Stop and swim in Lake Michigan. Feel a little tense and think depression is a little bit ahead of me. Kids want to stay and play in the sand and refuse to come when called. I absolutely blow my top in most

---

[1] Motor trip from Regina, Saskatchewan to Detroit, Michigan.

complete display of temper I can ever remember. I am startled and appalled by my emotion. It goes within a few minutes but leaves me in state of shock, shaking, and almost nauseous. Take 1 gram amide immediately.

1:50 PM. "Shock reaction persists, shakes, and near nausea. I've never felt a flood of pure rage like that before and hope I never feel it again. Think that I might have been capable of a triple axe murder if I'd had an axe!

2:00 PM. "Still shock, feel very tense and anxious. Waiting for ferry at the Straits and that doesn't help. Feel guilty over temper display.

2:30 PM. "Coming out of the shock reaction, now feel fatigued and just plain shaky. Emotional overtones are gone. Enjoy trip across Straits and apologize to kids.

5:00 PM. "Stop for food and coffee. I feel pretty good, not depressed, but am beginning to feel tired again. Take 1 gram amide, nap for about twenty minutes.

7:00 PM. "I feel tired but am not depressed. I am not irritable and feel moderately happy. There is none of the euphoria experienced earlier and things seem to be leveling off a bit. Colors have been normal for a long time.

Day 6—2:30 AM. "Arrive and finish unpacking the car. I am tired but not depressed, not irritable. Do not take any more amide before going to bed.

8:00 AM. "Up and ready to go again. Feel pretty good, not very tired or disorganized. Feel moderately happy. Know that I have a hard day ahead but am not disturbed by the knowledge.

8:15 AM. "On general principles, take 1 gram amide. Feel good, not sleepy, not dissociated, although physically tired.

10:00 AM. "Little change. Feel quite adequate and happy. No depression.

5:00 PM. "Get a drifting, floating feeling of being a little numb and cut off from the world. Have been studying like mad all day for prelims and can't decide whether it's the drug or just plain tiredness that is causing the sensations. No headache or depression with it.

5:10 PM. "Take 1 gram of amide to see what it will do. I am sure that this is just plain bone tiredness, not much of the drug effect since it is 119 hours since I took the adrenolutin. Feel unreal and quivery with sounds as though they were coming from another world across a little space, hands and legs shaky.

5:24 PM. "Feel a little less unreal and shaky. Can still concentrate well enough.

7:00 PM. "There is no great change in any direction. No euphoria, no depression, no nothing. I decide that I am just tired and that the drug has worn off.

10:00 PM. "In bed and go to sleep almost immediately.

Day 7—7:30 AM. "Up and away again. I feel completely normal now and am sure that the drug has been discharged in due order. I take no more niacinamide and get along about as expected.

"There is no question in my mind but that the drug had a definite and marked effect upon my behavior and mood. There is also no question in my mind but that the amide I took had a tremendous effect against the expected action of the drug. The drug produced depression, somasthetic sensations, and a feeling of dissociation, a frontal headache, and the distortion to color balance predominating in the reds. I could feel the effect of the drug coming on by definite symptoms or changes in feeling and perception. After taking the pill, I could feel the effects of the drug rolling back and experienced gayness and euphoria not to be expected under the circumstances of impending examinations and lack of sleep.

"The degree of euphoria experienced after nicotinamide seemed to be in inverse relation to the lapsed time since taking the drug. This would suggest that possibly one of the effects of the drug was to create within the body some biochemical reaction against the drug which, when the depressant effects of the drug were blocked by niacin, led to a supercharging of the system with the euphoriant material. This is parallel to the case with alcohol; blocking the depressant effect of the alcohol with niacin allows a long-lasting and extremely pleasant euphoriant condition to persist.

"It would be difficult to speculate on the action of the niacinamide in this particular case. I think that a parallel may be drawn to the LSD experience in that niacin in that case had only a selective effect. In other words, it did not rule out the LSD experience but controlled a portion of it, the perceptual, and thus modified the experience markedly. I would suggest that the amide taken did not reinstate creative processes or remedy the minor thought disorder resulting from the adrenolutin taken. I think that perhaps the niacin only controlled the depression and mood affect, the headache, the perceptual distortion, and the feelings of dissociation. I know that I was clear throughout the experience and capable of carrying out routine performances such as driving a car. I do not think that I could have done mental arithmetic or integrative reasoning much better after the amide than I did before.

"I was particularly impressed by the amount of amide required to keep a minor amount of change in hand. One gram of amide at a dose was minimum amount that would have any effect. I did not try any more than that although I would suggest that this should be done. When I purposely cut the dosage down to 0.5 gram I felt that I was on the edge of the drug effect and I had to soon take another 0.5 gram to pull myself out of it.

"My concluding comment is to the effect that, for further experimentation, I shall choose alcohol, LSD, and adrenolutin in that order. It was only when euphoria was in effect that I really had much fun out of the adrenolutin. Very dull stuff, indeed!"

Since these early experiments, we have given nicotinic acid or nicotinamide to subjects who had prolonged reactions to adrenolutin or to LSD.

Szatmari *et al.* (1955) reported that adrenochrome given to epileptics by injection produced major alteration in the EEG recordings. Eight of the epileptics received 50 mg of adrenochrome. All felt slightly sleepy or drowsy and two experienced a feeling that a seizure was developing. In two others, there were feelings of strangeness and unreality. Generally, the following EEG changes were recorded: (a) a decrease of 2 per second in the basic frequency, (b) an approximate decrease of 30% in voltage in some and a marked increase in others, (c) an increase in the dysrhythmic pattern and in hypersynchrony, and (d) an increase in activity of the focus.

Nicotinic acid was given intravenously after the adrenochrome effect had been determined. The dose was at least 400 mg. In normal controls, it produced a slight increase in frequency and a decrease in voltage. These results corroborated Darrow *et al.* (1951). With the epileptic patients, the adrenochrome effect was reversed. In every case, there was a shift in frequency to the fast side with a decreaes in voltage. The paroxysmal discharge was decreased in intensity but the focus continued with the same activity. It was less sensitive to hyperventilation. Subsequently, most epileptics felt more alert and fresh after receiving the nicotinic acid.

Anxiety and Adrenochrome

Early in our work with adrenochrome and adrenolutin we were recurrently surprised by the reduction or absence of anxiety in our normal volunteers who were given these hallucinogens. We expected that LSD-like reactions would result and in our experiences until 1955 we very seldom found that these psychotomimetic reactions contained much relaxation from anxiety. On the contrary, they were characterized by a good deal of anxiety, tension, and heightened awareness of the environment and self. But adrenochrome markedly reduced anxiety as did adrenolutin.

Anxiety and Adrenolutin

In our early studies, when 25–50 mg of adrenolutin were given orally to volunteers, nearly half of them felt much less anxious. Those who received a placebo continued to be more tense and anxious than those who had the adrenolutin. Eccles (1957) reports an interesting clinical finding noted by physicians many years ago, that 10 drops of adrenaline taken as a drink proved very effective in controlling the vomiting of pregnancy. This has been used recently with success. Adrenaline may have been converted into adrenolutin in the alkaline medium of the duodenum and this may well be the active factor.

Here are excerpts from the accounts of normal volunteers who took adrenolutin.

Subject L (psychiatrist):
I don't feel very talkative. I felt sort've contented and a little detached. As a matter of fact at that time you were talking to me and yet I didn't want to be left alone. It feels like I've had a mild sedative.

Subject H (psychiatric nurse): She became drowsy one half hour after taking 50 mg of adrenolutin by mouth. She tried to dispel this by walking up and down a long corridor but the drowsiness remained and lasted twenty minutes. Later, her arms felt more relaxed than the rest of her body and then she became completely relaxed. That evening at home, she felt unusually lazy and allowed her guests to straighten up her apartment after a party without helping them.

Subject C (psychologist): He had a general feeling of lassitude and apathy.

Subject C (psychiatrist):
I took 50 mg of the drug yesterday at 5:50 PM. I can remember quite clearly all that happened. Before taking the drug, I was aware of mild anxiety as I had no idea what was going to happen and I suspected that the experience might prove quite a terrifying one. My anxiety increased a little after taking the drug. At 6:05 PM, I recall being aware of my heart pounding a little. I looked at my watch and decided that this was unlikely to be the effect of the drug so soon after taking it. Then, over the next twenty minutes or so the anxiety steadily de-

creased until by about 6:30 PM it was replaced by a feeling of complete indifference. This feeling is difficult to describe. It was unlike anything I have experienced before. I felt peculiarly detached but quite well aware of what was going on. Also from this point on I think I became a very passive participant in the experiment. Previously I had felt a keen sense of interest, curiosity, and even slight apprehension about the experience; now I felt no urge to cooperate in volunteering information about my feelings. They put me through a few tests of perception of time and distance. These gave me no trouble and I felt mildly pleased at being able to do them. The tests required only short answers which was just as well as I did not feel any desire to talk for more than a few seconds. Although I was well aware of what was going on, I felt very little interest in it. At 7:30 PM I went to the EEG department. I remember contrasting this visit with the one in the afternoon before I took the drug.

During the afternoon I chatted away with the technician and was interested in all that was going on; now as a person he hardly existed for me. I felt no interest in him whatsoever. As he moved my head around to apply the band I remember thinking that was like one of the monkeys treated with Serpasil in a recent Ciba film-passive, compliant, emotionally flat but awake and well aware of what was going on. I know that if I communicated this thought with . . . he would ask for more details and I felt I could not be bothered pursuing the matter so I remained silent. Generally I think there was marked poverty of thought by this time. For long periods I would just be content to remain in the one position. I remember thinking while sitting in a chair in the EEG department that I would remain there for hours. Occasional thoughts passed through my mind while the EEG was being taken, e.g., that this was probably what a leucotomized patient, or perhaps a simple schizophrenic, felt like but I was quite incapable of pursuing or elaborating on this thought. I also remember feeling that I had lost the capacity to feel joy, sorrow, or indeed any powerful emotion. I thought of John Stuart Mill's remark 'better an unhappy man than a contented pig' which he made in discussing the qualities of pleasure but to continue any philosophical train of thought was beyond me. I did feel though that I had been reduced to a vegetative level.

For long periods, my mind was quite blank; I felt contented to lie and not think about anything. I realize this now—but about 8:20 PM when . . . said he was having to almost force answers out of me, I was mildly surprised and I did not seem to be as clearly aware of this change as I am now. I did not care about . . . remark as I had now no interest in the experiment, his feelings, or anything else. During the time the EEG was taken, I lay perfectly relaxed. I was mildly anxious to know what would happen when photic stimulation was applied. As it turned out the sensation was not particularly striking. I saw many colored dots in asymmetrical patterns. I think all the colors of the spectrum were there. Earlier in the afternoon I had merely seen concentric circles of light against a background which was first black then dark blue. While the EEG was in progress . . . came back into the room. For a moment his face looked much more dark and sombre than usual, almost threatening. So did . . . but the impression was momentary. Otherwise, I was unaware of any perceptual disturbance.

When I left the EEG department at 8:00 PM or thereabout, I was beginning to feel more 'alive.' On my way over to the Munroe Wing, I saw some patients playing croquet. I felt a transient rush of pleasure at the sight of the grass, trees, and the activities of the patients and recall realizing with a jerk just how automaton-like I had been feeling. I still felt dull and detached nevertheless, and not at all interested in talking to anyone. More tests of perception were now administered;

these I did without difficulty and then . . . gave me some of Sargent's Insight and Empathy Tests to do. For some reason, I felt most unwilling to do these. In the first place, I did not read the instructions properly and thought I was to tell a story around the theme mentioned. Then I noticed I was supposed to put myself in the position of the people mentioned. I found this hard to do. I felt no interest in the test. I did one question, then hoped . . . would forget about the other. When he did not I proceeded slowly with the second. It seemed to me that I merely applied previously acquired psychological knowledge to the situations. I did not really feel myself in them. I felt little interest and tried to make my answers as succinct as possible. I found this test involved a definite unpleasant sense of effort, whereas I rather enjoyed the perceptual ones. At 9:00 PM I left for home. I now felt much better. When I reached home my wife remarked that my pupils seemed somewhat dilated. She also noticed that I was slightly withdrawn. I now felt much better, however, but fatigued (which I had not noticed before). I was glad to turn into bed around 10:30 AM. Prior to that I was able to enjoy 'Pictures from an Exhibition' by Mussorgsky and Ravel though less intensely than usual. This morning after leaving home I felt rather dull and flat but the phenomenon was quite mild. Now (12 noon) I feel almost normal. This morning I carried out my usual duties without difficulty (including an LP); less interested in the patients than usual.

In summary, the outstanding features of the experience as I remember were:

1. Marked reduction in drive and interest with resulting poor concentration.

2. Inability to feel deeply. Diminished empathy towards others.

3. Complete absence of anxiety.

4. No gross perceptual anomaly. (The feeling about . . . face was slight, fleeting.)

5. Subjectively the intellectual functions seemed undisturbed but I seemed to lack the drive necessary to continue a thought out to its conclusion.

6. Lack of interest in myself and indifference to what others thought of me. Although clearly aware that a change had occurred in me, I found it hard to make a critical appraisal of this because I seemed to have lost the urge to do so.

The subject's account was in agreement with observations made of him by Dr. D. Blewett[2] and ourselves. Fifteen minutes after taking the drug, he had a "far-away feeling." At 20 minutes, he had a strong feeling of being far away or indifferent similar to the feeling he once had on very prolonged guard duty (36 hours). He had to fight physical exhaustion and fatigue. Toward the end of the duty, things appeared mechanical and far away. He had the same feeling now but without weariness or fatigue. At 35 minutes, when he was describing his feelings, Hoffer asked him "Have you ever felt this way when you were extremely anxious?" He replied, "Well, no, no." "I don't feel anxious at all now. I don't feel at all like that." At 45 minutes, he reported he was very relaxed and could stay where he was for long periods of time without becoming anxious.

When we conducted the double blind controlled comparison study of

[2] Supervising Psychologist, Psychiatric Services Branch, Department of Public Health, Regina, Saskatchewan.

adrenolutin against a riboflavin placebo (Hoffer, 1957a,b) special attention was given to anxiety, mood, and level of interest, since these are linked phenomena.

The effect of adrenolutin upon anxiety and other indices of mood changes have already been described.

5,6-Dihydroxy-*N*-methylindole

In 1957, Hoffer had the good fortune to meet Dr. Deltour, Medical Director of LABAZ, and Drs. Melander and Hellstrom of KABI at the psychopharmacology meeting in Milan. Dr. Deltour and Dr. Hoffer had a detailed private discussion of the properties of adrenochrome and its semicarbazide (adrenoxyl). Adrenoxyl is recommended for use as a hemostatic substance. There is no general agreement that its hemostatic activity is remarkable. However, many physicians use it regularly for their patients who have undergone surgery. Apparently this use is expanding. If its hemostatic properties are so uncertain why is it used? There are two possibilities: (a) that these physicians have blindly accepted the advertising claims and that their patients would do as well on placebo, or (b) that the physicians have observed that the patients either feel better or do better when given adrenoxyl. We prefer for the moment to accept the second possibility as more probable. If there is some improvement in the way these patients feel (most surgeons lean heavily on the subjective response of their patients and do not use objective tests) even though the increase in hemostatic ability is not remarkable, then there must be another reason. Perhaps adrenoxyl makes people feel better because, like Marsilid, it is a euphoriant. Their physicians would ascribe the improvement to the only known property of adrenoxyl which is its hemostatic action.

Pursuing this line of thought, Dr. Deltour remembered that some surgical patients did remark on their feeling of well-being after receiving adrenoxyl.

We have made a few preliminary trials with adrenoxyl on normal volunteers. It seems to have some euphoriant activity. It would not be very surprising if it inhibited amine oxidase for it is a semicarbazide and has some similarity in chemical structure to Marsilid and some newer analogs.

But adrenoxyl is normally not present in the body nor is it readily hydrolyzed. Our interest has been in naturally occurring antitension substances so we studied derivatives of adrenochrome which might be present in the body.

Discussions with Melander reinforced these possibilities. According to

Melander, adrenochrome and adrenolutin in small quantities produced changes in behavior in their animals. But if several times the amount of adrenochrome which will produce these changes in animals is treated with ascorbic acid and then all of this decolorized preparation is injected, no psychotomimetic changes are seen. This colorless substance was thought to be leucoadrenochrome which suggested that it, not being a psychotomimetic, might have some desirable properties, possibly as an antitension agent.

We could not explore this possibility until Heacock (1959) showed that "leucoadrenochrome" consists of several substances one of which is 5,6-dihydroxy-N-methylindole (DNMI).

This was synthesized and crystallized and became available for study late in 1958. Since then, we have run a substantial series of trials of this compound. Briefly, it has antitension or antianxiety properties when given in small dosages either sublingually or orally. These results with a case history will be given now.

Hoffer (1959a,b) examined the reaction of 10 mg of crystalline adrenochrome (from 1 adrenaline) given intravenously to 26 psychiatric patients. Each patient was informed this was a routine blood test. After the injection the patients were observed for changes in perception, thought and mood. The following changes were observed (see also Table 38).

TABLE 38

EFFECT OF ADRENOCHROME ON SEVERAL GROUPS OF SUBJECTS

Group	N	Tension			Visual changes	Other changes
		Increase	No change	Decrease		
Schizophrenic	13	3	4	6	8	10
Anxiety	5	0	0	5	2	1
Depression	3	1	0	2	0	2
Alcoholic	5	1	2	2	3	3
Total	26	5	6	15	13	16

Ten of the schizophrenics suffered an activation of their psychosis and six became less tense. Out of the other 13 nonschizophrenic patients, tension (anxiety) was decreased in 9.

These early observations led Hoffer (1957d) and Hoffer and Osmond (1960) to reconsider the role of adrenochrome in the body. As we pointed out adrenaline and noradrenaline are very toxic substances. As little as 1 mg of adrenaline has been known to kill an adult man when injected subcutaneously. Evolution was, therefore, faced with the interesting problem of how to dispose of such an essential toxic substance quickly. Not only were rapid detoxifying measures essential but these systems also had to be able to remove large quantities over long periods of time. The many reactive points on adrenaline have been reviewed. A change of any one would remove the main toxic quality.

But having detoxified the adrenaline it might be possible to use the metabolites as antiadrenalines or antitension compounds.

Hoffer and Osmond (1960) reviewed the antitension properties or 5,6-dihydroxy-N-methylindole. Normal subjects who were overly anxious, or tense, were usually relaxed a few minutes after they took this material sublingually. Depressed subjects also were benefited but it was impossible to predict by clinical criteria which subject would respond best. Some of our early subjects, tested in 1959, who did not respond later on were rediagnosed as malvaria, or schizophrenia. We will describe in detail only one case. This is the subject's own account.

Miss G. "The first depressive illness began when I was eleven years old. The symptoms, consolidated and categorized some ten years later, were: feelings of unhappiness and lack of worth, fear including a strong unreasoning fear of death, insomnia especially with early waking, loss of appetite, stomachaches, and tension which was manifested in restlessness and aching of skeletal muscles. This depression lasted four to six weeks, coming on suddenly and passing gradually as spring turned to summer.

"This depressed period was extraordinarily unpleasant for several reasons. More unpleasant than the physical discomfort was the fact that I had no explanation for this unhappy period and felt that I had no one in whom I could confide concerning my vague fears and general feelings of unhappiness and malaise. Symptoms are, after all, a physician's constructs. The patient has only a number of uncategorized feelings and changes in his physical state. Thus, the patient who consults his doctor about an illness, the nature of which he knows nothing about, may have great difficulty in describing his complaint and often may be reduced to statements like 'I don't know, doc, I just don't feel good.' Similarly a depressive, particularly a child, may see no connection between, for example, loss of appetite and feelings of unhappiness. Thus depressions may recur over a number of years before they are accurately diagnosed.

"The first depression I had been able to accept as an unpleasant experience similar to a nightmare. A year later, again in the spring, the second depressed period occurred. It was at this time, I think, that I began to question the nature of these depressions. The first thought was that these were a normal part of growing up, I began to read more widely—novels, biographies, autobiographies—to see if others mentioned these unhappy periods and to see how they coped with them. I watched my younger sister for signs of periodic unhappiness too, but she showed no evidence of them. At some point, I became aware of mental illness as a possible explanation. Like many people who know little about the subject, I assumed that mental illness dealt with changes in the mind and feelings only. Physical illness dealt with changes in the body. Understandably then, I split the symptoms into two groups and began to search for a physical basis for the tiredness and the stomach aches and for information on mental illness. Meanwhile the depressions increased from one a year at age 11 to two a year at age 13 and four a year by the time I was 17.

"During a late winter depression while I was 14, I had my first contact with a doctor since very early childhood. My mother became so worried about my complaints of stomachaches that I was hospitalized for a week for observation. The doctor was friendly, patted my arm, told me not to worry. She informed my mother that I had a nervous stomach. My fears were made worse—even the doctor could not diagnose my trouble. But some doctor must know the answer. In the next eight years I saw at least a dozen doctors, three psychiatrists and five psychologists, in an attempt to get, not so much a diagnosis but a course of action, some concrete way of dealing with this problem. I was told that I had ulcers, a hypothyroid condition, a nervous stomach, nothing wrong with me. The psychologists told me to stop worrying about my parents, not to study too hard, to apply myself to my studies more, to go out with more boys, to stop worrying. The psychiatrists told me very little at all, but it was suggested that I took things too seriously, had problems with my mother, was sexually inhibited, was jealous of my sisters. I gained a reputation for being hypochondriacal and neurotic. No one had asked me for the history of the depressions, told me what they were, given me any help in coping with them. And beyond answering their questions I could volunteer little information because I did not know what to tell them.

"Perhaps I should point out here that the patient has many sources of information. If he does not get an answer that is satisfactory to him from his doctor, he will look elsewhere for this satisfaction. He will read books and magazines, talk to other people, consult other professional persons, try to read over the shoulder of the doctor's receptionist or to overhear her conversation with the doctor. I, for example, learned that I was considered hypochondriacal by overhearing one nurse talking to another.

"This information, from whatever source, may be of little value to the patient. Unless it suggests some course of action, it is only confusing or disquieting. Let us take as an example the information given by the psychiatrist, that I was jealous of my sisters. What interpretations could be put upon this in relation to my illness?

1. I am depressed because I am jealous of my sisters, thus this has nothing to do with getting un-depressed.

2. I am jealous of my sisters because I am depressed. This has nothing to do with getting undepressed but it may suggest a way for becoming un-jealous.

3. I am depressed at least partly as a result of being jealous of my sisters. Getting un-depressed will be helped by becoming un-jealous.

4. I am depressed. I am jealous of my sisters. These propositions, though unrelated, are both interesting to the doctor.

"Unless the doctor spells out his interpretation, the patient and doctor may assume entirely different interpretations. The patient has consulted his doctor because he wants to know what to do to reduce his discomfort. If the doctor's information suggests no clear course of action to the patient, it serves only to increase the patient's fear and guilt,

"Inevitably these depressions caused changes in family relationships. A family may not realize that when one of its members becomes unhappy and tearful and does not seem to want to confide his troubles or to pull his load in the family, he is not being merely stubborn and hard to get along with, but is ill. A split occurred in our family. I became a member apart from the others, and my mother worried over the possible causes of this split. Over a period of years, she was told that I had a nervous stomach, that I took things too seriously, that I was jealous of my sisters. Yet the family, like the patient, requires a course of action, and information such as this, which did not suggest any definite course of action, only served to increase any guilt and worry already present, leading inevitably to further tension and disharmony within the family.

"At 17, I went for further schooling to a large city and was near a public library for the first time. In an old out-of-date book on mental illness I came upon a description of recurring elation and gloom called manic depressive psychosis. Though I was rarely elated and overcheerful, the description of depression did sound much like my own 'bad spells.' The outlook in this book was not at all good. I interpreted this information as meaning that my depressions would increase in number and severity until I had to be shut up (locked up) permanently in the 'looney house,' an irreparable family disgrace. For the first time I thought seriously of suicide; thereafter suicidal thoughts were often present during depressions.

"Because of these suicidal tendencies, I made a practice in the years that followed of confiding in one close friend in each town or city in which I lived. One girl in particular, a polio cripple who roomed next to me, had a very sensible attitude to the whole problem. During my depressions her door was always open. When I began to feel particularly unhappy I would go into her room. Rarely did she openly acknowledge my presence unless to offer me a cup of coffee, but I was not allowed to leave the house again that day unless in someone's company. Each night she would meet me after classes and we would walk home together. Such vigilance and matter-of-fact acceptance of these depressions helped greatly and almost certainly staved off several attempts at suicide.

"Such suicidal tendencies are not uncommon in depressives. I have mentioned the depressive's need for a definite course of action. Perhaps the great attraction of suicide for the depressive is just this, that it is something definite that the depressive can do about his illness. Yet even the depressed person usually realizes that suicide is a rather drastic solution to his depressed periods, a problem that will not last indefinitely. Thus the task of the depressed person and of his friends becomes one of providing alternatives or of delaying action until the depression passes. The depressed person must learn to recognize his suicidal tendencies as quite reasonable and therefore no cause for feeling guilty. Yet he must plan between times how to cope with these urges. Taking holidays at such times is most unwise; it is far easier to kill oneself in a lonely unfamiliar cabin in the Rockies than in one's own home among friends. Having a close friend one can talk to is invaluable. Often simply discussing these urges makes action unnecessary. At other times, the suicidal person may be too depressed to talk, and silent companionship is all that is needed. During a depression, a familiar routine among familiar surroundings does much to lessen suicidal tendencies.

"Anyone can help the depressed person who is feeling suicidal. From my own experience, the suidical periods are not present throughout the depressions, nor do they last for long periods of time. Furthermore, the depressed person knows when he is seriously considering suicide and when he is toying with the idea merely because he is feeling miserable. Any person who will act as an understanding nonjudgmental audience can help the suicidal depressive. If he can offer unobstrusive companionship, so much the better. Otherwise he should try to suggest someone who can provide this service. The depressive, after all, is not demanding at these times. It is not necessary and perhaps unwise to try to be amiable and to cheer him up. He cannot respond while he is ill and becomes tired and guilt-stricken or resentful if he tries and fails. The would-be cheerer is resentful of the depressive's apparent lack of gratitude and may cut off all relationships with him because of his un-responsiveness. Far better for both would have been a less effortful, less demanding relationship on the part of the cheerer. Silently walking the depressive home from work, offering him a cup of tea instead of cheery words, would be more rewarding for both parties. The main point is, after all, to keep in touch, to maintain some contact throughout the illness.

"I do not think most suicidal depressives consider the whole gamut of suicide methods. Most of them will settle for one or two, the choice depending upon the individual personality. To attempt to guard against all suicide methods is unnecessary and wholly frustrating for all concerned. I remember one occasion in which I was denied work in the ward kitchen of a mental hospital, a job which I had wanted to relieve the monotony of ward life and to keep my mind off my own problems. No explanation was given and I was thoroughly annoyed with the whole affair. Weeks later I learned that the staff considered me suicidal and were afraid to allow me access to the ward's one sharp knife. Yet I had always thought in terms of leaping off buildings or bridges and personally felt great distaste for such a gory method as throat-slitting or wrist-cutting.

"The depressive must avoid killing himself. He must also learn to live with his affliction. One of his major problems will be his choice of occupation. Slowly I realized that the incapacitating nature of these depressions each lasting several weeks and for which I had no treatment at that time, ruled out a number of vocations. These included all work involving numerous contacts with people, continuous daily applications of one's intellectual powers or tasks, involving continuous use of speed or manual dexterity. I was reasonably intelligent, so it appeared that research in one of the physical sciences would offer the greatest opportunities while still meeting the other requirements. The next task was to reach a high enough level in the field so that I could do most of the work on my own.

"Over a period of years I learned several other techniques for coping with the depressed periods. A rigid pattern of habits, a system of performing minor daily tasks proved extremely valuable. Even such details as getting up, brushing my teeth, making my bed, if done in the same order and same manner from day to day, tended to carry over into the depressed periods. Less thought and effort were required, leaving more energy for the other necessary tasks of existence. Fairly rigid patterns of sleeping hours and meal times made it easier to obtain what little sleep one could and gave some incentive for eating even when appetite was lacking. A tendency to overtidiness and neatness during well periods would prod one to make some effort to maintain outward appearances during depressions. Much has been written about the obsessional behavior of depressives yet perhaps the explanation simply lies in this fact, that many depressives find an ordered routine helps them to live with their illness. Rather than discouraging them from becoming obsessional then, depressives might better be encouraged to establish these routines which allow them to cope better when they are ill.

"I learned to avoid prolonged periods in bed when I found this often precipitated a depression or made a mild one worse. I learned to maintain a reasonable degree of physical activity from day to day. Yet I found that overtiring was not wise either, and to become overtired during a depression often meant an increase in suicidal tendencies. While I was depressed, I often found simple repetitive tasks to be very soothing. Almost ideal was the work of pricking thousands of seedlings into flats in the greenhouses. The work was in comfortable, quiet surroundings, usually with a silent companion, and required just enough effort to keep me occupied without being overtired.

"Friendships are a more difficult thing for the depressive than for the normal person. Inevitably his friends must consider him as different, whether they realize that he goes through periodic depressions or simply consider him odd and unpredictable. During depressions there is a lack of interest in other people and little energy to be put into maintaining friendships. If the depressive's companions recognize and accept this, so much the better. If they can realize that their depressive friend isn't capable of functioning normally at these times, that he probably will need silent support but prefers no sympathy or positive show of feelings, that this state will probably last only a few weeks with a gradual return to normal, then their friendship can be of real value. Yet often, because the depressive himself does not understand the nature of his illness or because he does not wish others to know, the problem is greatly confounded. The depressive must then put far greater effort into his relations with others. During his normal periods he must make his friendship so worthwhile and interesting to others that they will condone his inexplicable periodic lack of interest and avoidance of them. By developing a reputation for being erratic, by becoming a 'character,' he can maintain at least some semblance of normal human relationships.

"During my depressions up to the age of 17, I came to rely greatly upon my pets and particularly upon my horse. Often during these depressed periods I would go for long quiet rides or would sit petting her or watching her eat. Because our relationship did not depend on verbal communication as human relationships do to such a large extent, this relationship remained stable and served as a life line or reference point throughout these depressed periods. Perhaps depressives would be well advised to obtain a pet for this reason. The person who had set up permanent residence would probably have a wide choice of animals, but even the person who must move frequently could have a small dog, a bird, or a hamster. Such an idea is after all not new, for the Retreat Hospital in York, England, has encouraged its patients to keep pets since the 1790's.

"Twelve years after the first depression I had my first discussion about depressions as such, and about my depressions in particular, with a medical person. Much of the information that I had picked up through reading and observation during the intervening years was erroneous or misleading. From him I received a description of the probable course of the illness during my lifetime, the types of treatment now available, and certain precautions that may ward off a depressive episode. Half the battle was over. I now had a clear picture of the problem and could outline a good plan of action. Humans are, after all, singularly inept at battling with ghosts.

"I wonder if any thought has ever been given to developing a depressive's equivalent to A.A. Surely no one would know quite as well how to help a suicidal depressive as another person who has had a similar experience. The depressive does need companionship during his suicidal periods, and who could understand this better than someone who himself has been through suicidal episodes? I suspect that more than a few depressives feel guilty about their depressed periods, having been told from childhood that low spirits are simply an indication that the person needs to 'buck up' and 'snap out of it.' What could be more reassuring than to speak to someone who had had similar experiences? Such an organization could be reassuring to the ill, and through actively helping each other, the dangerous tendencies to self-invalidism and self-pity might be largely eliminated in the well."

Here follows the account of her response by H. Osmond.

Miss G. was, for her, moderately ill and from her history it seemed likely that her illness would continue for about another 3 weeks, and then it would slowly remit. During this period of remission she would have brief periods of tense elation followed by a return of depression. The main question was whether she could remain at work under supervision. There was some danger of suicide but she could talk about these fears so that I felt it would be safe to see her as an out-patient. I gave her a few slow release capsules of dexedrine and amytal. On August 22nd she took one of these with some transient benefit but on

August 22nd she was still severely depressed so that it was very difficult to sustain any conversation with her. On 8/24/58 when I saw her again she was in much the same state. It happened that I had a single 3-mg tablet of DNMI, one of about 12 which had been made as samples. Without much hope that it would help her I decided to try it, knowing that it could do no harm and this was, in fact, what she was told. "It can't harm you and it may help." At about 2:30 PM she put the tablet under her tongue. I did not question her at all closely because I did not want to suggest improvement, though I have never previously had any success from suggestion in depressions of this sort. In about an hour she seemed more relaxed and remarked spontaneously that "the muscles in the back of my neck feel easier." From this point she was clearly calmer, more cheerful and more spontaneous. She went on night duty and slept well later which she had not been doing before. Her appetite returned. Five days after she had received this single 3-mg tablet she still looked very well and remarked that her depression had lifted far more quickly and dramatically than usual. This first episode was so unexpected that I did not observe the crucial hour after taking the tablet as closely as I did later on. A remarkable change had undoubtedly occurred, but how far was leucoadrenochrome responsible for this? On the next two occasions when she needed leuco adrenochrome, which were September 4th and September 22nd, I was able to observe her far more closely. This is how she described her condition on September 22nd (1958):

> Very difficult to arouse enough interest to establish contact with people. Suicidal thoughts present. A dull, tight feeling just above and behind the eyes and at base of the skull. Colors dull. Could not become interested in surroundings even with exertion of will. Air of unreality about surrounding objects. Felt they did not exist. But could not rouse from apathy enough to be interested in them or to be affected by them. Felt like crying but also felt unable to summon enough energy to do so. At supper, almost started to cry when spoken to. Given DNMI by Dr. Osmond at approximately 9:15 PM. At 9:40, began to feel completely neutral, neither happy nor unhappy as though there has been a cessation of everything but existence. No desires or wishes. Conscious only of breathing, physical existence. 9:45: Suddenly felt like laughing, felt a need to move about, to break spell. Feeling of unreality. Giggled several times for no apparent reason. 9:50: Felt very much alive, cheerful, wished to smile. Conscious of sudden complete mood change including physical symptoms, and somewhat bewildered by it. Felt confident I could maintain a conversation. Somewhat talkative. Colors brighter. Interested and aware of surrounding. 10:30: Relaxed feeling of sleepiness setting in. Returned home. Cheerful, alert, self-confident. Chatted with several people. Very conscious of complete mood shift and inwardly pleased and excited about it. Eight hours quiet sleep. Excellent appetite. Finished book, light fiction, with enjoyment on September 23rd. Wished to study. No difficulty in concentration or comprehension. Realistic. Neither unduly optimistic or pessimistic attitude on problems.

My own notes taken at the time on the identical episode, written without reference to Miss G.'s notes, are: "She was clearly not well, looked tense, edgy, pallid—a tautness of the facial skin. Her words came slowly, her conversation was not spontaneous and I felt she might at any moment burst into tears. She had been well until September 20th. She said she did not feel tense, just depressed and described her condition as 'quite rough.'"

9:55 PM. I gave her 3 mg of my second batch of DNMI sublingually. I gave no special suggestion except to say what she already knew, that it had helped before. She sat on the chesterfield opposite me rather stiffly, as if she was a doll stuck on one position. Her expression and voice were all slightly wooden and it was an effort to talk with her.

10:10 PM. She made no comment and no questions asked. Shortly after this she began to look easier. The tautness seemed to have gone out of her face.

10:12 PM. I asked if DNMI had dissolved and she said yes.

10:15 PM. She laughed a little and picked up a book and began to read which she had not attempted to do before.

10:20 PM. She spoke much more spontaneously and said about herself: "This was an unpleasant happening, out of the frying pan into the sieve." She walked around the living room into our kitchen and began to laugh. I thought she might be crying at first but she was not. She returned to the living room at 10:25 saying, "It seems very stupid to laugh at nothing." She was clearly feeling much better.

10:30 PM. She was very talkative and cheery.

10:40 PM. She was much more talkative and easy. Much more relaxed. Her face beams and is more mobile. Her voice has a different timbre. Discusses the unfortunate happening as, "this very, very unpleasant business." She did not volunteer what this was and was not pressed to do so.

10:43 PM. Talkative, laughing, cheery, moving her hands freely.

10:45 PM. She is asked directly, "How are you feeling?" She then said that at about 22:15 [10:15 PM] there was this "indescribable lull. You don't feel happy or depressed. Nothing good or bad. Nothing right or wrong." However, this is a great improvement on her previous feeling. She now feels that she could concentrate which she could not do last night or earlier this evening. Colors look brighter.

H.O.: "When you are low they don't feel so bright?"
  G: "No, I no longer feel like crying."
H.O.: "How does this compare with the previous time?"
  G: "More like the first time I took it."
H.O.: "How?"
  G: "There was not the very sudden change I noticed the second time."
H.O.: "You were different?"
  G: "The second time I felt extremely tense but not depressed."
H.O.: "How does this compare with Dexamyl?"
  G: "The Dexamyl feels as if I were under sedation. You feel there was an artificial lid."
H.O.: "How does this feel?"
  G: "At the moment I feel there has been a rapid change."

She then added that she felt relieved and happy about this because she is not used to a change in mood upward at this speed. Mood change upward usually takes a day or more.

H.O.: "Different from Dexamyl?"
  G.: "Yes, definitely."
H.O.: "How about your feelings about this misfortune?"
  G.: "(confidently and smiling) "It will clear up."
H.O.: "How did you feel better?"
  G.: "I could realize it would straighten out but I didn't really believe this. (Spontaneously) Another thing suicide thoughts were very strong today, twice, and seemed to remain in the background. At the moment the whole thing seems pointless and there seems no good reason for wanting to do so."

11:00 PM. She was playing with the dog at this time and smiling easily.

H.O.: "What happens when you study?"
  G.: "Very little, it is very difficult to concentrate."

Reading assignments which should take half an hour would take a whole evening. Last night she read 2½ pages in three quarters of an hour which she would expect to do in 15 minutes.

11:45 PM. When she left she was cheerful and relaxed, friendly and talking freely. She said that she felt tired and needed a good night's sleep. She was clearly not depressed. Just before she left, she said, "I wondered whether it would work. The first time I was depressed and tense. The second time tense but not depressed. This time depressed and not tense." Clearly she had never gone from depression to normality so smoothly and quickly.

I think it proper to add that I was far from confident on this occasion but the result was clearcut and gratifying. There was no borderline improvement. In less than an hour a very depressed girl stopped being depressed. It was a dramatic and extremely convincing demonstration.

At 22:00 [10:00 PM] she was obviously depressed. At 22:30 [10:30 PM] she was obviously not depressed. The break-up of her depression came between 22:10 [10:10] and 22:25 [10:25]. It was like one of those speeded up films in which a flower suddenly unfolds in front of your eyes. It is the sort of thing one has never in fact seen before because it is not usually seen naturally and so is very disconcerting.

For the next 10 months Miss G. continued to take DNMI. Apart from unusual happenings, such as being confined to bed, she appears to need about one 3-mg tablet every 14 to 21 days. At the time of writing these notes, June 10, 1959, she has taken 30 tablets in 280 days. (Breakdown on tablets taken: Time: August 24, 1958–May 31, 1959, 280 days. Number of tablets: 30.[3]) In recent months she has not waited for her depression to develop fully but has taken the tablets when the first symptoms appear. She believes her life has altered substantially and she writes about her present condition in a recent note:

When I first started taking DNMI in August, 1958, it was used only when I was noticeably depressed or extremely tense, as a treatment for a condition already present. Now (June, 1959) I am using it at the onset of a depression to prevent a depression from developing.

Understandably, the use of DNMI has produced a marked change in my pattern of living. Over half my life (age 11–23) has been a pattern of recurrent depressions and longer or shorter intervening periods of normalcy. Thus, this past ten months has been a period unlike any other than I can clearly remember. Inevitably, it has been a period of unalloyed joy at having a 'magic cure' for an unpleasant illness. Though a physician may have an almost unbounded faith in the efficacy of his treatment, his patient may not. Where the condition recurs, as depressions do, there is uncertainty whether the treatment will always effect a cure, and there is always a period of testing the limits of a new treatment too. During the last ten months I have learned that DNMI is quite effective in controlling the mood drop that usually occurs when I spend any long period in bed, but that its efficacy may be affected by certain other drugs, the exact types of which are not clear.

Then there is the adjustment to a continuous normalcy—the reassessment of plans for one's vocation, another look at one's friendships and relations with other people, a settling down to a normal tempo of existence, that does not include preparation for periodic relative incapacity.

As I stated earlier I now use DNMI at the first indication of a depression's onset. I feel that I can distinguish the symptoms of depression from normal mood swings and thus am not using it unnecessarily. Thus, I may feel unhappy, or not sleep well one night after an exciting evening, or notice a sharp drop in my appetite due to fatigue or hot weather, or develop soreness in the muscles of my back, arms and legs after an upsetting evening and restless night's sleep; I may feel apathetic, and lacking in energy one day at work. None of these are, to me, indications of a need for DNMI. These are normal occurrences or personal idiosyncrasies. Only if several of these are present concurrently, and are accompanied by

[3] Including: 2 for car sickness, 6 in 19 days bedrest, and 4 in 2 double doses in 3 days.

some disturbance of thought patterns, do they indicate to me the onset of a depression.

DNMI has not brought about any leveling of what I consider to be normal mood swings. I may be particularly enthusiastic or happy one day, lose my temper on occasion, have days in which I may accomplish a good deal, others in which I may putter aimlessly. But through using leuco, essentially as a prophylactic, I am producing a protracted 'normal period' that I now expect to continue over a period of ten years.

Adrenochrome Monosemicarbazone

Adrenochrome monosemicarbazone (adrenoxyl), Statimo in Canada, Adrenosem in the United States, Adona (AC-17 in Japan) is relatively insoluble but has been solubilized by the addition of other substances. It is used widely as a hemostatic agent. This property easily demonstrated in animals is not as clear in human subjects. However, recently Burke *et al.* (1960) using a double blind controlled comparison study showed that Adrenosem and AC-17 reduced bleeding very substantially after transurethral resections. Whereas 48 patients given no treatment lost 256 ml of blood and 17 gm of tissue, 41 subjects given Adrenosem or AC-17 lost about 55 ml of blood and 4.5 gm of tissue.

We have already referred to our preliminary trials with this compound which suggested it was an euphorient substance. But our interest in 5,6-dihydroxyindole absorbed our interest and we did no more with it. However, when it became clear the dihydroxy-N-methylindole would not be generally available we once more turned our attention to adrenochrome monosemicarbazone.

Theoretically it could replace 5,6-dihydroxy-N-methylindole in our equation relating tension, adrenaline, and the dihydroxyindole. In addition, it was an azide and so might be expected to be an amine oxidase inhibitor like iproniazid, etc. Our earlier suggestion was corroborated spontaneously by Lucas (1964) who reported that while he was doing research on hemostasis his director conducted a controlled study of several hemostatic agents including Adrenosem. The experiment was carried out double blind. At the end of the experiment the project director was very concerned because the medications were not significantly different from each other for the control of bleeding. The only effect that was observed was that patients receiving Adrenosem became very happy, complained less, and had a much more pleasant postoperative course after dental surgery. No toxic reactions were seen.

Ernest and Agnew (1964) completed a carefully controlled double blind experiment comparing Adrenosem against matched placebo tablets containing the same ingredients present in the active tablets but without any Adrenosem. Normal volunteers were used and set was biased by careful preparation of the volunteers into a group who were allowed to remain neutral and a group who were made anxious. The dose was 50 mg of Adrenosem. It was hypothesized that Adrenosem would counteract tension, restlessness, dizziness, and irritability.

The results from self-rating scales indicated trends in the direction of mild stimulation by the drug. Some results reached significance. Out of 15 drug subjects who returned their questionnaires, 7 out of 15 showed evidence of stimulation. None of 12 placebo subjects were stimulated. ($P < 0.05$). Performance measures showed drug subjects performed less well on simple tasks, required more time on the word association test, and were slightly superior on more complex tasks. Their conclusion was that Adrenosem produced the subjective sensations of a stimulant drug and the performance effects of a depressant.

This was a very rigorous test since antidepressant drugs as a rule do not have as much effect on normal people as they have on those who are very anxious or depressed.

In contrast to adrenochrome its monosemicarbazone is an activator of glutamic acid decarboxylase, Deltour *et al.* (1959). This suggests that if semicarbazides could combine *in vivo* with adrenochrome they should be therapeutic for schizophrenia and should have antitension and antidepressive properties. But since semicarbazides are very reactive substances they would interfere at many metabolic sites and obscure any effect through GABA formation.

REFERENCES

Abood, L. G. (1957). "Conference on Biochemistry and Mental Illness." U.B.C., Vancouver.

Abood, L. G., Gibbs, F. A., and Gibbs, E. (1957). *A.M.A. Arch. Neurol. Psychiat.* **77**:643.

Akerfeldt, S. (1957a). *Science* **125**:117.

Akerfeldt, S. (1957b). "Serological Reaction of Psychiatric Patients to *N,N*-Dimethyl-*p*-Phenylenediamine." A.P.A. Meeting.

Alberty, J., and Takkunen, R. (1956). *Experientia* **12**:152.

Altschule, M. D. (1960). *J. Neuropsychiat.* **2**:71.

Altschule, M. D. (1962a). "Hyperaminochromia." A.P.A. Meeting, Toronto.

Altschule, M. D. (1962b). *Diseases Nervous System* **23**:592.

Amdisen, A. (1965). *Acta Psychiat. Neurol. Scand.* Suppl. 180, p. 411.

Angel, C., Leach, B. E., Martens, S., Cohen, M., and Heath, R. G. (1957). *A.M.A. Arch. Neurol. Psychiat.* **78**:500.

Angenent, W. J., and Koelle, G. B. (1952). *Science* **116**:543.

Anguiano, G., Villasana, A., Chavira, R. A., and Montano, C. (1958). *Bol. Inst. Estud. Med. Biol. (Mex.)* **16**:1.

Annals of the New York Academy of Sciences. (1965). **117**:647.

Ansley, H. R., Sheldon, W. H., Tenney, A. M., and Elderkin, R. D. (1957). *Diseases Nervous System* **18**:444.

Appel, K. E., Myers, J. M., and Morris, H. H. (1958). *In* "Schizophrenia: A review of the syndrome" (L. Bellak, ed.), p. 547. Logos Press, New York.

Armstrong, M. D., McMillan, A., and Shaw, K. N. F. (1957). *Biochim. Biophys. Acta* **25**:422.

Asher, R. (1949). *Brit. Med. J.* **II**:555.

Axelrod, J. (1964). *Biochim. Biophys. Acta* **85**:247.

Bacq, Z. M. (1949). *J. Pharmacol. Exptl. Therap.* **95**:1.

Bain, J. (1957). *Ann. N.Y. Acad. Sci.* **66**:459.

Bain, W. A., Gaunt, W. E., and Suffolk, S. F. (1937). *J. Physiol. (London)* **91**:233.

Ban, A., and Lehmann, H. E. (1965). *Can. Psych. Assoc. J.* **10**:112.

Banshikoff, V. M., and Stolaroff, G. V. (1963). *J. Neuropathol. Psychiat.* **63**:295.

Barsel, N. (1964). *Chem. Abstr.* **60**:506.

Bean, J. W. (1956). *Am. J. Physiol.* **187**:389.

Bean, J. W. (1965). *Ann. N.Y. Acad. Sci.* **117**:745.

Bean, J. W., and Johnson, P. C. (1955). *Am. J. Physiol.* **180**:438.

Beard, A. W. (1959). *Acta Psychiat. Neurol. Scand.* **34**:411.

Beauvillain, A., and Sarradin, J. (1948). *Bull. Ste. Chim. Biol.* **30**:472.

Bellak, L. (1948). "Dementia Praecox." Grune & Stratton, New York.

Bennett, P. B. (1963). *Am. J. Physiol.* **205**:1013.

Bergen, J. R., and Beisaw, N. E. (1956). *Am. Physiol. Soc.* **15**:15.

Billewicz-Stankiewicz, J., Szczekala, Z., and Tyburczyk, W. (1964). *Experientia* **20**:85.

Bischoff, A. (1952). *Monatsschr. Psychiat. Neurol.* **124**:211.

Blaschko, H., and Schlossmann, H. (1940). *J. Physiol. (London)* **98**:130.

Bleuler, M., and Zurgilgen, B. A. (1949). *Wien. Med. Wochschr.* **99**:357.

Bonasera, N., and Criscuoli, P. M. (1961). *Acta Neurol. (Naples)* **16**:329.

Boszormenyi-Nagy, I., and Gerty, F. J. (1955). *Am. J. Psychiat.* **112**:11.

Braines, C. H., Konev, C. B., Golubieva, G. P., Kuchino, E. B., and Kobrinckaio, O. J. (1959). *In* "Biophysical Research in Psychiatry" (C. H. Braines, ed.), p. 178. Inst. Psychiat., Acad. Med. Sci. U.S.S.R., Moscow.

Brenner, W., and Breier, A. (1949). *Z. Kinderheilk.* **66**:620.

Briggs, M. H. (1962a). Personal communication.

Briggs, M. H. (1962b). *Brit. Med. J.* **I**:1078.

Briggs, M. H., and Harvey, N. (1962). *Life Sci.* **2**:61.

Brodny, M. L. (1955). *A.M.A. Arch. Neurol. Psychiat.* **73**:410.

Brody, E. B., and Man, E. B. (1950). *Am. J. Psychiat.* **107**:357.

Buck, C. W., Carscallen, H. B., and Hobbs, G. E. (1950). *A.M.A. Arch. Neurol. Psychiat.* **64**:828.

Buck, C. W., Carscallen, H. B., and Hobbs, G. E. (1951). *A.M.A. Arch. Neurol. Psychiat.* **65**:197.

Bullough, W. S. (1952). *J. Endocrinol.* **8**:265.

Bullough, W. S. (1955). *Vitamins Hormones* **13**:261.

Bullough, W. S., and Rytomaa, T. (1965). *Nature* **205**:573.

Burke, D. E., Pogrund, R. S., and Clark, W. G. (1960). *Clin. Res.* 8:127.

Burn, J. H. (1952). *Brit. Med. J.* I:784.

Campbell, D. (1965). Week End Magazine, Calgary.

Cerletti, A. (1956). *Neuropharmacol., Trans. 2nd Conf., 1955* p. 9. Josiah Macy, Jr. Found., New York.

Claude, H., and Bernard, S. (1924). *Encephale* 19:1.

Cohen, G. (1959). *Federation Proc.* 18:378.

Cohen, G., and Hochstein, P. (1963). *Diseases Nervous System* 24: Monthly Suppl., 44.

Cohen, L. H. (1939). *Psychosomat. Med.* 1:414.

Connell, P. H. (1957). *J. Biochem.* 65:7.

Cousteau, J. Y., and Dumas, F. (1953). "The Silent World." Harper, New York.

Croot, J. R., Creveling, C. R., and Udenfriend, S. (1961). *J. Pharmacol. Exptl. Therap.* 132:269.

Danziger, L. (1958). *Diseases Nervous System* 19:374.

Danziger, L., and Kindwall, J. A. (1953). *Diseases Nervous System* 14:3.

Danziger, L., and Kindwall, J. A. (1954). *Diseases Nervous System* 15:35.

Darrow, C. W., Rosenthal, M. J., Arnott, G. P., and Brudo, C. (1951). *Electroencephalog. Clin. Neurophysiol.* 3:382.

Deltour, G. H., Ghuysen, J. M., and Claus, A. (1959). *Biochem. Pharmacol.* 1:267.

Denisoff, B. M. (1964). *Ukr. Biochem. J.* 36:711.

Dern, R. J., Glynn, M. F., and Brewer, G. J. (1963). *J. Lab. Clin. Med.* 62:319.

Derouaux, G., and Roskam, J. (1949). *J. Physiol. (London)* 108:1.

Donovan, C., and Osmond, H. (1963). *Mind* 1:42.

Doust, J. W. L., Husdan, H., and Salna, M. E. (1956). *Nature* 178:492.

Dumont, J. E., and Hupka, S. (1963). *Compt. Rend. Soc. Biol.* 156:1942.

Eade, N. R. (1954). M.Sc. Thesis, University of Saskatchewan, Saskatoon.

Eccles, O. (1957). *Lancet* 2:244.

Ehrensvard, G., Liljekvist, J., and Heath, R. G. (1960). *Acta Chem. Scand.* 14:2081.

Ellis, S. (1956). *Pharmacol. Rev.* 8:485.

Ernest, C., and Agnew, N. (1964). Personal communication.

Feldberg, W., and Myers, R. D. (1965). *J. Physiol. (London)* 177:239.

Feldberg, W., and Sherwood, S. L. (1954). *J. Physiol. (London)* 123:148.

Feldstein, A. (1958). *Science* 128:28.

Feldstein, A. (1959). *Am. J. Psychiat.* 116:454.

Fellman, J. H. (1958). *J. Neurol., Neurosurg., Psychiat.* [N.S.] 21:58.

Fenn, W. O. (1965). *Ann. N.Y. Acad. Sci.* 117:760.

Fischer, P., and Landtsheer, L. (1950). *Experientia* 6:305.

Fischer, P., and Lecomte, J. (1949). *Arch. Intern. Physiol.* 36:327.

Fischer, P., and Lecomte, J. (1951). *Bull. Soc. Chim. Biol.* 33:569.

Fischer, P., Derouaux, G., Lambot, H., and Lecomte, J. (1950). *Bull. Soc. Chim. Belges* 59:72.

Fitzpatrick, T. B., and Kukita, A. (1959). *In* "Pigment Cell Biology" (M. Gordon, ed.), p. 489. Academic Press, New York.

Fitzpatrick, T. B., and Lerner, A. B. (1954). *Arch. Dermatol. Syphilol.* 69:133.

Foley, J. M., and Baxter, D. (1958). *J. Neuropathol. Exptl. Neurol.* 17:586.

Foster, C. A., and Churchill-Davidson, I. (1963). *J. Appl. Physiol.* 18:492.

Friedhoff, A. J., Palmer, M., and Simmons, C. (1959). *A.M.A. Arch. Neurol. Psychiat.* 81:620.

Friedman, H., Becker, R. O., and Bachman, C. H. (1965). *Nature* 205:1050.

Frohman, C. E., Goodman, M., Luby, E. O., Beckett, P. G. S., and Senf, R. (1958). *A.M.A. Arch. Neurol. Psychiat.* **79**:730.

Frohman, C. E., Latham, L. K., Beckett, P. G. S., and Gottlieb, J. S. (1960). *A.M.A. Arch. Gen. Psychiat.* **2**:255.

Frohman, C. E., Beckett, P. G. S., and Gottlieb, J. S. (1965). *Recent Advan. Biol. Psychiat., 1964* p. 45. Plenum Press, New York.

Funkenstein, D. H. (1950). *Psychosomat. Med.* **12**:377.

Gamburg, A. L. (1962). *Excerpta Med., Sect. 8* **15**:608 (abstr.).

Gerschman, R., Gilbert, D. L., Nye, S. W., Price, W. E., and Fenn, W. O. (1955). *Proc. Soc. Exptl. Biol. Med.* **88**:617.

Gershenovich, Z. S., Krichevskaya, A. A., and Kalnitzky, G. (1955). *Ukr. Biokhim Zh.* **27**:3; *Chem. Abstr.* **49**:10470 (1955).

Gjessing, L. (1964). *J. Psychiat. Res.* **2**:123.

Gjessing, R. (1938). *J. Mental Sci.* **84**:608.

Gjessing, R. (1953). *Arch. Psychiat. Nervenkrankh.* **191**:191.

Goldenberg, M., Aranow, H., Smith, A. A., and Faber, M. (1950). *A.M.A. Arch. Internal Med.* **86**:823.

Goldschmidt, L., and Whittier, J. R. (1958). *J. Gerontol.* **13**:132.

Gornall, A. G., Eglitis, B., Miller, A., Stokes, A. B., and Dewan, J. G. (1953). *Am. J. Psychiat.* **109**:584.

Gornall, A. G., Eglitis, B., and Stokes, A. B. (1958). *In* "Psychoendocrinology" (M. Reiss, ed.), p. 152. Grune & Stratton, New York.

Green, D. E., and Richter, D. (1937). *Biochem. J.* **31**:596.

Green, S., Mazur, A., and Shorr, E. (1956). *J. Biol. Chem.* **220**:237.

Greig, M. E., and Gibbons, A. J. (1957). *Federation Proc.* **16**:302.

Greig, M. E., and Gibbons, A. J. (1959). *Am. J. Physiol.* **196**:803.

Greiner, A. C. (1965). Personal communication.

Greiner, A. C., and Berry, K. (1964). *Can. Med. Assoc. J.* **90**:663.

Greiner, A. C., and Nicolson, G. A. (1964). *Can. Med. Assoc. J.* **91**:627.

Greiner, A. C., Nicolson, G. A., and Baker, R. A. (1964). *Can. Med. Assoc. J.* **91**:636.

Grof, S., Vojtechovsky, M., and Horackova, E. (1961a). *Activitas Nervosa Super.* **3**:216.

Grof, S., Vojtechovsky, M., and Vitek, V. (1961b). *Activitas Nervosa Super.* **3**:209.

Grof, S., Vojtechovsky, M., Vitek, V., and Prankova, S. (1963). *J. Neuropsychiat.* **5**:33.

Gussion, P., Day, M. E., and Kuna, A. (1958). *Am. J. Psychiat.* **115**:467.

Halpern, B. N., Benacerraf, B., and Briot, M. (1952). *Proc. Soc. Exptl. Biol. Med.* **79**:37.

Harley-Mason, J. (1954). Adrenolutin given to A. Hoffer. London, England.

Harman, D. (1960). *J. Gerontol.* **15**:38.

Harman, D. (1961). *J. Gerontol.* **16**:247.

Harman, D. (1962). *Radiation Res.* **16**:753.

Harman, D. (1965). *J. Gerontol.* **20**:151.

Harris, A. (1942). *Lancet* **II**:125.

Harrison, W. H. (1963). *Arch. Biochem. Biophys.* **101**:116.

Haugaard, N. (1965). *Ann. N.Y. Acad. Sci.* **117**:736.

Heacock, R. A. (1959). *Chem. Rev.* **59**:181.

Heacock, R. A. (1965). *Advan. Heterocyclic Chem.* **5**:205.

Heacock, R. A., and Laidlaw, B. D. (1958a). *Nature* **182**:526.

Heacock, R. A., and Laidlaw, B. D. (1958b). *Chem. & Ind. (London)* p. 1510.

Heacock, R. A., and Mahon, M. E. (1958). *Can. J. Chem.* 36:1550.

Heacock, R. A., and Mattok, G. L. (1963). *Can. J. Chem.* 41:139.

Heacock, R. A., and Scott, D. (1959). *Can. J. Biochem. Physiol.* 37:1087.

Heacock, R. A., Nerenberg, C., and Payza, A. N. (1958). *Can. J. Chem.* 36:853.

Heacock, R. A., Mattok, G. L., and Wilson, D. L. (1963). *Can. J. Biochem. Physiol.* 41:1721.

Heath, R. G., and Leach, B. E. (1962). *Ann. N.Y. Acad. Sci.* 96:425.

Heath, R. G., Leach, B. E., Byers, L. W., Martens, S., and Fiegley, C. A. (1958). *Am. J. Psychiat.* 114:683.

Heath, R. G., Leach, B. E., and Cohen, M. (1959). *In* "The Effects of Pharmacologie Agents on the Nervous System" (F. J. Braceland, ed.), p. 397. Williams & Wilkins, Baltimore, Maryland.

Heath, R. G., Nesselhof, W., Bishop, M. P., and Byers, L. W. (1965). *Diseases Nervous System* 26:99.

Henneman, D. H., Altschule, M. D., Goncz, R. M., and Davis, P. (1955). *A.M.A. Arch. Internal Med.* 95:594.

Herjanic, M. (1965). Personal communication.

Hirsch, H. M. (1959). *In* "Pigment Cell Biology" (M. Gordon, ed.), p. 327. Academic Press, New York.

Hoagland, H., Rinkel, M., and Hyde, R. W. (1955). *A.M.A. Arch. Neurol. Psychiat.* 73:100.

Hoffer, A. (1954). *A.M.A. Arch. Neurol. Psychiat.* 71:80.

Hoffer, A. (1957a). *Hormones, Brain Function, Behavior, Proc. Conf. Neuroendocrinol., Harriman, N.Y., 1956* p. 181. Academic Press, New York.

Hoffer, A. (1957b). *In* "Tranquilizing Drugs," Publ. No. 46, p. 73. Am. Assoc. Advance. Sci., Washington, D.C.

Hoffer, A. (1957c). *J. Clin. Exptl. Psychopathol. & Quart. Rev. Psychiat. Neurol.* 18:27.

Hoffer, A. (1957d). *In* "Psychotropic Drugs" (S. Garattini and V. Ghetti, eds.), p. 10. Elsevier, Amsterdam.

Hoffer, A. (1959a). *In* "Molecules and Mental Health" (F. A. Gibbs, ed.), p. 44. Lippincott, Philadelphia, Pennsylvania.

Hoffer, A. (1959b). *Diseases Nervous System* 20:87.

Hoffer, A. (1955). Personal observations.

Hoffer, A. (1962a). Unpublished observations.

Hoffer, A. (1962b). *Intern. Rev. Neurobiol.* 4:307.

Hoffer, A. (1965). *Diseases Nervous System* 26:358.

Hoffer, A., and Callbeck, M. J. (1959). *Diseases Nervous System* 20:387.

Hoffer, A., and Kenyon, M. (1957). *A.M.A. Arch. Neurol. Psychiat.* 77:437.

Hoffer, A., and Mahon, M. (1961). *J. Neuropsychiat.* 2:331.

Hoffer, A., and Osmond, H. (1958). *J. Mental Sci.* 104:302.

Hoffer, A., and Osmond, H. (1959). *J. Nervous Mental Disease* 128:18.

Hoffer, A., and Osmond, H. (1960). "The Chemical Bases of Clinical Psychiatry." Thomas, Springfield, Illinois.

Hoffer, A., and Osmond, H. (1963). *Diseases Nervous System* 5:273.

Hoffer, A., Osmond, H., and Smythies, J. (1954). *J. Mental Sci.* 100:29.

Hoffer, A., Osmond, H., Callbeck, M. J., and Kahan, I. (1957). *J. Clin. Exptl. Psychopathol. & Quart. Rev. Psychiat. Neurol.* 18:131.

Hoffer, A., Smith, C., Chwelos, V., Callbeck, M. J., and Mahon, M. (1959). *J. Clin. Exptl. Psychopathol. & Quart. Rev. Psychiat. Neurol.* 20:125.

Holtz, P., and Westermann, E. (1956). *Naturwissenschaften* 43:37.

Horwitt, M. K., Meyer, B. J., Meyer, A. C., Harvey, C. C., and Haffron, D. (1957). *A.M.A. Arch. Neurol. Psychiat.* **78**:275.

Hoskins, R. G. (1932). *A.M.A. Arch. Neurol. Psychiat.* **28**:1346.

Hoskins, R. G. (1946). "The Biology of Schizophrenia." Norton, New York.

Hoskins, R. G., and Sleeper, F. H. (1929). *Endocrinology* **13**:459.

Hoskins, R. G., and Sleeper, F. H. (1931). *J. Psychiat.* **10**:411.

Hsia, D. Y. (1964). *In* "Diseases of Metabolism" (G. G. Duncan, ed.), p. 376. Saunders, Philadelphia, Pennsylvania.

Hutcheon, D. E., Lowenthal, J., and Eade, N. R. (1956). *Arch. Intern. Pharmacodyn.* **106**:90.

Inchiosa, M. A. (1959). Semiannual Report, p. 133. Biol. Med. Res. Div., Argonne National Lab.

Inchiosa, M. A., and Freedberg, A. S. (1961). *Federation Proc.* **20**:298.

Inchiosa, M. A., and Van Demark, N. L. (1958). *Proc. Soc. Exptl. Biol. Med.* **97**:59.

Iordanis, K. A., and Kuchino, E. B. (1959). *In* "Biophysical Research in Psychiatry" (C. H. Braines, ed.), p. 96. Inst. Psychiat., Acad. Med. Sci. U.S.S.R., Moscow.

Irvine, D. (1961). *J. Neuropsychiat.* **2**:292.

Jantz, H. (1956). *Zentr. Ges. Neurol. Psychiat.* **137**:141.

Kaliman, P. A. (1961). *Biochemistry* **26**:256.

Kaliman, P. A., and Koshlyak, T. V. (1962). *Biochemistry* **26**:636.

Kato, L., Gozsy, B., Lehmann, H. E., and Ban, T. A. (1962). *J. Clin. Exptl. Psychopathol. & Quart. Rev. Psychiat. Neurol.* **23**:75.

Kaufmann, H., and Koch, E. (1959a). *Rev. Ateroscler.* **1**:290.

Kaufmann, H., and Koch, E. (1959b). *Presse Med.* **67**:1141.

Kety, S. S. (1959). *Science* **29**:1528 and 1590.

Kisch, B. (1947). *Exptl. Surg.* **5**:166.

Koch, E. (1962). Personal communication.

Koch, E. (1966). *Intern. J. Neuropsychiat.* **2**:227.

Korzoff, B. A., and Kuchino, E. B. (1959). *In* "Biophysical Research in Psychiatry" (C. H. Braines, ed.), p. 206. Inst. Psychiat., Acad. Med. Sci. U.S.S.R., Moscow.

Krall, A. R., Siegel, G. J., Gozansky, D. M., and Wagner, F. L. (1964). *Biochem. Pharmacol.* **13**:1519.

Krupp, P., and Monnier, M. (1960). *Experientia* **16**:206.

Kuchino, E. B. (1959). *In* "Biophysical Rescearch in Psychiatry" (C. H. Braines, ed.), p. 105. Inst. Psychiat., Acad. Med. Sci. U.S.S.R., Moscow.

Laborit, H., Broussolle, B., and Perrimond-Trouchet, R. (1957a). *Compt. Rend. Soc. Biol.* **151**:868.

Laborit, H., Broussolle, B., and Perrimond-Trouchet, R. (1957b). *J. Physiol.* (*Paris*) **49**:953.

Langemann, H., and Koelle, G. B. (1958). *Experientia* **14**:303.

Lea, A. J. (1955). *J. Mental Sci.* **101**:538.

Leach, B. E., and Heath, R. G. (1956). *A.M.A. Arch. Neurol. Psychiat.* **76**:444.

Leach, B. E., Cohen, M., Heath, R. G., and Martens, S. (1956). *A.M.A. Arch. Neurol. Psychiat.* **76**:635.

LeBlanc, J., and Lemieux, L. (1961). *Med. Exptl.* **4**:214.

LeBlanc, J., Lemieux, L., Cote, F., Desbiens, A., and Blanchet, A. (1963). *Med. Exptl.* **8**:163.

Lecomte, J., and Fischer, P. (1951). *Arch. Intern. Physiol.* **58**:424.

Lemberg, R., and Legge, J. W. (1949). "Hematin Compounds and Bile Pigments." Wiley (Interscience), New York.

Lettre, H., and Albrecht, M. (1941). *Z. Physiol. Chem.* **271**:200.

Ling, N. S., and Blum, J. J. (1958). *Federation Proc.* **17**:98.

Lochner, K. H., Scheuing, M. R., and Flach, F. F. (1963). *Acta Psychiat. Neurol. Scand.* **39**:413.

Lucas, O. (1964). Personal communication.

Lucy, J. D. (1954). *A.M.A. Arch. Neurol. Psychiat.* **71**:629.

Lund, A. (1949a). *Acta Pharmacol. Toxicol.* **5**:231.

Lund, A. (1949b). *Acta Pharmacol. Toxicol.* **5**:75.

Lund, A. (1949c). *Acta Pharmacol. Toxicol.* **5**:121.

Lund, A. (1951). *Acta Pharmacol. Toxicol.* **7**:297.

Maas, J. W., Gleser, G. C., and Gottschalk, L. A. (1961). *Arch. Gen. Psychiat.* **4**:109.

Mall, G. (1962). *Arch. Psychiat. Nervenkrankh.* **200**:390.

Marrazzi, A. S., and Hart, E. R. (1956). *J. Nervous Mental Disease* **124**:388.

Martens, S., Vallbo, S., and Melander, B. (1959). *Intern. Rev. Neurobiol.* **1**:333.

Martin, G., Eriksen, N., and Benditt, E. P. (1958). *Federation Proc.* **17**:447.

Martin, G. J., Ichniowski, C. T., Wisansky, W. A., and Ansbacher, S. (1942). *Am. J. Physiol.* **136**:66.

Maslova, A. F. (1959). *Biokhymia* **24**:181.

Mason, H. S. (1955). *Advan. Enzymol.* **16**:105.

Mason, H. S. (1959). *In* "Pigment Cell Biology" (M. Gordon, ed.), p. 563. Academic Press, New York.

Mattok, G. L., and Heacock, R. A. (1965). *Can. J. Chem.* **43**:119.

Mattok, G. L., Wilson, D. L., and Heacock, R. A. (1966). *Clin. Chim. Acta* **14**:99.

Mayer-Gross, W. (1959). Personal communication to A. Hoffer.

Mefferd, R. B., Moran, L. J., and Kimble, J. P. (1960). *J. Nervous Mental Disease* **131**:354.

Meirowsky, E. (1940). *Brit. J. Dermatol. Syphilis* **52**:205.

Melander, B. (1957). Personal communication.

Melander, B., and Martens, S. (1958). *Diseases Nervous System* **19**:478.

Meyerhoff, O., and Randall, L. O. (1948). *Arch. Biochem.* **17**:171.

Miller, N. E. (1964). *Science* **148**:328.

Mollaret, P., Vic-Dupont, Pocidalo, J. J., and Monsallier, J. F. (1965). *Presse Med.* **73**:777.

Nicolaus, R. A. (1962). *Rass. Med. Sper.* **9**:1.

Nicolson, G. A., Greiner, A. C., McFarlane, W. J. G., and Baker, R. A. (1966). *Lancet* **I**:344.

Niswander, G. D., Haslerud, G. M., and Mitchell, G. D. (1963). *Arch. Gen. Psychiat.* **9**:229.

Noval, J. (1965). Personal communication.

Noval, J. J., Brande, B. L., and Sohler, A. (1959). *Federation Proc.* **18**:428.

Orstrum, A., and Skaug, O. E. (1950). *Nord. Psykiat. Medlemsblad* **4**:1.

Osaki, S., McDermott, J. A., and Frieden, E. (1964). *J. Biol. Chem.* **239**:364.

Osinskaya, V. O. (1957). *Biochemistry* **22**:496.

Osmond, H., and Hoffer, A. (1958). *J. Mental Sci.* **104**:302.

Osmond, H., and Hoffer, A. (1959). *Can. Med. Assoc. J.* **80**:91.

Osmond, H., and Smythies, J. (1952). *J. Mental Sci.* **98**:309.

Ostfeld, A. M., Abood, L. G., and Marcus, D. A. (1958). *A.M.A. Arch. Neurol. Psychiat.* **79**:317.

Ovshinsky, S. R. (1957). *J. Nervous Mental Disease* **125**:578.

Ovshinsky, S. R. (1958). *J. Nervous Mental Disease* **127**:180.

Ozek, M. (1957). *Arch. Psychiat. Z. Ges. Neurol.* **195**:408.

Palthe, P. M. van Wulfften, and Weeren, J. T. H. (1954). *Aeromed. Acta* 3:127.

Park, J. H., Meriwether, B. P., and Park, C. R. (1956a). *Federation Proc.* 15:141.

Park, J. H., Meriwether, B. P., Park, C. R., Mudd, S. H., and Lipmann, F. (1956b). *Biochim. Biophys. Acta* 22:403.

Pastan, I., Herring, B., Johnson, P., and Field, J. B. (1962). *J. Biol. Chem.* 237:287.

Payza, A. N., and Hoffer, A. (1959). *Bull. Fac. Med. Istanbul* 22:1096.

Payza, A. N., and Mahon, M. E. (1959). *Anal. Chem.* 31:1170.

Payza, A. N., and Mahon, M. E. (1960). *Anal. Chem.* 32:17.

Payza, A. N., and Zaleschuk, J. (1959). *Bull. Fac. Med. Istanbul* 22:1523.

Peck, R. E. (1963). *Diseases Nervous System* 24:84.

Peretz, D. I., Smythies, J. R., and Gibson, W. C. (1955). *J. Mental Sci.* 101:317.

Perot, P. L., and Stein, S. N. (1956). *Science* 123:802.

Pon, N. G. (1964). *Comp. Biochem.* 7:2.

Porter, C. C., Titus, D. C., Sanders, B. E., and Smith, E. V. C. (1957). *Science* 126:1014.

Pscheidt, G. R. (1964). *Intern. Rev. Neurobiol.* 7:191.

Raab, W., and Lepeschkin, E. (1950). *Exptl. Med. Surg.* 8:319.

Radsma, W., and Golterman, H. L. (1954). *Biochim. Biophys. Acta* 12:80.

Randall, L. O. (1946). *J. Biol. Chem.* 165:733.

Rangier, M. (1962). *Ann. Biol. Clin.* (*Paris*) 20:607.

Rawson, R. W., Koch, H., and Flach, F. F. (1957). *Hormones, Brain Function, Behavior, Proc. Conf. Neuroendocrinol., Harriman, N.Y., 1956* p. 221. Academic Press, New York.

Rees, L. (1957). *In* "Schizophrenia, Somatic Aspects" (D. Richter, ed.), p. 1. Macmillan, New York.

Reio, L. (1964). *Arkiv Kemi* 22:317.

Reiss, M., and Haigh, C. P. (1954). *Proc. Roy. Soc. Med.* 47:889.

Rice, E. W. (1962). *Am. J. Med. Sci.* 243:593.

Rigdon, R. H. (1940a). *Surgery* 8:839.

Rigdon, R. H. (1940b). *A.M.A. Arch. Surg.* 41:101.

Ritzel, G., Staub, H., and Hunzinger, W. A. (1957). *Ger. Med. Monthly* 2:110.

Roston, S. (1960). *J. Biol. Chem.* 235:3315.

Roston, S. (1962). *Nature* 194:1079.

Roston, S. (1963). *Nature* 197:75.

Roston, S. (1965). *Arch. Biochem. Biophys.* 109:41.

Rothman, S. (1942). *J. Invest. Dermatol.* 5:61.

Runge, T. M., Bohls, S. W., Hoerster, S. A., and Thurman, N. (1961). *Diseases Nervous System* 22:619.

Sackler, A. M., Sackler, R. R., Marti-Ibanez, F., and Sackler, M. D. (1956). *In* "The Great Physiodynamic Therapies in Psychiatry" (F. Marti-Ibanez *et al.*, eds.), p. 158. Harper (Hoeber), New York.

Sackler, M. D., Sackler, R. R., Sackler, A. M., La Burt, H. A., Van Ophuijsen, J. H. W., and Tui, C. (1951). *Psychiat. Quart.* 25:213.

Sackler, R. R., Sackler, M. D., Van Ophuijsen, J. H. W., Tui, C., and Sackler, A. M. (1951). *J. Clin. Exptl. Psychopathol.* 12:5.

Satanove, A. (1965). *J. Am. Med. Assoc.* 191:263.

Saunders, J. C., and Chipkiewicz, H. (1959). *J. Clin. Exptl. Psychopathol. & Quart. Rev. Psychiat. Neurol.* 20:7.

Scheid, K. F. (1938). *Klin. Wochschr.* 17:911.

Scheid, K. F., and Baumer, L. (1937). *Nervenarzt* 5:225.

Scheinberg, I. H., Morell, A. G., Harris, R. S., and Berger, A. (1957). *Science* **126**:925.

Schwarz, B. E., Sem-Jacobsen, C. W., and Petersen, M. C. (1956a). *A.M.A. Arch. Neurol. Psychiat.* **75**:579.

Schwarz, B. E., Wakim, K. G., Bickford, R. G., and Lichtenheld, F. R. (1956b). *A.M.A. Arch. Neurol. Psychiat.* **75**:83.

Sem-Jacobsen, C. W., Petersen, M. C., Lazarte, J. A., Dodge, H. W., Jr., and Holman, C. B. (1955). *Am. J. Psychiat.* **112**:278.

Shattock, F. M. (1950). *J. Mental Sci.* **96**:32.

Simonson, E., and Brozek, J. (1952). *J. Physiol. Rev.* **32**:349.

Sjovall, T. (1947). *Acta Psychiat. Neurol.* **47**:105.

Slocombe, A. G. (1956). *Federation Proc.* **15**:172.

Slocombe, A. G., Hoagland, H., and Tozian, L. S. (1956). *Am. J. Physiol.* **185**:601.

Sommer, R., and Osmond, H. (1960). *Am. Anthropologist* **62**:1051.

Stennett, R. G., and Callowhill, C. R. (1960). *Can. Psych. Assoc. J.* **5**:1.

Streifler, M., and Kornblueth, W. (1958). *In* "Chemical Concepts of Psychoses" (M. Rinkel and H. C. B. Senber, eds.), p. 257. McDowell, Obolensky, New York.

Sulkovitch, H. (1956). *Endocrinology* **59**:260.

Sulkovitch, H., and Altschule, M. D. (1958). *A.M.A. Arch. Gen. Psychiat.* **1**:108.

Sulkovitch, H., Perring, G. M., and Altschule, M. D. (1957). *Proc. Soc. Exptl. Biol. Med.* **95**:245.

Sundin, T. (1958). *Acta Med. Scand.* **161**:336.

Sweat, M. L., and Bryson, M. J. (1965). *Endocrinology* **76**:773.

Szatmari, A., Hoffer, A., and Schneider, R. (1955). *Am. J. Psychiat.* **111**:603.

Szepesey, A. (1962). *Gyogyszereszet* **6**:267.

Takahashi, Y., and Akabane, Y. (1960). *Arch. Gen. Psychiat.* **3**:674.

Taubmann, G., and Jantz, H. (1957). *Nervenarzt* **20**:485.

Taylor, D. W. (1958). *J. Physiol. (London)* **140**:23.

Tokusawa, K., Takahashi, H., Ashida, K., Kajitani, F., Fujiwara, S., and Matsuura, H. (1957). *J. Nervous Remedies* **6**:29.

Trevathan, R. D., and Tatum, J. C. (1954). *J. Nervous Mental Disease* **120**:83.

Tyler, D. B. (1955). *Diseases Nervous System* **16**:293.

Utevskii, A. M. (1963a). *Proc. 5th Intern. Congr. Biochem., Moscow, 1961* Abstr. commun. Pergamon Press, Oxford.

Utevskii, A. M. (1963b). *Proc. 5th Intern. Congr. Biochem., Moscow, 1961* Vol. 9, p. 13. Pergamon Press, Oxford.

Utevskii, A. M., and Osinskaya, V. O. (1957). *Ukr. Biokhim. Z.* **27**:401; *Intern. Abstr. Biol. Sci.* **6**:192 (1956).

Utevskii, A. M., and Osinskaya, V. O. (1964). *Chem. Abstr.* **60**:14790.

Utevskii, A. M., Osinskaya, V. O., and Kaliman, P. A. (1965). *Ukr. Biochem. J.* **37**:798.

Veech, R. L., Altschule, M. D., Sulkovitch, H., and Holliday, P. D. (1960). *Arch. Gen. Psychiat.* **3**:642.

Veech, R. L., Bigelow, L. B., Denckla, W. D., and Altschule, M. D. (1961). *Arch. Gen. Psychiat.* **5**:127.

Vencovsky, E., and Peterova, E. (1963). *Comprehensive Psychiat.* **59**:217.

Waelsch, H., and Rachow, H. (1942). *Science* **96**:386.

Wajzer, J. (1947). *Bull. Soc. Chim. Biol.* **29**:237.

Wakoh, T. (1959). *Mie Med. J.* **9**:351.

Walaas, O., Lingjaerde, O., Loken, F., and Hundevadt, E. (1954). *Scand. J. Clin. & Lab. Invest.* **6**:245.

Ward, J. (1965). Personal communication.

Watson, G., and Glaser, E. M. (1952). "Watson-Glaser Critical Thinking Appraisal." World Book, New York.

Weckowicz, T. E., and Hall, R. (1957). *J. Nervous Mental Disease* 125:452.

Weinstein, S., and Manning, R. J. (1935). *Proc. Soc. Exptl. Biol. Med.* 32:1096.

Van Der Wende, C., and Spoerlein, M. T. (1962). *Arch. Intern. Pharmacodyn.* 137:145.

Wiedorn, W. S. (1954). *J. Nervous Mental Disease* 120:1.

Wiedorn, W. S., and Ervin, F. (1954). *A.M.A. Arch. Neurol. Psychiat.* 72:321.

Wittman, P. (1948). *J. Clin. Psychol.* 4:211.

Wood, J. D., and Watson, W. J. (1963). *Can. J. Biochem. Physiol.* 41:1907.

Wood, J. D., and Watson, W. J. (1964a). *Can. J. Physiol. Pharm.* 42:277.

Wood, J. D., and Watson, W. J. (1964b). *Can. M. Physiol. Pharm.* 42:641.

Wood, J. D., Watson, W. J., and Clydesdale, F. M. (1963). *J. Neurochem.* 10:625.

Woodbury, D. M., and Vernadakis, A. (1958). *Federation Proc.* 17:420.

Yasunobu, K. T. (1959). *In* "Pigment Cell Biology" (M. Gordon, ed.), p. 583. Academic Press, New York.

Yuwiler, A., Jenkins, I. M., and Dukay, A. (1961). *Arch. Gen. Psychiat.* 4:395.

Chapter IV

Indole Hallucinogens Derived from Tryptophan

Introduction

l-Tryptophan is one of the essential amino acids. It is the only indole amino acid but not the only precursor of indoles, since substances derived from tyrosine may also be converted into indoles of another sort. Tryptophan is the potential precursor of the indole alkylamines, that is, compounds which include bufotenine, *N,N*-dimethyltryptamine, *N,N*-diethyltryptamine, serotonin, iboga, and harmala aklaloids, psilocybin, LSD, lysergic acid amide, and some yohimbe alkaloids. With the exception of serotonin all these compounds are hallucinogens and serotonin may be a neurohormone. All the compounds listed are found in plants and a few in animals in contrast to the adrenaline metabolite indoles derived from adrenochrome which occur only in animals, so far as we know.

These hallucinogens derive from tryptamine, an important metabolite of tryptophan, by the loss of a molecule of carbon dioxide. The enzyme is a decarboxylase. Because tryptamine is so quickly metabolized in the body, major increases in its concentration can be measured if the enzyme, amine oxidase, which metabolizes it further is inhibited, for example, by iproniazid. Tryptamine may be hydroxylated on the indole nucleus at one of the free positions 4, 5, 6, or 7, or it may be methylated or oxidized at the side-chain terminal nitrogen. Szara and Hearst (1962) observed 6-hydroxylation of *N,N*-dimethyl- and *N,N*-diethyltryptamine in the body. It seemed to be the major pathway. Tryptophan hydroxylases have been found in gastrointestinal mucosa and in nervous tissue but they probably are present in all tissues containing chromaffin cells.

5-Hydroxytryptamine (serotonin or 5-HT) may be acetylated to produce *n*-acetyl-5-HT which, in turn, is methylated to melatonin, apparently a hormone found in the pineal gland. A second hydroxyl group may be introduced to form 6-hydroxymelatonin.

1. The hydroxylation and methylation reactions lead to a series of new compounds which remain active physiologically, although the activity may be quite different. A series of degradation reactions occur which inactivate these indole alkylamines and produce apparently inactive compounds.

2. Oxidative deamination. Monoamine oxidase catalyzes the oxidation of these indoles to 5-hydroxyindoleacetic acid (5-HIAA) and other urinary indoles, such as indoleacetic acid, indolepyruvic acid, indolelactic acid, etc.

3. Formation of colored derivatives. Blaschko and Milton (1960) found that homogenates made from the gill plates of *Mytilus edulis* oxidized 5-hydroxytryptophan and serotonin took up oxygen and formed darkly colored derivatives. They suggested dihydroxyindoles or quinoneimines (similar to adrenochrome) were formed. Ceruloplasmin is an hydroxyindole oxidase which could form quinoneimine derivatives. Oxyhemoglobin is another oxidizing agent for 5-hydroxytryptamine and other hydroxyindoles. Pink-colored substances are formed.

4. *Part of the hydroxyindoles are broken open at one of the rings to form series of substances.* Little is known about them but some are involved in melanin formation.

Tryptophan

It has been known for some time that amino acids are toxic when given in excess. The accumulation of protein fractions, perhaps dipeptides or amino acids, has been considered responsible for the psychological changes which may culminate in coma in some patients with damaged livers; especially if they are on high protein diets. Gullino *et al.* (1956) gave 200-gm rats several amino acids and mixtures of 10 essential amino acids by IP injection. *l*-Tryptophan was the most toxic amino acid. It had an LD-50 of 8 mmole/kg. Isoleucine was the least toxic and one methyl donor, methionine, was somewhere in between. Tryptophan was the only amino acid where the levo isomer was much more toxic than the dextro or unnatural isomer. The mixture of all 10 amino acids was less toxic than was expected from its known composition. Winitz *et al.* (1956) reported that toxic doses of the amino acids produced hyperglycemia in rats. *d*-Tryptophan caused marked hyperglycemia in the rats at death. In contrast *l*-tryptophan, which was more toxic, produced hypoglycemia.

The Gullino *et al.* finding that mixture of amino acids were less toxic may account for Pfeiffer's (1960) observation that choline and *l*-tryptophan combined were not toxic for schizophrenic patients. The possibility choline protects against the toxic action of tryptophan should be examined. Sprince and Lichtenstein (1960) measured the activity of human serum pseudocholinesterase using indoxylacetate as a test substrate. Choline enhanced hydrolysis. Several hallucinogens (LSD, bufotenine) inhibited activity of the enzyme as did physostigmine, serotonin, and tryptamine. However, concentrations of choline within the physiological range protected the esterase against the inhibitory effects of these substances. It is, therefore, highly probable that choline did, indeed, protect one enzyme against some metabolites of *l*-tryptophan. However, it is possible alcoholics and schizophrenics have some biochemical constitution which protects them against *l*-tryptophan.

The first demonstration that *l*-tryptophan alone could produce toxic mental changes in man was made by Olson *et al.* (1960). They gave their subjects 10 gm of *dl*-tryptophan by mouth. All of the 16 normal comparison group experienced psychological symptoms such as changes in perception (lightheadedness, dizziness) and changes in mood, mainly euphoria. None of the 34 chronic alcoholics noted any symptoms.

About 5 years ago, Hoffer made the same observation. Five grams of *l*-tryptophan was taken by mouth several times over a period of days in order to measure the effect on some urine metabolites in which we were interested. At that time Hoffer was convinced that there would be no psychological effect since no changes of a psychological nature had been reported. In each case, within an hour, there was slight dizziness, a feeling of lightheadedness and some euphoria which was comparable to the effect of whisky (30% concentration). However, being somewhat inhibited by the criticisms against subjective experiments, and not thinking these findings were particularly significant, these changes were not reported. But we can corroborate the claims of Olson *et al.* since the changes were remarkably like those described by them in normal subjects. Their alcoholic subjects did not respond in the same way.

Smith and Prockop (1962) corroborated the observations of Olson *et al.* (1960). They gave *l*-tryptophan by mouth to 7 normal subjects. After receiving 2 gm (30 mg/kg) 5 of the 7 subjects became drowsy after 1 to 2 hours. The same number were drowsy after 4.5 gm (70 mg/kg) but after 6 gm (90/kg) all 7 became listless and yawned frequently. Five subjects slept for varying periods between testings. The 3 subjects whose EEG's were being recorded, were unable to remain awake for more than a few minutes. All were easily aroused, however, and then felt euphoric and were unusually voluble and overactive. One showed marked social disinhibition in his behavior.

At the two higher doses, subjects had nystagmus which was most prominent in the horizontal plane. At the highest dose, 2 subjects were clumsy in turning and tandem walking. One subject had a moderate frontal headache and one was dizzy without vertigo.

Smith and Prockop (1962) suggested that tryptophan could have produced these changes by increasing the concentration of tryptamine, 5-hydroxytryptamine and, perhaps, other derivatives shown in Fig. 10. The authors believe tryptamine might be the more active substance since, according to De Jong (1945), it was a very active substance for producing animal catatonia. Furthermore, tryptophan would increase tryptamine more than other metabolites since reactions further down the chain from tryptophan should be less affected theoretically. Zeller (1957, 1958, 1959), Lauer (1958) and Lauer *et al.* (1958) treated 7 schizophrenic patients daily with about 1 gram per day of *l*-tryptophan and with iproniazid for 6 weeks. On about the eleventh day the patients began to change. They became more active, improved their interpersonal relationships, and felt better. Toward the end of the treatment period withdrawn lethargic schizophrenics had, to some degree, become acutely anxious and active. No claims were made that they had been clinically improved, that is, less sick. Pfeiffer (1960) reported that he had given 6 gm of choline and 6 gm of *l*-tryptophan for 3 weeks, each day, to 7 mild schizophrenic patients. To his surprise none became worse but two were greatly improved. Kety (1959) was not impressed with this improvement.

However, a couple of years later, Pollin *et al.* (1961) also gave tryptophan to some schizophrenic patients treated with a monoamine oxidase inhibitor and observed changes similar to those first reported by Zeller and his colleagues, that is, extensive changes in mood and thus corroborated his psychological findings. They gave each person 15 gm/70 kg each day together with, first 50 mg iproniazid, and later 150 mg iproniazid per day. Slight changes were seen with the lower dose of amine oxidase inhibitor, but with the higher dose 7 out of 9 showed mild to marked changes. They reported an elevation of mood in these subjects, they increased their involvement in the ward and seemed to be more extroverted. These were essentially the changes observed by Zeller and his colleagues.

Another amino acid, *l*-methionine, with a dose of 20 gm/kg daily and 50 mg iproniazid daily for 7 days, produced some changes in 4 out of 9 subjects. From the description presented they seemed to have suffered a toxic or deliriod state.

The few reports reviewed show that *l*-tryptophan in doses of 5 gm/ day, or more, produced changes in normal subjects but not in alcoholics. When an amine oxidase inhibitor was also given, a similar change occurred in chronic schizophrenic patients. This suggests *l*-tryptophan

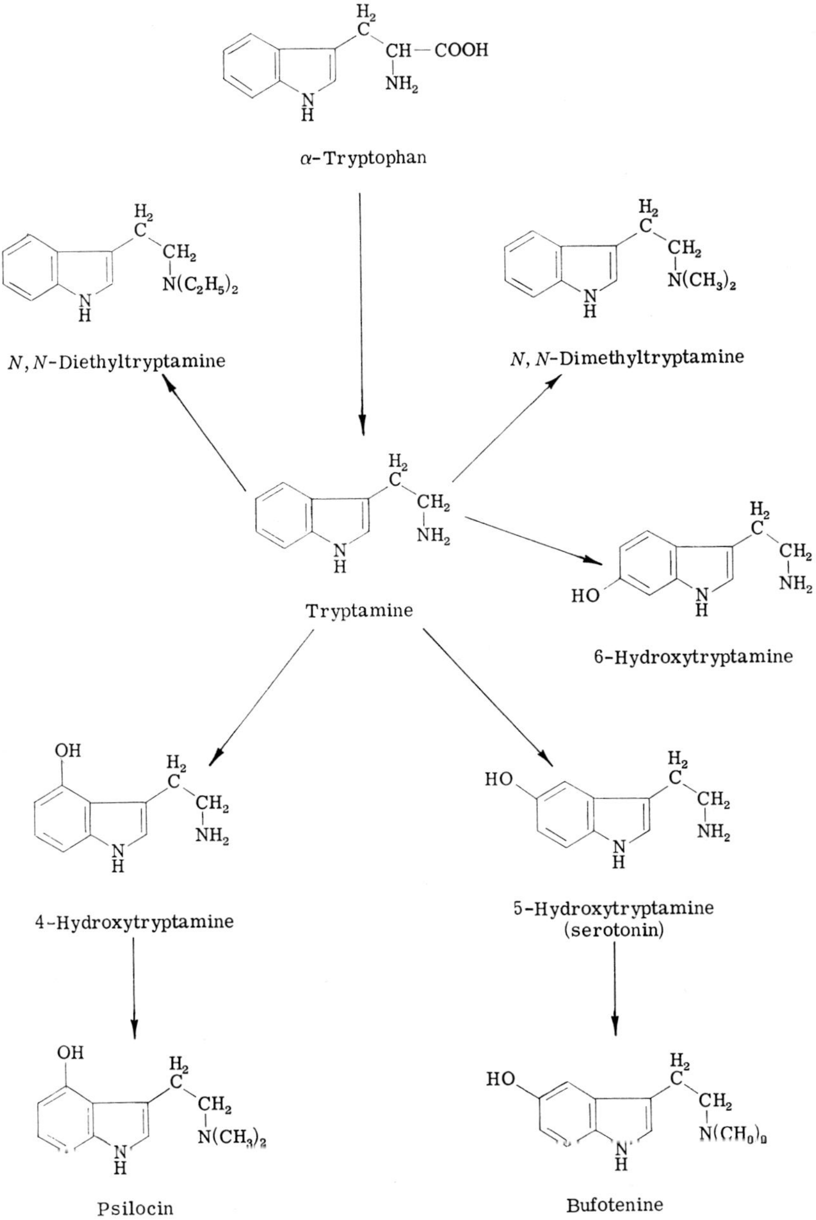

Fig. 10. Structures of hallucinogens related to tryptophan.

does not have any specific role in the etiology of schizophrenia unless other metabolic routes, not altered by amine oxidase inhibitors, are involved.

It is also possible that methionine which is a methyl donor could increase the production of toxic methylated derivatives of the kind described in this chapter, or could lead to the production of adrenochrome and adrenolutin from 5,6-dihydroxyindoles coming from tyrosine and dihydroxylphenylalanine.

Tryptamine

EFFECT ON ANIMAL BEHAVIOR

De Jong (1945) reasoning from the known increase in indoles in urine of pellagrins and from the catatonic changes seen in some pellagrins, gave tryptamine·HCl to his experimental animals. Some mice given 6–10 mg subcutaneously developed a mixture of catalepsy and paralysis. With a higher dose, rigid paresis developed.

De Jong gave seven 3-kg cats 100–150 mg of tryptamine intravenously. They developed autonomic changes (salivation, narrowing of the pupils) combined with negativism and catalepsy. When hung on a latticework they remained suspended. In contrast to the passing effects of other catatonic producing substances the syndrome induced by tryptamine lasted at least 4 days.

Ernst *et al.* (1961) gave 2–2.5 kg-cats 0.5–6.0 mg (in 0.1–0.2 ml) of 5-HT or tryptamine by suboccipital injection into the cisterna magna. Doses of 1–3 mg of tryptamine produced catatonia which lasted hours to several days and was characterized by hypokinesis, negativism, catalepsy, and often stupor. 5-HT produced parasympathetic symptoms only. 5-HT given after tryptamine abolished the catatonia within 30 minutes. Pretreatment with 5-HT partially protected them against tryptamine.

BIOCHEMISTRY

According to Erspamer, tryptamine inhibited peroxide formation in tissues slightly. It inhibited red cell cholinesterase but markedly activated hydrolysis of benzoylcholine by plasma cholinesterase. Neither 5-hydroxytryptamine (serotonin) tryptamine or *N,N*-dimethyltryptamine had this property.

Tryptamine was oxidized by monoamine oxidase. Thus the administration of iproniazid increased brain tryptamine levels fivefold. Corne and Graham (1957) reported that iproniazid altered the pattern of response to the infusion of intraarterial tryptamine more than it did to adrenaline or noradrenaline. They suggested amine oxidase played a more important role in metabolizing tryptamine than the catecholamines.

Bunag and Walaszek (1962) tested the effect of some indoles as antagonists of the depressor action of serotonin and tryptamine given to leghorn hens. Ergotamine, dihydroergotamine, LSD-25, BOL-148 ergonovine, and UML-491, in ascending order of potency, blocked the depressor action of both amines.

PHARMACOLOGY

Laidlaw (1912) completed the first report on the pharmacology of tryptamine. Cats and rabbits were given the compound. After 100 mg given subcutaneously very few behavioral changes were seen. The cats showed some uneasiness. With larger doses tryptamine produced a transient stimulant effect upon the central nervous system causing tremor of limbs and clonic and tonic convulsions. It had a direct stimulant action on plain muscle.

According to Erspamer, excess tryptamine left in contact with smooth muscle preparations abolished the effect of subsequent doses of serotonin. It prolonged sleeping time of chloral hydrate considerably and when given to rats intravenously it produced convulsions at 5 mg/kg or more. The convulsant effect was potentiated by amine oxidase inhibitors, antagonized by LSD, BOL, chlorpromazine and trifluoperazine.

The onset, duration, and relative intensity of clonic convulsions of rats pretreated with MAO inhibitors, correlated well with the increase in the concentration of tryptamine in the brain. An infusion of 1.5 mg/kg/min into rabbits pretreated with reserpine antagonized the ptosis, myosis, and depression induced by the reserpine. Iproniazid prolonged and potentiated this effect. Tryptamine depressed the geniculate response to optic nerve shock for 3–6 minutes. N,N-dimethyltryptamine and bufotenine produced depression for 30–60 minutes.

In rabbits 15 mg/kg IV flattened the electrocorticogram. Muscular hypertonia, diffuse tremors and arterial hypertension were seen.

Barlow (1961) found that tryptamine was a weaker antagonist of 5-hydroxytryptamine on rat fundus muscle strip than BOL, dimethyltryptamine, 2-methyldimethyltryptamine and 5-benzyldimethyltryptamine. At the concentrations used there was no inhibition of monoamine oxidase. They ascribed the differential character of this blocking action to interference with the transport of tryptamine through the cell wall coupled with the blocking of a receptor common to both tryptamine and serotonin.

Tedeschi *et al.* (1959) studied the action of several substances on the convulsant effect of intravenous tryptamine in rats. Iproniazid and methylphenythylhydrazine (JB-516) potentiated tryptamine but stimulants, like picrotoxin, caffeine *d*-amphetamine and several other compounds had no effect. LSD, BOL-148, and chlorpromazine prevented convulsions but phenobarbital, reserpine, morphine, 5-methoxytryptamine, stelazine, or Tofranil did not.

Cohoba, the Narcotic Snuff of Ancient Haiti

Safford (1916) reviewed the ancient and recent history of this narcotic snuff. There remained little doubt it was prepared from *Piptadena peregrina* and contained chemicals which produced remarkable changes when inhaled or snuffed.

The natives of Haiti already had the snuff habit when Columbus discovered the New World. It was inhaled through the nostrils through a bifurcated tube. There followed an intoxication accompanied by visions. At this time, priests were believed to communicate with unseen powers which allowed them to prophesy. Early writers tended to confuse the Cohoba snuff with tobacco and the snuffing tubes with nose pipes used for smoking.

The first written account dates from 1496 when Ramon Pane who accompanied Columbus on his second voyage described the beliefs and idolatries of the Indians. He stated "This powder they draw up through the nose and it intoxicates them to such an extent that when they are under its influence, they know not what they do." Safford quotes Las Casas: "The ends of these two canes inserted into the windows of the nostrils and the base of the flute into the powder on the plate, they would draw in their breath and snuffing up, would receive through the nostrils as much of the powder as they wished to take, which, when taken would go at once to the brain almost as though they had drunk strong wine, for they would become drunk or almost drunk."

This method of taking the finely ground powder is rather interesting for the chief route of absorption is from the nasal and pharyngeal mucosa although some of the powder would be swallowed. Anyone who has tried to inspire powders will realize that some experience and skill is required. It is likely that the quantity of snuff consumed will depend upon the explosiveness and force of the inhalation. One of the early authors, in describing the use of the snuff, stated, "The Omaguas (in South America) make use of the cane tube terminating in a fork of a Y-shaped form, each branch of which they insert into one of their nostrils. This operation, followed by a violent inspiration, causes them to make diverse grimaces." Another writer describing the habits of the

Mura Indians of the Rio Negro reported that they used tubes (which were not bifurcated) and blew the snuff into each other. "The partners . . . each in turn blowing this powder with great force through a hollow cane into the nostrils of his friend."

Piptadena is a shrub or tree which reaches up to 60 feet in height with a trunk about 2 feet in diameter. The bark is muricated but the branches and leaves are not. The leaves are bipinnate and resemble leaves of mimosas, with 15–30 pairs of pinnae and numerous small leaflets, these latter linear in shape and apiculate at the apex. The petiole at some distance from the base carries a conspicuous oblong nectar gland and on the rachis, between the last pair or, last 2 or 3 pairs of pinnae, there is usually a minute gland. The ovary contains several to many ovules and develops into a broadly linear, flat, leathery, or woody 2-valved legume, rough on the outer surface and thickened along the sutures, without pulp surrounding the seeds. The seeds are flattish and orbicular, green at first, at length black and glossy. Cohoba has been grown in Haiti, Porto Rico, Venezuela, North Eastern Peru, Southern Peru, Argentina, Guinea, and in many parts of Brazil.

According to Schultes (1963) Humboldt prepared the first scientific account concerning snuff or yopo in 1801. He saw the Otomaco pulverize seed of *P. peregrina,* mix it with quicklime and use it like snuff. This snuff is used in the orinoco basin of Colombia and Venezuela. Schultes described the yopo-snuffing habit as very dangerous. It was carried on by whole populations. The intoxication produced convulsive movements and distortions of face and body muscles, then a desire to dance and finally an inability to control their limbs. Then a violent madness or deep sleep overtook the user. Then they developed stupor. Many years ago it was used for special purposes, to induce bravery before battle, for producing prophetic visions, for clairvoyance, etc.

Fish *et al.* (1955a,b, 1956) and Fish and Horning (1956) showed that *P. perigrena* seeds had 5 indoles. The chief one was bufotenine. Also present were *N,N*-dimethyltryptamine, bufotenine oxide, *N,N*-dimethyltryptamine oxide, and an unidentified indole.

Jensen and Chen (1936) found bufotenidine in Ch'an Su and in the secretion of *Bufo bufo gargarizans, Bufo fowleri* and *Bufo formosus.* They found bufotenine in *Bufo vulgaris* and *Bufo viridis viridis.*

Wieland *et al.* (1953) extracted bufotenine from the poisonous mushrooms *Amanita mappa, A. muscaria,* and *A. pantherina.* Bufotenine was first found in the skin of several toad species and the dried secretion (Ch'an Su) of the Chinese toad has been known to be biologically active for centuries but there are no records of toad skin or its extract being used as hallucinogenic material. This suggests that there is too little bufotenine or that other substances which potentiates the effect of bufotenine are lacking in frog skin. We do not believe that Man has not sampled toad skin. Primitive man has been very adept at selecting those species of plants and animals which contained hallucinogenic compounds.

Only recently have chemists been able to produce hallucinogenic chemicals not already present in nature. Even a variety of fish produces hallucinations. Roughly (1960) described the dream fish present near Norfolk Island. The inhabitants stated consuming this fish would produce nightmares. In order to test this claim, Joe Roberts, National Geographic photographer, consumed some of the fish, broiled. The next morning he reported "It was pure science fiction." He saw a new kind of car, pictures of monuments to mark Man's first trip into space. The fish is *Kyphosus fuscus,* closely related to the silver drummer caught off New South Wales. The author, Roughly, also had tried the fish and also had weird dreams.

The fly-agaric mushrooms are the only other natural source of bufotenine. But they also contain three other main constituents (Buck, 1961). Muscarin which is a parasympathomimetic substance is present. It acts directly on effector organs, smooth muscle, and glandular cells. Atropine prevents most of the effects. Also present in some species of *Amanita* is a substance called pilzatropin which may be *l*-hyoscyamine. *dl*-Hyoscyamine is atropine. Finally a pilztoxin is present because even after the muscarine present is prevented from acting by pretreatment with atropine, there remains a psychological effect. Narcoticlike intoxication, convulsions, and death have followed in spite of adequate treatment with atropine.

Lewin (1931) described the use of the fly-agaric by the native tribes of North East Asia in Siberia. Lewin discussed briefly the suggestion Berserkers consumed this mushroom to produce their great rages. The fly-agaric was in constant demand and there was a well-established trade between Kamchatka where it did grow to the Taigonos Peninsula where it did not grow at all. The Koryaks paid for them with reindeer and Lewin reported one animal was sometimes exchanged for one mushroom.

The Kamchadales and Koryaks consumed from 1 to 3 dried mushrooms. They believed the smaller mushrooms with a large quantity of small warts were more active than the pale red and less spotted ones. Among the Koryaks, their women chewed the dried agaric and rolled the masticated material into small sausages which were swallowed by the men. Lewin does not report whether the women got some of the psychological response.

The Siberians discovered the active principle was excreted in the urine and could be passed through the body once more. As soon as the Koryak noted his experience was passing, he would drink his own urine which he had saved for this purpose. The same mushrooms could thus give one person several experiences or several people one experience. After several passages the urine no longer was able to produce the desired effect.

The response to the mushrooms varied from person to person and in the same person at different times. The mushrooms varied in potency and sometimes one mushroom was effective; at other times ineffective. The first response occurred in 1 to 2 hours beginning with twitching and trembling. Consciousness was maintained and during this induction phase the subjects were euphoric and contented. Then the visions came on. The subjects spoke to their visionary people and discussed various matters with them. They were quite calm but appeared entranced with a glassy stare.

Other subjects became very jolly or sad, jumped about, danced, sang or gave way to great fright. Their pupils were enlarged. Lewin believed this was responsible for the distortions in size which occurred. Small objects appeared much too large. This "deceptive perception is apt to influence his action" . . . "on the basis of his illusions the conclusion which he arrives at is very reasonable."

In large quantities more severe hallucinations and rages occurred. The initial excitation could become more and more severe leading to attacks of raving madness. In some cases motor excitation was dominant. The eyes became savage, the face bloated and red, the hands trembled and the individual danced or rushed about until exhausted when he apparently slept. But he then experienced more hallucinations. This could then be replaced by another spasm of overactivity followed by more hallucinations and fantasy.

Ramsbottom (1953) described in more detail the use of these mushrooms by the Berserkers. According to him, fly-agaric or bug-agaric were poisonous but not deadly and did not kill healthy people. The potency varied with district. In some districts of France these mushrooms are regularly eaten. S. Odman, in 1784, first suggested that Vikings used fly-agaric to produce their berserk rages. Ramsbottom cited 12 authors who referred to the use of these mushrooms by the Siberian tribes already mentioned. The Koryaks believed a person drugged obeyed the wishes of spirits residing in them.

Fabing (1956) and Fabing and Hawkins (1956) was convinced the Berserkers did, indeed, use fly-agaric. It is a very plausible explanation. Going beserk occurred as follows. The Norse took the mushrooms so that the effect came on during the heat of battle or while at work. During the berserk rage they performed deeds which otherwise were impossible. The rage started with shivering, chattering of the teeth, and a chill. Their faces became swollen and changed color. A great rage developed in which they howled like wild animals and cut down anyone in their way, friend or foe alike. Afterward their mind became dulled and feeble for several days. In 1123 AD a law was passed making anyone going berserk liable for several years in jail. It was not heard of since.

Fabing quoted Drew who described a modern reaction to *Amanita muscaria*. A patient ate some of the mushrooms at 10:00 PM. Two hours later he developed diarrhea, sweating, vertigo, and salivation. He fell asleep but was awake at 2:00 AM disoriented, irrational, and violent. On admission to hospital he was cyanotic, responded to pinpricks but not to deep pain. He was disoriented in all three spheres. Somnolence alternated with excitement. He thought he was in hell. He spoke continually and irrationally of religious matters. A physician was misidentified as Christ. When not in hell he was convinced he was in Eden. That evening his mental state cleared and next morning he was normal.

PSYCHOLOGICAL

Fabing and Hawkins (1956) gave bufotenine by intravenous injection to a series of healthy young convicts from Ohio State Penitentiary. All had been college students and had been mentally well. A dose of 1 mg produced a sensation of tightness in the chest and paresthesias of the face. Two mg caused a feeling of tightness in the stomach and a purple hue of the skin of the face. A feeling of weight and a state of relaxation was produced by 4 mg. This was followed by visual hallucinations of vivid red and black blocks, an inability to concentrate, and a feeling of great placidity with less anxiety. A sensation of lightheadedness, facial burning, a deep purple facial color and a sense of calm was caused by 8 mg. One subject saw some geometrical patterns in color. Six minutes after the end of the injection he felt relaxed and languid. After 16 mg these changes were more pronounced. During the injection the subject saw purple spots on the floor following each other in rapid succession. After the injection was over the visual changes were gone but space perception remained impaired. His face remained purple for 1 hour. Time and space perception remained grossly impaired.

Nausea was experienced early in the bufotenine changes. With the 16-mg dose the subject suffered retching. Nystagmus and mydriasis occurred in all cases. Pulse and blood pressure changes were minimal. All the subjects reported they were relaxed for up to 6 hours after the injection. They lay contentedly feeling pleasantly relaxed. Evarts (1958) reported that Isbell at Lexington had corroborated Fabing's findings that bufotenine was hallucinogenic for man.

Turner and Merlis (1959) attempted to produce psychological changes by inhaling Cohoba snuff but had difficulty retaining very much and they noted no reaction. They also quoted Isbel "No subjective or objective effects were observed after spraying as much as 40 mg of bufotenine creatinine sulfate."

However, bufotenine injected into schizophrenic patients did produce changes depending upon the rapidity of the injection. When they injected 20 mg over a 50-second interval there was an extreme reaction. The subject's face turned a plum color, the EEG slowed to 1 cycle per second with an increase in amplitude and some patients had intense salivation.

Pretreatment with reserpine or chlorpromazine made bufotenine much more active and after reserpine 2.5 to 5.0 mg was nearly fatal.

BIOCHEMISTRY

Axelrod (1961) found an enzyme in rabbit lung tissue which N-methylated 5-HT to bufotenine and tryptamine to N,N-dimethyltryptamine.

Bufotenine, like tryptamine and 5-HT, is oxidized by monoamine oxidase *in vitro* but the methyl groups on the terminal nitrogen slows this reaction (Govier *et al.*, 1953; Vane, 1959). Himwich *et al.* (1960) found that monoamine oxidase inhibitors potentiated the effect of bufotenine in dogs, which suggests but does not prove, bufotenine is oxidized by monoamine oxidases *in vivo*.

Fish *et al.* (1955b) found the microsome fraction of mouse liver homogenate converted N,N-dimethyltryptamine to its oxide. When incubation was carried out with whole homogenate the reverse change occurred. The microsome fraction also converted it and bufotenine, to β-indoleacetic acid.

Himwich *et al.* (1960) found that IV bufotenine increased the secretion of adrenaline from the adrenal medulla. But in dogs pretreated with another amine oxidase inhibitor, it increased adrenaline secretion two- to fivefold.

According to Erspamer, bufotenine inhibited human plasma cholinesterase more than serotonin. But on red cell esterase, tryptamine, and psilocybin had the same activity as serotonin. Bufotenine and gramine were 20 times as active. Hydrolysis of benzoylcholine by plasma cholinesterase was activated by tryptamine, but N,N-dimethyltryptamine was ineffective. Serotonin was 50 times as active as tryptamine or bufotenine in producing pain when placed on the exposed base of a cantharidin blister.

PHARMACOLOGY

Himwich *et al.* (1960) gave 0.5 mg/kg bufotenine IV to normal dogs. There was an immediate respiratory arrest following by panting. Then they observed slight weakness of the legs, ataxia, reduction of motor activity, salivation and piloerection. The animals recovered within 30 minutes. When dogs were pretreated with iproniazid (25 mg/kg) 5 times over a two-day period, the same quantity of bufotenine produced a much more severe reaction for a longer period of time. Female dogs were more sensitive to this combination.

Evarts (1958) found that 0.2 mg/kg of bufotenine in the carotid artery produced an effect similar to 30 μg/kg of LSD. There was an 80% decrease in amplitude of the postsynaptic lateral geniculate response to a single near-maximal optic nerve volley. In contrast to the response of the postsynaptic lateral geniculate area, the postsynaptic cortical response to stimulation of geniculate radiation fibers was very resistant to depression produced by bufotenine and LSD; 10 mg/kg via the left carotid had hardly any effect. Similarly the optic tract response to retinal photic stimulation was not depressed. Thus the geniculate relay seemed most sensitive and might be one of the target areas for bufotenine activity. *N,N*-dimethyltryptamine had a similar pattern of activity. Tryptamine had a transient inhibitory effect.

Walaszek (1960) studied the effect of topical application of adrenaline on the cerebral cortex of animals, or the CEPR. When adrenaline was applied to the cortex of the brain there was an elevation of blood pressure. Some substances (chlorpromazine, ergotamine, iproniazid, arecoline, physostigmine, and nicotine) diminished the CEPR. But two psychoactive drugs, reserpine (an indole), and tetrabenazine (an isoquinolizine), which may be formed in plants from adrenaline, potentiated the blood pressure response. Three hallucinogens, LSD, bufotenine, and adrenochrome were potentiators but mescaline and serotonin had no effect. Schizophrenic serum diminished the CEPR when the blood pressure measurements were made 3 hours or longer after the injection of serum. In a few experiments when the CEPR was studied 1–3 hours after the administration of the serum, there was an exaggerated CEPR. Apparently something in schizophrenic serum produced a response similar to LSD, bufotenine, and adrenochrome but this was destroyed in the rabbit body after 3 hours.

Weil-Malherbe *et al.* (1962) repeated Walaszek's work using a different method of injecting schizophrenic serum (5 ml intravenous instead of 2-ml subcutaneous in 4 days) and analyzed some brain tissues using a modification of the adrenolutin fluorescence method (whereas

Walaszek had used a bioassay technique). It is not surprising they found different results. But it is curious that even Weil-Malherbe *et al.* reported the following catecholamine levels for schizophrenic serum-injected and control serum-injected rabbits: adrenaline—in the hypothalamus 29.1 and 24.8 µg/kg, in the brain stem 12.6 and 8.8 µg/kg; noradrenaline—in the hypothalamus 1194 and 1143 µg/kg, in the brain stem 175 and 168 µg/kg. Dopamine levels were reversed as follows, hypothalamus 197 and 269 µg/kg, brain stem 117 and 156 µg/kg. The authors, using statistical techniques, found no significant differences but methods which can yield differences of means of 8.8–12.6 with N's over 27 must be very unreliable to yield insignificant differences. The ratio of the means of schizophrenic-treated rabbits over control-treated rabbits was as follows: for adrenaline (a) hypothalamus 1.18 (b) brain stem 1.43; for noradrenaline (a) hypothalamus 1.04 (b) brain stem 1.04. However, for dopamine the ratios were reversed, that is, (a) hypothalamus 0.73 and (b) brain stem 0.75. Weil-Malherbe's data, therefore, suggest that there was an increase in the conversion of dopamine to noradrenaline and adrenaline, and, furthermore suggest that if he had followed the original method more vigorously he might have corroborated with the results of the others. In any event his data do not have much bearing on the question. It is not difficult to use methods which do not work.

Marrazzi used the transcallosal cerebral synapses of the cat brain for measuring the effect of various substances. These were injected into the carotid artery which resulted in a transient high concentration of substance on the ipsilateral or recording side but it became diluted in the general circulation and exerted no peripheral effect. Adrenaline (10 µg/kg) and noradrenaline (150 µg/kg) caused somewhat similar inhibition. Serotonin was the most potent, being active in doses as low as 1 µg/kg, and was from 20 to 25 times more active than adrenaline. Bufotenine was even more active than serotonin. Adrenochrome and mescaline were similar to each other but were much less active as inhibitors.

RELATION OF BUFOTENINE TO SCHIZOPHRENIA

Bumpus and Page (1955) presented some evidence for the presence of bufotenine or something like it in human urine. Fish and Horning, as reported by Evarts, found tryptamine in human urine and another indole, possibly bufotenine, in small concentrations. Rodnight (1961) developed a method for measuring bufotenine in urine and in blood. He found no trace of bufotenine or any other methylated indole amine in urine from 8 mentally ill patients including 6 schizophrenic patients. On the other hand, Fischer *et al.* (1960, 1961a,b,c) developed a more sensitive method and they were able to corroborate the original findings of Bumpus and Page. They found a close relationship between the presence of bufotenine or some bufoteninelike substance and schizophrenia. Perry *et al.* (1962) also found bufotenine in urine in small quantities in normal children. Four children excreted bufotenine after monoamine oxidase blockade and one child excreted it normally. Blocking monoamine oxidase also increased the excretion of serotonin, tryptamine, normetanephrine, *p*-tyramine, and synephrine.

Dimethyl- and Diethyltryptamines

Fish *et al.* (1955a) found *N,N*-dimethyltryptamine in *Piptadena perigrina*. Some time after that Hochstein and Paradies (1957) also found it in *Prestonia amazonicum*, a member of the *Apocyanaceae*. According to Lewin (1931) the *Banisteria caapi* plant (which contains harmine) was prepared mixed with *Prestonia amazonicum*. "If the latter is added to the beverage, the character of the effects are different because this plant is extremely toxic."

Wilkinson (1958) extracted 5-methoxy-*N*-methyltryptamine from *Phalaris rundinacea* L. Sheep pastured on this grass developed staggers. Hordenine, psychologically inactive, was also present. Gallagher *et al.* (1964) reported that sheep grazing on pastures in southeastern Australia which contained *Phalaris tuberosa*, occasionally developed sudden collapse and death, or more chronically phalaris staggers. They saw 5 cases. Autopsy findings suggested a specific cardiopharmacological substances was involved. The major alkaloids in this plant were *N,N*-dimethyltryptamine and 5-methoxy-*N,N*-dimethyltryptamine with smaller quantities of bufotenine and traces of other indoles.

Parenteral administration of these substances or gramine-killed sheep, guinea pigs, rats, and mice due to acute heart failure. Pulse rates went up to 170–270 per minute. In the most severe form of acute phalaris staggers the sheep lay on their side with tetanic spasms and extensor rigidity of their legs. Their pupils were dilated and they had profound ropy salivation. Sheep affected less severely were hyperexcitable, walked with an incoordinated gait, and had convulsive spasms. All these changes were exaggerated by fright or enforced movement.

The same changes were seen in the laboratory. The most potent substance was 5-methoxydimethyltryptamine which produced changes when 0.1 mg/kg was given. These included hyperexcitability, salivation, head-nodding, ear-twitching, tail-twitching, dilatation of the pupils, circling movements, and incoordination. In sheep 5-hydroxydimethyltryptamine was less active and 0.5 mg/kg given intravenously caused similar changes plus hyperpyrexia. A dose of 1.5–2.0 mg/kg could be fatal.

Szara (1956, 1957) found that both N,N-dimethyltryptamine and N,N-diethyltryptamine were hallucinogenic for him, when he took them parenterally. They were inactive when taken by mouth.

From 3 to 4 minutes after the injection of 75 mg of dimethyltryptamine autonomic changes occurred including trembling, nausea, mydriasis, and elevation of blood pressure and the pulse rate. Simultaneously optical illusions and hallucinations appeared. These consisted of brilliantly colored moving oriental motifs and later, rapidly changing wonderful scenes. There was an elevation of mood leading to euphoria. At the height of the experience, Szara's attention was so firmly bound to the visual phenomena he could not describe them. After $\frac{3}{4}$ to 1 hour the symptoms had disappeared. Smaller doses produced less intense reactions.

The response to 60 mg of the N,N-diethyl derivative came on in 15 minutes, but when it occurred was similar to the effect of the simpler analog. The experience was over in about 3 hours.

In contrast to mescaline or LSD both compounds produced athetoid or choreiform movements.

Boszormenyi and Brunecker (1957) gave 1 mg/kg to 20 chronic schizophrenics and 4 normal subjects. The groups responded very differently. The schizophrenics responded more slowly and had fewer autonomic and psychological effects. Schizophrenics did not develop hallucinations.

Boszormenyi *et al.* (1959) studied the psychotomimetic properties of N,N-diethyltryptamine (DET). They experimented with 30 normal subjects and 41 psychiatric patients. The model psychoses, which developed by administration of 0.70–0.80 mg/kg given intramuscularly, resembled the action of a mescaline experience of mild to moderate severity. It caused the following changes: (a) Vegetative symptoms. These appeared 8–15 minutes after injection. They included dizziness, pupillary dilatation, nausea, tremor, increased pulse rate, and an increase of 10–40 mm Hg in blood pressure. Most of the unpleasant effects subsided in 40 minutes. (b) Neurological changes were less marked than with N,N-dimethyltryptamine. The main findings were paresthesia and transient reflex changes. Athetoid movements described for DMT did not occur. (c) Perceptual changes were prominent as with other hallucinogens. Auditory hallucinations occurred less frequently. In common with other hallucinogens the psychedelic experience also occurred. One subject reported, "The materialization of sounds varies all the time. Once ballet dancers, dressed in transparent silver-like clothes were dancing, sliding on ice, then blades danced, swords of different shapes broke through space, twinkling, shining, turning round and round. Then cliffs split apart, snow-covered peaks and blue ridges emerged from the ground toward the sky, then again there were many small ladders of glass and on them minute globules of sound were running up and down, dancing and jumping. Then again a small goldfish swam rapidly across an aquarium and the sound was the row of bubbles in its wake." (d) Perception of time was disturbed. (e) Associations were loosened or usually accelerated. During the latter part of the experience the subjects were more introverted. (f) Mood was usually euphoric. Transient anxiety was common. (g) Consciousness was clouded in the majority of cases. This was compared to being drunk or half asleep. Episodes of depersonalization occurred. Some subjects had a double awareness, that is, of themselves and of the environment. After the experience subjects were tired and had some headache, depression, and insomnia which lasted less than one day.

The effect of DET upon the EEG of 25 subjects was examined. Amplitude decreased and alpha rhythm was accelerated. The regularity of the alpha rhythm decreased. In general these changes paralleled the clinical changes in time. The major change came on at 50–80 minutes and produced an alert pattern. Under the influence of DET the majority of uncommunicative patients became more communicative. This was especially marked after the third hour.

DET was superior to intravenous barbiturates for exploring dynamics and for facilitating therapy. It appeared to be better than LSD or mescaline because the action did not last as long. Several subjects felt that DET experience was similar to deliria that they had experienced in the past with fever, or with trauma. The authors questioned whether fever deliria might be due to some abnormality in tryptophan metabolism.

Sai-Halasz (1962) gave about 1 mg/kg IM to a series of normal volunteers. They experienced an intense hallucinatory state for about 40 minutes. Some of the subjects were pretreated with 1 mg methylsergide (UML-491) a potent antiserotonin lysergic acid derivative 2 to 3 months later. They were then given the same quantity of DMT. The symptoms were intensified markedly. High doses of methysergide followed by DMT resulted in a profound estrangement from reality.

In a further study Sai-Halasz (1963) reported that a monoamine oxidase inhibition for several days with 100 mg of iproniazid decreased the human response to DMT. Seven subjects were given 100 mg of iproniazid for 4 days. This was followed by 2 days' rest and then 0.65–0.83 mg/kg of DMT on the seventh day. The reaction was less strong than they would have expected and consisted of two phases (a) an initial phase which lasted 14–24 minutes, similar to the usual DMT reaction but less intense, and (b) a following stage when no symptoms were present. However, the subjects were aware they were not normal. They still felt disinterested. After 70 minutes they were all normal. Sai-Halasz found the second phase comparable to schizophrenia.

Boszormenyi (1960) found an interesting sequel to the DET experience in many subjects. They had received from 0.70 to 0.80 mg/kg IM and had the usual reaction. But some time later several subjects began to show an interest in art and a renewed interest in writing. In our large series of normal subjects given LSD we have seen similar responses. Two of Boszomenyi's subjects began to paint whereas before the experience they had shown no inclination to do so. One of the subjects began to paint in order to better express his inexpressible experiences. Several professional authors compared their experience with spontaneous inspiration. Others were disappointed when no inspiration came to them. A young poet reported "The objects opened up their essence to me, I was feeling as if I knew them as they really are, I lived in them and was in direct contact with them. . . . I felt an enormous drive to write, to put down the marvelous feelings."

A painter reported "I felt as I did when I began to learn painting, when I tried to look at things consciously with a painter's eye . . . on a subject with normal mind this experience will certainly have an astonishing and marvelous effect. An artist with creative mind and phantasy will be less impressed." Boszormenyi suggested that the increase in creativity was due to the emergence of ancient desires and drives which forced the person to satisfy them by creating. This he explained was a temporary regression to childishness. One subject, a psychiatrist, wrote, "I felt as if I were discovering the world anew . . . like a small child staring at things."

There is much evidence that children and young adolescents do have a richer and less stable perceptual world than adults, and in this sense the psychedelic drugs do produce a temporary regression, at least in perception. Perhaps this is one of the dyanamic factors behind creativity. But we think an equally important factor is the increased awareness of new perceptual vistas and of the limitations of ordinary stable perception. This is more in line with Huxley's (1954) summation "the eye regains something of the unbiased look of childhood."

Effect of Bufotenine, Dimethyltryptamine (DMT), and Diethyltryptamine (DET) on Animal Behavior

Bufotenine (18–27 mg/kg IP) confused trained rats and changed their normal posture, that is, they dragged their abdomens on the floor. This is very similar to the effect of adrenochrome on rat behavior

(Weckowicz, 1961). Climbing time was prolonged up to 2 hours. LSD was 25 times more active but its effect was less prolonged. Bufotenine was about as active as adrenochrome. On repeated injections, tolerance developed to bufotenine. Pretreatment with 5-hydroxytryptophan protected the animals against both bufotenine and LSD.

Diethyltryptamine strongly affected rats and mice in doses of 30–50 mg/kg subcutaneously. It was also anticonvulsant and analgesic. One mg/kg completely counteracted the stimulating effect of 5 mg/kg subcutaneously of amphetamine. Pretreatment with reserpine partially blocked DET's effect (Pfeifer et al., 1961a,b,c).

DET (5–10 mg/kg IV) was neurotoxic to mice and rats (Borsy et al., 1961). As an analgesic it was midway in activity between LSD and mescaline. It enhanced the vasopressor activity of adrenaline on chloralose urethane narcotized cats. Himwich et al. (1959, 1960) injected bufotenine into the carotid artery of the vertebral artery which perfused the caudal portion of the brain. The behavioral reaction was intense. The cats developed reversible paraplegia, reflex oral movements, barking or howling, an apprehensive stare with bloodshot eyes, ataxia, weakness, and inappropriate behavior, for example, biting the wooden sides of the pen while wagging their tails.

Sai-Halasz and Endroczy (1959) found that 2-mg/kg DET produced the same activity in dogs as was reported for bufotenine. These were intense autonomic changes such as mydriasis and changes in respiration. The dogs appeared to hallucinate. During the 2 hours the drug was active the intensity fluctuated. There was also a decrease in performance of the conditioned response in trained animals.

Evarts (1956, 1958) compared the effect of bufotenine and LSD on the behavior of monkeys. Monkeys of weight 3–4½ kg were given 5 mg/kg IV bufotenine sulfate. The drug effect reached a maximum in 1 minute. For the next 20 minutes the animals did not walk or climb. They lay prone on the floor and when attempts were made to move them forcefully, returned to the prone position even though their muscle power was normal. After 20 minutes they began to move about and attempted to sit up. Their movements were ataxic. At 55 minutes there was still slight ataxia, but the animals showed a lack of response to pain and to visual stimuli. At 65 minutes the monkey remained blind and were unusually tame. They ran about the room without ataxia but headlong into objects. After normal vision returned, the animals remained unusually tame for 1½–2 hours when they appeared normal. Five mg/kg bufotenine produced an effect very similar to 1 mg/kg of LSD.

According to Gessner et al. (1960, 1961), bufotenine, serotonin, and 5-methoxytryptamine altered conditioned behavior in rats in the same way. The most active substance was 5-methoxy-*N,N*-dimethyltryptamine which was 3 times as powerful as bufotenine. In 10 trials, 0.05 mm/kg caused 10 mistakes. *O*-Methylation increased the potency of gramine, serotonin, and bufotenine in causing behavioral mistakes. *N,N*-Dimethylation of 5-methoxytryptamine increased the potency but *N*-acetylation inactivated it. They suggested that *o*-methylation of hydroxyindoles was not an inactivation mechanism for these indoles as it was for catecholamines. Melatonin was inactive in rats.

BIOCHEMISTRY

Erspamer (1955) and Szara (1957) found that 3-indolylacetic acid was the main metabolite of *N,N*-dimethyltryptamine in urine of rats. Szara (1957) found an increase in 5-hydroxyindolylacetic acid (a metabolite of serotonin). No unchanged dimethyltryptamine was found in urine or in blood after 10 minutes. Apparently, it was metabolized very quickly.

According to Szara (1961) both DMT and DET were metabolized by two main routes. One, as a result of dealkylation and oxidative deamination led to 3-indolylacetic acid. The other as a result of 6-hydroxylation, conjugation, then dealkylation and oxidative deamination led to 6-hydroxy-DMT or 6-hydroxy-DET. Szara *et al.* (1960) and Szara and Hearst (1962) found that 6-hydroxylation increased the psychological activity of these compounds. The hydroxylation occurred in liver and required reduced triphosphopyridine nucleotide (a nicotinamide containing enzyme) and oxygen.

DET injected IP into rats was partially converted into 6-HDET. They determined the behavioral threshold doses (BTS's) of DET and 6-HDET on rats. This was the minimum dose that brought about a significant increase in the number of electric shocks required after injection. This value was determinable within 1 mg/kg. An increase in dose by 1 mg produced a marked increase in shock at the critical level. The median point was taken as the BTS. Szara (1961) suggested mammalian tissue might produce more active 6-hydroxymethylated tryptamine derivatives.

However, a double blind comparison study by Rosenberg *et al.* (1963) did not support Szara's suggestion. They compared 6-hydroxy-*N*-dimethyltryptamine, *N*-dimethyltryptamine, and placebo in a number of subjects using the usual dose of DMT and 1 mg/kg of the 6-hydroxy derivative. DMT produced the usual psychotomimetic reaction but its 6-hydroxy derivative was not more active than placebo. They concluded the 6-hydroxy derivative could not be the active metabolite of DMT.

Many of these indoles are inhibitors of cholinesterase. Psilocybin and bufotenine inhibited human plasma cholinesterase more than serotonin. Tryptamine and psilocybin were as active as serotonin on red cell esterase, but bufotenine and gramine were 20 times more active. Tryptamine activated the hydrolysis of benzoylcholine by plasma cholinesterase but *N,N*-dimethyltryptamine was not active.

The ability to produce pain when placed on the exposed base of a cantharadin blister varied. Serotonin was 50 times more active than tryptamine or bufotenine.

Pharmacology

Both tryptamine and DMT depressed the geniculate response to optic nerve shock. The degree of inhibition was the same for these compounds and bufotenine but the tryptamine effect only lasted 3–6 minutes. The other two depressed the response 10 times as long. They did not reduce the cortical response to stimulation of the geniculate radiation.

Tryptamine (15 mg/kg IV) like serotonin flattened the electrocorticogram and produced a 30–40 cm/sec discharge in the rhinencephalon. infusion at a lower dose did not produce these changes.

Methyltryptamine injected in the vertebral artery of rabbits after ligation of the basilar artery produced EEG desynchronization. α-Ethyltryptamine produced an arousal pattern in the cat. Two fluorotryptamines were very active compounds. 5-Fluorotryptamine (0.25 mg) injected into the brain ventricles produced a stuporous state in mice. One mg/kg of 5-fluorotryptamine and 2 mg/kg of 5-fluoro-7-methyltryptamine placed in the brain ventricles of dogs produced a state of catatonia (Edery and Schatzberg-Porath, 1960).

Gessner *et al.* (1961) compared the oxytocic activity of several methoxyindole alkylamines. The most potent were 5-methoxygramine, *N*-acetyl-5-methoxytryptamine, 5-hydroxyindoleacetic acid, and 5-methoxyindoleacetic acid. Serotonin, 5-methoxy-*N,N*-dimethyltryptamine, and 5-methoxytryptamine and bufotenine were about 1/10,000 as active as vasopressor potentiators. Serotonin was most active followed by 5-methoxydimethyltryptamine, 5-methoxytryptamine, and bufotenine.

Apparently ortho methylation reduced the vasopressor activity of bufotenine but greatly increased oxytocic activity. *N*-acetylation of 5-methoxytryptamine inactivated it.

Cross-Tolerance of DMT

Rosenberg *et al.* (1964) investigated the cross-tolerance of DMT with LSD, mescaline and psilocybin. When DMT was given to subjects already tolerant to LSD they responded in the usual way to DMT. There was no cross tolerance as there is for LSD, mescaline and psilocybin. They also found no cross-tolerance to *d*-amphetamine, scopolamine, or JB-318.

α-Methyltryptamine

α-Methyltryptamine is an amine oxidase inhibitor with an oral LD-50 equal to 138 mg/kg in the rat according to Sandoz Inc., as reported by Murphree *et al.* (1961). They gave 12 inmates from a penitentiary 20 mg orally. The effect came on in about 3 to 4 hours and lasted 12 to 24 hours. In 2 subjects the changes continued 2 days. The majority reported that they were nervous, irritable, restless, and could not relax. Visual effects were not prominent. The subjects in general did not like the experience which they compared to a long-lasting LSD reaction. α-Ethyltryptamine was much less potent in its action, Szara (1961) found that 20 mg of *dl*-α-methyltryptamine was equivalent to 60 mg DET in psychotomimetic activity. There were more perceptual distortion but fewer autonomic reactivity.

Murphree *et al.* (1960) found *dl*-α-methyltryptamine at a dose of 20 mg produced a subjective action equivalent to 50 μg of LSD. The effect appeared later. The lag continued for up to 3 hours.

BIOCHEMISTRY

When it was incubated with rat liver microsomes, Szara (1961) found 3-indolyllacetone, 6-hydroxy-α-methyltryptamine and 6-hydroxy-3-indolyl-acetone. α-Methyltryptamine was about as active as α-ethyltryptamine as a monoamine oxidase inhibitor, but it also inhibited 5-hydroxy-tryptophan decarboxylase.

According to Gey and Pletscher (1962) α-methyl, α-ethyl, and α-dimethyltryptamine as well as harmaline were monoamine oxidase inhibitors *in vivo*. Given to rats, they increased serotonin levels in brain and heart after treatment with 5-hydroxytryptophan and inhibited the decrease of serotonin produced by tetrabenazine. The dimethyl derivative was the least active inhibitor.

PHARMACOLOGY

α-Methyltryptamine increased both systolic and diastolic blood pressure 3 hours after administration and increased pupillary diameter. In dogs it produced orthostatic hypotension. Himwich (1961) and Van Meter *et al.* (1960) found that α-methyltryptamine altered the EEG of rabbit preparations. It produced an amphetaminelike arousal pattern.

When the basilar artery was tied in the midpontine area, intracarotid injection also produced an immediate alerting. Posterior injections caused delayed activation probably due to the slower accumulation of serotonin.

α-Methyltryptamine, when applied electrophoretically to spinal neurones in lumbar segments of cats, did not alter the responses of the spinal interneurons (Curtis, 1962). This suggests tryptamine receptors are not of great significance in the operation of synaptic transmitters within the spinal cord.

α-Ethyltryptamine

α-Ethyltryptamine, better known as etryptamine or Monase, is a monoamine oxidase inhibitor which was released as an antidepressant compound but removed a short time later because of some toxicity.

PSYCHOLOGICAL

Murphree *et al.* (1961) gave 11 subjects 150 mg of α-ethyltryptamine by mouth. Within 30 to 90 minutes, 8 subjects reported that they felt intoxicated. Two were stimulated; later, 5 were lethargic, let down or sedated, and 4 had a hangover the next day. Usually the effects were of moderate duration. Six subjects reported anorexia and/or nausea. Three reported visual disturbances such as blurred vision or flashes of light. Only 2 subjects compared it to LSD.

α-Ethyltryptamine is not a powerful psychotomimetic but it is an antidepressant or euphorient. Robie (1961a,b), Turner and Merlis (1961a,b), and Kast (1961) reported that this substance had valuable antidepressant properties and many more observers, using ethyltryptamine, attested to this belief at the same symposium.

EFFECT ON ANIMAL BEHAVIOR

Greig *et al.* (1961) found that ethyltryptamine was as active as *d*-amphetamine in increasing motor activity of mice. Given before reserpine, it prevented any depression in mice. When mice were first treated with reserpine, ethyltryptamine later had no effect.

Matthews *et al.* (1961) gave ethyltryptamine to cats. Doses of 10 mg/kg produced definite changes in behavior. There was a decrease in spontaneous motor activity together with a stimulant central effect. Pupils were dilated. Nonpurposeful head movements occurred. Reflexes were intact but the animals could walk when prodded. When stimulated, the cat responded with hissing, spitting, piloerection, and a laying back of ears. The animals were normal in 24 hours.

Van Meter *et al.* (1960) reported that 10–20 mg/kg of α-methyl-tryptamine given intraperitoneally produced locomotor excitation and other behavioral changes in rats.

BIOCHEMISTRY

Ethyltryptamine is a competitive inhibitor of monoamine oxidase. *In vivo* it decreased brain and liver MAO activity and caused the accumulation of serotonin (Grieg *et al*, 1961). With ethyltryptamine alone serotonin increased 30% in rat brains but combined with 5-hydroxytryptophan the increase was 175%. There was only a slight inhibition of 5-hydroxytryptophan decarboxylase. Neither glutamic acid decarboxylase nor true cholinesterase were inhibited, but there was some inhibition of pseudocholinesterase. Brain noradrenaline levels were also increased by 8 mg/kg twice daily.

Eberts (1961) studied the distribution and excretion of ^{14}C-ethyltryptamine. In rats given 10 mg/kg IP, 73% appeared in the urine in 12 hours. Fecal excretion was minor. In rats and in dogs, the liver and organs of the gastrointestinal and genitourinary tract showed the greatest retention 24 hours after administration. There was no long term drug storage.

PHARMACOLOGICAL

Ethyltryptamine slowed the heart rate in human subjects and increased pupillary diameter (Murphree *et al.*, 1961). In dogs sedated with pentobarbital, ethyltryptamine did not produce any orthostatic hypotension (Grieg *et al.*, 1961).

Matthews *et al.* (1961) measured the action of ethyltryptamine on electrical transmission of stimuli. Ten mg/kg IV in cats depressed post-ganglionic spike potentials 30%. The depression was an initial response. It was maximal in 5 minutes but recovery was complete in 1 hour. Complete block was not found. The spinal and primary afferent pathways were not affected by doses which altered behavior. The EEG pattern of cerveau isole was not altered but in the intact animal there was sustained, low voltage, fast activity characteristic of arousal.

Himwich (1961) found that α-ethyltryptamine injected into rabbits produced an amphetaminelike arousal EEG pattern for about 25 minutes. This was then followed by a different type of alert pattern as it was occasionally interrupted by fleeting sleep reactions. This was due, they believe, to accumulation of serotonin and lasted about 1 hour. Steiner *et al.* (1963) repeated these findings and again found similar EEG changes and a 100% increase in brain serotonin. There was no change in noradrenaline levels in rabbit but a slight increase in rats. They concluded the ethyltryptamine had a direct stimulant effect and suggested there was no need to postulate an indirect action affecting serotonin or noradrenaline.

Methyl-2-methyltryptamine

Methyl-2-methyltryptamine is one of the newer antidepressants which was tested by Sandoz in Canada.

The 4-substituted indoles are interesting compounds and it is not surprising this compound was active. Its LD-50 for mice was 55 mg/kg given intravenously and 90 mg/kg given subcutaneously. The LD-50 for rabbits given intravenously was 6 mg/kg. It was less toxic than IT-290.

The 4-methyl derivative was a weak monoamine oxidase inhibitor. In rats it abolished the reserpine effect but had less synergistic effect with 5-hydroxytryptophan and α-dopa than did Catron.

Preliminary clinical investigations showed it was an antidepressant and was beneficial in two thirds of a small group of neurotic patients.

Iboga Alkaloids

The bark of the root of *Tabernanthe iboga* contains about 12 alkaloids (Downing, 1962). Of these the best known is ibogaine, a tryptamine derivative. This plant, named in 1889 by Baillon, was used by the natives of West Africa and the Congo to increase resistance against fatigue and tiredness and as an aphrodisiac. Dybowski and Landrin (1901) extracted the psychologically active alkaloid which they named ibogaine. They reported that the natives considered the plant equivalent or similar to alcohol, that it was a stimulant which did not disturb the thought processes of the user.

They wrote "l'Iboga avait sur eux une action identique a celle de l'alcool sans troubler la raison." Turner *et al.* (1955) believed this was a denial by the natives that ibogaine was psychotomimetic. But this is an interpretation based upon the belief that humans having perceptual changes must have some disorder of thought. Many unsophisticated subjects taking LSD, mescaline, or psilocybin do have changes in thought but after they became experienced with these compounds, changes in thought are rare. Native consumers of peyote, the *Psilocybe* mushrooms and, perhaps, iboga extract, can have vivid perceptual changes with no disturbance in thought.

According to Landrin (1905), Guien described the effect of chewing large quantities of roots on natives being initiated. They became very tense, developed an epilepticlike state during which they became unconscious and uttered words considered prophetic. An initiate would have a set toward initiation which combined with the iboga root could well produce these extreme states of excitement.

Dybowski and Landrin (1901) found ibogaine was as active psychologically as the whole root. Small doses produced states of excitation while massive doses were narcotic which they compared to massive quantities of alcohol. Haller and Heckel (1901) also extracted an alkaloid, probably the same one, which they called ibogaine.

Pouchet and Chevalier (1905) found that ibogaine given intravenously to dogs produced violent excitation motor incoordination, hallucinations, paraplegia, paralysis, and anesthesia. Tetanic convulsions occurred just before death. Death came from respiratory arrest and the heart stopped in diastole. They concluded ibogaine was a stimulant of the central nervous system. They found it was also a good surface anesthetic less intense than cocaine. There was a period of hyperesthesia before the anesthesia came on.

Animal Behavior

According to Lambert and Heckel (1901) subconvulsive doses produced marked changes in dogs. They developed a state of excitation and appeared to have hallucinations. The dogs crouched in a corner, growled and barked. After 1 hour they were normal. Phisalix (1901) gave dogs ibogaine by vein. A mild cerebral excitation was produced by 0.75 mg/kg. The dogs were more active and responded with alacrity to caressing. When 1 mg/kg was given, the dogs suffered incoordination and hallucinations. Ibogaine also produced excitation in other animals.

Lambert (1902) found ibogaine had a markedly cumulative effect in frogs. When 5 mg was injected, there was no noticeable effect, but the same dose given on succeeding days produced an increase in response, of the kind seen with higher initial doses. After several days the dose was toxic for some frogs. The toxic dose for frogs for one injection was 500 mg/kg. This suggests a different mode of activity for ibogaine than for LSD where toxicity does not accumulate.

Schneider and Sigg (1957) corroborated the findings of the early French scientists. They gave 2–10 mg/kg by vein to cats and dogs. In cats the effect came on immediately. They became very excited, began to develop a tremor, and developed rage reactions. The animals remained in one place, while hissing as if trying to frighten away an imaginary object. Often they tried to hide in a corner or to climb over the walls. At the height of the excitatory phase the animals had peculiar clinic extension of all the limbs which spread the limbs in all directions with the abdomen on the floor. The cats frequently mewed. Maximum excitement was reached in 10–20 minutes. Usually there were marked autonomic reactions including pupillary dilatation, salivation, partial piloerection, and tremor. After 1–2 the cats were normal.

Gershon and Lang (1962) also saw the marked excitatory properties of ibogaine. Dogs became more anxious and alert and did not recognize their regular handlers. Body tremor and shaking was noted in dogs and also in sheep. In dogs ibogaine caused a peculiar stance with legs apart and back arched.

In anesthetized dogs, cats, and sheep, ibogaine was analeptic and anesthesia was lightened.

Gershon and Lang (1962) and Schneider and Rinehart (1957) found that pretreatment with atropine prevented the rise in blood pressure produced in conscious dogs by ibogaine but according to the former the behavioral changes were not affected. Schneider and Rinehart (1957) suggested the increase in blood pressure produced by ibogaine was due to its stimulating effect on the reticular activating system. Anesthetized dogs, unable to respond to stimulation, suffered a decrease in blood pressure.

CHEMISTRY

Ibogaine had long been considered an indole because it reacted in color tests as an indole.

Another similar alkaloid voacangine present in *T. iboga* was first isolated from *Voacanga africana.* Renner *et al.* (1959) isolated 1 known and 4 new alkaloids from *C. durissima Stapf, Isovoacangine* (first found in *Stemmadenia* species by Walls *et al.*, 1958). The new compounds were conopharyngine, conodurine, conoduramine, and alkaloid E. Some alkaloids from iboga are tabulated below.

Alkaloid	R_1	R_2	R_3
Ibogaine	OCH_3	H	H
Ibogamine	H	H	H
Tabernanthine	H	OCH_3	H
Coronaridine	H	H	$COOCH_3$
Voacangine	OCH_3	H	$COOCH_3$
Isovoacangine	H	OCH_3	$COOCH_3$
Conopharyngine	OCH_3	OCH_3	$COOCH_3$

PHARMACOLOGY

Lambert and Heckel (1901), Phisalix (1901), Lambert (1902), Raymond-Hamet (1941a,b), Raymond-Hamet and Rothlin (1939), and Rothlin and Raymond-Hamet (1938) completed the early studies on the pharmacology of ibogaine.

When injected subcutaneously into the frog, voluntary movements and reflex activity were abolished, but muscles were still excitable. Respiratory movements were reduced for a time, but there was no effect on the heart rate. The toxic dose was about 0.5 gm/kg. In the guinea pig, rabbit, and dog, death occurred during convulsions.

In dogs, respiration was accelerated, the temperature became elevated, and the pupils became widely dilated and unresponsive to light.

Lambert and Heckel reported that sublethal doses produced an anesthetic effect around the area of the injection. They compared the surface anesthetic properties of ibogaine with cocaine. A few drops instilled in the eye abolished corneal sensation, although the solution produced a slightly caustic sensation in the eye.

Ibogaine inhibited contraction of the small intestine of the rabbit and the large intestine of the guinea pig. It decreased the inhibitor action of adrenaline but did not alter the effect of acetylcholine. Ergotamine reversed ibogaine's action. Ibogaine had no direct effect on the seminal vesicle of guinea pig but inhibited almost completely the motor effects of adrenaline and acetylcholine, that is, it antagonized adrenaline, acetylcholine, yohimbine, and atropine.

Schneider and Sigg (1957) studied the effect of ibogaine on the electroencephalogram of cats. Cats with cerveau isole and encephale isole preparations as well as curarized animals showed a typical arousal syndrome when a 2–5 mg/kg were given by vein. A slow frequency high-amplitude pattern was altered to a pattern of fast low-amplitude activity. It resembled the change during direct stimulation of the reticular formation. After ½–1 hour the patterns were normal. Pretreatment with atropine (2 mg/kg) blocked the arousal effect of ibogaine.

There were only slight changes in reflexes. The knee jerk reflex was reduced slightly. There was no effect on neuromuscular transmission. Ibogaine, in spite of its stimulant properties, had weak but definite anticonvulsant properties.

Iboga extract and ibogaine were weak cholinesterase inhibitors (Vincent and Sero, 1942). This is a property shared with many of the hallucinogenic indoles.

Gershon and Lang (1962) compared the effect of ibogaine in conscious and anesthetized dogs. In conscious dogs 5 mg/kg ibogaine accentuated the sinus arrhythmia by potentiating vagus effects. In anesthetized dogs the blood pressure fell and heart rate decreased. It also inhibited acetylcholine hypotensive response in anesthetized preparations, and potentiated the pressor response of both adrenaline and noradrenaline in conscious and anesthetized dogs. The serotonin pressor response was potentiated in both. Ibogaine did not alter heart rate changes induced by acetylcholine, histamine, or serotonin.

Salmoiraghi and Page (1957) compared the effect of bufotenine, mescaline, and ibogaine on the potentiation of hexobarbital hypnosis produced by serotonin and reserpine. Serotonin prolonged the hypnotic effect of hexobarbital as did reserpine. Large doses of LSD and BOL blocked this effect. Small doses of LSD and BOL potentiated the action of serotonin but not the reserpine potentiation. On the contrary this potentiation was blocked. Large doses of bufotenine blocked, and small doses enhanced the effect. Mescaline and ibogaine blocked the potentiation.

Harmine

Harmine is another one of the indole hallucinogens derived from native plant materials. It is found in the equatorial areas of western South America drained by the upper Amazon's tributaries and used by the tribes of Peru, Ecuador, Colombia, and Brazil, as an hallucinogenic substance. The *Banisteriopsis caapi* belongs to the family Malpighiaceae; mostly woody climbers. The same plant has various names, *Caapi ayahuasca, C. natema, C. nepe, C. pinde,* and *C. kahi* and the same name is applied to the beverage prepared from it. *Banisteriopsis* has been confused with *Prestonia Amazonica,* (*Haemadictyon Amazonicum*),

Yage, Jahi, Yahe, and Yaje which contains only *N,N*-dimethyltryptamine (Hochstein and Paradies, 1957).

Lewin (1931) reported that the natives often took both extracts simultaneously and that *P. Amazonica* extracts altered the psychological response. It is not difficult to understand how a combination of harmine compounds with *N,N*-dimethyltryptamine would produce a stronger and different experience. The native sorcerers added extracts from the wood and leaves of *P. Amazonica* to *Banisteriopsis* liquid which transposed their patients into states of ecstasy. Lewin considered that both types of extracts produced similar effects.

In order to prepare the active liquid the triturated solution derived from small pieces of wood was boiled in water for 2–24 hours. This was done in order to reduce the volume and increase the potency of the extracts. The Indians were given the extracts as a medicine, when they wished some guidance, for example, in choosing a new spouse or for having some revelation of the future, or when they desired the characteristic psychedelic experience sought by users of these and other hallucinogenic drugs.

When taken on an empty stomach the results came on more rapidly. Vomiting was very frequent after every new quantity of liquid was consumed. Vertigo occurred first, followed by a period of agitation, dancing, screaming, and then the complete experience. Subjects saw visionary images, pictures bearing on their own future, beasts in which demons were incarnated and other illusions and hallucinations.

Lewin reported that white travelers also reacted to *B. caapi*. Koch-Gruneberg experienced a peculiar scintillation of crude colors. When writing, shadows like red flames passed over the page. Another traveler saw beautiful landscapes, towns, towers, parks, and wild animals against which he defended himself.

Additional reports of the activity of *B. caapi* were given by Rusby (1924). Weiss and Schmidt described to Rusby the procedures used by natives in using *B. caapi* and showed him photographs. A movie film was made by G. MacCreagh of the entire ceremony and it was shown before the American Pharmaceutical Association at the Asheville meeting in 1923.

The plant was used differently in various regions. In Bolivia it was used as an exhilarating and stimulating beverage, like tea or coffee. Very small quantities were taken. In Colombia, its objective was to give courage and fortitude. Shortly after consumption there was a powerful circulatory effect and marked pallor. The subjects became restless and developed convulsive tremors. Then after a few minutes the skin became hyperemic and they became violently active. Fear and even caution were gone and they were ready to fight anything or anybody. This violent state was followed by exhaustion and somnolence. This account by Rusby is remarkably like the berserk reaction of the Vikings many centuries ago in a different country, using mushrooms.

Villalba (1925) reported that the Indians infused pieces of stem about 20 cm long. The liquid was concentrated by heat to one-tenth of its volume, diluted with water, and again concentrated. The liquor had a red color with a greenish hue which, on standing, changed to a topaz color with a bluish green fluorescence. The Indians used 60 ml or 0.5 gm of alkaloid. Under its influence they jumped, screamed, and ran about wildly but continued to take it for days to maintain the state of excitation. Villalba ingested the pure alkaloid and had no reaction to it, whereupon he concluded that other white people who had seen visions of the future, of things lost, and visions of distances and illusions, were exaggerating the effect. It is not unusual for people who have not seen, to be skeptical of the claims of others who have.

Chen and Chen (1939) reported further on the hallucinogenic properties of *B. caapi.* Thus they wrote,

> The most outstanding feature of Caapi seems to be its ability to produce visual hallucinations and dreams in men. The Caucasians who took this preparation apparently confirmed the Indians' claims. Thus Villavicencio experienced an aerial voyage, in which he saw the most beautiful sights, and Sprice quoted a Brazilian friend as saying that once, when he took a full dose of Caapi, he saw all the marvels that he had read about in the Arabian Nights pass rapidly before his eyes as a panorama; the final sensations and sights were horrible, as usual. Cardenas made seven observations on men, including himself, with the decoction in various doses. All the subjects appeared to have optical illusions of different degrees. No excitement was recorded in any case.

According to Schultes (1963) the most widely used species of *Banisteriopsis* are *B. caapi, B. inebriens,* and *B. rusbyana. B. quitensis* is also a major source. Schultes (1963) drank the hallucinogenic drinks prepared by the natives. He doubts that *Prestonia Amazonica* is mixed with *B. caapi.* But natives did often mix several species of *Banisteriopsis. B. rusbyana* (Chagro-panga or oco-yaje) was used to make yaje stronger. When he took the drink he had a pronounced reaction. The intoxication began with a feeling of giddiness and nervousness followed by nausea and profuse perspiration. Then he noted a period of lassitude during which colors increased in intensity. This later gave way to deep sleep interrupted by dreams. The only uncomfortable aftereffect the next day was severe diarrhea.

Various names have been given to the plant extracts: telepathine (Perrot and Raymond-Hamet, 1927); yageine (Villalba, 1925); and banisterine (Lewin, 1931). Hochstein and Paradies (1957) identified three alkaloids in *B. caapi*; harmine, harmaline, and 1,2,3,4-tetrahydro-harmine. Racemic 1,2,3,4-tetrahydroharmine is leptaflorine isolated from *Leptactina densiflora*. The structure of some harmine compounds is shown in Fig. 11.

Hendrickson (1961) suggested that mitragynine, the major alkaloid of the intoxicant *Mitragyna speciosa* of Borneo, is related to 1,2,3,4-tetra-hydroharmine and is a 4-methoxyindole.

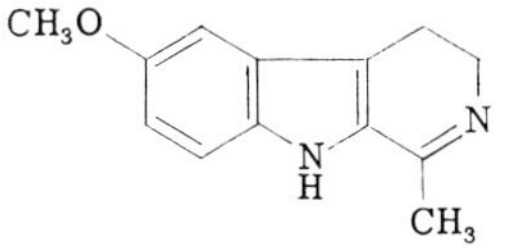

10-Methoxyharmalan

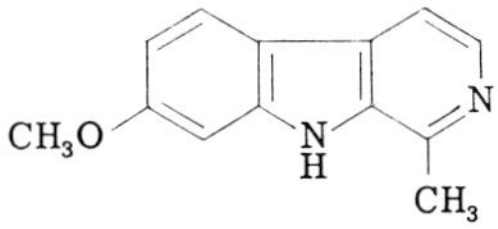

Harmine

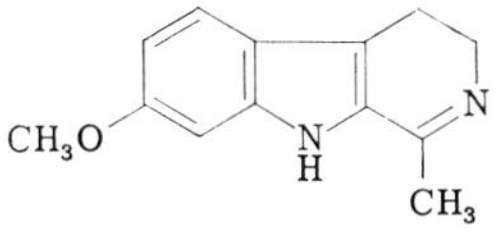

Harmaline

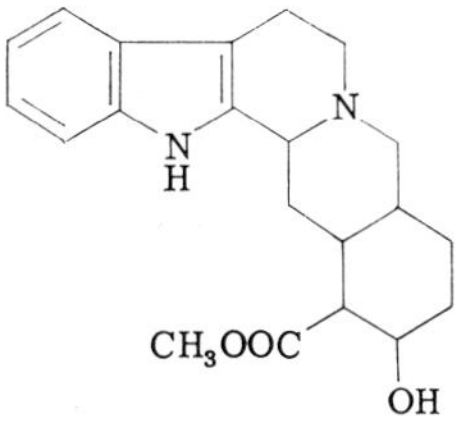

Yohimbine

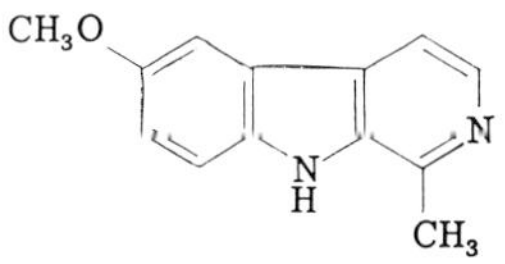

1-Methyl-6-methoxy-
2-carboline

FIG. 11. Some harmine analogs.

It is the first one to have been isolated and resembles psilocybin. According to Henry (1949) the leaves of *M. speciosa* called kratom are chewed as a narcotic in Siam. Mitragynine is a general depressant on plain muscle, facilitates the passage of autonomic impulses, and in some ways resembles cocaine. It would not be surprising if this alkaloid resembled psilocybin in its psychological activity.

O'Connell and Lynn (1953) also found harmine in *Banisteriopsis inebrians* Morton. This plant also is used by natives for ceremonial rites.

Harman, a degradation product of harmine, occurs in nature. It is found in the bark of *Symplocos racemosa* (it is identical with loturine) and in the bark of *Arariba rubra* (previously described as aribine). The alkaloid eleagnine is racemic tetrahydroharman (Marion, 1952).

PSYCHOLOGICAL

Pennes and Hoch (1957) gave harmine to mental patients: The majority were schizophrenic. The doses ranged from 20 to 960 mg oral, 40 to 70 mg SC, and 100–300 mg IV. Since normal subjects were not included, it is not possible to compare the effects of harmine as reported against LSD or mescaline. The authors reported harmine produced a similar effect but in addition there was some degree of clouding of consciousness. At low dosages slight drowsiness was produced. With medium and high doses the changes were like those produced by LSD. The reaction was semideliriod or like a cyclical confused state with intermittent drowsiness or sleep.

The major symptoms were impairment of contact, attention, grasp, responsiveness, and concentration and the subjects also had dreamy or twilight qualities. Perceptual disturbances were frequent. Hallucinations occurred with eyes closed. Subjects also noted some vertigo, lightheadedness, ataxia, and their speech was sluggish.

The threshold dose was 150–200 mg IV. With this dose 5 out of 11 subjects had visual hallucinations. No hallucinations were reported by the two other routes of administration. The subjects were free of all effects after 24 hours.

The chief differences between harmine and, for example, LSD, psilocybin, etc., as reported by these authors, was the presence of a deliriod-type reaction. Another major difference was that there was no report that any of the subjects had a pleasant or transcendental experience so commonly found with LSD. But it is premature to assume that this is a real drug difference. It is probably due to the differences in populations used, the different objectives, and the different settings. Schizophrenic patients generally do not have transcendental experiences unless they take LSD after they have recovered from the schizophrenia.

We have given LSD to a large number of patients (over 700) in 12 years and the uniform schizophrenic reaction (when they do react) is one of tension and fear in the presence of the other changes. We cannot recall even one schizophrenic who had the typical psychedelic experience. But about one half of all our other subjects, including alcoholics and normal subjects, did. The setting and objectives of the Pennes and Hoch (1957) research seem not to be conducive for these more desirable aspects of drug experience. Thus Hoch reported (1960) when discussing LSD that "actually in my experience no patient asks for it again." Denber supported Hoch's observations and none out of 200 subjects to whom he had given mescaline would have liked to have a second experience. These findings are quite opposite to our extensive findings in Saskatchewan and to those reported by all the growing group of investigators, who use the LSD experience as a treatment. We can only conclude that harmine will have to be tested by therapists who are accustomed to using LSD, etc., as therapy on patients who are not psychotic.

Effect on Animal Behavior

McIsaac *et al.* (1961) compared the effect of 10-methoxyharmalan against other similar compounds on rat behavior. They used rats conditioned to an avoidance-escape schedule. Melatonin at dose levels of 0.2 mmole/kg was inactive. 10-Methoxyharmalan (0.008 mmole/kg) caused errors. The dose response-error curve was linear to 0.25 mmole when they made 10 out of 10 errors. Harmaline was less active. Thus 10-methoxyharmalan was twice as active at 5-methoxy-N,N-dimethyl-tryptamine and 6 times as active as bufotenine.

Rats that were given 10-methoxyharmalan at doses of 2 mg/kg had a tremor for 1 hour but even at 10 mg/kg they were well able to walk. Harmine induced tremor in mice (Stern and Gasparovic, 1961). This was delayed by 5-hydroxytryptophan. Day and Yen (1962) induced tremor in mice with 50 mg/kg of harmine. The tremor was not produced in animals pretreated with nialamide, phenobarbital, chlorpromazine, meprobamate, or by LSD.

Villalba (1925) gave the alkaloid that was extracted to guinea pigs. The toxic dose was 0.2 gm/kg. After injection, the animals became restless, developed light tremors, and later the gait became peculiar and the hind limbs became extended. Later the animals were unable to stand and fell moving their limbs convulsively.

Chen and Chen (1939) reported harmine produced bodily trembling and an unsteady gait in monkeys. In larger doses they arched their back, stiffened their limbs, trembled all over, and had clonic convulsions. Gershon and Lang (1962) reported harmine in conscious dogs caused restlessness, anxiety, and apparent hallucinations.

In mice the LD-50 of harmine was 202 mg/kg. If 100 mg/kg sodium amytal was given intraperitoneally, the LD-50 was raised to nearly 600 mg/kg. Sodium amytal also produced rabbits against harmine.

CHEMISTRY

Harmine and harmaline are both crystalline and form crystalline salts with one equivalent of acid. Harmine crystallizes in needles, melting point 256–257°C, harmaline in platelets, melting point 238°C. Harmine is slightly soluble in water, alcohol, chloroform, and ether. Its hydrochloride salt is freely soluble in hot water. Harmaline is slightly soluble in hot alcohol and dilute acids, and forms blue fluorescent solutions.

A possible *in vivo* synthesis begins with 6-methoxytryptophan which condenses with acetaldehyde at pH 6.7 to yield 1,2,3,4-tetrahydro-harmine-2-carboxylic acid. On decarboxylation and oxidation, harmaline is formed which can be dehydrogenated to harmine (Downing, 1962).

McIsaac (1961a,b) synthesized 1-methyl-6-methoxy-1,2,3,4-tetrahydro-2-carboline from 5-methoxytryptamine. These are present in pineal gland tissue. McIsaac gave three rats radioactive 5-methoxytryptamine, iproniazid to inactivate amine oxidase, and disulfiram to block inactivation of acetaldehyde. Under. these conditions they found that some of the same substance was produced. They suggested a similar compound might be present in pineal tissue and that it might be adrenoglomerulotropin. McIsaac (1961a,b) and McIsaac *et al.* (1961) suggested some psychotic states could be due to endogenously produced harmalan alkaloids.

Melatonin is converted to 10-methoxyharmalan by the loss of one molecule of water (McIsaac *et al.*, 1961). The sequence of change (McIsaac, 1961a,b) was from melatonin to 10-methoxyharmalan which is similar to harmine or harmaline. McIsaac suggested that due to a peculiarity in metabolism, some serotonin could be converted to 5-methoxytryptamine and to a harminelike alkaloid or from serotonin to acetyl serotonin, melatonin, and then a harminelike toxic substance. Once produced, this would block monoamine oxidase, decrease the destruction of serotonin by a common pathway, and so increase the production of more psychotogen. This chemical reverberating system would perpetuate the illness (McIsaac, 1961a,b).

Lerner and Case (1960) reported that melatonin was also present in the peripheral nerves of man, monkeys, and cattle. It was present in the central nervous system of cattle and monkeys. They gave one subject 200 mg melatonin intravenously but saw only some mild sedation.

Harmine and harmaline were very potent inhibitors of monoamine oxidase *in vitro* and *in vivo*. They were nearly 100 times as active as iproniazid but the inhibition was of short duration. The long acting inhibitors are mainly hydrazine derivatives and may increase serotonin and noradrenaline levels in the brain for several days. Harmaline increased these amines for several hours. Pletscher and Besendorf (1959) found that rats and mice pretreated with harmaline were protected against iproniazid for up to 6 hours. After a longer interval there was no protection. Apparently the short-acting harmaline was adsorbed by monoamine oxidase and protected while the long acting inhibitor was excreted. Harmaline given after treatment with iproniazid was not an antagonist.

Woolley and Shaw (1957) reported harmaline was a serotonin antagonist. Using the isolated estrus rat uterus (McIsaac *et al.*, 1961) found that 0.2 μg of serotonin was completely blocked by 0.5 μg of LSD and 50 μg of harmine or harmaline added 5 minutes before. At higher levels they caused muscle contractions and later antagonism to serotonin was reduced. Methoxyharmalan was 25 times as active and 2 μg was as effective as 0.5 μg of LSD. Similar results were obtained on isolated guinea pig ileum. It seemed likely 10-methoxyharmalan and serotonin were competitive. The methoxyharmalan also antagonized the pressor effect of serotonin.

PHARMACOLOGICAL

In conscious dogs and sheep harmine increased arterial blood pressure and heart rate (Gershon and Lang, 1962). Blood pressure and heart rate fell in anesthetized animals. The pressor response to adrenaline was potentiated but the effect of noradrenaline was not altered. The blood pressure changes due to serotonin, were inhibited. Gerstner (1961) perfused the superior cervical ganglion with 10 μg/ml of harmine. The effect was similar to iproniazid, that is there was an immediate blocking followed by a progressive depression of transmission. The reversibility of the block with iproniazid was incomplete with harmine. When the ganglion was blocked for 1 hour with 10 μg/ml of harmine it was completely reversible but it occurred slowly. The harmine effect was independent of acetylcholine.

Harmaline protected mice against death from a combination of reserpine plus audiogenic convulsions (Lehmann and Busnel, 1961).

Harmaline is about twice as toxic as harmine to most laboratory animals (Henry, 1949). The minimum lethal doses of harmine, harmaline and tetrahydroharmine for rabbits were in the ratio 2 : 1 : 3. Changing harmine and harmaline to harmol and harmalol removed convulsant properties. The two phenols caused a progressive paralysis of the central nervous system.

Psilocybin

INTRODUCTION

Psilocybin is 4-phosphoryloxy-*N*,*N*-dimethyltryptamine, the active psychotomimetic present in the hallucinogenic mushrooms found in Mexico. These mushrooms known by Indians and used for many centuries were recently rediscovered by R. G. Wasson and V. P. Wasson in 1957. Their discovery brought Heim into this field who accurately described, identified, and named them. *Psilocybe* species, and the active hallucinogen was, therefore, named psilocybin. Psilocin is the dephosphorylated derivative. These compounds are the second type of natural indoles which contain either an hydroxyl or a phosphate group on position 4 of the benzene ring. The present interest in psilocybin as a psychotomimetic and psychedelic stems directly from the work of the Wassons and their collaboration with Professor Heim of Paris and Dr. A. Hofmann (1959), Sandoz Laboratories, Basle. This is an interesting example of pioneering research and exploration by two learned and enthusiastic mycophils, a curious mycologist and a biochemist, well-known for his work as the creator of lysergic acid derivatives. Nearly everything known about the *Psilocybe* mushrooms and psilocybin is available in the writings of these workers and their collaborators. Other scientists have done marginal research and have added some matters of detail. Recently R. G. Wasson (1962) has published a bibliography that is complete to July 1, 1962.

In primitive ages, the use of psychotomimetic mushrooms must have been widespread, especially in areas where Christianity was not yet firmly rooted. From the northern areas of Europe where the Vikings lived, eastward to the primitive tribes of Siberia, south to Borneo, and New Guinea and westward to Peru and meso-America there is evidence that these mushrooms were used in religious rites. But the use of the sacred mushrooms is dying. Even in the primitive world its survival is spotty and its arts known only to a few.

Christian white man has been remarkably intolerant of the use of any sacrament but liquors containing alcohol. The history of the native religions of the Americas can be written in terms of the conflict between Indian and white man as attempts were made to suppress these sacramental religions. The Mexicans also were forbidden the use of their sacred mushroom, nanacatl; the Indians of the southern USA were forbidden their use of peyote. Even today in many areas the use of peyote is illegal and in California some Indians were given suspended sentences for using peyote which was classed as a narcotic, although everyone who has studied it agrees it is not.

The Wassons have suggested that perhaps the idea of God arose from the accidental ingestion of these mushrooms as ancient man foraged for his food. "They may have served as a mighty detonation for early man's soul and mind and imagination" (R. G. Wasson, 1959, 1961; V. P. Wasson and Wasson, 1957).

If the Zapotec belief holds the key to the folkloric theme that we are examining, then the ancestors of all the various peoples that we have passed in review must have once known and used and worshipped the divine mushrooms. We must postulate a cultural theme of overwhelming subjective importance in pre-historic times, a period in early man's history, as he emerged from his lowly background, when the deep, disturbing powers of the hallucinatory mushroom served as an agent for the very fission of his soul, releasing his faculty for self-perception, as a stimulant for the imagination of the seer, the poet, the mystic, as a clinching argument for the existence of God. May not the hallucinatory mushrooms have been the most holy secret of the Mysteries? As the mushrooms are not addictives, we should suppose that by a progressive tabu the use was restricted to ever fewer persons, until in the end the secret was lost, except as it lingered on cryptically in myths without a remembered meaning, in obscure fossilized metaphors, and in the strange emotional rejection of all wild mushrooms that prevails to this day over much of Europe—a tabu so taken for granted by its victims that they usually perceive it not.

Our pattern of evidence is greatly strengthened by the survival into this century of the use of hallucinatory mushrooms among various remote tribes in Siberia—the Kamchadals, Korjaks, and Chukchees living on the Pacific Coast from Kamchatka to the northeastern tip of Siberia; the Yukaghirs further to the west; the Yenisei Ostjaks; and finally the Samoyed Ostjaks in the valley of the upper Ob. These people use the fly-amanita to achieve divine possession, and we discover this very mushroom potent with hallucinatory virtue, playing a role in a legend of the Chukchees that explains the origin of thunder and lightning. In the Chukchee tale as reported by Waldemar Bogoras, the lightning is a one-sided man who drags his one-sided sister along by her foot. The noise she makes as her back bumps along the floor of heaven is the thunder, and her urine is the rain. She is possessed by the spirits of the fly-amanita. Here then is the divine mushroom directly linked with the lightning-bolt, not now in Middle America but in Eurasia itself. Siberia is not the only region of the Old World where the hallucinatory mushroom is still used. We possess clear though tantalizing brief evidence that it is known to certain peoples of New Guinea and Borneo.

If true, it would be ironical that today God's religions as practiced by his White men are so antagonistic to the use of these substances which allow so many people a direct glimpse of the idea of divinity instead of having to depend upon the drier and less vivid word images described in his books.

The first record of the use of these hallucinogenic mushrooms dates from 1502, the year Montezuma was coronated. The whole city cele-

brated with nightlong dancing. Some Tlascalan princes captured by
Montezuma were given the mushrooms.

The Wassons documented all the sources describing the use of the
mushrooms. Of the 10 sources 6 were written by clerics or missionaries
of whom 3 were public officials. Only one was of Indian blood. Since
it was the official policy to suppress this religion there is some bias
in reporting. The best account was written by a Franciscan friar,
Bernardino de Sahagun who named these hallucinogenic mushrooms,
teonanacatl (sacred mushroom).

When Spain conquered Mexico the mushroom was in common use
from the Mexican valley south. It was an hallucinogenic or intoxicant
mushroom used with care and reverence in part of religious rites.
During the experience, divinatory revelations were experienced.

There was no widespread knowledge of these mushrooms this century.
This is a tribute to the care used by the Indians in withholding this
information from the white man. Safford (1915, 1921) claimed that the
mushrooms did not exist but that the Spanish priests had merely mistaken peyote buttons (*Lophophora Williamsie*) for mushrooms. This
scientific denial was rebutted by Reko (1919, 1923, 1949). In 1936,
Wertlaner (see Wasson and Wasson, 1957) found samples in Oaxaca
and sent them to Dr. Reko who sent them to the botanical group
at Harvard. Schultes (1937,1939,1940) identified some of the mushrooms
as *Panaeolus companulatus* L. var *sphinctrinus* (Fr.) Bresadola.

In 1938, 4 white people attended a mushroom rite (Johnson, 1939).
(See Wasson, 1962.) The Wassons took part in their first experience August 8, 1953, with a curandero and one other person. The curandero, or
healer, was the Mexican in charge of the religious rites where these
mushrooms were used. The Indians regarded the mushrooms as holy and
looked upon them as the key to communication with the Deity. They
were consumed behind closed doors in the night.

The nature and quality of the experience induced by hallucinogens
depended upon the setting, the personality, and the objectives of the
subject and, of course, the skill and experience of the conductor or the
curandero. The curandero had to be ceremoniously clean. The suppliant
had a specific problem. In contrast to peyote which was taken regularly every Saturday evening by members of the American Native
Church of North America, the mushrooms were only taken when a
grave problem needed to be resolved, such as a prophecy regarding the
outcome of a grave illness, or when news was lacking about a relative.

The striking contrast between the occasional use of hallucinogenic
mushrooms and the regular and frequent use of peyote has not received
much attention with respect to the toxicity of these substances when

used regularly. There is no doubt that peyote may be used safely as part of a well-established rite for many decades but this has not yet been established for the mushroom. There are no chronic toxicity trials with psilocybin. Since both substances are alike only in their hallucinogen-inducing properties but are different chemically one cannot conclude that psilocybin is also safe when used regularly. Since psilocybin is more like adrenolutin than is mescaline it might well, when used excessively, produce chronic toxic psychosis which will be very much like those we have seen with adrenolutin and schizophrenia.

The curandero preferred to use raw, unwashed, preferably fresh mushrooms but they could be preserved up to 6 months.

The Wassons described one ceremony or mushroom agape (love feast) at which 25 people were present. The adults were given 4, 5, 6, or 13 pairs of mushrooms. They were consumed by 10:40 PM. Their taste was acidic, like rancid grease, and unpleasant.

There were few unpleasant somatic changes. Some of the participants vomited several times. No one had any inclination to sleep. The Wassons first developed geometric patterns in rich colors which developed architectural oriental-like forms. The visions came in endless succession and did not include human beings. They had the sensation that the walls of their room vanished leaving their souls free in the universe. The visions seemed very significant and although they knew they were witnessing hallucinations the visions were sensed more clearly than had been the world before of normal reality. R. G. Wasson, on this occasion and on another, saw landscape visions which included the desert and camel caravans. When the landscape was interesting he approached it with the speed of light. For the first term "ecstasy" became meaningful.

The curandero chanted intermittently all night. She was helped by a daughter and several other people. She reported to the Wassons that it required from 3 to 5 experiences before one overcame the initial surprise. She also danced for 2 hours, clapped her hands, slapped her knees, and smacked her forehead. Every sound was resonant. The visions continued while attending to the auditory stimuli.

There was no erotic ideation. The Wassons had a very powerful feeling of brotherly affection. The sense of time passing was gone but memory was improved and all the impressions seemed engraved on memory. Throughout the ceremony the curandero spoke in a conversational tone. At that occasion the Wassons were concerned about their son whom they had left in New York. The curandero gave them some improbable information about their son's activities which later was found to be accurate.

Three days later they again took the mushrooms. This time R. G.

Wasson saw no geometric patterns. Instead the visual patterns consisted of artistic motifs of the Elizabethan and Jacobean periods of England, armor, family escutcheons, cathedrals, chairs, the landscapes were estuaries of immense rivers, and broad sheets of water blowing among reeds in pastel colors. After both experiences they slept well and awoke in the morning with a clear head.

The ceremony did not appear to be ritualized as is the peyote ceremony. In MIJE country the curandero did not eat the mushrooms— only the sick person did. The mushrooms were gathered, carried to the Church where God's blessing was invoked and then they returned home. The person who was to eat the mushroom was on a restricted diet for 4 days and remained sexually continent. The mushroom was consumed on an empty stomach. The same restricted diet was continued for 4 days after the ceremony. They did not give the mushrooms to pregnant women because they believed this would make them permanently mad.

The major difference between the mushroom and peyote users is in the frequency and timing. Peyote is used regularly once a week but the mushrooms are taken at irregular intervals when there is a great need for them. This may explain the differences in the ritual, for when the mushroom is used sparingly there is less need for a rigid ritual—more can be left to the ingenuity and resourcefulness of the curandero. But when the ceremony is conducted frequently there is more need for a clear and formalized ritual as is found in the Native American Church of America ritual described in this book. There are other differences. Peyote is taken every 7 days but the mushrooms may be taken even after 3 days. All the members of the peyote group take the peyote buttons but the curandero does not always take the mushrooms. Finally the detail of the rituals are much different as the peyote ceremony is conducted in a tepee half-filled with smoke and the air is full of the rhythmic beating of the water drum and the chanting of the peyote songs. Even the legends are different. There is a belief the mushrooms can leave someone permanently mad but we have not come across this belief about peyote.

Can it be that these differences are due to the chronic toxic effect of the mushrooms, or is it a matter of supply? Perhaps both factors play a role. For if a few subjects and the curanderos were to remain toxic after repeated use, there would soon be a tradition for not using it regularly.

R. G. Wasson (1959) believed the early use of hallucinogenic mushrooms was widespread. There is much evidence in folklore and in the vocabularies of European people which supports this view. He reports that Albertus Magnus (1250 A.D.) spoke of the insanity caused by certain fungi, not fly-amanita. In the past 150 years, 4 cases of accidental poisoning have been described. The 4 experiences were similar. They all lasted from 5 to 6 hours and were characterized by exaggerated hilarity and were similar to the mushroom experiences in Mexico. After the Wassons' article in *Life* magazine, three additional episodes of intoxication in the United States, Poland, and in the Fiji Islands were reported to him. McCawley *et al.* (1962) reported *Psilocybe* mushrooms grew in Milwaukee, Oregon, and Kelso, Washington.

The description of the effects of the mushrooms by Wasson is a model which has not been excelled. The major difference between the mushroom effect and pure psilocybin seems to be the dryness of the scientific accounts and the richness of the accounts of self-experimentation:

The sacred mushrooms of Mexico seize hold of you with irresistible power. They lead to a temporary schizophrenia, or pseudoschizophrenia, in which your body lies, heavy as lead, on the petate, or mat, and you take notes and compare experiences with your neighbor, while your soul flies off to the ends of the world and, indeed, to other planes of existence. The mushrooms take effect differently with different persons. For example, some seem to experience only a divine euphoria, which may translate itself into uncontrollable laughter. In my case I experienced hallucinations. What I was seeing was more clearly seen than anything I had seen before. At last I was seeing with the eye of the soul, not through the coarse lenses of my natural eyes. Moreover, what I was seeing was impregnated with weighty meaning: I was awe-struck. My visions, which never repeated themselves, were of nothing seen in this world: no motor cars, no cities with skyscrapers, no jet engines. All my visions possessed a pristine quality: when I saw choir stalls in a Renaissance cathedral, they were not black with age and incense, but as though they had just come, fresh carved, from the hand of the Master. The palaces, gardens, seascapes, and mountains that I saw had that aspect of newness of fresh beauty, that occasionally comes to all of us in a flash, I saw few persons, and then usually at a great distance, but once I saw a human figure near at hand, a woman larger than normal, staring out over a twilight sea from her cabin on the shore. It is a curious sensation: with the speed of thought you are translated wherever you desire to be, and you are there, a disembodied eye, poised in space, seeing, not seen, invisible, incorporeal.

I have placed stress on the visual hallucinations, but all the senses are equally affected, and the human organism as a whole is lifted to a plane of intense experience. A drink of water, a puff of the cigarette is transformed, leaving you breathless with wonder and delight. The emotions and intellect are similarly stepped up. Your whole being is aquiver with life.

Different regions of Mexico had species unique to the region. The sacred mushrooms belong chiefly to the genus *Psilocybe*. According to R. G. Wasson (1959) the following varieties are found:

Sierra Mazateca: (1) *Ps. mexicana* Heim; (2) *Ps. semperviva* Heim and Cailleux; (3) *Ps. caerulescens* Murrill var. Mazatecorum

Heim; (4) *Ps. yungensis* Singer & Smith; (5) *Strophana cubensis* Earle [synonym: *Ps. cubensis* (Earle Singer)]; and (7) *Conocybe siligineoides* Heim.

Slopes of Popocatepetl, Valley of Mexico: (8) *Ps. aztecorum* Heim.

Tenango del Valle: (9) *Ps. wassonii* Heim (synonym: *Ps. muliercula* Singer & Smith).

San Agustin Loxicha, in the Sierra Costera; (10) *Ps. zapotecorum Heim* (also No. 1, and two other species of unknown identity).

Mixerfa, region of San Juan Mazatlan: (11) *Ps. hoogshageni* Heim; (12) *Ps. cordispora* Heim; and (13) *Ps. mixaeensis* Heim (also No. 1).

Yaitepec, in the Chatino country, Sierra Costera: (14) *Ps. caerulescens* Murrill var. nigripes Heim (also Nos. 1 and 10).

Sochiapam in the Chinantla, No. 1?

The first psychological studies on pure psilocybin came from Hofmann's laboratory and using his first extracts (Gnirss, 1959; Rummele, 1959). These were summarized by Hofmann as follows:

The effect of psilocybin on human beings. Oral doses of a few milligrams lead, after 20 to 30 minutes, to changes in the psychic sphere. The psychic symptoms produced by small doses, i.e., up to 4 mg comprise effects on mood and environmental contact in that there frequently is a subjectively pleasant sensation of intellectual and bodily relaxation and divorcement from the environment. Not infrequently, these effects are associated with a pleasant feeling of physical tiredness and heaviness but sometimes they are accompanied by a feeling of extraordinary lightness, a bodily hovering. With higher doses, 6 to 12 mg more profound psychic changes are prominent and associated with alterations in spatial and temporal perception and with changes in the awareness of the self and the body image. Visual hypersensitivity is present and may lead to illusions and hallucinations. In the dream-like state long-forgotten memories, even some from early childhood, are often recalled.

The toxicity of psilocybin determined in animals is very slight by comparison with the doses effective in human beings. The LD-50 in the mouse is 280 mg/kg, i.e., psilocybin is 2.5 times less toxic than mescaline in the mouse although it is 50 times more powerful as a psychotomimetic in human beings.

CHEMISTRY

Hofmann *et al.* (1958) first extracted the active hallucinogen from the mushrooms, *Psilocybe mexicana* Heim grown in pure culture. Hofmann *et al.* (1959) also extracted psilocybin from *Strophana cubensis* Earle. Spores were collected in Mexico and grown in the laboratory. The methanol extract of dried powdered mushroom was treated with light petroleum ether, chloroform, and chloroform-ethanol to remove inert material. The psychological activity of the fractions was followed by giving them to the authors. Animals were unsatisfactory test organisms. More inert material was removed by dissolving the residue in water and precipitating with absolute ethanol. The solution was filtered, the solvent evaporated and the residue chromatographed on a cellulose column using water-saturated butanol as the developing solvent. The first fraction was dark colored and inactive. The fractions which followed gave blue to violet colors with Keller's reagent (glacial acetic acid and those containing ferric chloride and concentrated sulfuric acid). The later fractions were combined and again chromatographed on cellulose powder using water saturated butanol. Two zones were separated. A faster moving minor fraction gave a blue color with Keller's reagent. The second major fraction colored violet. The major fraction yielded an amorphous, highly active powder which was very soluble in water and contained a halogen. The aqueous solution was treated with silver carbonate and then the silver ion removed with hydrogen sulfide. The psilocybin crystallized from the concentrated solution as fine white needles. Yield was 0.4%. For final analysis, it was recrystallized from water or methanol.

Psilocybin is almost insoluble in organic solvents, ethanol, chloroform, or benzene. It is amphoteric. In aqueous ethanol pH is 5.2. The melting point is 185–195. $\alpha_B^{20} = 0°$ (0.02°). $C = 0.5$ in 50% methanol in a 20-cm tube. Crystallized from water it loses 25.4% of its weight (from methanol 10.4%) on drying in high vacuum at 100°C.

From 4 to 8 mg of pure psilocybin produced an experience similar to that induced by the mushrooms. After three-fourths of an hour the subjects felt drunk, physically relaxed, and psychically changed. There was no hangover. The symptoms varied with the subject but in general were similar to those produced by LSD and mescaline.

In addition to psilocybin, mushrooms contained very small quantities of psilocin. Hofmann (1961a,b) reported the synthesis of psilocybin in 10 stages from O-nitrocresol. This was a commercial synthesis and may be diagrammed as shown on p. 488.

According to Brack *et al.* (1961) tryptophan is a precursor of psilocybin in its biogenesis.

BIOCHEMISTRY

Blaschko and Levine (1960) found enzymes in the gill plates of *Mytilus edulis* which oxidized psilocin to a blue product which they thought might be an orthoquinoid compound. Horita and Weber (1961a,b) reported that intestinal phosphatase dephosphorylated psilocybin to psilocin. They also found that in the presence of KCN 5% kidney homogenate rapidly hydrolyzed psilocybin. The optimum pH

Psilocybin

was 9.0. In the absence of KCN or under anaerobic conditions no psilocin was found because it was rapidly oxidized to a dark blue compound. They suggested an ortho quinoid derivative was formed. Monoamine oxidase was not involved in the reaction. The oxidase was richest in heart and kidney tissue. Liver tissue had less. Rabbit brain had nearly as much as kidney and more than liver. In the guinea pig only the heart had more than brain. They believed a phenolase was involved. They have also observed dephosphorylation *in vivo* in rats.

Kalberer *et al.* (1962) synthesized psilocin-2′-^{14}C and N-methyl-^{14}C-psilocin. They gave 10 mg/kg of the first compound to rats by mouth. Within half an hour ¾ of the activity was in the gastrointestinal tract. In 1 hour it had decreased to 60% and in 4 hours to 50%. The concentration in tissue was highest after ½ hour and then decreased rapidly in 4 hours. Liver tissue, however, was richest in 1 hour and then decreased. The kidney had a higher concentration than any other organ and was followed by liver, brain and finally blood. The tissues which had higher concentrations than brain were the small intestine, skin, bone marrow, liver, lung, stomach, spleen adrenals, kidney, salivary glands, and thyroid. The tissues which had much less than brain were the colon, heart, testes, bone, muscle, and pancreas. The adrenal glands were richest in psilocin at all times except during one hour when the kidney had more. In 48 hours kidney had 3% of activity and liver 15%. In 24 hours 94% of the dose was excreted, 65% in the urine, and the rest in bile and feces.

Less than 10% was demethylated and deaminated. About 25% was excreted and unaltered. About 15% was metabolized to 4-hydroxyindole-acetic acid. The remainder was not accounted for. At 7 days they still found significant quantities of metabolites.

Woolley and Campbell (1962) found that in common with many other hallucinogens psilocybin and psilocin had serotoninlike and antiserotonin activity. As an antiserotonin it was as potent as the most potent known antiserotonin, but it was 100 times less potent than LSD.

Cerletti *et al.* according to Erspamer (1961) prepared psilocin derivatives which had more antiserotonin activity than psilocin. Thus

l-Benzylpsilocin   Psilocin benzoate

l-benzylpsilocin and psilocin benzoate had 10% and 18% of the anti-serotonin activity of LSD.

Hollister (1961) measured the effect of psilocybin on urinary phosphates, eosinophils, serum glutamic oxalacetic transaminase, serum alkaline phosphatase, serum pseudocholinesterase, and serum cholesterol.

There was a significant and substantial decrease of 30% in urinary phosphates (mean 0.55–0.38 mg P/mg creatinine) indicating a pronounced retention of phosphate. In this, psilocybin resembled LSD (Rinkel *et al.*, 1955), and adrenolutin (Hoffer and Osmond, 1959). Total eosinophils were decreased but none of the other chemical variables were altered. In a further report Hollister (1961) found that psilocybin significantly increased the three fatty acids of blood. (LSD-25 and mescaline were similar.)

Zsigmond *et al.* (1961) found that *in vitro* psilocybin inhibited plasma cholinesterase more than did serotonin but was the same as serotonin in inhibiting red blood cell or brain cholinesterase.

Boskovic and Przic (1961) compared the effect of some indoles on choline acetylase and coenzyme A. Adrenochrome was the most active indole; 5×10^{-7} M inhibited choline acetylase but 10^{-6} M potentiated. They were not active on coenzyme A at 10^{-6} M. BOL, serotonin, and medmain had no effect at 10^{-6} M on acetylase. But serotonin inhibited CoA at 10^{-7} M and BOL inhibited slightly at 10^{-6} M.

In concentrations up to 10^{-5} M, psilocybin had no effect on seminal vesicle, on duodenum and auricle of guinea pigs, or on rat uterus. There was no antagonism against adrenaline, acetylcholine, histamine, and nicotine.

PHARMACOLOGY

Weidmann and Cerletti (1959) found both psilocybin and psilocin facilitated the patellar reflex in the cat in IV doses as low as 5–10 μg/kg. With larger doses the reflex was inhibited.

In dogs anesthetized with amobarbital anesthesia 0.05–0.1 mg/kg IV produced a moderate but long-lasting drop in the mean arterial pressure and an increase in the heart rate. In cats anesthetized with urethan chloralose the same dose caused a brief but distinct elevation of blood pressure and bradycardia. This seemed to be due to a centrally mediated vasoconstriction. Small doses regularly caused contraction of the nictitating membrane in the anesthetized cat.

PHYSIOLOGICAL

When there were physiological changes they were very slight and usually only the autonomic nervous system was altered. Hollister (1961) found minimal changes in blood pressure or pulse rate. One borderline hypertensive patient had a substantial rise in blood pressure which increased over 25 mm/Hg. A constant feature was dilatation of the pupils. This was also the case for other hallucinogens. Deep tendon reflexes were increased.

On the other hand, Rummele and Gnirss (1961) reported a marked increase in autonomic symptoms such as bradycaria, increased blood pressure, and a decrease in blood pressure when psilocybin was given subcutaneously (6 mg). These are not major discrepancies compared to Hollister's work since the degree of anxiety will certainly vary with the overall feeling and setting of the experiment.

Maxwell *et al.* (1961) gave psilocybin intravenously (½ mg/kg) to dogs premedicated with morphine and Dial-urethan-nembutal anesthesia. The respiratory rate was depressed, as were oxygen saturation and cardiac output. This, of course, is a large dose and indicates psilocybin is very safe in clinical use. There was only a slight decrease in cardiac efficiency.

ACTION ON ANIMALS

A summary of the effect of psilocybin on some animals was prepared by Sandoz Laboratories.

Spontaneous Motor Behavior

No effect was seen in mice with subcutaneous doses below 10 mg/kg or in rabbits given 1 mg/kg IV. But with higher doses there was a reduction in activity in both species. Chauchard and Mazone (1961) found 1.5–3 mg of psilocybin (about 1–2 mg/kg) produced a brief period of increased activity followed by marked inhibition of activity for about 45 minutes. According to the Sandoz report 10 mg/kg fed to monkeys also produced a slight quietening effect.

Other Motor Changes

Psilocybin did not change the convulsive threshold in mice to electric stimulation or metrazole. But mice given psilocybin had a shorter reaction time to the hot plate test, that is, they responded more quickly to a warm plate.

Autonomic Effects

Mice were relatively resistant but 10 mg/kg subcutaneously produce pupillary dilatation and piloerection. Rabbits were more sensitive and reacted with a marked increase in heart and respiration rate. Doses as small as 0.02 mg/kg IV produced some fever. This increased slowly as the dose was increased. There was no evidence of tolerance after repeated doses. However, rabbits made tolerant to LSD did not respond with fever to psilocybin.

EEG

One to 2 mg/kg IV in curarized rabbits produced a regular low-voltage rhythm of 4–5 per second with nearly complete absence of slow waves and spindle-activity.

Adey *et al.* (1962) prepared cats with bipolar implanted electrodes in different parts of the deeper centers of the brain. Psilocin (0.25–1.0 mg/kg) given intraperitoneally produced pupillary dilation, vomiting, micturition, and rapid respiration. Affectionate behavior was not altered by either psilocin or psilocybin. The drug effect lasted from two to three hours. Doses of 0.25 mg/kg of psilocybin caused a pronounced slowing of electrical activity in the amygdala. With 1.0 mg/kg fast activity disappeared for many seconds from the amygdala and the visual cortex showed long runs of high amplitude slow waves. Psilocybin and psilocin produced similar activity but the psilocin effect was more transient.

Effect on Spiders

Christiansen *et al.* (1962) gave 150 mg/kg psilocybin by mouth, or 1 mg/kg mescaline to females of *Araneus diadematus* or *Araneus sericatus*. They increased their bodyweight 30%. Then they spun webs with shorter threads. The heavier spiders produced heavier threads but psilocybin did not do so. With higher doses it reduced the frequency of web building. At 6 gm/kg no webs were made. The mescaline effect was similar but psilocybin was 10 times more potent in terms of weight.

TOXICITY

The few studies which have been reported suggest that psilocybin is not very toxic for animals. Weidmann *et al.* (1958) gave mice up to 200 mg/kg intravenously with no lethal effect. A few animals died after 250 mg/kg. For mice it is much less toxic than bufotenine.

Psilocybin is relatively nontoxic for man. It may be argued that the psychological change is a toxic reaction but this is not the kind of toxicity we are discussing in this section.

Psilocybin was quite free of toxic effects when used in carefully controlled experiments. This also applied to the Indians who used it with discretion and not in a regular repetitive ritual as peyote was used for example. The observations of primitive man are in some instances more valuable than those of modern man and this cautious use of mushrooms suggests that the use of psilocybin on a chronic basis must be examined with great care. No chronic experiments on animals have been reported.

Cases of *Psilocybe* poisoning were reported in Oregon and Washington (McCawley *et al.*, 1962). The mushrooms were found growing in grass near conifers. Two adults and four children ingested these mushrooms. The usual psilocybin experience resulted but the children all developed a high fever (102°–106°F) and had convulsions. One child died. The mushrooms were identified as *Ps. balocystes* and chemical assays showed they contained psilocybin and psilocin.

TOLERANCE

Tolerance and cross-tolerance experiments suggest the toxicity of psilocybin is low but we have documented one case of a combined LSD and psilocybin intoxication which presented as a schizophrenic reaction.

Hollister (1961) gave one subject psilocybin every day for 21 days starting with 1.5 mg and finishing with 27 mg daily. There was hardly any reaction on the twenty-second day to 15 mg. After several weeks rest the same dose produced the expected reaction.

Isbell *et al.* (1961) studied the cross-tolerance of LSD and psilocybin on a series of volunteer opiate addicts serving sentences for violation of narcotic laws. They were all males between 25 and 35 years of age. The subjects were given adequate dosages of LSD or psilocybin for from 6 to 7 or 13 days. Then they were given the other drug. A high degree of tolerance to LSD developed in both experiments on both psychological and physiological parameters. Patients tolerant to LSD were also cross-tolerant to psilocybin. Direct tolerance to psilocybin did not develop as completely as did direct tolerance to LSD and patients on continuous psilocybin and tolerant to it were not as tolerant to a challenging dose of LSD. These findings of Isbell *et al.* (1961) suggest that chronic administration of psilocybin may not be as innocuous as chronic administration of LSD. Balestrieri (1960) also found some cross-tolerance from LSD to psilocybin but it was not as marked as from LSD to mescaline.

PSYCHOLOGICAL CHANGES

The psilocybin experience is similar to the mushroom experience already described by the Wassons. This suggests other mushroom chemicals exert little synergistic or inhibitory effect on the experience. Hofmann *et al.* (1958) were the first group to study the psychological properties of psilocybin on normal subjects. Delay *et al.*, in France (1959), were the first group to study psilocybin from a psychiatric view and Rinkel *et al.* (1960a) completed the first American studies. Both groups confirmed psilocybin's powerful psychological activity. Rinkel gave 5–10 mg sublingually to 4 male volunteers. These subjects reported minor changes in visual perception. Three noted changes in time perception and one was depersonalized. Thought was slowed but thought process was altered little. Speech was either slow or rapid and at times, slurred. All subjects experienced changes in mood with euphoria or dysphoria and two were more relaxed and sleepy. Somatic changes were slight and included the following: feeling of lightheadedness, nausea, pressure on the head, photosensitivity, and a feeling of weakness in the legs. These changes were not much different from those reported by Rummele and Gnirss (1961).

Hollister (1961) gave oral doses of 60–209 μg/kg and parenteral doses of 37–205 μg/kg to a group of psychologically sophisticated volunteers (graduate students, etc.). Most of the experiments were done in a single blind technique.

The intensity of the experience was dependent upon dose. A dose of from 115 to 160 μg/kg (about 10 mg per 135-lb person) seemed adequate to produce a definite effect. The lower level was the minimal threshold oral dose. The sequence of clinical changes is shown in Table 40.

Parental psilocybin produced similar experiences but they came on more quickly. Clinical changes started within 5 minutes. Subjects more often complained of difficulty in thinking, uncontrolled laughter, paresthesia and difficulty in breathing. Psychotic symptoms were infrequent. There were no paranoid delusions. A few reported auditory and visual perceptual changes but smell, taste, and tactile sensations were not altered. Many subjects felt they were more perceptive of other people's feelings and motivations. All were nearly normal after 5 hours and there were few aftereffects.

Two psychometric tests were given at hourly intervals. One consisted of a series of simple problems in arithmetic (Number Facility Test) and the other consisted of linear drawings which had to be copied (Flexibility of Closure). The number of problems completed was decreased by oral psilocybin at 1 hour only and by parenteral psilocybin at 1 and 2 hours. The performance on the other test was also inferior.

Personality is that personal quality by which a person is recognized as a unique individual by his fellows. It includes physical, psychological, and reactive attributes. It seems that early investigators believed drugs could impose a characteristic psychological experience on people which overrode their personality. But a moment's reflection must show that chemicals do not have personalities. They can only alter the function of the brain or mind in certain ways. But the nature of the experience which results must be determined by personality factors as well as by the kind of disturbance produced in the brain. No one should be surprised that each person given a drug reacts in his own peculiar way. The content of any chemically induced experience is more determined by personality than by chemistry. The fact that there is a disturbance is more determined by chemistry.

If common personality types are found, one might expect common responses to drugs, other factors being more or less equal. Dimascio *et al.* (1961) selected two types using the MMPI and interviews. These were the athletic type (mesomorphs) and the aesthetic intellectual type. The subjects were given 70 μg of LSD, 500 mg of mescaline, or 10 mg of psilocybin, in a double blind manner. In general, the changes already described for these hallucinogens were found. But the aesthetic types showed considerable more deterioration in simple mental function tests and this was most marked with LSD and mescaline. In self-ratings all "aesthetics" stated that they were confused, but one-third of the "athletics" felt they could think more clearly. A world of vivid and rhythmically undulating colored patterns was experienced by all athletics but only 20% of the aesthetics. Also, athletics more often experienced depersonalization, were more elated and euphoric. Athletics tended to become more tense after LSD, while in contrast aesthetics were less tense. One might summarize this work by stating that the mesomorphs or athletics tended to have psychedelic experiences, whereas the aesthetics or intellectual type (perhaps the ectomorphs) tended to have the psychotomimetic experiences.

Our own experience in Saskatchewan with several hundred subjects, tends to support these conclusions but there are very many exceptions and many subjects, having had one experience one time, will have the other on a second or third occasion. But we would agree that the athletic types would in general have more pleasant experiences.

COMPARISON OF PSILOCYBIN AND OTHER HALLUCINOGENS

Hoffer *et al.* (1954) classified as hallucinogens those substances which produced changes in perception, thought, and mood in the absence of changes in consciousness and disorientation. This definition was accepted by Hofmann (1961a,b). This excludes drugs like morphine, anesthetics, etc., which tend to produce more typical toxic changes where disorientation and levels of consciousness are altered. We would expect all hallucinogens should show rather similar psychological properties.

In general there are few major differences between these hallucinogens. Isbell (1959) compared the effect of psilocybin and LSD on a group of Negro male drug addicts in prison. They were given either placebo, LSD at a dose of 1 and 1½ μg/kg, or psilocybin at doses of 57, 86, and 114 μg/kg, by mouth.

The psilocybin reaction began within 15 minutes with mild anxiety and other vague changes. After thirty minutes, anxiety was definite and was expressed as a fear of something evil about to happen. There was some euphoria. Perception was altered, and vision was blurred,

TABLE 40

CLINICAL CHANGES PRODUCED BY PSILOCYBIN, IT-290, AND JB-329

Psilocybin	IT-290	JB-329
0–30 (minutes)	*0–30 (minutes)*	*0–30 (minutes)*
Dizzy, giddy	Euphoria	Dizzy, poor coordination
Nausea, abdominal discomfort	Nausea, heartburn	Nausea, dry throat, heartburn
Weakness, muscle aches and twitches, shivering	Yawning, drowsiness	Loss concentration, poor memory
Anxiety, restlessness		Blurred vision, decreased distance perception
Numbness of lips		Difficulty breathing
30–60 (minutes)	*30–120 (minutes)*	*30–120 (minutes)*
Visual effects (blurring, brighter colors, sharper outlines, longer afterimages, visual patterns with eyes closed)	Nausea, retching	Brighter colors, sharper outlines
	Dizzy, unsteady	Slurred, blocked, incoherent speech
Increased hearing	Euphoria, restlessness, jittery	Time sense distorted
Yawning, tearing, sweating, facial flushing	Yawning, lethargy	Body-image distorted
Decreased concentration and attention, slow thinking, feelings of unreality, depersonalization, dreamy state	Decreased concentration, silly, inappropriate smiling	Disorientation, confusion, memory loss
		Muscle spasms
Incoordination, tremulous speech	*120–240 (minutes)*	*120–240 (minutes)*
	Visual effects (blurring, apparent movement of objects, sharper outlines, brighter colors, longer afterimages, decreased depth perception)	Confusion, speech disorders continue
60–120 (minutes)		Apparent motion of objects, wave-like motion of surfaces
Increased visual effects (colored patterns and shapes, mostly with eyes closed)	"Drunk," euphoria, poor coordination	Decreased appetite
	Tremors, numbness of extremities	Tension, tremors, anxiety
Wave motion of viewed surfaces	*4–12 (hours)*	Weakness, lethargy, dreamy state
	Visual effects (patterns, eyes closed)	

Impaired distance perception
Euphoria, ruminative state, increased perception
Slowed passage of time

120–240 (minutes)

Waning and nearly complete resolution of above effects

4–12 (hours)

Usually normal

Later effects

Headache, fatigue, contemplative state

Less common effects

Uncontrollable laughter, paresthesia and synthesia, difficulty in breathing, decreased appetite, transient sexual feeling.

Muscle aching, shivering
Decreased appetite
Weakness, lethargy

Later effects

Continued stimulation, insomnia, fatigue, muscle aching, headache, heartburn, "hangover"

Less common effects

General malaise, salivation increased, paresthesia, dreamy state, mild depersonalization

Coughing
Mood change (usually depression)

4–12 (hours)

Some waning of above effects, if dose small; otherwise may persist

Later effects

Fatigue, lethargy, mental depression

Less common effects

Depersonalization, visual or auditory hallucinations

hearing was more keen and paresthesias were noted. After 1 hour, the reaction was definite. If the subjects were elated it was very marked and often accompanied by gales of laughter. All sensory perceptions were changed but visual changes were most prominent. None reported transcendental experiences. Isbell concluded that the psilocybin reactions were similar to the LSD reactions. Both cause autonomic changes, elevation of body temperature, dilatation of pupils, increased blood pressure and increased respiratory rate. These both increased central nervous system irritability (decreased knee jerk threshold). Psilocybin produced a shorter experience and in terms of dose is 100 to 150 times more potent.

Hollister *et al.* (1960) compared psilocybin against IT-290 (*dl-α*-methyltryptamine and JB-329—a mixture of two isomers: N-ethyl-2-pyrrolidylmethylphenylcyclopentyl glycolate hydrochloride and N-ethyl-3-piperidylphenylcyclopentyl glycolate hydrochloride). Psilocybin was given to 16 subjects (27 trials) orally with doses ranging from 60 to 209 μg/kg and parenterally 0.37 to 203 μg/kg. *dl-α*-Methyltryptamine was given to 8 subjects orally (384–810 μg/kg). JB-329 was given to 11 subjects orally (40–339 μg/kg). Data comparing them are shown in Table 40 (Hollister *et al.*, 1960).

The two indoles resembled each other most closely and of these, psilocybin was most likely LSD. It produced a dreamy introspective state with few somatic changes and hardly any impairment intellectually. The changes were shorter in duration than LSD. IT-290 had similar euphorient properties but it also induced lethargy, yawning, and dreaminess, somewhat like reserpine. The effects of large doses persisted up to 12 hours. On the other hand, JB-329 produced an experience more like a delirium analogous to atropine, scopolamine, or other belladonna alkaloids. Mental confusion, disorientation, memory loss, and changes in levels of awareness were prominent. This deliriod state lasted 12–24 hours.

Boszormenyi (1961) compared psilocybin, diethyltryptamine, and amphetamine. The psilocybin (6–11 mg parenterally) produced effects already described, but they noted fatigue, insomnia, altered moods, and eidetic visions for up to 3 days in some cases. The subjects were psychotic (16) or neurotic (8). Amphetamine, 15 mg given intravenously at the peak of the psilocybin experience, caused a reaction similar to that produced by diethyltryptamine alone, that is, there was more excitation.

Rinkel *et al.* (1960b) found little difference between LSD and psilocybin but mescaline produced stronger effects.

The psilocybin experience in many ways resembles the natural experience found in subjects by schizophrenia; it is, in fact, a good model but it is not an identity. One can find striking similarities or striking differences depending upon one's point of view and, of course, this can be said of any model. According to Delay (1962), the two experiences are similar enough to sometimes confuse even a well-trained psychiatrist. One would expect all chemically induced changes to be similar in process depending upon the degree and upon the site of action of the chemicals. All hallucinogens should be alike in that they produce changes in perception, thought, and mood. But they should produce experiences which differ in content since this will depend more upon the personality and intelligence of the subject. If, therefore, schizophrenia also produces a similar change in the mental processes, this suggests a chemical present is also involved and makes it difficult for those who see schizophrenia as a way of life (Adolf Meyer) or as a purely psychological alteration in personality to accept the model psychosis as having any similarity to schizophrenia.

There is little doubt that a psychiatrist who has had much experience with schizophrenia and with the model psychoses could, in most cases, distinguish between the drug experience and schizophrenia, especially if all other clues were not equalized. The duration of the experience alone would give it away, for an illness which has been present several weeks to several years, will bend a person differently as compared to an experience which started a couple of hours before. The experimental content of the experiences may give the code to the observer. But the changes in process will not, and there are some schizophrenic reactions which are very much like the ones induced by drugs. Hollister (1962) made this point very well and he concluded bluntly that a reasonably experienced clinical observer should easily distinguish between these states. Psychiatrists trained by him were able to select with better than chance success using selected portions of tape recordings from schizophrenics and from model psychoses. Hollister is, in fact, able to do so and apparently has passed this facility on to his colleagues. We prepared 20 pairs of mental status reports from the way 20 schizophrenics and 20 normal subjects having had LSD responded to the test (Hoffer and Osmond, 1961a,b). The two sets of scores had similar means and ranges. We have given these protocols to about 10 experienced psychiatrists and none of these were able to select the drug experience from schizophrenia. But when the test was sent to Hollister in 1962 he was able to select them with better than 95% success and one of his colleagues was about 75% successful.

Hollister has proven his point that there are differences and we have shown that the similarities are so marked it may be difficult to pick up the differences.

TREATMENT

Hallucinogenic drugs are well established as psychotherapeutic agents. They are used in two ways (a) as an aid to standard psychotherapies and psychoanalysis and (b) as a treatment in themselves where psychotherapy is used to bring about the most therapeutic experience. Probably no compound has been used more frequently than LSD. It is not surprising psilocybin which has a markedly similar effect should also be examined as a therapy in psychiatry. Delay and his colleagues examined psilocybin in this way. Reviewing the effects of psilocybin on 101 patients they concluded that the experience was valuable in getting at the individual's psychological and psychopathological state.

David and David (1961) and Fontana (1961) also used psilocybin as treatment aids. Fontana using hallucinogenic drugs since 1955 developed 4 main techniques:

1. In individual psychotherapy using mescaline, LSD or psilocybin as facilitating agents. The psychotherapeutic process was the same with, or without, the drug but the drug experience was more intense and disclosed deep-rooted mechanisms more readily. They obtained their best results in obsessive neuroses, character disorders, split personalities (we assume they mean schizoid patients, not schizophrenic), and anxiety neuroses.

2. In rapid psychotherapy following the method described for LSD by Sandison, their results were similar, that is, over 50% of 100 subjects were much benefited.

3. In group therapy they found these compounds particularly valuable for psychopathic, hypochondric, and adolescent acting-out patients.

4. In psychopathy of children.

Yohimbine

The main source of yohimbine is yohimbehe bark from a tree, *Pausinystalia yohimba* Pierre, syn *Corynanthe yohimbe* K. Schum, native to the French Congo and the Cameroons. Other *Corynanthe* species also contain yohimbine. Extracts contain yohimbine and several isomeric alkaloids. Quebrachine, the main alkaloid of *Aspidosperma quebracho-blanco*, is identical with yohimbine. Another isomer is mitraphylline found in *Mitragyna stipulosa* Kuntze. Rauwolscine is another isomer.

PHYSIOLOGICAL

A thorough study of yohimbine's autonomic effects was reported by Holmberg and Gershon (1961). It was given at a dose of 0.5 mg/kg. The initial response was facial blushing and an increase in heart rate. Then there followed perspiration, salivation, lachrymation, and pupillary dilatation and a rise of blood pressure. The heart rate increased to 48 beats per minute reaching its maximum immediately after the injection and returning to normal in 3–55 minutes. Systolic blood pressure rose 2–93 mm Hg. Diastolic pressure rose slightly.

Yohimbine pretreatment increased the heart rate response to 0.20 μg/kg/mm of adrenaline given intravenously over a three-minute period. Pretreatment with amobarbital prevented any of the yohimbine autonomic effects except blood pressure, which increased less. Librium partially blocked the yohimbine effect. Imipramine potentiated the action of yohimbine markedly in all the autonomic parameters measured. Emotional reactivity was rated. Subjects who had high base line levels reacted more strongly to yohimbine using heart rate as a measure but not for blood pressure changes. For the 15 schizophrenics tested, the correlation was 0.74. With 9 normal subjects it was 0.93. Holmberg and Gershon (1961) concluded yohimbine was both adrenergic and cholinergic in nature.

In conscious dogs and sheep, yohimbine elevated the mean arterial blood pressure, 60 mm Hg in dogs and 26 mm in sheep. In dogs the heart rate was elevated. In all anesthetized animals blood pressure fell and the heart rate increased less.

Yohimbine reversed adrenaline pressor response in anesthetized dogs; the pressor response of noradrenaline was reversed in some dogs. In conscious dogs the pressor response to adrenaline was reversed; response to noradrenaline was merely inhibited. The pressor response to serotonin was diminished in conscious animals and the response was transient. Yohimbine has antiserotonin properties (Woolley and Shaw, 1957).

PSYCHOLOGICAL

Holmberg and Gershon (1961) examined the autonomic and psychological effects of yohimbine hydrochloride. Sixty subjects, including 15 schizophrenic patients, were given IV injections of 0.5 mg/kg over a five-minute interval. The subjects became tense, irritable, restless, and anxious. The most anxious subjects were very reluctant to repeat the experiment. Five schizophrenic subjects were given yohimbine IM 3 times per week (20–40 mg/dose). Two showed a minimal response and became more active, alert, outgoing, and more responsive. The other three also became more active but the changes were not generally beneficial. One developed auditory hallucinations. All three were grossly disturbed for about 1 hour after each injection. They hallucinated, laughed, and spoke to their visual hallucinations. Later in the day they were more alert, active and responsive, and euphoric. One depressed patient was slightly improved for about 1 week only. Holmberg and Gershon concluded yohimbine was a powerful activator of anxiety, more active than adrenaline, and an activator of schizophrenic psychosis.

Premedication with amobarbital sodium completely abolished all the subjective effects of yohimbine. Librium also reduced anxiety and tension but not to the same degree as the amobarbital. In contrast, premedication with imipramine greatly increased the severity of the changes produced by yohimbine. The tremor and restlessness became so great in some cases it amounted to panic.

Effect on Animal Behavior

Gershon and Lang (1962) gave dogs and sheep 0.5 mg/kg of yohimbine. Dogs developed general body tremors, increased anxiety, restlessness, hypersalivation, diarrhea, and hyperventilation. Sheep became more alert but showed little further change.

How Tryptamine Hallucinogens Act

It is possible that these compounds have their remarkable central activity because they interfere with the proper function of natural substances whose turnover is basic for the normal operation of the brain. Since 1954 Woolley and his co-workers have studied the hypothesis that an interference with serotonin in the brain produced the disorganization of function experienced by the subject as the psychotomimetic or psychedelic experience. Their early evidence which led to the serotonin hypothesis of mental disease was that (a) many hallucinogens including LSD, harmine, and yohimbine were structurally analogous to serotonin, (b) they were antimetabolites, and (c) they produced mental changes. This serotonin hypothesis has received vigorous examination for the past 9 years, but there is, as yet, no consensus of opinion. Thus, there is no agreement between the two scientists chiefly responsible for isolating and determining the structure of serotonin. I. H. Page (1958) concluded, "It must be equally apparent that it probably participates in a wide variety of metabolic and physiologic functions, including that very intriguing area of brain and thought" although he found "the evidence that serotonin metabolism is disturbed in mental disease is not strong." On the other hand, Erspamer (1954) found this hypothesis rather fragile and 7 years later in 1961 he again concluded biogenic amines played an important role in normal functioning of the brain and that quantitative or qualitative changes in biosynthesis and metabolism may contribute to derangement of normal function. "However, for the present, this is all that can be said about these compounds." Since similar statements can be made about any brain constituent including glucose, calcium, sodium, even water, we wonder whether we are any closer to mental disease than we were in 1954 from the point of view of tryptophan derivatives. But the serotonin hypothesis is a valuable one and has resulted in a major expansion in biochemical research in psychiatry. It is, therefore, important to review the present state of the serotonin hypothesis since it may play a basic role in the function of all the compounds in this section, if not some of the other hallucinogens.

Serotonin

There have been many excellent reviews of serotonin (Maupin, 1961; Erspamer, 1954, 1961; I. H. Page, 1958). Erspamer's (1961) review covers over 1600 references to the literature.

Serotonin is present in all vertebrates especially in the intestine, but it is also present in some lower animal forms, for example, in the venom of some toads, in mollusks and in the sea anemone, etc. It is also present in some plants, for example, in the spicules of the stem of *Mucuna prurients*, in the hairs of the white nettle, and in relatively high concentrations in banana pulp.

Serotonin is present in all tissues except amniotic fluid. The digestive tract is richest containing about 3–6 μg/gm. The dog intestinal tract has 80% of all the serotonin of the body. The spleen is equally rich. Liver, lung, and skin have about 1 μg/gm. Nervous tissue has between 0.1 and 1 μg/gm. The distribution in the brain is similar to the distribution of noradrenaline. Serotonin is found chiefly in argentaffine cells, blood platelets, and mast cells. The argentaffine or enterochromaffine cells are the principal source. In the cells, it is apparently stored in cytoplasmic granules.

Serotonin is a metabolite from tryptophan. Tryptophan is hydroxylated to 5-hydroxytryptophan by tryptophan oxidase or hydroxylase. This is decarboxylated to serotonin. Serotonin does not cross the blood–brain barrier but 5-hydroxytryptophan crosses readily. When given to animals, it crosses into the brain and is rapidly decarboxylated to serotonin and may reach high concentrations. There is a high degree of parallelism between the distribution of serotonin and decarboxylase. Animals maintained on a low tryptophan diet have much less serotonin in brain.

A small portion of serotonin is excreted unchanged but most of it is metabolized. The main route is to 5-hydroxy-3-indolylacetaldehyde to 5-hydroxyindole-3-acetic acid to 5-hydroxyindoleaceturic acid. Amine oxidase is the main enzyme. Monoamine oxidase is found chiefly in the liver but also in brain and lung tissue. The administration of monoamine oxidase inhibitors causes an accumulation in tissues of serotonin.

Not all the serotonin oxidized by monoamine oxidase leads to 5-hydroxyindoleacetic acid. This may not be the major route and less than one-third may be so altered. Some of the 5-hydroxyacetaldehyde may form pigmented and fluorescent substances.

Another possible method of inactivation is via oxidation by ceruloplasmin to a *p*-quinone imine similar in structure to adrenochrome. Other pathways are *N*-acetylation yielding *N*-acetyl-5-hydroxytryptamine; conjugation with glycine forming 5-hydroxyindoleaceturic acid; and conjugation with glucuronic acid resulting in a glucuronide of serotonin.

The original hypothesis linking serotonin to mental disease resulted from a study of the antometabolites of serotonin. There are several classes of antagonists as follows: (a) indoxylalkylamines including gramine; (b) psychoactive alkaloids like LSD, harmine, yohimbine; (c) psychologically inactive alkaloids like Brom LSD; (d) some nitro-indole synthetics; and (e) some methylated serotonin derivatives.

RELATION OF SEROTONIN TO BRAIN FUNCTION

Brodie and Costa (1962) recently reviewed the relationship of serotonin to brain activity. Brodie and his colleagues suggested that both serotonin and noradrenaline were brain neurohormones. They both have certain essential properties of neurohormones, that is, they are readily available and are protected from enzymatic inactivation until after they have served their function. Both are associated in various areas of the brain except the limbic system which is high in serotonin and the corpus striatum which is high in dopamine.

Himwich and Costa (1960) pretreated dogs with monoamine oxidase inhibitors and 6 hours later gave them 5-hydroxytryptophan. There was a marked change in behavior. The first response was transient drowsiness in 10–15 minutes followed by extension of the toes of the hind legs and the hind limbs. Face licking and grimacing appeared intermittently. At 30–40 minutes, panting and hyperthermia sometimes developed. Then the dogs became more active and walked briskly around,

(40–50 minutes) and were very alert. Then locomotion became impaired by incoordination and a hunched back. They then developed a steppage gait. They marked time with their hind feet which exhibited rhythmic involuntary movements. Ataxia became marked and the dogs tended to keep near the wall. Finally, there was constant and aimless walking about until the animal was exhausted. They were then insensitive to light, sound, or touch. The reaction lasted 3–4 hours. Then there was a complete recovery. Larger doses prolonged the reaction but did not accelerate its onset and development.

Evidence that serotonin is a central neurohormone was listed by Costa *et al.* (1962). (a) It is localized in those parts of the brain that coordinate autonomic function with primitive patterns of behavior. (b) It is present in a bound form from which it can be released. (c) Monoamine oxidase is present wherever serotonin is, and is its main inactivation enzyme. (d) Increasing the concentration of serotonin in the brain produces changes in behavior. When low doses of 5-hydroxytryptophan are given which increase serotonin slightly, there is sedation and electroencephalographic sleep patterns. But when high doses are given there is uncoordinated excitation and electroencephalographic arousal.

It is unusually difficult to sort out the action of serotonin and noradrenaline. According to Costa *et al.*, one way of achieving this is by the use of substances which deplete brain of these amines.

Reserpine liberates serotonin by a direct cellular action on mechanisms that concentrate it in tissues without blocking formation. The effect of reserpine which includes tranquilization, decreased motor activity, lowered responsivity, depressed respiration, and increased parasympathetic activity, persist long after the reserpine is metabolized. But noradrenaline stores are also depleted. However, the depletion of serotonin seems more important. Rats stressed by exposure to cold and given reserpine did not release serotonin nor induce sedation, but their brain noradrenaline was depleted.

Two other compounds depleted brain noradrenaline levels without producing serotonin depletion and there was no sedation. One of them, α-methyl-*m*-tryosine, produces 90% depletion of noradrenaline for up to 16 hours. Serotonin levels were decreased transiently but were normal in about 4 hours. There was no sedation. In general only compounds which depleted serotonin 50% or more produced sedation.

Brodie *et al.* (1959) reviewed the hypothesis noradrenaline and serotonin controlled two functionally opposed brain systems. Noradrenaline was postulated to modulate the ergotropic system that integrates central sympathetic function. Increased activity is expressed as enhanced motor activity and increased responses to environmental stimuli. Sero-

tonin modulates the opposing trophotropic system that integrates parasympathetic function. These are expressed as increased parasympathetic
activity, drowsiness, sleep, decreased activity.

When mice were given α-methyl-*m*-tyrosine, which releases noradrenaline, and which is pretreated with a monoamine oxidase inhibitor
so that it is not destroyed, they were remarkably activated as if they
had been given amphetamine. There was frenzied hyperactivity, extreme exophthalmos, increased sensitivity to stimuli, and hyperthermia.

When both amines were released by reserpine and their degradation
was prevented by monoamine oxidase inhibitors, the mice were less
hyperexcitable than when noradrenaline alone was given. After the
release of serotonin alone there was no excitation, but sedation was not
as pronounced as after reserpine given alone.

Costa *et al.* concluded noradrenaline release was excitatory whereas
serotonin release was sedative in its action.

Drugs and Central Serotonin or Noradrenaline

Drugs could influence brain function by interfering with transmission
of stimuli across synapses, by decreasing energy production of brain
cells, that is, the neurons or the supporting cells, or by increasing or
decreasing the direct irritability of neurons.

INTERFERENCE WITH TRANSMISSION

Mimicking One of the Amines

The substance is a substitute for amine but will distort function because it may not match the receptors as well, may not be metabolized
and, therefore, be released as readily. If degradation is difficult due to
a lack of a specific enzyme the entire process of receptor adsorption
and release will be grossly altered.

Many congeners of noradrenaline penetrate the brain and produce the
well-known excitation mediated by the sympathetic nervous system.
Some of these substances are amphetamine and its analogs, deoxy-
ephedrine, methylphenidylacetate pipradol, tetrahydro-β-naphthylamine
and, perhaps, the phenylethylamine hallucinogens including mescaline
and LSD. However, the situation may be more complex in humans.
It is well known that amphetamine may produce a paradoxical sedation
in some subjects. A recent adrenalinelike substance, adrenaline methyl
ether (J. A. Page and Hoffer, 1964), produced a remarkable state of
sedation and tranquilization in a sophisticated subject who had previously reacted to amphetamine with excitation and to isopropyl-5,

6-diacetoxyindole with a sense of well-being. The tranquilization was so profound she refused to go on with the medication. Five milligrams acted as a sleeping preparation and kept her sedated 24 hours.

Further it is known that both noradrenaline and adrenaline placed within the brain ventricles of animals, produce sedation and narcosis and not excitation.

Blocking Action on Central Amine

Chlorpromazine apparently inhibits the physiological action of noradrenaline in brain. It produces sedation, decreased responsivity, decreases motor activity, and reduces central sympathetic outflow. It counters the action of the phenylethylamines including mescaline. It also seems to be more specific in its calming effect on manic states where there is a marked increase in the secretion of both noradrenaline and adrenaline.

Serotonin blockers should be stimulants since the depressant action of serotonin will not be exerted. In general, this appears to be the case, and some of these blocking agents are the tryptamines, including their methylated derivatives, the gramines, aminoindoles (methylmedmain) LSD and related substances including BOL-148, cyproheptadine (an antihistamine), Dibenamine, some sympathomimetic amines of which N-isopropylnoradrenaline is the most potent, adrenochrome and many others. There can be no direct relationship between blocking action and hallucinogenic activity for some powerful blockers like BOL-148 are not active psychologically, and some powerful hallucinogens are very weak blockers, for example, bulbocapnine. But in general, blockers are activators. Sulser *et al.* (1962) suggested that imipraminelike drugs may act as antidepressants because they are serotonin blocking agents.

Amine Stabilizers

These produce their action by inhibiting the enzymes which destroy the amines. Catecholamines are destroyed by monoamine oxidase, by methoxylases, by phenolases, and other methods. Monoamine oxidase appears to be the major intracellular brain enzyme for detoxifying these amines. Blocking agents increase the quantity of the amines and produce behavioral changes. Methoxylases seem less important in brain. The role of phenolases which lead to quinone indoles remains relatively unexplored. Payza and Hoffer (1959) found that brain tissue extracts were very rich in enzymes which quickly changed adrenaline to adrenochrome.

Several pig tissues were used for extracting adrenaline oxidase. One part of fresh tissue was homogenized with 20 parts of acetone chilled to $-20°C$. The homogenate was suction filtered and dried in air. The dry powder was stored at $-20°C$. One hundred milligrams of powder was treated with 5 ml of 0.02 *M* buffer (pH 5) for 1 hour at $0°C$ and adjusted to the required pH before use. When optimum conditions were used, pig brain was twice as active as kidney or lung at 30 minutes, 3 times as active as liver or spleen, and 50% more active than blood plasma.

Adrenaline is oxidized to adrenochrome as a rule more readily than is noradrenaline to noradrenochrome. This may be why very little adrenaline is found in brain tissue. If true, one would only find increased concentrations of adrenaline in brain when the adrenaline oxidase was blocked. The following substances were *in vitro* inhibitors of adrenaline oxidase; cysteine, sodium cyanide, sodium diethyldithiocarbonate, tris buffer, ascorbic acid, and ethylenediaminetetraacetate. Perhaps some of these substances given *in vivo* might result in elevated levels of brain noradrenaline and adrenaline.

Serotonin levels are also increased by monoamine oxidase blockers. There are a large number of these including iproniazid, isocarboxazide, trancylpromine, nialamide, hydrazines, harmine, etc.

Nerve End Depleters

These are compounds which release or irreversibly bind the amines into inactive compounds. Reserpine and other releasers have already been discussed. Amine oxidase activators, if known, could also deplete stores of serotonin.

For the catecholamines, activators of adrenaline oxidase could act as noradrenaline and adrenaline depleters. Payza and Hoffer (1959) found that *in vitro* semicarbazide, copper ion, and fresh hemoglobin were major activators of brain adrenaline oxidase. *O*-Cresol indophenol and iproniazid were less powerful activators. These compounds could act by increasing the conversion of the amines to noradrenochrome or adrenochrome. Excessive copper ions in brain produces Wilson's disease characterized by psychiatric and neurological changes. The tremor could be due to an increase utilization of dopamine which is now believed to play a role in the production of tremor (Barbeau, 1966).

Many unsubstituted hydrazides given in large amounts by any route produce convulsions (Reilly *et al.*, 1953; Pfeiffer *et al.*, 1956; Jenney and Pfeiffer, 1958; Pfeiffer, 1960). The convulsions resemble grand mal epilepsy and come on after a latent period of 1 to 2 hours. Other convulsant compounds act immediately if given intravenously, or if given orally produce continuous seizures. Hydrazides also lower the cerebral threshold for photic and auditory stimuli. Semicarbazide 40 mg/kg produces grand mal seizures in man but with photic stimulation 25 mg/kg produced convulsions.

Hydrazides have two known biochemical effects. They inactivate monoamine oxidase and react with carbonyl compounds. Semicarbazide combines irreversibly with adrenochrome to produce stable adrenochrome semicarbazone. Adrenochrome produces a marked change in the electroencephalogram of epileptics without itself producing convulsions (Szatmari *et al.*, 1955). These findings suggest that adrenochrome which, according to Marrazzi, is an inhibitor of synaptic transmission, may play a role in cerebral activity, if indeed it were present. Since many substances which inhibit monoamine oxidase are not convulsants, it appears likely that the convulsant activity of hydrazides may be more in their carbonyl trapping properties. If true, it would follow that the more active carbonyl trappers would have the greatest convulsant activity, other factors being equal. This possibility has not yet been examined. The best antidote against the hydrazide convulsions is pyridoxine. Other antagonists are acetone, phenurone, trimethadone, phenobarbital, α-ketoglutarate, pyruvate, and glucose in descending order.

These convulsant compounds which activate brain adrenaline oxidase and trap adrenochrome accelerate the conversion of noradrenaline and adrenaline to the chrome indoles and so produce their characteristic changes.

Synthetic Blockers

Very little is so far known about compounds which reduce the synthesis of brain amines.

Substances Which Interfere with Physiological Release

Bretylium and TMIO prevent the release of noradrenaline peripherally but do not enter the brain. No substances blocking release in brain are known.

A summary of the indoletryptamine hallucinogens discussed is shown in Table 41.

In general these compounds are acetylcholine esterase inhibitors, are serotonin antagonists, are synaptic inhibitors, and as well as being serotonin analogs can increase serotonin levels by blocking monoamine oxidase. Two of the monoamine oxidase inhibitors have been used as antidepressants but harmine has not been examined in this way. Some of the substances are convulsants, but one, harmine, is an anticonvulsant. All but DMT produce EEG arousal.

TABLE 41
THE INDOLETRYPTAMINE HALLUCINOGENS

	Trypto-phan	Trypta-mine	Sero-tonin	DMT	DET	α-Meth-yltrypt-amine	α-Ethyl-trypt-amine	Bufo-tenine	Harmine	Psilo-cybin	Ibo-gaine
Psychological											
animal	yes	yes	yes	yes	yes	yes	yes	yes	yes	yes	yes
man	yes	yes	no	yes	yes	yes	yes	yes	yes	yes	yes
Esterase inhibitor		yes	yes	yes	yes		yes	yes		yes	yes
Substrate for monoamine oxidases	no	yes	yes	yes	yes	no	no	yes	no	yes	no
Inhibitor glutamic acid decarboxylase		no	no	no	no	yes	no	no	no		
Serotonin antagonist		yes		yes	yes			yes	yes	yes	yes
Convulsant		yes	no	no	no			no	yes		no
Synaptic blocker		yes	yes	yes	yes	no	yes	yes	yes	yes	yes
Monoamine oxidase inhibitor		no	no	no	no	yes	yes	no	yes	no	
EEG arousal	yes	yes	no	yes	yes	yes	yes	yes	yes	yes	yes

REFERENCES

Adey, W. R., Bell, F. R., and Dennis, B. J. (1962). *Neurology* **12**:591.

Axelrod, J. (1961). *Science* **134**:343.

Balestrieri, A. (1960). *Psychopharmacologia* **1**:257.

Barbeau, A. (1960). *Neurology* **10**:446.

Barlow, R. B. (1961). *Brit. J. Pharmacol.* **16**:153.

Blaschko, H., and Levine, W. G. (1960). *Biochem. Pharmacol.* **3**:168.

Blaschko, H., and Milton, A. S. (1960). *Brit. J. Pharmacol.* **15**:42.

Borsy, J., Lenard, K., and Csizmadia, Z. S. (1961). *Acta Physiol. Acad. Sci. Hung.* **18**:83.

Boskovic, B., and Przic, R. (1961). *Biochem. Pharmacol.* **8**:33.

Boszormenyi, Z. (1960). *Conf. Psychiat.* **3**:117.

Boszormenyi, Z. (1961). *In* "Psilocybin and Diethyl Tryptamine: Two Tryptamine Hallucinogens" (E. Rothlin, ed.), Vol. 2, p. 226.

Boszormenyi, Z., and Brunecker, G. (1957). *In* "Psychotropic Drugs" (S. Garattini and V. Ghetti, eds.), p. 580. Elsevier, Amsterdam.

Boszormenyi, Z., Der, P., and Nagy, P. C. (1959). *J. Mental Sci.* **105**:171.

Brack, A., Hofmann, A., Kalberer, F., Kobel, H., and Rutschmann, J. (1961). *Arch. Pharm.* **4**:230.

Brodie, B. B., and Costa, E. (1962). *Psychopharmacol. Serv. Center Bull.* **2**:1.

Brodie, B. B., Spector, S., and Shore, P. A. (1959). *Pharmacol. Rev.* **11**:548.

Buck, R. W. (1961). *New Engl. J. Med.* **265**:681.

Bumpus, F. M., and Page, I. H. (1955). *J. Biol. Chem.* **212**:111.

Bunag, R. D., and Walaszek, E. J. (1962). *Arch. Intern. Pharmacodyn.* **135**:142.

Cerletti, A. (1959). *Proc. 1st Intern. Congr. Neuro-Pharm., Rome, 1958* p. 291. Van Nostrand, Princeton, New Jersey.

Chauchard, P., and Mazone, H. (1961). *Compt. Rend. Soc. Biol.* **155**:71.

Chen, A. L., and Chen, K. K. (1939). *Quart. J. Pharm. Pharmacol.* **12**:30.

Christiansen, A., Baum, R., and Witt, P. N. (1962). *J. Pharmacol. Exptl. Therap.* **136**:31.

Corne, S. J., and Graham, J. D. P. (1957). *J. Physiol. (London)* **135**:339.

Costa, E., Gessa, G. L., Hirsch, C., Kuntzman, R., and Brodie, B. B. (1962). *Ann. N.Y. Acad. Sci.* **96**:118.

Curtis, D. R. (1962). *Nature* **194**:292.

David, A. E., and David, J. M. (1961). *Acta Neuropsiquiat. Arg.* **7**:143.

Day, C. A., and Yen, H. C. Y. (1962). *Federation Proc.* **2**:335.

De Jong, H. H. (1945). "Experimental Catatonia." Williams & Wilkins, Baltimore, Maryland.

Delay, J. (1962). *Recent Adv. Biol. Psychiat.* **4**:111.

Delay, J., Pichot, P., and Nicolas-Charles, P. (1959). *Proc. 1st Intern. Congr. Neuro-Pharm., Rome, 1958* Vol. 1, p. 528. Van Nostrand, Princeton, New Jersey.

Dimascio, A., Rinkel, M., and Leiberman, J. (1961). *Proc. 3rd Congr. Psychiat., 1961*, Vol. 2, p. 933.

Downing, D. F. (1962). *Quart. Rev. (London)* **10**:133.

Dybowski, J., and Landrin, E. (1901). *Compt. Rend.* **133**:748.

Eberts, F. S. (1961). *J. Neuropsychiat.* **2**:S146.

Edery, H., and Schatzberg-Porath, G. (1960). *Experientia* **16**:200.

Ernst, A. M., Van Andel, H., and Charbon, G. A. (1961). *Psychopharmacologia* **2**:425.

Erspamer, V. (1954). *Pharmacol. Rev.* **6**:425.

Erspamer, V. (1955). *J. Physiol. (London)* **127**:118.

Erspamer, V. (1961). *In* "Progress in Drug Research" (E. Jucker, ed.), p. 151. Wiley (Interscience), New York.

Evarts, E. V. (1956). *A.M.A. Arch. Neurol. Psychiat.* **75**:49.

Evarts, E. V. (1958). *Res. Publ., Assoc. Res. Nervous Mental Disease* **36**:347.

Fabing, H. D. (1956). *Am. J. Psychiat.* **113**:409.

Fabing, H. D., and Hawkins, J. R. (1956). *Science* **123**:886.

Fischer, E., Liskowski, L., Fernandez, T. A., and Vazquez, A. J. (1960). *Prensa Med. Arg.* **47**:3188.

Fischer, E., Fernandez Lagravere, T. A., Vazquez, A. J., and Distefane, A. O. (1961a). *J. Nervous Mental Disease* **133**:441.

Fischer, E., Fernandez, T. A., and Vazquez, A. J. (1961b). *Semana Med. (Buenos Aires)* **118**:879.

Fischer, E., Vazquez, F. A., Fernandez, T. A., and Liskowski, L. (1961c). *Lancet* **I**:890.

Fish, M. S., and Horning, E. C. (1956). *J. Nervous Mental Disease* **124**:33.

Fish, M. S., Johnson, N. M., and Horning, E. C. (1955a). *J. Am. Chem. Soc.* **77**:5892.

Fish, M. S., Johnson, N. M., Lawrence, E. P., and Horning, E. C. (1955b). *Biochim. Biophys. Acta* **18**:564.

Fish, M. S., Johnson, N. M., and Horning, E. C. (1956). *J. Am. Chem. Soc.* **78**:3668.

Fontana, A. E. (1961). *Acta Neuropsiquiat. Arg.* **7**:94.

Gallagher, C. H., Koch, J. H., Moore, R. M., and Steel, J. D. (1964). *Nature* **204**:542.

Gershon, S., and Lang, W. J. (1962). *Arch. Intern. Pharmacodyn.* **135**:31.

Gerstner, S. B. (1961). *J. Pharmacol. Exptl. Therap.* **131**:223.

Gessner, P. K., Khairallah, P. A., McIsaac, W. M., and Page, I. H. (1960). *J. Pharmacol. Exptl. Therap.* **130**:126.

Gessner, P. K., McIsaac, W. M., and Page, I. H. (1961). *Nature* **190**:179.

Gey, K. R., and Pletscher, A. (1962). *Brit. J. Pharmacol.* **19**:161.

Gnirss, F. (1959). *AMA Arch. Neurol. Psychiat.* **84**:346.

Govier, W. M., Howes, B. C., and Gibbons, A. J. (1953). *Science* **118**:596.

Greig, M. E., Seay, P. H., and Freyburger, W. A. (1961). *J. Neuropsychiat.* **2**:S131.

Gullino, P., Winitz, M., Birnbaum, S. M., Cornfield, J., Otey, M. C., and Greenstein, J. P. (1956). *Arch. Biochem. Biophys.* **64**:319.

Haller, A., and Heckel, E. (1901). *Compt. Rend.* **133**:850.

Hendrickson, J. B. (1961). *Chem. & Ind. (London)* p. 713.

Henry, T. A. (1949). "The Plant Alkaloids," 4th ed. Blakiston, Philadelphia, Pennsylvania.

Himwich, H. E. (1961). *J. Neuropsychiat.* Suppl. 2, p. 136.

Himwich, W. A., and Costa, E. (1960). *Federation Proc.* **19**:838.

Himwich, W. A., Costa, E., and Himwich, H. E. (1959). *Federation Proc.* **18**:402.

Himwich, W. A., Costa, E., and Himwich, H. E. (1960). *Recent Advan. Biol. Psychiat., Proc. 14th Ann. Conv. Soc. Biol. Psychiat., Atlantic City, 1959* p. 321. Grune & Stratton, New York.

Hoch, P. (1960). *In* "The Use of LSD in Psychotherapy" (H. A. Abramson, ed.), p. 58. Josiah Macy, Jr. Found., New York.

Hochstein, F. A., and Paradies, A. M. (1957). *J. Am. Chem. Soc.* **79**:5735.

Hoffer, A., and Osmond, H. (1959). *J. Nervous Mental Disease* **128**:18.

Hoffer, A., and Osmond, H. (1961a). *J. Neuropsychiat.* **2**:306.

Hoffer, A., and Osmond, H. (1961b). *J. Neuropsychiat.* **2**:331.

Hoffer, A., Osmond, H., and Smythies, J. (1954). *J. Mental Sci.* **100**:29.

Hofmann, A. (1959). *Proc. 1st Intern. Congr. Neuro-Pharm., Rome, 1958* Vol. 1, p. 446. Van Nostrand, Princeton, New Jersey.

Hofmann, A. (1961a). *J. Exptl. Med. Sci.* **5**:31.

Hofmann, A. (1961b). *Indian Practitioner* **14**:195.

Hofmann, A., Heim, R., Brack, A., and Kobel, H. (1958). *Experientia* **14**:107.

Hofmann, A., Heim, R., Brack, A., Kobel, H., Frey, A., Ott, H., Petrzilka, T. H., and Troxler, F. (1959). *Helv. Chim. Acta* **42**:1557.

Hollister, L. E. (1961). *Arch. Intern. Pharmacodyn.* **130**:42.

Hollister, L. E. (1962). *Ann. N.Y. Acad. Sci.* **96**:80.

Hollister, L. E., Prusmack, J. J., Paulsen, J. A., and Rosenquist, N. (1960). *J. Nervous Mental Disease* **131**:428.

Holmberg, G., and Gershon, S. (1961). *Psychopharmacologia* **2**:93.

Horita, A., and Weber, L. J. (1961a). *Proc. Soc. Exptl. Biol. Med.* **106**:32.

Horita, A., and Weber, L. J. (1961b). *Biochem. Pharmacol.* **7**:47.

Huxley, A. (1954). "The Doors of Perception." Harper, New York.

Isbell, H. (1959). *Psychopharmacologia* **1**:29.

Isbell, H., Wolbach, A. B., Wikler, A., and Miner, E. (1961). *Psychopharmacologia* **2**:147.

Jenney, E. H., and Pfeiffer, C. C. (1958). *J. Pharmacol. Exptl. Therap.* **112**:110.

Jensen, H., and Chen, K. K. (1936). *J. Biol. Chem.* **116**:87.

Johnson, J. B. (1939). Editorial Cultural Mexico. See Wasson, 1962.

Kalberer, F., Kreis, W., and Rutschmann, J. (1962). *Biochem. Pharmacol.* **2**:261.

Kast, E. C. (1961). *J. Neuropsychiat.* **2**:S114.

Kety, S. S. (1959). *Science* **129**:1528 and 1590.

Laidlaw, P. P. (1912). *Biochem. J.* **6**:141.

Lambert, M. (1902). *Arch. Intern. Pharmacodyn.* **10**:101.

Lambert, M., and Heckel, E. (1901). *Compt. Rend.* **133**:1236.

Landrin, A. (1905). *Bull. Sci. Pharmacol.* **11**:319.

Lauer, J. W. (1958). *J. Clin. Exptl. Psychopathol. & Quart. Rev. Psychiat. Neurol.* **19**:110.

Lauer, J. W., Inskip, W. M., Bernsohn, J., and Zeller, E. A. (1958). *A.M.A. Arch. Neurol. Psychiat.* **80**:122.

Lehmann, A., and Busnel, R. G. (1961). *Biochem. Pharmacol.* **8**:8.

Lerner, A. B., and Case, J. D. (1960). *Federation Proc.* **19**:590.

Lewin, L. (1931). "Phantastica: Narcotic and Stimulating Drugs: Their Use and Abuse." Kegan Paul, London.

McCawley, E. L., Brummett, R. E., and Dana, G. W. (1962). *Proc. Western Pharmacol. Soc.* **5**:27.

McIsaac, W. M. (1961a). *Biochim. Biophys. Acta* **2**:607.

McIsaac, W. M. (1961b). *Postgrad. Med.* **30**:111.

McIsaac, W. M., Khairallah, P. A., and Page, I. H. (1961). *Science* **134**:674.

Marion, L. (1952). *In* "The Alkaloids" (R. H. F. Manske and H. L. Holmes, eds.), Vol. 2, p. 369. Academic Press, New York.

Matthews, R. J., Roberts, B. J., and Adkins, P. K. (1961). *J. Neuropsychiat.* Suppl. 1, p. 151.

Maupin, B. (1961). *Psychopharmacol. Serv. Center Bull.* **1**:15.

Maxwell, G. M., Kneebone, G. M., and Elliott, R. B. (1961). *Arch. Intern. Pharmacodyn.* **137**:108.

Murphree, H. B., Jenney, E. H., and Pfeiffer, C. C. (1960). *Pharmacologist* **2**:64.
Murphree, H. B., Dippy, E. H., Jenney, E. H., and Pfeiffer, C. C. (1961). *Clin. Pharmacol. Therap.* **2**:722.
O'Connell, F. D., and Lynn, E. V. (1953). *J. Am. Pharm. Assoc.* **42**:753.
Olson, R. E., Gursey, D., and Vester, J. W. (1960). *New Engl. J. Med.* **263**:1169.
Page, I. H. (1958). *Physiol. Rev.* **38**:277.
Page, J. A., and Hoffer, A. (1964). *Diseases Nervous System* **25**:558.
Payza, A. N., and Hoffer, A. (1959). *Bull. Fac. Med. Istanbul* **22**:1096.
Pennes, H. H., and Hoch, P. H. (1957). *Am. J. Psychiat.* **113**:887.
Perrot, E., and Raymond-Hamet, M. (1927). *Bull. Sci. Pharmacol.* **34**:417.
Perry, T. L., Shaw, K. N. F., Walker, D., and Redlich, D. (1962). *Pediatrics* **30**:576.
Pfeifer, A. K., Satory, E., and Pataky, I. (1961a). *Arch. Exptl. Pathol. Pharmakol.* **241**:196.
Pfeifer, A. K., Satory, E. P., and Vizy, E. (1961b). *Acta Physiol. Acad. Sci. Hung.* **18**:82.
Pfeifer, A. K., Satory, E., and Pataky, I. (1961c). *Acta Physiol. Acad. Sci. Hung.* **19**:225.
Pfeiffer, C. C. (1960). "Inhibitors of the Nervous System and γ-Aminobutyric Acid." Pergamon Press, Oxford.
Pfeiffer, C. C., Jenney, E. H., and Marshall, W. H. (1956). *Electroencephalog. Clin. Neurophysiol.* **8**:307.
Phisalix, M. C. (1901). *Compt. Rend. Soc. Biol.* **53**:1077.
Pletscher, A., and Besendorf, H. (1959). *Experientia* **15**:25.
Pollin, W., Cardon, P. V., Jr., and Kety, S. S. (1961). *Science* **133**:104.
Pouchet, D, and Chevalier, J. (1905). *Bull. Gen. Therap. (Paris)* **149**:211.
Ramsbottom, J. (1953). "Mushrooms and Toadstools. A Study of the Activities of Fungi." Collins, London.
Raymond-Hamet, M. (1941a). *Bull. Acad. Med. (Paris)* **124**:243.
Raymond-Hamet, M. (1941b). *Compt. Rend. Soc. Biol.* **135**:1414.
Raymond-Hamet, M., and Rothlin, E. (1939). *Arch. Intern. Pharmacodyn.* **63**:27.
Reilly, R. H., Killam, K. F., Jenney, E. H., Marshall, W. H., Tausig, T., Apter, N. S., and Pfeiffer, C. C. (1953). *J. Am. Med. Assoc.* **152**:1317.
Reko, B. P. (1919). *Mex. Antique* **1**:113.
Reko, B. P. (1923). Letter to J. N. Rose, U.S. National Museum. US National Herbarium. Herbarium Sheet No. 1745713, Washington, D.C.
Reko, B. P. (1949). *Bol. Soc. Botan. Mex.* **8**:9.
Renner, U., Prins, D. A., and Stoll, W. G. (1959). *Helv. Chim. Acta* **42**:1572.
Rinkel, M., Hyde, R. W., Solomon, H. C., and Hoagland, H. (1955). *Am. J. Psychiat.* **111**:881.
Rinkel, M., Atwell, C. R., Dimascio, A., and Brown, J. (1960a). *New Engl. J. Med.* **262**:295.
Rinkel, M., Dimascio, A., Robey, A., and Atwell, C. (1960b). *Neuro-Psychopharmacol.* **2**:273.
Robie, T. R. (1961a). *Diseases Nervous System* **22**:452.
Robie, T. R. (1961b). *J. Neuropsychiat.* **2**:531.
Rodnight, R. (1956). *Biochem. J.* **64**:621.
Rodnight, R. (1961). *Intern. Rev. Neurobiol.* **3**:251.
Rosenberg, D. E., Isbell, H., and Miner, E. J. (1963). *Psychopharmacologia* **4**:39.
Rosenberg, D. E., Isbell, H., Miner, E. J., and Logan, C. R. (1964). *Psychopharmacologia* **5**:217.

Rothlin, E., and Raymond-Hamet, M. (1938). *Compt. Rend. Soc. Biol.* **127**:592.

Roughly, T. C. (1960). *Natl. Geograph. Mag.* **118**:559.

Rummele, W. (1959). *Schweiz. Arch. Neurol., Neurochir. Psychiat.* **84**:348.

Rummele, W., and Gnirss, F. (1961). *Schweiz. Arch. Neurol., Neurochir. Psychiat.* **87**:365.

Rusby, H. H. (1924). *J. Am. Pharm. Assoc.* **13**:98.

Safford, W. E. (1915). *J. Heredity* **6**:291.

Safford, W. E. (1916). *J. Wash. Acad. Sci.* **6**:547.

Safford, W. E. (1921). *J. Am. Med. Assoc.* **77**:1278.

Sai-Halasz, A. (1962). *Experientia* **18**:137.

Sai-Halasz, A. (1963). *Psychopharmacologia* **4**:385.

Sai-Halasz, A., and Endroczy, E. (1959). *In* "Neuro-Psychopharmacology" (B. B. Bradley, P. Demker, and C. Radouco-Thomas, eds.), p. 405. Elsevier, Amsterdam.

Salmoiraghi, G. C., and Page, I. H. (1957). *J. Pharmacol. Exptl. Therap.* **120**:20.

Schneider, J. A., and Rinehart, R. K. (1957). *Arch. Intern. Pharmacodyn.* **110**:92.

Schneider, J. A., and Sigg, E. B. (1957). *Ann. N.Y. Acad. Sci.* **66**:765.

Schultes, R. E. (1937). *Botan. Museum Leaflets. Harvard Univ.* **5**:61.

Schultes, R. E. (1939). *Bot. Museum Leaflets. Harvard Univ.* **7**:37.

Schultes, R. E. (1940). *Am. Anthropologist* **42**:429.

Schultes, R. E. (1963). *Psychedelic Rev.* **1**:145.

Smith, B., and Prockop, D. J. (1962). *New Engl. J. Med.* **267**:1338.

Sprince, H., and Lichtenstein, I. (1960). *A.M.A. Arch. Gen. Psychiat.* **2**:385.

Steiner, W. G., Pscheidt, G. R., Costa, E., and Himwich, H. (1963). *Psychopharmacologia* **4**:354.

Stern, P., and Gasparovic, J. (1961). *Pharmacol.* **8**:26.

Sulser, F., Watts, J., and Brodie, B. B. (1962). *Ann. N.Y. Acad. Sci.* **96**:279.

Szara, S. (1956). *Experientia* **12**:441.

Szara, S. (1957). *In* "Psychotropic Drugs" (S. Garattini and V. Ghetti, eds.), p. 460. Elsevier, Amsterdam.

Szara, S. (1961). *Federation Proc.* **20**:885.

Szara, S., and Hearst, E. (1962). *Ann. N.Y. Acad. Sci.* **96**:134.

Szara, S., Hearst, E., and Putney, F. (1960). *Federation Proc.* **19**:23.

Szatmari, A., Hoffer, A., and Schneider, R. (1955). *Am. J. Psychiat.* **111**:603.

Tedeschi, D. H., Tedeschi, R. E., and Fellows, E. J. (1959). *Federation Proc.* **18**:450.

Turner, W. J., and Merlis, S. (1959). *A.M.A. Arch. Neurol. Psychiat.* **81**:121.

Turner, W. J., and Merlis, S. (1961a). *J. Neuropsychiat.* **2**:S69.

Turner, W. J., and Merlis, S. (1961b). *J. Neuropsychiat.* **2**:S73.

Turner, W. J., Merlis, S., and Carl, A. (1955). *Am. J. Psychiat.* **112**:466.

Vane, J. R. (1959). *Brit. J. Pharmacol.* **14**:87.

Van Meter, W. G., Avala, G. F., Costa, E., and Himwich, H. E. (1960). *Federation Proc.* **19**:265.

Villalba, A. M. B. (1925). *J. Soc. Chem. Ind. (London)* **44**:205.

Vincent, D., and Sero, I. (1942). *Compt. Rend. Soc. Biol.* **136**:612.

Walaszek, E. J. (1960). *Intern. Rev. Neurobiol.* **2**:138.

Walls, F., Collera, D., and Sandoval, A. L. (1958). *Tetrahedron* **2**:173.

Wasson, R. G. (1959). *Trans. N.Y. Acad. Sci.* [2] **21**:325.

Wasson, R. G. (1961). *Botan. Museum Leaflets. Harvard Univ.* **19**:137.

Wasson, R. G. (1962). *Botan. Museum Leaflets. Harvard Univ.* **20**:25.

Wasson, V. P., and Wasson, R. G. (1957). "Mushrooms, Russia and History." Pantheon Books, New York.

Weckowicz, T. (1961). Ph.D. Thesis, University of Saskatchewan.

Weidmann, H., and Cerletti, A. (1959). *Helv. Physiol. Pharmacol. Acta* **17**:46.

Weidmann, H., Taeschler, M., and Konzett, H. (1958). *Experientia* **14**:378.

Weil-Malherbe, H., Posner, H. S., and Waldrop, F. N. (1962). *Ann. N.Y. Acad Sci.* **96**:419.

Wieland, T., Motzel, W., and Merz, H. (1953). *Ann. Chem.* **581**:10.

Wilkinson, S. (1958). *J. Chem. Soc.* p. 2.

Winitz, M., Gullino, P., Greenstein, J. P., and Birnbaum, S. M. (1956). *Arch. Biochem. Biophyis.* **64**:333.

Woolley, D. W., and Campbell, N. K. (1962). *Science* **136**:777.

Woolley, D. W., and Shaw, E. N. (1957). *Ann. N.Y. Acad. Sci.* **66**:649.

Zeller, E. A. (1957). *J. Clin. Exptl. Psychopathol. & Quart. Rev. Psychiat. Neurol.* **19**: Suppl. 1, 106.

Zeller, E. A. (1958). *J. Clin. Exptl. Psychopathol. & Quart. Rev. Psychiat. Neurol.* **19**:106.

Zeller, E. A. (1959). *In* "Molecules and Mental Health" (F. A. Gibbs, ed.), p. 60. Lippincott, Philadelphia, Pennsylvania.

Zsigmond, E. K., Foldes, F. F., and Foldes, V. M. (1961). *Federation Proc.* **20**:393.

Chapter V

Hallucinogens Related to Parasympathetic Biochemistry

Introduction

Acetylcholine is one of the central parasympathetic chemicals and is one of the most interesting central nervous system chemical transmitters. When an impulse arrives at the nerve terminal a chemical transmitter is released, in this case, acetylcholine. The molecules diffuse across the synapse or gap between the nerve end and the closest neuron, or effector cell, and is adsorbed there by the receptor. This is an area on the neuron or effector cell which has a specific electrical configuration to which the transmitter is attracted or bound. This completes the process and another impulse is initiated in the cell housing the receptor.

Acetylcholine and noradrenaline are generally accepted as chemical transmitters, acetylcholine for the parasympathetic nervous system and noradrenaline for the sympathetic nervous system. Brodie proposed serotonin as a third chemical transmitter. This was discussed in the section on tryptophan hallucinogens. The chemical transmission hypothesis postulates an electrical circuit which is composed of conducting units connected by gaps which are bridged by slowly diffusing mediator molecules. Very little is known about the nerve terminal and just how the transmitters are released from their storage sites. Even less is known of the actual mechanism of transmitter diffusion to the receptor site but more is known about the nature of the receptor site and its combination with the chemical transmitter. A detailed examination of this problem is beyond the intent of this book.

Synthesis of Adequate Quantities of Acetylcholine

Inadequate synthesis is due to a shortage of either acetate or choline, or a shortage of acetylcholineacetylase, the enzyme which catalyzes their combinations, or inhibition of this acetylase will result in a scarcity of transmitter. The transmission across the synapse should, therefore,

517

be diminished with a consequent decrease of nervous activity. It is difficult to imagine an enzyme which has the "off-on" synthetic characteristics demanded by this theory but it is conceivable that, at the nerve ending which released acetylcholine, there is also an enzyme which binds both acetate and choline at an adjacent area. Thus synthesis would occur only after an impulse has released the acetylcholine molecule.

If too much acetylcholine were synthesized then there would be an increased leakage of acetylcholine across the synapse, and this would produce a more excitable effector or neuron.

The injection of acetylcholine or a similar substance would have the same effect.

STORAGE OF ACETYLCHOLINE

It is conceivable that a slight change in the nerve ending may either decrease or increase the affinity of the specialized storage site for acetylcholine. If the affinity is too great stimuli would have greater difficulty getting across the synapse because more energy would be required at the nerve ending to release the acetylcholine. If the affinity became too low acetylcholine might be released too readily, again increasing the excitability of the receptor.

DIFFUSION OF ACETYLCHOLINE ACROSS THE SYNAPSE

The time required for acetylcholine molecules to diffuse or travel across the synapse, depends upon the distance to be traveled, upon the concentration gradient from nerve terminal to receptor and upon the absence or presence of other chemicals in the synaptic fluid medium. In general, smaller molecules diffuse more rapidly than larger molecules and spherical molecules diffuse more rapidly than elongated molecules. Temperature is also important, and as temperature decreases, the rate of diffusion also should decrease.

Other molecules could theoretically interfere with the rate of diffusion simply by being there, that is, increasing the resistance to movement of the transmitter, or they could form an association with acetylcholine which, by markedly increasing the bulk of the coalesced molecules, would effectively reduce the diffusion time. These would decrease the effective transmission of stimuli across the synapse.

ADSORPTION ONTO THE RECEPTOR

The receptor might be free and able to bind acetylcholine avidly, or it may be partially blocked by the pressure of another molecule which would have to be displaced by acetylcholine, or it might be totally blocked by a molecule which has as great an affinity for the receptor as acetylcholine. In addition, the receptor site may be disfigured by injury or by some internal cellular defect so that it is less able to adsorb and be excited by acetylcholine.

We would expect that anything which slows the entire process would produce a state of inhibition or depression in the synapses affected. Conversely, factors which accelerate this process should bring about a state of increased excitation. The maximum state of excitation would be the convulsion or a major random discharge of electrical activity.

Factors Which Produce Synaptic Depression

1. Decreased synthesis of acetylcholine.
2. Increased affinity between acetylcholine and nerve terminal.
3. Lowered temperature.
4. Presence in the synapse of acetylcholine binders.
5. Decreased affinity of acetylcholine and receptor.
6. Blocking agents on receptors.

Factors Which Produce Excitation

1. Increased synthesis of acetylcholine or injection of acetylcholine or inhibition of acetylcholinesterase. Too great a concentration of acetylcholine should decrease the rate of diffusion of acetylcholine across the synapse since the diffusion gradient is relatively less. However, in fact, too much acetylcholine produces convulsions, the maximum state of excitation. This apparent paradox will be discussed later.
2. Decreased affinity between acetylcholine and nerve terminal.
3. Increased temperature.

There are many more methods for producing depression of transmission than there are methods of increasing transmission.

This, then, is a brief account of the chemical transmitter theory of synaptic transmission as applied to acetylcholine and the parasympathetic system. However, it does not appear to us that this theory accounts fully for the beautiful and smoothly functioning system which evidently exists. The chief objection is that the theory depends upon the diffusion of molecules as energy carriers which is a slow and unreliable method for transmitting information.

Until recently there was no known mechanism which would account any better than the diffusion theory. But few doubt that chemical transmitters are present and play a carrier role.

The function of the synapse is to act as an "off" or "on" switch. When "off" no current passes across, when "on" current must pass across freely and with as little time lag as possible. That is to say, the synapse is a switch in which the nerve terminal turns on the switch. A newer theory of synaptic transmission has been developed by Ovshinsky (1958) (see U. S. Patent No. 3,052,830 for technical description). Ovshinsky developed a chemical switch in which a small signal allows the transfer of large currents of electricity. The essence of his chemical switch are electrodes separated by a medium containing certain molecules. Normally these molecules are arranged or oriented in a random way. But when a signal is placed across the junction, the molecules orient themselves into a more or less parallel position and create numerous molecular chain conductors. The electrons are then transmitted across the electrodes by means of their molecular chains. As soon as the signal is removed that maintains the molecular alignment they immediately rotate into a random system again due to their kinetic energy and current ceases to flow. This switch does not depend upon moving or diffusing molecules to conduct current, but uses molecular chains which are made or broken by the signal given to it. This concept states that there is a polarity or an amphoteric quality which requires acceptors on a surface so that alignment can be brought about by an electric field generated at a distance from the surface where penetration takes place. With this penetration there also occurs simultaneously a change of impedance so that, for all intents and purposes, the membrane or film is impervious to certain ionic species but pervious to others.

Ovshinsky considers that there must be structural changes on the surfaces of the nerve cells caused by these electrochemical actions which can be initiated thermally, electrically, chemically, or even mechanically. These structural changes have to do with the amount of "amorphous" and crystalline structure which has a profound effect upon the electrical transmitting qualities. Therefore, substances which act as crystalline excitors have a profound meaning to synaptic conduction. Since polymeric substances alter their volume by the various types of phase changes that occur in them, it is even possible that there is a physical bridging between the nerve ends through the synapse.

Ovshinsky has postulated that a similar mechanism may operate at the synapse where the acetylcholine molecules would be randomly oriented so that no current could cross the synapse, until a signal came to the nerve terminal which would produce an electromotive potential. This would immediately orient the acetylcholine molecules into a molecular chain and the current would flow across the synapse to the receptor. This differs from the previous transmitter idea in that it is no longer necessary to postulate any diffusion of acetylcholine across the synapse.

This newer theory yields much the same predictions as does the diffusion theory. Thus there must be a nerve terminal portion which switches on the synapse. There must be a receptor at the other end to receive the signal and there must be sufficient molecules present to carry the current. The nerve terminal and the receptor may act as anchors for the acetylcholine molecular chains. Yet, there are many differences in the two theories. The molecular chain theory demands that there must be sufficient molecules of acetylcholine in the synapse from which the chains can be formed. With both systems too little acetylcholine is harmful. But when too much acetylcholine is present very different predictions are made. With the diffusion theory too much acetylcholine should decrease excitability since there would be a decrease in the rate of diffusion and signals should have more difficulty getting through. However, with the molecular chain theory, increasing numbers of acetylcholine molecules would mean that more molecular chains would be formed and more current carried across. It is possible that the number of acceptors limits the acetylcholine action in either case.

The diffusion theory requires periodic release of acetylcholine from nerve endings, whereas the molecular chain theory merely needs an optimum concentration of acetylcholine in the synapse. It seems to us to be more economical to have a chemical system in which enzymes are free to maintain an optimal concentration of acetylcholine molecules in the synapse and in which the nerve endings and receptors are left free to discharge and receive electrical impulses.

It may be possible to rule between these hypotheses by measuring the effect of temperature on electrical transmission. The effect of reducing temperature should be more marked in reducing diffusion than it should be in reducing orientation, that is, cooling on the diffusion theory, should be much more devastating on the functioning of the brain. This matter could be settled by cooling animals and measuring the effect on conductivity across synapses. If there is a marked reduction this would favor the diffusion theory. Of course, the effect of temperature on biochemical processes within the cell would also have to be considered. According to Ovshinsky, temperature can be a critical transition point for the structural changes that take place at the nerve endings.

The hallucinogens may act by interfering at any level with this complicated cycle for any distortion in the smooth flow of impulses would result in unusual information which would be experienced as changes in perception, thinking, and affect. It may be possible to classify hallucinogens by their effect upon the synapse.

Acetylcholine

Acetylcholine is a quaternary ammonium compound. The cationic head consisting of the nitrogen surrounded by four methyl groups is most important for acetylcholine's physiological activity. Reducing the number of methyl groups by replacing them with hydrogen markedly reduces its potency. The bond between the onium portion of acetylcholine and the receptor is ionic and may be essential to its activity. Another way to reduce the electronic charge of the onium head is to disperse it by the addition of more atoms. One ethyl group (CH_3—CH_2) on the nitrogen reduces physiological activity moderately. Two ethyl groups reduces activity markedly and three methyl groups completely alters the activity. The cationic head, because of the number of methyl groups, should be the hydrophobic end, that is, it is most likely the most important end of the molecule for anchoring it to the receptor which is a lipid-containing membrane and could have a strong attraction for the onium head.

The other end of the acetylcholine molecule is the alkyl chain or hydrophilic end because of the carboxylic ester linkage. Five atoms are present in the chains. When the chain is lengthened or an oxygen removed, the pharmacological activity is markedly decreased. Choline itself has all the activity of acetylcholine but a much greater concentration is required. It is easy to visualize orientation of acetylcholine on the neuron receptors with the onium head attracted to the receptor and the hydrophilic end pointing toward the nerve terminal. It is generally assumed that the acetylcholine is bound flat against the receptor, but this is not the only way.

It is clear that acetylcholine plays an important part in brain function. When dilute solutions are applied directly to cortical areas of the cerebrum, spiking activity is seen, which is completely countered by atropine. Topical applications of acetylcholine to the brain stem causes hyperpnea, nausea, vomiting, and pressor responses. The evidence that acetylcholine plays an important role in normal and abnormal brain functions is very powerful, that is increased concentrations of acetylcholine produces marked changes in behavior. Injections of acetylcholine into the ventricle of cats produced catatonic-like muscular changes (Feldberg and Sherwood, 1954). Injections into the ventricles of schizophrenic patients increased the severity of the illness (McCulloch, 1949). If these injections were followed by acetylcholinesterase injections the changes were rapidly reversed. Injections of cholinesterase into chronic schizophrenic patients produced prolonged remissions (Sherwood, 1955).

When patients were injected with atropine, neostigmine, and acetylcholine in that order, Szatmari and Schneider (1955), noted psychological changes and the electroencephalogram was activited. Some schizophrenic subjects developed a sleep EEG pattern without becoming sleepy. Others did not develop sleep activity but suffered reactivation of their earlier symptoms. Normal subjects became drowsy and showed sleep EEG changes. Epileptic subjects showed many EEG changes but did not become drowsy.

Cholinesterase inhibitors given alone increase acetylcholine concentrations and produce profound changes in behavior. But the degree of central activity depends upon the ease of penetration into the brain. Thus neostigmine is as potent as eserine in inhibiting esterase but eserine, an indole, has more central activity (Elkes *et al.*, 1954). On standing, eserine decomposes into a red pigment rubeserine which is similar in structure to adrenochrome. Hoffer (1962) found that one milligram of rubeserine placed in the ventricle of two cats produced less intense, but similar, activity to that produced by one milligram of adrenochrome. In one cat, mild change was observed. The other became less alert, less hostile, had much less motor activity, and showed no visible effect on its gait. There were no autonomic changes.

The effect of eserine pretreatment before injections of acetylcholine produced a different response compared with neostigmine. With eserine no somatic changes were observed, that is, there was no sense of constriction in the chest, no dyspnea, and no coughing. With neostigmine these changes were marked but transient. Eserine which produced very little change in the EEG did cause marked changes in the EEG following administration of acetylcholine. The changes were similar to the ones described by Szatmari and Schneider (1955). These were slow with high voltage waves which were much more pronounced.

Many of the hallucinogens are esterase inhibitors, for example, LSD, bufotenine, adrenochrome, etc. This role will be discussed further under the appropriate compound. Acetylcholine blocking agents produced central changes. These include atropine, benactyzine, etc., and will be discussed in detail.

Acetylcholinesterase

The enzymes which only split acetylcholine are called true cholinesterases or acetylcholinesterases. Other enzymes which also hydrolyze other organic esters are nonspecific or pseudo or butyrylcholinesterases.

Many chemicals are potent *in vivo* inhibitors of these esterases. There are 3 general kinds of anticholinesterases.

1. Alkyl or aryl carbamate derivatives of the type CH_3CH_2—O—CO—$N(CH_3)_2$.
2. Alkyl or aryl phosphates and fluorophosphates for example P—O—R where R is the organic radical.
3. Quaternary ammonium ions.

The mechanism of esterase inhibition is fairly well understood. An inhibitor is a compound which is attracted to either or both of the rectpro sites on the enzyme. This reduces the number of acetylcholine molecules which can be bound, activated, and split. Thus quaternary ammonium compounds may be bound to the anionic locus. Esters like neostigmine may be bound at the esterate site as well as at the anionic site. Binding may be reversible or irreversible, but this will vary depending upon the other chemicals present. Esterase inhibition results in an increase of acetylcholine with marked changes in physiology and in behavior.

Cholinesterases are regenerated slowly, and in the brain this may take three months, but peripheral esterases regenerate more quickly.

Anticholinesterases as Hallucinogens

Anticholinesterases are not remarkable for their hallucinogenic properties. This may be due to their intense central poisoning activity. Physostigmine (eserine) the alkaloid from the Calabar bean, is a very powerful anticholinesterase. When it is given quickly animals become weak and finally paralyzed due to the accumulation of acetylcholine at the motor end plates. Neostigmine is as potent an anticholinesterase but has less central activity. When large doses of eserine are given, there is an intense augmentation of brain activity. Atropine will block the central activity but not its activity on neuromuscular transmission. Rubeserine, the red quinone indole derived from eserine, is active when placed in the ventricles of cats but is not as potent, weight for weight, as adrenochrome. No human studies with rubeserine have been reported. We predict that it will be an hallucinogen. Sherwood (1958) reported that prostigmine taken by patients for treatment of myasthenia gravis occasionally produced psychotic episodes. Diisopropylfluorophosphate (DFP), once used to treat myasthenia gravis, also produced nightmares, mental confusion and hallucinations in some patients. Rowntree *et al.* (1950) found that DFP made schizophrenic patients more psychotic. With the increase in the common use of anticholinesterase insecticides the incidence of severe poisoning and even psychosis will undoubtedly rise.

Anticholinesterase inhibitors can not be classed as hallucinogens but the anticholinesterase activity of some hallucinogens may be very important for their activity.

Cholinergic-Blocking Hallucinogens

BELLADONNA ALKALOIDS

These are alkaloids extracted from *Atropa belladonna* (deadly nightshade), *Hyoscyamus niger* (black henbane), and *Datura stramonium* (Jimson weed, Jamestown weed, or Thornapple). The active alkaloids are *l*-hyoscyamine, *dl*-hyoscyamine (atropine), and *l*-scopolamine (as shown below).

Atropine   Scopolamine

The solanacea have been used as poisons and hallucinogens since the first records of history. Henbane was used in ancient Greece as a poison, to produce dementia, and to evoke prophecies. According to Louis Lewin the Arabs in the Near East smoked the dry feltlike leaves of *Hyoscyamus muticus* and developed a delirious psychosis. In the Punjab it was known as koki-bhang and smoked like Indian hemp. Thornapple was consumed by Antony's troops in 37 and 38 BC during their retreat from the Parthians. Many of them became psychotic before they died. During the Middle Ages these plants were reputedly used criminally for making people mad, for seducing women, etc.

There is no lack of accounts of belladonna psychosis. Standard psychiatric textbooks carry descriptions of them and even today an occasional patient will be admitted suffering from this drug-induced psychosis.

Roueche (1965) reported how a family became self-poisoned with atropine (hyoscyamine) from tomatoes. Tomato plants were grafted on to the Jimson weed where they grew well. Late in 1963 a family of 5 people ate these tomatoes. The tomatoes were later found to contain 6.36 mg per tomato. All five developed deliriod reactions of varying intensity and some had to be treated in hospital several days. This seems to be the first known instance of hallucinogenic tomatoes.

Not only are these compounds able to produce psychosis but they have been used to potentiate markedly the psychotomimetic actions of other substances such as hemp or poppy seeds. In India bhang and ganja were sometimes fortified with datura. Johnson (1953) quoted extracts from the Report of the Indian Hemp Drugs Commission 1893–1894. Hundreds of witnesses were examined. It was reported that datura mixed with hemp "causes a peculiar kind of delirium, something like delirium tremens: the man picks at his bedclothes and sees horrible objects like snakes, scorpions, etc. If the dose is a very large one he becomes drowsy and quite unconscious which might terminate in death, or temporary recovery and madness." Surgeon-major Quayle stated "Dhatura is mixed with ganja in excess and so taken the dhatura must affect the mental functions very powerfully, increasing the intoxicating effect and producing delirium and temporary insanity. In dhatura poisoning the person often tears off his clothes and wanders about quite out of his mind for one or two days." Atropine is believed to be a competitive inhibitor with acetylcholine for attachment to the receptor site. There it prevents the specific acetylcholine excitation of the receptor. It does not prevent the liberation of acetylcholine for attachment to the receptor site. It does not prevent the liberation of acetylcholine. Scopolamine acts in a similar way. Atropine has a specific blocking action on acetylcholine at the postganglionic junction, is transiently active at the ganglionic site and relatively inactive as a neuromuscular blocking agent. Scopolamine is a much stronger psychotomimetic; stupor and delirium are more prominent and excitement less evident. The narcotic action of scopolamine was used to control very excited psychiatric patients, to control delirium tremens, and in obstetrics to produce drowsiness with amnesia—a "twilight sleep."

When 1% atropine sulfate instillations in the eye were used commonly for postsurgical treatment of retinal detachment, postsurgical psychoses were not uncommon. Atropine of this strength contains 10 mg/ml of atropine. It is not surprising that sufficient atropine could be swallowed in tears to produce atropine psychosis. Some years ago it became fashionable to ascribe these psychotic changes to sensory deprivation; but when atropine eye drops were not used, these psychotic episodes apparently did not occur.

Baker and Farley (1958) described an acute confusional psychosis which followed the administration of 1% atropine sulfate drops in the treatment of retinal detachment. The patient recovered when given ECT. She remained emotionally labile and paranoid for a few days. Later when given a test dose of atropine, the psychosis returned. Hoefnagel (1961) described 5 additional cases. They were children given either atropine or homatropine eye drops. In these cases, and in most of the instances of atropine toxicity reported in the literature, psychiatric signs and symptoms were much more marked than perceptual changes. Ataxia occurred early and was sometimes so severe the children were unable to sit or stand unaided. Speech was dysarthric. They were very restless, overly active, muttered almost constantly, shouted or sang, and suffered great confusion, visual hallucinations, and often fright. Episodes of restlessness often alternated with periods of relaxation. When disturbed, violent and aggressive behavior occurred. Coma and convulsions have been reported. After recovery, retrograde amnesia was common. After withdrawal of atropine, recovery might take anywhere from several hours to several days. Homatropine was as toxic as atropine.

Case 2 (Hoefnagel) developed psychiatric changes after 2% homatropine eyedrops had been instilled. The prescription called for the instillation of 1 drop in each eye every 10 minutes for 6 administrations. After the first 2 drops the patient complained of a stuffy nose. After the sixth drop he became ataxic and developed hallucinations. He saw animals and people and spoke to them.

Atropine and scopolamine may act centrally by increasing parasympathetic activity which is expressed physiologically as an alert EEG pattern. Rinaldi and Himwich (1955) showed that intracarotid or IV injection of acetylcholine, or of DFP (0.05–0.3 mg/kg) produced an alert pattern in the EEG of curarized rabbits. This was reversed by atropine. When atropine was administered it produced a sleep spindle-slow wave pattern. At doses of from 3 to 6 mg/kg atropine abolished electrocortical responses to strong painful stimuli.

Atropine (1–3 mg IV) caused moderate to high voltage slow activity in EEG of curarized cats and monkeys. Wikler (1957) found atropine produced a dissociation between the sleep spindle-slow wave activity and the degree of alertness of the animal. Some animals appeared to be sedated but others were excited. Longo (1956) reported that atropine and also scopolamine produced sleep EEG patterns, abolished the awakening effect of high frequency electrical stimulation of the ascending reticular system as well as of all external stimuli except painful ones. But neither substance had an effect on the neurovegetative responses of the uncurarized rabbit to electrical stimulation of the anteromedial hypothalamus.

Scopolamine is now available in the sleeping preparation called "Sominex." Each tablet has 0.25 mg. Beach *et al.* (1964) reported 6 cases of severe scopolamine intoxication. The clinical picture included coma, convulsions, hallucinations, etc. The one person reported in detail suffered visual hallucinations, and severe disorientation for several hours.

The symptoms began to disappear in about 12 hours. Schultes (1956) discovered a new plant, apparently a member of the Solanaceae, in Columbia: *Methysticodendron amesianum,* in the Valley of Sibundoy. It is the most potent narcotic in the region, even stronger than datura. The intoxicant may be a tropane type of chemical. Witch doctors took it for very important cases of divination. The intoxication lasted from 2 to 4 days. The leaves were collected 1 hour before use, crushed and allowed to steep in cold water for 30 minutes. Just before consuming the infusion the mixture was agitated, warmed slightly, and strained. A large cupful was consumed over a 2-hour period.

Benactyzine

Benactyzine is a diphenylmethane compound introduced by Jacobsen and Sonne (1955) as an antidepressant. It is a central anticholinergic substance. Other diphenylmethanes are azocyclanol (Frenquel), hydroxyzine (Atarax), meclizine (Bonamine), and adiphenine (Trasentine).

Benactyzine is relatively nontoxic. Its LD-50 for mice, rats, guinea pigs, and rabbits is about 120 mg/kg IP.

Jacobsen (1958) found that benactyzine produced complete or partial blockage of the alpha rhythm of the EEG in man. Blockage began and ended simultaneously with the subjective changes. Subcutaneous doses of 5–6 mg produced changes in 5–10 minutes. These were dizziness, nausea or vomiting, muscular relaxation and thought blocking. Benactyzine appeared to reduce irritability in subjects. These early studies led to its introduction in psychiatry as an antidepressant agent, either alone or combined with meprobamate. Ayd (1957) found some psychotomimetic side effects on larger doses which included blurred vision, feelings of depersonalization, impaired concentration, and thought blocking. Raymond and Lucas (1956) found changes in perception in volunteers given 5 mg subcutaneously.

The recommended dosages for the treatment of anxiety neuroses and depression do not produce psychotomimetic effects. But when taken in doses about 20 times larger, benactyzine is a powerful hallucinogen and similar in its action to atropine or scopolamine.

Vojtechovsky and his colleagues were the first to describe the experimental psychoses due to high doses of benactyzine. In 1958, Vojtechovsky observed a patient who ingested 1300 mg of benactyzine. She suffered a short delirious psychosis with hallucinations, psychomotor restlessness, and a decreased level of consciousness. Following this observation, Vojtechovsky *et al.* (1958, 1960a,b), Vojtechovsky (1958),

Vinarova *et al.* (1958), and Grof and Vojtechovsky (1958), showed that doses of benactyzine of around 100 mg or overproduced experimental psychoses equivalent to those produced by LSD or mescaline. One of the authors, Dr. S. Grof, in a self experiment took 200 mg by mouth. After 15 minutes, visual illusions, weakness, and ataxia appeared. At the end of 1 hour he experienced marked hallucinations and illusions, derealization, disturbed consciousness, anxiety, dysarthria, and later, aphonia. Between the second and sixth hour during reduced level of consciousness, he observed massive visual hallucinations of animals and men. Auditory hallucinations were less common. His level of consciousness became normal at the seventh to ninth hour but the hallucinations, illusions, incoherence, and other changes continued to the twelfth hour. Vojtechovsky *et al.* (1960b) compared the delirium to atropine intoxication. With further research they were able to show that from 40 to 70 mg of benactyzine produced a psychotomimetic change in most normal volunteers. The experience caused by the reduced dose was qualitatively similar to the 200 mg experience, but it was less intense and consciousness was less disturbed. This experience began in half an hour and continued for about 6 hours reaching its peak at 1–4 hours. At this time there was a marked decrease in the excretion of 5-hydroxyindoleacetic acid and an increase in 17-oxysteroid excretion. (LSD had no effect on 5-hydroxyindoleacetic acid excretion.) At the height of the experience there was also marked disturbance in thinking. Association tests were performed badly and latency of associations was prolonged. There were marked changes in the EEG. Two hours after taking the benactyzine, the alpha rhythm disappeared and the theta rhythm of 5–6 cycles/second became dominant. When the subjects opened their eyes alpha activity was accentuated. Four hours after taking the drug alpha activity began to return. After 6 hours the pattern began to return to normal.

Vojtechovsky *et al.* (1960a) compared 200 mg of benactyzine with 500 mg of mescaline, and 150 μg of LSD. A summary of this comparison for one subject is shown in Table 42.

Trasentine is very similar in structure to benactyzine lacking only an hydroxyl on the carbon with the diphenyl groups, but so far no psychotomimetic experiences have been reported to result from it.

In mice, benactyzine produced hyperexcitability, and convulsions, and increased the mortality of electrically induced convulsions. In monkeys 1–6 mg/kg decreased locomotion. Large doses produced convulsions. Benactyzine in doses from 0.75 to 2.0 mg made the behavior of experimentally neurotic cats normal. It was superior to alcohol as a normalizer. Scopolamine and chlorpromazine were not effective.

TABLE 42

COMPARISON OF BENACTYZINE, LSD, AND MESCALINE ON ONE SUBJECT[a]

	Benactyzine	LSD	Mescaline
Induction period	15–20 min	45–50 min	20–30 min
Autonomic changes	Tachycardia, increase in b.p. mydriasis, dryness of mouth	Tachycardia, slight inc. b.p., nausea, mydriasis	Same as LSD
Motor changes	Ataxia, apraxia, aphonia, catatonia	Incoordination, mild ataxia	Slight unsteadiness walking
Perception changes			
1. Visual	Eidetic images, geometrical forms, less structural than with LSD, sensation of great illumination, hallucinations, illusions, micropsia, colored dreams, and eidetic images for several weeks	Eidetic images, formed scenes, colorful and well-formed kaleidoscopic visions	At beginning like LSD but toward end like benactyzine
2. Acoustic	Illusions and hallucinations	Illusions of music from monotonous stimuli, hyperacusis	Same as LSD
3. Tactile	Feeling of heaviness	Paresthesia, anesthesia, coenesthetic hallucinations	Same as LSD
4. Olfactory and gustatory	Hypernosmia, loss of taste	Same	Same as LSD
5. Time and space	Disorientation	Disturbed judgment of time and space, dimensions altered	Same as LSD

	Heavy feeling, depersonalization	Paresthesia, hyperalgesia, hypoalgesia, feelings of heaviness or lightness, depersonalization, changes in body image	Same as LSD, depersonalization, changes in body image
6. Proprioceptive	Heavy feeling, depersonalization	Paresthesia, hyperalgesia, hypoalgesia, feelings of heaviness or lightness, depersonalization, changes in body image	Same as LSD, depersonalization, changes in body image
Thought changes			
1. Consciousness	Clouding complete amnesia	Insignificant changes	Same as LSD
2. Thinking	Blocking incoherence, speech unintelligible, acalculia, unable to write or think	Autistic, strange ideas impaired, ambivalence	Autistic ideas less strange than LSD, difficulty in talking
Affective changes	Deep depression, anxiety	Euphoria	Depression at beginning
Changes in personality	Deep deterioration	No	No
Changes in behavior	Unable to move about at onset, later agitation and explosive actions, at end retardation	Reluctance to move about	Same as LSD
Duration	12–13 hours	5–6 hours	7½ hours
Peak	Third to fourth hour	2–3 hours	Fourth hour
Comparable diagnosis	Toxic delirium	Hebephrenic	Schizoid retardation

[a] From Vojtěchovsky *et al.* (1960).

In rats made anxious or tense by an electric shock and buzzer, benactyzine 0.25–1.0 mg/rat, reduced the tension and increased the number of conditioned avoidance responses (Jacobsen and Sonne, 1955).

Abood and his colleagues developed a large series of psychotomimetic anticholinergic substances. Their basic structure is shown in Fig. 12. These have been reviewed by Abood and Biel (1962).

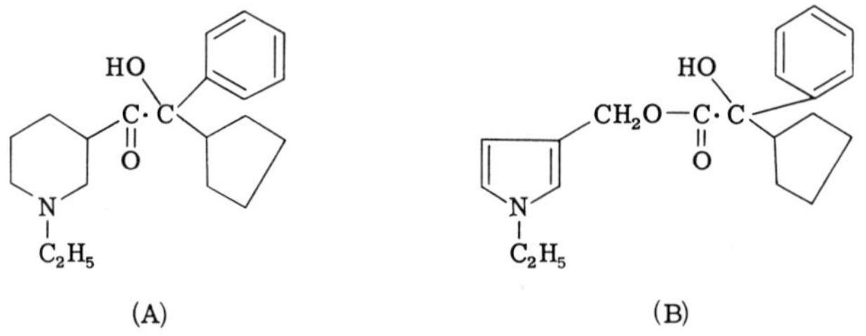

(A)   (B)

Fig. 12. Some anticholinergic psychotomimetic substances. Ditran contains 30% of N-ethyl-3-piperidyl cyclopentylphenylglycolate (A) and 70% of N-ethyl-3-pyrrolidylmethyl cyclopentylphenylglycolate (B).

RELATION OF STRUCTURE TO PSYCHOTOMIMETIC ACTIVITY

R_1 must be a lower alkyl group for maximum central activity. The degree of central activity of a series of compounds varying R_1 correlated very well with the hyperactivity produced in rats. The exception was the first member of the series when $R_1 = H$ which markedly reduced psychotomimetic activity but did not affect rat hyperactivity.

Maximum central activity was produced when R_2 was OH. An H or CH_3 group produced inactive compounds. A phenyl group on R_3 was required for maximum central activity. R_4 could be a phenyl, thienyl, cycloalkyl, or hydroxyalkyl group for central activity.

The position of the ester side chain or the size of the cycloalkylene imine ring did not markedly alter central activity provided the side chain was either a chemical bond or a methylene group. Increasing the length of the side chain or branching it markedly reduced activity. The 3-piperidyl esters were most active followed by 2-derivatives and finally 4-derivatives.

In general there was a low correlation between anticholinergic activity and central activity although all centrally active compounds were anticholinergic.

BIOCHEMISTRY

Abood and Rinaldi (1959) studied the distribution of labeled N-ethyl-3-piperidyl benzilate in the rat. More than 95% was excreted by the kidneys within two hours. About 0.1% was found in the brain after one hour, chiefly in the caudate nucleus, hypothalamus, and corpus callosum. A similar distribution was found in the rabbit brain. After 3 hours the activity was a small fraction of the half-hour activity.

The labeled substance was largely present in the mitochondria of the cells. In general the distribution was similar to the distribution of acetylcholine and this suggested the same receptor sites were involved.

Piperidyl glycolates had no specific inhibitory activity on numerous oxidases, glycolytic enzymes, phosphatases and esterases. Overall oxidative phosphorylation of rat brain mitochondria was not inhibited at concentrations 5×10^{-4} M. Neither was there any significant effect on the respiration of brain and liver slices. Neurons in tissue culture showed increased movement of cytoplasmic granules near the Nissl substance.

Physiological

The physiological changes were similar to those produced by anticholinergic drugs. Autonomic peripheral changes included mydriasis, dryness of the mouth, skin flushing, some tachycardia, and slight hypertension. Motor and somatic changes included slowness of speech and gait, tremors, and rigidity. Neurological changes included ataxia, aphasia, apraxia, dysarthria, dizziness, and nystagmus. Sometimes these neurological effects lasted from 2 to 4 days.

Fink (1960) found that the compounds which were psychotomimetic also produced desynchronization of the EEG pattern. Sleeplike spindle and slow waves were produced and the alerting response in the reticular formation was inhibited. Both the psychological changes and EEG changes were antagonized by chlorpromazine.

The piperidyl glycolates may produce heat loss due to the pronounced vasodilatation. Abood and Biel suggested the increased motor activity was a compensatory mechanism. When environmental temperature was increased from 0° to 40°C there was a decrease in spontaneous activity. But animals given these compounds maintained a constant rate of activity down to 20°C but activity declined suddenly between 20° and 30°C.

These substances tended to concentrate in the frontal lobe of the rat, an area involved in hypothalamic regulation in the corpus callosum which is associated with drowsiness, apathy, and memory changes, and in the dorsal medial nucleus of the thalamus.

With the use of smooth muscle as a test system the piperidyl glycolates were anticholinergic (10^{-7} M), antiserotonin (10^{-5} M), and antihistaminic (10^{-5} M). There was an increase in isometric contraction of isolated frog sartorius in Ringers solution. Spontaneous twitching in Ca-free solution was decreased. In Ringers solution lactate production was increased but in Ca-free EDTA solution, lactate production was decreased.

On isolated frog spinal ganglia these compounds increased negative after potential ($5 \times 10^{-7} M$), blocked the action potential ($10^{-5} M$) an increased oxidative glycolytic metabolism.

Effect on Animal Behavior

Doses of 5–10 mg/kg IP in rats produced gross behavioral changes. The rats developed greater motor activity with head bobbing, head swaying, jerky and hesitant body movements, hyperreactivity, hypersensitivity, and spontaneous squealing. With higher doses there was a generalized decrease in body tone, weakness and ataxia. Using more sensitive measures of drug response, Abood and Biel (1962) found that 0.25 mg/kg disrupted learned sequential responses. The degree of disruption was a function both of dose and of the complexity of the sequence.

Because the hyperactivity induced in rats was easily measured, Abood and Biel (1962) tested the action of a series of tranquilizer and antitension compounds as hyperactivity antagonists. The test compound was given to the animal 5 minutes before the piperidyl glycolate. The most potent tranquilizers, chlorpromazine, fluphenazine, perphenazine, trifluoperazine, and prochlorpromazine in doses of 10 mg/kg almost completely blocked the hyperactivity. Chlordiazepoxide was nearly as strong but reserpine, meprobamate, and piperidine were less effective. Tetrahydroaminoacridine was also an effective agent for blocking the animal hyperactivity.

Piperidine (100 mg/kg) had some of the central activity of N-methyl-3-piperidyldiphenyl glycolate. Biel *et al.* (1962) reported that several piperazinoalkyl esters, which had much less anticholinergic activity than the piperidyl compounds, had no central stimulant properties. They have the general structure shown in Fig. 12.

Y is a straight or branched lower alkylene group. When rats were premedicated with these compounds the central stimulant effect of one of the active N-methylated piperidyl derivatives was reduced.

Mode of Action

The piperidyl compounds could act by interfering with the acetylcholine cycle. Biel *et al.* summarized this as follows: (a) only piperidyl and pyrrolidyl glycolate esters exerted a profound stimulant effect on the central nervous system which were also potent anticholinesterases; (b) a potent cholinesterase inhibitor tetrahydroaminacrin reversed the psychotomime.ic effect; (c) Ditran was an effective anti-depressant; (d) these drugs exerted little effect on any other enzyme system in the body; (e) they accumulated in the hypothalamus and caudate nucleus.

Another mode of action has become possible, however, according to Abood *et al.* (1961). Piperidine was found in urine (von Euler, 1945) and in brain (Honegger and Honegger, 1960), and might have some normal function in regulation of brain activity. Piperidine is an antago-nist of the piperidyl psychotomimetics and has been useful in the treatment of some schizophrenic patients (Tasher *et al.*, 1960). When rabbits were given piperidine some appeared in the brain. The greatest concentration occurred in the caudate nucleus. Other regions of the diencephalon had half as much as regions close to the caudate. The quadrigemina had the most piperidine. The distribution between white and gray matter was equal. It is possible, as was suggested by Abood and his co-workers, that the psychotomimetic piperidyls interfere with the normal brain piperidine and so produce the disorganization of brain function. Perhaps nicotinic acid, slightly similar to piperidine, might also antagonize the activity of these compounds.

PSYCHOLOGICAL

In general, the psychotomimetic experience resembled that produced by the other hallucinogens but the vivid perceptual changes and con-fusion suggest that a delirium was produced rather than a truly schizo-phrenic-like disease. But there was no sharp demarcation as some acute severe schizophrenics also have states which are diagnosed initially as a delirium.

Piperidyl glycolates produced changes in perception, in thought, and in mood in the presence of changes in consciousness, disorientation, and memory. The hallucinations were predominantly visual and involved people, animals, vivid scenes, etc. Distortions of visual images and il-lusions were common. The Kluver form constants described under mescaline were present and particularly common. Auditory hallucina-tions usually involved musical instruments and voices, and subjects fre-quently carried on conversations with these voices. As subjects went more deeply into the experience they were not able to distinguish the hallucinations from reality. They often picked up phantom objects (three-dimensional hallucinations) such as cigarettes, cups of coffee, and reacted appropriately to the hallucination. Olfactory and taste hal-lucinations were also very common. Changes in thought included re-duced speed and accuracy in problem solving, inability to comprehend questions, changes in memory retrograde amnesia, and impaired ideation. They often spoke in a senseless rambling manner and occasionally had complete aphasia. According to Lebovitz *et al.* (1960) N-ethyl-3-piperidyl benzilate and LSD were not too different in their effect on several psychological tests. On the MMPI they were almost identical.

From the accounts we have seen of these experiences it does not appear likely psychedelic experiences will be produced. Abood *et al.* (1959) reported that LSD and piperidyl benzilates produced very different experiences. In their experiments LSD seldom produced dramatic visual or auditory hallucinations whereas with the piperidyls they were marked and also qualitatively different. Subjects lost contact more readily with the piperidyl compounds.

Gershon (1960) found that tetrahydroaminacrin, which is a cholinesterase inhibitor, was a specific antagonist of the central and peripheral effects of N-ethyl-3-piperidyl cyclopentylphenyl glycolate (Ditran). Succinate and several phenothiazines did not block the central and peripheral activity of Ditran. On the other hand tetrahydro-5-aminoacridine did not block the psychotomimetic effect of LSD or *l*-(1-phenylcyclohexyl) piperidine (Sernyl). Other cholinesterase inhibitors such as eserine, prostigmine, and DFP did not have this blocking action.

Ditran is a mixture of N-ethyl-3-piperidyl cyclopentylphenyl glycolate and 70% of N-ethyl-2-pyrrolidylmethyl cyclopentylphenyl glycolate. Abood and Meduna (1958) gave Ditran to 5 depressed patients as a treatment. In three cases the depression was lifted and the patients were discharged. The other two did not have the same good therapeutic result. In a further report Meduna and Abood (1959) treated a total of twenty cases. They were given 5–10 mg orally or IM. They then developed the typical hallucinogenic experiences. When the symptoms disappeared, the subjects suffered marked physical weakness for 10–24 hours. About 24–36 hours after administration of the drug their mood changed markedly. They observed slight hypomania accompanied by increased drive. Nine patients suffered from psychotic depressions. Of these, only two showed a satisfactory improvement. Ten of the patients were reactive depressives and 8 recovered sufficiently to resume their activities. One woman was given Ditran during a manic phase of her manic depressive psychosis and recovered. Ditran seemed to have a marked normalizing effect upon both depressed and excited patients. Abood and Biel (1962) summarized a series of clinical reports which corroborated the therapeutic effects of Ditran. Tasher *et al.* (1960) used cyclopentimine.

Fink (1959) reported that another anticholinergic substance, a phenothiazine, was a psychotomimetic. This substance diethazine (Diparcol) has pharmacologic properties similar to atropine. In animals it blocks the bradycardia, bronchospasm, salivation, and seizures induced by acetylcholine, DFP, and pilocarpine. Its structure is shown below.

Forty psychiatric patients were given from 2.8 to 4.0 mg/kg IV. Within 2–5 minutes subjects coughed and developed dry mouths and thick speech. They felt tired, heavy, and weak. Eighteen subjects reported visual illusions, feelings of unreality, and delusions. A few subjects developed severe panic. These changes were similar to those produced by LSD and mescaline. At the same time there was a decrease in voltage and desynchronization of all frequencies on the EEG. The behavioral changes lasted about 1½ to 4 hours.

Charatan (1959) reported that 250 mg diethazine given to chronic regressed schizophrenics at the height of their LSD reaction (200–400 μg) terminated the LSD reaction within 1 hour.

On the other hand, Denber (1959) found diethazine made 5 subjects who had been given ½ gm mescaline even worse. There was an increase in emotional and ideational reactivity, marked hyperpnea, restlessness, and motor agitation.

There was also a decrease in tactile sensibility and a decrease in response to pain, but no change in thermal sensation. The subjects had marked sensations of trembling which was not visible, but felt as keenly as if the body was composed of a vibration mechanism. Sometimes visual changes occurred. There was a sensation that exterior objects were displaced. General malaise, a state of vertigo, incoordination of speech, and difficulty in executing fine movements were noted. There was also difficulty in walking, muscle weakness, and finally prostration. During the period of prostration the patients had vivid dreams and hallucinations, although they were not asleep.

Fink (1960) compared several anticholinergic compounds. Diethazine (200 mg IV) produced a decrease in the EEG voltage and desynchronization. The patients coughed, and they were irritable, restless, tense, and excited. They had feelings of unreality, noted changes in color perception, saw halos around lights and were delusional. Win 2299 (2-diethylaminoethylcyclopentyl)(2-thienyl)glycolate HCl was very similar to diethazine. Pennes and Hoch (1957) found that Win 2299 in 2 mg doses was a sedative for 2 subjects. In four subjects 6.0 mg produced a confusional psychosis. They felt it was comparable to the mescaline experience with the superimposition of confusion. In one subject, 10 mg produced delirium, disorientation for time, place, and person, and visual and auditory hallucinations and loss of contact.

Fink (1960) further found that small quantities of benactyzine produced similar changes in the EEG without psychotic changes; atropine made the subjects drowsy and relaxed while two piperidyl benzilates, JB 318, and JB 336, produced both EEG and psychological changes. Active compounds appeared to act by desynchronizing the EEG.

Cholineacetylase Inhibitors as Antihallucinogens

If inhibition of acetylcholinesterase produces hallucinogenic changes by increasing the effective concentration of acetylcholine, it would not be surprising if compounds which prevented the synthesis of acetylcholine were antihallucinogens. Holan (1965) has found this to be true. He compared a series of cholineacetylase inhibitors for cholineacetylase inhibition and as antagonists to Ditran's effects on dogs. They found a correlation between inhibition and antihallucinogenic properties in dogs. Thus p-phenylmandelic acid, 3-phenanthrylglycolic acid, and benzilic acid all inhibited acetylase and antagonized Ditran. p-Phenoxy mandelic acid and p-chlormandelic acid did not inhibit acetylase and were not Ditran antagonists.

These interesting findings will undoubtedly be expanded to an examination of the effects of these substances as antagonists to other hallucinogens and as treatment for some schizophrenics, perhaps those who have deliriod psychosis. Other inhibitors of cholineacetylase are salicylic acid, benzaldehyde, piperidine, quinoline, indole, and camphor (Pfeiffer, 1959). Some natural inhibitors are alloxan, guanine, and uric acid.

Anesthetic Hallucinogens

SERNYL

Greifenstein *et al.* (1958) reported that *l*-(1-phenylcyclohexylpiperidine) (Sernyl) was a powerful analgesic in animals and in man. The infusion of a 0.1% solution at a rate of 5 ml per minute produced complete analgesia after 8–11 mg had been given, and was possible to perform surgery. EEG activity was definitely slowed which also became diffuse unlike that following the administration of barbiturates or normal sleep.

Sernyl was unsatisfactory for surgical procedures in one-fifth of a large group tested. Several of these subjects became severely excited and developed a state of near mania. Many of the patients were unmanageable in the postoperative period and also exhibited manic behavior. Most of the patients had retrograde amnesia for up to 24 hours. Some, on recovering, appeared mildly intoxicated.

Bodi *et al.* (1959) tried Sernyl as an antidepressant. It was moderately effective but the effective dose was too close to the toxic dose. Side effects were drowsiness, dizziness, and vivid dreams, each in 1 patient.

It is not surprising, therefore, that Sernyl turned out to be another psychotomimetic substance. Luby *et al.* (1959) reported that 0.1 mg/kg of Sernyl given IV produced marked psychological changes in normal subjects and in psychiatric patients. Their subjects reported changes in perception (body image, depersonalization, feelings of unreality, illusions of TAT cards becoming real, estrangement, and hypnagogic dreamlike visions while awake, loss of sense of time). Some of the hallucinations were reacted to as if true. Thus one student reported, "I felt as though I was in the midst of a horrible and dreadful nightmare. The walls at times became long." There were also changes in thought such as an inability to maintain a set, loss of goal ideas, concrete thinking, blocking, etc. Many subjects were hostile and negativistic. No clear account was given of changes in affect.

A few schizophrenic patients given Sernyl suffered a reactivation of their psychoses and an intensification of their symptoms. These authors concluded Sernyl was quite different in its activity from LSD or mescaline, and that it produced a psychotomimetic experience which was more like natural schizophrenia. Sernyl, they claimed, produced an experimental psychosis which brought out the primary symptoms of schizophrenia whereas LSD, etc., produced a condition in which the secondary symptoms were more dominant. Thus Sernyl increased thought disorder and potentiated the schizophrenic psychosis.

E. Bleuler arbitrarily divided the symptoms he found in schizophrenia into primary and secondary symptoms. His primary symptoms included difficulties in thought processes, for example, the presence of logically unrelated ideas (to the observer), use of symbols in a private way and disturbed associations. Secondary symptoms which presumably derived from the primary symptoms included hallucinations, delusions, negativism, stereotypes, and catatonia. Bleuler, and many others, since maintained that schizophrenics do not suffer from changes in perception but this idea is no longer tenable. E. Bleuler recognized that perceptual changes did occur, but he felt these were not really changes in perception but were projections of one's inner wishes and phantasies. He adopted Freud's simple analogy between the early nineteenth century picture projectors or lantern slides, and the displacement of these fantasies from nonvisual formless ideas to well-formed visual images somewhere out in space. The newer idea is that perception is disturbed in many schizophrenics, and we have suggested elsewhere that much of their symptomatology can be accounted for on the premise that their misperceptions are reacted to as if true. This makes them at times quite bizarre (Hoffer and Osmond, 1961, 1962, 1966; Fogel and Hoffer, 1962).

Thus, the classification of Sernyl, as primarily a substance which produces primary changes, will stand or fall only if it can be maintained that there are primary and secondary changes. But, even if we admit this to be true, it does not seem to us these authors have proven their claim. It is well known that the experience, which follows the ingestion of any psychotomimetic, depends upon numerous factors already listed. The experimenter and his objective can easily swing the experience from one which resembles schizophrenia, to one which resembles severe depression or even mania. Luby *et al.* found "primary" changes such as disturbances in association, etc., that is, thought disorder, but they also found the following "secondary" changes, hallucinations, delusions, negativism, and repetitive motor behavior (stereotypes). We have also seen these changes in subjects given mescaline and LSD. The fact that Sernyl intensified schizophrenic symptomatology is not as compelling as it might seem because a large number of compounds have the same property including the anticholinergic drugs (e.g., atropine), and stimulants (for example, Benzedrine), amine oxidase inhibitors, amino acids, etc. However, Sernyl may well be a schizophrenomimetic agent since schizophrenia is infinitely variable in its expression, and there are, undoubtedly, numerous compounds which can be similarly labeled.

Bakker and Amini (1961) gave Sernyl to seven normal subjects. The response was remarkably uniform. After several minutes they noted dizziness, strangeness, loss of time comprehension and when deeply intoxicated, total disorientation. The field of visual perception narrowed to tunnel vision, and subjects were unable to integrate information from their own body with that from the outer world. As well as a narrowing of perception there was an inability to attend selectively to information so all inflowing stimuli was responded to. All subjects had hallucinations and delusions, but Bakker *et al.* were not certain these were "real" because the subjects were aware that these responses were drug induced.

Sernyl produced an organic psychosis according to Bakker *et al.*, and thus did not resemble LSD. It appeared to alter the function of the nervous system but the content, or meaning of the communications, was much more personal and more related to his background and personality.

The psychological studies by Bakker and Amini showed Sernyl interfered with performance of digit span test, with word digit memory test, digit comparison test, Stroop test, digit symbol test and with performance on the progressive matrices. The mean response-time on the word association test was lengthened 20% but there was no qualitative change in the type of response.

Ban *et al.* (1961) gave 0.07 mg/kg IV in 7 minutes to 55 patients. In lower concentrations Sernyl disinhibited patients but it was not as good for this as sodium amytal or other barbiturates. The larger dose produced a reaction which was more pathologically specific than LSD or mescaline. Ban *et al.* observed that the Sernyl experience produced a maximal stress in terms of total self-organization. In recently recovered schizophrenics there was a return of their earlier symptomatology. The experience was very similar to the one described by Luby *et al.*, but an excellent account was given of the affective response which was lacking in Luby's first reports. Only 3 out of 55 subjects became euphoric, laughed, or expressed evidence of pleasure. What was very striking was that the Sernyl experience was uniformly unpleasant and extremely frightening. Patients spontaneously requested never to be exposed again. Patients who had received LSD and mescaline as well, invariably found Sernyl much more frightening. Preoccupation with death was common.

Ban *et al.* did not find the Sernyl experience was either psychotomimetic or schizophrenic-like. It seems to us that Sernyl did produce a good model of a delirium or toxic reaction and we would support Ban's evaluation. They pointed up a major difference between LSD and Sernyl. Sernyl did not produce a psychedelic experience and probably will not have any therapeutic value as an abreactive insight producing agent.

Cohen *et al.* (1960) and Pollard *et al.* (1960) found that Sernyl given to subjects under conditions of sensory deprivation produced an experience much less intense than when subjects were exposed to normal stimuli. Subjects remained more in control and less disturbed. A characteristic symptom was the feeling of "nothingness" and "emptiness." Pollard *et al.* gave it by mouth instead of parenterally as was done by the other investigators. A larger dose of 10 mg given this way was less effective in producing an experience. Under their conditions Sernyl caused a very slight reaction. On the other hand LSD and psilocybin under conditions of sensory deprivation did cause the usual psychotomimetic experience.

Cohen *et al.* (1962) reported Sernyl produced severe incapacity in symbolic cognition and sequential thinking. LSD and amobarbital sodium were much less active.

Beech *et al.* (1961) using 20 subjects found that 7.5 mg of Sernyl did not produce thought disorder as measured by Bannister's test. It rather resembled sodium amytal.

Lees (1962) found that Sernyl stimulated oxygen consumption by rat liver homogenates when succinate, α-ketoglutarate, β-hydroxybutyrate or citrate were substrates. Experiments with mitochondria gave similar results with succinate and ketoglutarate.

α-CHLORALOSE

Bercel (1953) gave a mixture of scopolamine and α-chloralose to three patients with psychomotor epilepsy. All three developed an acute psychosis. Monroe *et al.* (1956) gave 500 mg chloralose and 0.5 mg scopolamine to a large series of normal volunteers and psychiatric patients. Scopolamine was used because pure chloralose was not available but it was not needed, since it did not potentiate the experience. Chloralose activated the EEG in a large number of psychiatric patients. Of 48 patients with activation, 24 became psychotic. From 62 volunteers and neurologic subjects only 2 had severe disorientation and much confusion. In most cases the α-chloralose reactivated psychotic episodes previously experienced spontaneously. One subject was given LSD and mescaline as well. The first time she received chloralose she hallucinated her children and her husband and spoke to them. There was some disorientation. On a second occasion she experienced depersonalization only. With 100 μg of LSD, she hallucinated her children but this was transient. Later she was given 500 mg of mescaline sulfate IV and she did not hallucinate. However, she was given the mescaline 2 days after having had LSD and this may have moderated her experience. From the description of Monroe *et al.* there was little difference between chloralose and LSD or mescaline. Using the criterion of Luby *et al.* for a schizophrenomimetic drug we might class α-chloralose as one.

α-Chloralose was prepared by heating equal parts of chloral and glucose and seems to be a methylene bridge ether. Its formula is believed to be as shown.

It resembles morphine in its analgesic effect and is much used in animal anesthesia because respiration is not markedly altered.

It is doubtful whether anesthetic compounds such as α-chloralose or Sernyl should be classed as either psychotomimetic or hallucinogenic substances. Hoffer *et al.* (1954) were the first to define hallucinogenic substances. These were defined as substances which could produce psychological disturbances similar to those found in schizophrenia without causing clouding of consciousness, confusion, or gross physiological disturbances. We do not believe that either α-chloralose or Sernyl can be, therefore, called hallucinogens. Our definition was designed to eliminate anesthetic substances. It is well known that any anesthetic can produce similar changes as the subjects are swept from stage-one anesthesia through stage-two anesthesia. It seems likely any human stopped in stage-two anesthesia would, if examined carefully, have a psychotomimetic experience. Perhaps, Sernyl and α-chloralose are merely chemicals which take patients through stage-two anesthesia too slowly which is why they are not in general use as anesthetics.

L. Lewin described similar experiences in subjects inhaling chloroform, ether, and benzine. Here are excerpts from his account of these inebrienta as he called them. We believe inebrienta is still a good term for alcohol, chloroform, ether, Sernyl and α-chloralose, also laughing gas or nitrous oxide. Laughing gas was the popular psychedelic a century ago and was described by William James. Steinberg (1956) gave 50 subjects 30% nitrous oxide and oxygen inhalations. He observed 4 kinds of symptoms which resembled those found in some psychiatric patients. These were illusions and hallucinations, irrelevant or exaggerated thoughts and emotions, perseverations, and dissociated states.

In discussing chloroform Lewin wrote "In the great majority of cases, disturbances of the central nervous system occur. Their character is suspicious, irresolute, and capricious. They are irritable and occasionally they experience hallucinations which may be succeeded by a state similar to delerium tremens. Others are suddenly seized with persecution mania. The excitation assumes unusual proportions. Under the influence of excessively terrifying illusions and hallucinations of sight and hearing, the patients are seized with raving madness."

This seems not too different from Sernyl. The following account of an ether experience is much the same:

Illusions of sight and hearing, dreams of paradisal happiness, the hearing of pleasant music, visions, of beautiful women and lascivious situations and many other illusions may be experienced, enduring for some time and leaving behind them the remembrance of a wonderful dream.

More modern inebrienta are also used. Tolan and Lingl (1964) reported 2 subjects who got their psychotomimetic experiences from inhalation of gasoline fumes. The experience was very similar to the LSD reaction. Several gasoline tank sniffers have appeared in our hospital. They also sought the psychotomimetic experience. Perhaps model airplane glue sniffers have also found their psychedelic drug.

Lewin described the benzine reaction as follows:

Hallucinations appeared, the patient heard the unpleasant music of barrel-organs, and unharmonious singing by voices known to him; red ants crept about on his body, he saw several figures of animals and dwarfs, and once the whole room seemed to be full of colored silk threads which fluttered to and fro.

Benzine inhalations produced a similar effect. Margetts (1950) described a case of chloral delirium which occurred in a patient who used about 1 mg each day for three months and 2 mg per day for 5 days before admission. Upon admission, he had a typical delirium. The content of the delirium, the delusions, hallucinations, and illusions were readily related to his past. Auditory illusions were very prominent. His psychotic delusions were most active at night, after meals, during fatigue or after emotionally charged situations.

Modern pharmacology and thereapeutics have made us forget the effect of many potent chemicals on humans. One of the major problems facing surgeons and obstetricians was the deliria which occurred while anesthesia was being induced, and during recovery from the deep anesthesia. With chloroform, ether, and similar compounds, these were very common. Lewin and James were well aware of these changes and this information helped them shape their psychopharmacological hypothesis, but very few scientists in psychiatry have had any experience with these chemically produced deliria, for modern anesthetics take the subject through the delirious stage of anesthesia too quickly, both ways.

REFERENCES

Abood, L. G., and Biel, J. H. (1962). *Intern. Rev. Neurobiol.* 4:218.
Abood, L. G., and Meduna, L. J. (1958). *J. Nervous Mental Disease* 127:546.
Abood, L. G., and Rinaldi, F. (1959). *Psychopharmacologia* 1:117.
Abood, L. G., Biel, J. H., and Ostfeld, A. M. (1959). *In* "Neuropsychopharmacology" (P. Bradley, ed.), p. 433. Pergamon Press, Oxford.
Abood, L. G., Rinaldi, F., and Eagleton, V. (1961). *Nature* 191:201.
Ayd, F. J. (1957). *New Engl. J. Med.* 257:669.
Baker, J. P., and Farley, J. D. (1958). *Brit. Med. J.* II:1390.
Bakker, C. B., and Amini, F. B. (1961). *Comprehensive Psychiat.* 2:269.
Ban, T. A., Lohrenz, J. J., and Lehmann, H. E. (1961). *Can. Psychiat. Assoc. J.* 6:150.

Beach, G. O., Fitzgerald, R. P., Holmes, R., Phibbs, B., and Stuckenhoff, H. (1964). *New Engl. J. Med.* **270**:1354.

Beech, H. R., Davies, B. M., and Morgenstein, F. S. (1961). *J. Mental Sci.* **107**:509.

Bercel, N. A. (1953). *Electroencephalog. Clin. Neurophysiol.* **5**:297.

Biel, J. H., Nuhfer, P. A., Hoya, W. K., Leiser, H. A., and Abood, L. G. (1962). *Ann. N.Y. Acad. Sci.* **96**:251.

Bodi, T., Share, I., Levy, H., and Moyer, J. H. (1959). *Antibiot. Med. & Clin. Therapy* **6**:79.

Charatan, F. B. (1959). *In* "Biological Psychiatry" (J. H. Massermann, ed.), p. 195. Grune & Stratton, New York.

Cohen, B. D., Luby, E. D., Rosenbaum, G., and Gottlieb, J. S. (1960). *Comprehensive Psychiat.* **1**:345.

Cohen, B. D., Rosenbaum, G., Luby, E. D., and Gottlieb, J. S. (1962). *Arch. Gen. Psychiat.* **6**:395.

Denber, H. C. B. (1959). "Biological Psychiatry" (J. H. Massermann, ed.), p. 203. Grune & Stratton, New York.

Elkes, J., Elkes, C., and Bradley, P. B. (1954). *J. Mental Sci.* **100**:125.

Feldberg, W. S., and Sherwood, S. L. (1954). *J. Physiol. (London)* **123**:148.

Fink, M. (1959). *In* "Biological Psychiatry" (J. H. Massermann, ed.), p. 184. Grune & Stratton, New York.

Fink, M. (1960). *Electroencephalog. Clin. Neurophysiol.* **12**:359.

Fogel, S., and Hoffer, A. (1962). *J. Clin. Exptl. Psychopathol. & Quart. Rev. Psychiat. Neurol.* **23**:24.

Gershon, S. (1960). *Nature* **186**:1072.

Greifenstein, F. E., Yoshitake, J., DeVault, M., and Gajewski, J. E. (1958). *Anesthesia Analgesia, Current Res.* **37**:283.

Grof, S., and Vojtechovsky, M. (1958). *Csl. Psychiat.* **54**:369.

Hoefnagel, D. (1961). *New Engl. J. Med.* **264**:168.

Hoffer, A. (1954). *A.M.A. Arch. Neurol. Psychiat.* **71**:80.

Hoffer, A. (1962). *Intern. Rev. Neurobiol.* **4**:307.

Hoffer, A., and Osmond, H. (1961). *J. Neuropsychiat.* **2**:306.

Hoffer, A., and Osmond, H. (1962). *Can. Med. Assoc. J.* **87**:641.

Hoffer, A., and Osmond, H. (1966). *Intern. J. Neuropsychiat.* **2**:1.

Hoffer, A., Osmond, H., and Smythies, J. (1954). *J. Mental Sci.* **100**:29.

Holan, G. (1965). *Nature* **206**:311.

Honegger, C. G., and Honegger, R. (1960). *Nature* **185**:530.

Jacobsen, E. (1958). *Ugeskrift Laeger* **117**:1147.

Jacobsen, E., and Sonne, E. (1955). *Acta Pharmacol. Toxicol.* **11**:135.

Johnson, D. M. (1953). "The Hallucinogenic Drugs (The Insanity Producing Drugs: Indian Hemp and Datura)." Christopher Johnson, London.

Lebovitz, B. Z., Visotsky, H. M., and Ostfeld, A. M. (1960). *Arch. Gen. Psychiat.* **2**:390; **3**:176.

Lees, H. (1962). *Biochem. Pharmacol.* **11**:1115.

Longo, V. G. (1956). *J. Pharmacol. Exptl. Therap.* **116**:198.

Luby, E. D., Cohen, B. D., Rosenbaum, G., Gottlieb, J. S., and Kelley, R. (1959). *A.M.A. Arch. Gen. Psychiat.* **81**:363.

McCulloch, W. S. (1949). *J. Nervous Mental Disease* **119**:271.

Margetts, E. L. (1950). *Psychiat. Quart.* **24**:278.

Meduna, L. J., and Abood, L. G. (1959). *J. Neuropsychiat.* **1**:1.

Monroe, R., Jacobson, G., and Ervin, F. (1956). *A.M.A. Arch. Neurol. Psychiat.* **76**:536.

Ovshinsky, S. (1958). Personal communication.

Pennes, H. H., and Hoch, P. H. (1957). *Am. J. Psychiat.* **113**:887.

Pfeiffer, C. C. (1959). *Intern. Rev. Neurobiol.* **1**:195.

Pollard, J. C., Bakker, C., Uhr, L., and Feuerfile, D. F. (1960). *Comprehensive Psychiat.* **1**:377.

Raymond, M. J., and Lucas, C. J. (1956). *Brit. Med. J.* **I**:952.

Rinaldi, F., and Himwich, H. E. (1955). *A.M.A. Arch. Neurol. Psychiat.* **73**:396.

Roueche, B. (1965). "Annals of Medicine, Something a Little Unusual," p. 180. The New Yorker.

Rowntree, D. W., Nevin, S., and Wilson, A. (1950). *J. Neurol., Neurosurg., Psychiat.* **13**:47.

Schultes, R. E. (1956). *Bull. Narcotics U.N., Dept. Social Affairs* **8**:1.

Sherwood, S. L. (1955). *Lancet* **268**:900.

Sherwood, S. L. (1958). *In* "Chemical Concepts of Psychosis" (M. Rinkel and H. C. B. Denber, eds.), p. 268. McDowell, Obolensky, New York.

Steinberg, H. (1956). *Brit. J. Psychol.* **47**:183.

Szatmari, A., and Schneider, R. (1955). *J. Nervous Mental Disease* **121**:311.

Tasher, D. C., Abood, L. G., Gibbs, F. A., and Gibbs, E. (1960). *J. Neuropsychiat.* **1**:266.

Tolan, E. J., and Lingl, F. A. (1964). *Am. J. Psychiat.* **120**:757.

Vinarova, M., Vinar, O., and Vojtechovsky, M. (1958). *Casopis Lekaru Ceskych* **97**:1059.

Vojtechovsky, M. (1958). *Acta Psychiat. Neurol. Scand.* **33**:514.

Vojtechovsky, M., Vitek, V., Rysanek, K., and Bultasova, H. (1958). *Experientia* **14**:422.

Vojtechovsky, M., Grof, S., Vitek, V., Rysanek, K., and Bultasova, H. (1960a). *Wien. Z. Nervenheilk. Grenzg.* **17**:279.

Vojtechovsky, M., Rysanek, K., and Vitek, V. (1960b). *Psychiat. Neurol.* **139**:406.

von Euler, U. S. (1945). *U. S. Acta Pharmacol.* **1**:29.

Wikler, A. (1957). "The Relation of Psychiatry to Pharmacology." Williams & Wilkins, Baltimore, Maryland.

Chapter VI

Taraxein

Introduction

Taraxein is the only hallucinogen which has been extracted from humans. For this reason it is one of the most important substances known to students of schizophrenia and may lead us to the basic biochemical abnormalities of this great disease. It is generally unknown that taraxein is securely established among the hallucinogens, but, like adrenochrome and adrenolutin, it is also a schizogen—that is, a substance which reproduces schizophrenia better than the other hallucinogens described in this book.

Biochemistry of Taraxein

PREPARATION

The methods for extracting taraxein have been modified since the first report appeared in 1956. The original method was derived from methods which were then used for extracting ceruloplasmin. Blood serum was saturated with ammonium sulfate and centrifuged. The precipitate was dissolved and dialyzed against distilled water. All procedures were carried out at low temperatures between 2° and 10°C. Further extractions and column chromatography were then used to complete the isolation.

Taraxein is a very reactive substance and was easily destroyed under normal conditions of storage. As a result early attempts by Siegel *et al.* (1959) to corroborate taraxein failed. Siegel *et al.*, for example, stored their final preparation in a frozen state (temperature not given) up to seven days. Even taraxein prepared at Tulane, by Heath's laboratory, often arrived inactive after transshipment.

Hoagland *et al.* (1962) used a rat rope-climbing test for measuring the activity of taraxein. Their fractions rapidly lost activity on standing and on freezing. They used a zinc precipitation method which separated beta, gamma, and some alpha globulins as well as taraxein. This method requiring only 3 days for completion was less drastic so less material was lost. The fraction from nonschizophrenic subjects was active on the test rats, but schizophrenic taraxein was twice as active. When the active protein was stored under hydrogen in the presence of ascorbic acid it was much more stable. Their final method was as follows:

Plasma is separated promptly from the cells of whole blood by centrifugation. The plasma is diluted with an equal volume of cold (2°–4°C) 0.15 M sodium chloride solution containing 8 mmoles ascorbic acid adjusted to pH 6.4. To the diluted plasma is added zinc glycinate to give a concentration of 25 mmoles Zn. The mixture is adjusted to pH 6.8. After a period from two hours to overnight at from 2° to 4°C, the PGP is removed by centrifugation also at from 2° to 4°C. The PGP is dissolved in 0.5 M EDTA (ethylenediaminetetraacetic acid) solution, pH 7.0, a quantity of EDTA equivalent to the amount of added zinc being used. The dissolved PGP is dialyzed with stirring against large volumes of 0.15 M NaCl solution containing 4-mmoles ascorbic acid adjusted to pH 6.4 at from 2° to 4°C overnight.

BIOCHEMICAL PROPERTIES

Heath (1959b, 1961) concluded taraxein was a protein because it was heat labile, precipitated by ammonium sulfate, and was not dialyzable. The principal contaminant of early preparations was ceruloplasmin. Hoagland (1960) corroborated Heath's findings that schizophrenic plasma contained a toxic protein, and later, with his colleagues, showed that while taraxein did not dialyze, a small molecule attached to the larger protein molecule did. When active preparations were dialyzed with less active preparations there was a transfer so that the inactive side became more toxic and the active preparation became less toxic. Its molecular weight was thought to be less than 1000 and they felt it could be a polypeptide or an amine metabolite.

Hoagland *et al.* (1962) reported findings which suggest that taraxein produced physiological changes similar to those produced by lysergic acid diethylamide. Since the large protein moiety cannot cross semipermeable membranes it seems that the smaller molecule must have these LSD-like properties. They injected the protein into nonanesthetized rabbits and measured the cortical potentials evoked by light flashes. Taraxein was similar to LSD. Inactive protein fractions had no effect. Both taraxein and LSD decreased variability of the amplitude and wave pattern of repetitively evoked potentials. The LSD effect lasted 15 minutes and the taraxein effect 8 minutes; other work showed that taraxein was not a stimulant or inhibitor of peripheral autonomic nervous system in rabbits and cats.

This suggests that easily released noradrenaline or adrenaline are not available and so these amines are excluded as the small attached molecules.

Frohman *et al.* (1960a,b,c, 1962) followed the activity of the toxic protein extracts of chicken erythrocytes. They also stabilized the plasma with ascorbic acid. The plasma was then subjected to electrophoresis, precipitation with ammonium sulfate, and dialysis. The increase in activity was followed by observing the effect on the lactate–pyruvate ratios of the erythrocytes incubated in the various fractions. The active fraction was in the α-2 globulin area.

Latham and his co-workers found that the taraxeinlike material had the following properties: (a) It decreased the ratio of labeled 1 to 6 carbons of glucose converted into carbon dioxide. (b) It was unstable at pH below 6 or above 9. (c) It lost all activity after 12 hours at room temperature. (d) Ascorbic acid and hydrogen stabilized it. (e) Chickens reacted to protein fractions from control subjects and from schizophrenic subjects but control preparations produced an instantaneous reaction which was over in 15–20 minutes while the schizophrenic preparation exerted its effect up to 45 minutes after injection and it lasted from 30 minutes to 1 hour. (f) When they injected female spider monkeys with schizophrenic preparations marked behavioral changes appeared in 45 minutes. The monkeys became very quiet and motionless. They tucked in their limbs tightly against their bodies and lowered their heads. It was possible then to push, poke, and annoy them in other ways with no response. These changes, which are similar to those described by Heath and his colleagues, sometimes lasted up to four days. The comparable fraction from control subjects had no effect.

The small molecule that is adsorbed on the protein molecule may be noradrenaline, adrenaline, a similar amine, or derivatives of them. Thus, Hoagland (1964) found that although normetanephrine had little activity in altering rat behavior when 1 mg was added to the plasma globulin the preparation was remarkably potent. The injection of Marplan, the amine oxidase inhibitor, also potentiated the activity of the protein preparation in altering rat rope-climbing behavior. This suggests taraxein contains a catecholamine as a component.

Bergen (1965) again reported that taraxein was a complex of a protein carrier and a small molecule. The small molecule dialyzed into plasma but not into saline. Both metanephrine and normetanephrine markedly potentiated the activity of the active protein fraction. Active protein preparations produced a twin peak of activity in rats 30 minutes after injection. The only compound which produced a delayed peak within 30 minutes was 3,4-dimethoxyphenylethylamine. Adrenochrome produced a long delayed inhibition of climbing time that reached its maximum after 60 minutes.

It is possible that adsorbed amines would be oxidized to indoles such as adrenochrome or adrenolutin and so bound. Normetanephrine could be oxidized to similar methoxylated indoles. Taraxein might, therefore, consist of a complex of an active protein carrying sympathomimetic amines and their oxidized derivatives. Favoring this point of view is the following evidence: (a) Ceruloplasmin is a powerful binder of adrenolutin but not of adrenochrome. (b) Walaas and Walaas (1965) have shown *in vitro* that ceruloplasmin oxidizes noradrenaline and adrenaline to their chrome derivatives. Further they have suggested this is a model of what happens at the postsynaptic site of the synapse. (c) Pennell (1965) reported that in one experiment the isolation of active protein was interrupted for 2 days. When the procedure was renewed he found the material was red and its absorption spectrum was similar to that of adrenochrome. (d) Chemical procedures which sta-bilize the active protein are also those which stabilize adrenolutin. These are storage under hydrogen in the presence of ascorbic acid. These con-ditions would tend to reduce adrenochrome to adrenolutin and stabilize it. (e) Adrenochrome added to plasma proteins reproduces some of the physical chemical properties of schizophrenic plasma preparations. Thus Runge *et al.* (1961) reported that nearly half of 84 schizophrenic pa-tients had unusual infrared spectra. When adrenochrome was added to serum a similar spectrum was found with lyophilized normal serum.

Braines *et al.* (1959) measured the fluorescence spectra of plasma. When normal human and dog serum was irradiated with a beam of light it fluoresced. The spectrum had two main peaks, one at 2750 Å and a weaker one at 2440 Å. Schizophrenic plasma did not have the 2440 Å peak. When adrenochrome was injected into the blood of dogs *in vivo* the 2440 Å peak disappeared. Schizophrenic serum given to dogs in the same way also removed this peak. Thus adrenochrome added to normal plasma gave it a schizophrenic-like fluorescent spectrum.

Ceruloplasmin by binding adrenolutin would inactivate taraxein in the same way that dialyses by normal plasma would. Martens *et al.* (1959a) found, in fact, that Rhesus monkeys premedicated with 0.5 gm of ceruloplasmin did not respond at all to active taraxein extracted from 400 ml of schizophrenic serum. Normally this quantity would pro-duce characteristic catatonia and withdrawal. Ceruloplasmin also pro-tected animals against LSD and adrenolutin.

Recently Tsaune (1963) and Tsaune and Upenietse (1962) reported that toxicity in the proteinfree fractions prepared from schizophrenic blood was inversely proportional to ceruloplasmin levels, as would be expected. He used Macht's phytotoxic test. Contrary to this idea is Bergen's (1965) finding that a clam heart, which is sensitive to indoles, did not respond to active protein as if indoles were present. The force of contraction of the clam heart was decreased and this is its characteristic response to catecholamines. However, adrenochrome is not a typical indole and might affect clam heart preparations differently. It has a quinoid structure. Its activity on clam heart should be examined. Adrenolutin is an indole but it could be so firmly bound to its carrier it would exert no activity.

Psychological Properties

HUMAN STUDIES

By 1958, Heath *et al.* (1958a) had given taraxein to 20 volunteers. Of the volunteers 15 were prisoners, 2 were nonpsychotic volunteers, and 3 were recovered schizophrenics. In each case the dose was from 1½ to 5 ml, which was the quantity of taraxein solution extracted from 400 ml of schizophrenic serum. It was injected intravenously. These experiments were double blind and the controls were several substances including protein fractions extracted from normal subjects.

In no instance did a volunteer react to the control substances with psychotic behavior. All subjects given taraxein developed symptoms usually found in schizophrenic patients. Changes were found in the following areas:

Perception—Depersonalization and auditory hallucinations. Visual hallucinations characteristic of LSD were not reported.

Thought—Process changes included blocking, deprivation, autism, and content changes included referential ideas and delusions of persecution.

Mood—Catatonic stupor or excitement occurred.

These reactions lasted only several hours, but one of the three recovered schizophrenics reacted for four days. The other two were given smaller doses but reacted very strongly.

Professor Heath presented his findings to one of the Josiah Macy, Jr. meetings at Princeton in 1050b. The verbatim account of this meeting is most instructive, for here was a scientist reporting his results with taraxein to a particularly hostile group of critics. Yet he had carried out the double blind experiments so beloved by methodologists. He was not believed. It was suggested that his data were explainable as a placebo effect, but when Heath reported that he saw no placebo reactors who reacted this way, others inferred that he was extraordinarily naive. One of the few individuals who prepared to hear him, Frank Fremont-Smith stated "while others may over react because of the great potential significance of the findings it seems to me that four or five years from now it should be quite clear whether or not this is really an important breakthrough." But Dr. Fremont-Smith did not estimate correctly the powerful opposition which hurled itself at Heath so that even today the majority of psychiatrists are unaware that Heath has been corroborated by Hoagland and his colleagues (1962), Frohman *et al.* (1958, 1960a,b,c, 1962, 1965), Marrazzi (1962), Geiger (1957, 1958, 1960), Martens *et al.* (1959a,b), and others.

Silva *et al.* (1960) compared the psychotomimetic properties of taraxein against LSD, mescaline, and psilocybin. Four volunteers participated. Taraxein produced more typical schizophrenic reactions. In general, a subject who responded intensely to one substance responded markedly to the other compounds. The only human confirmatory study from another laboratory was reported by Melander and Martens (1958).

ANIMAL STUDIES

Heath and his colleagues injected taraxein into monkeys. Electrodes were implanted into deep areas of the brain. The animals were ideal test subjects since both EEG and behavioral changes were easily observed. Taraxein produced gross changes in behavior and in the EEG.

Ferguson and Fisher (1963) compared the effect of plasma and serum drawn from normal subjects, stressed subjects and schizophrenic subjects and schizophrenic subjects on *Cebus apella* monkeys. The animals were trained to perform a precision timing task. This was a well-controlled experiment. Plasma from stressed normals and schizophrenics was more toxic than serum.

Schizophrenic plasma produced the greatest toxicity. The mean total time required to complete the learned task was about 100 minutes for normal controls, between 125 and 140 minutes for stressed normal serum and plasma, and 200 minutes for schizophrenic plasma. The prolongation of time correlated with observable behavioral changes. Animals squatted in fixed positions often facing the discriminative stimulus panel, but failed to respond to it.

The experimental rat has probably been used more frequently than any other test animal. Taraxein produced marked behavioral changes in rats. The most easily quantified response was the prolonged effect on climbing time in the rope-climbing test of Winter and Flataker (1956, 1958). See Hoagland *et al.* (1962) for a brief review of the rat studies.

Mice also have been used. Mekler *et al.* (1958) prepared taraxein from schizophrenics using the Tulane method. After 1–2 hours all the mice given taraxein became immobile for 5 minutes at a time. Normal protein preparations produced much less immobility on a wire net; taraxein produced total periods of immobility of 27–40 minutes.

How Does Taraxein Work

Heath (1959a,b), Heath *et al.* (1957, 1958b, 1959), and Melander and Martens (1958) suggested that taraxein increased the permeability of the blood–brain barrier, thereby allowing toxic substances normally present in blood, but unable to get across into the brain to produce a toxic effect. Heath (1959a,b) reported that schizophrenic serum mixed with trypan blue increased penetration by this dye into the brain. Melander and Martens (1958) found that pretreatment of animals with taraxein markedly increased the activity of adrenolutin. Heath (1959a,b) found that a small dose of taraxein given to monkeys greatly increased the effect of a quantity of adrenolutin which was itself inactive. One monkey was killed by a usually nontoxic dose of adrenolutin.

Hoagland *et al.* (1962) were sympathetic to this view. Their work with dialysis of a small molecule suggested that a small active molecule bound to protein (as in taraxein) might be exchanged across the blood–brain barrier with a similar protein in the brain.

Heath (1959a,b) also suggested taraxein could be an allergen or antigen and in 1965 at the NATO Conference he amplified this idea.

REFERENCES

Bergen, J. (1965). *In* "The Molecular Basis of Some Aspects of Mental Activity." A NATO Advanced Study Institute, Drammen, Norway.

Braines, C. H., Konev, C. B., Golubieva, G. P., Kuchino, E. B., and Kobrinckaio, O. J. (1959). *In* "Biophysical Research in Psychiatry. Collected Papers" (Prof. C. H. Braines, ed.). Lab. Exptl. Pathol., Inst. Psychiat., Acad. Sci., Moscow.

Ferguson, D. C., and Fisher, A. E. (1963). *Science* 139:1281.

Frohman, C. E., Goodman, M., Luby, E. O., Beckett, P. G. S., and Senf, R. (1958). *A.M.A. Arch. Neurol. Psychiat.* 79:730.

Frohman, C. E., Latham, L. K., Beckett, P. G. S., and Gottlieb, J. S. (1960a). *A.M.A. Arch. Gen. Psychiat.* 2:255.

Frohman, C. E., Latham, K., Czajkowski, N., Beckett, P., and Gottlieb, J. (1960b). *Federation Proc.* 19:8.

Frohman, C. E., Czajkowski, N. P., Luby, E. D., Gottlieb, J. S., and Senf, R. (1960c). *A.M.A. Arch. Gen. Psychiat.* 2:263.

Frohman, C. E., Goodman, M., Beckett, P. G. S., Latham, L. R., Senf, R., and Gottlieb, J. S. (1962). *Ann. N.Y. Acad. Sci.* 96:438.

Frohman, C. E., Beckett, P. G. S., and Gottlieb, J. S. (1965). *Recent Adv. Biol. Psychiat.* 7:45.

Geiger, R. S. (1957). *Federation Proc.* **16**:44.

Geiger, R. S. (1958). *Federation Proc.* **17**:52.

Geiger, R. S. (1960). *J. Neuropsychiat.* **1**:185.

Heath, R. G. (1959a). *Intern. Rev. Neurobiol.* **1**:299.

Heath, R. G. (1959b). *Neuropharmacol., Trans. 4th Conf.* p. 37. Josiah Macy, Jr Found., New York.

Heath, R. G. (1961). *J. Neuropsychiat.* **3**:1.

Heath, R. G., and Leach, B. E. (1960). *Recent Adv. Biol. Psychiat.* **2**:285.

Heath, R. G., Martens, S., Leach, B. E., Cohen, M., and Angel, C. (1957). *Am. J. Psychiat.* **114**:14.

Heath, R. G., Martens, S., Leach, B. E., Cohen, M., and Feigley, C. A. (1958a). *Am. J. Psychiat.* **114**:917.

Heath, R. G., Leach, B. E., Byers, L. W., Martens, S., and Feigley, C. A. (1958b). *Am. J. Psychiat.* **114**:683.

Heath, R. G., Leach, B. E., and Cohen, M. (1959). *In* "Molecules and Mental Health" (F. A. Gibbs, ed.), p. 158. Lippincott, Philadelphia, Pennsylvania.

Hoagland, H. (1960). *Recent Adv. Biol. Psychiat.* **2**:281.

Hoagland, H. (1964). *Psychiat. Res. Rept.* **19**.

Hoagland, H., Pennell, R. B., Bergen, J. R., Saravis, C. A., Freeman, H., and Koella, W. (1962). *Recent Adv. Biol. Psychiat.* **4**:329.

Marrazzi, A. (1962). *Ann. Meeting Am. Psychiat. Assoc.*, Toronto.

Martens, S., Vallbo, S., and Melander, B. (1959a). *Intern. Rev. Neurobiol.* **1**:333.

Martens, S., Vallbo, S., Andersen, K., and Melander, B. (1959b). *Acta Psychiat. Neurol. Scand.* **34**:361.

Mekler, L. B., Lapteva, N. N., and Lozovsky, D. V. (1958). *Zh. Nevropatol. i Psikhiatr.* **58**:703.

Melander, B., and Martens, S. (1958). *Diseases Nervous System* **19**:478.

Pennell, R. B. (1965). *In* "The Molecular Basis of Some Aspects of Mental Activity." A NATO Advanced Study Institute, Drammen, Norway.

Runge, T. M., Bohls, S. W., Hoerster, S. A., and Thurman, N. (1961). *Diseases Nervous System* **22**:619.

Siegel, M., Niswander, G. D., Sachs, E., and Stavrus, D. (1959). *Am. J. Psychiat.* **115**:819.

Silva, F., Heath, R. G., Rafferty, T., Johnson, R., and Robinson, W. (1960). *Comp. Psychiat.* **1**:370.

Tsaune, M. K. (1963). *Zh. Nevropatol. i Psikhiatr.* **63**:748.

Tsaune, M. K., and Upenietse, M. (1962). *Zh. Nevropatol. i Psikhiatr.* **61**:1222; *Excerpta Med., Sect. 15,* **5**:617.

Walaas, O., and Walaas, E. (1965). *In* "The Molecular Basis of Some Aspects of Mental Activity." A NATO Advanced Study Institute, Drammen, Norway.

Winter, C. A., and Flataker, L. (1956). *Proc. Soc. Exptl. Biol. Med.* **92**:285.

Winter, C. A., and Flataker, L. (1958). *A.M.A. Arch. Neurol. Psychiat.* **80**:441.

Chapter VII

Animal Studies of Hallucinogenic Drugs

T. WECKOWICZ

Introduction

In recent years, the studies of the effects of drugs on the behavior of animals have been playing an increasingly important role. Animal studies have an advantage over studies with human subjects because of a better control of all experimental variables and a possibility of using a wider range of the doses. It is also permissible to administer toxic compounds to animals. One can interfere surgically with various parts of the central nervous system while investigating the effects of the drugs. The whole field of comparative psychopharmacology has been recently reviewed (Brady, 1959; Brady and Ross, 1960; Miller, 1957).

Brady and Ross (1960) in reviewing the methodology of animal drug studies stress the importance of: (a) standardization of test situations to provide quantitative measurement techniques; (b) comparative evaluation of drug effects in different animal species and strains, and (c) development of behavior profiles of different drugs. The behavior profile is particularly important since it gives some insight into the total effect of the drug on an organism. Brady and Ross also stress the importance of understanding the behavioral mechanism which is being influenced by a drug. They believe that "operant conditioning" is the most useful technique because it allows the greatest number of variables to be controlled both outside the animal and inside the animal.

Miller (1957) stresses the importance of separating the effects a drug may have on motor function from that of perception and motivation. He considers well-planned studies of the effect of various drugs on motivation of animals particularly relevant to psychiatry. He also advocates using diverse tests on the same animals in order to indicate the basic effect of the drug in contrast to its side effects. In case of hallucinogenic compounds it is very important to separate the effects on perception, learning, and specific motivation from side effects due to general toxicity of these compounds.

The animal studies with hallucinogenic drugs can be divided into three groups. To the first group belong unsystematic and incidental observations on the behavior of animals made by biochemists, physiologists, and pharmacologists in the course of their studies of metabolic effects of these drugs. To the second group belong standardized tests for the presence of these substances. These tests have a character of bioassay. They are limited to establishing a typical relation between a small quantity of a drug in question and characteristic change in the animal behavior. To the third group belong the most recent studies where the effect of the drug on a certain aspect of behavior is investigated in a systematic manner and the explanation of the effect is sought in the framework of behavioral theory or/and the motor functioning of the nervous system. Various conditioning experiments with higher animals are particularly important in this connection. The animal studies with various hallucinogenic substances will now be reviewed systematically.

Studies in Invertebrates

Among all hallucinogenic substances by far the greatest number of invertebrate animal studies have been carried out with LSD.

Spiders

In spiders the effect of LSD and other hallucinogens was studied by Witt (1951, 1952, 1956). He found that the web-spinning activity of spiders, belonging to species *Zilla-X-notata, Meta reticulata,* and *Arenea diadema* is very sensitive to various pharmacological agents even in minute quantities. For most of his work he has used *Zilla-X-notata* and with this species he has developed a standardized test based on measurements of the relative sizes of various parts of the spider web. He found that LSD in higher doses (0.1–0.3 per animal) produced the following changes:

1. Slight reduction in catching area of the web.
2. Longer, vertical dimension in relation to horizontal dimension.
3. Slight reduction in the regularity of the angles between the radial threads of the web.

Lower doses of LSD (0.03–0.05 per animal) showed the following effects.

1. Decrease in the frequency of web making.
2. Reduction in the number of oversized sectors.
3. Increased regularity of the angles between the radial threads of the web.
4. Increased regularity of the sticky spiral thread.

The increase in the regularity of the web is particularly interesting. According to Witt, the regularity of the web pattern is determined by the spider taking the path that is shortest, and that demands the least effort when spinning the thread. Slight irregularity occurring in a normal web is due to distracting external stimuli that make the spider swerve from the shortest path. LSD in spiders seems to reduce the sensory input and make them less susceptible to extraneous stimuli. The effect on the spider web produced by LSD is different from that produced by other hallucinogenic substances such as mescaline and adrenochrome. Mescaline given in the dose of 100 μg per animal reduced the frequency of web spinning, reduced the regularity of the angles between the radial threads of the web, and reduced the number of coils and the regularity of the sticky spiral thread. The effect of mescaline was the same as that of increasing the weight of the spider, by attaching to it small pieces of lead.

Adrenochrome in the dose 4 μg per animal produced marked reduction of the size of the total web, particularly that of the catching area. There was a marked distortion of the symmetry of the entire web with the displacement of the hub from the central position, marked irregularity of the radial angles, and irregularity of the spiral thread. Christiansen *et al.* (1962) investigated the effect of mescaline and psilocybin on the web-spinning activity of the female spiders (*Aranea diadema*); psilocybin was found to have an effect similar to mescaline, but to be 10 times more potent. Thus substances which have similar hallucinogenic effects in human beings have a very different effect on the web-spinning activity of the spiders, which suggests that the mechanisms involved in production of hallucinogenic effects in man may be different in the cases of different drugs. Reider (1957) reported that butanol and chloroform extract from the urine of schizophrenic patients produced a distortion of symmetry and radial angle irregularity of the web, when given to *Zilla-X-notata*, while the extract from the urine of controls did not have the same effect. Witt (1958) could not confirm these findings.

WORMS

In other invertebrates the effect of hallucinogens on the patterns of movements of lower worms (Nematoda and Trematoda) was studied.

Mansour (1956, 1957) reported that both serotonin and LSD in concentrations of 10^{-1} M stimulated the rhythmical movements of liver fluke (*Fasciola hepatica*). Mescaline in higher concentration had a similar effect, while bromolysergic acid diethylamide (BOL) depressed the rhythmic movement, and antagonized the effects of serotonin and LSD. Low concentrations of LSD (5×10^{-9} to 5×10^{-8} M) temporarily reduced rhythmic activity of the worm.

GASTROPODA

The effect of LSD on the behavior of snails was studied by Abramson and Jarvik (1955) and Jarvik (1957). They reported that the Mystern snail (*Ampularia cuprina*) responded to LSD (in solutions of 0.01, 0.1, and 1 μg/ml) with a typical persistent movement of the gastropod. The snail opens its operculum and extends its tentacles, proboscis, and gastropod. The movement of the gastropod consists of a rather wild waving muscular movement, which prevents the snail from adhering to any surface. These disorganized movements have been observed to last for 36 hours. BOL-148 has an opposite effect. It causes shutting of the snail's operculum and immobility. Serotonin stops temporarily the effect of LSD. Salanski and Koschtojantz (1962) investigated the effect of 5-hydroxytryptamine, LSD, and various catecholamines on the tonus of the posterior closing muscle of the fresh water mussel (*Anodouta cygnea*). The tonus of this muscle shows diurnal variation. LSD produced a gradual but quite marked inhibition of the muscle tone, while serotonin, tryptamine, and adrenaline caused rapid termination of the tonic contraction of the muscle.

These invertebrate studies are more of pharmacological than behavioral or psychological interest because of marked differences between the primitive invertebrate and more complex vertebrate nervous systems.

Lower Vertebrates

FISHES

In lower vertebrates there has been a series of studies on the effect of LSD and other substances on the behavior of various fishes; mainly, that of Siamese fighting fish (*Betta splendens*). Abramson and Evans (1954) reported the characteristic effects of LSD water solution in concentrations from 1 mg/ml to 50 mg/ml of the subsequent behavior of the Siamese fighting fish (*B. splendens*) in fresh water. The fish were kept in LSD solution for 6 hours and their behavior was observed upon their removal from LSD solution into fresh spring water. The following behavior effects were observed in these fish:

1. Backward movements accomplished almost entirely by the pectoral fin
2. "Head up-tail down" position with the body suspended in the vertical plane or of some angle from the vertical
3. "Cartesian diver" effect; the fish sinks or rises very slowly in the near vertical plane without visible body movement except by means of pectoral fins
4. "Barrel-roll" effect, or change of a position or location occurs by a peculiar rolling of the fish upon its long axis in the vertical plane
5. "Trancelike" effect; motionless position is maintained for minutes at a time at the peak of the drug effect
6. All movements of the treated fish are slow and deliberate as compared with the typical swift and sudden movements of normal fish
7. A treated fish exhibits a typical "kinking" of its body, easily observed from above
8. There often occurs a "lateral display" involving ventral and dorsal fins, less often the tail as well
9. There occurs a pigmentation effect, best exhibited in juvenile fish (which are more susceptible to LSD). The immediate effect is darkening of the body color which fades slowly as recovery occurs

The fish under the influence of LSD shows rheotropic movements, but to a lesser extent than untreated fish. It can also be aroused from the stupor by an attacking fish and it can even counterattack, but after a brief battle, there is an immediate relapse into the stuporous state.

In a subsequent study Evans *et al.* (1956) investigated, using the method described by Abramson and Evans, the effect of various analogs of LSD and other hallucinogenic agents on Siamese fighting fish. BOL-148 and LAE-32, both LSD analogs, produced a most similar effect to LSD, which could be, however, distinguished from that of the latter drug. Mescaline and mepedrinehydrochloride (Demarol) were completely inactive.

Abramson and his group tried to discover the physiological and biochemical mechanisms involved in the effect of LSD on the Siamese fighting fish. They tried to find out whether the well-known enzyme blocking poisons would produce a similar effect on the fish as LSD, thus providing a model of the action of this substance.

Weiss *et al.* (1958) and Abramson *et al.* (1958) investigated the effect of KCN (potassium cyanide) sodium azide, and hydrazine on the behavior of Siamese fighting fish. All these substances are inhibitors of oxidizing enzymes in the cells. In addition the action of oxidation reduction indicator systems and other dyes has been explored, KCN and sodium azide in nonlethal concentrations of approximately 1 mg per ml in the water act similarly to LSD. Negative results were obtained with hydrazine sulfate and hydroxylamine hydrochloride. The action of KCN was reversible with the fish recovering more rapidly than under a similar concentration of LSD. Lack of oxygen in the water or high concentration of certain dyes like methylene blue, Bindschelder's green and sodium-2,6-dichlorobenzeneindophenol produced effects similar to that of LSD.

There is a possibility that the effect of LSD in the fish may be due to an inhibition by this substance of the oxidizing metal–enzyme systems. Trout (1957) investigated the effect of controlled stress situations involving hypoxia on Siamese fighting fish under the effect of LSD. A glazed ceiling under the water surface in the tank prevented the fish to surface to fill the accessory air sac or labyrinth. The duration of quiescent periods before the fish attempted to surface and the duration of the intensity of the fighting periods were measured. LSD depressed the duration and intensity of fighting activity, whereas serotonin increased it. LSD and serotonin, however, had the same effect in reducing the duration of almost continuous activity. When the two drugs were added together serotonin potentiated the effect of LSD. Apart from serotonin the effect of other compounds which could possibly antagonize LSD and prevent its effect was investigated.

Turner (1956a,b) reported that Frenquel had no effect on LSD phenomena in the Siamese fighting fish. Abramson (1957) and Abramson *et al.* (1957a,b) reported that crude Siamese fighting fish brain extract, prepared by the method of Florey (Florey and McLennan, 1955) if given prior to LSD prevented the latter substance from having its effect. The following concentrations of the brain extracts were used: 2 mg, 0.2 mg, and 0.02 mg in 200 ml of water. Both the 2 mg and 0.2 mg inhibited the reaction of the fish to LSD, while following similar procedure with serotonin was not effective. If the blocking of the LSD effect occurred inside the fish and not in the water, this was apparently the first time that blocking effect (not a symptomatic depressant) of behavior changes, engendered by LSD had been produced by a biologically derived substance. That the substance which protects the organism from the effect of LSD is not specific to the *Betta splendens* brain was shown by Abramson *et al.* (1957a,b). These workers reported that beef brain extract prepared by the method of Florey had the same effect as the *Betta splendens* brain extract. The substance responsible is not serotonin, nor any of the several amino acids which were tried. Smith and Moody (1956) replicated the findings of Abramson and his group on the effects of LSD on *Betta splendens*. In addition these workers also investigated the effect of concentrated urine from schizophrenic patients on the behavior of the fish. No difference was found between the urine from the schizophrenic patients and the normal controls. The effect of LSD and its analogs on other species of fish has been investigated. Thus, Turner (1956a,b) explored the action of 60 pharmacological agents on 22 species of fresh water fish (*Betta splendens, Aequidens latifrans, Aequidens helleri, Trichogaster sumatrans, Trichogaster leeri, Platypocillus maculatus, Tachynichtys albonibes, Mocropodus viridi aureatus, Lebistes reticulatus, Peryphyllum scalare, Barbus titteya, Haplochromis multicolor, Pristella raddlei, Carrasius aureatus, Cichlosoma meeki, Corydorus aeneas,* and *Barbus sumatrans*). LSD has specific action on *Betta splendens* which is found to a much lesser degree in other species. The author speculates on the possibility that the action of LSD on *Betta splendens* could be due to an action of this substance on the neurones of the visual pathway whereby the spatial and visual organization of the impulses, which encode information to the tectum and thence to other parts of the nervous system suffers distortions. The effect of LSD was found by him to be potentiated by hyoscine and counteracted by pilocarpine.

Abramson *et al.* (1961) investigated the effect of LSD in the surfacing behavior of the carp. They found that LSD and LAE-32 when added to the water in the same concentrations as in the experiments with Siamese fighting fish produced the surfacing behavior of the carp.

Abramson *et al.* (1960) reported a similar effect with psilocybin and psilocin as that of LSD when these substances were fed to goldfish. Keller and Umbreit (1956) described the effect of LSD on guppy (*Lebister reticulatus*) when the fish were placed in a solution containing LSD (4 mg/ml at pH 6.5–7.5 and 25°C–28°C) for 1 hour and then transferred to fresh water, They responded with characteristic vibrating movements. This consisted of a rapid swimming until the wall of the container was reached at which point the fish continued to make swimming movements apparently unaware that it was not making any progress. Serotonin had no effect on the LSD response of the guppy. Indole and tryptamine followed by LSD prolonged the effect of the last substance as long as 1 week. Courtship pattern was disturbed. Indole and tryptamine alone had no effect. Indole given together with LSD produced even a longer lasting or apparently permanent disturbance of behavior, which could be counteracted by reserpine. Cutting *et al.* (1959) investigated the effect of LSD, bulbocapnine and mescaline on the behavior of guppy (*Lebistes reticulatus*), Mexican blind fish (*Anoptichtys hubbsi*), and goldfish (*Carrassius aureatus*). The drugs were added into the water. After adding LSD in concentrations of 2 mg/ml guppies turned dark within 10 minutes. The effect lasted 1 hour during which the experimental animals could be differentiated from the controls. Goldfish exposed to the same solution reacted by dropping the dorsal fin and floating to the surface. Rheotaxis was reduced and they tended to swim backward, however, they exhibited normal fear reaction. Mexican blind cave fish responded to the same concentration by swimming in very small circles, followed by increased movement in all directions, and then after 10–15 minutes by a return to normal. It took this fish about 5 times as long as controls to swim through the maze.

Bulbocapnine (in solution, 25–100 mg/ml) increased activity of the guppies and goldfish, this increased activity lasted 15–40 minutes. Mescaline in the concentration 100 mg/ml did not produce any effect.

Saxena *et al.* (1962) investigated the effect of mescaline, LSD, and thiopropazate, and their interaction with serotonin and dopa on fighting response in males of the species *Colisa calia*. Both LSD and mescaline when injected intramuscularly produced disturbed behavior and stopped the fighting response for several hours. This effect was counteracted in the case of mescaline by a previous injection of serotonin and in the case of LSD by a subsequent injection of dopa. Fishes when injected with mescaline or LSD on repeated occasions tended to develop tolerance. Wilber (1958) investigated the effect of LSD on the activity of melanophores in a sea fish species (*Fundiclus heteroclitus*). LSD was administered either by adding it to the water of the aquarium or by injecting it into the fish. In all experiments light-adapted fish became darker; the melanin concentrated in the center of the melanophores was dispersed. The degree of dispersal was directly related to the dose as a log function. Apparently the drug exerted a depressant action on the specific loci in the brain from which the melanophore-concentrating fibers originate. This action allows the melanophore-dispersing fibers to darken the fish. The fish displayed some behavioral abnormality, they swam to the surface, showed signs of air hunger, and showed peculiar vibratory movement on contact with the glass wall of the aquarium. Similar effect of LSD on chromatophores in the female guppy (*Lebistes reticulatus*) was reported in an earlier paper by Cerletti and Berde (1955). These authors reported that this effect of LSD could be prevented by serotonin.

AMPHIBIA

Another study on the effect of LSD on melanophores in lower vertebrates is that of Burgers *et al.* (1958). These authors studied the effect of LSD on the pigmentation of the toad (*Xenopus laevis*). Among the lower vertebrates investigated so far *Xenopus laevis* is the only species which reacts with pigment concentration instead of pigment dispersion following injection of LSD. It is assumed by the authors that LSD does not act directly on the melanophores of the toad, but indirectly through the pituitary gland by inhibiting the production of secretion of the melanophore controlling hormone by the intermediate lobe of this gland.

These studies on lower vertebrates indicate that different hallucinogenic compounds produce different disturbances of behavior in different species. LSD was found to produce behavioral changes most consistently even if given in minute doses. These drugs disrupt instinctive patterns of behavior in many species very often without producing markedly toxic symptoms.

Higher Vertebrates

Studies with higher vertebrates, particularly mammals, are of greater interest than studies with invertebrate and lower vertebrates because of greater similarity of the nervous system of these animals to that of man and because of better techniques to control behavioral situations, particularly learned behavioral patterns. These studies can be divided into noncontrolled observations of behavior and sutdies where certain aspects of behavior are observed and measured under strictly controlled conditions.

General Effect of Hallucinogenic Drugs Introduced Intrasystemically

There have been many studies in which the effect on behavior of hallucinogenic drugs injected intraperitoneally, intramuscularly, or intravenously, was observed. In most of these studies the pharmacological or electrophysiological properties of these drugs were investigated and the observations made on behavior were incidental. Various species ranging from mice and pigeons to the Asiatic elephant have been used.

BIRDS

Rosen and Jovino (1963) reported that LSD (in the dose of 0.2 mg/ kg b.w.[1]) given intraperitoneally inhibited the nesting behavior of male

---

[1] Abbreviation b.w., by weight.

pigeons, which was not due to a motor inhibition, but probably was caused by an inhibition of the secretion of prolactin, controlled by the hypothalamus.

Hoffer and Wojicki (1957) described similar inhibition in pigeons of courting, nest protecting, and brooding behavior by sublethal doses of adrenochrome and adrenolutin. These disturbances of patterns of instinctive activity in pigeons are probably due to the effect of the hallucinogenic drugs on the lower brain centers. Probably inhibition by LSD in pigeons of apomorphine-induced pecking behavior is also of this nature, as reported by Dhawan (1961).

MAMMALS

Several noncontrolled behavioral studies were carried out on mice. Woolley (1955) reported that mice injected intraperitoneally with LSD (in the dose of 100 mg/kg) behaved in a very similar way to normal mice when placed on a level surface and faced with the prospect of sliding down an inclined plane. The mice spread forelegs and fingers in order to "resist" movement forward and started walking backward on the level surface. The author believes that the drug induced in mice a hallucination of sliding down on an inclined plane. This abnormal behavior could be prevented in some animals by injection of serotonin plus carbamoylcholine into the lateral ventricle. LSD, also produced characteristic shaking of the head and the whole body, reddening of the ears and piloerection, absent in the normal reaction of mice to sliding down.

Keller and Umbreit (1956) confirmed the latter observation. In mice injected intravenously with LSD (0.25–5 mg/kg) they described violent head shaking when any area about the back of the head was lightly touched. This characteristic head-shaking response appeared from 5 to 10 minutes after the injection and lasted for intervals which varied from 10 minutes to 2 hours. The length of the interval was proportional to the dose of LSD used. Mescaline, yohimbine, and serotonin did not elicit this response. A permanent effect in some cases lasting a few months, was obtained in mice pretreated with an injection of indole (1.5 mg/kg) followed immediately with an injection of LSD. This permanent head-shaking condition could be cured by injections of reserpine. This potentiating effect of indoles on reserpine was also reported by the same authors in fish (*Lebister reticulatus*) (see previous section). Day and Yen (1962) found that LSD could prevent tremors produced in mice by injections of harmine, nicotine, and by a mixture of iproniazid and 5-HTP. Brown (1957), using the Dews method (Dews, 1956), investigated the effect of various drugs on spontaneous activity of mice. LSD (dose 10 mg/kg to 80 mg/kg) increased spontaneous activity without producing ataxia. This effect was antagonized by serotonin and reserpine. These two substances cause prolongation of sleep induced by hexobarbital. The latter effect is antagonized by LSD. The interactions between LSD and other substances depend very much on the dose used. Thus, the depression of spontaneous activity in mice produced by serotonin is converted into increased spontaneous activity by a noneffective dose of LSD. Teaschler and Cerletti (1957) reported that the excitatory effect of LSD in mice is markedly enhanced by pretreatment by small doses of reserpine. BOL, an equipotent inhibitor of serotonin does not produce increase in spontaneous activity of mice. Tripod (1957) has found that mescaline increases spontaneous motility in mice to a greater extent than LSD does. Mescaline had no effect on metrasol convulsions in mice, but inhibited andiogenic convulsions in rats. Fellows and Cook (1957) reported that mescaline administered orally in the dose of 20–100 mg/kg produced increased scratching in mice. This scratching response is antagonized by chlorpromazine, reserpine, serotonin, and morphine. It may be due to cutaneous paresthesias (hallucinations) produced in mice by mescaline; Greenblatt and Oesterberg (1961) reported this of various stimulating drugs having a tendency to sustain a high motor (exploratory) activity of mice placed in an actometer. Mescaline did not sustain this high activity. Some workers tried to standardize behavioral situations in order to investigate the effects of various drugs on the behavior of mice. Smythies (1959) investigated the effects of LSD, adrenochrome, adrenolutin, and bufotenine, on the pole climbing in mice separately, and in combination. The criterion measure was the time taken by mice to climb the pole. It was found that LSD increased the climbing time. The effect was at its maximum 10–15 minutes after the injection, but was still appreciable after 30 minutes. Neither bufotenine nor adrenochrome had this effect. Adrenolutin had no effect by itself, but it antagonized the delaying effect of LSD. In further experiments the author found that some derivatives of LSD produced a marked sedation in mice and caused a delay in the descending time from the pole. This sedative effect could be overcome by motivation and training. Morpholide derivatives of LSD were less active. Jacob and Blazowski (1961) could not find any determinable effect of LSD in doses 0.5, 1.0, and 2.5 mg/kg on the escape reaction by jumping from a hot metal surface (temperature 65°C). Laborit *et al.* (1957a,b) found that adrenochrome and adrenochrome semicarbazone increased the tendency for convulsions in mice. LSD had no effect, serotonin protected the mice against convulsions, and glutamic acid gave also some protection.

There is a hereditary-degenerative disease of the nervous system in mice which produces marked cerebellar ataxis manifesting itself in constant circling "waltzing" movements. The strain of mice possessing this "waltzing" anomaly was used in drug investigations. Rothlin and Cerletti (1952) and Rothlin (1953) reported that LSD and LAE (monoethylamide of lysergic acid) inhibited waltzing activity by increasing the general excitation and activity of animals. The increased spontaneous activity suppressed the waltzing movements. Hydergine also inhibited the waltzing movement, however, in an absolutely different manner. It produced an inhibition of the activity of the mice. Natural alkaloids of ergotamine did not have any effect. Thuillier and Nakajima (1957) described a technique of producing artificially the "waltzing" syndrome in normal mice by injecting imino-β-β-dipropionitrile. The symptoms obtained are indistinguishable from those occurring in the inherited condition. They persist indefinitely without further administration of the compound.

The IDPM mouse, as the preparation is called, can be used for "screening" tests of various pharmacological compounds. Psychotropic drugs modify the behavior of IDPM mice in a characteristic manner. From these characteristics it is possible to classify psychotropic drugs into "narcoleptics," "tranquilizers," "hypnotics," and "stimulators," of the autonomic nervous system. LSD was found to stop circling movements. It produced also generalized trembling, clonic jerks, general agitation, and copious salivation. Widlocher et al. (1957) reported further that both LSD and LAE in doses greater than 1 mg/kg inhibited the circular movements in IDPM mice. This effect was produced by doses which did not cause a general motor excitement. Delay et al. (1959) compared the effect of psilocybin on the IDPM and normal mice with that of LSD and LAE (monoethylamide). Psilocybin produced more profound inhibition of waltzing movements of the mice, than two other compounds, without affecting their reactivity to painful stimuli. At the same time it produced less-pronounced autonomic reaction and trembling. In normal mice, psilocybin in doses of 5–50 mg/kg b.w. had a strong sedative effect without abolishing sensitivity to nociceptive stimuli. Woolley and Van Der Hoeven (1963) reported that an excess of cerebral serotonin decreased maze ability of adult mice, while a deficiency of serotonin and catecholamines increased it slightly.

West and Pierce (1962) attempted to inject LSD in an Asiatic elephant in the dose 0.1 mg/kg. The elephant is the only animal which under normal conditions suffers from a profound aberration of behavior, the so-called "musth" madness. The elephant goes "berserk" and attacks everything it encounters. These attacks of madness occur only in male elephants and are associated with a profuse discharge of sticky fluid from the temporal glands. The authors were interested in finding out whether LSD would produce a similar aberration of behavior, which would suggest that "musth" madness in elephants was produced by some toxic substance similar to LSD. The dose of LSD which was used produced the death of the elephant in about one hour after the injection. This study draws attention to the great difference in the tolerance to the same dose of the drug per kilogram body weight by different species. Small rodents particularly can tolerate doses which are lethal to carnivors and primates. Evarts (1956) reported that a rhesus monkey required from 0.5 to 1.0 mg/kg b.w. of LSD to cause temporary blindness and loss of balance, while the cats require higher doses to cause even a transient rage reaction. In humans, 0.02 mg/kg b.w. of LSD produces profound toxic symptoms. Baruk *et al.* (1958) investigated the effect of LSD in pigeons, guinea pigs, and mice. In pigeons LSD in doses from 2 to 7 mg/kg b.w. produced a loss of balance, a posture with widely spread legs, and a tendency to fall forward, at the lower doses. In guinea pigs various doses of LSD, ranging from 2 to 30 mg/kg b.w. produced increasing degrees of ataxia and paralysis of the hind quarters, which were dragged behind. The animals moved forward with the front legs. There was an episthotonos and myoclonic convulsions. The dose of 30 mg/kg b.w. killed the animals. In mice the dose 1–10 mg/kg did not produce much effect. The dose 20–30 mg/kg produced fine myoclonic cramps, tremor, and hyperexcitability. The mice survived the dose of 50 mg/kg, while in rhesus monkeys 5 mg/kg b.w. produced coma and death. One mg/kg b.w. of LSD produced generalized hypertonia, hyperextension of the head. There was a period of muscular paralysis followed by long lasting muscular weakness. Delay (1953; Delay *et al.*, 1952) reported cataleptic phenomena in rabbits injected intraperitoneally with 50 mg/kg b.w. LSD. With larger doses there was a catatonic stupor without paralysis. Shore and Brodie (1957) reported that administration of reserpine to rabbits pretreated with iproniazid (a monoamine oxidase inhibitor) caused excitation and sympathomimetic effects similar to those observed after administration of LSD or high doses of 5-hydroxytryptophan. These effects are apparently associated with the presence of high concentration of free serotonin in the brain, released from the bound form by reserpine and prevented from oxidation by blocking of monoamine oxidase by iproniazid. The LSD-like effect is produced by blocking parasympathetic synapses by the free seronotin, thus producing sympathetic overactivity. Most of the studies with the white rats have been carried out in more controlled situations, dealing with learned behavior and will be discussed further on. However, some general observations will be reviewed now. Winter and Flataker (1957) while investigating the effect of LSD on rope climbing in rats made the following general observation. After an intraperitoneal injection of LSD the animals appeared to be confused and explored the cage more busily than usual. After 2–3 minutes of this activity the animals stopped and started shaking their heads violently (a symptom described in mice). This shaking sometimes was so pronounced that it involved the entire body. After 3–5 minutes the animals had occasional periods during which all four legs were flexed so that the abdomen touched the floor of the cage and the animals crawled on the floor. After 5–10 minutes hyperactivity subsided and the animals became unusually quiet. They withdrew to the back of the cage and remained nearly motionless for prolonged periods. After 15 minutes the animals salivated profusely and were less responsive to external stimulation.

Doepfner (1962) reported that combined intravenous injection of LSD and Doseril in female rats produced hyperactivity, general body tremor, and convulsive movements. Speck (1957) studied the effect of mescaline on rats in acute and chronic experiments. In the acute experiment, after the animals were returned to their cages they groomed themselves, huddled together, and stood on their hind legs without moving for 10–20 minutes. They were hyperactive to noises for several hours after injection. A weakness of the hind legs, exophthalmos, trembling, and hyperreactivity to a tap on the spine were frequently recorded. Chewing, sniffing, and sneezing was noted in all animals given mescaline. The following day the rats were drowsy and slept much of the time. In the chronic experiment all of the animals that received mescaline had ruffled coats, squealed when they were handled, and generally seemed more apprehensive than normal animals. Auditory stimuli, for example, key jangling, produced excitement, but no convulsions. After the first week there was no apparent increase in the sensitivity to noise. Friedhoff and Goldstein (1962) by using radioactive carbon-marked mescaline in combination with iproniazid (a monoamine oxidase inhibitor) showed in rats and rabbits that intermediates of mescaline metabolism such as 3,4,5-trimethoxyphenylacetic acid and 3,4,5-trimethoxyphenylethanol had a more profound behavior and pharmacological effect than mescaline itself. Brimblecombe (1963) studied the effects of LSD, mescaline, harmine, N-methyl-3-piperidyl benzilate hydrochloride, dimethyltryptamine, dipropyltryptamine and methyltryptamine, bufotenine bioxalate, and pheniclidine on the behavior of rats in the open field. These drugs produced a significant increase in emotional defecation. Parker and Hilderbrand (1962) reported that dibenamine prevents overt signs of mescaline intoxication in cats. Fuller (1962) investigated the effect of mescaline (50 mg/kg b.w.) and *dl*-amphetamine (2 mg/kg) in chronic experiments on groups of pups reared in complete isolation or in normal conditions. The pups were 3–11 weeks old at the beginning of the experiment. The drugs and a control dextrose were administered per os. The isolation group was kept in complete isolation for 11 weeks. The drug test began on the fifth week. Subjects receiving amphetamine were indistinguishable from those treated with dextrose. Mescaline produced "stuporous depression," disorientation, bizarre postures, and apathy. There was a difference between the animals reared in isolation and in normal conditions in their reaction to mescaline. The animals reared in normal conditions remained responsive to external stimuli in spite of large doses of mescaline, while the animals reared in isolation were unresponsive.

Evarts (1956) investigated the effects of LSD and bufotenine on the behavior of rhesus monkeys. LSD in the dose 1 mg/kg b.w. and bufotenine in the dose of 5 mg/kg b.w. injected intravenously produced a syndrome characterized by a gross sensory disorder with normal muscular power. The animals became very tame. They assumed prone (froglike) positions for the first 20 minutes after injection. Later on they developed ataxia, insensitivity to painful stimuli and blindness. Baruk *et al.* (1962) investigated the effect of LSD on the psychomotor behavior of monkeys. LSD produced experimental catatonia which was counteracted by serotonin. The monkeys developed flacidity, lack of initiative, and restlessness.

Lagutina *et al.* (1964) examined the effect of LSD upon adult male baboons, ages 4 to 7. They were observed during free movement and various conditioned reflexes were examined. Doses of from 2 to 5 µg/kg had a marked effect on these animals for 30–60 minutes. There was a loss of individual and all conditioned reflexes but unconditioned reflexes remained normal. Doses of 10–40 µg per kg caused more profound changes for 3 hours. The animals were watchful, moved about less, and their gait was uncertain. They were hyperexcitable but often they remained in the same position for unusually long periods of time. They sometimes caught at things in the air, jumped about the chamber and tried to escape as if they had hallucinations.

Buscaino and Frougia (1953) injected 1 and 10 mg/kg intravenously into dogs. The animals developed psychomotor excitement, followed by depression. In chronic experiments (4 mg/kg b.w. intravenously over 23 days) the animals developed psychomotor excitement, but were soon normal. Gershon and Lang (1962) studied the effect of various indole alkaloids on the behavior of dogs. They reported that yohimbine, harmine, and ibogaine produced different cardiovascular responses in conscious animals as compared to anesthetized animals. In conscious animals these alkaloids produced marked anxiety, tenseness, and alertness. After ibogaine and harmine the dogs showed lack of recognition of their regular handlers and of their environment. There was a pronounced body tremor and shaking. After the ibogaine the dogs adopted a peculiar stance with their legs apart and backs arched. Schneider and Sigg (1957) described similar excitatory effect in cats after the injection of 2–10 mg/kg b.w. of ibogaine. The animals became very agitated and showed marked signs of fear, arousal, and sympathetic discharge. Chen and Chen (1939) reported that harmine when injected into monkeys caused trembling of the body, unsteady gait and a tendency to stay in one corner of the cage. When given large doses the monkeys showed arching of the back, stiffening of the legs, shaking, and chronic convulsions. There are two early reports of hallucinations produced in dogs by harmine (Lambert and Heckel, 1901; von Ferdinand, 1929).

There are several nonsystematic observations on the effect of adrenochrome and adrenolutin on the behavior of animals. Eade (1954) in the course of his study of adrenochrome toxicity noticed that albino rats injected daily with 1 or 2 mg of adrenochrome intraperitoneally had typical chronic convulsions of the hind legs. There was a loss of muscular coordination and a resultant dragging of the hind legs. This observation was confirmed by Weckowicz (1962). Eade also reported a state of pronounced apathy in rats after adrenochrome injection. Noval *et al.* (1959) reported that adrenochrome produced the de Jong type of catatonia in rats and in higher doses convulsions and death. With smaller doses the rats were disinclined to move about; when placed alongside a Bunsen burner the animals grasped the burner with their forelegs and clung until they sank slowly to the table, doubled up, apparently exhausted but still clinging. Pretreatment with LSD made the adrenochrome four times as effective. Vallbo (1957) reported that adrenolutin, when given intravenously, produced catatonic-like symptoms, some muscular relaxation, and stupor in rats, rabbits, and monkeys. Krupp and Monier (1960) observed an increased sensitivity to external stimuli in rabbits injected intravenously with from 3.5 to 6 mg/kg b.w. of adrenochrome. Melander and Martens (1958, 1959) reported that adrenochrome in the doses of 2 mg/kg b.w. produced drowsiness and muscular relaxation in monkeys pretreated with taraxein or LSD. Heath *et al.* (1959) reported that adrenolutin was effective in monkeys only if they were pretreated with taraxein. In contrast to these general observations some workers investigated the effect of hallucinogenic drugs using more systematic observational techniques.

Norton (1957) and Norton and Tamburo (1958) developed a scoring system (rating scale) for quantitative rating of sociability, contentment, excitement, defensiveness, and aggression. They studied the effect of several drugs on the behavior of cats, hamsters, and monkeys. LSD produced in cats and hamsters an increase in excitement and both aggressive and defensive hostility. There was also a decrease in contentment or sociability. Chlorpromazine had, in general, an opposite effect. It produced an increase in contentment and sociability. Mescaline had a similar effect in cats to that of LSD. There were only minor differences in the patterns of behavior changes produced by the hallucinogenic drugs in the three species studied.

Elder and Dille (1962) injected 400 mg/kg b.w. LSD intravenously into cats. The behavior of animals was observed and a rating scale was used to rate the autonomic responses, spontaneous activity and responses to visual, auditory, and tactile stimuli. The cats displayed a marked autonomous discharge, rage reaction and excitement. Phenoxybenzamine and chlorpromazine antagonized the behavioral effects induced by LSD. Surgical sympathectomy and adrenal demedulation did not have any effect on behavioral changes produced by the drug. Reserpine did not prevent the behavioral changes induced by LSD but caused the animals so treated to develop a catatonic-like state instead of excitement.

Intracerebral Effect of Hallucinogenic Drugs

Hallucinogenic drugs were also introduced directly into the cerebral ventricles of the mice. Haley (1956a,b, 1957) studied the response made by conscious mice after intracerebral injection of hallucinogenic and other psychotomimetic agents. The effects were produced at doses ineffective by other routes of administration. Intracerebral administration of 5 mg of LSD produced hyperexcitability and aggressiveness. Rapid, jerky movements were induced by light touch or sound. Aggressiveness consisted in a direct attack upon any object placed in front of the animals. There was also marked "Straub" tail phenomenon. These effects were followed by a stuporous condition lasting about 12 hours. Mescaline in the dose of 10 mg produced tachypnea, flattening of the ears against the head, extension of the tail. The mice were aggressive attacking all objects in front of them. Paroxysmal ear scratching was also observed. Later the animals were depressed for approximately 10 minutes. Increasing the dose of mescaline to 50 mg resulted in a more profound depression of 1–2 hours duration and a complete absence of the aggressive tendency. The paroxysms of ear scratching persisted. Serotonin caused an autonomic nervous system discharge followed by a central depression. Chlorpromazine produced alternating sedation and hyperexcitability with clonic seizures. Acetylcholine produced sedation and an akinetic seizure. Adrenaline produced hyperexcitability and death from a pulmonary edema. Bulbocapine caused catatonic symptoms.

The method of introducing hallucinogenic compounds directly into cerebral ventricles or other parts of the brain has been used with other species of animals, mainly with cats and dogs.

De Jong (1945) carried out many early studies on the effects of bulbocapnine and mescaline introduced into the third ventricle or intravenously on the behavior of dogs. He described a syndrome which he called "experimental catatonia." After intraventricular administration of mescaline, dogs showed diminished motor activity. Spontaneous movements completely disappeared but there was no paralysis. The animals displayed "negativism" as measured by resistance to a change of position. They assumed bizarre postures. They maintained the front legs in a crossed position with their hind legs rigidly extended and their heads bent low. The animals maintained such postures for long periods and could be pulled "en masse" along the floor on all fours. The animals did not respond to visual, auditory, and pain stimuli; also, while under the influence of mescaline the dogs displayed characteristic chewing movements. More recently this "catatonia"-producing property of mescaline given intraventricularly to dogs was confirmed independently by Hosko and Tislow (1956), and by Sturtevant and Drill (1956). Haley and his associates (Haley, 1956a,b; Haley and McCormic, 1956; Haley and Gupta, 1958) investigated the effect of LSD administered intraventricularly into conscious dogs. Using an implanted cannula (Haley, 1956b) LSD in doses of 1.6–10 mg/kg was injected into the third ventricle of unanesthetized dogs. The following symptoms were observed: violent shaking of the head, salivation, licking the chops, slightly later there was retching, nausea, emesis, tachypnea, and micturitions. The dogs were ataxic, had dilated pupils which reacted to lights. Recovery occurred after 15–20 minutes. Throughout this period the animals appeared frightened, but there was no impairment in their ability to follow simple commands. The most interesting effect was that the dogs regressed from an adult behavior pattern to that of a puppy, which resembled to some extent the changes observed in humans (Forrer and Goldner, 1951). Some of the symptoms were due to a massive autonomic discharge due probably to a stimulation of the posterior hypothalmus and the reticular activating system.

Feldberg and Sherwood (1954) described a technique of implanting cannules permanently into the cerebral ventricles of cats for testing the effects of various compounds administered directly into the brain. This method was used to test the effect of various hallucinogenic compounds on the behavior of cats. Thus, Schwartz *et al.* (1956) investigated the effect of LSD, mescaline, adrenochrome, and adrenolutin. They found that while LSD (15 mg) produced restlessness and increased activity, mescaline, adrenochrome, and adrenolutin produced catatonic-like states with stupor, immobility, and decreased sensitivity to pain. Rice and McColl (1960) using a similar technique obtained sympathetic rather than parasympathetic stimulation with adrenochrome and mescaline. The animal became aggressive and developed epileptoid seizures. Gaddum and Vogt (1956) observed "sham rage" in cats after 800 mg of LSD administered intravertebrally. Sturtevant *et al.* (1956) injected LSD into the lateral ventricle of cats; there was marked salivation emesis and generalized depression, bordering on catatonia when lower doses of LSD (5–50 mg) were given. Higher doses of LSD (100 mg) produced hypersensitivity to both auditory and visual stimuli. The animals did not show "sham rage," but appeared to be irritable and fearful. Sturtevant and Drill (1956) also investigated the effect of mescaline (in doses 1–3 mg) on the behavior of cats when given intraventricularly. Immediately after the injection the cats started making continuous yowling noises. During the next 20 minutes there was marked salivation, tachypnea, retching, lacrimation, defecation, urination, and mydriasis. The cats displayed little interest in the environment and could be aroused only with difficulty. Body movements were slowed and somewhat ataxic when the cats were forced to jump or walk. They tended to remain stuporous and immobile. The cats lost their aggressivity towards mice, they "fondled" a mouse, instead of attacking it. All these studies show that although undoubtedly there is an overlap between the symptoms produced in cats by intraventricular injection of mescaline and LSD, there are also consistent differences. Both substances produce an autonomic, predominantly sympathetic discharge and an irritation to the cerebral ventricles. However, LSD tends to produce greater excitation, fearfulness, irritability, and increased sensitivity to external stimuli, while mescaline produces predominantly depression, stupor, and catatonic symptoms. Adrenochrome seems to be more similar to mescaline in its effect, than to LSD. The effect of drugs depends very much on its dose and exact place of application of the drug in the cerebral ventricles. Schain (1962) on the basis of the study of the effect of various substances when introduced into cerebral ventricles obtained amazing variety of symptoms and came to the conclusion that the paraventricular region is an area of very high pharmacological sensitivity with various parts of this area being sensitive to specific drugs.

The effect of the drug may be completely different when the drug is introduced into the nuclei in the vicinity of the third ventricle rather than into the ventricle itself. Thus, Wood *et al.* (1958) made observations on the effects of various compounds on the behavior of conscious cats, when these substances were injected into various subcortical nuclei by permanently fixed cannula. LSD injected into the ventromedial nucleus of the hypothalamus produced a depressed state in which the animals became quiet and unresponsive. Reserpine and serotonin when injected into this region produced immediate increase in activity and vocalization. An increase in aggressive behavior toward other animals and an increase in rough behavior was also observed with these LSD antagonists. Fazio and Sacchi (1957) reported that serotonin produces catalepsy in cats when introduced into the third ventricle, but this can be prevented by pretreating the animals with LSD.

Apart from LSD and mescaline other hallucinogenic compounds or their analogs have been investigated by injecting them intracerebrally. Hoffer (1962) did a systematic study of the effects of introducing the following compounds into the brain ventricles of cats by a permanent cannula: adrenochrome, 5,6-dihydroxy-N-methylindole, adrenochrome methylether, adrenolutin, N-ethylnoradrenochrome, N-isopropylnoradrenochrome, rubeserine and 3,4-methylenedioxy-α-aminomethylbenzyl alcohol oxalate. Saline was used as a control. He found that when 0.5 mg of adrenochrome was introduced intraventricularly to the cat the animal became docile, apathetic, indifferent, and alertness and motor activity was much decreased; its gait became awkward and unsteady. Other substances were not effective. Kanai *et al.* (1962) injected 5 mg/kg O-methylbufotenine intraventricularly into cats. The cats became apprehensive, showed autonomic overactivity, ataxia, catatonic postures and mixed reactivity to sensory stimuli. These effects were reduced by lobotomy, section of optic nerves, tranquilizers, and anesthetics. Response to pain was diminished. The similar effects were produced by intravenous injection of O-methylbufotenine. Wada (1962) studied the effect of bulbocapnine (1–6 mg), psilocybin (0.5–2 mg), adrenaline (30–50 mg) and acetylcholine (0.25–5 mg) injected intraventricularly into two freely moving rhesus monkeys. The behavioral changes were correlated with electrocorticograms. Intraventricular bulbocapnine induced synchronization of thalamocortical system and desynchronization of the midbrain reticular system, which manifested itself in behavior by immediate excitement followed by cyclic episodes of stupor and arousal. Adrenaline, acetylcholine, and psilocybin produced similar effects which bore a certain verisimilitude to the onset of natural sleep.

These studies in which compounds are introduced intracerebrally have been concerned with the catatonic-like symptoms produced by even minute quantities of hallucinogenic drugs. The main interest has been possible similarity between the effects produced in animals by these drugs and some symptoms occurring in schizophrenic patients.

Behavioral Correlates of Electrophysiological Effects of Hallucinogens

There are several studies in which the effect of various hallucinogenic compounds on the patterns of electrical activity of various parts of the brain was tested. Some of these studies were carried out on conscious animals and an attempt was made to correlate the electrical activity of the brain with the animal behavior.

Since this review is concerned with the effect of hallucinogenic drugs on behavior and not with electrophysiological changes these studies will be mentioned only briefly.

Bradley (1953) recorded electrical activity from the cortical and subcortical regions of the conscious cat, using permanently implanted electrodes. LSD and amphetamine both produced electrical activity typical of the reticular activating system arousal. These electric changes were accompanied by alerting of the animals. Adey *et al.* (1962) studied the effect of LSD, psilocybin, and psilocin in cats with electrodes chronically implanted in the amygdala, parts of hippocampus entorhinal cortex, the thalamic nucleus ventralis anterior, rostral midbrain reticular formation, and the primary visual cortex. Certain characteristic changes in general behavior followed administration of LSD in doses of 25–100 mg. The animals adopted a wide-based "kangaroo" sprawling posture with the claws and tail extended. They exhibited head shaking and a staring gaze. There was a loss of normal effective responses. At the doses around 25 mg/kg brief seizurelike episodes were seen in the EEG records: they were maximal in amplitude and longest in duration in dorsal hippocampal and entorhinal cortex and appeared variably in the thalamus and midbrain reticular formation. These seizures occurred more often when visual and auditory stimulation was reduced. Psilocybin and psilocin resembled LSD in their general effects, but differed in the brevity of their action and frequent occurrence of severe autonomic reactions.

Chauchard (1961) reported that in white rats psilocybin had a diphasic action. A period of excitation was followed by a period of marked inhibition of activity. Psilocybin possesses a definite calming and narcoleptic effect mediated through the regulatory centers at the base of the brain which is not possessed by LSD, serotonin, or reserpine.

Marazzi and Hart (1955) studied the effect of LSD on the evoked cortical response of a transcallosal preparation of a cat. Injection of 8

mg/kg b.w. of LSD reduced the amplitude of the postsynaptic component of the transcallosal response. Some studies were concerned with
the effect of hallucinogenic compounds on the electric activity of the
limbic system in relation to the neocortex. Thus, Brown (1961) reported
that LSD, administered intravenously in cats altered hippocampal
"theta" waves and caused frequent rhythmic bursts in the neocortex.
It also produced dissociation between the cortical and subcortical alerting response. There was also some dissociation between the recorded
electrical patterns and the behavior of the animals. The effect of LSD
injected intraventricularly was opposite to that effect when injected
intravenously.

Brücke (Brücke et al., 1961) reported that high doses of LSD given
intravenously to rabbits abolished both slow wave activity and the hippocampal unit firing. This effect was tentatively attributed to the blocking effect of LSD on the axondendritic synapses.

Stumpt et al. (1962) also reported that in conscious rabbits LSD
acts directly on the hippocampus abolishing the "theta" rhythm without
changing the septal electric activity. McGough et al. (1963) reported
that LSD (0.01–0.05 mg/kg) suppressed in rabbits instrumental and
discriminative response without producing synchronization of EEG.
Monroe and Heath (1961) used 6 conscious rhesus monkeys with chronically implanted electrodes over the frontal and occipital cortex and in
the septal, caudate and hippocampal regions. The effects of LSD, several of its analogs, and mescaline, were studied. The behavior of animals
was correlated with the subcortical electrograms. Disturbed catatonic-
like or agitated behavior was associated with rhinencephalic, paroxysmal,
hypersynchronous activity. This activity, particularly in the septal region,
was related to abnormal behavior. Ursin (1962) induced in cats, by
unilateral electrical stimulation of the amygdaloid nuclear complex, an
attention response directed to the opposite side. The threshold of this
attention response was tested before and after IV or IP injection of
LSD (5–200 mg/kg b.w.). The threshold was found to be unaltered
by LSD while chlorpromazine blocked this response. The author concluded that the LSD effect is not due to an inability to attend to the
stimulus but to an interference the sensory inflow to the CNS. This
supports the findings of Evarts et al. (1955) who reported that LSD
and bufotenine block the transmission of the nerve impulses in the lateral
geniculate nucleus of the cat, thus interfering with the animal's visual
system. Adey (1961) correlated the pattern of wave activity arising
primarily in the temporal lobe system with certain clearly defined behavioral patterns. He used cats and monkeys as subjects. He showed
that temporal wave process itself is intimately concerned with informa-

tion handling processes. The role of the subthalamus was studied in the performance of a discrimination task and its relation to hippocampal wave pattern. The effects of LSD (50–250 mg/kg b.w.) and cyclohexamine (1–3 mg/kg b.w.) on the wave pattern and learned performance in a "T"-maze (in cats) were studied. LSD did not impair the performance, but produced a hippocampal seizure discharge pattern between the performances with evidence of hallucinations. During the performance itself, this seizure discharge disappeared to return when the performance was over.

The temporal lobes appear to play an important role in the mechanism by which hallucinogenic agents produce their effect. This was indicated quite clearly by the study of Baldwin *et al.* (1959). These authors reported that LSD reaction (60 mg/kg b.w.) in young chimpanzees consisting of excitement, wild screaming, panic state, and visual hallucinations was prevented by bilateral temporal lobotomy. A bilateral prefrontal lobotomy had no effect on LSD reaction. Lateral temporal cortex was found to be essential for psychic LSD reaction in these animals. (Some autonomic nervous system symptoms, such as dilation of the pupils and piloerection could be evoked by LSD even after bilateral temporal lobotomy.)

Ochs *et al.* (1962) applied directly 1% solution of mescaline to the cortices of anesthetized rabbits and cats. It produced a pattern of convulsive activity in both the intact cortex and isolated portions of the cortical tissue. The mescaline spikes could be blocked by IV pentobarbital.

The only generalizations which one can make from these uncontrolled observations of the animal behavior under the influence of various hallucinogenic agents are as follows:

1. The effects produced by different compounds differ from species to species. There are marked differences among animals of the same species.

2. Since the effect of a hallucinogenic drug on the behavior of an animal depends to a great extent on the dose and on the time interval of the observation after the administration of the compound, it is very important to use several doses of the drug and several time intervals between the administration of the drug and the observation of the animal.

3. All hallucinogenic drugs tend to produce sympathetic discharge. However, LSD produces much more motor excitement than mescaline, while this latter drug tends to produce more motor inhibition and more pronounced catatonic symptoms than LSD.

4. Temporal lobes particularly the lateral cortex and limbic system

appear to play particularly important roles in the mechanism by which the psychotomimetic symptoms are produced.

Effects of Hallucinogenic Drugs on Learning and Other Higher Cognitive Functions

Another group of the studies of a greater interest from the psychological point of view than the uncontrolled observations of behavior, are studies which have used strictly controlled conditions for the investigation of the effects of hallucinogenic drugs on the behavior of animals. These studies make it possible to separate the effects of the drug on various aspects of behavior, such as motor activity, motivation, perception, learning, memory, and performance. In this way they offer a better insight into specifically hallucinogenic or psychotomimetic properties of these drugs in human beings. Learning and conditioning are the most suitable techniques because they provide precise criterion measures of behavior. These studies are more recent and less numerous than those reviewed previously in this chapter.

SENSORY PROCESSES

The studies of the effects of hallucinogenic drugs on sensory processes and perception are of the greatest theoretical interest because the main effects of these drugs in human beings are perceptual abnormalities and distortion. Also electrophysiological studies suggest that hallucinogenic compounds interfere with the sensory afferent pathways and subcortical centers, producing distortion of the sensory input. Blough (1957a,b,c) developed an objective method of measuring absolute and differential visual thresholds in pigeons. Pigeons are trained in a Skinner box to peck one key when a spot of light is visible and another key when this spot of light is not visible. Pecking of the key rewarded when the spot is visible causes a decrease in the brightness of the spot, while pecking of the other key causes an increase. In this way absolute visual threshold could be measured in pigeons objectively. LSD at doses from 100 mg/kg b.w. to 300 mg/kg b.w. elevated the absolute visual threshold. In a complex task when the pigeons had to discriminate between two keys, one darker and one brighter, by pecking at the brighter key when the partition between the keys was illuminated and at the darker one when the partition was dark, LSD in the dose 200 mg/kg b.w. improved the discrimination. It also, in the dose 50 mg/kg b.w. improved the performance of pigeons on even more complex tasks. The pigeons had to match after a 0–5 second delay the flickering or steady signal light by choosing between two keys, one with a flickering light and one with a steady light. This effect of LSD was quite specific, since alcohol, barbiturates, and chlorpromazine in all doses impaired the performance of birds. These findings were not confirmed by the study of Berryman *et al.* (1962). These authors trained four female pigeons in "matching" responses. The pigeons had to respond by pecking green, red, or blue illuminated keys in accordance with the color of the signal light. LSD produced an initial period of inactivity during which the birds did not respond to experimental task. After this initial period of inactivity there was no evidence of either improvement or impairment in the discrimination.

Furster (1957) trained rhesus monkeys to recognize stereometric objects exposed tachistoscopically. He was interested in the effect of arousal on perception. The arousal was produced by introducing loud noises during the test performance or direct stimulation by implanting electrodes of the reticular activating system. He also investigated the effect of LSD (dose 5–10 mg/kg b.w.) on the exposure threshold, reaction time, and number of errors. LSD produced impairment in the recognition of the figures and lengthening of the reaction time. Stimulation of the reticular formation with a mild current (100 mA, 300 cps) improved the performance and shortened the reaction time. This suggests that the effect of LSD on perception is not through the reticular formation discharge produced by this drug.

Asfield and Johnson (1961) reported that LSD interferes more with nonvisual cues than visual cues in maze-learning rats. They trained blind and normal rats in the Hebb-Williams mazes, injecting half of the animals with LSD (dose from 0.03 to 0.25 mg/kg b.w.) and half with water. Thus, there were four groups of animals: LSD-blind, LSD-seeing, water-blind, and water-seeing. There was definite interaction between blindness and LSD. Blind animals took a longer time and made more errors with higher doses of LSD. Seeing rats which had learned to run the maze with other than visual cues were more severely affected by LSD. The disorientation induced by LSD was ameliorated by the presence of visual cues. This is surprising in view of the electrophysiological finding that LSD affects mainly the subcortical visual centers. However, this latter observation was made on cats. In these animals, vision plays a much more important role and visual centers are better developed than in rats. The latter animals make a greater use of maze learning by sensation of touch from the skin and vibrissae. Thus, LSD may affect in different animal species different and most highly developed sensory centers.

Key (1961, 1962) reported that LSD in cats affects auditory discrimination learning. It produces greater generalization and abolishes differentiation inhibition. Since these studies were also concerned with other aspects of conditioning they will be reviewed in greater detail later on.

LEARNING AND CONDITIONING

There have been several studies on the effect of hallucinogenic drugs on conditioning and learning motor tasks. Rats, cats, and monkeys were used as subjects. Winter and Flataker (1951, 1957) used a test, described earlier by them (Winter and Flataker, 1951) to investigate the effect of various drugs on the performance of a learned simple behavior in white and hooded rats. In this test the rats are trained to climb a rope in order to receive a reward (usually food). LSD, given in dosages from 0.175–0.5 mg/kg b.w., produced signs of confusion and markedly prolonged the time of climbing. The method of climbing used by rats, while under the influence of LSD, was different from that used by normal animals. In the normal animals both forepaws at once were followed by both hindpaws, so that they appeared to be literally leaping up the rope. The intoxicated animals advanced one paw at a time. They would climb a short distance then stop and remain motionless, staring into space. When they reached the top they refused to eat food. This effect of the drug lasted one to two hours. There was straight linear function between the climbing time and the log of the dose of LSD. Pretreatment with reserpine (50 mg/kg b.w. daily for 5 days), chlorpromazine (1–5 mg/kg b.w., 30 minutes before LSD), or indole (2 mg/kg b.w.) potentiated the effect of LSD in trained rats. The effect of LSD was antagonized by meprobamate (20 mg/kg b.w.) and benactizine (2.5-5 mg/kg b.w.).

Freedman *et al.* (1958) confirmed the Winter and Flataker findings. They also reported that repeated injections both of LSD and of mescaline produced tolerance for the effect on rope climbing. This tolerance developed faster for LSD than for mescaline.

Marazzi (1961) and Oakley and Marazzi (1961) investigated the effects of LSD and other compounds the ability of rats to press a bar for water in a Skinner box. It was discriminant operant learning. The water was available when a tone was sounded. LSD, in the dose 0.1 mg/kg b.w. intraperitoneally, inhibited bar pressing in thirsty rats. Chlorpromazine (dose 0.3 mg/kg b.w.) given prior to LSD antagonized the effect of LSD. Slightly larger doses of chlorpromazine enhanced the effect of LSD. Still larger doses of chlorpromazine inhibited bar pressing even when LSD was omitted. In more complex situations in which the subject had to discriminate between two signals and had to choose the correct one to obtain the reward, small doses of LSD

(0.01 mg/kg b.w.), mescaline (10 mg/kg b.w.), and amphetamine had little effect on the correct bar pressing. Inhibition by LSD and mescaline appeared to impair the ability to select the correct signal. Larger doses blocked performance completely. Weckowicz (1962) reported that adrenochrome, in the dose 25 mg/kg b.w. in rats, reduced the rate of bar pressing for food and water in a Skinner box.

Braines *et al.* (1959b) reported studies of the effect of LSD, chlorpromazine, adrenochrome, amenazine, tryptophan, tyrosine and blood serum of schizophrenic patients on the behavior of rats, dogs, monkeys, and chimpanzees. All these substances, if given in a sufficient dose, produced catatonic states in animals. In smaller doses these substances did not produce catatonic symptoms, but suppressed learned habits (conditioned reflexes).

An important method of studying the effect of drugs on behavior is that of avoidance conditioning. In this method the animals learn to escape from a pain producing stimulus. They also learn further to associate a preceding neutral stimulus with the nonsusceptible stimulus and to avoid the latter. Thus we can separate the reactivity to painful stimuli from that to a neutral stimulus which has become a sign of danger.

Cook and Weidley (1957) developed a method for testing avoidance response with rats, which has been used widely in drug studies. The rats have to learn to climb a pole when a "warning" signal (conditioned stimulus) is displayed in order to avoid a painful electric shock (unconditioned stimulus) to the grid floor of the cage. Cook and Weidley (1957) reported that LSD, in the dose 1.5 mg/kg b.w., blocked specifically the response to the conditioned stimulus with minimal effect on the response to the unconditioned stimulus. Higher doses of LSD blocked both the conditioned and unconditioned responses. However, even blocking of escape response did not incapacitate the pole climbing activity. Serotonin (dose 0.5–40 mg/kg b.w.), chlorpromazine (dose 10 mg/kg b.w.), and reserpine (25 mg/kg b.w.) blocked conditioned responses. This effect could be counteracted by very small doses (0.1–0.5 mg/kg b.w.) of LSD which did not have any effect when given alone. In case of meprobamate (dose 500 mg/kg b.w.), which inhibited both conditioned and unconditioned responses, LSD counteracted only the blocking of unconditioned responses. It had no effect on blocking produced by morphia. Mescaline (dose 10–100 mg/kg b.w.) had no blocking effect on conditioned and unconditioned responses and did not antagonize other agents. Wada *et al.* (1963) reported that 5-hydroxytryptophan, a precursor of serotonin, impairs the performance of both conditioned avoidance and approach responses in cats and monkeys. This effect could be counteracted by pretreatment with atropine.

Yakugaku (1961) reported that both LSD and mescaline showed a weak antagonistic action to the inhibitory effect of the conditioned avoidance response in rats, which was produced by perphenazine (a tranquilizing agent of phenothiazine group) and reserpine.

Mahler *et al.* (1958) using the same technique compared the effects of bufotenine on the avoidance of responses of rats with that of LSD. They used smaller doses of LSD (0.3–0.5 mg/kg b.w.) than previous authors. The dose of bufotenine was from 8.0 to 27.0 mg/kg b.w. Both LSD and bufotenine increased markedly the latency of conditioned response. The effect produced by bufotenine lasted longer than that produced by LSD. Both substances soon after the injection produced characteristic changes in the posture. The animals were crawling, dragging their abdomens on the cage floor. Another technique used for investigation of the effect of drugs on conditioned avoidance responses is that of "shuttle box." The animals which have been used in connection with this method are rats, cats, and dogs. A shuttle box is a cage separated by a barrier. The animals have to learn to escape from the electrified part of the cage by jumping over the barrier to the other side. They also have to learn to avoid shock (unconditioned stimulus) when the "warning" stimulus, usually a buzzer or light (conditioned stimulus), is displayed. Several substances have been investigated. McIsaac *et al.* (1961) and also Gessner and Page (1962) investigated the effect on avoidance conditioning in rats, using a shuttle box with the following compounds: LSD, bufotenine (5-hydroxy-*N,N*-dimethyltryptamine), other tryptamine derivatives (harmaline and 10-methoxyharmalin) and also melatonin (substance isolated from pineal gland). All these compounds are powerful serotonin antagonists, and all of them, even in small doses, suppressed conditioned avoidance responses in rats. The authors point to the significance of this finding, for the theory that mental illness is caused by an abnormality of the tryptophan metabolism.

Hamilton (1960) investigated the effect of LSD on the running speed of rats in an escape from a shock situation. Over the dose level used (0.13–1.0 mg/kg b.w.) an increased speed of running was consistently observed. There was no evidence to indicate the development of tolerance to these effects after seven daily injections. Amphetamine produced similar results. Studies of conditioned avoidance response indicated higher percentages of avoidance in rats under LSD and amphetamine than under the control conditions. Pawlowski (1962), on the other hand reported that rats injected with LSD (50–800 μg/kg b.w.)

showed an impairment of conditioned avoidance response of jumping at the CS (buzzer) to avoid UCS (electric shock). It appears that small doses of LSD enhance conditioned responses while higher doses abolish them. Key (1961, 1962) compared the effect of LSD and chlorpromazine on generalization, discrimination, and extinction of conditioned avoidance responses of cats to tones in a shuttle box situation. LSD (15 μg/kg b.w.) produced a significant decrease in the rate of extinction of conditioned avoidance response to the tone of 600 cm/sec. There was an increase in generalization of avoidance responses to the tones ranging from 200 to 2000 cm/sec. LSD also abolished differentiation between two tones established previously. The animals started responding to both reinforced and nonreinforced tones; chlorpromazine (5 mg/kg b.w.), on the other hand, produced in comparison with the controls an increased extinction of conditioned responses and decreased the number of generalized responses which could be evoked, however, without altering the generalization gradient.

This was not confirmed by McGough *et al.* (1963) who carried out electroencephalographic and behavioral analysis of the effect of LSD on an instrumental reward discrimination in rabbits. The rabbits were trained to discriminate a continuous buzzer which was followed by a reward and an intermittent buzzer which was not followed by a reward. LSD (dose 0.01–0.05 mg/kg b.w.) blocked concomitantly the discrimination and instrumental responses. During the blocking of the response the EEG showed no signs of synchronization. In an earlier paper Key and Bradley (1958) investigated the effect of various compounds in cats on arousal pattern, as evidenced by the electrocorticogram. The effects of habituation to novel stimuli and the effects of pairing a neutral stimulus (a sound) with an electric shock were investigated. Habituation did not occur to a novel stimulus, which had been paired with an electric shock. LSD injected intraperitoneally in the dose of 5 mg/kg b.w. lowered the threshold of arousal to unconditioned stimuli (electric shocks) without affecting the conditioned arousal responses. Similarly the stimuli to which the animal had been habituated started evoking a marked response. The intensity of stimuli needed to produce this effect was also much lower than the original level. Chlorpromazine and reserpine produced opposite effects to LSD. Thus LSD appeared to increase arousal to most sensory stimuli to a level similar to that achieved by conditioning for any given stimulus. This perhaps would explain the increased "significance" and "meaning" of perceived objects reported by human subjects who have taken LSD; a symptom occurring also in schizophrenia. Tranquilizers have the opposite effect. The effects of mescaline on conditioned avoidance responses in a shuttle box are not the same as that of LSD. Chorover (1961) reported that mescaline, in the dose 25 mg/kg b.w. intraperitoneally, suppressed conditioned avoidance responses in white rats. Escape responses and spontaneous locomotor activity in an open field test were unaffected by the drug at this dose level. Orienting responses to conditioned stimulus showed that the animals heard the buzzer signal after the drug administration. Lewis (1961) found that mescaline, in the dose of 25 mg/kg b.w. intraperitoneally, caused a rapid extinction of conditioned avoidance response to a sound in albino rats. In higher doses (25–50 mg/kg b.w.) mescaline depressed spontaneous activity and impaired performance of previously learned conditioned avoidance responses to auditory or visual stimuli. Bridger and Grantt (1956) using conditioning technique instead of a shuttle box investigated the effect of mescaline on conditioned responses in dogs. The dog was conditioned to flex a leg to a tone (conditioned stimulus) in order to avoid an electric shock (unconditioned stimulus). This situation should be regarded as both being avoidance instrumental learning—flexion of the leg, and classical conditioning—visceral responses to the conditioned stimulus. Mescaline produced an interesting dissociation between the motor responses (leg flexion) and visceral responses (cardiac rate). At low doses of mescaline, motor component of the conditioned response (leg flexion) was present while the visceral components were absent. At both dose levels the animals lost the ability to differentiate between conditioned and unconditioned stimuli. They responded by whining to both the tone (conditioned stimulus) and the electric shock (unconditioned stimulus). A difference in reaction to conditioned and unconditioned stimuli is usually quite striking in well-established conditioned avoidance response. The authors attach a great importance to this lack of differentiation between the signal and the signaled event and explain on this basis both the symptoms of mescaline intoxication and schizophrenia in human subjects. From the point of view of the present discussion the most interesting finding is suppression by mescaline of visceral response before motor response, an effect opposite to that which LSD seems to possess.

Other hallucinogenic compounds seem to produce a similar effect on conditioned avoidance response as mescaline. Wada (1962) reported that small doses of bulbocapnine and psilocybin suppressed avoidance responses in cats in the shuttle box situation without impairing their motor coordination. Grof et al. (1963) studied the effect of adrenochrome on avoidance in rats. The conditioned stimulus was a low intensity light. The unconditioned stimulus was an electric shock delivered to a grid from which the rats could escape by climbing a net. Adrenochrome increased markedly the latency of the avoidance response. Weckowicz (1962) reported that adrenochrome, in the dose from 6.25 mg/kg to 25.0 mg/kg b.w. administered intraperitoneally, affected both the acquisition of a conditioned avoidance response by white rats in the shuttle box and the performance of learned avoidance responses. Adrenochrome produced also a very fast extinction of avoidance responses learned prior to its injection. There was no interference with the escape response at this dose level of the compound. There was also a strong tendency for adrenochrome to inhibit conditioned emotional response in the Skinner box situation. Another interesting finding was that adrenochrome interfered with consolidation of long-term memory "engrams."

A conclusion can be made that mescaline and adrenochrome appear to leave almost identical effect on avoidance conditioning. Both these compounds appear to have in many ways an opposite effect to that of LSD and a similar effect to that of tranquilizers, for example, chlorpromazine and reserpine. In the case of mescaline and adrenochrome conditioned avoidance responses are affected by a reduced arousal to the conditioned stimulus and an increased speed of extinction, while in the case of LSD conditioned avoidance responses are probably affected by a confusion produced by overarousal and overgeneralization.

In another type of experiment on producing conditioned avoidance responses an animal has to press a bar with certain frequency or to hold a lever in certain positions to avoid an electric shock. This latter technique is particularly often used with monkeys to investigate the effect of various compounds on avoidance conditioning. Clark *et al.* (1962) investigated in rhesus monkeys the effects of LSD (dose 10 mg/kg b.w.) and also some barbiturates, tranquilizers, and stimulants on conditioned avoidance responses. The monkeys had to hold the lever in certain positions against a pull of weight in order to avoid an electric shock. Both LSD and Pentothal caused a recurrent pattern of slow release of the lever to the point where a shock was received followed by a rapid recovery to a safe position. A similar effect was obtained by increasing the weight load of the lever. Thus, it is difficult to say whether the effect was due to a muscular weakness or lowering of the drive level (fear).

Iordanis and Kuchina (1959) reported the effect of chlorpromazine, adrenochrome, and schizophrenic serum on the behavior of chimpanzees. Both adrenochrome and chlorpromazine suppressed in chimpanzees complex conditioned reflexes (the so-called "stereotypes"). The animals had to perform a specific succession of different actions, for example, pulling a lever, pressing a button, or pressing a pedal in order to obtain food. These complex habits were particularly sensitive to small doses

of LSD and adrenochrome. This indicates that hallucinogens may dis-
organize temporal order of response and affect their timing. Braines
et al. (1959a) reported that adrenochrome impaired learning of complex
mazes in rats, particularly when given at the stage when the responses
are combined in complex spatial and temporal pattern. Maffi and
Constantini (1961) investigated the effects of LSD and several other
pharmacologically active compounds on the timing behavior of rats. The
rats, in order to be rewarded, had to make responses at certain time
intervals. Both too infrequent and too frequent responses were penal-
ized. Stimulants, for example, amphetamine, produced an increased
rate of responding. Tranquilizers, for example, pheniprazine, depressed
the rate of responding. LSD at the dose 0.1 mg/kg b.w. had no effect;
at the dose of 0.5 mg/kg b.w. completely eliminated all evidence
of timing behavior. Jarvik and Chorover (1958) investigated the effect
of LSD on delayed alternation tasks in eight Macaque monkeys. It
was found that the doses of LSD, as low as 0.01 mg/kg b.w., produced
a marked decrement in accuracy with relatively little effect on the
rate of performance. At higher doses (0.05–0.1 mg/kg b.w.) the rate
was also depressed. This was in contrast to findings in the same test
with chlorpromazine, amphetamine, and pentobarbital, all of which
produced changes in the rate of performance with relatively little effect
on the accuracy. Thus LSD seems to effect the temporal organization
required by alternate responses. Stewart (1963) separated the delay
responses, while LSD but not chlorpromazine, produced a significant
decrease in accuracy in the double alteration task. The results of the
study suggested that LSD disrupted the ability of the monkeys to utilize
cues supplied by previous responses, but did not affect their capacity
to retain information afforded by visually presented cues in simple
delayed response testing.

A new method in psychopharmacology was introduced by Olds
(1958). Using the technique of self-stimulation (Olds and Milner, 1954)
Olds investigated the effect of various drugs and hormones on the rate
of self-stimulation in rats. He found that with electrodes placed in the
hypothalamus and its vicinity the effect of LSD on the rate of self-
stimulation depended on whether the electrodes were placed in the
anterior or the posterior part of the hypothalamus. If the electrodes
were placed in the posterior part of the hypothalamus, LSD reduced
markedly the rate of self-stimulation, but this effect of LSD was antagonized by serotonin. An analog of LSD, BOL, had no effect with this
placement of electrodes.

If electrodes were placed in the anterior part of the hypothalamus,
LSD also suppressed the rate of self-stimulation. However, in this case

its effect was not antagonized by serotonin and BOL had the same effect as LSD.

Mogenson (1962) in a study of the effect of adrenochrome on self-stimulation in rats found a similar interaction between the electrode placement and the effect of the drug. Adrenochrome significantly decreased the rate of self-stimulation when the electrodes were placed in the posterior part of the hypothalamus, but had no effect when the electrodes were placed in the anterior part of the hypothalamus.

The studies of the effect of the hallucinogenic drugs on experimentally produced conflict and neuroses in animals are of special psychiatric interest because they afford an insight into the mode of action of these drugs on motivation. There is also a possibility of better understanding of a possible relationship between conflict and maladjustment on one hand and possible endogenous toxic, hallucinogenic substances, produced by the body in case of a psychotic illness on the other. These studies also could offer a better understanding of possible use of hallucinogenic drugs as therapeutic agents. Braines (1959), for instance, found that a condition of fear may produce catatonic reaction in dogs. In a milder state of fear, which does not produce catatonic systems, introduction of a small dose of bulbocapnine, which by itself was not sufficient to produce a catatonic-like state, produced catatonic symptoms in the animal. Adrenochrome produced similar results. A dose of this drug which was not by itself sufficient to produce catatonic-like symptoms, was introduced into an animal in a mild environmental stress, catatonic symptoms were produced. In this way there is a possibility of formation of a vicious circle: Environmental stress through conditioning may produce disturbance of metabolism of neurohormones which act in a similar way as hallucinogenic compounds. The abnormal neurohormones may produce a further abnormality in conditioning and further stress. The most simple conflict situation in which an animal can find itself is an approach–avoidance conflict. The animals have to perform certain acts to be rewarded by food or water at the same time the performance of the same cat is punished by a painful shock.

Marazzi (1962) and Ray and Marazzi (1961, 1962) found that LSD inhibited much more conditioned approach behavior, than conditioned avoidance behavior. In one experiment (Ray and Marazzi (1961), rats were trained to press in a Skinner box the same bar to obtain milk and to avoid a shock. An auditory signal was used as a discriminandum between the period when pressing of the bar produced milk and the period when pressing of the bar prevented the electric shock. These periods were presented in random order. LSD (dose 0.08–0.125 mg/kg b.w.) blocked the bar pressing for milk, but had no effect, apart from a slight increase in the latency of response, on the bar pressing to avoid shock. Mescaline (dose 11.0–15.0 mg/kg b.w.) had a similar effect as LSD. The effect of mescaline lasted longer than the effect of LSD, 60–90 minutes, as against 20–60 minutes. In another experiment (Ray and Marazzi, 1962) rats were trained in a Skinner box to press a lever for water reward during 20-second periods during which a light was flashing. If the flashing of light was accompanied by a tone the rats could obtain 4 times as much water as when only the light was flashing. However, each reward in the presence of the tone was accompanied by a painful electric shock delivered to the animal's feet. In this way a typical approach–avoidance conflict was produced. LSD in smaller doses reduced the bar pressing during the periods when the flashing of light was accompanied by the tone, which signaled the conflict situation. In higher doses it also reduced the bar pressing, when only the light was flashing and water could be obtained without the painful shock. Both meprobamate and pentobarbital produced an opposite effect from LSD. This increased the rate of bar pressing in the conflict situation, in spite of the painful shock. Chlorpromazine and reserpine had no effect.

Maier (1949) described a technique by which fixated stereotyped behavior is produced in rats by frustration. The rats had to learn to jump in the Lashlay jumping stand to one of the two doors. The correct door could be opened and the rat received food reward. The wrong door could not be opened and the rat received a painful bump on the head and fell to a net situated below. In Maier's experiment, however, the problem was not soluble and the rat could be rewarded only 50% of the time. In case rats refused to jump in such a situation they were forced off the stand by a blast of air. As a result of this procedure the rats developed a fixated, stereotyped positional habit, which could not be modified even when the problem became solvable. The author believed that stereotyped patterns of behavior are an important element in most forms of mental illness.

Liberson *et al.* (1961, 1962) investigated the effect of various compounds on behavior fixation in rats and in guinea pigs. Motor coordination, sensory and symbolic discrimination, reaction times during approach, avoidance and escape behavior, behavior variability, compulsive rigidity, and various learning patterns were studied. LSD (1 mg/kg b.w.) blocked goal directed behavior and temporarily disorganized both avoidance and approach behavior in rats. Iproniazid (20 mg/kg b.w.) shortened the latency of jumping to the rewarding window, but affected the response to the punishing window to a lesser degree. It produced also some delay in the learning of discrimination. Phenilprazine (1 mg/

kg b.w.) in fixated rats decreased the latency time of jumping to the rewarding window, while increasing the latency time for jumping to the punishing window with finally suppressing the avoidance reaction of air blast.

Murphree and Peters (1956) used an unsolvable "T"-maze problem with random reward and punishment. In this situation rats tended to develop fixed, stereotyped behavior. The effects of various agents such as ESC (electric shock convulsions), chlorpromazine, reserpine, and LSD (13–40 mg/kg b.w.) were studied on the fixation of behavior. ESC decidedly reduced the fixation and increased the variability of behavior. Chlorpromazine caused only a slight increase in variability. LSD in the doses used did not increase the variability of behavior.

As far as the effects of hallucinogenic substances on learning are concerned it is very difficult to make any generalizations. Again there seems to be a contrast between LSD and other hallucinogenic substances. In some experiments LSD had the effect of a stimulant not unlike that of amphetamine, while the other hallucinogenic drugs seemed to have the effect similar to that of depressant drugs. However, in view of frequent contradictory findings any conclusions which can be drawn are only tentative.

Summary and Conclusions

In ending this review of the effects of hallucinogenic compounds on animal behavior one should draw certain general conclusions. However, the whole field of research with hallucinogenic compounds seems to be in a flux, full of contradictory reports and very often premature claims. Therefore, in drawing any general conclusions utmost caution is indicated.

One conclusion seems to be justified: The effects of so-called hallucinogens vary considerably with the particular compound being investigated, the dose used, and the species experimented on. Particularly, a difference in the dose may produce opposite effects. A development of standardized behavioral techniques for investigating various compounds seems to be extremely important. As a tentative generalization one would like to point out the following:

1. There is a difference between LSD and other hallucinogenic compounds. LSD seems in small doses to act as a stimulant not unlike amphetamines, in larger doses it seems to possess a depressant effect. Other hallucinogenic compounds tend to have depressant effects at all the dose levels.

2. There seems to be an association between the function of the

temporal lobes and the limbic system in higher animals on one hand and the effect of hallucinogenic compounds on the other. Further research into this relationship will be rewarding.

3. It is extremely important to separate the effect of various hallucinogenic substances on sensory functions from that on motivation and memory before a better understanding of the mechanisms involved is achieved.

4. Further research should concentrate on a few standardized techniques such as classified conditioning, which can be easily quantified and combined with electric brain recording, rather than to proliferate uncontrolled observations on new species of animals.

REFERENCES

Abramson, H. A. (1957). *Neuropharmacol., Trans. 3rd Conf., Princeton, New York, 1957* p. 9. Josiah Macy, Jr. Found., New York.

Abramson, H. A., and Evans, L. T. (1954). *Science* **120**:990–991.

Abramson, H. A., and Jarvik, M. E. (1955). *J. Psychol.* **40**:337–340.

Abramson, H. A., Sklarofsky, B., Baron, M. O., and Gettner, H. H. (1957a). *A.M.A Arch. Neurol. Psychiat.* **77**:439–445.

Abramson, H. A., Sklarofsky, B., Baron, M. O., and Gettner, H. H. (1957b). *Science* **125**:397–398.

Abramson, H. A., Weiss, B., and Baron, M. O. (1958). *Nature* **181**:1136–1137.

Abramson, H. A., Rolo, A., Sklarofsky, B., and Stache, J. (1960). *J. Psychol.* **49**:151–154.

Abramson, H. A., Gettner, H. H., Hewitt, M. P., and Dean, G. (1961). *J. Psychol.* **52**:445–455.

Adey, W. R. (1961). *Trans. 6th Res. Conf. Coop. Chemotherapy Studies Psychiat. Broad Res. Approaches Mental Illness, 1961.*

Adey, W. R., Bell, F. R., and Dennis, B. J. (1962). *Neurology* **12**:591–602.

Asfield, P. J., and Johnson, J. J. (1961). *Am. Psychologist* **16**:452.

Baldwin, M., Lewis, S. A., and Bach, S. A. (1959). *Neurology* **9**:469–474.

Baruk, H., Launay, J., Berges, J., Perles, R., and Conte, C. (1958). *Ann. Med.-Psychol.* **42**:413–414.

Baruk, H., Launay, J., Berges, J., and Perles, R. (1962). *In* "Annals moreau de Tours" (H. Baruk and J. Launay, eds.), p. 275. University of France, Paris.

Berryman, R., Jarvik, M. E., and Navin, J. A. (1962). *Psychopharmacologia* **3**:60–65.

Blough, D. S. (1957a). *In* "Psychotropic Drugs" (M. S. Garattini and V. Ghetti, eds.), p. 110. Elsevier, Amsterdam.

Blough, D. S. (1957b). *Ann. N.Y. Acad. Sci.* **66**:733–739.

Blough, D. S. (1957c). *Science* **126**:304–305.

Bradley, P. B. (1953). *3rd Intern. Electroencephalog. Congr., 1953* p. 21.

Brady, J. V. (1959). *In* "Psychopharmacology" (J. O. Cole and R. W. Gerard, eds.), p. 46. Natl. Res. Council, Washington, D.C.

Brady, J. V., and Ross, S. (1960). *In* "Drugs and Behaviour" (L. Uhr and J. G. Miller, eds.), p. 232. Wiley, New York.

Braines, C. H., ed. (1959). *In* "Problems of Experimental Pathology." Inst. Psychiat., Acad. Med. Sci. U.S.S.R., Moscow.

Braines, C. H., Kobrinska, Q. J., and Schneider, J. A. (1959a). *In* "Problems of Experimental Pathology" (C. H. Braines, ed.), p. 164. Inst. Psychiat., Acad. Med. Sci., U.S.S.R., Moscow.

Braines, C. H., Kavierznieva, E. D., Kotsoff, B. A., and Kuchina, E. B. (1959b). *In* "Problems of Experimental Pathology" (C. H. Braines, ed.). Inst. Psychiat., Acad. Med. Sci. U.S.S.R., Moscow.

Bridger, W. H., and Grantt, H. W. (1956). *Am. J. Psychiat.* 113:352–360.

Brimblecombe, R. W. (1963). *Psychopharmacologia* 4:139–147.

Brown, B. B. (1957). *Ann. N.Y. Acad. Sci.* 66:677.

Brown, B. B. (1961). *Federation Proc.* 20:320.

Brücke, F., Gogolak, G., and Stumf, C. (1961). *Arch. Exptl. Pathol. Pharmakol.* 240:460–468.

Burgers, A. C. J., Leemreis, W., Dominiczak, T., and van Oordt, G. J. (1958). *Acta Endocrinol.* 29:191–200.

Buscaino, F. A., and Frougia, N. (1953). *Acta Neurol.* (*Naples*) 8:641.

Cerletti, A., and Berde, B. (1955). *Experientia* 11:312.

Chauchard, P. (1961). *Compt. Rend. Soc. Biol.* 155:71–72.

Chen, A. L., and Chen, K. K. (1939). *Quart. J. Pharmacol.* 12:308 (quoted by Gershon and Lang, 1962).

Chorover, S. L. (1961). *J. Comp. Physiol. Psychol.* 54:649–655.

Clark, R., Jackson, J. A., and Brady, J. V. (1962). *Science* 135:1132–1133.

Christiansen, A., Baum, R., and Witt, P. N. (1962). *J. Pharmacol. Exptl. Therap.* 136:31–37.

Cook, L., and Weidley, E. (1957). *Ann. N.Y. Acad. Sci.* 66:740–752.

Cutting, W., Baslow, M., Read, D., and Furst, A. (1959). *J. Clin. Exptl. Psychopathol. & Quart. Rev. Psychiat. Neurol.* 20:26–32.

Day, C. A., and Yen, H. C. Y. (1962). *Federation Proc.* 21:335.

De Jong, H. H. (1945). "Experimental Catatonia." Williams & Wilkins, Baltimore, Maryland.

Delay, J. (1953). *Electroencephalog. Clin. Neurophysiol.* 5:130.

Delay, J., Lhermitte, F., and Verideaux, G. (1952). *Rev. Neurol.* 86:81.

Delay, J., Thuillier, J., Nakajima, H., and Duradin, M. C. (1959). *Compt. Rend. Soc. Biol.* 153:244–248.

Dews, P. B. (1956). *Ann. N.Y. Acad. Sci.* 65:268–281.

Dhawan, B. N. (1961). *Brit. J. Pharmacol.* 16:137–145.

Doepfner, W. (1962). *Experientia* 18:256–257.

Eade, N. R. (1954). Unpublished M.Sc. Thesis, University of Saskatchewan, Saskatoon.

Elder, J. T., and Dille, J. M. (1962). *J. Pharmacol. Exptl. Therap.* 136:162–168.

Evans, L. T., Geronimus, L. H., Kornetsky, E., and Abramson, A. H. (1956). *Science* 123:26.

Evarts, E. V. (1956). *A.M.A. Arch. Neurol. Psychiat.* 75:49–53.

Evarts, E. V., Laudau, W., Freygang, W., and Marshall, W. H. (1955). *Am. J. Physiol.* 182:594–598.

Fazio, C., and Sacchi, U. (1957). *In* "Psychotropic Drugs" (S. Garattini and V. Ghetti, eds.), p. 104. Elsevier, Amsterdam.

Feldberg, W., and Sherwood, S. L. (1954). *J. Physiol.* (*London*) 123:147–171.

Fellows, G. J., and Cook, L. (1957). *In* "Psychotropic Drugs" (S. Garattini and V. Ghetti, eds.), p. 397. Elsevier, Amsterdam.

Florey, F., and McLennan, H. (1955). *J. Physiol.* (*London*) 192:384.

Forrer, G. R., and Goldner, R. D. (1951). *A.M.A. Arch. Neurol. Psychiat.* **65**:581–588.

Freedman, D. X., Aghajanian, G. K., Ormitz, E. M., and Rosner, B. (1958). *Science* **127**:1173–1174.

Friedhoff, A. J., and Goldstein, A. J. (1962). *Ann. N.Y. Acad. Sci.* **92**:5–13.

Fuller, J. L. (1962). *Ann. N.Y. Acad. Sci.* **96**:199–204.

Furster, J. M. (1957). *Federation Proc.* **16**:43.

Gaddum, J., and Vogt, M. (1956). *Brit. J. Pharmacol.* **11**:175–179.

Gershon, S., and Lang, W. J. (1962). *Arch. Intern. Pharmacodyn.* **135**:31–56.

Gessner, P. K., and Page, I. H. (1962). *Am. J. Physiol.* **203**:167–172.

Greenblatt, E. N., and Oesterberg, A. C. (1961). *Federation Proc.* **20**:397.

Grof, S., Vojtechovsky, M., Vitek, V., and Prankova, S. (1963). *J. Neuropsychiat.* **5**:33.

Haley, T. J. (1956a). *20th Intern. Physiol. Congr., Brussels.* pp. 386–387.

Haley, T. J. (1956b). *J. Am. Pharm. Assoc., Sci. Ed.* **45**:604.

Haley, T. J. (1957). *Acta Pharmacol. Toxicol.* **13**:107–112.

Haley, T. J., and Gupta, G. R. (1958). *Arch. Intern. Pharmacodyn.* **113**:296–301.

Haley, T. J., and McCormic, W. G. (1956). *Federation Proc.* **15**:433.

Hamilton, C. L. (1960). *A.M.A. Arch. Gen. Psychiat.* **2**:104–109.

Heath, R. G., Leach, B. E., and Cohen, M. (1959). *In* "The Effects of Pharmacological Agents on the Nervous System" (F. J. Braceland, ed.), p. 397. Williams & Wilkins, Baltimore, Maryland.

Hoffer, A. (1962). *Intern. Rev. Neurobiol.* **4**:307.

Hoffer, A., and Wojicki, H. (1957). Personal communication.

Hosko, M. J., and Tislow, R. (1956). *Federation Proc.* **15**:440.

Iordanis, K. A., and Kuchina, E. B. (1959). *In* "Problems of Experimental Pathology" (C. H. Braines, ed.). Inst. Psychiat., Acad. Med. Sci. U.S.S.R., Moscow.

Jacob, J., and Blazowski, M. (1961). *Arch. Intern. Pharmacodyn.* **133**:296–309.

Jarvik, M. E. (1957). *Trans. 3rd Conf. Neuropharmacol.* Josiah Macy, Jr. Foundation, New York.

Jarvik, M. E., and Chorover, S. (1958). *Federation Proc.* **17**:381.

Kanai, T., Misrahy, G., and Clark, L. C. (1962). *Federation Proc.* **21**:322.

Keller, D. L., and Umbreit, W. W. (1956). *Science* **124**:723–724.

Key, B. J. (1961). *Psychopharmacologia* **2**:352–363.

Key, B. J. (1962). *2nd Meeting Coll. Intern. Neuropharmacol.* Elsevier, Amsterdam.

Key, B. J., and Bradley, P. B. (1958). *Nature* **182**:1517–1519.

Krupp, P., and Monnier, M. (1960). *Experientia* **16**:206–209.

Laborit, H., Broussolle, B., and Perrimond-Trouchet, R. (1957a). *J. Physiol.* (*Paris*), **49**:953–962.

Laborit, H., Broussolle, B., and Perrimond-Trouchet, R. (1957b). *Compt. Rend. Soc. Biol.* **151**:863–872.

Lagutina, N. I., Laricheva, K. A., Mil'shtein, G. I., and Norkina, L. N. (1964). *Federation Proc.* **23**:T737.

Lambert, M., and Heckel, E. (1901). *Compt. Rend. Soc. Biol.* **133**:1236.

Lewis, C. S. (1961). Unpublished Ph.D. Thesis, University of Washington.

Liberson, W. T., Kafka, A., and Schwartz, E. (1961). *Biochem. Pharmacol.* **8**:15–16.

Liberson, W. T., Paul, E., Schwartz, E., Wilson, A., and Gagon, V. P. (1962). *Neuropsychiatry* **3**:298–303.

McGough, J. L., Le de Baran, M. D., and Long, V. G. (1963). *Psychopharmacologia* 4:126–138.

McIsaac, M., Khairallah, P. A., and Page, I. H. (1961). *Science* 134:674–675.

Maffi, G., and Constantini, D. (1961). *Biochem. Pharmacol.* 8:61–62.

Mahler, D. J., Hummoller, F. L., and Dunn, A. L. (1958). *Federation Proc.* 17:103.

Maier, N. R. F. (1949). *In* "Frustration, the Study of Behaviour without a Goal." McGraw-Hill, New York.

Mansour, T. E. (1956). *Federation Proc.* 15:454–455.

Mansour, T. E. (1957). *Brit. J. Pharmacol.* 12:406–409.

Marazzi, A. S. (1961). *Ann. N.Y. Acad. Sci.* 92:990–1003.

Marazzi, A. S. (1962). *Ann. N.Y. Acad. Sci.* 96:211–226.

Marazzi, A. S., and Hart, E. R. (1955). *Science* 121:365–367.

Melander, B., and Martens, S. (1958). *Diseases Nervous System* 19:478–479.

Melander, B., and Martens, S. (1959). *Acta Psychiat. Neurol. Scand.* 34: Suppl. 136, 344–348.

Miller, N. E. (1957). *In* "Psychotropic Drugs" (S. Garattini and V. Ghetti, eds.), p. 83. Elsevier, Amsterdam.

Mogenson, G. (1962). *Can. Psychol. Assoc. Conv., Hamilton, 1962.*

Monroe, R. R., and Heath, R. G. (1961). *J. Neuropsychiat.* 3:75–82.

Murphree, O. D., and Peters, J. E. (1956). *J. Nervous Mental Disease* 124:78–83.

Norton, S. (1957). *In* "Psychotropic Drugs" (S. Garattini and V. Ghetti, eds.), p. 73. Elsevier, Amsterdam.

Norton, S., and Tamburo, J. (1958). *J. Pharmacol. Exptl. Therap.* 57:122.

Noval, J. J., Brande, B. L., and Sohler, A. (1959). *Federation Proc.* 18:428.

Oakley, R. S., and Marazzi, S. A. (1961). *Science* 133:1705–1706.

Ochs, S., Dowell, A. R., and Russell, I. J. (1962). *Electroencephalog. Clin. Neurophysiol.* 14:878–887.

Olds, J. (1958). *Science* 127:315–324.

Olds, J., and Milner, P. (1954). *J. Comp. Physiol. Psychol.* 47:419–427.

Parker, J. M., and Hilderbrand, N. (1962). *Lancet* II:246.

Pawloski, A. A. (1962). *J. Neuropsychiat.* 4:81–86.

Ray, O. S., and Marazzi, A. S. (1961). *Am. Psychologist* 16:453.

Ray, O. S., and Marazzi, A. S. (1962). *Federation Proc.* 2:415.

Reider, H. P. (1957). *Psychiat. Neurol.* 134:378–396.

Rice, W. B., and McColl, J. D. (1960). *Arch. Intern. Pharmacodyn.* 128:249.

Rosen, E., and Jovino, A. (1963). *Nature* 197:614–615.

Rothlin, E. (1953). *19th Intern. Psychol. Congr., Montreal, 1953* Abstr. commun., pp. 948–949.

Rothlin, E., and Cerletti, A. (1952). *Helv. Physiol. Pharmacol. Acta* 10:319–327.

Salanski, J., and Koschtojantz, C. S. (1962). *Acta Physiol. Acad. Sci. Hung.* 20:45.

Saxena, A., Battacharaya, B. K., and Mukerji, B. (1962). *Arch. Intern. Pharmacodyn.* 140:327–335.

Schain, R. J. (1962). *World Neurol.* 3:706–714.

Schneider, J. A., and Sigg, E. B. (1957). *Ann. N.Y. Acad. Sci.* 66:765–776.

Schwartz, B. I., Wakim, K. G., Bickford, R. C., and Lichtenheld, F. R. (1956). *A.M.A. Arch. Neurol. Psychiat.* 75:579–587.

Shore, P. A., and Brodie, B. B. (1957). *Proc. Soc. Exptl. Biol. Med.* 94:433–435.

Smith, K., and Moody, A. C. (1956). *Diseases Nervous System* 17:327–328.

Smythies, J. R. (1959). *Nature* 183:545–546.

Speck, L. B. (1957). *J. Pharmacol. Exptl. Therap.* 119:78–89.

Stewart, C. N. (1963). *Eastern Psychol. Assoc. Meeting, New York, 1963.*

Stumpt, C., Petsche, H., and Gogolak, G. (1962). *Electroencephalog. Clin. Neurophysiol.* **14**:212–219.

Sturtevant, F. M., and Drill, V. A. (1956). *Proc. Soc. Exptl. Biol. Med.* **92**:383–387.

Sturtevant, F. M., Drill, V. A., and Searle, G. D. (1956). *Anat. Record* **125**:607.

Teaschler, M., and Cerletti, A. (1957). *J. Pharmacol. Exptl. Therap.* **120**:179–183.

Thuillier, J., and Nakajima, H. (1957). *In* "Psychotropic Drugs" (S. Garattini and V. Ghetti, eds.), p. 136. Elsevier, Amsterdam.

Tripod, J. (1957). *In* "Psychotropic Drugs" (S. Garattini and V. Ghetti, eds.), p. 437. Elsevier, Amsterdam.

Trout, D. L. (1957). *J. Pharmacol. Exptl. Therap.* **121**:130–135.

Turner, W. J. (1956a). *Diseases Nervous System* **17**:193–197.

Turner, W. J. (1956b). *Diseases Nervous System* **17**:198–204.

Ursin, H. (1962). *Psychopharmacologia* **3**:317–330.

Vallbo, S. (1957). Personal communication (cited by Hoffer, 1962).

von Ferdinand, F. (1929). *Muench. Med. Wochschr.* **76**:112 (quoted by Gershon and Lang, 1962).

Wada, J. A. (1962). *Ann. N.Y. Acad. Sci.* **96**:227–250.

Wada, J. A., Hill, D., and Wrinch, J. (1963). *J. Neuropsychiat.* **4**:413–415.

Weckowicz, T. E. (1962). Unpublished Ph.D. Thesis, University of Saskatchewan.

Weiss, B., Abramson, H. A., and Baron, M. D. (1958). *A.M.A. Arch. Neurol. Psychiat.* **80**:345–350.

West, L. J., and Pierce, C. M. (1962). *Science* **138**:1100–1103.

Widlocher, D., Nakajima, H., and Thuillier, J. (1957). *Compt. Rend. Soc. Biol.* **151**:668.

Wilber, C. W. (1958). *Am. J. Physiol.* **194**:488–490.

Winter, C. A., and Flataker, L. (1951). *J. Pharm. Exptl. Therap.* **101**:156.

Winter, C. A., and Flataker, L. (1957). *J. Pharmacol. Exptl. Therap.* **119**:194.

Witt, P. N. (1951). *Experientia* **7**:310.

Witt, P. N. (1952). *Behaviour* **4**:172–189.

Witt, P. N. (1956). *In* "Die Wirkung von Substanzen auf den Netsban der Spinne als biologischer Test." Springer, Berlin.

Witt, P. N. (1958). *In* "Psychopathology a Source Book" (C. F. Reed, J. E. Alexander, and S. S. Tomkins, eds.), p. 660. Harvard Univ. Press, Cambridge, Massachusetts.

Wood, C. D., Stone, J. E., and Seager, L. D. (1958). *Federation Proc.* **17**:420.

Woolley, D. W. (1955). *Proc. Natl. Acad. Sci. U.S.* **41**:338–344.

Woolley, D. W., and Van der Hoeven, T. (1963). *Science* **139**:610–611.

Yakugaku, K. (1961). *Japan. J. Pharm. & Chem.* **33**:47.

Author Index

Numbers in italics refer to the pages on which the complete references are listed.

A

Aaronsen, B. S., 227, 235, *252*
Abbott, D. D., 63, *75*
Abood, L. G., 139, *252*, 309, 314, 326, *439*, 532, 534, 535, 536, *544, 545, 546*
Abramson, H. A., 93, 103, 114, 120, 123, 139, 150, 208, 209, 213, *252, 253, 257, 259, 260,* 558, 559, 560, 561, *590, 591, 594*
Adey, W. R., 491, *511,* 575, 576, *590*
Adkins, P. K., 466, 467, *513*
Aghajanian, G. K., 30, 77, 580, *592*
Agnew, N., 196, 207, 223, *253,* 433, *435*
Akabane, Y., 332, *441*
Akerfeldt, S., 314, 325, 326, *433*
Alberty, J., 295, *433*
Albrecht, M., 316, *438*
Alema, G., 115, *253*
Alexander, F., 217, *264*
Alles, G. A., 46, 47, *75*
Amidisen, A., 304, *433*
Altschule, M. D., 64, *76,* 274, 339, 340, 341, *437, 441*
Amini, F. B., 540, *544*
Anastasopoulos, G., 100, *253*
Andersen, K., *261,* 552, *554*
Anderson, E. W., 150, *253*
Angel, C., 314, *434,* 553, *554*
Angenent, W. J., 333, 337, *434*
Anguiano, G., 332, *434*
Ansley, H. R., 306, *434*
Ansbacher, S., 336, *439*
Antopol, W., 221, *257*
Appel, K. E., 275, *434*
Apter, N. S., 508, *514*
Apter, J. T., 93, *253*
Aranow, H., 339, *436*
Arendsen-Hein, G. W., 177, *253*
Armstrong, J. J., 176, *253*
Armstrong, M. D., 325, *434*
Arnold, O. H., 207, *253, 258*
Arnott, G. P., 415, *435*
Aronson, H., 122, 123, *253*

Asfield, P. J., 579, *590*
Asher, R., 300, *434*
Ashida, K., 318, *441*
Atwell, C. R., 41, *80,* 493, 498, *514*
Avala, G. F., 465, 467, *515*
Axelrod, J., 22, 33, 77, 89, *253, 256,* 281, 331, *434,* 455, *511*
Ayd, F. J., 528, *544*

B

Bach, S. A., 577, *590*
Bachman, C. H., 312, *435*
Bachtold, H. P., 74, *79*
Bacq, Z. M., 267, 332, *434*
Bain, J. A., 207, 213, *253,* 303, *434*
Bain, W. A., 304, *434*
Baird, K. A., 201, *253*
Baker, J. P., 526, *544*
Baker, R. A., 289, 311, *436, 439*
Bakker, C. B., 540, 541, *544, 546*
Baldwin, M., 577, *590*
Balestrieri, A., 30, 42, *76,* 139, *253,* 493, *511*
Ball, J. R., 176, *253*
Ban, A. A., 289, 304, 320, *434*
Ban, T. A., 317, *438,* 541, *544*
Banshikoff, V. M., 322, *434*
Barbeau, A., 508, *511*
Barber, B., 198, *253*
Barger, G., 1, *76*
Barlow, R. B., 449, *511*
Baron, M. O., 208, *253,* 559, 560, *590, 594*
Barrios, A. A., 230, *253*
Barsel, N., 318, 319, *434*
Baruk, H., 567, 569, *590*
Baslow, M., 562, *591*
Battacharaya, B. K., 562, *593*
Baum, R., 36, *76,* 492, *511,* 557, *591*
Baumer, L., 308, *440*
Baxter, D., 286, 332, 333, *435*
Baxter, R. M., 56, *80*
Beach, G. O., 527, *545*
Bean, J. W., 289, 294, *434*

Beard, A. W., 311, *434*
Beauvillain, A., 285, *434*
Becke, F., 17, *80*
Becker, A. M., *254*
Becker, R. O., 312, *435*
Beckett, P. G. S., 307, 308, 326, *436*, 549, 552, *553*
Beech, H. R., 542, *545*
Beisaw, N. E., 91, *254*, 277, *434*
Belden, E., 169, 231, *254*
Bell, F. R., 491, *511*, 575, *590*
Bellak, L., *254*, 303, *434*
Belleville, R. E., 176, 208, *259*
Belsanti, R., 139, *254*
Benacerraf, B., 295, *436*
Bender, L., 90, 178, 214, 225, 233, *254*, *263*
Benedetti, G., 150, 155, *254*
Benditt, E. P., 322, *439*
Benington, F., 33, *80*, 213, *255*
Bennett, P. B., 293, *434*
Bercel, N. A., 542, *545*
Berde, B., 562, *591*
Bergen, J. R., 74, *76*, 91, 209, *254*, 277, *434*, 547, 548, 549, 551, 552, 553, *553*, *554*
Bergen, S., 210, *259*
Berger, A., 314, 326, *441*
Berges, J., 567, 569, *590*
Beringer, K., 4, 5, *76*
Berlin, L., 127, *254*
Bernard, S., 300, *435*
Bernheim, F., 20, *76*
Bernheim, M. L. C., 20, *76*
Bernsohn, J., 446, *513*
Berry, K., 289, *436*
Berryman, R., 579, *590*
Bertino, J. R., 104, 207, 209, 210, *254*, *259*
Besendorf, H., 74, 79, 479, *514*
Bhattacharya, B. K., 35, *80*
Bickford, R. G., 40, 41, 43, *80*, 91, 206, *263*, 313, 348, *441*, 573, *593*
Biel, J. H., 139, *252*, 532, 534, 536, *544*, *545*
Bigelow, L. B., 340, *441*
Billewicz-Stankiewicz, J., 329, 335, *434*
Bin, H., 75, *76*
Birnbaum, S. M., 444, *512*, *516*
Bischoff, A., *434*

Bishop, M. P., 335, *437*
Blanchet, A., 320, *438*
Blaschko, H., 24, *76*, 332, *434*, 444, 487, *511*
Blazowski, M., 565, *592*
Bleuler, M., 275, *434*
Blewett, D. B., 136, 137, 158, 163, 195, 227, *254*, *255*, *265*
Block, K., 23, *76*
Block, W., 23, *76*
Blough, D. S., 578, *590*
Blum, J. J., 322, *439*
Boardman, W. K., 120, *254*
Bodi, T., 539, *545*
Bohls, S. W., 25, *80*, 280, *440*, 550, *554*
Bolton, W. B., 234, *254*
Bonasera, N., 326, *434*
Bonner, J. F., 89, *254*
Borsy, J., 32, *76*, 77, 462, *511*
Boryczka, A., 223, *257*
Boskovic, B., 490, *511*
Boszormenyi, Z., 459, 461, 498, *511*
Boszormeyi-Nagy, I., 273, 307, *434*
Bourne, G. H., 222, 225, *261*
Boyd, E. S., 89, *254*
Brack, A., 486, 487, 493, *511*, *513*
Bradley, C. A., 25, *76*
Bradley, P. B., 91, 210, 219, *254*, 523, *545*, 575, 583, *590*, *592*
Brady, J. V., 555, 585, *590*, *591*
Brady, O., 89, *253*
Braines, C. H., 279, *434*, 550, *553*, 581, 586, 587, *590*, *591*
Brande, B. L., 363, *439*, 570, *593*
Braude, M. C., 49, 50, 51, *81*
Braun, D. L., 206, *254*
Breier, A., *434*
Brengelmann, J. C., 139, 209, *254*
Brenner, W., *434*
Brewer, G. J., 306, *435*
Bridger, W. H., 584, *591*
Briggs, M. H., 286, *434*
Brimblecombe, R. W., 568, *591*
Briot, M., 295, *436*
Brodie, B. B., 217, 219, *254*, *255*, 504, 505, 507, *511*, *515*, 567, *593*
Brodny, M. L., 274, 302, *434*
Brody, E. B., *434*
Broer, H. H., 90, 221, 223, *263*
Brousseau, E. R., 184, *264*

Broussolle, B., 289, *438*, 565, *592*
Brown, B. B., 206, *254*, 564, 576, *591*
Brown, J., 493, *514*
Brown, M. L., *76*
Brozek, J., 370, *441*
Brudo, C., 415, *435*
Brücke, F., 576, *591*
Brummett, R. E., 485, 492, *513*
Brune, G. G., 217, *255*
Brunecker, G., 459, *511*
Bryson, M. J., 332, *441*
Buck, C. W., 297, 298, *434*
Buck, R. W., 452, *511*
Bullough, W. S., 274, 316, 317, 332, 333, *434*
Bultasova, H., 528, 529, *546*
Bumpus, F. M., 457, *511*
Bunag, R. D., 218, 220, *255*, 449, *511*
Bunnell, S., 45, *80*
Burgers, A. C. J., 563, *591*
Burke, D. E., 432, *435*
Burn, J. H., 324, *435*
Burstein, S., 35, *77*
Burton, R. M., 219, *255*
Buscaino, F. A., 569, *591*
Busch, A. K., 131, 149, 150, *255*
Busnel, R. G., 479, *513*
Buzard, J. A., 74, *76*
Byers, L. W., 315, 335, 363, *437*, 553, 554
Byrne, V. P., 137, 160, 163, *260*

C

Calder, J., 165, *255*
Callaway, E., 49, 50, 51, *81*, 104, *259*
Callbeck, M. J., 125, 169, 183, 195, 209, 233, *258*, 300, 320, 328, 400, *437*
Callowhill, C. R., 326, *441*
Cameron, K., 177, *255*
Campbell, D., 291, *435*
Campbell, N. K., 489, *516*
Cantril, H., 64, *76*
Cardon, P. V., Jr., 446, *514*
Care, C. M., 209, *254*
Carl, A., 467, *515*
Carscallen, H. B., 297, 298, *434*
Caruso, P. L., 219, *263*
Case, J. D., 478, *513*
Casey, T. M., 139, *259*
Castells, C., 91, *257*

Cates, N., 90, 221, 223, *263*
Cattell, J. P., 38, *78*, 128, 139, 144, *258*
Cerletti, A., 73, *76*, 85, 93, 95, 214, 222, 255, *258*, 296, *435*, 490, *511*, *516*, 562, 565, 566, *591*, *593*, *594*
Chandler, A. L., 150, *255*
Charatan, F. B., 537, *545*
Charbon, G. A., 448, *511*
Chassan, J. B., 69, *76*, 202, *254*, *255*
Chauchard, P., 491, *511*, 575, *591*
Chaudhury, S. S., 56, *76*
Chavira, R. A., 332, *434*
Cheek, F. E., 110, 178, *255*
Chen, A. L., 474, 477, *511*, 570, *591*
Chen, K. K., 451, 474, 477, *511*, *513*, 570, *591*
Cherkas, M. S., 235, *255*
Chevalier, J., 469, *514*
Chipkiewicz, H., 326, *440*
Cholden, L. S., 139, 206, *255*, *263*
Chorover, S. L., 31, 32, *76*, 584, 586, *591*, *592*
Christiansen, A., 36, *76*, 492, *511*, 557, *591*
Christomanos, A. A., 49, *76*
Churchill-Davidson, I., 294, *435*
Chwelos, N., 136, 137, 158, 163, 195, *254*, *255*
Chwelos, V., 328, *437*
Clark, L. C., 574, *592*
Clark, L. D., 139, 206, 210, 213, *255*
Clark, L. S., 139, 210, *255*
Clark, R., 585, *591*
Clark, W. G., 432, *435*
Claude, H., 300, *435*
Claus, A., 24, *77*, 433, *435*
Cline, H. S., 139, *255*
Clydesdale, F. M., 289, *442*
Cobrinik, L., 178, 225, *254*
Cochin, J., 22, *76*
Cohen, B. D., 539, 541, 542, *545*
Cohen, G., 304, 305, 306, *435*
Cohen, L. H., 300, *435*
Cohen, M., 313, 314, *434*, *437*, *438*, 551, 552, 554, 570, *592*
Cohen, S., 88, 96, 98, 99, 101, 110, 114, 116, 118, 120, 135, 150, 163, 164, 196, 201, *255*, *256*, *260*
Cole, J. O., 199, 200, 201, 203, *255*
Collera, D., 471, *515*

Collier, D., 209, *254*
Collins, V. J., 90, 236, *259*
Condrau, G., 128, 139, *255*
Connell, P. H., 46, 77, 335, *435*
Conner, W. R., 184, *264*
Constantini, D., 586, *593*
Conte, C., 567, *590*
Contrera, J. F., 21, *78*
Cook, L., 28, 77, 565, 581, *591*
Cook, W. B., 85, 240, *255*
Cooper, H. A., 206, *255*
Corne, S. J., 448, *511*
Cornfield, J., 444, *512*
Costa, E., 26, *76*, 217, 219, 224, *254,
    255, 257*, 455, 456, 462, 465, 467,
    468, 504, 505, *511, 512, 515*
Cote, F., 320, *438*
Cousteau, J. Y., 291, *435*
Craig, J. O., 63, *77*
Creveling, C. R., 325, *435*
Criscuoli, P. M., 326, *434*
Cronheim, G. E., 32, 61, *78*
Croot, J. R., 325, *435*
Csak, Z., 32, *77*
Csizmadia, Z. S., 32, *76*, 462, *511*
Curtis, D. R., 27, 77, 466, *511*
Cutting, W., 562, *591*
Czajkowski, N., 549, 552, *553*

D

Dale, H. H., 1, 49, *76, 77*
Daly, J., 22, 33, *77*
Dana, G. W., 485, 492, *513*
Dandiya, P. C., 56, 77, *80*
Danziger, L., 300, *435*
Darrow, C. W., 415, *435*
Das, P. K., 56, *77*
David, A. E., 500, *511*
David, J. M., 500, *511*
Davidson, J. M., 223, *257*
Davies, B. M., 542, *545*
Davis, P., 274, *437*
Davis, R., 27, *77*
Day, C. A., 477, *511*, 564, *591*
Day, M. E., 326, *436*
Dean, G., 561, *590*
de Giacomo, U., 128, 139, *255*
de Jong, H. H., 19, 32, 33, 34, 74, 75,
    77, 446, 448, *511*, 572, *591*

Delay, J., 128, 139, *255, 256,* 493, 499,
    511, 566, 567, *591*
Delfour, G. H., 24, 77, 433, *435*
De Maar, E. W. J., 104, *256*
Denber, H. C. B., 25, 39, 42, 44, 77,
    537, *545*
Denckla, W. D., 340, *441*
Dengler, H. J., 25, *77*
Denisoff, B. M., 279, *435*
Dennis, B. J., 491, *511,* 575, *590*
Denson, R., 183, *256*
De Onorato, A. C., 139, *263*
Der, P., 459, *511*
Dern, R. J., 306, *435*
De Ropp, R. S., 25, *77*
Derouaux, G., 332, 339, 384, *435*
Desbiens, A., 320, *438*
Deshon, H. J., 91, 128, 129, 139, *256,
    262*
DeVault, M., 538, *545*
Dewan, J. G., 300, *436*
Dews, P. B., 564, *591*
Dhalla, N. S., 56, *77*
Dhawan, B. N., 564, *591*
Dille, J. M., 206, 209, 210, *256,* 571, *591*
Dimascio, A., 41, *80,* 105, *256,* 493, 495,
    498, *511, 514*
Dippy, E. H., 464, 466, 467, *514*
Distefane, A. O., 457, *512*
Ditman, K. S., 96, 98, 99, 101, 135, 150,
    196, 204, *255, 256*
Dodge, H. W., Jr., 314, *441*
Doepfner, W., 93, *255,* 568, *591*
Dominiczak, T., 563, *591*
Donovan, C., 296, *435*
Doust, J. W. L., 139, *264,* 295, *435*
Dowell, A. R., 27, 79, 577, *593*
Downing, D. F., 468, 478, *511*
Drill, V. A., 572, 573, *594*
Dukay, A., 326, *442*
Dumas, F., 291, *435*
Dumont, J. E., 299, *435*
Dunn, A. L., 582, *593*
Duradin, M. C., 566, *591*
Dusen, W. V., 106, *256*
Dybowski, J., 468, 469, *511*

E

Eade, N. R., 269, 295, 296, *435, 438,*
    570, *591*

Eagleton, V., 535, *544*
Eberts, F. S., 467, *511*
Ebin, E. V., 178, *256*
Eccles, O., 416, *435*
Edery, H., 464, *511*
Edwards, A. E., 112, 114, 116, 118, 120, *255, 256*
Eglitis, B., 300, *436*
Ehrensvard, G., 287, *435*
Eisner, B., 150, 163, 164, *255, 256*
Elder, J. T., 206, 209, 210, *256*, 571, *591*
Elderkin, R. D., 306, *434*
Elkes, C., 523, *545*
Elkes, J., 91, 210, *254, 256*, 523, *545*
Elliott, R. B., 490, *513*
Ellis, H., 3, 77, 106, *256*
Ellis, S., 297, *435*
El-Meleghi, M., 100, *261*
Endroczy, E., 462, *515*
Eriksen, N., 322, *439*
Ernest, C., 433, *435*
Ernst, A. M., 34, 35, 77, 448, *511*
Erspamer, V., 217, *256*, 463, 489, 503, *511, 512*
Ervin, F., 316, 335, *442*, 542, *545*
Evans, J., 46, 77
Evans, L. T., 558, *590, 591*
Evarts, E. V., 89, 91, 92, *253, 256*, 454, 456, 462, *512*, 567, 569, 576, *591*
Ewald, A. T., 120, 123, *253, 259*

F

Faber, M., 339, *436*
Fabing, H. D., 43, 77, 206, *256*, 453, 454, *512*
Fadiman, J., 137, 152, 196, *261, 263*
Fang, A. Ding, 139, 150, *259*
Faretra, G., 178, 225, *254*
Farley, J. D., 526, *544*
Fazio, C., 574, *591*
Feigley, C. A., 315, 363, *437*, 551, 553, *554*
Fekete, M., 32, 76, 77
Feld, M., 151, *256*
Feldberg, W. S., 296, 313, *435*, 522, *545*, 572, *591*
Feldman, R. G., 206, *254*
Feldstein, A., 341, 349, *435*
Fellman, J. H., 286, 332, 333, *435*

Fellows, E. J., 28, 77, 449, *515*, 565, *591*
Fenn, W. O., 289, 291, *435, 436*
Ferguson, D. C., 552, *553*
Ferguson, M. W., *253*
Fernandez, T. A., 457, *512*
Fernberger, S. W., 4, 77
Ferrer, S., 91, *257*
Feuerfile, D. F., 541, *546*
Fichman, L., 150, *255*
Field, J. B., 299, 305, 332, *440*
Fink, M., 533, 536, 537, 538, *545*
Fischer, E., 457, *512*
Fischer, P., 339, 340, 342, *435, 438*
Fischer, R., 25, 77, 157, 211, *256*
Fischer, R. A., 202, *256*
Fish, M. S., 451, 455, 458, *512*
Fisher, A. E., 552, *553*
Fitzgerald, R. P., 527, *545*
Fitzhugh, O. G., 63, 79
Fitzpatrick, T. B., 285, 287, *435*
Flach, F. F., 299, 301, 302, 303, *439, 440*
Flataker, L., 552, *554*, 568, 580, *594*
Flores, S. E., 85, 252, *262*
Florey, F., 560, *591*
Fogel, S., 227, 229, 235, *256*, 540, *545*
Foldes, F. F., 221, 222, *265*, 490, *516*
Foldes, V. M., 221, 222, *265*, 490, *516*
Foley, J. M., 286, 332, 333, *435*
Fontana, A. E., 151, *256*, 500, *512*
Fontanari, D., *76*, 139, *253*
Forrer, G. R., 131, 139, 150, *256*, 572, *592*
Foster, C. A., 294, *435*
Fox, R. P., 213, *255*
Fraser, H. F., 176, 208, *259*
Frederking, W., 40, 45, 77, 150, 151, *256*
Freedberg, A. S., 273, *438*
Freedman, A. M., 178, *256*
Freedman, D. X., 30, 77, 218, *256*, 580, *592*
Freeman, H., 139, 210, *255, 259*, 547, 548, 552, 553, *554*
Fremont-Smith, F., 208, *253*
Freter, K., 89, *256*
Frey, A., 486, *513*
Freyburger, W. A., 466, 467, *512*
Freygang, E., 92, *256*
Freygang, W., 576, *591*

Fried, G. H., 221, *257*
Frieden, E., 325, *439*
Friedhoff, A. J., 21, 22, 31, 77, 78, 326, *435*, 568, *592*
Friedman, H., 312, *435*
Friedman, O. M., 35, 77
Frohman, C. E., 307, 308, 326, *436*, 549, 552, 553
Frougia, N., 569, *591*
Frumin, M. J., 92, *262*
Fujiwara, S., 318, *441*
Fuller, J. L., *592*
Funk, A., 164, 174, *261*
Funkenstein, D. H., 296, *436*
Furgiele, A. R., 61, 78
Furst, A., 562, *591*
Furster, J. M., 579, *592*

G

Gabrio, B. W., 21, 38, *80*, *81*
Gaddum, J. H., 217, *257*, 573, *592*
Gagon, V. P., 588, *592*
Gajewski, J. E., 538, *545*
Galkin, V. A., 47, 77
Gallagher, C. H., 458, *512*
Galvin, J. A. V., 206, *260*
Gamburg, A. L., 332, *436*
Ganong, W. F., 223, *257*
Gasparovic, J., 477, *515*
Gastaut, H., 91, *257*
Gatty, R., 62, 77
Gaunt, W. E., 304, 434
Gautam, S. R., 56, *76*
Geiger, R. S., 212, *257*, 552, *554*
Genest, K., 85, 238, *257*
Georgi, F., 25, 77, 157, *256*
Geronimus, L. H., 213, *257*, 559, *591*
Gerschman, R., 289, *436*
Gershenovich, Z. S., 288, 339, *436*
Gershon, S., 76, 470, 472, 478, 479, 501, 502, *512*, *513*, 536, *545*, 569, *592*
Gerstner, S. B., 479, *512*
Gerty, F. J., 273, 307, *434*
Gessa, G. L., 219, *255*, 505, *511*
Gessner, P. K., 462, 464, *512*, 582, *592*
Gettner, H. H., 560, *590*
Gey, K. R., 465, *512*
Ghuysen, J. M., 24, 77, 433, *435*
Giarman, N. J., 218, *256*

Gibbons, A. J., 214, *257*, 278, 332, 333, *436*, 455, *512*
Gibbs, E., 309, 314, 325, *433*, 535, 536, *546*
Gibbs, F. A., 309, 314, 325, *433*, 535, 536, *546*
Giberti, F., 206, *257*
Gibson, W. C., 45, 79, 370, *440*
Gilbert, D. L., 289, *436*
Gilfoil, T. M., 220, *260*
Ginzel, K. H., 208, *257*
Gjessing, R., 300, *436*
Gjessing, L. R., 300, 302, *436*
Glaser, E. M., 370, *442*
Gleser, G. C., 326, *439*
Glynn, M. F., 306, *435*
Gnirss, F., 486, 490, 494, *512*, *515*
Gogerty, J. H., 206, 209, 210, *256*
Gogolak, G., 576, *591*, *593*
Gold, E., 90, 218, *263*
Goldberger, M., 222, *257*
Goldenberg, H., 222, *257*
Goldenberg, M., 339, *436*
Goldenberg, V., 222, *257*
Goldfeen, A., 223, *257*
Goldner, R. D., 131, 139, 150, *256*, 573, *592*
Goldschmidt, L., 178, 233, *254*, 326, *436*
Goldstein, A. J., 568, *592*
Goldstein, L., 91, *257*, *262*
Goldstein, M., 21, 31, 77, 78
Goldstone, S., 120, *254*
Golterman, H. L., 273, *440*
Golubieva, G. P., 279, *434*, 550, 553
Goncz, R. M., 274, *437*
Gonzales-Monclus, E., 139, 207, *262*
Goodell, H., 127, *254*
Goodman, J. R., 151, *256*
Goodman, M., 326, *436*, 549, 552, 553
Gorin, M. H., 208, *253*
Gornall, A. G., 300, *436*
Gorodetzky, G. W., 93, *257*
Gottlieb, J. S., 307, 308, *436*, 539, 541, 542, *545*, 549, 552, 553
Gottschalk, L. A., 326, *439*
Govier, W. M., 455, *512*
Gozansky, D. M., 273, *438*
Gozsy, B., 317, *438*
Grace, G. S., 26, 78
Graham, J. D. P., 139, *257*, 448, *511*

Grantt, H. W., 584, *591*

Green, D. E., 269, 273, 331, *436*

Green, R. C., 49, *78*

Green, S., 308, 332, 339, *436*

Greenblatt, E. N., 32, *78*, 565, *592*

Greenstein, J. P., 444, *516*

Gregoretti, L., 206, *257*

Greifenstein, F. E., 538, *545*

Greig, M. E., 214, *257*, 278, 332, 333, *436*, 466, 467, *512*

Greiner, A. C., 289, 311, *436, 439*

Grelis, M. E., 222, *264*

Grinker, R. R., 135, 204, *257*

Grof, S., 122, *257*, 314, 349, 351, 397, *436*, 528, 529, *545, 546*, 584, *592*

Grover, B., 150, *255*

Grunberg, F., 227, *259*

Guido, J. A., 151, *256*

Gullino, P., 444, *512, 516*

Gunn, J. A., 31, 48, *78*

Gupta, G. R., 572, *592*

Gurd, M. R., 31, 48, *78*

Gursey, D., 445, *514*

Gussion, P., 326, *436*

Guthrie, T., 127, *254*

Guttmann, E., 4, *78*, 150, *257*

Guzak, S. V., 25, *80*

H

Haffron, D., 326, *438*

Haigh, C. P., 302, *440*

Halbach, A., 208, *261*

Halevy, A., 223, *257*

Haley, T. J., 28, *78*, 219, *257*, 571, 572, *592*

Hall, R., 295, *442*

Hall, R. W., 226, 227, *259, 265*

Haller, A., 469, *512*

Halpern, B. N., 295, *436*

Hamilton, C. L., 582, *592*

Hance, A. J., 91, 219, *254*

Handa, K. L., 56, *76*

Hansen, W. H., 63, *79*

Harley-Mason, J., 21, *78*, 270, *436*

Harman, D., 312, *436*

Harman, W. W., 137, 152, 164, 196, *257*, *263*

Harris, A., 284, *436*

Harris, G. W., 219, *257*

Harris, R. S., 314, 326, *441*

Harrison, W. H., 340, *436*

Harrisson, J. W. E., 63, *75*

Hart, E. R., 61, *78*, 92, 220, *260*, 294, *439, 575, 593*

Hartman, M. A., 114, 150, *255, 257*

Hartwich, C., 237, *257*

Harvey, C. C., 326, *438*

Harvey, N., 286, *434*

Harwood, P. D., 95, *257*

Haslerud, G. M., 312, *439*

Haugaard, N., 290, *436*

Hawkins, J. R., 453, 454, *512*

Hayman, M., 196, 204, *256*

Heacock, R. A., 64, *78*, 85, 87, 214, 238, *257*, *264*, 268, 269, 270, 271, 278, 285, 340, 420, *436, 437, 439*

Heard, G., 233, *257*

Hearst, E., 443, 463, *515*

Heath, R. G., 27, 43, 44, *79*, 92, 219, 223, *257*, *261*, 287, 313, 314, 315, 325, 326, 328, 334, 335, 363, *434, 435, 437, 438*, 548, 551, 552, 553, *554*, 570, 576, *592, 593*

Heckel, E., 469, 471, *512, 513*, 570, *592*

Heffter, A., 17, *78*

Heim, R., 486, 493, *513*

Hendrickson, J. B., 475, *512*

Henneman, D. H., 274, *437*

Henner, K., 74, *78*

Henry, T. A., 476, 479, *512*

Herjanic, M., 304, *437*

Herman, M., 46, *78*

Herran, J., 85, 252, *262*

Herring, B., 299, 305, 332, *440*

Hewitt, M. P., 93, *253*, 561, *590*

Hildebrand, N., 44, *79*, 568, *593*

Hill, D., 75, *81*, 581, *594*

Himwich, H. E., 26, 43, *78, 81*, 206, *262*, 455, 456, 462, 465, 467, 468, *512, 515*, 527, *546*

Himwich, W. A., 217, *257*, 455, 456, 462, 504, *512*

Hirsch, C., 219, *255*, 505, *511*

Hirsch, M. W., 103, 114, 120, 123, 208, *253, 259, 336, 437*

Hitchen, R., 169, 231, *254*

Hoagland, H., 90, 91, 222, 233, *258*, *262*, 277, 312, *437, 441*, 489, *514*, 547, 548, 549, 552, 553, *554*

Hobbs, G. E., 297, 298, *434*

Hoch, P. H., 38, 42, 43, 44, 78, 104, 128, 129, 139, 144, 151, 205, 206 258, 476, 477, *512, 514,* 538, *546*
Hockstein, F. A., 458, 473, 475, *512*
Hochstein, P., 305, 306, *435*
Hodge, H. C., 89, *254*
Hoefnagel, D., 526, *545*
Hoerster, S. A., 25, *80,* 280, *440,* 550, *554*
Hoff, H., 207, *258*
Hoffer, A., 48, 64, 65, 66, 78, 79, 91, 100, 102, 116, 124, 125, 129, 136, 149, 157, 158, 163, 169, 180, 181, 183, 184, 188, 190, 195, 196, 202, 207, 209, 210, 214, 215, 217, 220, 223, 225, 227, 229, 233, 235, 253, 255, 256, 257, *258, 261, 264,* 268, 276, 278, 281, 284, 285, 290, 293, 296, 300, 306, 313, 315, 319, 320, 321, 322, 325, 326, 327, 328, 333, 335, 336, 337, 342, 343, 348, 363, 387, 398, 400, 415, 419, 420, 421, *437, 439, 440, 441,* 489, 495, 499, 506, 507, 508, 509, *512, 513, 514, 515,* 523, 540, 543, *545,* 564, 574, 592
Hofmann, A., 85, 88, 89, 93, 238, *258, 264,* 480, 486, 487, 493, 495, *511, 513*
Hofmann, G., 207, *253*
Hogben, L., 202, *258*
Holan, G., 538, *545*
Holliday, P. D., 340, *441*
Hollister, L. E., 25, 78, 114, 128, 139, *258,* 489, 490, 493, 494, 498, 499, *513*
Holman, C. B., 314, *441*
Holmberg, G., 501, *513*
Holmes, R., 527, *545*
Holtz, P., 278, 289, *437*
Honegger, C. G., 535, *545*
Honegger, R., 535, *545*
Horackova, E., 314, 397, *436*
Horita, A., 487, *513*
Horning, E. C., 451, 455, 458, *512*
Horwitt, M. K., 327, *438*
Hoskins, R. G., 300, 302, 319, *438*
Hosko, M. J., 572, *592*
Housepian, E. M., 92, *262*
Howes, B. C., 455, *512*
Hoya, W. K., 534, *545*
Hsia, D. Y., 304, *438*

Hubbard, A. M., 137, 159, 160, 163, *258, 260*
Hughes, M. A., 152, 163, *263*
Hummoller, F. L., 582, *593*
Hundevadt, E., 274, *441*
Hunt, W. A., 63, 64, 76, *79*
Hunter, W., 39, *79*
Hunzinger, W. A., 315, *440*
Hupka, S., 299, *435*
Husdan, H., 295, *435*
Hutcheon, D. E., 269, 295, 296, *438*
Huxley, A., 13, 78, 236, *258,* 461, *513*
Hyde, R. W., 90, 91, 128, 139, 178, 222, 233, *258, 262, 264,* 277, *437,* 489, *514*

I

Ichniowski, C. T., 336, *439*
Igert, C., 40, *80*
Inchiosa, M. A., 273, *438*
Ingraham, L. J., 213, *257*
Inskip, W. M., 446, *513*
Iordanis, K. A., 332, 333, *438,* 585, *592*
Irvine, D., 102, 157, 180, 233, *259,* 336, *438*
Isbell, H., 30, *81,* 86, 93, 139, 176, 206, 208, 250, *257, 259, 262,* 463, 464, 493, 495, *513, 514*
Izumi, K., 234, *259*

J

Jackson, D. D., 231, *259*
Jackson, J. A., 585, *591*
Jacob, J., 565, *592*
Jacobsen, E., 528, *545*
Jacobsohn, D., 219, *257*
Jacobson, G., 542, *545*
Jacques, L. B., 95, *260*
James, W., 125, *259*
Jameson, D., 217, *264*
Janiger, O., 196, *259*
Jantz, H., 343, 348, *438, 441*
Jarman, R. C., 234, *259*
Jarvik, M. E., 103, 114, 120, 123, 208, *253, 259,* 558, 579, 586, *590, 592*
Jenkins, I. M., 326, *442*
Jenney, E. H., 91, 139, *261, 262,* 465, 466, 467, 508, *513, 514*
Jensen, H., 451, *513*
Jensen, S. E., 115, 163, 195, *259*
Jimenez, F. G., 85, 252, *262*

Johnson, C., 131, 149, 150, *255*
Johnson, D. M., 526, *545*
Johnson, J. B., 482, *513*
Johnson, J. J., 579, *590*
Johnson, N. M., 451, 455, 458, *512*
Johnson, P., 299, 305, 332, *440*
Johnson, P. C., 289, *434*
Johnson, R., 552, *554*
Jovino, A., 563, *593*

K

Kablson, G., 219, *257*
Kafka, A., 588, *592*
Kahan, I., 183, 233, 258, 300, 400, *437*
Kayitani, F., 318, *441*
Kalberer, F., 487, 488, *511, 513*
Kaliman, P. A., 332, 339, *438, 441*
Kalnitzky, G., 288, 339, *436*
Kanai, T., 574, *592*
Kast, E. C., 90, 236, *259*, 466, *513*
Kato, L., 317, *438*
Katz, M. M., 199, 200, 201, 203, *255*
Katzenelbogen, S., 139, 150, *259*
Kauffman, D., 25, *77*
Kaufman, M. R., 114, 123, *253, 260*
Kaufmann, H., 340, 341, *438*
Kavierznieva, E. D., 581, *591*
Keller, D. L., 561, 564, *592*
Keller, F., 61, 62, *78*
Kelley, R., 539, *545*
Kelm, H., 115, 227, *259*
Kendel, S. I., 56, *80*
Kenna, J. C., 99, 100, 120, 145, *259, 263*
Kenyon, M., 328, 342, *437*
Kety, S. S., 215, *264*, 325, *438*, 446, *513, 514*
Key, B. J., 579, 583, *592*
Khairallah, P. A., 462, 477, 478, 479, *513*, 582, *593*
Khalidi, A. I., 139, *257*
Kieland, W. F., 85, 240, *255*
Killam, K. F., 508, *514*
Kimble, J. P., 310, *439*
Kindwall, J. A., 300, *435*
Kinross-Wright, V. J., 86, 250, *259*
Kisch, B., 332, *438*
Klee, G. D., 104, 120, 122, 123, 127, 207, 209, 210, 231, *253, 254, 259, 263, 265*
Klohs, M. W., 61, 62, *78*

Kluver, H., 4, 9, 11, 16, *78*, 106, *259*
Knauer, A., 4, 14, *78*
Kneebone, G. M., 490, *513*
Kobel, H., 486, 487, 493, *511, 512*
Kobrinckaio, O. J., 279, *434*, 550, *553*
Kobrinska, Q. J., 586, *591*
Koch, E., 340, 341, *438*
Koch, J. H., 303, *440*, 458, *512*
Koella, W. P., 26, *80*, 547, 548, 552, *553, 554*
Koelle, G. B., 282, 286, 332, 333, 337, *434, 438*
Konev, C. B., 279, *434*, 550, *533*
Konzett, H., 492, *516*
Kornblueth, W., 273, *441*
Kornetsky, C., 114, 123, 215, *253, 264*
Kornetsky, E., 559, *591*
Korzoff, B. A., 332, *438*
Koschtojantz, C. S., 558, *593*
Koshlyak, T. V., *438*
Kotsoff, B. A., 581, *591*
Kovaleva, V. I., 56, *79*
Krall, A. R., 273, *438*
Krantz, J. C., 49, 50, 51, *81*
Kreis, W., 488, *513*
Kreuter, W. F., 25, *80*
Krichevskaya, A. A., 288, 339, *436*
Krupp, P., 312, *438*, 570, *592*
Krus, D. M., 139, 209, 210, *254, 259, 264*
Kuchino, E. B., 279, 332, 333, *434, 438*, 550, *553*, 581, 585, *591, 592*
Kukita, A., 287, *435*
Kuna, A., 326, *436*
Kuntzman, R., 219, *255*, 505, *511*
Kuo-Chang, K., 75, *76*
Kurland, A., 139, 206, *255*

L

Laborit, H., 289, *438*, 565, *592*
La Burt, H. A., 295, *440*
Lagravere, T. A., 457, *512*
Lagutina, N. I., 569, *592*
Laidlaw, B. D., 285, *436*
Laidlaw, P. P., 449, *513*
Laird, A. H., 21, *79*
Lam, K., 74, *81*
Lambert, M., 469, 471, *513*, 570, *592*
Lambot, H., 339, *435*
Landau, W., 92, *256*, 576, *591*
Landis, C., 63, 64, *79*, 131, 226, *259*

Landrin, A., *513*
Landrin, E., 468, *511*
Landtsheer, L., 339, 342, *435*
Lang, W. J., *76*, 470, 472, 478, 479, 502, *512*, 569, *592*
Langemann, H., 282, 286, 332, 333, *438*
Langs, R. J., 124, 128, *260*
Lapteva, N. N., 552, *554*
Laricheva, K. A., 569, *592*
Latham, L. K., 307, 308, *436*, 549, 552, 553
Lauer, J. W., 446, *513*
Launay, J., 567, 569, *590*
Laverty, S. G., 139, *254*
Lawrence, E. P., 451, 455, *512*
Lazarte, J. A., 314, *441*
Lea, A. J., 282, 295, *438*
Leach, B. E., 223, 257, 287, 313, 314, 315, 325, 327, 328, 363, *434*, *437*, *438*, 551, 553, *554*, 570, *592*
LeBlanc, J., 296, 320, *438*
Lebovits, B. Z., 139, *259*, *261*, 536, *545*
Lecomte, J., 339, 340, 342, *435*, *438*
Le de Baran, M. D., 576, 583, *593*
Lees, H., 542, *545*
Leemreis, W., 563, *591*
Legge, J. W., 341, *438*
Lehmann, A., 479, *513*
Lehmann, H. E., 289, 304, 317, 320, *434*, *438*, 541, *544*
Leiberman, J., 105, *256*, 495, *511*
Leiser, H. A., 534, *545*
Lemberg, R., 341, *438*
Lemieux, L., 296, 320, *438*
Lemperiere, T., 139, *256*
Lenard, K., 462, *511*
Lennard, H., 93, *253*
Leon, N., 237, *259*
Lepeschkin, E., 318, *440*
Lerner, A. B., 285, *435*, 478, *513*
Leserre, N., 91, *257*
Lettre, H., 316, *438*
Leuner, H., 152, *259*
Leupold-Lowenthal, H., 207, *253*
Levine, A., 114, 123, *253*, *260*
Levine, W. G., *511*
Levy, C. K., 26, 33, *80*
Levy, H., 539, *545*
Lewin, L., 1, 3, 4, 47, 57, 59, *79*, 106, *260*, 452, 458, 473, 475, *513*

Lewis, C. S., 584, *592*
Lewis, D., 139, *254*
Lewis, J. L., 24, 79, 213, *260*
Lewis, S. A., 577, *590*
Leyton, G., 73, *79*
Lhamon, W. T., 120, *254*
Lhermitte, F., 567, *591*
Liberson, W. T., 588, *592*
Lichtenheld, F. R., 313, 348, *441*, 573, 593
Lichtenstein, I., *515*
Liddell, D. S., 222, *260*
Liebert, R. S., 139, *260*
Liljekvist, J., 287, *435*
Lindemann, E., 64, 79
Ling, N. S., 322, *439*
Lingjaerde, O., 274, *441*
Lingl, F. A., 544, *546*
Linton, H. B., 124, 128, *260*
Lipmann, F., 273, *440*
Liskowski, L., 457, *512*
Llewellyn, R. C., 27, 43, 44, 79, 92, *261*
Lochner, K. H., 299, 301, 302, *439*
Locke, J., 168, *260*
Logan, C. R., 176, 206, 208, *259*, 464, 514
Lohrenz, J. J., 541, *544*
Loken, F., 274, *441*
Long, E. L., 63, 79
Longo, V. G., 527, *545*, 576, 583, 593
Lorenz, A. A., 184, *264*
Lowenthal, J., 269, 295, 296, *438*
Lozousky, D. V., 552, *554*
Luby, E. D., 326, *436*, 539, 541, 542, *545*, 549, 552, 553
Lucas, C. J., 528, *546*
Lucas, O., 432, *439*
Lucas, O. N., 95, *260*
Lucy, J. D., 295, 320, *439*
Luduena, F. P., 20, 79
Lund, A., 270, 336, 341, *439*
Lushnat, K., 91, *257*
Lynn, E. V., 476, *514*

M

McAdam, W., 128, 157, 206, 213, *261*
McCawley, E. L., 485, 492, *513*
McColl, J. D., 573, *593*
McCormic, W. G., 572, *592*
McCubbin, J. W., 218, *262*

McCulloch, W. S., 522, *545*
McDermott, J. A., 325, *439*
MacDonald, D. C., 137, 160, 163, *260*
MacDonald, J. M., 206, *260*
McFarlane, W. J. G., 311, *439*
McGeer, E. G., 75, *81*, 219, *260*
McGeer, P. L., 75, *81*, 219, *260*
McGlothlin, M. S., 196, 201, *260*
McGlothlin, W. H., 196, 201, *260*
McGough, J. L., 576, 583, *593*
Machover, K., 139, *260*
McIlwain, H., 24, 79, 213, *260*
McIsaac, W. M., 462, 464, 477, 478, 479, *512, 513*, 582, *593*
Maclay, W. S., 150, *257*
Maclean, J. R., 137, 160, 163, *260*
McLennan, H., 560, *591*
McMillan, A., 325, *434*
Maas, J. W., 326, *439*
Maffezzoni, G., 221, *262*
Maffi, G., 586, *593*
Mahler, D. J., 582, *593*
Mahon, M. E., 85, 100, 180, 214, 233, 238, 257, 258, 264, 270, 328, 337, 340, 342, *437, 440*
Maier, N. R. F., 588, *593*
Makita, K., 212, *261*
Malhotra, C. L., 56, 77
Mall, G., 300, *439*
Maloney, W. J. M. A., 4, 14, 79
Man, E. B., 302, *434*
Mandell, A. J., 217, *260*
Manning, R. J., *442*
Manske, R. H. F., 74, 79
Mansour, T. E., 558, *593*
Marcovitz, E., 49, 79
Marcus, D. A., 314, *439*
Margetts, E. L., 544, *545*
Margolis, L. H., 202, *260*
Marion, L., 476, *513*
Markham, S., 123, *260*
Marrazzi, A. S., 26, 32, 61, *78, 79, 80*, 92, 220, *260*, 294, *439*, 552, *554*, 575, 580, 587, 588, *593*
Marshall, W. H., 92, *256*, 508, *514*, **576**, *591*
Martens, S., 210, 215, 223, *260, 261*, 314, 315, 362, 363, *434, 437, 438, 439*, 550, 551, 552, 553, *554*, 570, *593*
Marti-Ibanez, F., 295, *440*

Martin, G., 322, *439*
Martin, G. J., 336, *439*
Martin, J., 176, *261*
Marti-Tusquets, J. L., 139, 207, *262*
Maslova, A. F., 340, *439*
Maslow, A. H., 155, 201, *261*
Mason, H. S., 280, 281, 287, 322, 337, *439*
Matefi, L., 40, 79
Matsuura, H., 318, *441*
Matthews, R. J., 466, 467, *513*
Mattok, G. L., 220, *261*, 268, 278, 334, *437, 439*
Matussek, N., 208, *261*
Maupin, B., 503, *513*
Maxwell, G. M., 490, *513*
Mayer-Gross, W., 4, 14, 79, 128, 157, 206, 208, 213, *257, 261*, 348, *439*
Mazone, H., 491, *511*
Mazur, A., 308, 333, 339, *436*
Meduna, L. J., 536, *544, 545*
Mefferd, R. B., 310, *439*
Meirowsky, E., 280, 332, 333, *439*
Mekler, L. B., 552, *554*
Melander, B., 209, 210, 215, 223, *260, 261*, 315, 316, 362, 363, *439*, 550, 552, 553, *554*, 570, *593*
Menon, M. K., 56, 77
Meriwether, B. P., 273, *440*
Merlis, S., 39, 77, 79, 93, *253*, 455, 466, 469, *515*
Merz, H., 451, *516*
Meyer, A. C., 326, *438*
Meyer, B. J., 326, *438*
Meyer, H. J., 49, 62, 79
Meyer-Burg, J., 62, 79
Meyerhoff, O., 273, 307, *439*
Mickle, W. A., 27, 43, 44, 79, 92, *261*
Miller, A., 300, *436*
Miller, A. I., 104, 207, 210, *256, 261*
Miller, E., 16, 79
Miller, N. E., 296, *439*, 555, *593*
Milner, P., 586, *593*
Mil'shtein, G. I., 569, *592*
Milton, A. S., 444, 487, *511*
Miner, E. J., 30, *81*, 463, 464, 493, *513, 514*
Mironychev, A. V., 47, 77
Miner, E. J., 139, 259, *262*
Misrahy, G., 574, *592*

Mitchell, G. D., 312, *439*
Mitchell, S. W., 3, 79, 106, *265*
Miura, T., 212, *261*
Miya, T. S., 25, *76*
Mogar, R. E., 152, 163, 196, *261, 263*
Mogenson, G., 587, *593*
Mokrasch, J. C., *81*
Mollaret, P., 290, *439*
Moller, A. G., 21, 79
Monnier, M., 312, *438*, 570, *592*
Monroe, R. R., 27, 43, 44, 79, 542, *545,*
    576, *593*
Monsallier, J. F., 290, *439*
Montanari, G., 127, *264*
Montano, C., 332, *434*
Monroe, R. R., 92, *261*
Moody, A. C., 561, *593*
Mooney, J., 3, 79
Moore, R. M., 458, *512*
Moran, L. J., 310, *439*
Morell, A. G., 314, 326, *441*
Morgan, F. P., 3, 79, 80
Morgenstein, F. S., 542, *545*
Morin, R., 213, *255*
Morimoto, K., 178, *264*
Morris, H. H., 275, *434*
Morselli, G. E., 29, 79
Motskus, D. V., 56, 79
Motzel, W., 451, *516*
Moyer, J. H., 539, *545*
Mudd, S. H., 273, *440*
Mukerji, B., 35, *80*, 562, *593*
Muller, J., 20, *80*
Murphree, H. B., 91, 139, 206, 207, 210,
    257, 261, 262, 465, 466, 467, *514*
Murphree, O. D., 589, *593*
Myers, J. M., 275, *434*
Myers, R. D., 296, *435*

N

Nagler, S. H., 46, *78*
Nagy, P. C., 459, *511*
Nakahara, A., 212, *261*
Nakajima, H., 566, *591, 594*
Nakazwa, T., 212, *261*
Nandy, K., 222, 225, *261*
Navin, J. A., 579, *590*
Nelson, A. A., 63, 79
Nerenberg, C., 270, *437*
Nesselhof, W., 335, *437*

Nevin, S., 524, *546*
Nichols, F., 169, *261*
Nicolas-Charles, P., 139, *256*, 493, *511*
Nicolaus, R. A., 280, 287, 311, 337, *439*
Nicolson, G. A., 289, 311, *436, 439*
Niswander, G. D., 312, *439*, 547, *554*
Norkina, L. N., 569, *592*
Norton, S., 571, *593*
Noval, J. J., 295, 363, *439*, 570, *593*
Nuhfer, P. A., 534, *545*
Nunes, E. P., 139, *261*
Nye, S. W., 289, *436*
Nytch, P. D., 74, *76*

O

Oakley, R. S., 580, *593*
Ochs, S., 27, 79, 577, *593*
O'Connell, F. D., 476, *514*
Oesterberg, A. C., 565, *592*
Olds, J., 586, *593*
Oliva, L., 237, *261*
Olsen, N. W., 214, *262*
Olson, R. E., 445, *514*
O'Neill, F. J., 93, *253*
O'Reilly, P. O., 163, 164, 174, 207,
    229, *261*
Ormitz, E. M., 580, *592*
Ornitz, E. M., 30, 77
Orstrum, A., 307, *439*
Osaki, S., 325, *439*
Osinskaya, V. O., 340, *441*
Osmond, H., 36, 48, 65, 78, 79, 84, 86,
    91, 100, 102, 106, 110, 121, 124, 128,
    129, 132, 134, 135, 157, 163, 181, 183,
    195, 202, 215, 217, 223, 225, 227,
    233, 234, 238, 241, *258, 261, 264,*
    268, 276, 284, 285, 293, 296, 300,
    306, 313, 321, 322, 325, 328, 343,
    348, 350, 363, 400, 420, 421, *435,*
    437, 439, 441, 489, 495, 499, *512,*
    540, 543, *545*
Osterberg, A. C., 32, 78
Ostfeld, A. M., 139, *259, 261*, 314, *439,*
    536, *544, 545*
Otey, M. C., 444, *512*
Ott, H., 486, *513*
Ovshinsky, S. R., 308, *439*, 520, *546*
Owens, H., 26, 78, 223, *262*
Ozek, M., *439*

P

Page, I. H., 188, 217, 218, *261, 262,* 457, 462, 464, 472, 477, 478, 479, 502, 503, *511, 513, 514, 515,* 582, *593*
Page, J. A., 64, 65, 79, *261,* 506, *514*
Palmer, M., 326, *435*
Palthe, P. M. van Wulfften, 369, *440*
Paradies, A. M., 458, 473, 475, *512*
Parameswaran, K. N., 35, 77
Park, C. R., 273, *440*
Park, J. H., 273, *440*
Parker, C. M., 217, *264*
Parker, J. M., 44, 79, 568, *593*
Parkman, E. W., 63, *75*
Pastan, I., 299, 305, 332, *440*
Pataky, I., 462, *514*
Patzig, B., 23, *76*
Paul, E., 588, *592*
Paul, I. H., 124, *260*
Paulsen, J. A., 498, *513*
Pawloski, A. A., 582, *593*
Payne, R. B., 50, *79*
Payza, A. N., 270, 315, 316, 321, 326, 327, 328, 335, 336, 340, 342, *437, 440,* 507, 508, *514*
Peck, R. E., 320, *440*
Peerman, D., 133, *261*
Pennell, R. B., 547, 548, 550, 552, 553, *554*
Pennes, H. H., 38, 78, 128, 139, 144, *258, 261,* 476, 477, *514,* 538, *546*
Perles, R., 567, 569, *590*
Peretz, D. I., 45, 79, 370, *440*
Perezamador, M. C., 85, 252, *262*
Perlin, S., 215, *264*
Perot, P. L., 294, *440*
Perrimond-Trouchet, R., 289, *438,* 565, *592*
Perring, G. M., 340, *441*
Perrot, E., 475, *514*
Perry, T. L., 458, *514*
Peterova, E., 321, *441*
Peters, J. E., 589, *593*
Petersen, M. C., 314, *441*
Petrzilka, T. H., 486, *513*
Petsche, H., 576, *594*
Pfeifer, A. K., 462, *514*
Pfeiffer, C. C., 91, 92, 104, 139, *253, 256, 257, 261, 262,* 444, 446, 465, 466, 467, 508, *513, 514,* 538, *546*

Phibbs, B., 527, *545*
Phipps, E., 218, *263*
Phisalix, M. C., 469, 471, *514*
Photiades, H., 100, *253*
Pichot, P., 128, 139, *255, 256,* 493, *511*
Pierce, C. M., 95, *265,* 566, *594*
Pigulevskii, G. V., 56, *79*
Pincus, G. G., 209, *254*
Pletscher, A., 28, 74, 79, 217, *254,* 465, 479, *512, 514*
Pocidalo, J. J., 290, *439*
Pogrund, R. S., 432, *435*
Polanyi, M., 198, *262*
Polatin, P., 144, *258*
Pollard, J. C., 541, *546*
Pollin, W., 446, *514*
Poloni, A., 209, 221, *262*
Pomerantz, S., 21, *78*
Pon, N. G., 305, *440*
Pool, J. L., 92, *262*
Porter, C. C., 322, *440*
Posner, H. S., 456, *516*
Pouchet, D., 469, *514*
Power, F. B., 49, *79*
Prankova, S., 122, *257,* 349, 351, *436,* 584, *592*
Prentiss, D. W., 3, *79, 80*
Price, W. E., 289, *436*
Prins, D. A., 470, *514*
Prockop, D. J., 445, 446, *515*
Purpura, D. P., 92, *262*
Prusmack, J. J., 498, *513*
Przic, R., 490, *511*
Pscheidt, G. R., 217, *255,* 335, *440,* 468, *515*
Putney, F., 463, *515*

Q

Quastel, J. H., 24, 43, *80*
Quetin, A. M., 139, *256*

R

Raab, W., 318, *440*
Rachow, H., 277, *441*
Radema, W., 273, *440*
Rafaelsen, O. J., 25, *80*
Rafferty, T., 552, *554*
Rajotte, P., 25, *77*
Ramsbottom, J., 453, *514*
Ramsay, R. W., 115, *259*

Randall, A. H., *262*
Randall, L. O., 273, 307, *439, 440*
Rangier, M., 281, 340, *440*
Ransohoff, J., 92, *262*
Ratcliffe, J., 21, *80*
Rawnsley, K., 150, *253*
Rawson, R. W., 303, *440*
Ray, O. S., 32, 61, 78, *80*, 587, 588, *593*
Raymond, J. C., 528, *546*
Raymond-Hamet, M., 471, 475, *514, 515*
Read, D., 562, *591*
Redlich, D., 458, *514*
Rees, L., 275, *440*
Reich, G., 163, 207, 229, *261*
Reider, H. P., 557, *593*
Reilly, R. H., 508, *514*
Reio, L., 340, *440*
Reiss, M., 302, *440*
Reko, B. P., 482, *514*
Renner, U., 470, *514*
Reti, L., 16, 17, 19, *80*
Rice, E. W., 311, *440*
Rice, W. B., 573, *593*
Richards, T. W., 29, 42, *80, 81*
Richter, D., 21, *80*, 269, 273, 331, *436*
Rigdon, R. H., 281, 333, 340, *440*
Rinaldi, F., 206, *262*, 527, 532, 535, *544, 546*
Rinehart, R. K., 470, *515*
Rinkel, M., 41, *80*, 90, 91, 105, 115, 128, 129, 139, 222, 233, *256, 258, 262*, 277, *437*, 489, 493, 495, 498, *511, 514*
Ritzel, G., 316, *440*
Roberts, B. J., 466, 467, *513*
Robertson, M. C., 91, *262*
Robey, A., 41, *80*, 498, *514*
Robie, T. R., 466, *514*
Robinson, W., 552, *554*
Rodnight, R., 77, 457, *514*
Rolo, A., 139, *253*, 561, *590*
Rome, H. P., 40, 41, 43, *80*, 91, 206, *263*
Rosen, E., 563, *593*
Rosenbaum, G., 539, 541, 542, *545*
Rosenberg, D. E., 139, *262*, 463, 464, *514*
Rosenquist, N., 498, *513*
Rosenthal, M. J., 415, *435*
Roskam, J., 332, 384, *435*

Rosner, B., 580, *592*
Ross, S., 555, *590*
Rostafinski, M., 128, *262*
Roston, S., 279, 285, 332, *440*
Rothlin, E., 89, 93, 95, 221, *254, 262*, 471, *514, 515*, 566, *593*
Rothman, S., 285, *440*
Roueche, B., 525, *546*
Roughly, T. C., 452, *515*
Rovetta, P., 27, *80*
Rowntree, D. W., 524, *546*
Rudolph, G. G., 214, *262*
Ruiz-Ogara, C., 139, 207, *262*
Rummele, W., 486, 490, 494, *515*
Runge, T. M., 25, *80*, 280, *440*, 550, *554*
Rutschmann, J., 257, 487, 488, *511, 513*
Rusby, H. H., 473, *515*
Russell, I. S., 27, *79*, 577, *593*
Rysanek, K., 528, 529, *546*
Rytomaa, T., 317, *434*

S

Sacchi, U., 574, *591*
Sachs, E., 547, *554*
Sachs, I., 31, 48, *78*
Sackler, A. M., 223, *262*, 295, *440*
Sackler, M. D., 295, *440*
Sackler, R. R., 295, *440*
Safford, W. E., 237, *262*, 450, 482, *515*
Sai-Halasz, A., 460, 462, *515*
Salmoiraghi, G. C., 218, *262*, 472, *515*
Salanski, J., 558, *593*
Salna, M. E., 295, *435*
Salomon, K., 21, *80*
Salvay, A. H., 49, *79*
Sampaio, B. A., 40, *80*
Sanchez, A. J., 43, *81*
Sanders, B. E., 322, *440*
Sandison, R. A., 150, 151, 206, 232, *262, 263*
Sandler, M., 209, *254*
Sandoval, A. L., 471, *515*
Sankar, D. B., 90, 218, 221, 223, *263*
Sankar, D. V. S., 90, 178, 214, 218, 221, 223, 233, *254, 263*
Santesson, C. G., *263*
Saravis, C. A., 547, 548, 552, 553, *554*
Sargant, W., 201, 230, *263*
Sargent, T., 45, *80*
Sarradin, J., 285, *434*

Satanove, A., 289, *440*
Sato, K., 212, *261*
Satory, E., 462, *514*
Saunders, J. C., 326, *440*
Sauri, J. J., 139, *263*
Savage, C., 127, 137, 139, 150, 152, 163, 165, 196, 201, 206, 232, 255, *261*, *263*
Savage, E., 137, 152, *263*
Sawyer, C. H., 219, *263*
Saxena, A., 35, *80*, 562, *593*
Schain, R. J., 573, *593*
Schaltenbrand, G., 74, 75, 77
Schatzberg-Porath, G., 464, *511*
Scheid, K. F., 308, *440*
Scheinberg, I. H., 314, 326, *441*
Scheuing, M. R., 299, 301, 302, *439*
Schlossmann, H., 332, *434*
Schneider, J. A., 470, 471, *515*, 570, 586, *591*, *593*
Schneider, R., 223, *264*, 278, 313, 398, 415, *441*, 509, *515*, 523, *546*
Schopp, R. T., 25, *80*
Schmiege, G. R., 149, 232, *263*
Schueler, F. W., 24, 43, *80*
Schultes, R. E., 48, 50, *80*, 85, 239, *263*, 451, 474, 482, *515*, 528, *546*
Schwarz, B. E., 40, 41, 43, *80*, 91, 206, *263*, 313, 314, 348, *441*
Schwartz, B. I., 573, *593*
Schwartz, E., 588, *592*
Scott, B. D., 64, 78
Scott, D., 285, *437*
Seager, L. D., 574, *594*
Searle, G. D., 573, *594*
Seay, P. H., 466, 467, *512*
Sedman, G., 99, 100, 120, 145, *259*, *263*
Seevers, M. H., 22, 76
Selye, H., 219, *263*
Sem-Jacobsen, C. W., 314, *441*
Senf, R., 326, *436*, 549, 552, *553*
Serko, A., 4, *80*
Sero, I., 472, *515*
Share, I., 539, *545*
Sharma, J. D., 56, *77*, *80*
Shattock, F. M., 299, *441*
Shaw, E. N., 212, 217, *265*
Shaw, K. N. F., 325, *434*, 458, 479, *501*, *514*, *516*
Sheldon, W., 105, *263*

Sheldon, W. H., 306, *434*
Shellard, E. J., 252, *263*
Shelton, J., *263*
Sherwood, J. N., 137, 164, 196, *263*
Sherwood, S. L., 313, *435*, 522, 523, 524, *545*, *546*, 572, *591*
Shore, P. A., 217, *254*, 505, *511*, 567, *593*
Shorr, E., 308, 332, 333, 339, *436*
Shulgin, A. T., 45, 55, *80*
Siegel, G. J., 273, *438*
Siegel, M., 547, *554*
Sigg, E. B., 470, 471, *515*, 570, *593*
Silva, F., 552, *554*
Silverstein, A. B., 120, 122, 123, 127, 253, *263*, 265
Simmons, C., 21, 78, 326, *435*
Simonson, E., 370, *441*
Simpson, C. R., 84, *263*
Sjovall, T., 307, *441*
Skaug, O. E., 307, *439*
Sklarofsky, A. B., 139, 208, 209, *253*, 560, *590*
Slater, I. H., *254*
Slater, P. E., 178, *264*
Sleeper, F. H., 300, *438*
Sloane, B., 139, *264*
Slocombe, A. G., 312, *441*
Slotkin, J. S., 153, 155, *264*
Slotta, K. H., 20, *80*
Smith, A. A., 339, *436*
Smith, B., 445, 446, *515*
Smith, C. M., 65, *80*, 136, 158, 160, 163, 195, 207, 229, 255, *264*, 328, *437*
Smith, E. V. C., 322, *440*
Smith, K., 561, *593*
Smith, M. G., 4, *80*
Smith, P., 21, *80*
Smythies, J. R., 21, 26, 33, 36, 45, 78, 79, *80*, 129, *258*, *261*, 268, 293, 313, 321, 325, 343, 370, *437*, *439*, *440*, 495, *513*, 543, *545*, 565, *593*
Snedeker, E. H., 25, 77
Sohler, A., 363, *439*, 570, *593*
Sokoloff, L., 215, *264*
Sollero, L., 218, *262*
Solms, H., 87, 93, *264*
Solomon, H. C., 90, 91, 128, 129, 139, 262, 489, *514*
Solomon, K., 38, *81*

Sommer, R., 227, *265*, 350, *441*
Sonne, E., 528, *545*
Spath, E., 17, 19, *80*
Speck, L. B., 28, *80*, 568, *593*
Spector, E., 21, 23, *81*
Spector, S., 505, *511*
Spencer, A. M., 150, 151, 178, *264*
Spiegel, H. E., 25, *77*
Spoerlin, M. T., 331, *442*
Sprince, H., 217, *264*, *515*
Stache, J., 139, *253*, 561, *590*
Staub, H., 316, *440*
Stavrus, D., 547, *554*
Steel, J. D., 458, *512*
Stefaniuk, B., 110, 121, *264*
Stein, H., 4, 14, *79*
Stein, S. N., 294, *440*
Steinberg, H., 543, *546*
Steiner, W. G., 468, *515*
Steinmetz, E. F., 57, 61, 62, *81*
Stennett, R. G., 326, *441*
Stern, P., 477, *515*
Stevenson, I. P., 29, 42, 43, *80*, *81*, 232, *264*
Stewart, C. N., 586, *593*
Stockings, G. T., 4, *81*
Stokes, A. B., 300, *436*
Stolaroff, G. V., 322, *434*
Stolaroff, M. J., 137, 164, 196, *263*
Stoll, W. A., 83, 88, 103, 128, 139, *264*
Stoll, W. G., 470, *514*
Stone, J. E., 574, *594*
Streifler, M., 273, *441*
Stuckenhoff, H., 527, *545*
Stumf, C., 576, *591*, *594*
Sturtevant, F. M., 572, 573, *594*
Suffolk, S. F., 304, *434*
Sulkovitch, H., 340, *441*
Sulser, F., 507, *515*
Sundin, T., 297, *441*
Swan, H. J. C., 64, *81*
Sweat, M. L., 332, *441*
Sykes, E. A., 73, *80*
Szara, S., 40, *81*, 443, 459, 463, 465, *515*
Szatmari, A., 223, *264*, 278, 313, 398, 415, *441*, 509, *515*, 523, *546*
Szczekala, Z., 329, 335, *434*
Szepesey, A., 280, *441*

T

Tabachnick, I. I., 222, *264*
Taber, W. A., 85, 87, 238, *264*
Taeschler, M., 492, *516*
Takahashi, H., 318, 332, *441*
Takahashi, Y., *441*
Takeo, Y., 26, *81*
Takkunen, R., 295, *433*
Takumi, A., 209, *265*
Tamburo, J., 571, *593*
Tasher, D. C., 535, 536, *546*
Tatum, J. C., 296, *441*
Taubmann, G., 348, *441*
Tausig, T., 508, *514*
Taylor, D. W., 289, *441*
Teaschler, M., 565, *594*
Tedeschi, D. H., 449, *515*
Tedeschi, R. E., 449, *515*
Teller, D. N., 25, *77*
Tenney, A. M., 306, *434*
Terrill, J., 110, 165, *264*
Thale, T., 21, 38, *80*
Thomas, W. D., 95, *265*
Thompson, R. H. S., 221, *264*
Thuillier, J., 566, *591*, *594*
Thurman, N., 25, *80*, *440*, 550, *554*
Tickner, A., 221, *264*
Tislow, R., 572, *592*
Titus, D. C., 322, *440*
Titus, E. O., 25, *77*
Tobin, J. M., 184, *264*
Toekes, M. I., 61, *78*
Tokusawa, K., 318, *441*
Tolan, E. J., 544, *546*
Tolentino, I., 46, *81*
Tonini, G., 127, 221, *264*
Tozian, L. S., 312, *441*
Tremere, A. W., 84, *264*
Trendelenburg, V., 220, *264*
Trevathan, R. D., 296, *441*
Tripod, J., 42, 44, *81*, 565, *594*
Trout, D. L., 560, *594*
Troxler, F., 486, *513*
Truitt, E. B., 49, 50, 51, *81*
Tsaune, M. K., 550, *554*
Tscherter, H., 85, *258*
Tsujiyama, Y., 212, *261*
Tuchweber, B., 219, *263*
Tui, C., 295, *440*

Turner, W. J., 93, *253,* 455, 466, 469, *515,* 560, 561, *594*
Tyburczyk, W., 329, 335, *434*
Tyhurst, J. S., 198, *264*
Tyler, D. B., 371, *441*

U

Udenfriend, S., 325, *435*
Uhr, L., 541, *546*
Unger, S. M., 134, 201, *264*
Umbreit, W. W., 561, 564, *592*
Upenietse, M., 550, *554*
Urbina, M., 237, *264*
Ursin, H., 576, *594*
Utevskii, A. M., 340, 341, *441*

V

Vallbo, S., 215, *260, 261,* 315, 362, 363, *439,* 550, 552, *554,* 570, *594*
Van Andel, H., 448, *511*
Van Demark, N. L., 273, *438*
Van der Hoeven, T., 566, *594*
Vane, J. R., 455, *515*
Van Meter, W. G., 26, 78, 465, 467, *515*
van Oordt, G. T., 563, *591*
Van Ophuijsen, J. H. W., 295, *440*
Vazquez, A. J., 457, *512*
Veech, R. L., 340, *441*
Vencovsky, E., 321, *441*
Verideaux, G., 567, *591*
Vernadakis, A., 278, *442*
Vester, J. W., 445, *514*
Vic-Dupont, 290, *439*
Villalba, A. M. B., 474, 475, 477, *515*
Villasana, A., 332, *434*
Vinar, O., 529, *546*
Vinarova, M., 529, *546*
Vincent, D., 472, *515*
Vining, L. C., 85, 87, *264*
Visotsky, H. M., 139, *259, 261,* 536, *545*
Vitek, V., 122, 257, 314, 349, 351, 397, *436,* 528, 529, *546,* 584, *592*
Vizy, E., 462, *514*
Vogel, V. H., 43, *81*
Vogt, M., 23, *81,* 573, *592*
Vojtechovsky, M., 122, 257, 314, 349, 351, 397, *436,* 528, 529, *546,* 584, *592*
von Euler, U. S., 535, *546*
von Ferdinand, F., 570, *594*

W

Wada, J. A., 75, *81,* 219, *260,* 574, 581, 584, *594*
Waelsch, H., 277, *441*
Wagner, B. M., 63, *75,* 253
Wagner, F. L., 273, *438*
Wajzer, J., 331, *441*
Wakim, K. G., 313, 348, *441,* 573, *593*
Wakoh, T., 300, *441*
Walaas, E., 550, *554*
Walaas, O., 274, *441,* 550, *554*
Walaszek, E. J., 218, 220, *255,* 449, 456, *511, 515*
Waldrop, F. N., 456, *516*
Walker, D., 458, *514*
Walker, J. W., 128, 157, 206, 213, *261*
Walls, F., 471, *515*
Wapner, S., 139, 210, *259, 260, 264*
Ward, J., 335, *442*
Wasson, R. G., 126, *264,* 480, 481, 482, 484, 485, *515*
Wasson, V. P., 126, *264,* 480, 481, 482, *515*
Watermann, C. E., 122, *253*
Watson, G., 370, *442*
Watson, W. J., 289, 290, *442*
Watts, J., 507, *515*
Waud, R. A., 74, *81*
Waxenberg, S. E., 114, 123, *253*
Weber, L. J., 487, *513*
Weber, R., 25, 77, 157, *256*
Webster, G. R., 221, *264*
Weckowicz, T. E., 112, 226, 227, 234, 265, 295, *442,* 462, *516,* 570, 580, 585, *594*
Weeren, J. T. H., 369, *440*
Weider, A., 127, *254*
Weidley, E., 581, *591*
Weidmann, H., 490, 492, *516*
Weil-Malherbe, H., 222, *260,* 456, *516*
Weinstein, S., *442*
Weintraub, W., 104, 122, 207, 209, 210, 254, 259, 265
Weiss, B., 559, *590, 594*
Weltman, A. S., *223, 262*
Wende, Van Der, C., 331, *432*
Werner, H., 139, *260*
West, E., 84, *263*
West, L. J., 95, *265,* 566, *594*
Westermann, E., 278, 289, *437*

Weyl, B., 128, 150, *265*
Wheatley, A. H. M., 24, 43, *80*
Whitaker, L. H., 152, 207, *265*
Whitelaw, J. D. A., 150, 151, 206, *263*
Whittier, J. R., 326, *436*
Whittlesey, J. R. B., 196, 204, *256*
Widlocher, D., 566, *594*
Wiedorn, W. S., 316, 335, *442*
Wieland, T., 451, *516*
Wikler, A., 26, *81*, 139, 176, 208, *259*, 493, *513*, 527, *546*
Wilber, C. W., 562, *594*
Wilder, J., 103, *265*
Wilkinson, S., 458, *516*
Williams, H. L., 104, 207, 210, *256*
Williams, R. E., 61, 78
Wilson, A., 524, *546*, 588, *592*
Wilson, D. L., 220, *261*, 268, 334, *437*, 439
Wilson, E. A., 178, *256*
Winitz, M., 444, *512*, *516*
Winkle, E. V., 22, 77
Winter, C. A., 552, *554*, 568, 580, *594*
Wisansky, W. A., 336, *439*
Witkop, B., 22, 33, 77, 89, *253*, *256*
Witt, P. N., 36, *76*, 492, *511*, 556, 557, *591*, *594*
Wittman, P., 275, *442*

Wojicki, H., 564, *592*
Wolbach, A. B., 30, *81*, 139, *259*, *262*, 493, *513*
Wolff, H. G., 127, *254*
Wood, J. D., 289, 290, *442*, 574, *594*
Woodbury, D. M., 278, *442*
Woods, L. A., 22, *76*
Woolley, D. W., 212, 216, *265*, 479, 489, 501, *516*, 564, 566, *594*
Wrinch, J., 75, *81*, 581, *594*

Y

Yakugaku, K., 582, *594*
Yamada, T., 209, *265*
Yasunobu, K. T., 336, *442*
Yen, H. C. Y., 477, *511*, 564, *591*
Yim, G. K. W., 25, *76*
Yoshitake, J., 538, *545*
Yuwiler, A., 326, *442*

Z

Zaleschuk, J., 315, 316, 326, 327, 328, 440
Zeller, E. A., 446, *513*, *516*
Zender, K., 222, *265*
Zetler, G., 224, *255*
Zsigmond, E. K., 221, 222, *265*, 490, *516*
Zurgiligen, B. A., 275, *434*

Subject Index

A

Acetylcholine, 522–523
  adsorption of, 518–519
  brain function and, 522
  diffusion of, 518
  intracerebral effect of, 572, 574
  LSD and, 222
  storage of, 518
  synthesis of, 517–518
Acetylcholinesterase, 523–525
  inhibition of by adrenochrome, 277–278
Activity, changes in due to LSD, 126
Acuity, auditory, LSD and, 117
Adjuvant, LSD as, 149–153
Adrenaline, 17
  conversion of into adrenochrome, 281
  electrograms and, 312
  formation of adrenochrome and, 332–337
  hypothermia and, 297
  intracerebral effect of, 215, 572, 574
  LSD and, 220
  oxygen toxicity and, 288–289, 293
  pulmonary function and, 321
dl-Adrenaline, adrenochrome from, 361–362
l-Adrenaline, adrenochrome from, 343–361
Adrenaline metabolism, LSD and, 222–223
Adrenaline methyl ether, 64–73
  treatment using, 65–70
Adrenaline oxidase, 325–331
Adrenaline oxidase inhibitors, formation of adrenochrome and, 336–337
Adrenochrome,
  anxiety and, 415–416
  ascorbic acid and, 284–286
  biochemical properties of, 272–321
    acetylcholinesterase inhibition and, 277–278

Adrenochrome—*Continued*
  biochemical properties of—*Continued*
    allergies and, 295–296
    amino acids and, 278–280
    antithyroid properties and, 299–303
    brain inhibitor factor and, 278
    carbohydrate metabolism and, 273–277
    cardiovascular system and, 318–321
    ceruloplasmin and, 314–316
    copper metabolism and, 308–312
    electrograms and, 312–314
    erythrocyte metabolism and, 304–308
    hypothermia and, 296–299
    iron metabolism and, 308–312
    melanin pigmentation and, 280–288
    mitosis and, 316–317
    mucopolysaccharides and, 317–318
    oxygen toxicity and, 288–295
    pulmonary function and, 321
  blood and, 224–225, 318–321
  blood-brain barrier and, 215–216
  brain and, 24, 213, 220, 573, 574
  chemical properties of, 269–272
    oxidation and, 272
    rearrangement and, 271
    reduction and, 271–272
  clinical changes and, 349–361
    mood and, 351, 360–361
    perception and, 349–350, 360
    thought and, 350–351, 360
  conditioning and, 584–586, 587
  feces and, 324
  formation of, 269–270, 322–323
    adrenaline and, 281, 332–337
    dl adrenaline and, 361–362
    l-adrenaline and, 343–361
    adrenaline oxidase inhibitors and, 336–337
    body and, 331–342
    malvaria and, 337–339

613

Adrenochrome—*Continued*
  formation of—*Continued*
    monoamine oxidase inhibitors and, 335–336
    schizophrenia and, 337–339
    sulfoesterase inhibitors and, 336
  glutamic acid decarboxylase and, 289–290, 293
  intracerebral effect of, 573, 574
  intrasystematic effect of, 564, 565, 570
  LSD and, 169, 210, 220, 330–331, 363–366
  metabolism of, 323–331
    enzymes and, 323–331
    monoamine oxidase and, 324–325
    tolerance curves and, 224–225, 342–343
  oxygen toxicity and, 288–295
  phenolic hydroxyls and, 325
  potentiation of action of by LSD, 363–366
  prolonged reactions to, 397–399
  psychological properties of, 343–366
    dl-adrenaline and, 361–362
    l-adrenaline and, 343–361
    potentiation of action and, 210, 362–366
  saliva and, 324
  schizophrenia and, 325–331
  sweat and, 324
  sympathetic nervous system and, 223
  taraxein and, 215
  toxicity of, 288–295
  urine and, 324
Adrenochrome monosemicarbazone, 419, 432–433
  allergies and, 295
Adrenochrome reaction, reversal of, 400–415
Adrenolutin, 366–397
  anti-insulinase activity of, 303–304
  anxiety and, 369, 373–374, 378, 385–386, 387, 416–419
  ceruloplasmin and, 223
  clinical observations and, 368–369
  EEG and, 370
  flicker fusion frequency and, 370, 380–382
  hypothermia and, 296

Adrenolutin—*Continued*
  insight and, 369, 376–377
  insulin and, 303–304
  interest and, 374–375, 378
  intracerebral effect of, 573, 574
  intrasystematic effect of, 564, 565, 570
  mood and, 369, 374, 378, 387
  phosphate excretion and, 276–277
  physiological tests and, 370–377, 380–397
  potentiation of by LSD and, 210
  preparation of, 270
  prolonged reactions to, 399–415
  psychological changes and, 377–380
    tests used, 369–370
  sociability and, 369, 375
  sympathetic nervous system and, 223
  thought and, 368, 370–373, 378, 382–384, 386, 387
  visual perception and, 370, 375–376, 380–382
Adrenoxyl, *see also* Adrenochrome monosemicarbazone, 419
Affect, lack of, LSD and penicillamine and, 169–176, 229–230
Afterimage, changes in induced by mescaline, 14
Age, reaction to LSD and, 106
Alcoholics,
  delirium tremens and, 153–155
  LSD experience and, 115, 130
  malvarian, 157, 181–183
    treatment of, 183–196
  nicotinic acid in treatment of, 183–196
  psychotherapy with LSD and, 136–137, 153–169, 179–196
  treatment of as schizophrenics, 183–196
Allergies,
  adrenochrome and, 295–296
  adrenochrome monosemicarbazone and, 295
  schizophrenia and, 295–296
Amines, sympathomimetic, 63–75
  LSD and, 220–221
Amino acids, adrenochrome and, 278–280
Amphetamines, 46–47
  electrophysiological effect of, 575

Amphetamines—*Continued*
khat, 47
LSD compared to, 139
motor tasks and, 581, 582
potentiation of effect of LSD and, 210
psilocybin compared to, 498
Amphibia, hallucinogenic drugs and, 563
Anesthetic hallucinogens, 538–544
α-chloralose, 542–544
sernyl, 538–542
Animal(s),
adrenochrome and, 584–586, 587
amphetamines and, 581, 582
benactyzine and, 534
bufotenine and, 461–463, 582
bulbocapnine and, 584
chlorpromazine and, 581, 583, 585–586, 588, 589
diethyltryptamines and, 462–463
dimethyltryptamines and, 463–464
harmine and, 477–478
iboga alkaloids and, 469–470
invertebrate, 556–558
LSD and, 89–90, 95–96, 580–581, 582–584, 585, 586, 587–589
mescaline and, 30, 31–36, 581–582, 583–584, 585, 588
nutmeg and, 50
psilocybin and, 491–492, 584
tryptamine and, 448
vertebrate, 558–563
yohimbine and, 502
Antihallucinogens, 293
cholineacetylase inhibitors as, 538
Anti-insulinase activity, adrenolutin and, 303–304
Antithyroid properties, adrenochrome and, 299–303
Anxiety,
adrenochrome and, 415–416
adrenolutin and, 369, 373–374, 378, 416–419
Apparent movement, mescaline and, 14–15
Asarone, 55–56
mescaline and, 56
Ascorbic acid,
adrenochrome and, 223, 284–286

Ascorbic acid—*Continued*
LSD and, 209, 224
penicillamine and, 223
reduction of LSD experience and, 209
schizophrenia and, 284–286
Atropine, 525–528
Auditory aids, reaction to LSD and, 110
Auditory discrimination, LSD and, 579–580
Auditory perception, *see* Perception, auditory
Autism, psychotherapy with LSD and, 178–179

B

Barbiturates, antagonization of mescaline and, 42–43
Behavior,
animal,
benactyzine and, 534
bufotenine and, 461–463
diethyltryptamines and, 462–463
dimethyltryptamines and, 463–464
harmine and, 477–478
iboga alkaloids and, 469–470
mescaline and, 31–36
nutmeg and, 50
psilocybin and, 491–492
tryptamine and, 448
yohimbine and, 502
electrophysiological effects of drugs and, 575–578
motor, psilocybin and, 491
Behavior problems, psychotherapy with LSD and, 176–177
Belladonna alkaloids, 525–528
Benactyzine, 528–538
animal behavior and, 534
biochemistry of, 532–533
mode of action of, 534–535
physiology of, 533–534
psychological effects of, 535–538
psychotomimetic activity and, 532
Birds, hallucinogenic drugs and, 563–564
Blood,
adrenochrome and, 224–225, 318–321
circulation of in brain, effect of LSD on, 215

Blood—*Continued*
LSD and, 89–90
mescaline and, 22
Blood-brain barrier,
ceruloplasmin and, 215
effect of LSD on, 212, 215–216
Blood pressure,
LSD and, 224
schizophrenia and, 319–321
Body image, LSD and, 119
Body temperature, 222
schizophrenia and, 297–298
Brain,
adrenochrome and, 24, 213, 220, 573, 574
interference with transmission in, 506–510
intracerebral introduction of drugs and, 571–575
LSD and, 91–92, 211–212, 221–223, 571, 572, 573–574
mescaline and, 24–25, 26–28, 571, 572, 573
spontaneous activity in, effect of LSD on, 91–92
Brain cells, effect of LSD on, 212–214
Brain circulation, effect of LSD on, 215
Brain function,
acetylcholine and, 522–523
alteration of by LSD, 116
serotonin and, 504–506
Brain inhibitor factor, adrenochrome and, 278
Bufotenine,
animal behavior and, 461–463
biochemistry of, 455
cohoba and, 451–452
conditioning and, 582
intrasystematic effect of, 565, 569
pharmacology of, 456–457
psychological effects of, 454–455
schizophrenia and, 457–458
Bulbocapnine, 73–75
conditioning and, 584
intracerebral effect of, 572
intrasystematic effect of, 562

C

Cactus alkaloids, *see also* Mescaline, 16–19

Carbohydrate metabolism, adrenochrome and, 273–277
Cardiovascular system, adrenochrome and, 318–321
Cerebral activity, spontaneous, effect of LSD on, 91–92
Ceruloplasmin, 325–331
adrenochrome and, 314–316
adrenolutin and, 223
blood-brain barrier and, 215
reduction of LSD experience and, 209, 223
schizophrenia and, 314–316, 325–331
Children,
autistic, psychotherapy with LSD and, 178–179
verbal, LSD and, 179
α-Chloralose, 542–544
Chlorpromazine,
conditioning and, 581, 583, 585–586, 588, 589
intracerebral effect of, 571–572
oxygen toxicity and, 289
reaction to LSD and, 206, 580
serotonin and, 218
Choline acetylase inhibitors, as antihallucinogens, 538
Cholinergic-blocking hallucinogens, 525–528
belladonna alkaloids as, 525–528
Cholinesterase, inhibition of by LSD, 221–222
Cohoba, 450–458
biochemistry of, 455
bufotenine and, 451–452
experience under, 453–455
pharmacology of, 456–457
psychological effects of, 454–455
schizophrenia and, 457–458
sources of, 451–452
Color,
LSD and, 114
mescaline and, 12–13
Comprehension, LSD and, 117, 121, 122
Conditioning, effect of hallucinogenic drugs on, 580–589
Congeners, LSD and, 208–209
Convolvulaceae, taxonomy of, 239–240
Convolvulaceous resins, 252

Copper, schizophrenia and, 309–312
Copper metabolism, adrenochrome and, 308–312
Creativity, LSD and, 126–127

D

Death, LSD and, 235–236
Delirium tremens, LSD experience as model of, 153–155
Depression,
  LSD and, 96–97, 100, 126
  synaptic, factors producing, 519
Dibenamine, antagonization of mescaline and, 44
Dibenzylin, reduction of LSD experience and, 209
Diethyltryptamines, 458–461, 462–463
  animal behavior and, 462–463
  psilocybin compared to, 498
Digit span, LSD and, 122
5,6-Dihydroxy-N-methylindole, 419–432
3,4-Dimethoxyphenylethylamine, 17
Dimethyltryptamines, 458–461, 463–464
  animal behavior and, 463–464
  cross-tolerance of, 464–465
  intrasystematic effect of, 568
Discrimination, auditory, LSD and, 579–580
Drug(s),
  electrophysiological effect of, 575–578
  reaction to LSD and, 108
Drug addicts, LSD and, 176, 235

E

Education, reaction to LSD and, 105
Electroconvulsive therapy, mescaline and, 44
Electrophysiological effect, behavioral correlates of, 575–578
Electroretinograms, effect of LSD on, 93
Emotion, lack of, LSD and, 125, 169–176, 229–230
Ephedrine, 17
Epilepsy, mescaline and, 39–40
Ergot, as source of LSD, 84
  ololiuqui from, 85–87
Ergot alkaloids,
  psychotomimetic activity and, 93–95

Ergot alkaloids—*Continued*
  taxonomy of convolvulaceae containing, 239–240
Ergotism, 84
Erythrocyte metabolism, adrenochrome and, 304–308
α-Ethyltryptamine, 466–468
  biochemistry of, 466
  pharmacology of, 466–468
Euphoria, LSD and, 124
Excitation, factors producing, 519–522
Expectation, reaction to LSD and, 106–107

F

Fear, LSD and, 125–126
Feces, adrenochrome and, 324
Fishes, hallucinogenic drugs and, 558–562
Flicker fusion frequency, adrenolutin and, 370, 380–382
Frenquel, 293
  antagonization of mescaline and, 43
  reaction to LSD and, 206, 560

G

Gastropoda, hallucinogenic drugs and, 558
Glucose, reduction of LSD experience and, 206–207
Glucose metabolism, substances which modify, 206–208
Glucosides, 240–241
Glutamic acid, reduction of LSD experience and, 207
Glutamic acid decarboxylase, adrenochrome and, 289–290, 293
Group dynamics, LSD and, 235
Group psychotherapy, LSD and, 160–162
Growth, schizophrenia and, 274–275

H

Hallucinations, LSD and, 114, 117
Hallucinogens, *see also* d-Lysergic acid diethylamide; Mescaline; etc.
  anesthetic, 538–544
  α-chloralose, 542–544
  sernyl, 538–542

Hallucinogens—*Continued*
  cholinergic-blocking, 525–528
  experience with, reaction to LSD and,
      107, 108–109
  invertebrates and, 556–558
  learning and, 578–589
    conditioning and, 580–589
    sensory processes and, 578–580
  psychotherapy and, 150
  tryptamine, 502–503
Harmine, 472–480
  animal behavior and, 477–478, 570
  chemistry of, 478–479
  intrasystematic effect of, 564, 568,
      570
  pharmacology of, 479–480
  psychological effects of, 476–477
Health, reaction to LSD and, 106
Histamine,
  brain function and, 219–220
  LSD and, 208, 209, 219–220
  serotonin and, 220
Heart, adrenochrome and, 318–321
Homosexuality, psychotherapy with
    LSD and, 176–177
Hydroxymescaline, 19
Hyoscyamine, 525–528
Hypothermia,
  adrenaline and, 297
  adrenochrome and, 296–299
  adrenolutin and, 296

                    I

Iboga alkaloids, 468–472
  animal behavior and, 469–470
  chemistry of, 470–471
  pharmacology of, 471–472
Illusions, LSD and, 114, 117
Imagery, LSD and, 111–112
Indole hallucinogens,
  bufotenine, 450–458
  cohoba, 450–458
  diethyltryptamines, 458–461, 462–
      463
  dimethyltryptamines, 458–461, 463–
      464
  α-ethyltryptamine, 466–468
  harmine, 472–480
  iboga alkaloids, 468–472
  methyl-2-methyltryptamine, 468

Indole hallucinogens—*Continued*
  α-methyltryptamine, 465–466
  psilocybin, 480–500
  serotonin, 506–510
  tryptamine, 448–450
  tryptophan, 444–448
  yohimbine, 500–502
Indoles, 217
  intrasystematic effect of, 561–562,
      564
  potentiation of LSD and, 580
Insight, adrenolutin and, 369, 376–377
Insulin,
  adrenolutin and, 303–304
  schizophrenia and, 303–304, 307
Intellectual function, LSD and, 123–124
Interest, adrenolutin and, 374–375, 378
Invertebrates, hallucinogenic drugs and,
      556–558
Iron metabolism, adrenochrome and,
      308–312

                    K

Kat, *see* Khat
Kava kava, 57–62
  botany of, 57–58
  ceremony attached to, 59
  clinical uses of, 62
  geographical distribution of, 57
  harvesting of, 58
  pharmacology of, 61–62
  preparation of, 58
  psychological activity of, 59–61
    chewing and, 59–60
    grating and, 60–61
  toxicity of, 62
Khat, 47
Kinesthesis, changes in due to LSD,
      118–119

                    L

Learning,
  effect of hallucinogens on, 578–589
    conditioning and, 580–589
    sensory processes and, 578–580
  LSD and, 122–123
Light,
  LSD and, 114
  mescaline and, 12–13

Lobotomy, mescaline and, 44
LSD, *see* *d*-Lysergic acid diethylamide
Lungs, adrenochome and, 321
Lysergic acid alkaloids, 241
  activity of, 93–95
Lysergic acid amide, psychological properties of, 87
d-Lysergic acid diethylamide,
  adrenaline metabolism and, 220, 222–223
  adrenochrome and, 169, 210, 220, 330–331, 363–366
  adrenolutin and, 210
  amphetamines and, 139, 210
  ascorbic acid and, 209, 224
  biochemistry of, 90–91
  blood and, 89–90, 224
  brain and, 91–92, 211–212, 221–223, 571, 572, 573–574
  ceruloplasmin and, 209
  chemistry of, 88–89
  chlorpromazine and, 206
  cholinesterase and, 221–222
  complications arising from use of, 96–103
    reasons for, 98–103
  comprehension and, 117, 121, 122
  congeners and, 208–209
  contraindication for, 99–103, 144
  delirium tremens and, 153–155
  depression and, 96–97, 100, 126
  dibenzylin and, 209
  direct action of, 212–221
    antagonism of serotonin and, 216–219
    blood-brain barrier and, 215–216
    brain cells and, 212–214
    brain circulation and, 215
    histamine and, 219–220
    sympathomimetic amines and, 220–221
    transmission of stimuli and, 216
  dosage and, 103–104, 161
  electrograms and, 92, 312–313, 314
  electrophysiological effect of, 575–577
  frenquel and, 206
  glucose and, 206–207
  indirect action hypothesis and, 224–225

d-Lysergic acid diethylamide–*Continued*
  indirect activity to, 221–224
    parasympathetic nervous system and, 221–222
    sympathetic nervous system and, 222–224
  intracerebral effect of, 571, 572, 573–574
  intrasystematic effect of, 558–571
  lack of affect and, 169–176, 229–230
  mechanisms of, 211–232
    biochemical, 211–225
    clinical, 229–232
    psychological theories and, 225–229
    synaptic transmission and, 216
  model of schizophrenia and, 128–129, 131, 132, 180, 225
  modifiers of experience with, 205–211
    activators, 210
    reducers, 205–210
  motor tasks and, 580–581, 582–584, 585, 586, 587–589
  neurophysiological effects of,
    electroretinograms and, 93
    spontaneous cerebral activity and, 91–92
    synaptic transmission and, 92–93
  nicotinic acid and, 207–208
  noradrenaline and, 118
  normal subjects and, 104–127
    activity changes and, 126
    auditory perception and, 117–118, 228
    body image and, 119
    comprehension and, 121, 122
    creativity and, 126–127
    digit span and, 122
    fear and, 125–126
    intellectual function and, 123–124
    kinesthetic changes and, 118–119
    learning and, 122–123
    mental testing and, 121–124
    mood changes and, 124–126, 169–176
    problem solving and, 121–122
    proverbs and, 121
    tactile changes and, 118
    taste changes and, 118
    thought changes and, 120–124
    time passage and, 119–120

d-Lysergic acid diethylamide—*Continued*
  normal subjects and—*Continued*
    variables influencing reaction and,
        104–110
    visual perception and, 111–117
  penicillamine and, 169–176
  personality change and, 196–197
  pharmacology of, 89–90
  prolonged experiences with, 99–103
  psilocybin compared to, 138–139,
      495–498
  psychedelic experience and, 131–139,
      153–169
    other nonergot hallucinogens and,
        138–139
  psychiatry and, 232–236
    architecture and, 234
    death and, 235–236
    drug addicts and, 235
    group dynamics and, 235
    philosophy and, 235
    religion and, 234–235
    Synanon and, 235
    teaching and, 234
  psychological activity and, 103–104
    mescaline compared to, 40–41,
        138–139
  psychotherapy and, 96–97, 148–196
    alcoholics and, 115, 130, 136–137,
        153–169, 179–196
    autistic children and, 178–179
    criticisms of, 197–205
    drug addicts and, 176
    group, 160–162, 177–178
    homosexuality and, 176–177
    malvaria and, 180–196, 225
    penicillamine and, 169–176, 229–230
    psychedelic use of, 153–169
    psychoadjuvant use of, 149–153
    psychopaths and behavioral prob-
        lems and, 176–177
    verbal children and, 179
  psychotomimetic activity of, 214, 215
  psychotomimetic reaction to, 128–131
    aftermath of, 130–131
    experience and, 130
    prodromal phase of, 129–130
    recovery and, 130
  reaction to,
    age and, 106

d-Lysergic acid diethylamide—*Continued*
  reaction to—*Continued*
    auditory aids and, 110
    drugs and, 108
    education and, 105
    expectation and, 106–107
    experience with hallucinogens and,
        107
    health and, 106
    meals and, 108
    number of people present and, 110
    personality and, 104–105
    physical setting and, 109–110
    premedication and, 108
    previous psychiatric treatment and,
        107–108
    somatotype and, 105
    therapist and, 96, 98, 108–109, 153,
        158, 159–160, 230
    time and, 108
    visual aids and, 110, 137
    vocation and, 105–106
  reserpine and, 118, 206, 218
  schizophrenic patients and, 139–148
    acute florid, 145
    malvaria and, 140–143
    pseudoneurotic, 144–145
    recovered, 146–148
  sedatives and, 205–206
  sensory deprivation and, 116
  serotonin and, 35, 209, 212, 216–219
  sources of, 83–88
    ergot and, 84
    morning glory and, 84–88
  steroid hormones and, 209–210
  stimulus hierarchy and, 230–231
  succinic acid and, 207
  synaptic transmission and, 212, 216,
      221
  tension and, 135–138, 148–149, 174
  tolerance and, 30
  toxicology of, 95–96
  uses for, 132–135

M

Malvaria, 233
  alcoholics and, 157, 181–183
    treatment of, 183–196
  diagnosis of, 180–181

Malvaria—*Continued*
   formation of adrenochrome and, 337–339
   LSD and, 102–103, 140–143, 180–196, 225
   psychotherapy with LSD and, 180–196
   relationship of to schizophrenia, 102–103, 140–143, 147
Mammals, hallucinogenic drugs and, 564–571
Mauve factor, *see also* Malvaria, 102
Melanin pigmentation,
   adrenochrome and, 280–288
   schizophrenia and, 282–284
Mental testing, LSD and, 121–124
Mescaline, 1–45
   antagonization of, 42–45
      barbiturates and, 42–43
      dibenamine and, 44
      electroconvulsive therapy and, 44
      frenquel and, 43
      lobotomy and, 44
      succinate and, 43
      tranquilizers and, 43–44
   asarone and, 56
   biochemistry of, 20–25
   blood and, 22
   brain and, 24–25, 26–28, 571, 572, 573
   electrograms and, 313, 314
   electrophysiological effect of, 577
   extraction and isolation of, 16–19
   intracerebral effect of, 571, 572, 573
   intrasystematic effect of, 559, 562, 564, 565, 568–569, 571
   LSD compared to, 138–139
   motor tasks and, 581–582, 583–584, 585, 588
   physical properties of, 17
   physiology and, 25–28
   potentiation of, 42
   prolonged reactions to, 29–30
   psilocybin compared to, 498
   psychological changes produced by, animals and, 31–36
   psychological effect of on humans, 36–45
      epileptics and, 39–40
      LSD compared to, 40–41

Mescaline—*Continued*
   psychological effect of on humans—*Continued*
      repeated administrations and, 41–42
      schizophrenia and, 21, 22, 25, 36–39
      sensory deprivation and, 40
   psychotherapy using, 45
   schizophrenia and, 21, 22, 25, 36–39
      brain and, 27–28
      visual imagery and, 38
   serotonin and, 35
   tolerance and, 29, 30
   toxicology of, 28–30
   urine and, 20–22, 23
   visual changes induced by, 11–15
      afterimages and, 14
      apparent movement and, 14–15
      color and, 12–13
      form constants and, 12
      illumination and, 12–13
      transformations and, 15
      visual patterns and, 13–14
Mescaline analogs, 45–46
   3,4,5-trimethoxyamphetamine, 45–46
3-Methoxy-4,5-methylenedioxyamphetamine, 55
Methylenedioxyamphetamines, 47–55
   3-methoxy-4,5-methylenedioxyamphetamine, 55
   nutmeg, 48–55
Methyl-2-methyltryptamine, 468
Methyltryptamine, intrasystematic effect of, 568
α-Methyltryptamine, 465–466
   biochemistry of, 465
   pharmacology of, 465–466
Mitosis, adrenochrome and, 316–317
Monoamine oxidase, metabolism of adrenochrome and, 324–325
Monoamine oxidase inhibitors, formation of adrenochrome and, 335–336
Mood,
   adrenochrome and, 351, 360–361
   adrenolutin and, 369, 374, 378, 387
   LSD and, 124–126, 169–176
Morning glory, as source of LSD, 84–88
Motor behavior, psilocybin and, 491
Motor tasks, 580–589

Mucopolysaccharides, adrenochrome and, 317–318
Mushrooms, psilocybin and, 480–486
Myristicin, *see* Nutmeg

N

Nervous system,
  parasympathetic, 221–222
  sympathetic, 222–224
Nicotinic acid,
  psychotherapy and, 152
  reduction of LSD experience and, 207–208
  treatment of alcoholics and, 183–196
Noradrenaline,
  electrograms and, 312
  interference with transmission and, 506–510
  reduction of by LSD, 118
  serotonin and, 505, 506–510
Nutmeg, 48–55
  animal behavioral changes and, 50
  pharmacology of, 50
  psychotomimetic properties of, 51–55
  toxicology of, 49–50

O

Ololiuqui,
  chemistry of, 240–241
    glucosides and, 240–241
    lysergic acid alkaloids and, 241
  history and identification of, 237–239
  psychological properties of, 241–252
    convolvulaceous resins and, 252
    dosage and, 243–244
    experiments and, 244–248
    ololiuqui glucoside and, 250–252
    ololiuqui seeds and, 241–242
  source of, 85–87
Ololiuqui glucoside, 250–252
Oxygen toxicity,
  adrenaline and, 288–289, 293
  adrenochrome and, 288–295
  chlorpromazine and, 289

P

Parasympathetic nervous system, indirect activity to LSD, 221–222

Penicillamine, LSD and, 169–176, 209
  lack of affect and, 169–176, 229–230
Perception,
  adrenochrome and, 349–350, 360
  auditory, LSD and, 117–118, 228, 579–580
  visual,
    adrenolutin and, 370, 375–376, 380–382
    changes in, *see* Visual changes
    LSD and, 110, 111–117, 228, 578–579
    mescaline and, 12–15, 38
Performance tests, LSD and, 123
Personality, LSD and, 104–105, 196–197
Peyote, *see also* Cactus alkaloids, 482–483
  alcoholism and, 155
Phenolic hydroxyls, adrenochrome and, 325
Phenylpropanolmethylamine, 17
Phosphate excretion, *see also* Urine
  adrenolutin and, 276–277
  LSD and, 91
Plant β-phenethylamines,
  adrenaline methyl ether, 64–73
  amphetamines, 46–47
  anhaline, 19
  asarone, 55–56
  bulbocapnine, 73–75
  candicine, 19
  coryneine, 19
  N-dimethylmescaline, 19
  hordenine, 19, 20
  3-hydroxytyramine, 19
  kava kava, 57–62
  khat, 47
  mescaline, 1–45
  3-methoxy-4,5-methylenedioxyamphetamine, 55
  methylenedioxyamphetamines, 47–55
  N-methylphenylethylamine, 19
  myristicin, 48–55
  nutmeg, 48–55
  phenylethylamine, 19, 28, 33
  safrole, 62–63
  sympathomimetic amines, 63–75
  3,4,5-trimethoxyamphetamine, 45–46
Problem solving, LSD and, 121–122

Psilocybin, 480–500
  animals and, 491–492
  biochemistry of, 487–490
  chemistry of, 486–487
  conditioning and, 584
  electrograms and, 313, 491–492
  electrophysiological effect of, 575
  intracerebral effect of, 574
  intrasystematic effect of, 561, 566
  LSD compared to, 138–139
  other hallucinogens and, 138–139,
    495–500
  pharmacology of, 490
  physiological effects of, 490–491
  psychological changes and, 493–495
  schizophrenia and, 499–500
  tolerance to, 30, 493
  toxicity of, 492
  treatment and, 500
Psychedelic experience,
  LSD and, 131–139, 153–169
    other nonergot hallucinogens and,
    138–139
  research on, 135–138
Psychiatric treatment, *see also* Electro-
    convulsive therapy; *d*-Lysergic acid
    diethylamide, psychotherapy and
  previous, reaction to LSD and, 107–
    108
Psychiatry, consequences of LSD for,
    232–236
  architecture and, 234
  death and, 235–236
  drug addicts and, 235
  group dynamics and, 235
  philosophy and, 235
  religion and, 234–235
  Synanon and, 235
  teaching and, 234
Psychopaths, LSD and, 176–177
Psychotherapeutic agent, mescaline as,
    45
Psychotherapy,
  alcoholics and, 136–137, 153–169,
    179–196
  LSD and, *see d*-Lysergic acid diethyl-
    amide, psychotherapy and
  nicotinic acid and, 152, 183–196
Psychotomimetic activity,
  benactyzine and, 532

Psychotomimetic activity—*Continued*
  ergot alkaloids and, 93–95
  LSD and, 214, 215
  nutmeg and, 51–55
Psychotomimetic reaction, LSD and,
    128–131
  aftermath of, 130–131
  experience and, 130
  prodromal phase of, 129–130
  recovery and, 130
Pulmonary function, adrenochrome and,
    321

R

Religion, LSD and, 234–235
Reserpine,
  indoles and, 564
  potentiation of LSD and, 118, 206,
    218, 580
  serotonin and, 218, 505
Rorschach test, LSD and, 124

S

Safrole, 62–63
Saliva, adrenochrome and, 324
Schizophrenia,
  acute florid, LSD and, 145
  adrenochrome and, 325–331, 337–339
  alcoholics treated as, 183–196
  allergies and, 295–296
  ascorbic acid and, 284–286
  blood pressure and, 319–321
  body temperature and, 297–298
  bufotenine and, 457–458
  ceruloplasmin and, 314–316, 325–331
  chronic, LSD and, 145
  cohoba and, 457–458
  contraindication for LSD, 99–103,
    144
  copper and, 309–312
  growth and, 274–275
  hypothesis of, 226–229
  insulin and, 303–304, 307
  LSD and, 139–148
  malvaria and, 102–103, 140–143, 147
  melanin pigments and, 282–284
  mescaline and, 21, 22, 25, 36–39
    brain and, 27–28
    visual imagery and, 38

Schizophrenia—*Continued*
  model of, 128–129, 131, 132, 180, 225
  nicotinic acid and, 183–184
  phosphate excretion and, 276–277
  pseudoneurotic, LSD and, 144–145
  psilocybin and, 499–500
  recovered, LSD and, 146–148
  thyroid medication and, 299–302
  tryptophan and, 446–447
Scopolamine, 525–528
Sedatives, reduction of LSD experience by, 205–206
Sensory deprivation,
  LSD and, 116
  mescaline and, 40
Sensory processes, 578–580
Sernyl, 538–542
Serotonin, 503–506
  brain function and, 504–506
  chlorpromazine and, 218
  electrograms and, 312
  interaction of with mescaline, 35
  interaction of with LSD, 35
  interference of transmission and, 506–510
  intracerebral effect of, 574
  intrasystematic effect of, 560, 562, 564, 565, 566
  LSD and, 35, 209, 212, 216–219
  noradrenaline and, 505, 506–510
  physiology of, 28
  reduction of LSD experience and, 209
  reserpine and, 218, 505
  tryptamine and, 449
Set, reaction to LSD and, 106–107
Similarities tests, LSD and, 122
Sociability, adrenolutin and, 369, 375
Somatotype, reaction to LSD and, 105
Sound, LSD and, 117–118
Space, three-dimensional, LSD and, 111, 112
Spiders,
  effect of hallucinogens and, 556–557
  psilocybin and, 492
Steroid hormones, reduction of LSD experience and, 209–210
Stimulus, transmission of, effect of LSD on, 216

Stimulus hierarchy, LSD and, 230–231
Succinate, antagonization of mescaline and, 43
Succinic acid, reduction of LSD experience and, 207
Suicide, LSD and, 96–97
Sulfoesterase inhibitors, formation of adrenochrome and, 336
Sweat, adrenochrome and, 324
Sympathetic nervous system,
  adrenochrome and, 223
  adrenolutin and, 223
  indirect activity to LSD and, 222–224
Sympathomimetic amines, 63–75
  adrenaline methyl ether, 64–73
  bulbocapnine, 73–75
  LSD and, 220–221
Synanon, 133
  LSD and, 235
Synaptic depression, factors producing, 519
Synaptic transmission, 519–522
  LSD and, 92–93, 212, 216, 221

T

Tactile changes, LSD and, 118
Taraxein, 547–553
  adrenochrome and, 215
  biochemistry of, 547–551
    biochemical properties and, 548–551
    preparation and, 547–548
  electrograms and, 313
  mode of action of, 553
  psychological properties of, 551–553
Taste, changes in due to LSD, 118
Teaching, LSD and, 234
Tension, reduction of by LSD, 135–138, 148–149, 174
Testing,
  adrenolutin and, 369–370
  LSD and, 121–124
Tetrahydroisoquinolines, 17
Therapist, reaction to LSD and, 96, 98, 108–109, 153, 158, 159–160, 230
Therapy, *see also d*-Lysergic acid diethylamide, psychotherapy and; Psychiatric treatment; Psychotherapy
  electroconvulsive, mescaline and, 44

Therapy—*Continued*
  psychedelic experience with LSD and,
    135–138, 148–149, 174
Thought,
  adrenochrome and, 350–351, 360
  adrenolutin and, 368, 370–373, 378,
    382–384, 386, 387
  LSD and, 120–124
Thyroid medication, schizophrenia and,
  299–302
Time, reaction to LSD and, 108, 119–
  120
Tolerance,
  adrenochrome and, 342–343
  LSD and, 30
  mescaline and, 29, 30
  psilocybin and, 30, 493
Toxicity,
  adrenochrome and, 288–295
  kava kava and, 62
  LSD and, 95–96
  mescaline and, 28–30
    acute, 28–29
    chronic, 29
    prolonged reactions and, 29–30
    tolerance and, 30
  nutmeg and, 49–50
  oxygen,
    adrenaline and, 288–289, 293
    adrenochrome and, 288–295
    chlorpromazine and, 289
  psilocybin and, 492
Tranquilizers,
  antagonization of mescaline and, 43–
    44
  reduction of LSD experience by, 205–
    206
Transcendental reaction, LSD and, 125
3,4,5-Trimethoxyamphetamine, 45–46
Tryptamine, 448–450
  animal behavior and, 448, 561–562
  biochemistry of, 448–449
  pharmacology of, 449–450
  serotonin and, 449
Tryptamine hallucinogens, activity of,
  502–503
Tryptophan, 444–448
  indole hallucinogens derived from,
    bufotenine, 450–458
    cohoba, 450–458

Tryptophan—*Continued*
  indole hallucinogens derived from—
    Continued
    diethyltryptamines, 458–461, 462–
      463
    dimethyltryptamines, 458–461,
      463–464
    α-ethyltryptamine, 466–468
    harmine, 472–480
    iboga alkaloids, 468–472
    methyl-2-methyltryptamine, 468
    α-methyltryptamine, 465–466
    psilocybin, 480–500
    serotonin, 506–510
    tryptamine, 448–450
    tryptophan, 444–448
    yohimbine, 500–502
  schizophrenic patients and, 446–447

U

Urine, *see also* Phosphate excretion
  adrenochrome and, 324
  diagnosis of malvaria and, 180–181
  LSD and, 91
  mescaline and, 20–22, 23
  schizophrenic patients and, 561

V

Vertebrates,
  higher, hallucinogenic drugs and, 563
  lower, hallucinogenic drugs and, 558–
    563
Visual aids, reaction to LSD and, 110,
  137
Visual changes,
  adrenolutin and, 370, 375–376, 380–
    382
  LSD and, 111–117
    blurring and, 111
    changes in three-dimensional space
      and, 112
    closed eyes and, 115–117
    color and, 114
    faces and, 112–113
    hallucinations and, 114, 117
    illusions and, 114
    imagery and, 111–112
    light intensity and, 114
    objects and, 113–114, 115
    visual perseveration and, 115

Visual changes—*Continued*
  mescaline and, 11–15
    afterimages and, 14
    apparent movement and, 14–15
    color and, 12–13
    form constants and, 12
    illumination and, 12–13
    transformations and, 15
    visual patterns and, 13–14
Visual patterns, 13–14
Visual perception, *see* Perception, visual
Visual perseveration, LSD and, 115
Visual threshold, LSD and, 578–579

Vitamin C, *see* Ascorbic Acid
Vocation, reaction to LSD and, 105–106

W

Word association test, LSD and, 122
Worms, hallucinogenic drugs and, 557–558

Y

Yohimbine, 500–502
  animal behavior and, 502
  intrasystematic effect of, 564, 569–570
  physiological effects of, 501
  psychological effects of, 501–502